Saudi Arabia Enters
the Twenty-First Century

Other Books by Anthony H. Cordesman

The Lessons of Afghanistan: War Fighting, Intelligence, and Force Transformation (Washington, DC: CSIS, 2002)

Iraq's Military Capabilities in 2002: A Dynamic Net Assessment (Washington, DC: CSIS, 2002)

Strategic Threats and National Missile Defenses: Defending the U.S. Homeland (Westport, CT: Praeger, 2002)

A Tragedy of Arms: Military and Security Developments in the Maghreb (Westport, CT: Praeger, 2001)

Peace and War: The Arab-Israeli Military Balance Enters the 21st Century (Westport, CT: Praeger, 2001)

Terrorism, Asymmetric Warfare, and Weapons of Mass Destruction: Defending the U.S. Homeland (Westport, CT: Praeger, 2001)

Cyber-threats, Information Warfare, and Critical Infrastructure Protection: Defending the U.S. Homeland, with Justin G. Cordesman (Westport, CT: Praeger, 2001)

The Lessons and Non-Lessons of the Air and Missile Campaign in Kosovo (Westport, CT: Praeger, 2000)

Transnational Threats from the Middle East: Crying Wolf or Crying Havoc? (Carlyle, PA: Strategic Studies Institute, 1999)

Iraq and the War of Sanctions: Conventional Threats and Weapons of Mass Destruction (Westport, CT: Praeger, 1999)

Iran's Military Forces in Transition: Conventional Threats and Weapons of Mass Destruction (Westport, CT: Praeger, 2000)

U.S. Forces in the Middle East: Resources and Capabilities (Boulder, CO: Westview, 1997)

Perilous Prospects: The Peace Process and Arab-Israeli Military Balance (Boulder, CO: Westview, 1996)

The Lessons of Modern War, Volume IV: The Gulf War, with Abraham R. Wagner (Boulder, CO: Westview, 1995; paperback 1999)

US Defence Policy: Resources and Capabilities (London: RUSI Whitehall Series, 1993)

After the Storm: The Changing Military Balance in the Middle East (Boulder, CO: Westview, 1993)

Weapons of Mass Destruction in the Middle East (London: Brassey's, 1991)

The Lessons of Modern War, Volume I: The Arab-Israeli Conflicts, with Abraham R. Wagner (Boulder, CO: Westview, 1990)

The Lessons of Modern War, Volume II: The Iran-Iraq Conflict, with Abraham R. Wagner (Boulder, CO: Westview, 1990)

The Lessons of Modern War, Volume III: The Afghan and Falklands Conflicts, with Abraham R. Wagner (Boulder, CO: Westview, 1990)

The Gulf and the West: Strategic Relations and Military Realities (Boulder, CO: Westview, 1988)

NATO's Central Region Forces: Capabilities, Challenges, Concepts (London: RUSI/Jane's, 1987)

Western Strategic Interests in Saudi Arabia (London: Croom Helm, 1986)

The Gulf and the Search for Strategic Stability: Saudi Arabia, the Military Balance in the Gulf, and Trends in the Arab-Israeli Military Balance (Boulder, CO: Westview, 1984)

Jordanian Arms and the Middle East Balance (Washington, DC: Middle East Institute, 1983)

Imbalance of Power: An Analysis of Shifting U.S.-Soviet Military Strengths, with John M. Collins (Monterey, CA: Presidio, 1978)

Saudi Arabia Enters the Twenty-First Century

The Political, Foreign Policy, Economic, and Energy Dimensions

ANTHONY H. CORDESMAN

Published in cooperation with the
Center for Strategic and International Studies,
Washington, D.C.

Westport, Connecticut
London

Library of Congress Cataloging-in-Publication Data

Cordesman, Anthony H.
  Saudi Arabia enters the twenty-first century: The political, foreign policy, economic, and energy dimensions / Anthony H. Cordesman.
    p. cm.
  Includes bibliographical references (p.) and index.
  ISBN 0–275–97998–9 (alk. paper)—ISBN 0–275–98091–X (set : alk. paper)
    1. Saudi Arabia—Politics and government—20th century. 2. National security—Saudi Arabia. 3. Petroleum industry and trade—Saudi Arabia. I. Title: Political, foreign policy, economic, and energy dimensions. II. Title: Saudi Arabia enters the 21st century. III. Title.
  DS244.52.C67 2003
  953.805′3—dc21   2002044974

British Library Cataloguing in Publication Data is available.

Copyright © 2003 by the Center for Strategic and International Studies

Library of Congress Catalog Card Number: 2002044974
ISBN: 0–275–98091–X (set)
      0–275–97997–0 [Military]
      0–275–97998–9 [Political]

First published in 2003

Praeger Publishers, 88 Post Road West, Westport, CT 06881
An imprint of Greenwood Publishing Group, Inc.
www.praeger.com

Printed in the United States of America

The paper used in this book complies with the
Permanent Paper Standard issued by the National
Information Standards Organization (Z39.48–1984).

10 9 8 7 6 5 4 3 2 1

Contents

Chapter 2 Foreign Relations and External Security   41

Chapter 3 Politics and Internal Stability   131

Illustrations

Preface

The assessment of Saudi Arabia's strategic position in this volume includes an analysis of the trends in Saudi society, foreign policy and strategic issues, domestic politics and opposition elements, economic trends and challenges, demographics, and energy. A companion volume looks at the military dimension and internal security.

Both volumes are a product of the Saudi Arabia Enters the 21st Century Project of the Center for Strategic and International Studies (CSIS). This project has been supported by the Smith Richardson Foundation and builds on the work done for the CSIS Strategic Energy Initiative, the CSIS Net Assessment of the Middle East, and the Gulf in Transition Project. It is being conducted in conjunction with a separate—but closely related—study called the Middle East Energy and Security Project.

The project uses a net assessment approach that looks at all of the major factors affecting Saudi Arabia's strategic, political, economic, and military position and future implications of current trends. It examines the internal stability and security of Saudi Arabia, social and demographic trends, and the problem of Islamic extremism. It also investigates the changes taking place in the Saudi economy and petroleum industries, the problems of Saudisation, changes in export and trade patterns, and Saudi Arabia's new emphasis on foreign investment.

The resulting assessment of Saudi Arabia's strategic future includes an analysis of its possible evolution in the face of different internal and external factors—including changes in foreign and trade policies toward Saudi Arabia by the West, Japan, and the Gulf states. Key issues affecting Saudi

Arabia's future, including its economic development, relations with other states in the region, energy production and policies, and security relations with other states will be explored as well.

SOURCES

The text of this book points out that many of its statements and statistics are highly uncertain. As the notes make clear, this book relies primarily on both Saudi and U.S. government publications, and on material from the international agencies like the World Bank and the UN. It also uses material from leading research institutes like the International Institute for Strategic Studies (IISS). While academic and private estimates of key data and trends have been reviewed extensively, few such data are incorporated in the text. This was done both to ensure some degree of consistency and comparability in the data, and to ensure that the data involved were as reliable and up-to-date as possible.

A major effort has been made to provide a range of data based on official sources and to graph and chart the different trends and data affecting key issues. It is important that the reader understand, however, that much of the information used in this book is derived from informal comments based on the working drafts of the manuscript reviewed by Saudi officials, private individuals, and other experts on Saudi Arabia, as well as on interviews in the Kingdom and elsewhere.

The author has frequented Saudi Arabia for several decades, and was able to visit the Kingdom several times over a three-year period during the drafting of this book. During each of these visits, various drafts of the manuscript were circulated to Saudi officials, military, academics, and other experts, as well as U.S., British, and French officials who were serving in Saudi Arabia or had served in it in the past. In addition, the book was placed on the CSIS Web site for comment, and copies were sent to various U.S., British, and French officials, military officers, intelligence officers, and other experts. Some provided detailed comments on the text, and the text was constantly revised as a working document on the basis of such input.

Most of these interviews and comments are not cited because most of those involved did not want their contributions acknowledged in any form. The few exceptions are made at the request of those contributing. It should be noted, however, that most of the updates covering the period from 1999 onward depend heavily on field research, interviews, and outside comments, rather than on formal written sources.

Media sources, including Internet material, translations of broadcasts, newspapers, magazine articles, and similar materials, have also been used extensively. These are referenced in most cases, but some transcribed broadcasts and much of the Internet material did not permit detailed attribution. The use of media sources presents obvious problems in terms of reliability, but the author has not found that academic or official sources are more reliable than the media sources used in this book, and extensive cross-comparisons have been made of most such material.

The Internet and several online services were used to retrieve data on U.S. and Saudi government reporting and policy. Since most of the databases involved are dynamic and either change or are deleted over time, there is no clear way to footnote much of this material. Recent press sources are generally cited, but are often only part of the material consulted.

While the use of the computer database developed for this study allowed some cross-correlation and checking of conflicting sources, citing multiple sources for each case is often not possible. Personal and location names also presented a major problem. No standardization emerged as to the spelling of various names. Differences emerged in even in the transliteration of terms and names into English by the Saudi government, and in the signatures used by Saudi officials and members of the royal family in different correspondence. A limited effort has been made to standardize some of the spellings used in this text, but many names are tied to databases where the preservation of the original spelling is necessary to identify the source and tie it to the transcript of related interviews that cannot be referenced in the notes because of an agreement not to reveal the source.

METHODS

No book can resolve all of the major uncertainties in analyzing Saudi Arabia with the available data. As a result, comparative data are provided where possible, and graphs and tables are used to help illustrate the differences in both the data and resulting trends. In some cases, the author adjusted figures and data on a "best-guess" basis, drawing on some thirty years of experience in the field. In most situations, the original data provided by a given source were used without adjustment to ensure comparability. This leads to conflicts in dates, place names, force strengths, and the like, within the material presented. In such cases, it seemed best to provide contradictory estimates to give the reader some idea of the range of uncertainty involved.

The reader should also understand that this book is not designed to prove some theory about Saudi Arabia or to reflect a given view of Saudi culture—although the author obviously is not a Saudi, Arab, or Muslim and cannot avoid having a perspective shaped by his own culture and country. It is intended as an analytic description of the basic forces and trends at work in Saudi Arabia and how these trends are likely to develop over time. It also deliberately explores the complexity and uncertainly of the major issues addressed, rather than summarizes trends or ignores such details.

Where judgments and recommendations are made, they are intended to be pragmatic assessments of the options available, and the reader should understand that in most cases there is no one valid solution to such problems. It is all too easy to write summary conclusions. In the real world however, little is simple and notions must cope with the full complexity of the issues they face.

Anthony H. Cordesman
Arleigh A. Burke Chair in Strategy
Center for Strategic and International Studies

Acknowledgments

The author would like to thank Kevin Wein, Uzma Jamil, Carolyn Mann, Daniel Berkowitz, Andrew Li, Jeffery Leary, and Jennifer Moravitz for their assistance in researching and editing this study, and John Duke Anthony, David Long, Natif Obeid, and Saint John Armitage for their comments and insights. He would also like to thank the many Saudis who made comments and suggestions that cannot be formally attributed them, as well as the officials in the U.S., British, and French governments.

Chapter 1

Introduction

Saudi Arabia enters the twenty-first century as a nation in the midst of major political, social, economic, and military transitions. External transitions include the reemergence of Iraq as a major force in Gulf security and the world oil market, with grave uncertainties over a possible U.S. and British invasion to drive Saddam Hussein from power. They include Iran's uncertain shift toward political moderation and regional cooperation, and the failure of the Southern Gulf states to develop meaningful collective security arrangements. They also include the tensions caused by the breakdown of the Arab-Israeli peace process, creeping proliferation in much of the Middle East, and the need to redefine Saudi dependence on the United States for security. At the same time, the Kingdom is part of a global economy affected by continuing uncertainties in the world energy market.

The most visible internal transitions are political. King Fahd's health continues to deteriorate, and Crown Prince Abdullah continues to take on added responsibilities as his successor. For the first time since 1982, Saudi Arabia is likely to have a king who is not one of the "al-Fahd"—who are also known as the "Sudairi Seven." Almost inevitably, these changes have focused the world's attention on how Prince Abdullah will govern, how long a man already in his seventies will rule, and how the Saudi regime will change in the future.

This fascination with the succession issue is not without cause, but the Saudi royal family has long shown that it can maintain its cohesion and resolve internal disputes. In fact, a coalition of the royal family and Saudi Arabia's technocrats has led most political and economic change in what

Map 1.1

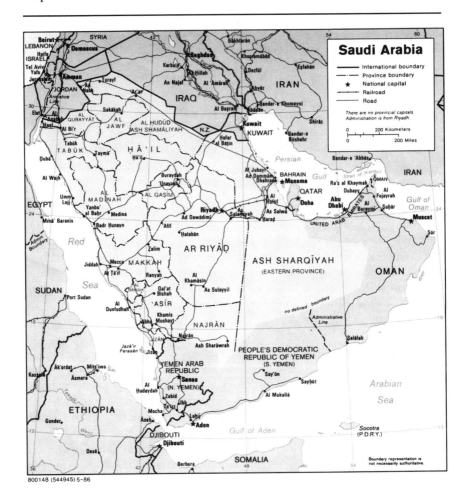

800148 (544945) 5-86

is still an intensely conservative society. The changes in the political role and importance given princes may have great internal impact within the Saudi royal family, but it is far from clear that near-term changes will have a major impact on Saudi internal politics, external relations, or social change.

In practice, it is the social, economic, and military transitions within Saudi Arabia, and not the politics of the ruling family, that are likely to have primary importance in shaping the Kingdom's future. The Saudi Arabia of the twenty-first century must deal with massive ongoing social changes, growing demographic problems, and the need to fundamentally restructure and diversify the Saudi economy. It must find new solutions to encourage foreign and domestic direct investment. It must create a far stronger private sector and one far less dependent on oil and gas exports, service industries, and imports. It must develop and implement a long-term energy structure to manage massive changes in the production and use of oil and gas and the scale and character of downstream operations.

Saudi Arabia must replace its dependence on foreign labor with jobs for Saudis, and Saudi labor and investment must become more productive and globally competitive. The Kingdom's economy must absorb a near-"explosion" of young Saudis and expand its educational system, infrastructure, and job market accordingly. At the same time, it must adapt its traditional culture, religious customs, education, and political structure to maintain its Saudi character and become a modern nation.

The problems such transitions pose should not be exaggerated. Saudi Arabia has demonstrated its resilience and adaptability in the past, and it seems to be committed to doing so in the future. Crown Prince Abdullah and the Saudi government have already set forth policies to deal with many of these changes. In fact, some of these policies are already being given tangible form through the restructuring of the Saudi government, the actions of various ministries, and the goals set as part of the Seventh Development Plan (2000–2004).

Nevertheless, the challenges the Kingdom faces are more serious than any it has seen since the days of Nasser and the period before it acquired real oil wealth. Saudi Arabia can only be successful in meeting these changes if it begins serious economic and social reforms, and then proceeds to implement them steadily over a period of decades. Such progress will impose a continuing burden on Saudi capacity for political, social, and economic change. It cannot be successfully accomplished at the traditional pace of Saudi culture, and plans and good intentions will be no substitute for effective and timely implementation. While this need for change has been broadly recognized by the senior members of the royal family, Saudi technocrats, and Saudi intellectuals, it will not come easily and will involve massive investments and substantial risks.

At the same time, Saudi Arabia will not have the luxury of being able to concentrate on internal change at the expense of external security. It must plan for the reemergence of the Iraqi threat and the uncertainty surrounding Iran's future intentions and military capabilities. It must adapt its military forces to deal with the growing threat of asymmetric warfare, the probability of the steady buildup of weapons of mass destruction and long-range delivery systems in the Northern Gulf, and less direct dependence on United States and other Western military forces. It must cope with other security problems: the backlash from the Arab-Israeli conflict, and the near-certainty that neither the Gulf Cooperation Council (GCC) nor any other form of regional security structure can provide an effective deterrence and defense against potential threats from the Northern Gulf. At least for the foreseeable future, Saudi Arabia's de facto alliance with the United States and the West can evolve, but it cannot be replaced with any substitute approaching the same degree of military capability.

OIL AND SAUDI PROGRESS

Saudi Arabia has dealt with many challenges in the past, having already coped with massive social and economic change. In 1973, before the beginning of the oil boom, Saudi Arabia was a nation of roughly 6.8 million people. It had a gross national product (GNP) of less than $10 billion in market prices, and a per capita income of less than $2,500.[1] It was largely rural or nomadic and largely preindustrial in character. Although no precise figures are available, its population growth rate was probably under 2.7%, and less than 30% of its population was under fourteen years of age.[2]

Chart 1.1 shows just how dramatically the Saudi economy and national budget were altered by the massive rise in the value of Saudi oil exports that followed the October War in 1973 and the oil embargo of 1974. At the same time, Chart 1.1 shows that other external events like the fall of the Shah of Iran in 1979, the Iran-Iraq War of 1980–1998, Iraq's invasion of Kuwait and the Gulf War in 1990–1991, and sudden swings in the world oil market since 1995 have also had major impacts on the Kingdom.

In fact, the one constant in Saudi Arabia is continuing and dramatic change. The oil boom that began in 1974 transformed Saudi Arabia into a heavily urbanized welfare state. Its economy became so different in the process that it is difficult to make direct statistical comparisons of its GNP before and after this oil boom. According to World Bank estimates, however, its GDP reached $46.8 billion in 1975 in current U.S. dollars, $86.7 billion in 1985, $125.5 billion in 1995, and $143.4 billion in 1998.[3]

No source disputes these broad trends, but there are sharp differences over the level of growth and how to estimate Saudi Arabia's GDP in purchasing power parity terms. These differences illustrate how difficult it is to make accurate estimates of any aspect of the Kingdom's economic be-

Chart 1.1
The Impact of Oil Wealth on the Saudi GDP and Government Expenditures,
1970–1999

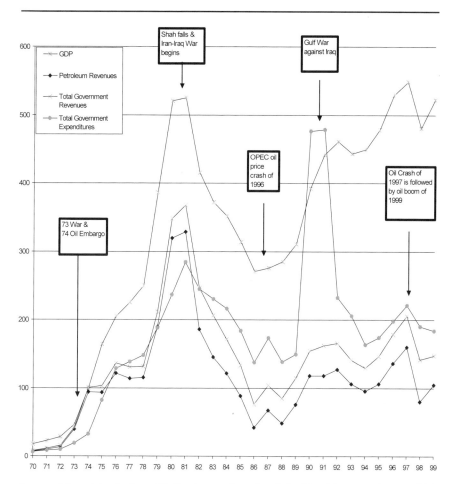

Source: Adapted by Anthony H. Cordesman from Saudi Arabian Monetary Agency, *36th Annual Report-1421H (2000G)* (Riyadh: SAMA, 2001), pp. 343–346, 360–361, 393–395. Note that the Saudi budget cycle was changed in 1990, and that the period from 1990–1991 is reported as a single year.

havior. The CIA estimated that the Kingdom's GNP was $186 billion in 1998, and that its per capita income was around $9,000.[4] The Department of Energy estimated that the GNP was $137.7 billion in 1999.[5] The U.S. Embassy in Riyadh estimates that the Saudi GDP was $130.1 billion in

1998, and $140.9 billion in 1999. In contrast, the IISS estimates that Saudi Arabia had a GDP of $133 billion in 1998.[6] These figures reflect a range of uncertainty of at least 40% for the year 1998 alone.

Population estimates show a similar pattern of radical change and uncertainty. U.S. government estimates indicate that the total population increased from 6.8 million people in 1973 to 7.3 million in 1975, 9.3 million in 1980, 13.2 million in 1985, 15.9 million in 1990, and 18.7 million in 1995.[7] The CIA estimated that Saudi Arabia became a nation of over 22 million people in 2000, but rose so quickly that it had a population of 23.5 million in 2002, including 5.36 million nonnationals.[8] The World Bank estimate that Saudi Arabia's population was 20.2 million people in 1999; the IISS estimated that it was 22 million in 2000.[9] The Saudi Plan organization estimated it at 22.31 million in 2000, including 5.7 million foreigners.

Regardless of these uncertainties, it is clear that Saudi Arabia's population increased by at least 300% between 1973 and 2000. It is also clear that Saudi population growth produced a virtual "youth explosion." Saudi Arabia's average life expectancy climbed to over seventy years of age after 1975, its population growth rate averaged well over 3.4%, and its infant mortality rate dropped sharply. As a result, the CIA estimates that roughly 42.5% of the Kingdom's population was fourteen years or younger in 2002.[10] Equally important, other estimates indicate that the native population was even younger. Some 35% of the total population of fifteen years of age or more consisted of foreign nationals. Only a token percentage of the group below that age was foreign.[11] Saudi figures provide a similar picture. Estimates of the age distribution of the total population in 1999 indicated that 40.8% were fourteen years and under. The figure for the native Saudi population, however, was 46.2%.

These trends ensure that Saudi Arabia will face major future population growth even if the birth rate should drop sharply over time. A steady increase in the number of youths entering the job market will put growing pressure on the economy's ability to employ them for most of the next two decades, and the pressures on the Saudi job market are already considerable. Saudi estimates indicate that there are 1.9 million native males and 2.1 million native females in the age group from fifteen to twenty-nine years. This is 26.8% of the population. The previous "generation," now in the age group from thirty to forty-nine, totals only 17.6% of the population.[12]

The resulting combination of economic and demographic change has already affected virtually every aspect of Saudi life. The urban population increased from less than one million in 1973 to 6.2 million in 1980, and 17.2 million in 1999. Hyperurbanization reached the point where nearly 20% of Saudi Arabia's total population was located in one city in 2000. This change alone is forcing the Kingdom to convert from a rural, tribal society to an urban-dwelling society of extended families that retains its tribal ties but is increasingly dependent on individual family units and the ability to compete in a modern economy.[13]

Between 1973 and 2000, the Saudi labor force shifted from a society in which 64% of the total worked at manual labor in agriculture to a society in which the total percentage was only 5%—and even that 5% was highly subsidized. By 2000, 40% of the labor force—almost all Saudi—worked in office jobs in government. As for the rest of the Saudi labor force, some 25% worked in industry and oil, and 30% worked in services. Little of the Saudi portion of this workforce did manufacturing or manual labor. A subsistence society with little foreign labor and that had been dependent on hard work became a welfare society dependent on foreign labor for its manual labor. Roughly 20% of all its personal income came from government grants, services, and subsidies.[14]

Many of the changes in Saudi Arabia have had positive effects. Table 1.1 provides a statistical overview of the progress in many areas of the Saudi economy, social welfare, and education. It shows that oil wealth not only lifted Saudi Arabia's native population out of a subsistence economy, but also created the infrastructure of a modern state. It allowed Saudi Arabia to spend some $1.124 trillion dollars on development between 1970 and 1995.

Saudi Arabia had 8,000 kilometers of paved roads in 1970, but 44,104 kilometers in 2001; it had 64,300 kilometers of unpaved and asphalted roads in 1974, but 102,420 in 2001.[15] The number of registered vehicles rose from 112,000 in 1974 to 5,078,000 in 1999. It had 27 wharves (berths) at its seaports in 1970, and 183 in 2000.[16] Its cargo-handling capacity rose from 3,652,000 tons to 252,500,000. It had twenty-five modern airports in 1999, including three international airports. Air passenger traffic rose from 17 to 153 million kilometers and incoming air cargo rose from 248,000 tons to 2,898,000. Rail freight tons rose from 34 million in 1970 to 822 million in 2000, and passenger kilometer miles rose from 39 million to 288 million.[17]

Saudi Arabia had 3,283 elementary schools in 1970, 21,854 in 1995, and 22,770 in 1999. Only 61% of school-age Saudi males ever entered primary school when the oil boom began, but the percentage rose to over 80% by 1990. The percentage for females rose from 39% to 48%. Literacy in the population as a whole rose from 15% to over 60% by 1995, and well over 63% by 1999. Total enrollment in Saudi schools rose from 547,000 in 1970 to roughly 2,000,000 in 1982, and 4.8 million in 2000. The number of students receiving intermediate and secondary education rose from 77,000 to 1.8 million, and the number of students receiving higher education rose from 7,000 to 387,000.[18]

A near-revolution took place in the education of women. The total number of female students in school rose from 311,000 in 1974 to 2,351,000

Table 1.1
Progress in Saudi Arabia: The Ministry of Planning Estimate—Part One (Costs in Billions of Current Saudi Riyals Unless Otherwise Stated)

	1970	1974	1979	1985	1990	1995	1999	2000
GDP in Producer's Values								
In Current Riyals	16.9	120.8	326.2	310.0	392.0	478.7	535.4	649.3
In Constant 1994 Riyals	132.8	258.7	379.2	328.0	400.0	452.7	470.5	492.6
Percentage from oil sector	46.3	57.2	46.2	18.1	29.2	32.6	30.3	31.7
Government Expenditures and Revenues								
Total Expenditures	6.1	32.0	188.3	184.0	210.4	173.9	183.8	203.0
Total Revenues	5.7	100.1	211.2	133.6	154.7	146.5	147.5	248.0
Percentage from oil sector	90.3	94.1	89.6	66.2	76.4	77.2	70.8	—
Domestic Fixed Capital Formation								
In Current Riyals	2.7	13.0	85.2	76.3	74.8	93.6	95.6	102.7
In Constant Riyals	19.2	44.7	125.4	97.2	70.7	67.9	93.4	98.0
Exports	10.9	126.2	213.2	99.5	166.3	187.4	190.1	295.9
(Petroleum, Minerals, Chemicals, Plastics)	(10.89)	(126.0)	(211.5)	(96.8)	(160.4)	(179.3)	(181.6)	(287.5)
Imports by Major Commodity Groups	3.2	10.1	81.5	85.6	90.1	105.2	105.0	113.2
Desalinized Water Output (Millions of U.S. Gallons)	4.4	11.0	31.9	355.3	437.2	440.5	492.4	491.6
Storage Capacity of Dam (Millions of Cubic Meters)	60.3	62.4	83.1	370.9	433.6	433.6	765.4	809.5

Factories in Operation								
Number of Factories	199	357	734	1,293	1,800	2,725	3,163	3,207
Total Capital (Billions of Riyals)	2.8	6.3	21.1	96.5	150.1	217.0	231.2	231.9
Manpower (in 1,000s)	14	28	75	145	183	221	292	294
Power Sold (Millions of KWh)	1,690	3,400	13,499	41,904	58,973	85,889	105,612	110,511
Production of Industrial Products								
Cement (1,000s of Tons)	667	1,057	2,648	12,599	13,696	15,773	16,313	18,293
Chemical Fertilizers (1,000s of Tons)	24	175	290	916	2,186	4,012	4,364	5,120
All Petroleum Products (millions of BBL)	225	237	304	415	557	529	581.5	602.2
Agricultural Production (1,000s of tons)								
Cereals	213	299	340	2,191	4,138	2,670	2,445	2,300
Vegetables	—	674	705	1,443	2,201	2,690	1,836	1,903
Meat	43	87	87	348	456	592	635	702
Agricultural Loans (Billions of Riyals)	0.02	0.15	1.13	2.32	1.0	0.4	0.9	1.1
Communications								
Telephones Operating (1,000s)	29	90	277	936	1,278	1,568	2,706	2,963
Mobile Telephones (1,000s)	—	—	—	—	—	160	837	1,376
Outgoing Telegrams (Millions)	1.9	4.3	6.2	3.1	1.1	1.0	0.9	—
Domestic Letters (Millions)	19	32	61	116	194	251	306	311

continued

9

Table 1.1 (Continued)
Progress in Saudi Arabia: The Ministry of Planning Estimate—Part Two (Costs in Billions of Current Saudi Riyals Unless Otherwise Stated)

	1970	1974	1979	1985	1990	1995	1997	1998	1999	2000
Number of Students (Men and Women; in 1,000s)										
Total	547	984	1,462	2,280	3,135	4,044	4,467	4,605	4,774	4,824
(Women only)	135	311	511	932	1,403	2,020	2,222	2,292	2,369	2,351
Secondary	16	42	93	172	291	452	608	672	734	756
(Women only)	2	10	29	72	132	232	309	337	368	366
Higher & Technical	8	23	70	116	154	204	300	349	377	337
(Women only)	—	3	13	41	62	87	138	174	181	198
Overseas	2	5	10	8	3	4	4	5	7	7
Number of Schools	3,283	5,634	11,070	15,093	17,038	21,854	22,301	22,678	22,770	23,435
Number of Teachers (1,000s)	23	44	78	151	209	281	325	334	355	363
Health and Medical (Ministry of Health Only)										
Number of Hospitals	47	58	67	105	163	175	180	182	186	183
Number of Health Centers	519	609	824	1,306	1,668	1,724	1737	1,751	1,756	1,766
Hospital Beds	7.195	9.070	10,978	20,796	25,835	26,737	27,054	27,428	27,794	27,854
Number of Doctors (1,000s)	0.79	1.9	3.4	9.3	13.0	15.5	15.5	14.4	14.8	15.04
Total Medical Personnel (1,000s)	4.4	8.8	13.7	40.1	57.4	70.7	69.6	71.1	73.34	74.6
Government Subsides—Dispersed	0.017	1.2	3.9	9.0	8.3	7.4	6.5	5.6	5.3	5.3
Social Security										
Regular & Emergency in Billions of Riyals	0.042	0.358	1.1	1.5	1.3	2.6	2.9	3.0	3.0	3.1
Public/Private Employees Covered (1,000s)	145	226	1,346	3,616	3,267	2,495	2,513	2,529	2,539	2,557

Pilgrims from Abroad (1,000s)	431	919	863	920	775	918	1,018	1,133	1,057	1,268
Roads and Vehicles										
Paved (1,000s of Kilometers)	8.0	9.7	18.9	32.9	38.5	42.7	44.1	45.2	45.5	45.3
Unpaved (1,000s of Kilometers)	3.5	6.8	20.1	57.5	80.4	99.0	102.3	104.4	106.3	107.9
Vehicles Registered (1,000s)	60	112	290	136.7	167.0	249.5	246.1	466.2	507.8	—
Railways										
Freight Ton Kilometers (Million)	34	192	397	733	743	1,008	1,251	923	900	822
Passenger Kilometers (Million)	39	67	89	67	151	165	208	209	267	288
Ports										
Berths	—	—	95	168	174	182	183	183	183	183
Cargo Handling Capacity in 1,000 Weight/Tons	1,837	3,652	31,1000	52,000	245,000	252,200	252,200	252,500	252,500	232,200
Airlines										
Arriving Passengers (Millions)	0.8	1.7	7.2	11.4	10.5	12.4	13.1	13.3	14.4	15.8
Incoming Cargo (1,000s of Tons)	10.3	24.8	58.8	229.8	206.8	240.3	274.0	280.4	289.5	239.8

Sources: Adapted by Anthony H. Cordesman from material provided by SAMA: and Ministry of Planning, *Kingdom of Saudi Arabia: Achievements of the Development Plans 1390–1418 (1970–1998), Facts and Figures,* 16th Issue (Riyadh: Ministry of Planning, 1999); Kingdom of Saudi Arabia, Ministry of Planning, *Achievements of the Development Plans 1970–2000, Facts and Figures* (Riyadh: Ministry of Planning, 2000), Part One (F), p. 20; and data provided to the author by Saudi officials on April 17, 2002. Additional data are available on the Web at *http://www.sama.gov.sa/kf/eachievements.htm,* but use a different statistical base of 1982, and do not allow different comparisons with the above data.

in 2000. The number of males graduating annually from secondary school rose from 2,437 in 1970 to 68,643 in 1999, while the number of female graduates rose from 369 to 98,145. Female graduates were only 15% of total graduates in 1970, but they were 143% of total graduates in 1999. The number of males graduating annually from foreign and domestic universities rose from 795 in 1970 to 21,229 in 1999, while the number of female graduates rose from 13 to 21,721—ending in a total that slightly exceeded the total of male graduates.[19] At the same time, the number of women in business rose to 25% of commercial registrations.

A similar revolution occurred in the use of modern communications. In the process, Saudi society became far more exposed to the world's media. Saudi Arabia had over six million television sets in 1999, and over 260 television sets per 1,000 people. Most educated Saudis now have satellite dishes. Over 95% of the Saudi people have exposure to radio. The number of operating telephones increased from 29,400 in 1970 to 2,965,000 million in 2000, plus 1.376 million additional cell phones.[20] Saudi Arabia has also become a major user of the Internet, and had forty-two Internet service providers in 2001.[21]

Major advances took place in medical services. During 1970–2000, Saudi Arabia more than quadrupled its number of hospitals from 74 to 318, its major hospitals from 47 to 188, and raised the number of beds from 9,039 to 27,864 (45,729 counting smaller hospitals and clinics). The number of Ministry of Health community health centers rose from 519 to 1,766. The number of doctors in the Kingdom increased from 1,172 in 1972, to 6,649 in 1982 and 32,475 in 2000—an average annual growth rate of well over 12%; nursing staff increased from 3,261 to 65,526.[22]

Water became something Saudis can—and do—waste. The Kingdom increased the output from its desalination plants from 21,500 cubic meters per day (4.4 million U.S. gallons per day) in 1970 to 2.4 million cubic meters per day (491.6 million gallons per day) in 2000—an average growth rate of 17% million gallons. It raised its electric generation capacity from 344 megawatts to more than 17,400 megawatts in 1995, and 20,647 megawatts in 1999. Electricity consumption increased by 315% during 1982–2000, and rose to 110,611 million kilowatt hours.

A slow, but steady, growth took place in the manufacturing sector. Saudi Arabia had 119 factories in 1970; 2,303 in 1995, with an invested capital of $40.7 billion; and 3,163 in 1999, with an invested capital of $85.7 billion. The total was 3,381 in 2000, with an invested capital of 239 billion riyals.[23]

The oil boom changed Saudi Arabia's strategic position as well. Saudi Arabia became one of the largest and most powerful states in the Gulf, and a key supplier of world oil imports. In 2000, the Kingdom had 260 billion barrels of proven oil reserves, more than one-fourth of the world's total. It was the world's largest oil producer, with an average output of 7.5 million barrels of oil (MMBD) per day, and a total production capacity of 10.2 to 11.4 MMBD.[24] This surplus capacity made Saudi Arabia the world's largest "swing" producer, and its ability to increase production to meet a crisis means that it plays a critical role in ensuring moderate and stable oil prices.

Saudi Arabia became the only Southern Gulf power able to develop military forces strong enough to play a major role in defending itself against Iran and Iraq and capable of playing a significant role in military action in the Red Sea area. As it showed during the Gulf War, Saudi Arabia was the Southern Gulf power with enough air power and armor to play a major war-fighting role in a U.S.-led coalition; its development of advanced air bases, ports, and facilities made it critical to any Western effort to project military power into the Gulf.

HISTORICAL ORIGINS

Saudi Arabia faces foreign as well as domestic challenges, and the political and religious character of Saudi history will do much to determine how well it can meet this mix of challenges. Although it is impossible to do justice to the Kingdom's past in an analysis focused on its future, at least some introductory analysis is necessary to provide the proper perspective to those who are not familiar with the Kingdom's history.

Arabia played only a relatively limited role in history before the rise of Islam. However, the civilizations of the Gulf and the Arabian Peninsula date back for several millennia. The recorded history of the region traces its origins to the ancient culture of Dilmun, a major trading link between Mesopotamia and the Indus River valley, and to Arabia Felix, a confederation of states in southern Arabia that formed a network of trade routes between India and Africa. Caravan routes between Arabia Felix and Egypt created trading cities in the Hijaz region, of which the most prominent were Mecca and Medina.[25]

It was the rise of Islam in the Arabian Peninsula, however, that played the most important role in shaping the character of modern-day Saudi Arabia. In A.D. 570, the Prophet Muhammad was born in Mecca. By the time of the Prophet's death in 632, most of the Arabian Peninsula had become united under Arab rule, with Mecca and Medina as important centers of Islam. The unity of Islam in Arabia dissolved in later centuries, however, and Arabia became the scene of shifting power struggles between various tribes and families. Even under the nominal suzerainty of the Ottoman Empire that began in the sixteenth century, the Arabian Peninsula remained a largely undeveloped tribal battleground.

It was the Saud family that began to bring unity to Arabia in modern times, and there have been three Saudi states up to the present. An alliance between a spiritual reformer, Muhammad ibn Abd al-Wahhab, and a political leader and warrior, Muhammad ibn Saud, laid the foundation for the first Saudi state in 1744. Al-Wahhab was born in 1703 into a prominent intellectual family in 'Uyayna—a small oasis in the province of Najd—and showed remarkable intellectual prowess at an early age. He traveled widely about the peninsula during his studies but returned to 'Uyayna in 1744 and began preaching against the lax behavior of the townspeople and their disregard for Islamic law. He was quickly expelled from the town and sought refuge in the nearby town of Dar'iya, where he was invited to stay by the local emir, Muhammad ibn Saud.

Al-Wahhab preached a return to the strict, puritanical practices of Islam in the time of Muhammad. His revival movement, later known as in the West as Wahhabism, was based on the Islamic doctrine of *tawhid* (strict monotheism) and condemned several local practices, including the veneration of holy men and the visitation of their tombs, as polytheistic practices and desecrations to the sovereignty of God. The movement also drew inspiration from the writings of Ibn Taymiyya, an early reformer from the Hanbali School of Islamic law.[26] The Hanbali School is the most conservative of the four recognized law schools with regard to personal law.

The alliance that arose between al-Wahhab and the Saud clan set the stage for the rise of the first Saudi state. Strengthened by the military and political leadership of the Sauds, the Wahhabi movement quickly attracted converts, many of whom were desert warriors. Under the banner of Wahhabism, they began to convert the neighboring Najdi tribes and transform the traditional Bedouin warfare into a holy crusade. By the time of Muhammad ibn Saud's death in 1765, most of the Najd was under the control of the Sauds. Under Emir Muhammad's son and grandson, the domains were expanded to include most of the Arabian Peninsula and by 1801, included parts of Iraq and Syria. By 1806, the Sauds had taken over the Hijaz, including Mecca and Medina. Thus, the first Saudi state was at its peak in the early 1800s.

These developments brought the Sauds into conflict with the Turks. In response to the expansion of the Wahhabi movement, the loss of control over Islam's holy places, and the resulting decline in tribute, the Ottoman Empire sent an army to Arabia under Muhammad Ali Pasha of Egypt. Muhammad Ali dispatched an army under his son Tusun in 1811. His first offensive retook the cities of Mecca and Medina, but was not able to subjugate the Sauds. In 1816, Muhammad Ali sent his second son, Ibrahim Pasha, to invade the Najd. In 1818, Ibrahim Pasha entered Dar'iya. The city was totally destroyed by Ibrahim's forces and the first Saudi state was crushed.

The Wahhabi forces had also gradually expanded into what is present-day Oman, forced the sultan to pay tribute, attacked shipping in the waters of the Southern Gulf. The Turkish victories in 1816 forced the Sauds to withdraw from Oman and the Gulf coast. In December 1819, as part of an attempt to fight piracy, a large British naval and land force took control of the town of Ras al-Khaymah, a stronghold of local Wahhabis; a General Treaty of Peace followed a month later. This led to the creation of a network of treaties with the coastal cities in the Southern Gulf that eventually created the Trucial State and gave Britain hegemony in the area.[27]

The birth, rise, and fall of the second Saudi state followed a pattern similar to the first. In 1824, Turki bin Abdullah assembled a garrison and drove the Egyptian forces from Dar'iya. He established himself in Riyadh and assumed the Emirship of the Najd.[28] In 1834, Turki was assassinated and his place assumed by his son, Faisal. In 1838 the Egyptians again invaded Najd and installed a puppet government under the leadership of Khalid bin Saud. In 1843, Faisal returned, restored order to Najd, and expanded his domains north to the Jabal Shammar and south to the borders of Oman. Faisal's death in 1865, however, was followed by a period of violent interfamily struggle, during which the state again began to collapse. In 1871, the Ottomans invaded Al-Hasa to the east, Oman and the Trucial States freed themselves from Saudi control, and the Jabal Shammar revolted. The Saudi lands fell largely under the control of a rival family from the north, the Rashids. Unable to escape Rashidi hegemony, the Saudi ruling family escaped to Kuwait in 1891, and the second Saudi state thus came to a close.

The modern Kingdom of Saudi Arabia traces its roots to the return of Abd al-Aziz al-Saud from exile and his subsequent founding of the third, and present, Saudi state. In 1902, Abd al-Aziz al-Saud (also known as Ibn Saud) attacked Riyadh with a small band of followers. He was able to seize the main fortress in the town and attract a large number of new followers, and gradually regained power over the region. In the process, he launched another Wahhabi revival. In late 1911 and early 1912, he inaugurated a fanatical force of Islamic warriors—the Ikhwan—which numbered in the thousands and whom he placed in settlements in the Najdi oases. By 1912, Ibn Saud had expelled the Rashids from the region and become the ruler of the Najd and central Arabia. By the start of World War I, Ibn Saud also controlled Qatif and the Al-Hasa coast, although the Hijaz and western Arabia still acknowledged Ottoman rule.

The West initially paid little attention to these developments, but World War I forced the British to become interested in countering German influence in the eastern Arab provinces of the Ottoman Empire. The British were primarily concerned with reducing the Turkish threat to the Suez Canal and driving the Turks out of the Levant. As a result, they sponsored an Arab uprising in the Hijaz in western Arabia. The British promised Hussein bin Ali, the Hashemite Sharif of Mecca, support for Arab independence if he would incite his people to revolt against the Turks, which led to a broad Arab revolt against the Turks in 1916. Hussein bin Ali proclaimed independence, declared war on the Ottoman Empire, and claimed the title of "King of the Arab Lands" in November 1916. Two months later, Britain, France, and Italy recognized him as "King of the Hijaz." The British, however, also provided some money and arms to the Sauds. In 1915, Abd al-Aziz met with Sir Percy Cox, the British Resident in the Gulf, who formally recognized Ibn Saud as Sultan of Najd and Al-Hasa and gave him a lump sum of £2,000 and 1,000 rifles.

The division of much of Arabia between Saud and Hashemite rule led to a growing rivalry between Abd al-Aziz and Hussein after World War I. This rivalry turned into a war when Hussein proclaimed himself the caliph of Islam in 1924. Abd al-Aziz invaded the Hijaz, forcing Hussein to abdicate, and conquered Mecca and Jeddah in 1926. In 1927, the British recognized Ibn Saud as King of the Hijaz and Sultan of the Najd and its Dependencies, and in 1930, Abd al-Aziz expanded his rule to include much of western and southeastern Arabia. On September 23, 1932, Abd al-Aziz al-Saud created Saudi Arabia in its modern form and decreed that his country should be known as the Kingdom of Saudi Arabia.[29]

Since that time, there have been five kings in Saudi Arabia: Abd al-Aziz, and then his four sons, Saud, Faisal, Khalid, and the present ruler, King Fahd. King Saud came close to creating a new threat to the Kingdom's existence at the time when Nasser and Pan Arabism seemed likely to dominate the Arab world. When Abd al-Aziz died in 1953, his eldest son, Saud, succeeded him and reigned for eleven years. King Saud's rule was well-intended but he seriously mismanaged the country's political and financial affairs. His unchecked spending on luxury items and lack of financial planning depleted the nation's coffers, and helped strengthen the pro-Nasser movement.

Saud's erratic foreign policy led the Kingdom into growing tension with Nasser at a time when civil war in Northern Yemen had brought Egyptian forces into the Arabian Peninsula. This, and Saud's mismanagement of the Saudi budget, led to a long struggle between King Saud and his half-brother, Crown Prince Faisal bin Turki bin Abdulaziz. Faisal's conservative attitude towards politics and the budget were a strong contrast to Saud's profligate spending.

In 1958, Saud's inability to manage the Kingdom's financial and political affairs led the royal family to take action. A meeting of a powerful and secretive body of senior princes known as the *ahl-aqd wal hal*, "those who tie and untie," forced King Saud to delegate direct conduct of Saudi government affairs to Prince Faisal and make him prime minister.[30] Faisal took control of the Kingdom's foreign and internal affairs, initiated an austerity program in 1959, balanced the budget, stabilized the currency, and reduced the national debt.

The reductions Faisal made to the royal household budget led King Saud to fight back. He regained control of the government in 1961, and Faisal and his Council of Ministers tendered their resignations. King Saud attempted to organize the country's affairs by appointing a new cabinet of progressive, Western-educated commoners, but he could not win the support of the royal family and Saudi Arabia's ruling elite or bring the budget under control.

In March 1962, Faisal returned to office as prime minister in all but name. By October 1962, his status was confirmed, and Saud was publicly said to be in "ill health." Faisal began many new projects, including the establishment of local government and the formation of an independent judiciary with a supreme council composed of both modernist and traditionalist members. In 1964, senior royal family members and religious leaders proclaimed Faisal king, and Saud left the country for Greece, where he died in exile in 1969.[31]

King Faisal proved to be a highly competent ruler and dealt effectively with a series of foreign policy crises. These included the Six-Day (Arab-Israeli) War of June 1967; the Yemeni Civil War, which became a proxy war between Saudi Arabia and Egypt; and the 1973 Arab-Israeli War. It was Faisal who organized the Arab oil boycott that followed the 1973 war, and it was this "oil embargo" that led to a sudden massive increase in oil prices, Saudi oil wealth, and Saudi political influence.

Faisal also chose a middle ground between religious conservatism and modernization. He attempted to preserve the Kingdom's religious character and to mitigate the adverse effects of modernization. Although Faisal felt some aspects of foreign influence were undesirable, he realized that Saudi Arabia had to modernize many aspects of its economy and society. He spent the Kingdom's growing oil revenues on social welfare and investments designed to stimulate growth. He also began massive education programs and introduced Western technology at a careful pace.

A mentally ill nephew assassinated King Faisal in 1975, but the royal family dealt with the succession smoothly. It quickly appointed Faisal's half-brother Khalid as king and prime minister. Khalid's brother Fahd was appointed as crown prince and first deputy prime minister, with the understanding that the next in line for this position would be the traditionalist Prince Abdullah, one of Prince Fahd's half-brothers by a different mother.[32]

Khalid did not possess Faisal's sophistication. He had been educated in the palace and could not converse in English. His visits outside the country had been limited to state visits or trips to the United States for medical care. Nevertheless, his leadership proved to be effective. He was more liberal in terms of informing the press of the rationale behind foreign-policy decisions and allowed his policymakers more latitude in decision making within their separate areas of specialty.

King Khalid also empowered Crown Prince Fahd to oversee many aspects of the government's international and domestic affairs. He presided over the continuation of Saudi Arabia's rapid economic development, and the Kingdom maintained an influential role in both regional political and international economic and financial matters. Otherwise, there was little basic change in government policies and programs from the course set under Faisal's reign.

King Khalid died in June 1982, and Fahd assumed the throne. Prince Abdullah, the commander of the National Guard, was named crown prince and first deputy prime minister, and Prince Sultan bin Abdulaziz was named second deputy premier and second in the line of succession. King Fahd accelerated some aspects of Saudi Arabia's modernization and gave the expansion of Saudi military forces a higher priority. He also took a more flexible stand on Israel and supported the Arab-Israeli peace process. In broad terms, however, he followed the same path that Khalid and Faisal maintained for running the country. He continued to maintain friendly relations with the United States, as illustrated by American involvement in the Gulf War.

Since the mid-1990s, Crown Prince Abdullah has played a major role in ruling the Kingdom because King Fahd has often been weakened or incapacitated by his physical condition. In 1996, Fahd suffered a major stroke, and Abdullah was named regent for seven weeks while Fahd recovered. Abdullah was also de facto ruler for ten weeks in 1999, when King Fahd went to Spain for a vacation.[33] While Prince Abdullah is a traditional Saudi leader in many ways, he has actively faced Saudi Arabia's current political and economic challenges. He has developed an extensive reform program, and has indicated that further changes need to occur in the near future. Some of these changes include the addition of technocrats and nonroyal ministers to the cabinet and a program of economic liberalization that will allow the country to fulfill requirements to membership in the WTO.[34]

Although such a capsule history cannot do real justice to the Kingdom—and the following chapter provides extensive additional details on the Kingdom's history in specific areas—it does make several important points. The history of Saud rule is considerably longer than many outsiders realize, and its religious underpinnings are sincere and longstanding. The Saudi royal family has dealt with many crises, and proved flexible in doing so. It has outlasted Pan Arabism, Arab Socialism, and serious internal struggles. Moreover, it has usually led to Saudi Arabia's modernization rather than resisted it. While the Western stereotype of Gulf monarchies is often one of conservative and selfish rule challenged by a progressive intellectual elite tied to the people, the reality in Saudi Arabia has been that it is a coalition of the Saud family, moderate clerics, and technocrats that have pushed for evolutionary change. If the result has not moved forward as quickly as some Saudi intellectuals and businessmen would like, it has generally moved faster than the majority of the clergy and large numbers of Saudi traditionalists have desired.

THE POLITICAL AND FOREIGN POLICY CHALLENGES OF THE TWENTY-FIRST CENTURY

Even though Saudi Arabia has a long history of evolutionary change and adaptation, and seems to be making a smooth transition to a new king, the twenty-first century presents the Kingdom with serious challenges. It must deal with a wide range of potential foreign threats and foreign policy problems, and with a small, violent Islamic extremist minority that commits acts of foreign and domestic terrorism. It must find ways to adapt its dominant Wahhabi faith to economic and social change. Saudi Arabia is rapidly approaching a generational change in leadership, not only in age but also in terms of background and experience. As David Long states, "It will mean the assumption of power by a new generation with a totally different outlook—a generation that is Western-educated, has nearly always known affluence, and has never had to toil just to survive."[35]

The political and economic changes needed to move Saudi Arabia into the twenty-first century with stability and security will require that future rulers make difficult decisions about the nature and role of the Saudi state. It remains to be seen whether the younger generation possesses such resolve. The next generation of leaders will have to walk the same fine line between tradition and modernity as their predecessors. Although the Kingdom has formed several fledgling institutions for wider political participation and expression, leadership must ensure that these institutions grow into useful, effective bodies at a pace that the country can tolerate.

The change from a closed political system to one of greater representation and participation cannot and should not happen too quickly, lest the stability of the nation be jeopardized. The creation of stable political parties, improving the rule of law, and the expanded protection of human rights have at least the same priority as "democratization" per se. However, it is more likely that the country's traditional and Islamic forces will delay the necessary pace of change, rather than let it happen too rapidly. The real challenges to the royal family and Saudi Arabia's leadership elite is to ensure that these same forces do not prevent change from occurring at the pace necessary to meet Saudi Arabia's social, demographic, and economic needs.

As has been touched on earlier, the key to Saudi Arabia's political success will not be "democratization" or establishing political "legitimacy" in the Western sense. Rather, it will be transforming Saudi Arabia from a largely patriarchical welfare economy, dependent on oil wealth and foreign labor, to a diversified, largely private economy, in which its citizens do the work and take a major role in shaping the nation's future. Saudi Arabia must move beyond its former reliance on petroleum, service-based economy, and subsidized welfare state, and attempt to curb the excessive spending and extravagances of the royal family and its wealthier citizens. Meeting these challenges will involve both changing Saudi customs and traditions and changing a welfare-driven social contract that has now existed for decades. It will encounter internal opposition, but giving the Saudi people a more direct means of expressing their grievances and problems can help win their support during these changes. Instant democracy is far more likely to divide the country and paralyze change than serve the nation's need.

THE COMING DOMESTIC CHALLENGES

In spite of its past accomplishments, Saudi Arabia faces other challenges that will be difficult to meet. Saudi Arabia must deal with the social and economic impacts of its explosive population growth at a time when much of its oil wealth has diminished in relative terms. Saudi Arabia must shape an energy strategy that will maintain its position as the world's preeminent oil exporter while developing its gas resources and diversifying its economy.

The same wealth that transformed other aspects of Saudi society helped raise the average population growth rate to 4.0% during 1980–1999, and it averaged 4.4% during 1990–1998. Saudi experts initially estimated that this growth rate declined to an average of 3.3% during 1995–2000, although some estimates indicate that it was still 3.8%.[36] The Saudi Ministry of Planning projects that the Saudi birth rate will drop to 2.6% by 2005, but there is little evidence as yet that this decrease will occur. The World Bank forecasts that Saudi Arabia's population will grow by about 2.9% per year during 1999–2015. Even this rate, however, would mean a total Saudi population of 32.1 million people in 2015, and 46 million in 2030.

A combination of explosive population growth and slow real growth is creating a Saudi economy that needs massive restructuring to absorb increasing numbers of young Saudis entering the labor market.[37] Since the early 1980s, Saudi Arabia's oil wealth has declined in both absolute and per capita terms. Saudi Arabia's population has grown explosively while oil prices have remained nearly constant. The World Bank estimates that Saudi Arabia's population rose from roughly 9.4 million in 1980 to 19 million in 1999—an increase of 104%. In contrast, the World Bank estimates that Saudi Arabia's GDP dropped from $156.5 billion in 1980, in current dollars, to $125.5 billion in 1995. This is a drop of nearly 20% in current dollars and well over 35% in constant dollars. U.S. estimates are similar, but the World Bank estimates that the Saudi GNP dropped by over 35% during the same period.[38]

The Kingdom has failed to create Saudi jobs and to adequately diversify its economy. The U.S. Energy Information Agency (EIA) estimated that oil revenues still made up 90% to 95% of Saudi Arabia's total export earnings, 80% of its state revenues, and 40% of its gross domestic product in 2001.[39] This dependence on the petroleum sector makes it extremely difficult for Saudi Arabia to manage its economy and development because of the major swings that take place in oil prices and revenues. For example, Saudi oil revenues rose from $19.3 billion in 1972, in constant 2000 dollars, to $223.2 billion in 1980, then dropped to $31.2 billion in 1986. The boom and bust cycle in world oil prices increased Saudi oil income to $58.2 billion in 2001 in current dollars. This total was nearly double the $29.4 billion oil revenues in 1998, and a 52% rise from its revenues of $38.3 billion in 1999, but was over one-third of Saudi Arabia's peak earnings in 1980 in constant dollars.[40]

Many of the Kingdom's earnings from its petroleum product and downstream operations have been offset by the high investment costs for facilities and by the concealed cost of the subsidized diversion of crude oil and gas to feedstock. For example, Saudi gas is sold at prices that are only 54% to 60% of the market price of gas in other Gulf countries. Domestic energy use has been wasteful, and much of Saudi Arabia's GDP now consists of service industries whose only real function is to increase and meet the demand for imports. Trade is virtually all in petroleum-related exports and in imports financed by these exports.[41] Trade makes up nearly 50% of the Saudi GDP today, but less than one percent of Saudi exports are manufactured.

While estimates differ, virtually all outside analysts agree that Saudi Arabia's per capita income has declined to around 40% of its peak at the height of the oil boom, and has been static or declining for most of the last decade. The World Bank estimates that Saudi Arabia's per capita income dropped by an annual average of 2.9% during 1970–1995, and by a total of nearly 20% during 1985–1995. During the same period, however, Saudi Arabian private consumption rose from $34.5 billion to $52.0 billion. This growth in consumption reflected both the impact of population growth and an increasing social dependence on imports and services. Private consumption rose from 22% of the GDP in 1980 to 41% in 1998, while government consumption rose from 16% to 32%. At the same time, gross domestic investment during that period dropped slightly from 22% to 21%, and gross domestic savings dropped precipitously from 62% of GDP to 26%.[42]

Saudi Arabia also faces serious social challenges as a result of its rapid social and economic evolution. These challenges range from the need to modernize religious practices and the legal system to the "culture shock" resulting from placing a highly traditional society in continuing contact with a secular West. The most serious of these challenges, however, is to create a meaningful future for Saudi youth.

In spite of the massive increase in literacy and the number of students educated, most of Saudi Arabia's young population is not yet properly educated to compete in the modern world economy, and nearly half of its labor force is foreign. While over 85% of young Saudi males and females reached grade four in 1997, only 5% of males and 2% of females moved on to secondary school. Much of Saudi education lacks focus on training students for real-world jobs and contains a disproportionate amount of religious teaching. Vocational training increased from 578 students in 1970 to 12,287 in 1999, but this is a token increase in terms of the total labor force; less than half of these students graduated. Students in technical schools increased from 840 to 33,800 during 1970–1999, but the number of annual graduates totaled less than 6,000.[43]

Recent increases in education spending have done far too little to change the character and quality of Saudi education, much of which is unfocused, religious in character, reliant on rote learning without instruction in problem solving and creative reasoning, provided by low-quality teachers, and lacking in standards that ensure a proper level of teacher quality and student performance. As a result, Saudi youth will have very uncertain prospects of finding real, productive employment unless Saudi Arabia radically restructures its educational system and economy. The Kingdom must shift from an inadequate and traditional education style to one capable of supporting a knowledge-based economy if Saudi youth is to be able to compete in global terms and support a diversified economy, and it cannot do this simply by replacing or supplementing bad foreign teachers with underqualified native Saudi teachers.

The Saudi labor force is seriously distorted by disguised unemployment in a swollen state sector and by overdependence on foreign labor. Government employment has increased to the point where it consumes 40% of Saudi Arabia's labor force and more than half of its native labor force. The Saudi government costs over $50 billion a year and government spending accounts for 36% of GDP. The spending leads to excessive dependence on welfare and has created far too many meaningless government and government-related jobs. This, combined with reliance on foreign labor, has left native Saudi youth without jobs and a work ethic, while declining per capita oil revenues mean the Kingdom cannot hope to sustain its past pattern of disguised unemployment and subsidies.

Saudi Arabia also faces major labor productivity problems because of the social constraints on the role of women. Although female workers rose from 3% of the labor force in 1980 to 7% in 1999, these percentages are lower than in most other Gulf states and far lower than the percentages of female labor in most of the developing world.[44] Saudi Arabia must reduce unproductive employment in government jobs and restructure its economy to deal with declining per capita oil wealth and the need to rely on native, rather than foreign, labor. It must transform its society to compete in a world where oil wealth alone is not enough to keep its per capita income from dropping steadily lower, and do so without losing its Islamic and Arab character.

Increasing domestic capital formation and encouraging foreign and domestic private investment will be another challenge. During the coming decades, Saudi Arabia not only must invest to create a large diverse private sector, but it must make massive new investments to maintain its status as a petroleum power. It must make equally massive investments in the national infrastructure to support its rapidly growing population. These investments almost certainly will cost in excess of one-third of a trillion dollars and this may be a greater sum than the Kingdom can self-finance, even if it shifts from dependence on state investment to dependence on private financing.[45]

Saudi Arabia may be able to meet this mix of internal challenges, but the task will not be easy. Restructuring Saudi society and the economy present the most serious challenges of all, and change must come at a time when Islamic extremism is a serious concern and Saudi Arabia's oil income is not sufficient to meet its social and economic needs. While Western critics may call for "democratization," Saudi Arabia's real needs are to match educational and social reform with economic reform. At present, Saudi society is too conservative, welfare-oriented, and lacking in political experience and modern economic institutions for "democratization" to push the Kingdom in the right direction or meet its social needs. More representative and pluralistic institutions must come, and steady, gradual progress is important. The Kingdom's other needs, however, are far more urgent.

Saudi Arabia must simultaneously deal with major strategic challenges. The Kingdom faces very real external threats from Iran and Iraq, and its military forces are not strong enough to defend itself from Iran and Iraq without U.S. military aid. Saudi Arabia also faces a growing threat from Iraqi and Iranian proliferation and the risk that the use of weapons of mass destruction may shape a future major conflict in the Gulf. It has not been able to catalyze effective collective security efforts within the GCC. Although Saudi Arabia has made a serious effort to improve its relations with Kuwait, Oman, and Yemen, change comes slowly in the Gulf and tensions still exist with other Gulf states.

In the past, Saudi Arabia has met these external challenges by maintaining a strategic partnership with the United States and other Western countries. However, Saudi Arabia's strategic partnership with the West involves inevitable differences in national interest and culture. Its partnership with the United States presents a problem: the United States is not an Islamic power and many in the Kingdom resent any form of U.S. military presence in a nation with Islam's holiest shrine. The rise of the Second Intifada has made these challenges much worse because the United States is Israel's closest ally and there is little immediate prospect of a full Arab-Israeli peace. The Saudi alliance with the United States also presents problems in burden sharing, counterterrorism, and prepositioning, and in defining a stable and equitable division of effort.

THE ECONOMIC AND DEMOGRAPHIC CHALLENGES OF THE TWENTY-FIRST CENTURY

Saudi Arabia will remain a massive oil power for the foreseeable future. It has vast oil reserves—261 billion barrels of proven oil reserves, not including the Saudi-Kuwaiti "Neutral Zone" (more than one-fourth of the world total) and up to one trillion barrels of ultimately recoverable oil. As Chart 1.2 shows, Saudi Arabia is almost certain to make major further increases in its oil production capacity over the coming years, and in its oil export income. Nevertheless, Saudi Arabia still can only meet its people's needs if it restructures its economy and cuts its population growth and dependence on foreign labor.

Saudi Arabia's oil revenues and strategic importance are virtually certain to increase with time. While oil company projections are usually more conservative, estimates by the Department of Energy (DOE) indicate that Saudi oil production capacity will rise from 8.6 MMBD in 1990, 10.6 MMBD in 1995, and 11.4 MMBD in 1998, to a capacity of 12.5 MMBD in 2005, 14.6 MMBD in 2010, 18.2 MMBD in 2015, and 22.1 MMBD in 2020. This is a cumulative rise of 11.5 MMBD, or 108% between 1995 and 2020. U.S. estimates indicate that Saudi Arabia will account for nearly half of the total 21.2 MMBD increase in Gulf oil production the DOE projects for the period between 2000 and 2020. The DOE estimates that Gulf oil exports must rise from 6.0 MMBD to 24.7 MMBD, and will total over 80% of all worldwide petroleum trade by 2020.[46]

Oil, however, can be a curse as well as a blessing. Saudi Arabia is now so dependent on a petroleum-based economy that it is sharply vulnerable to changes in the world oil market.[47] The Kingdom relies on oil revenues for around 90% of its total export earnings, about 70% of state revenues, and 40% of its GDP. The massive swings in annual oil revenues shown in Chart 1.3—worse than those in the total for OPEC—illustrate the risks this dependence on oil revenues has created in a nation whose budget revenues depend almost solely on the income from its petroleum sector.

"Oil Crash" and "Oil Boom" in 1996–2001: A Case Study

The sudden shift to oil crash and oil boom that took place between 1996 and 2001 illustrates just how serious the impact of these swings can be. Chart 1.3 shows that the value of Saudi oil and petroleum-related exports suddenly dropped from $45.5 to $54.7 billion in 1997 in current dollars to $29.4 to $34.2 billion in 1998, rose back to $38.3 to $43.9 billion in 1999, leaped to $66 to $75.3 billion in 2000, and then dropped to $58.2 to $63.1 billion in 2001.[48]

Chart 1.2

The "Swing State": Saudi Petroleum Production Capacity Relative to Gulf and World Capacity During 1973–2020 (EIA Reference Case in MMBD)

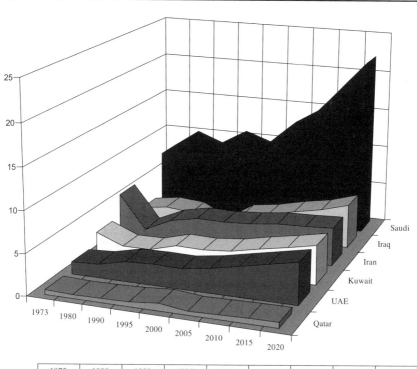

	1973	1980	1990	1995	2000	2005	2010	2015	2020
Qatar	0.57	0.472	0.5	0.6	0.9	0.5	0.6	0.7	0.7
UAE	1.533	1.709	2.5	2.6	2.5	3	3.7	4.4	5.1
Kuwait	3.02	1.656	1.7	2.6	2.5	2.8	3.5	4.1	4.8
Iran	5.8	1.662	3.2	3.9	3.8	4	4.4	4.5	4.7
Iraq	2.018	2.514	2.2	0.6	2.6	3.1	3.9	4.5	5.5
Saudi	7.596	9.9	8.6	10.6	9.4	12.5	14.6	18.2	22.1

Total Gulf	—	18.7	—	21.7	25.9	30.7	36.4	42.9	
Saudi Arabia as % of Total	—	45.95	—	43.35	48.2	47.6	50.0	51.53	
Total OPEC	—	27.2	—	31.4	38.4	44.8	52.0	60.2	
Total World	—	69.4	—	77.4	88.0	98.4	109.8	121.3	
Saudi Arabia as % of Total	—	12.4	—	12.1	14.25	14.8	16.6	18.21	

Sources: Adapted by Anthony H. Cordesman from EIA, *International Energy Outlook, 1997* (Washington, DC: DOE/EIA-0484 [97], April 1997), pp. 157–160, and EIA, *International Energy Outlook, 2002* (Washington, DC: DOE/EIA-0484 [2002], March 2002), Table D1.

Chart 1.3
Swings in Saudi Oil Export Revenues (in $U.S. Current and 2000 Constant Billions)

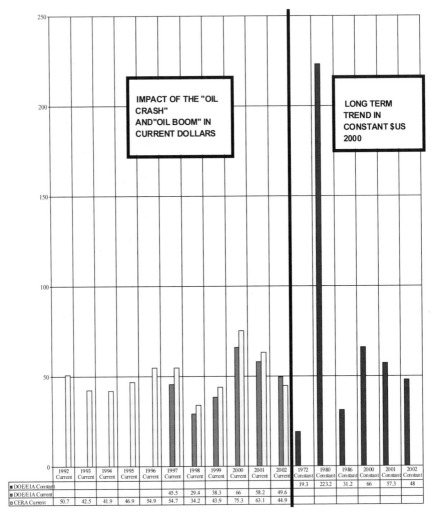

	1992 Current	1993 Current	1994 Current	1995 Current	1996 Current	1997 Current	1998 Current	1999 Current	2000 Current	2001 Current	2002 Current	1972 Constant	1980 Constant	1986 Constant	2000 Constant	2001 Constant	2002 Constant
■ DOE/EIA Constant												19.3	223.2	31.2	66	57.3	48
■ DOE/EIA Current						45.5	29.4	38.3	66	58.2	49.6						
□ CERA Current	50.7	42.5	41.9	46.9	54.9	54.7	34.2	43.9	75.3	63.1	44.9						

Note: EIA data are for crude oil exports. CERA data are for total petroleum exports.
Sources: Adapted by Anthony H. Cordesman from data provided by the EIA as of March
2001 and December 2001 (*www.eia.gov/emeu/cabs/opecrev2.html*) and in Cambridge
Energy Research Associates, "OPEC Tilts to Market Share," *World Oil Watch* (Winter
2002), p. 28.

Chart 1.4
Pressures on the Saudi Budget: The Impact of the Recent "Oil Crash" and "Oil Boom" (in Billions of Saudi Riyals)

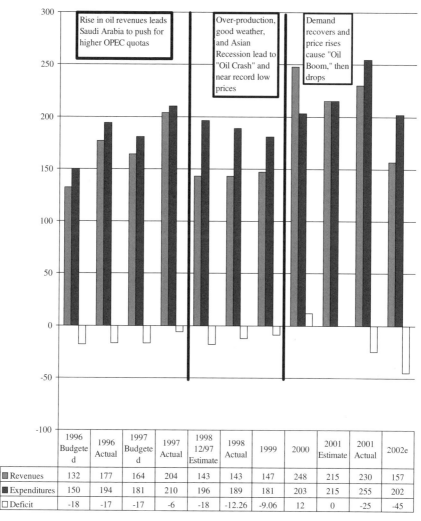

	1996 Budgeted	1996 Actual	1997 Budgeted	1997 Actual	1998 12/97 Estimate	1998 Actual	1999	2000	2001 Estimate	2001 Actual	2002e
Revenues	132	177	164	204	143	143	147	248	215	230	157
Expenditures	150	194	181	210	196	189	181	203	215	255	202
Deficit	-18	-17	-17	-6	-18	-12.26	-9.06	12	0	-25	-45

Text within chart:
- Rise in oil revenues leads Saudi Arabia to push for higher OPEC quotas
- Over-production, good weather, and Asian Recession lead to "Oil Crash" and near record low prices
- Demand recovers and price rises cause "Oil Boom," then drops

Sources: Adapted by Anthony H. Cordesman from *US–Saudi Business Brief* (Winter 1998), p. 1; Reuters, December 28, 1998, 1728; data provided by the Saudi Information Office in Washington, D.C., in March 2001; and Brad Bourland, *The Saudi Economy in 2002* (Riyadh: Saudi American Bank, February 2002), p. 10.

These swings occurred because good weather and an Asian financial crisis had triggered an oil crash that began in 1997. From January 1998 through March 1999, the price of Saudi oil averaged between $9 and $13 per barrel, down sharply from late 1997, and the lowest in inflation-adjusted terms for any sustained period of time since 1973. This decline in oil prices came just as the Saudi economy appeared to be recovering from the adverse impacts of the Gulf War of 1990–1991, and seriously hurt Saudi Arabia's economic and financial situation and ability to invest in infrastructure and petroleum development and facilities.[49] It cut total Saudi oil export revenues from $45.5 to $54.7 billion in 1997, in current U.S. dollars, to only $29.4 to $34.2 billion in 1998. As stated earlier, prices stayed low through most of 1999, limiting oil revenues to $38.3 to $43.9 billion.[50]

The Saudi GDP only had a nominal growth of 0.4% in 1999.[51] Chart 1.4 shows that Saudi Arabia had to adopt an austerity budget for 1999 that included spending cuts of almost 16%, and do so without any new taxes or other measure to increase revenues. Low oil prices forced Saudi Aramco—the state oil and gas company, whose expenditures account for around 6% of Saudi GDP—to reassess its capital expenditure program, delay a series of upstream and refining projects (at an estimated savings of $2 billion in 1998), and defer bidding on the $150 to $200 million Haradh (phase 2) crude oil production increment project. In October 1998, a planned $800 million upgrade of the Rabigh oil refinery was cancelled, leaving Saudi Arabia with only one major energy project under bidding— the $2 billion Hawiya natural gas processing plant (part of an ambitious expansion plan for the Saudi Master Gas System).[52]

In December 1999, Saudi Arabia issued a budget for 2000 that called for only a 2% increase in government spending and that was based on conservative assumptions about oil revenues. In early January 2000 Saudi Arabia announced the creation of an eleven-member Supreme Council for Petroleum and Minerals Affairs to help oversee the restructuring of its economy and accelerate private sector involvement in the country's energy sector.[53]

Ironically the "manic depressive" cycles in the oil market unexpectedly improved Saudi Arabia's situation strikingly after early 1999. Saudi oil prices increased sharply following OPEC's March 23, 1999, cutback agreement and drove prices up to well over $30 per barrel. The sharp increase in oil revenues that followed significantly improved Saudi Arabia's economic situation. Saudi Arabia earned about $66 to $75.3 billion from oil exports in 2000, more than double its oil export revenue in 1998.[54]

As Chart 1.5 shows, these cycles had a major impact on the growth of the Saudi GDP and Saudi GNP per capita. The chart provides World Bank estimates, but the Kingdom's estimates are similar. Saudi Arabia estimates that its GDP increased from $142.7 billion in 1999 to $173.1 billion in 2000—well over a 40% increase in the oil sector in current prices. The private-sector GDP increased by only 3.1% between 1999 and 2000, but

Chart 1.5
Saudi Annual Growth in GDP and GNP Per Capita: 1966-1999 (in Percent)

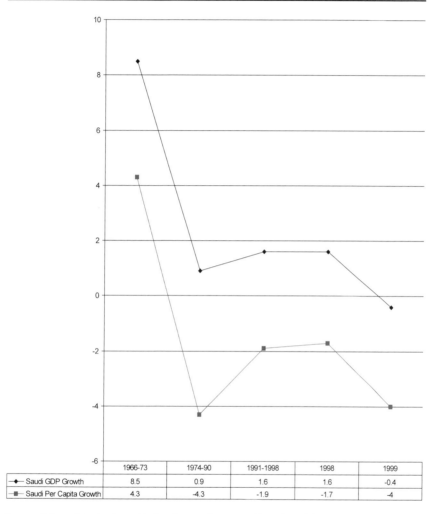

	1966-73	1974-90	1991-1998	1998	1999
Saudi GDP Growth	8.5	0.9	1.6	1.6	-0.4
Saudi Per Capita Growth	4.3	-4.3	-1.9	-1.7	-4

Source: Adapted by Anthony H. Cordesman from World Bank, *Global Economic Prospects: 2000* (Washington, DC: World Bank, 2000), pp. 152–153.

the non-oil industrial sector increased by 7% and the value of the Saudi stock market index increased by 13% as investment and demand resumed. The increase in oil revenues produced the first current account surplus in three years, which totaled $6.06 billion, and non-oil exports (which include petroleum product) rose from $5.8 billion to $6.4 billion.[55]

The pressures on the Saudi budget also eased sharply. The oil crash in late 1997 had more than offset Saudi efforts to bring its budget back into balance. Saudi Arabia had budget deficits of $9.28 billion in 1994, $7.31 billion in 1995, $5.07 billion in 1996, $4.21 billion in 1997, $12.27 billion in 1998, and $9.07 billion in 1999. However, the sudden rise in oil prices in 2000 led to the first real Saudi budget surplus in many years. This surplus totaled an estimated $6.06 billion even though total Saudi expenditures rose from $48.3 billion in 1999 to $62.8 billion in 2000. Saudi Arabia announced in January 2001 than it planned a budget of $215 billion for the year, which was intended to be a balanced budget with neither a surplus nor deficit.[56]

Unfortunately, booms are no more predictable or enduring that busts, and Saudi Arabia must try to break out of the cycle of the Kingdom's violent swings in its revenues and economy. Its $66 to $75 billion in earnings in 2000 dropped to $58.2 to $63.1 billion in 2001. The Kingdom's oil revenues are also likely to be at its peak earning level in the near-term, but they compare with total earnings of $223.2 billion in 1980 constant dollars. As a result, they are less than one-third of the earnings the Kingdom had at the peak of its true oil boom in the 1980s. The U.S. Energy Information Administration (EIA) also forecasts a 17% cut in real Saudi oil revenues in 2002. The EIA expects Saudi Arabia to earn approximately $49.6 billion in oil export revenues in 2002, which is down from $58.2 billion in 2001.[57] The Kingdom can only fund its present welfare state and the reforms called for in its Seventh Development Plan (2000–2004), however, if it consistently receives real oil revenues as high as or higher than those it received in 2000.

The Impact of Demographics: A Rising Population Means Declining per Capita Oil Income

The uncertainties in Saudi oil income interact with the certainty of massive population growth. Chart 1.6 provides a World Bank estimate of Saudi population growth, based on relatively conservative assumptions about future Saudi population growth, which still shows that the Kingdom is projected to have some of the fastest population growth in the Arab world, and indeed the entire world. Even though the World Bank projections call for a significant future decrease in the Saudi population growth rate, they still project that Saudi Arabia will grow from a nation of 21.7 million people in 2000 to over 46 million in 2030.

The actual impact of demographic pressure may be much worse. Chart 1.7 shows estimates by the U.S. Census Bureau. These estimates indicate that that Saudi Arabia will grow from 22.0 million in 2000 to 30.5 million in 2010, 41.9 million in 2020, 55.8 million in 2030, 72.3 million in 2040, and 91.1 million in 2050. These increases take place even though the

Census Bureau estimates that the population growth of Saudi Arabia will decline from 3.3 % during 1990–2000 to 3.3% in 2000–2010, 3.2% in 2010–2020, 2.9% in 2020–2030, 2.6% in 2030–2040, and 2.3% in 2040–2050.[58]

The population growth shown in Charts 1.6 and 1.7 has already sharply reduced per capita oil export earnings. As Chart 1.8 shows, population growth and limited oil revenues have already made massive cuts in Saudi Arabia's per capita income relative to the "boom" years of the late 1970s and early 1980s. They have also forced Saudi Arabia to spend an increasing proportion of its budget on welfare and entitlements at the expense of investment. Any projections about the future involve so many assumptions about future oil production and prices and demographics that they can be little more than guesswork. It seems likely that per capita export income from crude oil and gas will drop by another 40% to 60% in real terms by 2030.[59]

The Ongoing Saudi Response

These pressures help explain why Crown Prince Abdullah has continued to warn that a period of a potential "economic crisis" lays ahead. They also help explain why Saudi Arabia's government continues to support the need to reduce state involvement and increase private sector—including foreign—participation and investment in the economy.[60]

Crown Prince Abdullah stated that privatization must be a "strategic choice," and has shown his support for reforms through measures like the creation of the Supreme Economic Council. This council was created in September 1999, and charged with boosting investment, creating jobs for Saudi nationals, and promoting the private sector. As Chapters 4 and 5 analyze in depth, the government is making important changes to the rules governing foreign investment and creating a wide range of incentives for domestic investment as well. In one move in this direction, international investors have been permitted to invest in local shares through established open-ended mutual funds. In another, the Kingdom issued an amended foreign investment act on April 10, 2000, and created the Saudi Arabian General Investment Authority to encourage foreign and private domestic investment.[61]

Saudi Arabia's desire to join the World Trade Organization (WTO) is another example of the efforts at reform. The Saudi government says that it is seeking WTO membership partly to attract foreign investment and partly to help find new markets for the country's petrochemical industry, but it also clearly sees such membership as a way of forcing Saudi industry to become more competitive on a global basis. King Fahd stated that "the world is heading for . . . globalization" in November 1999, and that "it is no longer possible for [Saudi Arabia] to make slow progress."

Chart 1.6
Living in a Crowded Desert: Saudi Population Growth Compared to Trends in Other
Gulf Countries—Part One: The World Bank Estimate (Population in Millions)

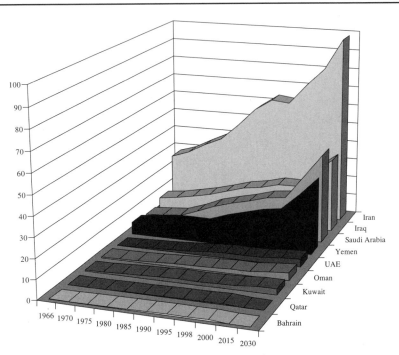

	1966	1970	1975	1980	1985	1990	1995	1998	2000	2015	2030
☐ Bahrain	0.18	0.22	0.3	0.4	0.4	0.5	0.6	0.6	0.6	NA	NA
■ Qatar	0.07	0.09	0.14	0.3	0.3	0.4	0.5	0.6	0.7	NA	NA
■ Kuwait	0.5	0.8	1	1.4	1.7	2.1	1.7	1.9	2.3	2.9	3
☐ Oman	0.6	0.7	0.8	1.1	1.5	1.8	2	2.3	2.3	3.3	4
■ UAE	0.2	0.3	0.7	1	1.6	2.3	2.8	2.7	2.8	3.7	4
■ Yemen	6.1	7.2	8.3	8.5	8.4	11.6	14.1	16.6	17.8	26.6	36
☐ Saudi Arabia	4.8	5.4	6.2	9.4	13.2	15.9	18	20.7	21.7	33.7	46
☐ Iraq	8.2	9.4	11.1	13	15.7	18.4	19.9	22.3	22.3	31.3	38
☐ Iran	26.8	30.1	34.9	39.1	47.6	56.9	63.1	61.9	72.7	82.1	98

Source: Adapted by Anthony H. Cordesman from data provided by the U.S. State Department
and the World Bank database for *World Development Indicators, 2000* (Washington, DC:
World Bank, 2000), pp. 40, 44. The World Bank does not report on Bahrain and Qatar.
World Bank figures are otherwise used for 1980, 1998, 2015, and 2000.

The king has also emphasized the importance of regional unity among Gulf
states—economically, politically, and militarily. One example is a proposal
for a customs union among the GCC countries. It is important to note, however, that there is only limited comparative advantage in trade within the

Chart 1.7
Living in a Crowded Desert: Saudi Population Growth Compared to Trends in Other
Gulf Countries—Part Two: The U.S. Census Bureau Estimate (Population in Millions)

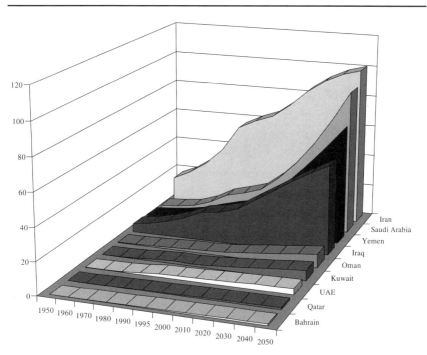

	1950	1960	1970	1980	1990	1995	2000	2010	2020	2030	2040	2050
☐ Bahrain	0.11	0.16	0.22	0.35	0.5	0.57	0.63	0.74	0.83	0.9	0.95	0.97
■ Qatar	0.03	0.05	0.11	0.23	0.48	0.61	0.74	0.97	1.1	1.2	1.2	1.2
☐ UAE	0.07	0.1	0.25	1	2	2.2	2.4	2.8	3.1	3.4	3.5	3.7
■ Kuwait	0.15	0.29	0.75	1.4	2.1	1.6	2	2.8	3.7	4.6	5.5	6.4
■ Oman	0.49	0.6	0.78	1.2	1.8	2.1	2.5	3.5	4.7	5.9	7.2	8.3
■ Iraq	5.2	6.8	9.4	13.2	18.1	19.6	22.7	29.7	36.9	43.9	50.5	56.4
■ Yemen	4.5	5.5	6.6	8.5	12	14.9	17.5	24.6	34.2	45.5	58	71.1
☐ Saudi Arabia	3.7	4.7	6.1	9.9	15.8	18.6	22	30.5	41.9	55.8	72.3	91.1
☐ Iran	16.4	21.6	28.9	39.3	55.7	61.5	65.6	73.8	84.2	91.7	96.9	100.2

Source: Adapted by Anthony H. Cordesman from data provided by the U.S. State Department
and the World Bank database for *World Development Indicators, 2000* (Washington, DC:
World Bank, 2000), pp. 40, 44. The World Bank does not report on Bahrain and Qatar.
World Bank figures are otherwise used for 1980, 1998, 2015, and 2000.

GCC, and little near-term prospect that comparative advantage and trade will
increase in the future. Saudi annual non-oil trade with all of the GCC states
is still very limited. Saudi figures show less than 10 billion riyals in annual
imports, and less than 7.5 billion riyals in exports, during 1997–1999. This

Chart 1.8
The Demographic Squeeze: Saudi Arabia's Population Growth in Millions versus per Capita Income in Constant $U.S. (Population in Millions; Per Capita Income in Thousands of Constant 1997 $US)

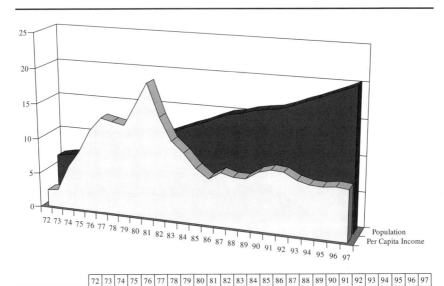

	72	73	74	75	76	77	78	79	80	81	82	83	84	85	86	87	88	89	90	91	92	93	94	95	96	97
☐ Per Capita Income	2.4	2.6	6.3	8.6	12	14	13	13	16	19	15	11	9.8	7.9	6.6	7.7	7.2	7.2	8.3	8.8	8.7	7.8	7.3	7.2	7.4	7.3
■ Population	6.5	6.8	7	7.3	7.7	8.2	8.8	9.5	10	11	11	11	12	13	13	14	15	15	16	16	16	17	17	18	19	20

Source: Adapted by Anthony H. Cordesman from data in various editions of the *World Military Expenditures and Arms Transfers* database.

is about 10% of Saudi imports, but much of the total consists of reexports. It is a significant share of Saudi non-oil exports, but less than 5% of all Saudi exports, and much of the Saudi export total consists of reexports of goods or parts bought outside the GCC.[62]

Saudi Arabia is taking other steps toward enlarging its private sector and the eventual creation of a structured system of utilities based on real market prices. Both of these measures could increase revenues and fund development projects. Reducing the Kingdom's heavy reliance on subsidies would aid Saudi Arabia's attempts to open its economy in order to participate in the WTO.[63]

Setting the Pace of Implementation

So far, however, reform is moving far too slowly to meet the nation's needs. No one who has studied the Kingdom's history, and the number of times outsiders have issued exaggerated warnings about a coming political or economic crisis, can afford to ignore its adaptability. Nevertheless, the Saudi government has yet to properly practice what it preaches. This may be because of its fear of job losses for Saudi citizens, and because of resistance within part of the private sector and by some members of the Saudi royal family.[64] Even during the worst point of the oil crash in 1997–1998, the Kingdom was slow to cut government subsidies, although it increased the price of gasoline by 50%—to about $0.90 per gallon—in May 1999. It raised electricity prices and then reversed them after relatively mild prices, and continued to charge only about 5% of the market price for water. Since that time, the government has been equally slow to increase taxes, reform the financial sector, and open up the economy to foreign and private domestic investment on competitive terms.

Much depends, therefore, on Saudi ability to implement structural economic reform at a much faster pace. In the past, Saudi leaders have tended to halt economic reforms as soon as the signs of prosperity return, and the steps Saudi Arabia has taken so far are clearly not adequate to make the changes in its economy that will meet its future needs. As the following chapters show, such delays are creating growing political and social risks. The government lacks the resources to return a policy of employing Saudis in meaningless government positions rather than face the prospect of large masses of unemployed youth who are dissatisfied with their government. Only a massive increase in employment in the private sector and downstream petroleum production can ensure that Saudi Arabia remains economically stable and that sufficient revenue is available to fund social projects for its growing population.

THE SECURITY CHALLENGES OF THE TWENTY-FIRST CENTURY

Saudi Arabia not only must cope with massive internal changes, it must also deal with serious external threats. Saudi Arabia is the richest single prize in the Middle East and possesses the largest oil reserves of any country in the world. Oil wealth makes Saudi Arabia a natural target of radical political movements and ambitious states throughout the Middle East, as well as the natural target of other oil exporting states that seek to restrict the volume of world oil exports and raise world oil prices.

Territory, Strategic Depth, and Vulnerabilities

Saudi Arabia must defend a total of 2,510 kilometers of coastline on the Gulf and Red Sea. The Saudi Gulf coast is within five minutes flying time of Iran by jet fighter, and a causeway connects Saudi Arabia with Bahrain, a small island state that Iran has claimed in the past. The Kingdom's ports on the Red Sea make it a major Red Sea power and link its politics and security position with that of Egypt, the Sudan, Ethiopia, and Djibouti.

Saudi Arabia must guard against threats to maritime traffic through the Red Sea, and against any spillover of the continuing political upheavals and conflicts in the Horn of Africa.[65]

Saudi Arabia's large territory gives it strategic depth, but its most important oil fields and many of its key ports, facilities, and cities are clustered along the upper Gulf coast opposite Iran and Iraq. The Kingdom's size also prevents strategic concentration. It must cope with the fact that its population is dispersed into cities that are separated by long distances and vulnerable to attacks on their infrastructure. Saudi Arabia offers many high-value targets in terms of oil and gas facilities, as well as central power grids. Also, it is heavily dependent on secure maritime and air traffic for imports and exports.

Saudi Arabia's forces must defend the territory of a nation with a total area of 1,960,582 square kilometers, roughly one-fourth the size of the United States. Saudi forces must either help defend Kuwait in its entirety or at least its 222-kilometer border with Kuwait, as well as defend an 814-kilometer boundary with Iraq. The Kingdom also has a 728-kilometer border with Jordan, a 676-kilometer border with Oman, a 457-kilometer border with the UAE, a 60-kilometer border with Qatar, and a 1,458-kilometer border with Yemen.[66]

Strategic Concerns and Military Requirements

Unlike the other Southern Gulf states, Saudi Arabia cannot shape its strategy only around potential threats in the Northern Gulf. Saudi Arabia faces a radical Sudan across the Red Sea and the prospect of continuing instability in the other Red Sea states. While Saudi Arabia has consistently tried to distance itself from military involvement in the conflicts between Israel and its Arab neighbors, it can never be certain that it will not be threatened by the escalation of an Arab-Israeli conflict or pressure from one of the confrontational Arab states.

This strategic position forces Saudi Arabia to disperse its limited military resources to forward bases throughout the country, leaving it with limited forces on any given front. It has also led Saudi Arabia to make a major effort to build up its military forces. It has transformed its army from a small and lightly mechanized force, concentrated near existing urban areas, to a heavily armored force, deployed in new military cities near its strategic borders. Saudi Arabia has built up a small coast guard into the nucleus of a two-fleet navy, and has transformed a small showpiece air force into one of the largest and best-equipped air forces in the developing world.

This modernization effort has cost Saudi Arabia nearly $300 billion (in constant 2000 dollars) in military expenditures over the last decade, of which nearly $70 billion has been spent on arms transfers.[67] The modernization of Saudi forces, however, is still very much an ongoing process. The Saudi Army is still in the process of developing the capability to fight independent maneuver and armored warfare against potential foes like Iraq, the Saudi Air Force has lost readiness and effectiveness since the Gulf War, and the Saudi Navy is far from being ready to directly challenge the Iranian Navy or deal with a serious submarine and mine warfare threat.

The Problem of Strategic Dependence on the West

Creating effective Saudi military forces is not easy. Air power offers Saudi Arabia a potential means of compensating for the weakness and dispersal of its land and naval forces. However, Saudi Arabia can only use air power decisively if it has significant land and naval capabilities and its Air Force is a combat-ready and true war-fighting force. In practice, this means the Air Force must meet five key criteria: (a) its limited first-line fighter strength has the range and refueling capability to mass quickly, (b) its air units can maintain a decisive technical and performance edge over threat forces, (c) it can provide sufficient air defense capability to provide air cover for Saudi ground forces, naval forces, and key targets, (d) it can provide sufficient dual capability in the attack mission to offset its limited ground strength and give it time to reinforce its army units, and (e) its air units are cumulatively strong enough to provide at least limited coverage of the Northern Gulf or Red Sea front while facing an active threat on the other front.

Even the most effective process of military modernization cannot, however, give Saudi Arabia the strength and war-fighting capability it needs to deal with Iran and Iraq and the threat of proliferation. No matter how Saudi Arabia shapes its military forces, it cannot meet the threat from the Northern Gulf alone, or in combination with the other Southern Gulf states.

As a conservative monarchy, Saudi Arabia now lacks the population and skills to create military forces large enough to defend its territory or regional position. It is dependent on Western power projection capabilities to check Iran and Iraq, and contain any spillover of an Arab-Israeli conflict. Yet, this same dependence confronts Saudi Arabia with the problem of maintaining close security ties to the United States, even though the United States is a secular democracy and Israel's greatest ally. The events of the last few years have made it all too clear that changes have to occur in this aspect of U.S. and Saudi relations, as well as in Saudi military relations with other Western countries.

NOTES

1. This estimate is based on data in ACDA, *World Military Expenditures and Military Transfers, 1972–1982*, Table I, April 1984.

2. Based on the Bureau of Arms Control (formerly ACDA), U.S. State Department database for *World Military Expenditures and Military Transfers*, and unclassified CIA estimates.

3. World Bank, Country Profile, "Saudi Arabia,"URL: *www.ifc.org/camena/saudi.htm*, and various editions of *World Bank Atlas*.

4. CIA, *World Factbook, 1999* (Washington, DC: GPO, 1999), "Saudi Arabia."

5. *www.eia.doie.gov/emeu/cabs/saudi.html*. January 2000, World Bank, *World Development Indicators* (Washington, DC: World Bank, 2000), p. 184

6. Economist Intelligence Unit, *Saudi Arabia—Country Profile*, 1st Quarter, 1995.

7. Based on the Bureau of Arms Control (formerly ACDA), U.S. State Department database for *World Military Expenditures and Military Transfers*.

8. Working estimate by CIA analysts.

9. IISS, *Military Balance, 2000–20001*; World Bank, *World Bank Atlas, 2000*; World Bank, *World Development Indicators, 2001*, p. 46.

10. CIA, *World Factbook, 2002*, "Saudi Arabia."

11. CIA, *World Factbook, 2002*, "Saudi Arabia," IISS, *Military Balance, 2001–2002*; World Bank, *World Development Indicators, 2002*, p. 40.

12. Saudi Arabia Monetary Agency (SAMA), *Thirty-Sixth Annual Report (1421H (2000G)* (Riyadh: SAMA, 2000), pp. 253–255.

13. Interviews with the Saudi five-year plan staff in April 2000, and World Bank, *World Development Indicators 2001*, 3.10.

14. World Bank, *World Development Indicators, 1997*, pp. 16, 68, 116, 286; CIA, *World Factbook, 2001*; World Bank, *World Bank Atlas, 1997*, pp. 36–37; Kingdom of Saudi Arabia, Ministry of Planning, *Achievements of the Development Plans 1970–2000, Facts and Figures*, (Riyadh: Ministry of Planning, 2000), Part One (F); data provided by Saudi officials on April 18, 2002; and Kingdom of Saudi Arabia, Ministry of Planning, *Achievements of the Development Plans 1970–2001, Facts and Figures* (Riyadh: Ministry of Planning, 2002),19th Issue.

15. CIA, *World Factbook, 2001*, "Saudi Arabia."

16. Kingdom of Saudi Arabia, Ministry of Planning, *Achievements of the Development Plans 1970–2000, Facts and Figures*, Part One (F); *http://www.sama.gov.sa/kf/eachievements.htm* accessed April 19, 2002; data provided by Saudi officials on April 18, 2002; and Kingdom of Saudi Arabia, Ministry of Planning, *Achievements of the Development Plans 1970-2001, Facts and Figures*.

17. Ibid.

18. Ibid.

19. Ibid.

20. World Bank, *World Development Indicators, 2000*; CIA, *World Factbook, 2002* "Saudi Arabia."

21. Khaled Abdullatif al-Arfaj, *The Information Industry in Saudi Arabia* (Riyadh: King Fahd National First Series, 1997); World Bank, *World Development Indicators, 2000*;, interviews, February 2001; CIA *World Factbook 2002*, "Saudi Arabia."

22. Kingdom of Saudi Arabia, Ministry of Planning, *Achievements of the Development Plans 1970–2000, Facts and Figures*, Figure 48 and supporting text; and Kingdom of Saudi Arabia, Ministry of Planning, *Achievements of the Development Plans 1970–2001, Facts and Figures*.

23. *Saudi Arabia* (March 1997), p. 3; Ministry of Planning, *Kingdom of Saudi Arabia: Achievements of the Development Plans 1390–1418 (1970–1998), Facts and Figures* (Riyadh: Ministry of Planning, 1999), 16th Issue; Kingdom of Saudi Arabia, Ministry of Planning, *Achievements of the Development Plans 1970–2000, Facts and Figures*, Part One (F). p. 20; and Kingdom of Saudi Arabia, Ministry of Planning, *Achievements of the Development Plans 1970–2001, Facts and Figures*.

24. Energy Information Administration (EIA), "Saudi Arabia," Department of Energy, January 2000, URL: *www.eia.doe.gov/emeu/cabs/saudi.html*.

25. This section draws heavily from David Long's book, *The Kingdom of Saudi Arabia* (Gainesville: University Press of Florida, 1997), pp. 22–33.

26. Ibid., p. 45.

27. From comments by St. John Armitage.

28. Saudi Information Resource, "History of Saudi Arabia," URL: *http://www.saudinf.com*.

29. Ibid.

30. Robert Cullen, "Uneasy Lies the Head That Wears a Crown," *Nuclear Energy* (Third Quarter 1995), p. 24.

31. Robert Lacey, *The Kingdom* (New York: Harcourt Brace Jovanovich, 1981), p. 378.

32. *The Estimate*, January 5, 1996, p. 11.

33. Reuters, September 29, 1999; Saudi Press Agency Information Release, October 18, 1999.

34. *The Estimate*, June 4, 1999, p. 9.

35. Long, *The Kingdom of Saudi Arabia*, p. 129.

36. The World Bank, *World Development Indicators, 2000* and *2001* (Washington, DC: World Bank, 2001), Table 2.1.

37. The World Bank, *World Development Indicators, 2000*, Table 2.1.

38. World Bank, *World Development Indicators, 1997*, pp. 136, 294; *2000*, p. 40; *2001*, p. 46; historical data base for Table I, Bureau of Arms Control (formerly ACDA), U.S. State Department, *World Military Expenditures and Arms Transfers*, various editions.

39. EIA "Saudi Arabia," January 2002, URL: *www.eia.doe.gov/emeu/cabs/saudi.html*, and EIA "OPEC Revenues Fact Sheet," December 2001, URL: *www.eia.doe.gov/emeu/cabs/opecrev.html*.

40. EIA "OPEC Revenues Fact Sheet."

41. World Bank, *World Development Indicators, 1997*, pp. 136, 294.

42. World Bank, *World Development Indicators, 1999*, p. 222; CIA, *World Factbook, 1997*, "Saudi Arabia."

43. Kingdom of Saudi Arabia, Ministry of Planning, *Achievements of the Development Plans 1970–2000, Facts and Figures*, Figures 45 and 46, and supporting text; and Kingdom of Saudi Arabia, Ministry of Planning, *Achievements of the Development Plans 1970–2001, Facts and Figures*.

44. World Bank, *World Development Indicators, 2001*, p. 50.

45. No precise estimate is possible and some private Saudi estimates for water, electricity, energy, roads, housing, facilities, and rehabilitation and improvement of existing infrastructure would exceed one trillion $U.S. between 1995 and 2015.

46. EIA, *International Energy Outlook, 1999* (Washington, DC: GPO, March 1999), p. 32, and EIA, *International Energy Outlook, 2000*, Table D1.

47. EIA "Saudi Arabia," January 2000.

48. Figures drawn from various versions of the EIA "OPEC Revenues Fact Sheet," March 2000 and April 2002, URL: *www.eia.doe.gov/emeu/cabs/opecrev.html*; and from data provided by Cambridge Energy Research Associates (CERA). The lower figure only includes crude exports. The higher figure in the range includes total petroleum exports.

49. Ibid.

50. Ibid.

51. EIA "Saudi Arabia," January 2000.

52. EIA "OPEC Revenues Fact Sheet," March 2000 and April 2002; and data provided by CERA. The lower figure only includes crude exports. The higher figure in the range includes total petroleum exports.

53. EIA "Saudi Arabia," January 2000.

54. EIA "OPEC Revenues Fact Sheet," March 2000 and April 2002; and data provided by CERA. The lower figure only includes crude exports. The higher figure in the range includes total petroleum exports.

55. *Saudi Arabia*, vol. 18, no. 1 (January 2001), pp. 2–5.

56. Ibid., p. 5.

57. EIA "OPEC Revenues Fact Sheet," various editions.

58. U.S. Census Bureau, "IDB Summary Demographic Data for Saudi Arabia," estimated accessed as of May 7, 2001, URL: http://www.census.gov/ipc/www/idbsum.html.

59. These are back-of-the-envelope calculations based on the World Bank population growth estimate and EIA estimates of future Saudi and Gulf exports and oil prices in the *International Energy Outlook, 2000* (March 2000), online edition.

60. EIA "Saudi Arabia," January 2000.

61. EIA "Saudi Arabia," January 2001.

62. SAMA, *Thirty-Sixth Annual Report, 1421H (2000G0)* (Riyadh: SAMA, 2000), pp. 152–166.

63. EIA "Saudi Arabia," January 2000.

64. Ibid.

65. CIA, *World Factbook, 2002*, "Saudi Arabia."

66. Ibid.

67. Bureau of Arms Control (formerly ACDA), U.S. State Department, *World Military Expenditures and Arms Transfers, 1993–1994*, pp. 80, 128.

Chapter 2

Foreign Relations and External Security

Saudi Arabia plays a major diplomatic role in the Gulf and the Middle East, is an important voice in OPEC and world energy policy, and has large military forces by Southern Gulf standards. At the same time, Saudi foreign relations are heavily influenced by external security issues.

The Kingdom demonstrated during the Gulf War that it could bear a large portion of its own defense, and that it could be an important strategic partner of the West. Saudi Arabia played a key part in organizing the Arab side of the UN Coalition and commanded both of its Arab task forces, Joint Forces Command (East) and Joint Forces Command (North).[1] These forces were organized under the command of Lieutenant General Prince Khalid bin Sultan al-Saud.[2] By the time the Air/Land phase of the Gulf War began, the Saudi ground forces in the theater totaled nearly 50,000 men, with about 270 main battle tanks, 930 other armored fighting vehicles, 115 artillery weapons, and over 400 anti-tank weapons.[3] The Saudi Air Force flew a total of 6,852 sorties between January 17 and February 28, 1991—about 6% of all sorties flown—ranking it second after the United States in total air activity.[4]

Saudi Arabia, however, could not have defended itself against Iraq without massive Western aid. Many aspects of its military capabilities have declined since the Gulf War, and it continues to face many strategic and military challenges from several of its neighbors. Its primary threats are Iran and Iraq, but the Kingdom still faces a potential threat from Yemen in spite of recent improvements in Saudi-Yemeni relations. Its long coast along the Red Sea means that it cannot ignore the constant turmoil in the Horn of

Africa. Its western border with Jordan—and its close proximity to Egypt, Israel, and Syria—means that it must pay close attention to the risk of a new Arab-Israeli conflict and the failure to reach a comprehensive peace settlement.

At the same time, Saudi Arabia faces challenges in dealing with its friends, including its Southern Gulf neighbors. The Kingdom has resolved many of the lingering border disputes and other tensions that affected its relations with these state in recent years. However, there has been only limited progress in developing effective collective security arrangements in the Southern Gulf since the Gulf War. The GCC remains largely a political, rather than military, alliance and Saudi Arabia often has different interests from those of its Southern Gulf neighbors.

Saudi Arabia also faces a continuing crisis because of the failure of the Arab-Israeli peace process, and its conversion into a "war process," once the Second Intifada began in September 2000. The Kingdom does not face a direct military threat from Israel, but it cannot distance itself from the Arab world and the Palestinian cause. Key Saudi leaders like Crown Prince Abdullah and Foreign Minister Prince Saud al-Faisal have long supported the cause of Palestinian statehood, and the Second Intifada and the suffering of the Palestinians has aroused more feeling among the Saudi people than any issue in decades. It is the one issue since the time of Nasser that has led to serious public demonstrations, and demonstrations have taken place in spite of government efforts to halt them.

These pressures interacted with other tensions between Saudi Arabia and its most important military ally, the United States. While Saudi Arabia has long been dependent on the United States as its ultimate defense against Iran and Iraq, it has resisted major U.S. deployments or repositioning on Saudi soil. While the Iran-Iraq War and Gulf War demonstrated the importance of U.S. power projection capability to Saudi security, the deployment of large U.S. forces on Saudi soil after Iraq's invasion of Kuwait has aroused significant opposition from Saudi Islamists and violent opposition from the Islamist extremists at the fringe of the Saudi political spectrum.

The continuing U.S. air presence in Saudi Arabia after the Gulf War—and ongoing U.S., British, and French operations against Iraq to enforce the southern no-fly zone—quickly became an issue for some Sunni Islamist opposition groups as well as for Iranian-backed Shi'ite extremists. These tensions led to a number of low-level incidents, and then to two major terrorist attacks: the bombing of the Saudi National Guard Training Center in Riyadh on November 13, 1995, and the bombing of the U. S. Air Barracks at Al-Khobar on June 25, 1996. In addition, violent extremist groups like al Qaeda, led by Osama bin Laden, not only accused the United States of deploying forces in Saudi Arabia's "holy places" but organized Saudi and other terrorist groups to attack U.S. targets outside the Kingdom, including the U.S. embassies in Kenya and Tanzania on August 7, 1998. and the U.S.S. *Cole* in the port of Aden on October 12, 2000.

The start of the Second Intifada in September 2000, and differences between the United States and Saudi Arabia over how to deal with Iran and Iraq, made these problems worse. Spontaneous popular Saudi boycotts of U.S. firms began in the spring of 2001 in opposition to U.S. support of Israel. Saudi Arabia reached a rapprochement with Iran while the United States chose to isolate and sanction it. There were serious differences between Saudi Arabia and the United States over the use of forces to enforce UN sanctions on Iraq during the Clinton administration. The election of George W. Bush in November 2000 brought to power a U.S. administration that actively advocated the useuse of force to overthrow Saddam Hussein. In contrast, the Saudi government not only questioned whether such action was necessary, but whether a new Iraqi regime would come to power that could hold the country together, and/or would not be dominated by Shi'ites sympathetic to Iran.

The events of September 11, 2001, brought these Saudi and U.S. tensions to the point of crisis. The al Qaeda attack on the World Trade Center and the Pentagon involved fifteen Saudis out of nineteen direct participants. It suddenly exposed the role Saudi Arabia had played in Pakistan and central Asia. It also exposed weaknesses in the Saudi internal security services and government control over the end-use of both Saudi aid efforts overseas and the flow of private donations. Equally important, it triggered a flood of U.S. media criticism of the Saudi royal family, Saudi social and political behavior, and Saudi "fundamentalism" in ways that confused conservative Wahhabi practices with extremism and terrorism. This triggered a responding wave of Saudi media criticism of the United States, much of it equally unfair, exaggerated, and uninformed.

Almost inevitably, these events also led the leaders of both countries to reexamine Saudi and U.S. ties and the size and role of U.S. forces in Saudi Arabia. This debate was heightened by Saudi reluctance to offer the use of Saudi bases for the U.S. war against the Taliban and al Qaeda that followed the September 11th attacks. While the United States did make limited use of Saudi command facilities and air space, it deployed most of its forces to Qatar, the UAE, and Oman. Both Saudi Arabia and the United States carried out a quiet effort to determine ways to further reduce the U.S. military presence in the Kingdom.

The potential threat to Saudi Arabia from Iran and Iraq has scarcely vanished, but the problem of Islamic extremism and terrorism is now a critical problem in Saudi foreign relations, and is likely to remain one. The steady increase in the fighting between Israel and the Palestinians poses a constant problem for Saudi-U.S. relations, in spite of Crown Prince Abdullah's presentation of an eight-point plan for full Arab-Israeli peace in March 2002. For example, the Israeli reoccupation of Palestinian cities in the West Bank in April 2002 sharply increased Saudi public hostility to U.S. support of Israel. President Bush and Crown Prince Abdullah met in Texas that same month, and declared that Saudi and U.S. strategic relations had not changed, but it was clear that the Second Intifada continued to undermine U.S. and Saudi relations.

IRAN AND IRAQ: THE PRIMARY THREATS

Iran and Iraq are natural rivals of Saudi Arabia for power and influence in the Gulf. The struggle to preserve the balance of power in the region requires a constant Saudi effort to balance Iran against Iraq and vice versa. It requires an equally constant Saudi effort to maintain the kind of ties to the United States and the West that will counterbalance the threat from both states. Today, Iraq is by far the most serious potential threat. Saudi relations with Iran have steadily improved over the last few years and Saudi Arabia may actually show the way for similar improvements in U.S.-Iranian relations. There are no certainties in the Gulf, however, and the continuing internal political turmoil forces Saudi Arabia to continue to perceive Iran as a potential threat.

The Problem of Iran

Saudi relations with Iran have never been easy. Tensions have existed between the Wahhabi and Shi'ite clerics for over two centuries. The founder of the Wahhabi movement, Muhammad abd al-Wahhab, felt that Shi'ite Islam was an apostate version of Islam; Wahhab led raids into Shi'ite southern Iraq to raze the shrine of al-Hussein, one of the most important leaders in Shi'ite theology. Since then, tension has existed between those who hold strongly and conservatively to the Wahhabi and Shi'ite creeds. This religious tension is unlikely to be resolved any time soon.

The two states were more rivals than friends while the Shah remained in power. Following the Iranian Revolution in 1979, Iran became actively hostile to Saudi Arabia. Khomeini and other Iranian leaders often violently attacked the character and religious legitimacy of the Saudi regime. Iran attempted to fly combat aircraft into Saudi air space during the Iran-Iraq War, and threatened tanker traffic to Kuwait and Saudi Arabia in an effort to force Saudi Arabia to reduce its support for Iraq. Iran also sponsored riots and unrest during the sacred pilgrimage to Mecca, the Hajj.

Unlike the United States, however, Saudi Arabia never severed diplomatic relations with Iran even during the worst periods of tension following the fall of the Shah. Saudi Arabia never ignored the potential threat from Iran, but continued to maintain diplomatic relations with Iran during the Iran-

Iraq War and sought to find ways to reach a modus vivendi with its revolutionary regime.

These Saudi efforts began to pay off after the death of the Ayatollah Khomeini. Iran's new president, Ali Akbar Hashemi Rafsanjani, made the first attempt to improve relations. Saudi Arabia reacted favorably to what became a series of Iranian speeches calling for improved relations, such as those of Iranian Foreign Minister Ali Akbar Velayati in March 1997. As a result, Foreign Minister Velayati visited Saudi Arabia in the spring of 1997—his first visit in four years.

Iran pulled back from efforts to encourage Saudi Shi'ite unrest and terrorism, halted its attacks on the Saudi royal family, and stopped supporting riots and protests during the Hajj. Iran and Saudi Arabia began to cooperate in key areas like oil policy. They made a joint effort to persuade the Organization of Petroleum Exporting Countries (OPEC) to cutback oil production in June 1997.[5] Contacts between the countries increased in the areas, and Iran Air resumed flights to Saudi Arabia in September 1997.[6] Prince Sultan, Saudi Arabia's minister of defense, stated in July 1997 that "ties between Saudi Arabia and Iran will never be severed."[7] King Fahd sent Minister of State Abdulaziz bin Abdullah Khoweiter to Tehran with messages from the king and Crown Prince Abdullah, and responded favorably to Iran's invitation to send a senior official to the Organization of the Islamic Conference (OIC) in Tehran in December 1997.

The Iranians acted to break out of a growing isolation in the Gulf, to create a diplomatic alliance that would help check Iraq, and because of a growing scale of their internal political and domestic problems. The Saudis acted in spite of years of tension, and incidents like Al-Khobar, for similar reasons. Iran was a potential check on Iraq, and rapprochement offered an end to Iranian sponsored internal security problems. Many senior Saudis saw Ali Muhammad Khatami's election as president of Iran on August 3, 1997, as an indication that Iran might be evolving into a state with which Saudi Arabia could have "correct," and possibly "friendly" relations, and that the new Iranian regime would focus on domestic issues rather than on regional and ideological ambitions. They believed that they might be able to reach an accommodation with Iran that traded Saudi support for better relations between Iran and the Arab world, for Iranian non-interference in Saudi affairs, and an easing of the Iranian military buildup in the lower Gulf.[8]

Saudi Arabia held high-level talks with the Iranian government. For example, in November 1997, Saudi Oil Minister Ali al-Naimi met with his new Iranian counterpart Bijan Zanganeh before an OPEC meeting in Jakarta. On November 26, 1997, King Fahd was invited to visit Iran. The Iranian officials who invited him did so knowing that the king was ill, but that Crown Prince Abdullah had already privately agreed to come.

As a result, Crown Prince Abdullah led a delegation to the OIC in Tehran in December 1997. In a statement before the opening session of the conference, Prince Abdullah called on the OIC to focus on resolving the problems of the Islamic community and promoting unity: "The relationship between a Muslim and another Muslim has to be founded on amity, cooperation and giving counsel on a reciprocal basis. . . . [W]e have to eliminate the obstacles which block the way and be aware of the pitfalls which we may come across as we make our way towards a better future."

Prince Abdullah also praised his Iranian hosts: "With the immortal achievements credited to the Muslim people of Iran and their invaluable contributions . . . it is no wonder that Tehran is hosting this important Islamic gathering." During the course of the conference, the crown prince also held two rounds of private talks with President Muhammad Khatami. During the second round of talks, President Khatami departed from protocol by calling on the Saudi leader in his suite for a meeting that lasted forty-five minutes.

Yet, Prince Abdullah was also careful to qualify his remarks. He attacked terrorism and extremism in the Islamic world. He also stated that,

> I do not think it would be difficult for the brotherly Iranian people and its leadership and for a big power like the United States to reach a solution to any disagreement between them. . . . There is nothing that will make us more happy than to see this sensitive part of the world enjoy stability, security and prosperity. . . . If the United States asks us we will not hesitate to contribute to efforts to bring stability to the region.[9]

In February 1998, former Iranian president Hashemi Rafsanjani visited Saudi Arabia for ten days. Rafsanjani, who had been Iran's president for eight years before Khatami took over in August 1997, headed Iran's powerful policy-making Expediency Council that played an important policy role and advised supreme leader Ayatollah Ali Khamenei.

Saudi Arabia's King Fahd and Rafsanjani met in Riyadh to discuss regional and bilateral ties and the problem of falling oil prices. The official Iranian news agency, IRNA, issued the following statement: "The Saudi king told Ayatollah Rafsanjani that Iran and Saudi Arabia as two important nations of the world and also of the region must collaborate in every issue of their mutual interest including oil, OPEC, and regional matters." The INRA release said that King Fahd "promised that his country would have closer cooperation with Iran for maintaining oil prices at reasonable rates in the future." At the same time, IRNA quoted Rafsanjani as saying, "mutual good understanding between petroleum exporting countries would certainly prevent a downturn in oil prices," and that Rafsanjani, "observed that the Muslim world can rely on its own indigenous resources to solve those problems without the involvement of non-Muslim alien powers."

Prince Saud al-Faisal was quoted as saying, "The Iranians used last December's Islamic summit in Tehran to give the world a message, not one of shadows but one of substance, that they want to improve relations." The editor of *Asharq al-Awsat*, a Saudi daily, also remarked that "the future is bright for Saudi-Iranian relations."

Iran issued this praise of the visit even though a Saudi cleric made derogatory remarks about Shi'ite Islam and Iran's 1979 Islamic revolution at Friday prayers during Rafsanjani's minor pilgrimage to the Islamic holy city of Medina. The Ayatollah Ahmad Jannati, a senior Iranian Shi'ite Muslim cleric, said in a sermon following Rafsanjani's visit that while some opposed rapprochement, Saudi Arabia and Iran should work to overcome their differences:

> Rafsanjani had a good trip to Saudi Arabia except for that one incident at Friday prayers. . . . We have had differences with Saudi Arabia in the past but these cannot remain. . . . Of course, there are those within Saudi Arabia who don't want us to improve relations but we should work together and join as Moslem brothers. . . . We Moslems must wake from our slumber and join together.

Both countries continued to cooperate in oil policy. Rafsanjani's visit occurred at a time when oil prices had dropped to their lowest levels in nearly four years because of a combination of higher OPEC supplies, Asia's economic crisis, a mild winter in the northern hemisphere, and the return of Iraqi exports under a UN oil-for-food deal. The drop also occurred because Saudi Arabia, with the aid of Kuwait and the UAE, led OPEC ministers in November to increase the eleven-member group's output ceiling by 10% to 27.5 million barrels per day (bpd).

Iranian Oil Minister Bijan Namdar Zanganeh and other officials who met with Saudi Oil Minister Ali Naimi accompanied Rafsanjani. They issued a joint statement expressing willingness to work together towards correcting a sharp decline in oil prices but voiced their concern over quota violations by other member states:

> The two sides [Iran and Saudi Arabia] are prepared to coordinate their efforts with other members of OPEC to bring back stability to the oil market if meaningful efforts are taken by quota-violating member countries. They reaffirmed their conviction that the responsibility for re-stabilizing oil prices falls upon all exporting countries.[10]

Saudi Arabia steadily improved its contacts with Iran during 1998. For the first time in many years, the two nations cooperated during the annual pilgrimage to Mecca. Saudi Arabia increased the quota for Iranian pilgrims in February 1998. The two governments took steps to keep any Iranian demonstrations during the pilgrimage peaceful, and when Iranian pilgrims complained of Saudi treatment during the early stages of the pilgrimage in March 1998, the Iranian minister of the interior, Abdullah Nouri, flew to Saudi Arabia to work things out with his Saudi counterpart, Interior Minister Prince Nayeff bin Abdulaziz.[11]

The resulting dialogue between Minister Nouri and Prince Nayef scarcely solved every problem. The Ayatollah Muhammad Mohammadi Reyshahri, Iran's top official at the Muslim Hajj pilgrimage in Saudi Arabia, accused "suspicious and backward elements" in the Saudi holy city of Medina of insulting Iranians and expelling them from shrines. He then told Iranian pilgrims that they should denounce the United States and Israel as "devils." On March 29, 1998, Iranian television reported that the Ayatollah spoke to an audience of Iranian pilgrims, called for a Saudi-banned rally, and stated that, "The disavowal of infidels is the realization of the political dimension of Hajj . . . which makes the pilgrimage real and complete."

Reyshahri said a ritual at the climax of Hajj, in which pilgrims throw stones at pillars symbolizing Satan, was a "symbol of struggle against America and its illegitimate procreation Israel. . . . America is today at the forefront of all devils." At the same time, this exercise in rhetoric was relatively private, and far from the kind of crisis that occurred in 1987, when 402 people, mostly Iranians, died in clashes with Saudi security forces at an Iranian-led rally. This crisis led Iran to boycott the Hajj during 1988–1991. Iranian pilgrims have limited their actions to holding low-key rallies inside their own tent compounds in recent years, and Saudi authorities have not intervened.[12]

Saudi Arabia followed up in early April 1998 by inviting President Khatami to visit Saudi Arabia for the annual pilgrimage as a further sign of improving relations between the two countries. Khatami declined the invitation to the pilgrimage, which started April 6, but said that he would come "as soon as possible."[13] At the end of the Hajj, Iran's supreme leader, Ayatollah Ali Khamenei, acknowledged that Iran's ties with Saudi Arabia were improving and this year's pilgrimage to Mecca was a success. Khamenei's remarks, quoted by Iranian television, gave clear backing to the more conciliatory approach to the Hajj that Iranian officials adopted this year, reflecting last year's election of moderate President Khatami.

Khamenei stated that Iranian pilgrims should continue to hold their anti-Western "Disavowal of Infidels" rally, which had caused serious friction in the past, during the Hajj. Speaking to Iran's top Hajj officials, Khamenei praised the pilgrimage as "very good and successful . . . and performed in peace and without apprehension," and also said, "We do not give up our basic beliefs at any price and cannot forgo the Disavowal at Hajj ceremonies—we try rather to perform it as much as possible." He went on to say ties with Saudi Arabia were "good" and expressed his hope that political relations would improve "day by day within an acceptable framework."[14] Both governments discussed ways to minimize the religious tensions between the Shi'ites in Saudi Arabia's eastern province and its vast majority of Wahhabis. While many tensions remained, this kind of dialogue had been unthinkable since the fall of the Shah until 1997—a period of nearly two decades.

In May 1998, Saudi Arabia and Iran signed an agreement on cooperation in the power and power-generating sectors as well as in other joint-investment projects.[15] The agreement defined cooperation in economic, commercial, technical, scientific, cultural, and sports fields, and also covered cooperation in providing consular services, expansion of communications services, air and sea transport, and environmental issues.[16]

A two-day visit to Iran in April 1999 by Saudi foreign minister Prince Saud al-Faisal produced further warming of relations. In May 1999, Saudi Defense Minister Prince Sultan made a five-day visit to Iran in what was the first visit by a Saudi defense minister to the country since 1979. Prince Sultan and Iranian Vice President Hassan Habibi discussed upgrading trade and cultural ties and signed an agreement to increase flights between the two countries. President Khatami made a landmark visit to Saudi Arabia as part of a regional tour in May 1999.[17]

It was reported during this meeting that the two countries were improving their security relations as well. While Prince Sultan was quoted as saying, "Military cooperation is not easy between two countries who did not have ties for years," the two countries did agree to exchange military attaches.[18] Iran and Saudi Arabia also agreed on a cooperation in internal security measures and mutual non-interference in the other state's internal affairs. On April 18, 2001, the Saudi minister of the interior, Prince Nayef, and his Iranian counterpart, Abdolvahed Mousavi-Lari, signed an agreement in Tehran on internal security cooperation. The agreement addressed efforts to fight organized crime, terrorism, and drug trafficking.[19] Mousavi-Lari stated during a press conference following the signing, "This agreement promises peace and friendship and Iran has always reached out a hand of friendship to its neighbors." The agreement did not cover extradition, however, and Prince Nayef was forced to deny that this omission was because of the Al-Khobar bombing during the same press conference.[20]

Saudi and Iranian relations do continue to have problems. In the case of oil policy, for example, tensions still remained over many petroleum issues including Iran's poor compliance with OPEC quotas and Saudi Arabia's rising oil exports to South Africa, where Iran is the leading OPEC supplier.[21] During OPEC meetings in March 1999, however, Saudi Arabia made a significant effort to resolve the dispute over Iran's compliance. An agreement was finally reached, delimiting the baseline for Iran's share of OPEC cutbacks at 3.9 million barrels per day, rather than 3.6 million barrels per day as argued by other OPEC member states. Although Iran faced the same 7.3% reduction as other member states, in actuality Iran's cuts were smaller due to the amended baseline.

While Saudi Arabia and Iran did not agree on oil strategy at the OPEC meeting in March 2000, they did not openly split. Saudi Arabia called for a major increase in the OPEC production quotas both to stabilize prices and to take advantage of its large amounts of surplus production capacity. Iran was near full production and perceived any increase to have the potential to lead to a cut in oil prices and revenues—a critical concern for a state almost as dependent on oil exports as Saudi Arabia and for whom a shift of a dollar in oil prices is worth nearly $800 million in oil revenues a year. As a result, Iran resisted any increase in oil production, although it eventually followed the Saudi lead.

These differences, however, did not lead to name calling or political hostility. Saudi Arabia and Iran continued their dialogue on OPEC policy in 2000, 2001, and 2002. Saudi policymakers, do however, have few illusions about the uncertainties they face in dealing with Iran. They realize that there are deep divisions between the "pragmatists" and "hardliners" in Iran, which could become more hostile in the future; religious tensions are still a serious problem. Many believe that Saudi Arabia will still have to compete with Iran for regional influence even if a pragmatic regime does eventually emerge as the stable and dominant political faction in Iran because problems will likely arise over oil prices and quotas. Many feel that Saudi Arabia will continue to have to deal with Iranian efforts to intimidate Saudi Arabia or its neighbors and attempts to win influence with Saudi Arabia's Shi'ites.

Saudi officials and military planners recognize that Saudi Arabia must continue to plan to meet military threats from Iran's conventional forces, unconventional forces, and its weapons of mass destruction until a new Iranian regime has proven its moderation over a period of years. They continue to be concerned about Iran's attempts to build up the military capability to threaten tanker and other shipping through the Gulf. They note that Iran has provoked unrest within the Saudi Shi'ite community in the past and deliberately caused unrest among Shi'ite and other pilgrims during the Hajj. Saudi security forces remember clashes with pro-Iranian demonstrators in 1987 that resulted in the death of over 400 people, mostly Iranian pilgrims, and Iran and Saudi Arabia severing diplomatic relations.

Iran's hostility to the United States creates additional problems for Saudi Arabia. Iran openly opposes the presence of the United States and other Western forces in the Gulf. Moreover, serious questions still remain about the role of the Iranian government in past acts of terrorism. Saudi intelligence officials privately make it clear that they believe Iranian officials played at least an indirect role in terrorist attacks on U.S. and Saudi facilities in Saudi Arabia, and that the attack on the U.S. Air Force housing complex in Al-Khobar that killed 19 Americans in June 1996 may have been authorized at the highest levels of the Iranian government.[22] They also fear that Iran may provide indirect support for Saudi Sunni Islamic extremists who attack the legitimacy of the Saudi royal family and its interpretation of Islamic law and religious practices.

Saudi Arabia has denied that the Al-Khobar issue has been the subject of formal discussions with Iran since Saudi Arabia asked Iran to provide background data on some aspects of the investigation on behalf of the United States in 1999. For example, it denied that the Saudi and Iranian foreign ministers discussed the issue when they met in May 2001.[23] The Iranian Foreign Ministry also stated in May that "[t]hese baseless claims are published by circles that are worried about the development of relations between the Islamic Republic of Iran and Saudi Arabia."

This denial took place, however, after the publication of an article in the *New Yorker* that said FBI Director Louis Freeh had handed the Bush administration a list of suspects that included senior Iranian officials.[24] Previous reports had mentioned Ahmad Sherrif, a senior official in the Iranian Revolutionary Guards, as having been involved in the planning of the Al-Khobar bombings. A major London-based Saudi newspaper, *al-Hayat*, also claimed that the disappearance of two Saudis and one Lebanese believed to have planned the bombing may have initially fled to Iran although investigation has since indicated they were not there.

Saudi Arabia has never made testimony of the two Saudis arrested for the bombing—Hani al-Sayegh and Mohammed Qassab—public.[25] The Saudi government has never formally denied that Iran may be connected to the Al-Khobar bombings, but Foreign Minister Saud al-Faisal did state that it "is not a good thing to launch accusations here and there reporting a matter on which the investigation has not been completed," shortly after the *New Yorker* article appeared.[26]

The U.S. indictment of fourteen suspects in the Al-Khobar bombing on June 21, 2001, has added a new dimension to this problem. The text of the U.S. indictment repeatedly mentioned Iran. While it did not include any Iranians in the list of those indicted, it was clear that the United States was effectively naming Iran as a major suspect. As a result, it confronted Saudi Arabia with the dilemma of having to try to preserve its rapprochement with Iran, or supporting its closest military ally. Senior Saudi officials like Minister of the Interior Prince Nayef and Minister of Defense Prince Sultan reacted by stating that such indictments were an interior Saudi matter and that the United States had failed to consult and present its evidence.

So far, Saudi Arabia, Iran, and the have avoided a formal confrontation over the issue, but they have scarcely established a stable basis for avoiding one in the future. Any firm evidence showing links between Iran and the Al-Khobar bombings could freeze progress in Saudi-Iranian relations, sever them, or lead to a massive confrontation between the United States and Iran.

Moreover, Iran continues to occupy Abu Musa and the Greater and Lesser Tunbs, two islands claimed by the UAE. The Saudi government has consistently supported the UAE position on the issue at the twenty-first GCC summit in December 2000.[27] Saudi Arabia is also deeply concerned with Iran's buildup of forces that can threaten naval traffic passing through the Straits of Hormuz and the lower Gulf.

Nevertheless, Saudi Arabia is almost certain to continue to maintain its rapprochement with Iran unless the Al-Khobar bombing or some new crisis forces it to change this policy. The Kingdom will do so to reduce the risk of military and political confrontation with Iran, to allow Saudi Arabia to use Iran as a counterbalance to Iraq, to ease Saudi Arabia's internal problems with its Shi'ites, and to reduce the backlash from Saudi Arabia's military dependence on the United States.

The Problem of Iraq

Saudi Arabia faces far more severe problems in dealing with Iraq than with Iran. Privately, Saudi officials see Iraq as the greatest single political and military threat the Kingdom faces. At the same time, Saudi officials feel they must live with Saddam's regime. In spite of efforts during 2001 and 2002 by senior U.S. officials like Vice President Cheney and Secretary Rumsfeld to persuade the Kingdom to support efforts to remove Saddam from power, Saudi Arabian officials have little confidence in U.S. efforts to bring down Saddam Hussein's regime.

While Saudi officials are divided over whether the United States could, or should, have done this in 1991, few believed as of mid-2002 that the United States had yet shown that a U.S.–British-led invasion would solve Saudi Arabia's problems with Iraq, or that the United States had a convincing plan to drive Saddam from power and reshape Iraq once he was gone. Although Saudi officials realized that U.S. and British military action could produce radical changes in the Iraqi threat, they still felt that Saudi Arabia must plan to live with Saddam Hussein and prepare for a time when Iraq will eventually break out of sanctions. Moreover, some Saudi policymakers were not confident that a post-Saddam Iraq would ultimately be a friendly state, and felt that any successor regimes might do just as much to try to expand Iraq's regional influence and oil revenues at the expense of its neighbors.

Saudi Arabia has pursued a policy of limited political accommodation with Iraq while planning for the risk of war and continuing to support U.S. efforts to contain Iraq. Saudi Arabia felt that it must try to find some kind of modus vivendi with Iraq, and established "correct" relations with the country during the Arab foreign ministers meeting in April 2002. It has sought to avoid provocation where possible, and wants to minimize the risk of driving Iraq toward better ties with Iran. The Kingdom has been careful to show overt concern for the suffering of the Iraqi people, has placed limits on cooperation with the United States and Britain in the event of U.S.

and British enforcement of the southern no-fly zone, and has conspicuously avoided any visible support of U.S. efforts to overthrow Saddam Hussein.

Trying to Live with the "Enemy"

Saudi Arabia has never advocated political tolerance of Iraq's defiance of the UN. King Fahd made this clear in several statements in early 1998, and Crown Prince Abdullah reiterated this point during a visit to Cairo to discuss the Iraqi crisis with President Hosni Mubarak: "I call on President Saddam Hussein to listen . . . to the voice of reason and political awareness and to implement the UN Security Council's resolutions and spare the Iraqi people the coming threat. . . . The Iraqi people will suffer more if reason is ignored and previous experiences are not remembered."[28]

Saudi Arabia has continued to support the enforcement of UN sanctions and demands that Iraq allow the return of UN inspectors. Ever since the late 1990s, however, Saudi Arabia has refused to support major U.S. military action against Iran. Despite intense lobbying by U.S. Secretary of State Madeleine Albright and Secretary of Defense William Cohen, however, Saudi Arabia has refused to support U.S. threats to strike Iraq if it did not allow UNSCOM to operate freely. On February 2, 1998, a senior Saudi official stated, "Saudi Arabia will not allow any strikes against Iraq, under any circumstances, from its soil or bases in Saudi Arabia, due to the sensitivity of the issue in the Arab and Muslim world." Prince Abdullah reiterated these same points during his visit to Cairo.

On February 16, 1998, Information Minister Fouad al-Farsi bin Abdul-Salam bin Muhammad Farisi was quoted by the official news agency SPA as saying, "King Fahd restated that the Kingdom is eager for all diplomatic means to be exhausted to find an appropriate solution to the current crisis." In addition, according to Information Minister Farisi, King Fahd "affirmed that the Kingdom's position is based on the desire to put an end to the suffering of the Iraqi people and the desire for peace in Iraq and its territorial integrity." At the same time, he said that King Fahd also blamed the crisis on the Iraqi government's failure to implement UN Security Council resolutions, "especially those related to the mission of the Special Commission charged with dismantling weapons of mass destruction."[29]

There has been little popular Saudi support for military action against Iraq at any time during the long crisis over UN inspections. Public opinion polls are a rarity in Saudi Arabia and most are anything but scientific. However, a poll of 330 Saudi men and women conducted in 1998 and published by the London-based Arabic-language newspaper *Asharq al-Awsat* found that 90.3% of respondents were against a military strike while only 5.5% supported an attack. The remaining 4.2% gave no response. The poll was conducted in the Saudi capital of Riyadh, and *Asharq al-Awsat* concluded that "the Saudis who got used to the atmosphere of war seven years ago . . . do not hesitate now to show opposing views to what their stands were in the early 1990s." When asked to explain their stance, 69% of those opposed to an attack cited sympathy with the Iraqi people as one of their primary reasons. Approximately one third said they saw no justification for such an attack, while according to the paper, 22.5% of those opposed to an attack explained their views by what they deemed a double standard in the United States' treatment of Iraq and Israel.[30]

Saudi Arabia maintained a cautious attitude throughout the crisis over the continuation of UNSCOM inspections that continued through December 1998. Visits by both Secretary Albright and Secretary Cohen failed to convince the Saudis to permit the use of air bases inside Saudi Arabia in the event of a U.S.-led attack against Iraq. While the Saudis issued a joint warning with the United States to Iraq that it would be responsible for the consequences of its actions, Crown Prince Abdullah made it clear in a speech that Saudi Arabia opposed the use of force: "We will not agree and we are against striking Iraq as a people and as a nation." They also joined many of the other Arab states in calling for an ease in sanctions on Iraq.

On February 22, 1998, King Fahd expressed hope that the mission of UN Secretary-General Kofi Annan would help spare the country and its people more suffering. The official Saudi Press Agency reported that the king, "expressed his hope for the success of the mission of UN Secretary-General Kofi Annan to find a diplomatic solution to spare Iraq and the Iraqi people more tragedies." The king made similar comments during talks with Iran's former president, Akbar Hashemi Rafsanjani.[31]

Saudi Arabia did, however, support U.S. and British efforts to create a "smart sanctions" policy toward Iraq that eases the sanctions affecting Iraq's economy while maintaining or tightening the sanctions on military and "deal use" imports. Saudi officials also consistently recognized that they face a serious threat from a revanchist Iraq.

The Kingdom did reach a tentative agreement with Iraq on the partition of their neutral zone in 1981 as well as a full border settlement in 1983, but Saudi Arabia sized its military buildup around possible war with Iraq and never felt it could trust the Iraqi regime. Saudi Arabia was one of Iraq's strongest backers during the Iran-Iraq War, and provided it with massive financial and military aid. The end result was not gratitude, however, but Iraq's invasion of Kuwait in 1990. Iraqi forces massed on the border and posed a major threat to Saudi Arabia. This conflict became the Gulf War and created a legacy of Saudi-Iraqi hostility that may long outlive Saddam Hussein.

Any post–Gulf War "rapprochement," has been more façade than real. Saddam Hussein and senior Iraqi officials have continued to issue sporadic statements attacking Saudi Arabia for supporting the United States, cooperating with the West in military operations against Iraq, and overproducing oil. They did so in spite of efforts to improve Saudi-Iraqi relations at the Arab Foreign Ministers meeting in April 2002. Iraq continued to accuse Saudi Arabia of "aggression" for allowing U.S. and British air units to enforce the southern no-fly zone from bases in the Kingdom. Iraqi officials and the Iraqi government press sometimes urged Saudis and other Arabs to rebel against their regimes and to revolt against the presence of foreign troops on Saudi soil. Iraq has also attacked Saudi Arabia for holding military meetings of the GCC.[32]

While Iraq paid lip service to its recognition of Kuwait at the Arab foreign ministers meeting in April 2002, it previously had taken previous steps that show it did not accept the new border that the UN demarcated between Iraq and Kuwait. Saddam's sons, Vice President Taha Yassin Ramadan, and other senior Iraqi officials issued statements that imply that Kuwait remains a missing province of Iraq.[33] Most notably, Saddam's eldest son, Uday, printed a working paper he had submitted to parliament in November 2000 in his paper *Babil* on January 15, 2001. He declared that "the current map of Iraq, which is the emblem of the National Assembly, does not include all Iraq's borders as known by the people in all their components, namely Kuwait City." He then called upon the National Assembly to "prepare a map of the whole of Iraq, including Kuwait City as an integral part of Iraq." The next day in Cairo, Vice President Ramadan stated that these views were shared by 99% of the Iraqi people.[34]

During interviews in 2000, 2001, and 2002, Saudi officials quietly made it clear that they recognized all of these issues. They saw no near-term prospects for truly reintegrating Iraq into the "family of nations." They made it clear that Saudi Arabia has been the target of a continuous stream of hostile statements from Iraq since 1990, and that these attacks have, for the most part, increased since the United States and Britain carried out Operation Desert Fox in December 1998. They have made it equally clear since September 2000 that they feared the backlash from Iraq's ability to exploit the new wave of Israeli-Palestinian violence that began in September 2000, Iraq's improving relations with Syria, and Iraq's growing influence in Jordan.

While Saudi officials made it clear that they believed that much of the present degree of Iraqi hostility was unique to Saddam Hussein, few seemed to feel that the Kingdom would be able to trust a new Iraqi regime, even if it did appear to be moderate. The fear that such a regime would still seek to reacquire weapons of mass destruction and pursue Iraqi hegemony still remains. Most indicated that it would take years of proven moderation by a new Iraqi regime before Saudi Arabia could relax its guard.

Saudi Arabia has had continuing reasons to examine possible Iraqi attacks on Saudi Arabia and Kuwait and make such contingencies a key priority for national security planning. On June 5, 2001, for example, Saudi Arabia accused Iraq of staging eleven raids on Saudi border outposts in the previous few months and warned the U.N. Security Council that more such attacks could have "grave consequences." It stated that an Iraqi soldier was killed in one attack on May 23, and that "a number" of Saudi soldiers were wounded when an Iraqi patrol moved 437 yards inside Saudi territory and fired on Saudi border forces near the Sahn al-Sharqiyah post in the Uwayqilah sector. The Kingdom stated that Iraq had carried out ten other raids between March and April, when Iraqi soldiers fired on Saudi outposts from their side of the border and did not enter Saudi territory.[35]

Ambassador Fawzi bin Abdul Majeed Shobokshi sent a letter to the UN Security Council revealing that although Saudi Arabia initially believed the attacks were isolated incidents "that might be overlooked," they concluded that the attacks' persistence "demonstrate[d] that the Iraqi authorities [were] responsible for them." Saudi Arabia appealed "to the Security Council to urge Iraq to desist from its violations of Saudi Arabia's international boundaries, and . . . assert the inalienable right of the Kingdom to take whatever measures it deems appropriate to protect its security and its borders." Saudi Arabia alerted the members of the United Nations "to the grave consequences of the continued violation by the Iraqi authorities of the territory of Saudi Arabia, which jeopardizes security and peace in the region."

Saudi officials do not oppose U.S. and British operations in support of the southern no-fly zone, such as the new round of U.S. strikes on Iraq that took place on January 16, 2001, at the start of George W. Bush's term of office.[36] The Kingdom has been notably silent about the series of strikes that have occurred since that time. In short, the Saudi policy of "living with Saddam" has never meant trusting Saddam or believing that he can eventually be integrated into the community of nations. At the higher levels of the Saudi security apparatus there is also some fear that Saddam Hussein's regime will try to take political revenge and possibly use terrorism and proxy warfare, maybe involving at least the tacit threat of using weapons of mass destruction. Saudi Arabia must consider the threat that both Iraqi and Iranian "creeping proliferation" pose to the Kingdom, the risk of new missile attacks, and the need for both some form of defense and some form of deterrent. This also means that Saudi opposition to U.S. military intervention to overthrow Saddam Hussein's regime is relative. Saudi Arabia distrusts the uncertain character and fears the political costs of war, but would scarcely shed tears if the United States proved successful. It may yet give way to U.S. pressure to provide Saudi facilities and would certainly seek to take advantage of Saddam's fall.

The Threat of Iraqi Invasion

Part of the reason for Saudi concern is that the Iraqi military threat to Saudi Arabia differs fundamentally from that posed by Iran. Iran does not share a common border with the Kingdom and has very limited amphibious capabilities. It can pose an air or missile threat, attack shipping and Saudi facilities in the Gulf, and threaten to use weapons of mass destruction. Iraq, however, does share a common border with Saudi Arabia and is the only power with land forces strong enough to pose a major threat of invasion to the Kingdom's key cities and oil facilities.

The threat of such an invasion should not be exaggerated; Iraq has not had any significant arms shipments or resupply of munitions and spare parts since the summer of 1990, and its military forces took massive losses during the Gulf War. Its Air Force is of relatively limited quality, and clashes like Desert Fox have shown that Iraq would have to be willing to take extreme risks to engage in any conflict that involves U.S. air and missile forces. Iraq also cannot rebuild its conventional forces quickly. It will be years after UN sanctions on Iraqi arms imports are finally lifted before any credible combination of Iraqi arms imports and military production efforts can give the country enough capability to deliberately initiate a conflict with Saudi Arabia as long as it is allied with Britain and the United States.

Nevertheless, Iraq does have near-term contingency capabilities that might allow it to exploit the limits to Saudi and U.S. capabilities. Iraq's land forces still retain significant war-fighting capabilities and much of the force structure that made Iraq the dominant military power in the Gulf after its victory over Iran.

Iraqi land forces still make Iraq a major military power by Gulf standards and those forces could still seize Kuwait in a matter of days or occupy part of Saudi Arabia's Eastern Province if they did not face immediate opposition from U.S., Kuwaiti, and Saudi forces. The IISS and U.S. experts indicate that the Iraqi Army had a total of around 375,000 full-time actives (including 100,000 recalled reserves) in mid-2002, and a total of seven corps, with six Republican Guards corps and three regular army corps. Iraq had a total of twenty-three divisions; these divisions included six Republican Guard divisions (three armored, one mechanized, and two infantry) and one Presidential Guard/Special Security Force division.[37] There were also fifteen independent Special Forces or commando brigades. This compares with thirty-five to forty divisions in the summer of 1990, and sixty-seven to seventy divisions in January 1991—just before the Coalition offensives began in the Gulf War.[38]

Experts indicate that Iraq's divisions were arrayed north-to-south in early 2002, with a mix of regular and Republican Guards divisions. All of the divisions near the Kuwait border were regular, although some Republican Guard divisions could move to the border relatively rapidly. All Republican Guards divisions were located above the 32-degree line. Several additional Republican Guards divisions were located around Baghdad to play a major role in internal security, and a number of Republican Guards divisions were located north of Baghdad closer to the Kurdish area.[39]

At least twelve Iraqi divisions seemed to be effective enough to be used in an attack on Kuwait and/or Saudi Arabia, or intensive combat operations against Iran. There were five regular divisions—three relatively combat-ready—in Iraq's southern border region north of Kuwait. There were two more Republican Guards divisions south of Baghdad that could be rapidly deployed to support the three more capable regular divisions in an attack on Kuwait that USCENTCOM labeled the "Basra breakout."[40]

Iraq did, however, face significant limits on its operational capabilities. Iraq would encounter major problems in assembling and deploying its forces into any kind of coherent invasion force. It would lack both modern air defense weapons and high-quality air support. The Iraqi Air Force had a total of roughly 35,000 to 40,000 men in mid-2002, including some 15,000 to 17,000 air defense personnel.[41] U.S. estimates indicate that the Iraqi Air Force had 330 to 370 combat aircraft in inventory. IISS estimates indicate that Iraq had at least 316 combat aircraft, including 6 bombers, 130 fighter-ground attack aircraft, and 180 fighters. However, most experts agreed that many of the Iraqi aircraft counted in this total had limited or no operational combat capability, and Iraqi training and readiness standards are poor.

In fact, some aspects of Iraq's military infrastructure were better than its combat forces. Iraq has been able to rebuild many of the shelters and facilities it lost during the war, as well as much of the Air Force C[4]I/BM system. This C[4]I/BM system included an extensive net of optical fiber communications, a TFH 647 radio relay system, a TFH tropospheric communications system, and a large mix of radars supplied by the Soviet Union. Iraq had rebuilt most of the air bases damaged during the Gulf War, and a number of bases received only limited damage. This gave Iraq a network of some twenty-five major operating bases, many with extensive shelters and hardened facilities.[42] Iraq had also greatly improved the integration and survivability of the C[4]I/BM system for its land-based air defenses.

Saudi Arabia too has important weaknesses. The Saudi Army has reverted to a static defensive force that has limited effectiveness above the company and battalion level. Although it claims to have 75,000 full-time regulars in the Army, plus 75,000 active members of the National Guard, actual manning levels are significantly lower. Some of its M-1A2 tanks are still in storage, plus about 145 of its 290 obsolescent AMX-30s. As a result, Saudi Arabia relies heavily on its 450 M-60A3s. This is still a significant amount of armor, but it is dispersed over much of the Kingdom and Saudi Arabia lacks the training, manpower quality, sustainability, and C[4]I/SR capabilities for effective aggressive maneuver warfare and forward defense.

While the GCC has rapid reaction force on paper, the reality is a few hollow allied battalions. The so-called GCC rapid deployment force is largely a political fiction with no meaningful real-world combat capability against Iraqi heavy divisions. Moreover, the new GCC agreements that were signed in 2000 and 2001 to strengthen this force will do nothing substantive to change what is little more than a military façade.[43]

The United States can bring decisive force to bear, but this normally takes time. Delays in U.S. power projection capability normally limit U.S. ability to exploit its advantages in military technology and the land elements of the "revolution in military affairs." Nevertheless, the successes in U.S. and allied air power in the Gulf War, "Desert Fox," and U.S. operations in Afghanistan show that Iraq would be acutely vulnerable to U.S. and British air and cruise missile power.

One thing is certain, a Saudi–U.S.-led coalition's ability to deal with a sudden Iraqi attack on Kuwait (or Saudi Arabia) depends on U.S. ability to mass offensive air and missile power, and its ability to use it immediately against Iraq the moment major troop movements begin without first seeking to win air superiority or air supremacy. It will also depend on U.S. willingness and ability to couple strikes against Iraqi leadership and strategic targets to this offensive in an effort to halt Iraq, and U.S. ability to deter, defend, and retaliate against any Iraqi use of weapons of mass destruction.

At the same time, much still depends on Saudi Arabia and the other Gulf states. The United States will require the full support of Saudi Arabia in committing its Army and Air Force to the defense of Kuwait and the Saudi border area, and on the Kingdom, Bahrain, Qatar, the UAE, and Oman to assist in the deployment and basing of U.S. forces in the region. The United States used some twenty-three air bases and airports in the Gulf War in 1990–1991, and eleven were in Saudi Arabia. It will also necessitate Kuwaiti willingness to allow the United States and Saudi Arabia to employ force against Iraq before its forces can deploy to the Kuwaiti border area.

Much will also depend on the quality of Saudi–U.S. military relations, regional perceptions of the long-term resolve of the United States, the ability of the Southern Gulf states to act quickly in a crisis, and the willingness of the Southern Gulf states to show that they will support a firm U.S. response to Iraq, even at some risk. Equally important will be the ability of Iraq's leadership to set achievable demands and avoid open confrontation. In broad terms, it seems likely that Iraq's ability to intimidate will slowly improve over time, but there is no way to predict how quickly or by how much.

Iraq and Asymmetric Warfare

Unlike Iran, Iraq has never demonstrated great capability to conduct "proxy wars" by training, arming, and funding Arab extremist movements. Iraq does sponsor some extremist and terrorist groups, and Iraqi intelligence has long maintained contact with terrorist movements, but the end result has done little for Iraq. Iraq also lacks Iran's bases, training centers, and staging facilities in other countries, and the political support of third nations like the Sudan and Syria that are close to the scene of such proxy conflicts. Similarly, Iraq can only hope to win proxy wars fought against vulnerable governments. Attempts to fight such wars will have little impact on a successful Arab-Israeli peace settlement, or in sustaining civil conflict in the face of a government that demonstrates that it has the capacity to govern and deal with its social problems.

Iraq has some capability for information warfare and cyber-terrorism, but it seems very unlikely that it is capable of advanced attacks on protected U.S. military and U.S. government systems. Iraq also probably has little capability to attack the U.S. private sector and the systems of Gulf states. It is, however, steadily improving the defense of its own systems. Most are redundant, rely heavily on buried land-links and optical fibers, and isolated from netted or open systems.

Iraq also has a strong revanchist motive to use proxy warfare against Israel, Saudi Arabia, and the United States. The continued failure of the Arab-Israeli peace process, Iraq's efforts to exploit its support of the Palestinian cause, and any new instability in the regimes in the Gulf and the region might allow Iraq to make more successful use of proxy wars in the future. So would the creation of a radical Arab regime in Jordan, Egypt, or Syria, which might turn to Iraq for support. Similarly, Iraq may seek to covertly improve its capabilities for unconventional warfare, including the use of chemical and biological weapons. The practical problem that Iraq faces will then be to find a place and contingency where it could exploit such capabilities that offer more return than using proxies, and that allows Iraq to act at an acceptable level of risk so that the United States and its allies would not retaliate.

Iraq and Weapons of Mass Destruction

Iraq has a much more serious history as a proliferator than Iran. Iraq has seen proliferation as a counter to conventional superiority since the late 1960s. It began to seek weapons of mass destruction in the early 1970s, long before the Gulf War showed what the "revolution in military affairs" (RMA) and U.S. conventional superiority could accomplish. As a result, it is hardly surprising that Iraq sees proliferation as its key potential method of countering the U.S. advantage in conventional forces and the RMA, and has been willing to pursue such options in the face of massive economic costs, UNSCOM and IAEA efforts to destroy its remaining capabilities, and the remaining extension of UN sanctions.

In spite of the Gulf War, and nearly eight years of UNSCOM efforts before Iraq forced an end to the UN inspection effort, Iraq still presents a major threat in terms of proliferation. It is also all too clear that Iraq may have increased this threat since active UNSCOM and IAEA efforts ended in December 1998.

Iraq's present holdings of chemical and biological weapons now seem to be limited to the point where they do not impose major constraints on

U.S. freedom of action, or do much to intimidate Iraq's neighbors. It seems unlikely that Iraq can reach the point, in the near-term, where its capabilities are great enough to change Saudi, U.S., British, Iranian, Israeli and/or Southern Gulf perceptions of risk to the point where they would limit or paralyze outside military action. Furthermore, it seems unlikely that Iraq can openly build up major production and deployment capabilities without provoking strong U.S. counterproliferation programs, including retaliatory strike capabilities. The same is true of a response by Iran and the Southern Gulf states. As a result, Iraq's acquisition of weapons of mass destruction may end simply in provoking an arms race even when UN sanctions are lifted.

Nevertheless, no one can be certain of Iraq's holdings and capabilities, and Iraq's possession of such weapons inevitably affects Saudi, other Southern Gulf states, U.S., British, and Israeli perceptions of the risks inherent in attacking Iraq. Once UN sanctions on Iraq are lifted, Iraq may be able to rebuild its strategic delivery capabilities relatively quickly, and any sustained conflict involving weapons of mass destruction could have drastic consequences. Even today covert and asymmetric attacks present a threat. This would be particularly true if Iraq could develop advanced biological weapons with near-nuclear lethality, or assemble nuclear devices with weapons-grade fissile material bought from an outside source. There might be little or no warning of such strategic developments.

As is the case with Iran, there are several other developments that might allow Iraq to use proliferation to pose a near-term threat to U.S. conventional capabilities in the region:

- A successful Iraqi attempt to buy significant amounts of weapons-grade material. This could allow Iraq to achieve a nuclear breakout capability in a matter of months. Both the United States and the region would find it much harder to adjust to such an Iraqi effort than to Iraq's slow development of nuclear weapons by creating fissile material. It seems likely that the United States could deal with the situation by extending a nuclear umbrella over the Gulf, but even so, the Southern Gulf states might be far more responsive to Iraqi pressure and intimidation. Most, after all, are so small that they are virtually "one-bomb states."

- A change in the United States and regional perception of biological weapons. Biological weapons are now largely perceived as unproven systems of uncertain lethality. Regardless of their technical capabilities, they have little of the political impact of nuclear weapons. Iraq might, however, conduct live animal tests to demonstrate that its biological weapons have near-nuclear lethality, or some other power might demonstrate their effectiveness in another conflict. The successful mass testing or use of biological weapons might produce a rapid "paradigm shift" in the perceived importance of such weapons and of Iraq's biological warfare programs.

- Iraq might break out of UN sanctions and reveal a more substantial capability than now seems likely. Paradoxically, such an Iraqi capability would help to legitimize Iran and Israel's nuclear, biological, and chemical programs and the escalation to the use of such weapons.

- Iraq might use such weapons through proxies or in covert attacks with some degree of plausible deniability. Terrorism and unconventional warfare would be far more intimidating if they made use of weapons of mass destruction.

The Saudi Approach to "Dual Containment" and the Overthrow of Saddam Hussein

Given this background, it is clear why Saudi Arabia has not taken the same approach toward either Iran or Iraq as the United States. Saudi officials have no illusions about the threat or the military problems they would encounter in dealing with either Iran or Iraq. They recognize that Saudi Arabia needs strong military forces and support from the United States, and that the Kingdom must plan to provide for both the security of smaller and more vulnerable neighbors like Bahrain and Kuwait and for the waters of the Gulf and Gulf of Oman. At the same time, most Saudi officials do not support U.S. policies that sanction both Iran and Iraq or American adventures in regime change in Iraq.

Saudi policymakers feel that Saudi foreign policy must address the best way to live with two very different regimes that it feels can be contained militarily, but that cannot be isolated economically and politically. As a result, the Saudi approach to dealing with the very different regimes in Iran and Iraq has sought to use the modernization and expansion of its own forces and its alliance with the United States to develop the military means to deter and contain Iran and Iraq, but also to create a dialogue and diplomatic relations with Iran. Saudi Arabia has taken the approach that Iran might at least act as a "moderate" state if it is given support in developing its economy and energy exports and if it does not feel encircled and threatened by a combination of Iraq, the United States, Israel, and the Southern Gulf states.

At the same time, Saudi policymakers have sought to ease the threat from Iraq by finding ways to reduce the political backlash from the hardships that sanctions imposed on the Iraqi people, and have tried to find ways to create some form of rapprochement with Saddam Hussein. They have also sought to reduce the political visibility of Saudi Arabia's role in providing military support for U.S. and British air operations and strikes against Iraq, and have distanced themselves firmly from any U.S. efforts to support outside Iraqi opposition groups.

It is important to note in this respect that Saudi Arabia, like virtually all Arab states, sees the preservation of Iraq's unity as a primary objective in spite of Saddam Hussein's regime. Rightly or wrongly, Saudi Arabia prefers to see Iraq remain under Sunni rule, and has little interest in trying to restructure Iraq to increase the rights of its Shi'ites or Kurds. Iraq's ethnic and religious diversity is seen as a threat to Saudi interests, one that might under worst cases greatly strengthen Iran if Iraq was ever to become a Shi'ite-dominated state. This is at least possible: The CIA estimates that Iraq is 75% to 80% Arab, 15% to 20% Kurdish, and 5% Turkoman, Assyrian, and other. It also estimates that it is 60% to 65% Shi'ite, 32% to 37% Sunni, and 3% Christian. All of the major Iraqi outside opposition groups are largely Shi'ite, and the group that has conducted the most actual operations against Saddam's regime is a religious faction supported by Iran.[44]

THE SOUTHERN GULF AND YEMEN

Saudi diplomacy has made a major effort to reassure the Kingdom's smaller neighbors that it at most seeks the status of first among equals, rather than that of a politically dominant power. Saudi Arabia has also made increasing use of the GCC as a political, economic, and security forum where all of the Southern Gulf states can discuss issues as "equals."

Saudi Arabia has largely resolved the border disputes that have long been a source of tension in the Southern Gulf, although history of such disputes is scarcely forgotten. Saudi Arabia's present boundaries with Jordan, Iraq, and Kuwait were established as the result of British efforts to limit Saudi military expansion in the 1920s and 1930s. The Saudi-Yemeni border area grew out of a war in the 1930s, and Saudi Arabia had more recent border disputes with Oman, Qatar, and the UAE. However, as a result, Saudi Arabia is so clearly the largest power in the Southern Gulf that some of the smaller Gulf states see the Kingdom as a potential hegemon or threat. It will take time to fully lay the fears to rest that Saudi Arabia seeks to dominate the Arabian Peninsula.

Relations with Yemen

Saudi Arabia's most serious problems with other states in the Arabian peninsula have been with Yemen. The two countries have had long-standing political differences dating back to the battles that forged Saudi Arabia as a modern state until the unification of North and South Yemen in 1990. Saudi Arabia saw South Yemen as a source of Marxist radicalism and terrorism and saw North Yemen as a potential threat to its southeast. Unification removed the more radical elements in South Yemen from power, but Saudi Arabia still regarded Yemen as a serious potential threat until the late 1990s and still plans for possible conflict.

Part of the reason for these Saudi concerns is that Yemen is an extraordinarily poor state with a population that nearly equals that of Saudi Arabia. The U.S. Census Bureau estimated that Yemen had a population of 18.7 million in 2001 versus 23.5 million for Saudi Arabia, and that Yemen's population will grow to 45.5 million by 2030 versus 55.8 million for Saudi Arabia.[45] The World Bank projects that Yemen's population will increase from 17.5 million in 2000 to 26.6 million by the year 2015, and 36 million by the year 2030.[46] These figures compare with estimates of 33.7 million for Saudi Arabia in 2015 and 46 million in 2030.

Unless the economic conditions change, an impoverished Yemen may well contribute to regional instability in spite of improvements in Saudi-Yemeni relations. The country's ongoing failure to develop, coupled with major population growth will put a growing pressure on an already difficult situation. Yemen's population is crowded into a resource-poor country that has long had to export labor to Saudi Arabia and that has limited oil and gas reserves. It has a territory of some 528,000 square kilometers versus 1,960,000 square kilometers for Saudi Arabia. The CIA estimates that Yemen had a GDP per capita of approximately $820 in purchasing power parity terms in 2002, versus $10,600 for Saudi Arabia.[47] Saudi Arabia has feared that Yemen's sheer poverty might lead it to spill over into Saudi Arabia.

Yemen still has significant military forces, although a series of civil wars and the breakup of the Soviet Union, have made Yemen a far less serious military threat than it was in the late 1980s. In 2002, Yemen's military force had 54,000 full-time actives. Its Army had 910 tanks, although these were worn and largely obsolete. Its Air Force had seventy-one active combat aircraft and eight attack helicopters, although its modern combat aircraft were limited to five MiG-29s.[48]

Saudi planners do not ignore the history of a long series of clashes over contradictory Saudi and Yemeni claims in their 1,460-kilometer-long border area, and here some historical background is useful. North Yemen became independent from the Ottoman Empire in 1918, and its Imam claimed much of the territory that Ibn Saud felt he had acquired in conquering southern Arabia. This led to war in the early 1930s, when the Imam of Yemen invaded Saudi Arabia's southeastern border area. Saudi Arabia won this war and Yemen was forced to sign the Taif Agreement of 1934, which gave Saudi Arabia control of the territory that Yemen had claimed, plus additional territory in the Jizan, Asir, and Najran regions. Ever since, Yemeni leaders and nationalists have indicated that they would like to reverse the Taif Agreement.

New tensions arose between Saudi Arabia and North Yemen in the early 1960s. In 1962, civil war erupted between Yemeni Royalists and Republicans. Egyptian forces entered North Yemen to support the new Republican government, while Saudi Arabia backed the Royalists. Egypt was forced to withdraw its troops from North Yemen in 1967 because of its defeat in its war with Israel. Nevertheless, the Republicans won the civil war in North Yemen, leaving a continuing potential threat. This led to long-lasting Saudi tension with the government of North Yemen. Although Saudi Arabia provided North Yemen with aid and allowed nearly a million Yemenis to work in Saudi Arabia, it also continued to interfere in North Yemeni affairs and constantly attempted to divide North Yemen's tribes and prevent a strong central government from emerging.

A different kind of threat developed in South Yemen. The British had created a protectorate area around the southern port of Aden in the 19th century composed of a number of different tribal groups. The Yemenis in the port area became politically radicalized during the 1930s–1950s and launched a low-intensity war against the British and the more conservative tribal groups outside of Aden. The British withdrew in 1967 and the protectorate became South Yemen. Three years later, battles within the southern government defeated a pro-Nasser faction and South Yemen became a radical Marxist state. This triggered a massive exodus of hundreds of thousands of Yemenis from the south to the north, contributing to two decades of hostility between the two Yemens. While South Yemen posed more of a threat to Oman and North Yemen than it did to Saudi Arabia, Saudi Arabia could not ignore either state. During the 1970s and 1980s, Saudi Arabia fought repeated clashes with Yemen, partly over control of the potential oil reserves in their border area.

A bloody civil war took place in South Yemen in the late 1980s that destroyed many of its most radical factions. South Yemen was so impoverished that it was practically forced into unification with North Yemen in 1990. However, the newly unified Republic of Yemen sided with Iraq in 1990, which led to severed relations between Saudi Arabia and Yemen. As a result, the Yemeni Embassy ordered Yemenis to leave Saudi Arabia, prompting a mass exodus of tens of thousands of Yemeni expatriate workers from the country. This hostility increased after the unification of North and South Yemen in 1990. Saudi Arabia then backed factions in South Yemen against the central government in the Yemeni Civil War of 1994, only to see South Yemen defeated. A new series of border clashes then took place in the Najran region, once again in areas with potential oil reserves.

In late 1994, however, Saudi Arabia and Yemen began to mediate their border disputes. Yemen became more accommodating after it had been weakened by civil war, the loss of Soviet support following the breakup of the former Soviet Union (FSU), and the virtual cut-off of external Arab aid following its decision to side with Iraq after Saddam Hussein's invasion of Kuwait. This change in Yemen's position helped lead to more successful negotiations, even though incidents continued, such as Yemeni fire on Saudi aircraft believed to be violating Yemeni airspace in January 1995. As a result, both countries signed a Memorandum of Understanding (MOU) in Mecca on February 26, 1995. The eleven-point agreement was negotiated by Prince Sultan, Saudi Arabia's second deputy prime minister and minister of defense and aviation, and Sheik Abdullah al-Ahmar, the speaker of the Yemeni House of Representatives, and approved by King Fahd and President Ali Abdullah Saleh of Yemen.[49]

The agreement recognized the validity of most of the borders set forth in the Taif Agreement of 1934 while clearly defining the remaining areas of uncertainty and dispute. Saudi Arabia and Yemen set up a joint committee to use "modern technology" to establish border markers in the area from Raseef Al-Bahr (Ral Al-Mewaaj Shami) to Radeef Qrad (between Meedi and Al-Mosem) and then to a point near Al-Thar mountain, after which they would demarcate the remaining borders. Additional joint committees were established to demarcate marine borders along the Red Sea Coast, guarantee nonmilitary movements or establishments in the border area, and promote economic and cultural ties. A higher committee was set up to oversee and facilitate the work of the other committees. Both countries also agreed to prohibit the use of their territory for hostile acts against the other, to refrain from hostile propaganda, and to report all actions in official minutes of meetings signed by officials of both countries.

King Fahd and President Saleh reinforced this agreement at a meeting on June 6, 1995. Saudi Arabia agreed to allow more Yemeni workers into the Kingdom and provide some aid. Senior Saudi officials—including Prince Sultan, Foreign Minister Saud al-Faisal, and Minister of the Interior Prince Nayef bin Abdulaziz—then made a three-day visit to Sana'a in late August, 1996, and met with the President Saleh and Prime Minister Abdul Aziz Abdul Ghani. Prince Sultan and the speaker of the Yemeni Parliament, Sheikh Abdullah al-Ahmar, chaired a meeting of the Saudi-Yemeni Higher Joint Committee. The end result was a joint communiqué stressing the commitment of both sides to the Taif Agreement of 1934, and a new agreement to promote economic, commercial, technical, and investment cooperation. Saudi Arabia and Yemen also signed new agreements on July 29, 1996, that dealt with security cooperation and fighting drug trafficking. The security agreement established security liaison groups and an extradition agreement.[50]

Further negotiations—led by Minister of the Interior Prince Nayef, rather than Saudi Arabia's traditional negotiator, Minister of Defense Prince Sultan—took place in July 1997. Prince Nayef brought new settlement proposals sent by King Fahd and President Saleh announced, "The gap between Yemen and Saudi Arabia has been narrowed to a great extent." Saudi Arabia did not, however, agree to Yemen's proposal to accept arbitration, and considerable differences remained.[51] Those issues included Saudi plans for a possible oil pipeline corridor across Yemeni territory to be controlled by Saudi Arabia and a land dispute over the Wadi'ah and Sharurah areas that lie between the 17th and 18th parallels of latitude adjacent to the Hadhramaut region of northeastern Yemen.

Minor clashes occurred in spite of the negotiations. Violence erupted along the Saudi-Yemeni border in August 1997 when Saudi border police fired automatic weapons at Yemeni soldiers near the Rub al-Khali, wounding eight Yemeni soldiers. In November, tensions flared again when two Saudis were killed in border clashes with Yemeni forces. Tensions between the two countries were also exacerbated after a Syrian on trial for bombings in Yemen claimed that he was recruited by Saudi intelligence to assassinate Yemen's foreign minister. In light of these developments, the Yemeni president declared in late December that talks with the Saudis were deadlocked and called for a postponement. One source in the region claimed that Sallah stated in a telephone call with Saudi Crown Prince Abdullah ibn Abdulaziz, "If there is no will on the part of our Saudi brothers to settle the border question at the present time it is possible to adjourn these negotiations until it fully convinced and wants to pursue these talks."

Even so, the two sides continued to meet and made further progress. Yemeni officials announced in early April 1998 that Yemen and Saudi Arabia would resume talks. Yemen's speaker of parliament, Sheikh Abdullah bin Hussein al-Ahmar, stated on March 4, 1998: "In the coming days the serious and positive dialogue between the two countries will be resumed." Ahmar said he had discussed the dispute with Saudi Defense Minister Prince Sultan in February. "When I visited Prince Sultan . . . I felt from him the desire to continue dialogue between Yemen and Saudi Arabia and to continue border negotiations in order to reach a satisfactory solution." At the same time, Ahmar said major differences remained between the two sides over border demarcation.[52]

Relations between the two countries worsened again after a July 1998 incident in which Saudi and Yemeni forces clashed on the island of Duwaima, one of three islets in the Red Sea claimed by both countries.[53] Saudi Arabia claimed 75% of the island and maintains that only the remaining 25% is Yemeni, while Yemen claimed the whole island as part of its sovereign territory.[54] In a conflict that lasted five hours, Saudi warships fired at the island, reportedly in self-defense, killing three Yemenis and wounding nine. By the end of July, however, the two countries reached a new agreement calling for talks to resolve outstanding issues.

Saudi Arabia's long series of negotiating efforts seems to have finally paid off in 2000. On June 12, 2000, Saudi Arabia and Yemen signed a border agreement that covered both the border delineated under the Taif Agreement and issues that had not yet been resolved. The line was to run from Al-Thar mountain to the latitude of 19 degrees North and the longitude of 52 degrees East, where the borders of Saudi Arabia, Oman, and Yemen meet. The settlement was relatively generous to Yemen; Yemen received some 40,000 square kilometers in the dispute area in the eastern sector and approximately 3,000 square kilometers in the Red Sea area, including four of the disputed islands. The exact boundaries in disputed areas near Oman could not be resolved, but agreement was reached on seventeen border coordinates, and an agreement was reached in principle that the remaining disputes were to be demarcated in detail by the internationally recognized

German survey group Hansa Luftbild. At the same time, Saudi Arabia received Yemen's reaffirmation of the Taif Agreement of 1934, which had transferred these provinces from Yemen to Saudi Arabia, and which Yemen had sometimes claimed was a "temporary" settlement. Furthermore, Article 5 of the Taif Agreement required that all military forces be withdrawn from sectors of five kilometers from each side of the border.[55] The Saudi and Yemeni governments began to withdraw troops from the border region in February 28, 2001, following a February 15, meeting of the Joint Demarcation Committee in Riyadh.

Problems remained despite support for the new border agreement by Crown Prince Abdullah and President Saleh. In January 2001 government-controlled newspapers in Yemen ran stories claiming that Saudi troops had crossed twenty kilometers into Yemeni territory and were still building garrisons on the Yemeni side of the border. One paper went so far as to describe the Saudi forces as "evil" and trying to create unrest in pro-Yemeni tribes in the border areas. Reports of such military action, however, have not been independently verified and the incident involved may have been a Saudi countersmuggling–illegal immigration effort rather than a clash between the two countries.[56]

Some continuing tensions are natural. The new agreement created several problems similar to those that had kept the border from being demarcated by the British and the Ottomans. Any border settlement had to cut across areas the territory of some individual tribes, and the border settlement in the area from the Red Sea to the Jebal Al-Thar split the territory of some tribes with what they consider to be an arbitrary line.[57] The border also crossed areas involving tribal disputes. The resulting problems were made worse by the fact that the Saudi and Yemeni government had backed various tribal sheikhs in the other's country in the past in order to gain political leverage over the other country. This escalated tribal tensions in the border, and certain sheikhs that Saudi Arabia had supported found themselves on the Yemeni side of the border, which placed them in hostile territory without Saudi support. This prompted some of these sheikhs to secure funding from what they describe as "wealthy Saudi business interests," and others to seek support from Osama bin Laden.[58] So far, however, these tribal problems have only amounted to a minor internal security concern for Yemen and have not led to significant clashes across the new border.

Stability is in the national interest of both countries. Yemen badly needs Saudi foreign aid and is seeking a Saudi commitment to added economic cooperation, budgetary support, energy development, and Yemen's membership in the GCC. On February 23, 2001, Saudi Arabia pledged $300 million in aid, and it rescheduled some $250 million of Yemeni debt in March—roughly 70% to 80% of the debt Yemen had accumulated over the last forty years. These sums can scarcely speed Yemen on the road to development, but even limited foreign aid offers Yemen more than war.[59]

Saudi Arabia needs stability on its southern borders and Red Sea coast to concentrate on the far more serious military threat in the Gulf, and Yemeni economic development and stability is critical to easing the pressure on Yemenis to immigrate and find jobs in Saudi Arabia. This helps explain why Crown Prince Abdullah made state visits to Yemen in June 2000 and May 2001, and President Saleh of Yemen visited Saudi Arabia in May 2001—visits that made a major political statement of Saudi Arabia's commitment to better relations with Yemen.[60]

Nevertheless, the underlying demographic, economic, and social pressures on Yemen have not changed. Yemen has few prospects for stable economic development unless significant numbers of Yemenis can work in Saudi Arabia, and the border is peaceful enough to allow Yemen to develop its oil resources. Yemen's experience during the Gulf War is a good case in point. The World Bank estimates that Yemen's per capita income only totaled $540 in 1991, after the cut-off in aid following Yemen's support of Saddam Hussein. It also estimates that Saudi Arabia's expulsion of Yemeni workers during the Gulf War led to a sudden 8% increase in the population, while the combined price of reductions in aid and worker remittances cost Yemen over $1 billion a year. These developments produced a more than 15% cut in Yemen's GDP during 1990–1992.[61] Official Yemeni estimates indicated in September 1998 that nearly 7 million Yemenis were dependent on remittances from Yemenis working in Saudi Arabia to meet their essential living requirements.[62]

In short, it is too early to talk about a lasting ability to maintain good relations. Saudi Arabia continues to try to manipulate Yemen's politics. At the same time, Yemen creates problems of its own. For example, in March 1999, Yemen banned the Saudi-owned, London-based *Asharq al-Awsat* newspaper from entering the country, citing a February article that accused Yemen of siding with Eritrea in its war with Ethiopia and providing military equipment to Somalia.[63]

Saudi Arabia does perceive Yemen to be less of a "danger" today than in the past, but it has not dropped Yemen from its list of threats. The Kingdom maintains a large part of its military forces near Yemen, and makes defense against Yemeni invasion a major aspect of its contingency planning. Saudi Arabia has also begun the construction of a new military city at Jizan, near the Red Sea and the Saudi-Yemeni border. The new facility will include a naval base, an air base, and a dry dock. This adds naval and air capability in an area where Saudi Arabia already has a massive military city at Abha, which it uses to base its land forces, and a major air base at Khamis Mushayt. While Saudi Arabia has never announced figures for the cost of the new base at Jizan, it is almost certain to be several hundred million dollars. It has not been a casual effort at a time when the Kingdom has faced major budget deficits.[64]

Relations with Oman

Saudi Arabia has also had a history of tension and conflict with Oman. Saudi Arabia once made extensive claims to Western Oman; skirmishes occurred over control of that area and the Buraimi Oasis area claimed by Abu Dhabi during the 1950s. The Saudis occupied the area by force, but were expelled by the British and the Trucial Oman Scouts. Relations slowly improved in the 1960s, however, and Saudi Arabia officially recognized Sultan Qabus as "His Majesty" in 1971. The border dispute over the Buraimi Oasis area was resolved in 1974, when the UAE made a complex local trade that gave Saudi Arabia territory along the coast between Qatar and Saudi Arabia in return for Saudi willingness to give up its claims to the Buraimi Oasis and territory in the area of what has become the city of Al Ain.

These improvements in Saudi-Omani relations have allowed the two countries to resolve the rest of their border disputes. In 1990, Saudi and Omani negotiators reached an agreement that demarcated 657 kilometers of their border and set terms for negotiating the rest. On July 9, 1995, these negotiations resulted in the signature of an agreement in Riyadh that finally demarcated the entire border.[65] Although there have been some petty incidents over the display of Saudi maps that still show the Kingdom's earlier claims to Omani territory, there have been no real tensions over the new border and no signs that border issues of territorial claims will lead to some future conflict.

Oman and Saudi Arabia have, however, been occasional rivals for the leadership of the Southern Gulf and the GCC. Sultan Qabus of Oman has played a growing role in mediating between the smaller Gulf states—a role that proved to be critical during the tensions between Qatar and the other Gulf states in 1995 and 1996. Oman has maintained close relations with Qatar and has taken the lead in normalizing relations with Israel. Saudi Arabia has resented some of these Omani actions, particularly the rate at which Oman improved its relations with Israel.

Saudi Arabia and Oman disagreed in the past over Sultan Qabus's call for the creation of an integrated 100,000-man GCC force and other Omani efforts to strengthen the military integration of the GCC. Saudi Arabia felt that such efforts would result in making Omani military manpower a major force within the GCC while forcing the other GCC states to provide Oman with significant military aid. Saudi Arabia also tacitly opposed Oman's past efforts to develop a GCC-wide approach to funding gas and oil pipelines to Omani ports on the Indian Ocean in order to reduce dependence on tanker traffic through the Gulf.

These tensions, however, have eased since 1995. Both countries have cooperated in less ambitious efforts to strengthen the GCC and collaborate in a number of other areas. The Saudi government is reported to be more willing to encourage GCC development activity in Oman and the creation of pipelines and Omani ports on the Indian Ocean. Nevertheless, few Saudis and Omanis seem to predict that there will be an end to their low-level rivalry for influence in the region.

Relations with Qatar

Saudi Arabia has had disputes with Qatar, some territorial and some political. The territorial disputes initially centered on the control of Khaur al-Udaid, a long, winding inlet at the base of the eastern side of the Qatari peninsula, and control over the territory behind it. The al-Thani family of Qatar and the al-Nihayan family of Abu Dhabi had long quarreled over control of the Khaur al-Udaid. This dispute broadened in 1935, however, when Saudi Arabia asserted its own claims to the area, along with claims to much of the rest of Qatar and Abu Dhabi.[66]

Most of these disputes were resolved in 1965 when Qatar gave up its claims to the Khaur al-Udaid in return for territorial concessions at the base of the Peninsula. Under the terms of this agreement, Saudi Arabia and Qatar reached agreement on the border from Duhat as-Salwa to Khwar al-Udaid, although Britain and Abu Dhabi did not recognize the new border because Abu Dhabi claimed some of the territory involved. Qatar also signed a bilateral security agreement with Saudi Arabia in 1982. However, like many other border "settlements" in the Gulf, many of the details were not fully covered. This situation was further complicated in 1974 by the same agreement that resolved the Saudi dispute with Oman over the Buraymi Oasis. The UAE gave Saudi Arabia a fifteen-mile stretch along the coastline between Qatar and the UAE that resolved most of the Saudi-UAE differences, but the new agreement did not involve Qatar.[67]

A seemingly minor incident turned these unresolved issues into a crisis in the early 1990s. Qatar felt that Saudi Arabia was infringing on its territory by building roads and facilities in the border area. A confrontation between roving Bedouins caused a minor clash between Saudi Arabia and Qatar on September 30, 1992. This clash took place at a small outpost at Al-Khofuous, about eighty miles southeast of Doha. Qatar claimed that Saudi Arabia attacked a Qatari border post, while Saudi Arabia claimed the incident was simply a clash between Bedouins from the two different countries. Two Qataris were killed in the incident, and a third taken prisoner. Qatar reacted by canceling its participation in the GCC's ongoing Peninsular Shield exercises, which practice the defense of Kuwait and the Saudi border against Iraq.[68]

The clash ended when new talks took place between King Fahd and the then-Emir of Qatar, Sheik Khalifa bin Hamad al-Thani in December 1992. However, tensions continued. A brief incident in October 1993 resulted in several more deaths. Five Qatari-Saudi border skirmishes occurred during

1994, as well as a diplomatic row in which Qatar boycotted the November 1994 GCC summit conference. In December 1994, Qatar and Saudi Arabia considered the formation of a joint committee to investigate the conflicts but no real progress took place. The ruling elites of both countries remained divided over the issue and showed considerable private distrust of the other's position. The Qataris tended to see such disputes as a symbol of Saudi pressure to dominate the smaller Gulf states, whereas their Saudi counterparts tended to see them as a result of Qatari provocation.[69]

Tensions between Qatar and Saudi Arabia grew notably worse after Sheikh Hamad bin Khalifa al-Thani deposed his father in the spring of 1995 and became Qatar's new emir. Saudi Arabia was quick to recognize Sheikh Hamad as emir, but some members of the Saudi royal family regarded the new emir's father as a long-standing friend. They had long felt that Sheikh Hamad was deliberately challenging Saudi leadership in the Gulf and provoking differences between Saudi Arabia and the other Southern Gulf states. One senior Saudi prince privately described the new emir and his new foreign minister, Sheik Hamad bin Jassim bin Jabr al-Thani, as a "dangerous and disruptive influence."

These tensions reached a crisis point when the two nations clashed over the appointment of a new secretary-general to the GCC in December 1995. Qatar accused Saudi Arabia of forcing a Saudi secretary-general, Ambassador Jamil al-Hujailan, on the GCC. Although the GCC had no formal rules regarding the nationality of the secretary-general, Qatar felt that custom dictated that the secretary-general should be chosen through alphabetical rotation. The previous secretaries-general had been Kuwaiti and Omani, which would have meant that the new secretary-general should be a Qatari candidate. The situation was made still worse when the emir and foreign minister of Qatar walked out of the GCC meeting. Saudi Arabia, Bahrain, and the UAE felt that Qatar had failed to observe the normal courtesies between GCC states in handling the dispute, and that Qatar had insulted Sheikh Zayed bin Sultan al-Nuhayyan of the UAE when he attempted to mediate.

Saudi Arabia retaliated for the Qatari walkout by joining Bahrain and the UAE in receiving the emir's deposed father, Sheikh Khalifa bin Hamad, who made it clear during his visits that he was actively seeking to regain power. The UAE received Sheikh Khalifa bin Hamad on December 21, 1995. Sheikh Khalifa then announced that he would set up "temporary quarters" in Abu Dhabi until he returned to power in Doha and pledged that he would improve relations between Qatar and its neighbors if he resumed power.[70] Sheikh Khalifa then went on to visit Cairo and Damascus and again announced he was seeking to resume the throne.

Qatar's new emir, Hamad bin Khalifa al-Thani, responded by visiting Egypt, Jordan, and Oman to demonstrate that he had influence in other Arab states, and gave an interview indicating that he hoped to solve Qatar's border disputes with Saudi Arabia in a "brotherly way." He clarified his position on the selection of a new secretary-general of the GCC by stating,

> If people thought what happened in Muscat was a result of the border [dispute with Saudi Arabia], that is not right at all. . . . We don't mind the Secretary-General being a Saudi . . . [but all] six countries have to agree on this issue. We don't mind Saudi Arabia coming in with its candidate. The way they . . . did it was not a way we can accept. It was a way that did not happen before in the GCC.[71]

The exact nature of what happened next is still a subject of debate within the Gulf states. Qatar's leadership felt that Bahrain, Saudi Arabia, and the UAE allowed Sheikh Khalifa bin Hamad to prepare a coup attempt. They claimed the coup was planned to combine Qataris loyal to the deposed emir with a force of up to 2,000 Yemeni and other Arab mercenaries, which was to assemble on the Saudi side of the border. They also claimed that this force was under the leadership of a French officer who had commanded Sheikh Khalifa bin Hamad's personal guard and had previously been one of the leaders of the French special forces that suppressed the uprising at the Grand Mosque in Mecca. They accused Bahrain, Saudi Arabia, and the UAE of allowing the deposed emir to prepare the force in their countries, of allowing the plotters to stage two Transall transports to move the forces involved, and even of plans to provide air cover for the coup.

It is clear that Qatar took these events seriously enough to mobilize the Emiri Guard on February 17, 1996, and carry out several hundred arrests. Beyond this, the details of what happened remain unclear. Bahrain, Saudi Arabia, and the UAE deny that a coup attempt ever reached the point where Sheikh Khalifa bin Hamad assembled any significant forces on their soil and deny that a major recruiting effort ever took place. They accuse Qatar of making false charges to deliberately embarrass them and provide an excuse for its arrests.

The views of other Gulf states are ambiguous. Oman denounced the coup attempt, but Kuwait was silent. No buildup prior to the coup attempt was detected by U.S. intelligence, but several senior U.S. officials in the Gulf felt that a coup attempt was being mobilized. The United States encouraged the Southern Gulf states to resolve their differences peacefully, and supported Qatar in a call for a special summit meeting to deal with the issue. Both France and the United States also carried out exercises with Qatar to help show their support.[72]

In any case, the situation improved in March and April 1996, and Qatar and its neighbors reached a compromise over the GCC. In March 1996, Qatar agreed with the other GCC states that the secretary-general of the GCC would now be selected from each Gulf state in alphabetical order and that a secretary-general could only serve for a maximum of two three-year terms. This compromise seemed to support Qatar's original position, but the fact that the GCC had just selected a Saudi meant that Qatar would now only receive its turn after a secretary-general had served from every other Gulf state. The de facto result was a Saudi victory over the GCC.

In return, Bahrain, Saudi Arabia, and the UAE endorsed the rule of Emir Hamad. Bahrain also agreed to accept the International Court's jurisdiction over the Hawar Islands dispute, while Qatar stopped allowing the Bahraini opposition to make statements attacking the Bahraini government from Qatari soil. Furthermore, Saudi Arabia and Qatar agreed in November 1996 to sign a contract to have the international division of the French Institut Geographique National demarcate their land and maritime borders. An agreement was signed in Riyadh in which both countries agreed that the mapping would be binding on both governments.[73] Saudi Arabia also played a prominent role in arranging a conciliatory meeting in Riyadh between President Mubarak of Egypt and the emir of Qatar at which al-Thani was reported to have expressed regret over what happened between the two countries.

These compromises and agreements restored the image of unity, but the royal families of Qatar and Saudi Arabia have remained somewhat at odds. The Saudis continued to see the Qatari emir and foreign minister as brash and willing to revoke unnecessary controversy. In April 1997, Saudi Arabia conspicuously withdrew from the economic summit in Doha that was planned for November 1997. Saudi Arabia's public reason for its withdrawal was that "Jerusalem was being lost and swallowed," and that no summit should be held that included Israel when so little progress was being made in the Arab-Israeli peace process. At the same time, it was a convenient excuse to deprive Qatar of the status that holding a successful summit would have provided.[74] In contrast, members of the Qatari royal family sometimes describe the Saudis as bullies who attempt to dominate the GCC and a nation led by a generation that is too old to adapt to the changes in the Gulf.

There are some religious and political level issues as well. Although both states adhere to the Wahhabi sect of Islam, the Saudis see the Qataris as slack and as deviating somewhat from the dictates of Wahhabi beliefs, while the Qataris see the Saudis as accommodating Islamic extremists by adopting exaggerated and overly rigid religious practices.

The main political differences between Saudi Arabia and Qatar now seem to focus on the Saudi feeling that Qatar's emir is making democratic and social reforms too quickly, and that Qatar's foreign minister is sometimes a disruptive influence. The Saudis also resent Qatar's tolerance of a relative free and often critical—if not hypercritical—media. Ironically, the most serious source of irritation to the Saudis is Qatari TV station, Al-Jazeera, that broadcasts widely throughout the Gulf. It was originally formed out of staff that the BBC had recruited to run a news station in Saudi Arabia.

One must be careful, however, about exaggerating the importance of these remaining differences. Senior Saudi officials and members of the royal family seem more tolerant of Qatar's actions than Saudi mid-level officials and clerics. The idea that the Saudi royal family opposes all reform in neighboring states is simply incorrect. If anything, some senior Saudi officials feel that Qatar acts as a useful stimulus for evolutionary reform in Saudi Arabia and as a counterbalance to the region's Islamists.

Nevertheless, relations between Qatar and Saudi Arabia have continued to improve. Some Saudi officials attribute this shift to Saudi Foreign Minister Prince Faisal and Prince Abdullah. Saudi Arabia and Qatar initialed maps in 1999 that showed a new land boundary and a division of their coastal waters in the area called Dohat Salwa that some feel has offshore oil and gas resources. The Saudi and Qatari foreign ministers signed a border agreement recognizing these new boundary lines on March 21, 2000, in a ceremony in Doha, and Saudi Arabia has supported the appointment of a Qatari to a top position in the GCC.[75]

Relations with Kuwait

Saudi Arabia has generally had better relations with its other Southern Gulf neighbors. This is particularly important in the case of Kuwait and Bahrain because the defense of the Saudi border with Iraq, and of the key Saudi oil fields and facilities in the Upper Gulf, is dependent on close cooperation between these three states.

Although Saudi Arabia and Kuwait had some border disputes in the 1950s, there have been no serious clashes between the two nations since Britain prevented Saudi conquest of Kuwait at the peak of Ibn Saud's conquests well over half a century ago. The Saudi-Kuwaiti "Neutral Zone" was partitioned for administrative purposes in 1971. Each state continued to equally share the petroleum resources of the zone, which the Saudi government now calls the "Divided Zone."

Saudi Arabia and Kuwait continued to dispute ownership of Qaruh and the Umm al-Maradim Islands and offshore areas, but both states entered into new negotiations after the Gulf War, and demarcated the rest of their borders in July 1995.[76] They also established a Joint Technical Committee to resolve the remaining border issues. This committee made little real progress until 2000, when its work was rushed forward due to disputes both countries had with Iran over its drilling activity in the nearby Dorra gas field in an undesignated area in the Gulf and their concern over Iraqi claims in the area.

Saudi Arabia and Kuwait signed an agreement on the borders affecting the islands and offshore borders of the Neutral Zone in July 2000, and deposited agreed maps with the GCC, Arab League, and UN. This settlement gave Kuwait sovereignty over the islands of Umm al-Maradim and

Quruh and a one-mile radius around each island. It also stipulated that the offshore gas resources in the Dorra gas field, estimated to be in excess of 370 billion cubic meters, would be shared by the two countries. The two countries exchanged documents formally ratifying the new border on January 23, 2001.[77] Iran did not protest this settlement, but Iraq announced it would not recognize any settlement in the area that did not take account of Iraqi rights.

The Neutral Zone contains about 5 billion barrels of proven oil reserves. Within the Neutral Zone, Japan's Arabian Oil Co. (AOC) operated two offshore fields (Khafji and Hout) until the fields were transferred to Aramco in the spring of 2000. (The AOC concession on the Saudi side expired on February 27, 2000, and in January 2003 on the Kuwait side. Texaco operates three onshore fields: Wafra, South Fawaris, and South Umm Gudair.)[78]

Saudi Arabia and Kuwait have cooperated with the United States in developing their defenses against Iraq since the Gulf War. Saudi Arabia and Kuwait have begun to conduct air and land exercises that are more realistic than in the past. The Saudi and Kuwaiti air forces have cooperated closely with U.S. air units and have improved their capability to cooperate in mission planning and battle management using advanced command and control systems like the AWACS and JSTARS. Further, the Saudi and Kuwaiti armies began common brigade-level combined arms command post exercises in 1995, supported by battalion-level field exercises.

Unfortunately, this cooperation has failed to develop anything like an effective and coherent military response to the threat posed by Iraq. The Saudi Army is not organized to concentrate and deploy rapidly to the border or into Kuwait and fight an aggressive war of maneuver in defending its northern border area. It is overdispersed, favors static defense, and is poorly organized and trained for maneuver warfare. The links between the Saudi air defense control and warning system and Kuwait are relatively primitive considering the probable intensity of any joint effort.

Saudi offensive air power is still poorly organized for attacks on Iraqi forces if they advance on Kuwait. Saudi Arabia would be also totally dependent on the United States for intelligence, targeting, advanced command and control/battle management, joint warfare planning, and air-land and combined warfare. While broad conceptual plans exist for the United States to perform this role, and some progress has been made at the tactical level, detailed contingency planning is weak to nonexistent. Few realistic major command and field exercises have taken place to prepare Saudi Arabia and Kuwait for the demands of this kind of coalition warfare.

There are also some political and social tensions between Saudi Arabia and Kuwait on political grounds, although the perception in some Western circles that Saudi Arabia sees Kuwait's National Assembly as a symbol of a destabilizing tolerance for political dissent may be incorrect. Some experts feel that the Saudi leadership has seen the Kuwaiti National Assembly as a useful experiment.

As for social issues, many Saudis see Kuwaitis as arrogant and as refusing to cooperate in many areas. Kuwaiti officials, in turn, see Saudi Arabia as attempting to preserve outdated political and social customs, as defending an interpretation of Islamic law and custom that is too conservative to function in the modern world, and as attempting to interfere in Kuwaiti domestic matters. If Saudi Arabia sometimes sees Kuwait as slow to cooperate, Kuwait sees Saudi Arabia as a power that sometimes attempts to intimidate its neighbors and is careless of their sensitivities. These tensions do not block cooperation between the two states, but they cannot be disregarded.

Relations with Bahrain

Saudi Arabia has long had good relations with Bahrain, and the causeway that links Bahrain with Saudi Arabia is virtually a symbol of the closeness of the two countries.[79] The foreign policies of both Bahrain and the UAE often coincide with that of Saudi Arabia, and Saudi Arabia has also given Bahrain extensive economic aid. The Kingdom has cooperated closely with Bahrain in security exercises since 1975.[80]

Bahrain, however, has been a troubled country. It has suffered from deep divisions between its ruling Sunni elite and a largely Shi'ite population. The CIA estimates that the total population is 70% Shi'a Muslim and 30% Sunni Muslim, but these figures are not based on a census and most experts feel the portion of Shi'a is at least 80%. Poor labor and immigration policies—and deliberate efforts to exploit low-cost foreign labor even at the price of native unemployment—have created a total population that is 63% Bahraini, 19% Asian, 10% other Arab, and 8% Iranian.[81]

Bahrain has serious economic problems. Although Bahrain was one of the first nations in the Gulf to develop an oil economy, its oil reserves are largely depleted and it has become more of a service economy whose success has depended on the oil wealth of its neighbors. It was hit hard by the major drop in oil revenues in 1986, the drop in oil revenues and economic activity during and following the Gulf War, and the new oil crash in 1997. High unemployment has continued in 1999 and 2000—especially among young Shi'ites—in spite of high oil revenues. While its per capita income was still $15,900 in 2001, at least as measured in purchasing power parity terms, this income was poorly distributed.[82] Much of it was concentrated in a small cadre of elite citizens, many of them Sunni. In contrast, many Shi'ites have been squeezed out of the middle-class position that they occupied during the past, when Bahrain was still earning significant oil revenues.

Bahrain has been the target of past Iranian political pressure, although both the shah and Khomeini renounced Iran's past claims to Bahrain. Iran supported a Shi'ite coup attempt in the early 1980s and continued to back Shi'ite opposition groups, some of which had extremist and violent elements. It is important to note, however, that most native Bahraini Shi'a activist demands were peaceful and focused on the return of an elected National Assembly, better distribution of the nation's income, more social and political equity, and reductions in Shi'ite unemployment.[83]

In fact, during the 1980s and much of the 1990s, Bahrain often used Iranian sponsorship as an excuse for domestic Shi'ite unrest that was actually provoked by the failure of the government's economic policies and unwillingness to grant Shi'ites a fair share of the nation's wealth and share of political power. The royal family was slow to recognize the need for change and reform. Prime Minister Khalifa bin Salman al-Khalifa, who served for many years, was particularly prone to exporting blame to Iran when internal reform was needed. His intransigence and failure to deal fairly with the Shi'ite problem was almost certainly a significantly greater threat to Bahrain than Iran.

Fortunately, a new and younger emir, Hamad bin Isa al-Khalifa, came to power in March 1999. Both the new emir and his son and heir apparent—Crown Prince Salman bin Hamad—have since made important economic and political reforms, worked to improve relations with the Shi'a community, moved toward elections. They understand the need to heal Bahrain's internal differences and its economic priorities. The new emir promised a "new political era" in a speech on October 3, 2000, after he had appointed a new consultative council (Shura) with nineteen new members out of forty. These included one Jew, an Indian-Bahraini, and four women. He also stated that elections for the Shura would be held for the first time in 2004.[84] Since that time, the emir has continued his reform efforts and attempted to reach out to the nation's Shi'ites. While Bahrain still has serious economic problems, it also has improved its economic reform efforts.

As might be expected, Saudi Arabia has been deeply concerned with the Shi'ite unrest in Bahrain. It has long given Bahrain the oil it needs to operate its refinery, and the output from the Saudi half of the oil field the two countries share, in an effort to relieve economic pressures on Bahrain and improve its political stability. At the same time, some Saudi security officials did recommend that Bahrain's government take a strong, if not repressive, approach to dealing with dissent during the 1980s and most of the 1990s.[85]

Some Bahrainis, including several senior officials, feel that Saudi Arabia's influence helped delay necessary political reforms during much of the 1990s and made it more difficult for the Bahraini government to reach a settlement with the country's Shi'ites. They feel that Saudi Arabia failed to provide the economic aid and support Bahrain needs and has concentrated on repression to the exclusion of peaceful solutions to the problem. Saudi Arabia has also been ambivalent about Bahrain's social tolerance of secular customs, including tourism and the ability to buy alcohol. Although many Saudis take holidays in Bahrain and take advantage of Bahrain's liberal social customs, the Saudi government sometimes attempts to push Bahrain toward more stringent "Islamic" behavior. In contrast, Bahraini officials feel that many Saudis use Bahrain as a social outlet in order to obtain relief from the increasingly strict interpretation of Wahhabi Islam adhered to by Saudi Arabia and do so with the tacit acceptance of the Saudi government.

These tensions have diminished since the new emir came to power. Moreover, many of the pro-reform and modernization members of the Saudi royal family, as well as senior Saudi officials and technocrats, take a favorable stand toward Bahrain's present reforms. Rather than seeing such change as threatening, they see it as creating pressure for evolutionary change inside Saudi Arabia and as setting examples the Kingdom can follow.

Saudi economic aid to Bahrain has been significant. Bahrain's economy is heavily dependent on the operation of its Sitra refinery, which has a throughput of some 256,000 to 262,000 barrels per day, and which produces some 94 million barrels of product a year, almost all of which is exported. Bahrain's own oil reserves are almost totally exhausted, and its onshore Awali field produces only 37,000 to 38,000 barrels of crude a day. Bahrain's only other source of oil is its Abu Safah offshore field, which it shares with Saudi Arabia. The field is owned 50-50 by the two countries and produces around 140,000 barrels of Arab medium crude per day. Production was split equally between the two countries until 1992, when Saudi Arabia allowed Bahrain to overlift its share of the field, and in September 1992, Saudi Arabia allowed Bahrain to increase its share of the total output from 70,000 to 100,000 barrels per day. On April 1, 1996, Saudi Arabia agreed to allow Bahrain to lift all 140,000 barrels per day. Saudi Arabia also seems to have made concessions to Bahrain that help it import some 220,000 to 225,000 barrels per day to keep its refinery operating near full capacity.[86]

The scale of Saudi aid to Bahrain's military and internal security efforts is less clear. There are reports that Saudi Arabia and Bahrain have agreed on contingency plans to rapidly deploy Saudi security and/or National Guard forces to Bahrain if there should be any kind of Shi'ite uprising, and that Saudi Arabia has quietly provided substantial funding to Bahrain to help build its military bases and acquire some military equipment. As is often the case in the Gulf, it is nearly impossible to obtain accurate data to put these reports in perspective.

What is clear is that Saudi Arabia encouraged Bahrain to reach a border settlement with Qatar. This settlement has greatly improved relations between two critical countries that share a common border with Saudi Arabia and that have a strategic position in the Gulf. The two countries disputed claims to islands and reefs in the offshore areas between them, and Bahrain claimed Zubara, a small enclave in Qatar. While the disputed area involved potential oil and gas reserves, the main reason for the dispute was a long-standing feud, with roots in the 17th century, concerning the ruling al-Khalifa family in Bahrain, which had lost its territory in Qatar to the al-Khalifa family when it took control of all of Qatar between 1850 and 1860.

The dispute over one reef, the Fasht al-Dibal, led both countries to the brink of a serious military clash in 1986. The Saudis offered to mediate at this point, and made repeated efforts to bring the two sides together until 1991. Qatar saw the Saudis as biased in favor of Bahrain, however, and pressed for the issue to be turned over to the International Court of Justice (ICJ) in The Hague, while Bahrain pushed for regional mediation. As a result, the quarrel festered until 1991, when Qatar took its case to the ICJ. New tensions between the two countries flared in 1997, but Bahrain eventually agreed to give the ICJ jurisdiction and to abide by its decision. It is not clear exactly what role Saudi Arabia played in this decision, but senior Saudi officials say that the Kingdom did counsel Bahrain to accept a judgment by the ICJ.

The ICJ reached a decision on March 16, 2001, that gave both countries much of what they wanted. Bahrain got control of the Hawar islands and the island or reef called Qit'at Jarada. Qatar got control of Zubara—the enclave on its territory, a reef called the Fash al-Dibal, two islands called Janana and Hadd Janana, and the right of innocent passage between the Hawar Islands and Bahrain. The emirs of both countries claimed victory in ways that made it clear they were more interested in improved relations than continued tension. They began to discuss cooperation in exploring the offshore oil and gas resources between them.[87]

The way in which the two emirs dealt with the court's decision was clearly far more the result of their own decisions than any intervention by Saudi Arabia. Nevertheless, Saudi officials do seem to have played a constructive role, and one that may facilitate Saudi security cooperation with both Bahrain and Qatar.

Relations with the UAE

Relations between Saudi Arabia and the United Arab Emirates are good, although, some Saudi officials complain that the UAE has become over-liberal in dealing with foreigners and has failed to properly enforce Islamic customs. They admire Sheikh Zayid as a man and a leader, but feel the UAE has done too little to support Gulf security and help integrate the oil policies of the

Southern Gulf states. There are also some residual tensions over past border disputes. Senior officials in Abu Dhabi still resent what they feel was an unfair border settlement in 1974 and they claim Abu Dhabi only agreed to it because of the lingering Saudi military threat to the Buraymi Oasis area.

As has been touched on earlier, Saudi Arabia had attempted to occupy parts of the area by force in the 1950s and 1960s. While British and the Trucial Oman Scouts expelled the Saudis, British withdrawal from the Gulf in 1971 left Abu Dhabi and the other six Emirates that combined to form the UAE militarily weak and somewhat exposed. As a result, the UAE (in reality Abu Dhabi) reached a secret agreement in 1974 that gave Saudi Arabia substantial territory along a fifteen-mile stretch of the coast between Qatar and the UAE in return for Saudi Arabia recognizing the UAE's sovereignty of the area around the Buryami Oasis and Al Ain. This same agreement gave Saudi Arabia rights to a large oil field in the disputed area called the Shaybah field that some estimates put as high as 14 billion barrels.[88]

Although the UAE announced that the settlement was the result of the "generosity" of the UAE's president, Sheikh Zayid bin Sultan al-Nuhayyan, UAE officials privately made it clear that they felt the agreement was forced on the UAE by Saudi "arrogance" and the Saudi "threat." Saudi officials, in return, felt that the Kingdom ended in losing territory to the UAE because of British interference and colonialism.

No significant tension surfaced over the remaining problems in demarcating the Saudi-UAE border. Saudi Arabia fully demarcated the remaining part of its border with the UAE in 1999 as part of its settlement with Qatar. This settlement—combined with the Saudi border settlement with Kuwait and Yemen—left only one significant "border" issue unresolved between Saudi Arabia and its neighbors—the demarcation of the offshore boundary with Iran.[89] Moreover, it left only two major territorial disputes of any kind in the Gulf region affecting other countries: Iraq's claims to part or all of Kuwait and a dispute between the UAE and Iran over three islands in the Gulf.

Some senior UAE officials do feel, however, that Saudi Arabia should share the output of the Shaybah field, which has estimated reserves of up to 14 billion barrels of oil. In spite of the demarcation of their border, the UAE and Saudi Arabia still do not have a precisely defined border in the desert separating them, and the Shaybah field straddles territory claimed by both countries. Saudi Arabia began production from the Shaybah field in late 1998, and the UAE has demanded an agreement to share production.[90] The UAE boycotted a Saudi-hosted meeting of the GCC oil minister in March 1999, in part because it coincided with Prince Abdullah's opening of major production from the field and in part because it felt that improving Saudi relations with Iran had led the Kingdom to tilt in Iran's favor in regard to a dispute between the UAE and Iran over the ownership of the Gulf islands of Abu Musa, Greater Tunbs, and Lesser Tunbs.[91]

While the origins of this latter dispute over Abu Musa and the Tunbs date back to British withdrawal from the Gulf in 1971, more recent Iranian actions have made control over the islands a major foreign-policy issue. This dispute also has considerable strategic importance because the three islands occupy a position so close to the main shipping lanes through the lower Gulf. [92]

Iran effectively seized all three islands from the nominal control of Ras al-Khaimah when the British left the Gulf in 1971, and did so with at least tacit British compliance. Ras al-Khaimah, which later became part of the UAE, was given a face-saving compromise and jurisdiction over the small Arab population on Abu Musa. The island dispute was then further complicated by the development of Mubarak field in the Gulf, which is located six miles off Abu Musa and began producing gas-rich oil in 1974.

The UAE did not, however, formally accept this compromise, and its position may be summarized as follows:[93]

Documents provide evidence of the use, presence, administration and display of authority of the Qawassim of Sharjah and Ras al-Khaimah on Abu Musa and the Tunbs from the early to mid-1700s. Abu Musa was in the possession of Sharjah while the Tunbs fell under the jurisdiction and control of Ras al-Khaimah.

Sharjah's right to Abu Musa and Ras al-Khaimah's claim to the Tunbs was frequently asserted, defended, and exercised on behalf of the Qawassim by British officials from the 1800s until 1971. Persia did not begin to assert specific claims to the Tunbs until the late nineteenth century or to Abu Musa until the early twentieth century, and its claims over the following decades were relatively infrequent.

On the eve of the creation of the United Arab Emirates and the British withdrawal from the Gulf, Iran occupied the Greater and Lesser Tunb by force and seized it from Ras al-Khaimah on November 30, 1971. Earlier that month, Sharjah and Iran had signed a Memorandum of Understanding (MoU) regarding Abu Musa. There are indications that the MoU was signed under duress, since the Shah had indicated that he would take Abu Musa by force if necessary. During this period, Ras al-Khaimah was also pressed to sign an agreement involving a permanent lease to Iran, but refused. This seems to have triggered the Iranian occupation.

The MoU on Abu Musa states that "neither Iran or Sharjah will give up its claim to Abu Musa nor recognize the other's claim." Referring to the Iranian arrival on the northern half of the island, the MoU acknowledges that "within the agreed areas occupied by Iranian troops, Iran will have full jurisdiction. . . ." The MoU's language on Sharjah's presence on the island is that "Sharjah will retain full jurisdiction over the remainder of the island." Thus, the MoU is essentially an interim arrangement between a state that came to occupy part of the island and a state that was already on the island and retained its position on part of it.

Sharjah exercised all aspects of sovereignty over the remainder of the island over the ensuing years, including flying its and the UAE flag as well as providing public services. This despite the fact that in 1983 Iran began encroaching on Sharjah's zone, and in 1987 briefly occupied the zone after hearing rumors of a coup in Sharjah. Since 1992, Iran has been violating the MoU when it took over the entire island and evicted all UAE nationals from it.

With the establishment of the UAE in 1971, the island dispute between the emirates of Sharjah and Ras al-Khaimah and Iran became a federal UAE issue. Since that time, the UAE has tried unsuccessfully to recover the sovereignty over the islands by peaceful means. The UAE has advocated direct negotiation, mediation, or taking the case to the ICJ. Iran has refused all these measures; will only consider discussing the case of Abu Musa, to which it refers to as a "misunderstanding"; and repeatedly states that all three islands are an inseparable part of Iran.

Even so, the awkward combination of de facto Iranian sovereignty, plus a limited UAE role in the islands, survived the Iranian Revolution and continued throughout the Iran-Iraq War. It came as a surprise to the UAE, therefore, when Iranian troops effectively occupied all three islands in 1992. In 1995, the Iranian Foreign Ministry went further and claimed that the islands were "an inseparable part of Iran." Iran then rejected a GCC proposal GCC made in 1996 that the dispute should be resolved by the ICJ. In early 1996, Iran took further steps to strengthen its hold on the disputed islands. These actions included starting up a power plant on Greater Tunb, opening an airport on Abu Musa, and announcing plans for construction of a new port on Abu Musa.[94]

The UAE has repeatedly reasserted its claims to sovereignty since 1992, has sought support from bodies like the GCC, and has continued to try to bring the issue to the ICJ. Iran, in contrast, has resisted any efforts to internationalize the dispute and has continued to take a firm position that the islands are sovereign Iranian territory—a position it also took under the shah.

At the same time, UAE officials have chosen not to try to escalate the dispute in ways that would lead to the use of force and have supported the GCC's calls for mediation or a settlement by the ICJ. They have done so in fact partly because of the risk that a major confrontation between the UAE and Iran could lead to conflict, partly because of the UAE's military weakness, and partly because none of the UAE's allies have seen the dispute as either a case of naked aggression or worth a conflict. In fact, Iran has remained one of Dubai's major trading partners, accounting for 20% to 30% of Dubai's business.

This background helps explain why the UAE was deeply disturbed at the warming of relations between Iran and Saudi Arabia during 1988–1999; it feared this might weaken Saudi support for the UAE's claims to Abu Musa and the Tunbs. The UAE government made this position public after a visit of Iran's President Khatami to Saudi Arabia in May of 1999. The UAE accused Saudi Arabia of bidding for closer ties with Iran at the expense of its regional allies. A long verbal battle followed in the press and the UAE was rumored to be reconsidering its role in the GCC alliance. Iran, for its part, expressed a willingness to improve its relations with the UAE, though it refused to agree to the preconditions proposed by the UAE for a set agenda and timetable to be included in discussions.[95]

Nevertheless, Saudi Arabia has remained publicly supportive of the UAE's claims but has done little in practical terms. For example, in July 1999, a committee made up of Saudi Arabia, Qatar, and Oman, was set up to work on the dispute but has made little headway.[96] Saudi Arabia does not seem to have taken any serious unilateral action to try to resolve the issue during its dialogues with Iran, although it does seem to have asked Iran to turn the dispute over to the ICJ.

Saudi Arabia and the GCC

Saudi Arabia has played a key role in the GCC since its founding following an Arab summit meeting in November 1980. The Kingdom hosted the formal creation of the GCC at a meeting in Riyadh on February 4, 1981, and helped draft the charter that the members of the GCC approved in May 1981. It has pushed for increased cooperation in the political, economic, and security areas, and hosts the organization's political and military headquarters. At the same time, it has been careful to advance its own interests, to act as a prima inter pares, and to assure that the GCC does not infringe on its sovereignty.

The Kingdom has supported collective efforts by the GCC to discuss trade agreements and the WTO with the European Community, cooperation in energy policy, creation of a Customs Union, and slow movement toward the GCC equivalent of a Common Market.[97] It has supported the coordination of banking, monetary, and financial policies and the idea of moving toward a common currency. It has also supported the idea of uniform standards, retail trade regulations, and common commercial codes, as well as cooperation in sharing data on suspected terrorists, criminals, and political extremists and taking a GCC-wide census of citizens to assess the impact of foreign labor and ways to increase jobs for native citizens.[98]

Both King Fahd and Crown Prince Abdullah have given repeated speeches at meetings of the GCC Summit Council calling for added cooperation. For example, Crown Prince Abdullah gave an address to the council meeting in December 1998 stating, "We cannot live isolated from the world, which is at present facing a strong and overwhelming current, the current of globalization, that advocates the opening of borders and the removal of obstacles to the free movement of peoples, ideas, capital, and goods."[99]

At the twenty-first meeting of the GCC Summit Council on December 30, 2000, Crown Prince Abdullah called on the members to develop clear priorities for a common strategy on comprehensive development at the economic, cultural, and social level. Prince Abdullah also asked the members to cooperate in developing an "efficient capability" to deter any possible attack on any GCC member-state as a key priority, "This requires all GCC countries to move decisively toward improving their collective defense capabilities to enable them to confront current and potential challenges."[100] Saudi Arabia continued to advance these themes.

At the same time, Saudi Arabia has never had any illusions about how quickly progress can be made, about the level of real unity within the GCC, or the difference between reality and diplomatic and economic rhetoric. Crown Prince Abdullah was careful to lay out the limits of the GCC at the same meeting of the Summit Council. He stated that it was unwise to talk about a unified military coalition when there was no unified and cohesive political front and when so many statements and remarks never found their way to implementation.[101]

Like all of the Southern Gulf states, Saudi Arabia finds the GCC useful but does not see it as a substitute for reliance on national diplomatic, economic, and internal security efforts. The most senior Saudi officials also see developments like the GCC's December 2000 Manama Declaration as largely an exercise in political and diplomatic symbolism. The Manama Declaration called for greatly enhanced cooperation in creating power projection capabilities, and for increasing the Peninsula Shield Force deployed near Hafr al Batin in northwestern Saudi Arabia from 5,000 men to 25,000 men, largely as a political gesture, and the GCC announced new efforts to expand the force in 2001 and 2002. However, senior Saudi officials have made it clear that this "expansion" consists of little more than earmarking existing units with little prospect that they will be given real mobility, sustainability, effective war-fighting training, and the necessary command and control assets. They also make it clear that the non-Saudi elements of the existing Peninsula Shield Force are severely understrength and have little heavy armor and artillery.[102]

Saudi Arabia has, however, continued to hold other meetings with GCC states to discuss security issues like defensive against Iraq. One such meeting in Hafr al-Batin on April 5, 2001, included senior military and intelligence officials from all of the GCC states; Iraq denounced it as "an act of provocation and threat" in its official press.[103] Although Saudi Arabia has been cautious about sharing command and control, sensor, and intelligence data with its neighbors, it has supported the creation of a common early warning system and common secure communications. These efforts have included the creation of a $160 million secure fiberoptic link between the ministries of defense of all six states, called the Hizam al-Taawun (Belt of

Cooperation). The system was completed by Raytheon of the United States and Ericson of Sweden and became operational in February 2001.

Still, this effort represents the only major GCC cooperative program to have been implemented since the GCC was founded in 1980. According to some reports, completion of the system was also delayed for several years by internal political squabbling in Kuwait, and escalated in cost from an original estimate of $70 million. At present it is little more than a glorified "hotline" for communicating messages and radar data primarily between ministries of defense. What the GCC states actually need is a fully integrated air defense and maritime surveillance system with real-time capability to assist in air-to-air combat and land-based air defense operations. Such a full-scale command and control system is now "planned," but "plan" is not an encouraging substitute for "execute." The military staffs of the GCC first began discussing such a system in 1982—nearly two decades before the first elements of the Hizam al-Taawun became operational.

It is also important to note that Saudi Arabia, Kuwait, and Bahrain still do not have command and control, intelligence, sensor and radar, air defense, and maritime surveillance systems that they can fully integrate for war-fighting purposes, even though they are the front-line states that must defend against Iraq. Much of the Saudi and Kuwaiti systems were designed to be autonomous, even though it has long been clear that integration was vital to dealing with air attacks from both Iraq and Iran, and no concerted effort has yet been made to fund a matching and integrated system in Bahrain. This failure is partly the fault of Saudi parochialism, but disputes within the Kuwaiti government and parliament have also played a major role and Kuwait has delayed procurement of even an effective national system for years.[104]

RELATIONS WITH ISRAEL AND POLICY TOWARD THE ARAB-ISRAELI CONFLICT

Saudi Arabia's attitudes toward Israel have shifted with time and have become increasingly dependent on the progress in the Israeli-Palestinian peace settlement and the tension and violence between Israel and Palestine. During the reign of King Faisal, Saudi Arabia was one of Israel's strongest opponents. Since that time, the Kingdom has become progressively more concerned with its own security and has adopted a policy of trying to decouple Saudi foreign policy from the Arab-Israeli conflict. As a result, Saudi Arabia strongly supported the Arab-Israeli peace process when it made progress and when Israel's relations with the Palestinians and/or Syria seemed to be improving under the leadership of Prime Ministers Rabin, Peres, and Barak.

On the other hand, the Kingdom strongly condemned Israel when the peace process slowed, or when Israel attacked Arab states or clashed with the Palestinians. It joined other Arab nations in condemning former Prime Minister Benjamin Netanyahu for failing to consider Palestinian and Arab sensitivities. It has been a leader in supporting the Palestinians against Prime Minister Ariel Sharon. In the process, it provided Saudi funds to violent Palestinian movements like Hamas. Saudi Arabia has not, however, abandoned the peace process, and Crown Prince Abdullah advanced a new peace proposal in March 2002.

The Saudi Shift Toward Peace

Saudi attitudes toward Israel eased significantly after the death of King Faisal and again after the Gulf War. Saudi Arabia effectively ended support of the second Arab boycott of Israel after Prince Saud al-Faisal, the Saudi foreign minister, attended some of the ceremonies relating to Israel's peace settlement with the Palestinians following the Oslo Accords in 1994.

Saudi Arabia supported efforts to achieve a comprehensive peace settlement. At the same time, it generally kept a low public profile in dealing with Israel and the peace process, and lagged behind Gulf states like Oman and Qatar in improving relations with Israel. The Saudi government continued to take the position that East Jerusalem should come under Arab and Islamic jurisdiction and that Israel be held accountable for its killing of Palestinians through a war crimes tribunal.

This stance can be explained by several factors. First, the Saudi royal family has made its commitment to Arab and Islamic causes, one of the foundations of its legitimacy. Second, the Wahhabi dominance of the Saudi Ulema makes Muslim control over Islamic holy sites a major Saudi concern. The Wahhabi worldview excludes external control of mosques by non-Muslims, and at least some Wahhabi preaching and writing has an anti-Semitic and anti-Christian character. Change in the Wahhabi position is very unlikely given the importance of Haram al-Sharif to Muslim history. Third, Saudi and Arab public opinion is strongly pro-Palestinian and the Saudi ruling elite has always been sensitive to public opinion, particularly when meeting public demands does not affect the Kingdom's strategic interest.

Israel has remained the target of many of Saudi Arabia's Islamists, and the anti-Semitism of Saudi extremists is far more direct than that of mainstream Wahhabi preachers. Some opposition-oriented Islamists have used attacks on Israel and a "Zionist" U.S. as an indirect way of attacking the Saudi regime. Nevertheless, Saudi government support for the Palestinian cause has never meant uncritical support of the Palestinian leadership. The relationship between the Saudi leadership and Yasser Arafat and the Palestinian Authority has always been an uncertain one, and there seems to be little mutual admiration and respect. Saudi officials have also been disconcerted with the Palestinian Authority's tendency to squander aid and failure to capitalize on its opportunities for a just peace. They are far more sympathetic to the Palestinians than to Arafat and many officials in the Palestinian Authority.

Saudi Arabia was initially cautious when Prime Minister Netanyahu came to power on May 29, 1996. Once it became clear that he did not give peace the same priority as Rabin and Peres, however, Saudi Arabia became more openly critical. Saudi Arabia strongly opposed new Israeli settlements in Jerusalem, in part because this was a critical issue for the Kingdom's Islamists, but also because Saudi Arabia has always seen the problem of Jerusalem as part of the Palestine issue.

Saudi Arabia stepped up its criticism of the Israeli government in October 1996, when the Israeli mayor of Jerusalem opened a tunnel in the area near the main mosque in Jerusalem, the al-Aqsa Mosque or "Dome of the Rock." The bloody riots that followed caused the death of fifty-five Palestinians and fourteen Israelis. King Fahd attacked Israel for "practices which will not only sabotage the peace process but will greatly harm the world's stability and prosperity. . . . Israeli changes to the nature of al-Aqsa which aim at suppressing the identify of Islamic holy [sites] are a flagrant deviation from international laws and norms."[105]

In March 1997, King Fahd spoke out about the deterioration of the peace process: "Saudi Arabia is following with extreme concern the repeated acts of aggression of the Israeli authorities against the city of Jerusalem. . . . Such actions are in defiance of all international resolutions and conventions." Saudi Arabia announced in April 1997 that it would not attend the fourth Middle Eastern economic summit because it was inappropriate to do so when the peace process was in near-paralysis. Saudi Crown Prince Abdullah stated in an interview in June 1997 that Saudi Arabia had advised Qatar to cancel the summit because, "Jerusalem is being lost and swallowed."[106]

At a meeting of the Arab League in September 1997, Prince Said al-Faisal the Saudi foreign minister and chairman of the session, said that the "general attitude among Arab countries was linking participation in Doha to progress in the peace process." Despite U.S. pressure, Saudi Arabia did indeed eschew the conference and joined most other Arab countries in a show of protest over the lack of progress in the peace process.

During the Iraqi crisis in late 1997, Saudi Arabia expressed its dismay over what it perceived to be a double standard whereby Israel was allowed to disregard UN Security Council resolutions while Iraq was threatened with military action. Saudi Foreign Minister Saud al-Faisal called Israel's policy toward the Palestinians, "[T]he greatest destabilizing element in the Middle East and the cause of all other problems in the region."

On April 9, 1998, King Fahd and Crown Prince Abdullah issued a joint statement addressed to Muslims attending the Hajj pilgrimage condemning Israeli expansionism and calling for the return of Arab land so the region could concentrate on economic development.[107]

> Given its importance and strategic position, the Middle East must be guarded from tensions and conflicts caused by Israeli expansionist ambitions. This aggressive move, founded on racism and oppression, must be subject to international law . . . in order to restore all occupied Arab territories and establish a Palestinian state with Jerusalem as its capital. This must be achieved quickly and without dilly-dallying so that all countries in the region can concentrate their efforts on economic and social development.

In March 1999, the Kingdom criticized Israel for undermining the peace process by its continuing raids on Palestinian and Hezbollah targets. The remarks were made after a cabinet meeting that reviewed Israel's attacks on the Palestinians in the occupied territories and the latest raids on Lebanon. The Saudi Press Agency said King Fahd "called on the international community to exert pressure on Israel to implement international resolutions and commitments to peace agreements with various Arab parties, in line with international law."[108]

Saudi Arabia was cautiously optimistic about Ehud Barak's victory over Benjamin Netanyahu in May 1999. It then supported peace negotiations between Syria and Israel, and the Palestinians and Israel, until the peace process collapsed in September 2000. The Saudi government did, however, blame Israel for the lack of progress in the peace process and Palestinians' economic problems even before the outbreak of the Second Intifada in September 2000.

Peace and the Second Intifada

Both the Saudi government and Saudi people have become steadily more critical and angry since September 28, 2000 when Ariel Sharon visited the Al-Aqsa mosque/Temple Mount and the cycle of violence that has become the "Second Intifada" began. Crown Prince Abdullah, in particular, took a progressively firmer stance in calling for an end to Israeli attacks on Palestinians and for collective Arab and GCC action to push for an end to violence and a peace settlement favorable to the Palestinians.[109]

Ariel Sharon's election and the steady escalation of Israeli-Palestinian violence since September 2000 have pushed Saudi Arabia to increasingly challenge not only Israel's actions but those of the United States. Since September 2000, the Saudi government has been steadily more critical of Israel, more willing to support joint Arab action against Israel, and more willing to provide financial and political aid to the Palestinians. It has rarely condemned Palestinian terrorism, has put increasing pressure on the United States to intervene, and has distanced itself from public ties to U.S. policy even at the cost of weakening its strategic ties with the United States.

By the spring of 2001, Saudi anger toward Israel had reached the boiling point for reasons that had little to do with traditional anti-Semitism or Islamic extremism. This triggered a popular boycott of American products by Saudi youth and led many Saudis to attack U.S. policies and see the United States as unfair to the Arab world. The Saudi government had come to see the Israeli-Palestinian struggle as the most destabilizing and threatening force in the Middle East. On June 5, 2001—after another cycle of Israeli-Palestinian violence and a two-day visit to Syria—Crown Prince Abdullah stated,

> The Israeli side has gone too far in its aggression, use of force and arrogance; Israeli bullets have assassinated old men, women and even toddlers. Let Sharon do whatever he wants because today might be his day but tomorrow—God willing—will be ours and every drop of Arab blood that has been spilled on our Arab land will be paid for by those who spilled it. . . . [V]iolence only breeds violence. . . . We urge all honest people in the world to contribute actively and with no bias to achieve just and comprehensive peace and we call upon the United States, Europe and the whole world to meet their historic commitments towards the peace process.[110]

The Crown Prince followed up with steadily more serious letters to President Bush. By August, he reached the point of warning the president that unless the United States became more active n the peace process, there would be a major crisis in Saudi-U.S. relations. It is important to note, however, that the Crown Prince's statement focused on advancing the cause of peace and not on making threats of war, which has been a consistent theme of recent Saudi policy.

Saudi Arabia has not opposed Israel's right to exist since the time of King Faisal. Although Saudi Arabia did not support the Camp David accords, King Fahd did put forth a peace plan in 1981 designed to encourage peace without committing Saudi Arabia to taking a stand that might lead to sharp criticism from other Arab states. The plan was presented to the Arab League Summit in Morocco. It was fervently criticized by many Arab states, particularly Iraq, Syria, Algeria, and Mauritania, and denounced by Libyan leader Moammar Qaddafi as "a betrayal of [the] Arab cause."[111] Even so, a "watered-down version" of King Fahd's plan was accepted one year later—only to be lost in the furor over Israel's invasion of Lebanon. Since that time, a number of Saudi princes and officials have played an active behind-the-scenes role in the peace process.

The Saudi government has reacted to both the royal family's concern with Jerusalem and the Palestinian people and increasing pressure from Saudi public opinion. On October 9, 2000, the Saudi royal family opened an Al-Quods fund for the "support of Al-Quods (Jerusalem) Intifada," beginning with a 30-million-riyal ($U.S. 8 million) donation from King Fahd.[112]

Within three days of the opening of the fund, the televised donation campaign had raised 150 million riyals ($U.S. 40 million) from private Saudi citizens.[113]

By May 2002, according to the Royal Saudi Embassy in Washington, D.C., the Kingdom's donations to the Al-Quods foundation had totaled nearly 201 million riyals ($U.S. 53.67 million) since the foundation was established in October 2000. The Saudi government has contributed approximately 1,376 million riyals ($U.S. 367.42 million) in aid since the beginning of the Intifada, in addition to the 11.25 riyals ($U.S. 3.0 million) donated to the Al-Quods Beit-al-Mal Agency.

The Kingdom also donated 938 million riyals ($U.S. 250.47 million) as its "share in the budget of [the] Al-Quods Intifada and the Al-Aqsa Fund in line with the decision taken at the . . . Arab Summit in Cairo in 2000, plus an additional 78.75 million riyals [$U.S. 21.03 million] as a result of the decision reached at the Arab Summit held in Beirut in March 2002."[114] It was also agreed at the Arab Summit that during the first quarter of fiscal year 2002, Saudi Arabia's share in the budget of the Palestinian Authority would be 169 million riyals ($U.S. 45.13 million), and another 12 million riyals ($U.S. 3.2 million), would be allocated to the assistance to the Intifada.[115]

Overall, the Saudi government and private Saudi citizens contributed approximately 9.78 billion riyals ($U.S. 2.61 billion) to the Palestinian people from September 2000 to May 2002[116]—providing much of the humanitarian support to the Palestinians.[117] Despite allegations by Israeli Prime Minister Ariel Sharon in May 2002 that Saudi Arabia has been encouraging terrorism through this monetary assistance to the Palestinians, the government of Saudi Arabia has consistently denied accusations that Saudi donations (both by its government and its people) have ever been knowingly allocated to help finance suicide bombers or terrorist groups.[118] Some of the Saudi money may, in fact, have been passed on to terrorist groups, but no evidence has yet surfaced to contradict those Saudi claims.

Yet the Saudi government also began to take a more open and realistic approach to seeking a peace. Initially, Saudi Arabia took a relatively rigid stand after the outbreak of the Second Intifada. Prince Saud al-Faisal, the foreign minister, stated in October 2000, "All bonds that link Israel with the Arab world should be revised. . . . The Kingdom of Saudi Arabia will never accept anywhere other than Jerusalem as the capital the Palestinian state."[119] This statement is consistent with Saudi attitudes that had their roots in the Wahhabi foundation of the Saudi state.

Crown Prince Abdullah's Peace Proposal

In early 2002, however, Crown Prince Abdullah took a new and far more courageous approach. This decision may have been related to other issues.

It came after a year fraught with escalating violence between the Israelis and Palestinians, the attacks on the United States on September 11, 2001— in which fifteen of the nineteen airline hijackers were from Saudi Arabia— and Saudi Prince al-Walid bin Talal bin Abdulaziz's subsequent warnings to the United States as to the urgency in altering U.S. policies toward the Palestinians, citing them as motivation behind the attacks.[120] All of these factors led to deteriorating Saudi Arabia-U.S. ties.

In February 2002, during an interview with *New York Times* veteran reporter Thomas Friedman, Crown Prince Abdullah revealed his intent to help bring the Israelis and Palestinians out of their deepening quagmire. At the time, the peace process had all but subsided—yet another causality of seventeen months of ensuing violence resulting in 1,200 deaths by February 2002.[121]

Friedman's article conveyed, for the first time to the world, the Saudi Crown Prince's ideas that later served as a basis for an eventual proposal presented at the 2002 Arab League Summit in Beirut.[122] Deliberately elusive and based on a thirty-five-year-old concept, the model was all too familiar: land for peace.[123] There was no discussion of Palestinian refugees and the right of return—which would be an essential component to any viable proposal for the Palestinians. There was no mention of defined state borders for Israel and a Palestinian state. These provisions, the prince believed, should be left to Israeli, Palestinian, Syrian, and Lebanese negotiators.[124]

The plan did, however, call for the "full withdrawal [of Israeli personnel] from all the occupied territories, in accord with U.N. resolutions, including in Jerusalem, for full normalization of relations."[125] The report suggested that the entire Arab world would commit to "normalized" peaceful relations with Israel (implying normalized economic, political, and social relations) in exchange for an Israeli withdrawal from land in the West Bank, Gaza Strip, Golan Heights, and East Jerusalem that it captured during the 1967 Six-Day War.

Abdullah's proposal was not totally dissimilar to several previous Saudi initiatives: King Fahd's 1981 peace plan, like those proposed later by former President Clinton and former Israeli Prime Minister Ehud Barak in 2001, were somewhat similar to Abdullah's attempt at peace.[126] The new proposal did, however, allow the Kingdom to avoid clashing with the more conventional Palestinian/Arab position while also offering Israel—for the first time—collective recognition by the Arab world and an alternative negotiating partner beyond Palestinian Chairman Yasser Arafat—two things that Israel has long sought.[127]

It also had special significance because of the "timing" of the proposal and the rank of its "messenger." The timing was important for two reasons. First, the proposal came precisely when negotiations between the Israelis and Palestinians had reached a momentous impasse. Both sides viewed the peace proposal as a "way out of the impasse"[128] that gave "a new lease of life to diplomatic efforts to bring calm to the Middle East."[129] Second, diplomatic relations between the United States and Saudi Arabia had been deteriorating. As has been discussed earlier, the events of September 11, 2001, and its aftermath strained bilateral relations. This led some to perceive the proposal as a public relations ploy and a "conciliatory gesture to repair relations with the United States."[130]

Some alleged that the plan spoke "volumes about Saudi concern over anti-Arab and Muslim backlash after the terrorist attacks last September [2001] in the United States."[131] Others were skeptical of Crown Prince Abdullah's intentions because Abdullah revealed the proposal to the *New York Times* before notifying foreign state officials—leading skeptics to believe, that it was a "good indication that their [Saudi Arabia's] motivation . . . [was] to improve public relations with the United States."[132]

Yet Crown Prince Abdullah has never been an opportunistic "messenger," or one likely to take such a stand simply to please the United States in the face of his own convictions, Saudi public opinion, or Arab opposition. The fact that he extended such an olive branch made the proposal all the more significant. His authorship acted to "give [other Arab states] crucial religious cover to making peace with [Israel]."[133]

The very fact that Saudi Arabia initiated such a proposal gave it added credence to the rest of the Arab world and to Israel. Although a similar plan had been put forth by Libyan officials during a "closed-door meeting" at the Arab League Summit in Amman, Jordan in 2001 and League officials designated a committee to review the proposal it had no credibility or momentum.[134] Libya did not possess the clout necessary to advance such a proposal beyond its nascent stages.

Crown Prince Abdullah's proposal received a warm reception from the United States, Russia, the European Union, several Arab states, and both Palestinian and Israeli officials alike—including Palestinian Authority Chairman Yasser Arafat, Israeli Foreign Minister Shimon Peres, and Israeli President Moshe Katsav.[135] Soon after the proposal was made public, Javier Solana, foreign affairs chief to the European Union, announced that he would travel to Riyadh to find out more about Abdullah's plan. The plan quickly gained momentum.

Before visiting Riyadh, Solana discussed the proposal with Israeli Prime Minister Ariel Sharon. Solana revealed to the press that, according to Sharon, Israeli officials "would be willing to meet anybody from Saudi Arabia, formally, informally, publicly, discreetly, whatever, to get better information about the significance of this idea."[136] While Sharon's interest seemed encouraging, the Saudi state-run newspaper *Al-Watan* reported that "no Israeli-Saudi visits could take place until a Mideast peace agreement had been reached."[137] If members of the Saudi government were to meet with Israeli government officials before such a plan was accepted, it might signify a "normalization" of relations between the two countries, which might devalue the Arab bargaining tool.

White House spokesman Ari Fleisher did make initial comments that "the initiative did not represent a breakthrough."[138] Yet he was referring to the situation on the ground and not the proposal's value as a new opportunity for genuine peace negotiations. In contrast, U.S. President Bush telephoned Crown Prince Abdullah and signaled his approval by commending the proposal. According to a later statement by Fleisher, President Bush "praised the crown prince's ideas regarding the full Arab-Israeli normalization once a comprehensive peace agreement has been reached."[139]

Syrian President Bashar Assad, with some notable reservations, then affirmed his support for Crown Prince Abdullah's vision "for a comprehensive and just solution for the conflict in the region."[140] His avowal helped bring the Arab world closer than it had ever been to recognizing Israel's right to exist.[141] Similarly, Lebanese Prime Minister Rafik Hariri endorsed the initiative and believed that "the initiative received wide support because it is based on UN resolutions, called for by the Arabs, and because what the Israeli prime minister, Sharon, is doing has brought the region to an impasse and this proposal is a way out of the impasse."[142]

Ironically, Libyan leader Moammar Qaddafi openly expressed his opposition to the Saudi peace initiative. He described the proposal as "shocking" and was discouraged because he considered "Saudi Arabia [to be] . . . the [Arab world's] reservoir, the one country that did not indulge in cheap bargaining."[143] In response to Abdullah's proposal, Qaddafi offered an alternative: "Israel must allow Palestinian refugees living in other Arab nations the right of return, dispose of its weapons of mass destruction, and establish a combined Palestinian-Israeli state called 'Isratine' with Jerusalem being a place where people from all religions can gather."[144] Furthermore, Qaddafi threatened to withdraw Libya from the Arab League; only after a visit and much persuasion by the spokesman for the Arab League, Secretary-General Amr Moussa, did he rescind this threat.

On March 10, 2002, less than one month after *New York Times* reporter Thomas Friedman publicized Abdullah's ideas for a proposal, Saudi Arabia's foreign minister, Saud al-Faisal, offered the most detailed Saudi remarks on its overture to Israel before the summit meeting. He linked "'complete peace' to the creation of an independent Palestine with Jerusalem as its capital"—both expanding upon and complicating the initial proposal.[145] For those that sought a "trouble-free" end to the impasse, this presented yet another stumbling block to sealing the deal.

The Arab Summit: Beirut, Lebanon, 2002

On March 27 and 28, 2002, Crown Prince Abdullah sought broad endorsement for his Middle East peace initiative at the Arab Summit in Beirut,

Lebanon. Underlings occupied just more than half of the seats reserved for the twenty-one heads of state and Palestinian Chairman Arafat. This was due partly to illness, as was the case for Saudi Arabia, and partly due to cited diplomatic or domestic reasons.[146] Although barriers to an "Arab world," at least in political terms, were at an all-time high, officials seemed united when it came to a collective concern for the Palestinian situation. As a whole, the Arab world felt antipathy regarding Chairman Arafat's inability to travel to the summit due to Israeli travel restrictions and the concern that he may not be able to return once he left his compound in Ramallah. Moreover, all were united in opposition to the possibility of a U.S. military strike against Iraq.[147]

The first day of the summit was fraught with internal strife, a walkout by the Palestinian and UAE delegations to protest the refusal of Lebanon to permit a speech by Chairman Arafat to be televised live via satellite,[148] and the absence of two key leaders—Egyptian President Hosni Mubarak, who stayed in Egypt to show his solidarity with Arafat, and Jordanian King Abdullah, fatigued after his return from a foreign trip. Without these important leaders present, combined with the atmosphere at the summit, many feared that the plan's momentum would be lost and that the impact any decision would have on a global scale would be tapered due to these circumstances. In spite of these concerns, Saudi Crown Prince Abdullah and delegation presented and endorsed the proposal at the summit's opening session.

The Crown Prince declared that "Israel, and the world, must understand that peace and the retention of the occupied Arab territories are incompatible and impossible to reconcile and achieve."[149] He went on to say to the Israeli people, "[I]f their government abandons the policy of force and oppression and embraces genuine peace, we [Arab states] will not hesitate to accept the right of the Israeli people to live in security with the people of the region."[150]

The Saudi foreign minister was more negative and more direct. Foreign Minister Prince Saud al-Faisal asserted that the proposal "is a very clear equation. . . . If Israel refuses, the peace process will not go on. This is it. We return toward violence. We return toward the threat of widening conflict."[151] His statements notwithstanding, a shadow was cast on the historic prospect of the proposal after a Hamas-sponsored suicide bomber attack in Netanya, Israel, which killed twenty people at a Passover dinner.

Despite the lack of top-level leadership present at the summit, the infighting at the meeting, and a continuation of suicide bombings in Israel, the League unanimously endorsed the Saudi proposal on March 28, 2002, titling it the "Arab Initiative." This signified at least a partial transformation in the Arab world's approach to the state of Israel. The endorsed plan was, however, slightly different than the original for three main reasons. First, the initial offer of "full normalization," implying broad diplomatic, economic, and social ties with Israel, was replaced with the phrase "normal relations" in order to gain unanimous Arab approval. Israel openly deemed this term "too vague for interpretation" and continued to be committed to the conditions implied by "normalization."[152]

Second, the initiative stipulated East Jerusalem to be the capital of the future state of Palestine, thereby dividing the city—another stumbling block for Israel. Third, the initiative called for a "just solution" for Palestinian refugees, which connotes either the right of return or financial reparations for an unspecified number of refugees. The Israeli government was cautioned to accept such a provision because there are currently more than 3 million refugees, with an exceptionally high birth rate, that would fall into this category. At the time, Jews comprised 80% and Arabs nearly 20% of a population of approximately 6 million people.[153] If taken literally, as perceived by Israel, the right of return could mean the end of a Jewish majority in the state of Israel.

These differences, and the additional demands outlined by the initiative, not only conflicted with Israeli Prime Minister Sharon's platform but Israel's historical position.[154] Although it received praise from various camps, these differences also made it difficult, if not impossible, for Israel to accept the plan in the form endorsed by the Arab League.

Furthermore, the first communiqué issued by the summit "encouraged continued Palestinian terrorism" and even "pledge[d] to fund it."[155] The communiqué also "affirm[ed] an Arab commitment to ostracize Israel until it agrees to the Arab League's demands," which included the expectation that Israel comply with the League's perceptions of both UN resolutions 1948 and 1949—effectively recommending the return of Palestinian refugees to Israel.

The Arab Peace Initiative

The Arab Initiative was agreed to on March 28, 2002; and contained the following text: [156]

The Council of Arab States at the Summit Level at its 14th Ordinary Session,

- Reaffirming the resolution taken in June 1996 at the Cairo Extra-Ordinary Arab Summit that a just and comprehensive peace in the Middle East is the strategic option of the Arab countries, to be achieved in accordance with International Legality, and which would require a comparable commitment on the part of the Israeli Government.

- Having listened to the statement made by His Royal Highness Prince Abdullah bin Abdulaziz, the Crown Prince of the Kingdom of Saudi Arabia in which his Highness presented his Initiative, calling for full Israeli withdrawal from all the Arab territories occupied since June 1967, in implementation of Security Council Resolutions 242 and 338, reaffirmed by the Madrid Conference of 1991 and the land for peace principle, and Israel's acceptance of an independent Palestinian State with East Jerusalem as its capital, in return for the establishment of normal relations in the context of a comprehensive peace with Israel.

- Emanating from the conviction of the Arab countries that a military solution to the conflict will not achieve peace or provide security for the parties, the council:

  1. Requests Israel to reconsider its policies and declare that a just peace is its strategic option as well.

  2. Further calls upon Israel to affirm:

     a. Full Israeli withdrawal from all the territories occupied since 1967, including the Syrian Golan Heights, to the lines of June 4, 1967 as well as the remaining occupied Lebanese territories in the south of Lebanon.

     b. Achievement of a just solution to the Palestinian Refugee problem to be agreed upon in accordance with UN General Assembly Resolution 194.

     c. The acceptance of the establishment of a sovereign independent Palestinian state on the Palestinian territories occupied since June 4, 1967 in the West Bank and Gaza Strip, with East Jerusalem as its capital.

  3. Consequently, the Arab countries affirm the following:

     a. Consider the Arab-Israeli conflict ended, and enter into a peace agreement with Israel, and provide security for all the states of the region.

     b. Establish normal relations with Israel in the context of this comprehensive peace.

  4. Assures the rejection of all forms of Palestinian patriation which conflict with the special circumstances of the Arab host countries.

  5. Calls upon the government of Israel and all Israelis to accept this initiative in order to safeguard the prospects for peace and stop the further shedding of blood, enabling the Arab countries and Israel to live in peace and good neighborliness and provide future generations with security, stability and prosperity.

  6. Invites the International Community and all countries and organizations to support this initiative.

  7. Requests the Chairman of the Summit to form a special committee composed of some of its concerned member states and the Secretary General of the League of Arab States to pursue the necessary contacts to gain support for this initiative at all levels, particularly from the United Nations, the Security Council, the United States of America, the Russian Federation, the Muslim states and the European Union.

Ironically, the Palestinians as well as the Israelis had reservations about the initiative. According to a poll commissioned by Independent Media Review (IMR) and the Zionist Organization of America (ZOA) and conducted by the Palestinian Center for Public Opinion, approximately 62% of the 1,181 Palestinians surveyed were against the Arab Initiative and merely 24% were in favor, with a 2.85% margin of error.[157] In addition, only 12.1% of Palestinians surveyed disagreed that Fatah Tanzim and other illegal militias should relinquish weapons if asked to do so by the Palestinian Authority.[158]

A similar Smith Institute poll commissioned by the IMR and ZOA determined that only 22% of the 501 Israelis surveyed favored the initiative, while 73% opposed it when the territories to be handed over were mentioned (with a 4.5% margin of error).[159] Likewise, when the "right of return" was included in the question, a mere 9% of Israelis surveyed approved the plan and an overwhelming 87% were opposed.[160] Furthermore, at the time, only 16% of Israelis favored an Israeli withdrawal to the 1967 lines in return for broad peace with the Arab world.

RELATIONS WITH EGYPT

Saudi attitudes toward Egypt, Jordan, and Syria vary with time and are based largely on intelligent Saudi self-interest. They often have little to do with the Pan-Arab rhetoric that is normally used by all four countries. Egypt and Saudi Arabia cooperate in many areas, but a rich, ultra-conservative Saudi monarchy and a poor, secular Egypt differ in many ways and scarcely have identical interests. Saudi Arabia also perceives Egypt as a natural rival for power and influence in the Arab world.

The relationship between Saudi Arabia and Egypt has involved considerable tension and conflict in past years. Saudi Arabia and Egypt were de facto enemies during most of Nasser's rule, and fought a proxy war in Yemen. Saudi Arabia did improve its relations with Egypt when Sadat came to power, but then distanced itself from Egypt after Camp David. Saudi Arabia never supported the efforts of some Arab leaders to isolate Egypt, however, and the Kingdom improved relations once Mubarak came to power.

Saudi Arabia and Egypt cooperated closely during the Gulf War, but Saudi Arabia did not support Egypt's efforts to create a common military command and obtain major Saudi subsidies for a large Egyptian power projection force to defend the Gulf after the war. Senior Saudi officials strongly deny that they ever indicated to Egypt or Syria that the Damascus Accords, signed after the Gulf War, would lead to more than the creation of a small headquarters in the Gulf and the stationing of a limited number of Egyptian and Syrian officers at that headquarters. They make it clear that Saudi Arabia does not want a significant Egyptian or other Arab military presence on its soil during peacetime, and sees any such relationship with Egypt as a potential financial burden and a complication in Saudi relations within the GCC.

Some Saudi military officers went further and criticized Egypt's performance during the Gulf War. They feel that Egypt was slow to deploy, showed only limited skills in power projection, required massive aid in terms of support, and did not organize well for the offensive phase of Desert Storm. They claim that the Egyptian Air Force lacked the training and technical capability to operate in the complex and demanding air combat environment over the Kuwaiti Theater of Operations. They also feel that Egyptian land forces delayed unnecessarily during the crossing of the Iraqi forward line, when Egyptian intelligence claimed it detected preparations of a nonexistent Iraqi counterattack. They believed that Egypt showed little aggressiveness and only met its military objectives because other Coalition forces had driven virtually all Iraqi forces out of the Egyptian line of advance. As a result, they see little prospect that Egypt can develop the military effectiveness to match or replace Western forces in the defense of the upper Gulf.[161] Other Saudi officers, however, feel that Egypt confronted major problems in power projection for which it was not well trained and equipped, and did well under the circumstances.

At the same time, Saudi Arabia fully recognizes Egypt's influence in the region. It has a strong national interest in Egyptian stability and in good relations with a moderate, secular regime such as that of President Mubarak. Saudi Arabia understands the political value of support from Egypt and the role Egypt plays in reducing the risk of Saudi involvement in the problems created by the Arab-Israeli conflict. It is hardly surprising under these circumstances that Crown Prince Abdullah flew to Damascus for a two-day mini-summit with Presidents Mubarak and Assad just after Prime Minister Netanyahu's victory on May 29, 1996.[162] Saudi Arabia has consulted closely with Egypt on other major issues since that time, and made a special effort to obtain President Mubarak's support for Crown Prince Abdullah's Arab-Israeli peace proposal in 2002. Like Saudi-Syrian cooperation, Saudi-Egyptian cooperation on Arab-Israeli issues greatly reduces the risk that Saudi Arabia might be singled out for its lack of support for the "Arab nation."

Saudi Arabia recognizes that it might need military support from Egypt in some future contingency as a demonstration of Arab solidarity, and continues to conduct limited military exercises with Egypt. For example, the Egyptian and Saudi navies cooperate in the Coral-3 series of exercises in the Red Sea. These exercises not only strengthen their ability to cooperate in the Red Sea, but have included minesweeping exercises and ASW exercises involving Egypt's Romeo-class submarines that seem tailored to improve Saudi capabilities to defend against Iran.[163]

RELATIONS WITH SYRIA

Saudi Arabia has long maintained friendly relations with Syria and has provided Syria with substantial aid. This Saudi effort initially stemmed largely from both its opposition to Israel and the fear Syria might support radical political movements inside Saudi Arabia. Over time, however, Prince

Abdullah developed close relations with President Hafez Assad of Syria, and Saudi Arabia began to see Syria as a strategic counterweight to Iraq. Abdullah played a key role in this relationship as a result of his maternal connection with the Shammar tribe and its Syrian allegiance.[164]

Saudi Arabia actively sought Syrian support during the Gulf War as part of joint Saudi-Egyptian-Syrian cooperation, and provided both aid and political support for Syrian intervention in Lebanon. Syria's military deployments to the Gulf, however, exhibited much less power projection capability than Egypt, and Syria sent forces that played a largely passive role. As a result, Syria's military performance and initial reluctance to cooperate with the Americans did little to impress either members of the royal family or Saudi military officers with Syria's ability to support Saudi Arabia in the defense of the upper Gulf.

Saudi Arabia has continued to maintain good relations with Syria. Crown Prince Abdullah has repeatedly visited Saudi Arabia since Hafez Assad's death and Basher Assad's ascent to power.[165] However, Saudi Arabia currently sees little prospect that Syria can play a major role in supporting any of the radical groups that threaten Saudi and Gulf internal security, and has not provided Syria with any significant military or economic aid since 1992. While it helped broker Syria's intervention in Lebanon, it has been careful to distance itself form Syria's support of the Hezbollah, and has had mixed feelings about the improvement in Syrian-Iraqi relations that has taken place since 2000.

RELATIONS WITH JORDAN

Saudi Arabia has a strong strategic interest in the independence of Jordan, and in Jordan's remaining under the control of a moderate, largely pro-Western monarchy. It also has a strategic interest in a Jordanian peace with Israel that can buffer Saudi Arabia from being dragged into any kind of military involvement in an Arab-Israeli conflict or having to deal with a radicalized state on its western border. At the same time, the Saudi royal family has a long history of tension with the Hashemite royal family of Jordan. The al-Sauds were the rival of the Hashemites in seeking control over the territory that has become modern Saudi Arabia. Although that rivalry has sharply diminished since the decisive Saud victory that drove the Hashemites out of the Hejaz and Arabia in the 1920s, there still are vestiges of such tensions in the relations between Saudi Arabia and Hashemite-ruled Jordan.

Saudi Arabia did provide aid to Jordan as part of the Arab-Israeli conflict and allowed many Jordanians and Jordanian Palestinians to work in Saudi Arabia, yet relations between the two regimes have never been close. Saudi and Jordanian relations also deteriorated sharply at the time of the Gulf War; Saudi Arabia abruptly halted all aid and expelled most workers with Jordanian passports in 1990 when King Hussein of Jordan lent his support to Iraq. Saudi Arabian intelligence also concluded that Jordan provided Iraq with significant arms shipments and support during the period immediately before Desert Storm—a perception that worsened relations during 1991.

The two nations slowly rebuilt their relations after 1992, and Saudi Arabia began to provide token amounts of aid. Relations improved still further in 1995, after King Hussein broke more openly with Saddam Hussein. In August 1996, King Hussein flew to Jeddah to meet with King Fahd— the first real meeting between the two heads of state in six years. It came after two abortive attempts by King Hussein to arrange such a meeting. The resulting communiqués essentially ended the Gulf War tension between the two countries.[166] In a follow-up meeting, King Hussein flew to Jeddah in January 1997 to discuss ways of consolidating Saudi-Jordanian relations and developments in the Middle East peace process. In June, the Saudi foreign minister visited Jordan and in September the Jordanian crown prince made his first visit to the Kingdom in ten years. Concern by both countries for the faltering Middle East peace process has led to improved relations between them.

Since that time, Saudi Arabia has become increasingly supportive of Jordan, in part because it has become increasingly concerned over Jordan's future stability, its future relations with Iraq, and the destabilizing effect of the Second Intifada. Saudi policymakers recognize that they have a strategic interest in a stable Jordan, in the continued rule of the moderate Hashemite regime, and in the success of the Jordanian-Israeli peace process.

The Kingdom has openly supported King Abdullah since he assumed power after his father's death on February 7, 1999. Crown Prince Abdullah, attending the funeral services in place of King Fahd, said, "We have respect for Jordan's monarchy, officials and people and will never hesitate in extending support to Jordan."[167] Saudi officials recognize that good relations with Jordan are another way of defusing the impact of the Arab-Israeli problem on Saudi Arabia and ensuring that Jordan will act as a buffer between the Kingdom and Israel and Iraq. At the same time, Saudi policymakers show little current interest in military cooperation with Jordan and have uncertain faith in a stable long-term relationship. Saudi aid levels scarcely do much to help Jordan develop or deal with its economic problem.

RELATIONS WITH THE GREATER ARAB WORLD

Saudi Arabia seeks to maintain a broader regional balance of power that helps to secure it against Iran and Iraq, as well as relations with the greater Arab and Islamic world that strengthen its legitimacy as both the custodian of the Islamic holy places and a leading Arab state. In the process, Saudi Arabia must play a five-sided game in which it does its best to neutralize any threat from Iran, Iraq, and Yemen; avoid any backlash from the Arab-Israeli conflict; and use its ties to the United States to counter-balance the military strength of its northern neighbors without alienating its own fundamentalists and the Arab world.

Saudi Arabia must preserve its interests in dealing with its Southern Gulf neighbors—Bahrain, Kuwait, Oman, Qatar, and the UAE. In the case of Bahrain, this is increasingly a client relationship in which Saudi Arabia provides the oil necessary to sustain Bahrain's economy and an ultimate security guarantee against its Shi'ites and interference from Iran. In the case of Kuwait, Saudi Arabia is caught up in an awkward and poorly defined security relationship that must deal with the threat from Iraq. In the case of Oman, it must seek to overcome past tensions, contain what it feels are the regional ambitions of Sultan Qabus, and still maintain "friendly rela-tions." In the case of Qatar, it must deal with lingering Qatari resentment and fear of a powerful southern neighbor. In the case of the UAE, it must deal with lingering tensions over border disputes; its primary concern, how-ever, is the unity of the UAE and ensuring that it does not become vulner-able to Iran.

Saudi ties to the rest of the Arab world are based on a real concern for Islamic values, the Palestinian people, and Arab development. At the same time, the Kingdom has learned the hard way in recent years that efforts to create "Islamic" political movements are a two-edged sword that may turn on the Saudi regime. Saudi Arabia was careless at best in funding extremist and sometimes-violent Islamist causes in much of the Arab world. Since September 11, 2001, it has begun to exercise more care about the transfer of funds to Islamic and Arab movements than in the past. However, pri-vate Saudi citizens still are a major source of money for extremist move-ments and "charities" that use "Islam" as their ideological rationale. Saudi support for the Palestinians is not matched by any real affection for either Arafat and the other leaders of the Palestinian Authority or for rival move-ments like Hamas and the Palestinian Jihad, but the Second Intifada has sustained a flow of official and private Saudi money to violent elements in the Palestinian movement in Lebanon, Gaza, the West Bank and elsewhere in the Arab world.

Saudi relations with North Africa vary by country. Relations are good with Morocco and Tunisia; although Saudi Arabia has sharply reduced its foreign aid levels since the end of the oil boom and seeks to minimize any financial obligations. Saudi relations with Algeria are correct, but the King-dom has no desire to become involved in taking sides in the Algerian Civil War and conflicts between its secular government and "Islamic" extremists.

Saudi Arabia has sought to improve its relations with Libya, as evidenced by its involvement in mediating the turnover of suspects in the Lockerbie case in 1999. In his visit to Libya in June of the same year, Crown Prince

Abdullah emphasized the unity and close ties between Saudi Arabia and Libya.[168] In September 1999, Saudi businessman and billionaire Prince al-Walid bin Talal met with Moammar Qaddafi to discuss joint economic investment in Libya and Middle Eastern tourism and hotel projects.[169] Improved relations could be of mutual benefit to both countries. The lifting of ten years of economic sanctions has left Libya in need of foreign investment to revitalize its economy. Even limited Saudi investment and political support for Qaddafi pushes him toward moderation, limits the risk the Kingdom will become a target of his political attacks, and reduces the possibility that he will support Saudi extremists.

These relationships change with time, and it is important to understand that it is the practical realities of regional power politics that govern Saudi relations with the greater Arab world, and not the Kingdom's occasional references to other Arab leaders as "brothers" or Pan-Arab rhetoric. Saudi Arabia continues to seek prestige and influence throughout the Arab world and to define its legitimacy as the Arab custodian of Mecca, Medina, and the site of the pilgrimage. It does not, however, define its security or trade relations in terms of ties to Arab states outside the Gulf. This is likely to be an enduring reality. It may not endear itself to Arabists, but it must be treated as such.

RELATIONS WITH THE UNITED STATES AND THE WEST

Two very different nations, with different cultures and political structures, have been thrust together by oil and security. Saudi Arabia depends on the United States for security and many aspects of its development. The United States depends on Saudi Arabia to provide oil exports, use its swing production capacity to help stabilize the oil market, and provide basing and military support for U.S. power projection in the Gulf. Over the years, this mutual dependence has often benefited both countries and created a climate of friendship.

At the same time, oil economics have long made the states competitors as well as allies. Both nations have limited tolerance for the other's social and religious practices. A conservative and cautious monarchy and an interventionist democracy have inevitable differences. The American alliance with Israel and Saudi support for Arab causes have led to several periods of serious tension between the two countries. They have also sometimes had a serious impact on Saudi security due to the unwillingness of the United States to provide Saudi Arabia with modern arms.

The United States has pressed for "democratization" without sufficient concern for the internal political and social dynamics of Saudi society. The need exists to couple increased political pluralism to the development of stable political parties and to consider other Saudi needs, such as economic reform, human rights, and an improved rule of law. On the other hand, the constant tension between the Saudi royal family and technocrats and the more conservative Wahhabi Ulema over modernization has increasingly interacted with a Wahhabi and Islamist extremist resentment of the impact of Western secularism in general and of the United States in particular. While mainstream Wahhabi practices tend to be relatively tolerant, there are hard-line and extremist elements that resent or oppose any overt Western presence in the Kingdom, particularly the presence of U.S. and British military forces.

The events of September 11, 2001, have combined with the backlash from the Second Intifada to create the worst period in Saudi-U.S. relations since the oil embargo of 1973. The fact so many young Saudis were involved in the attacks on the World Trade Center and the Pentagon on September 11, and in Osama bin Laden's al Qaeda organization, has dramatized the tensions in Saudi-U.S. relations in ways that have led in both countries to ignore a history of friendship and the underlying reasons for a long-standing de facto U.S.-Saudi alliance.

This situation has not been helped by the steady escalation of the Second Intifada since September 2000. Far too many outsiders see the resulting popular Saudi anger at the United States as coupled to Islamic or Wahhabi extremism. In practice, the reality is very different. Religious extremism is at the margin of Saudi society, but the constant images of Palestinian suffering in the Arab media have had a major impact on all aspects of Saudi society, particularly young Saudis who have little meaningful contact with Americans. Long before September 11, there were spontaneous student boycotts of American products as a result of the Second Intifada, and the level of Saudi popular anger reached a new peak at the time of the Israeli Army's reoccupation of Palestinian cities in the West Bank in the spring of 2002. It is fair to say such anger and resentment interacts with Islamic extremist criticism of the United States, just as it is fueled by the more extreme one-sided coverage of much of the Arab media available by satellite. However, confusing Saudi anger over the Second Intifada with Islamic extremism in Saudi Arabia—as has been done in many U.S. press reports and in interpreting the results of several badly structured opinion polls—does nothing to put the real issues in proper perspective.

It is a cliché of diplomacy that nations have no permanent allies, but only permanent interests. Certainly, Saudi diplomacy is as subject to such *realpolitik* as is the diplomacy of the United States—a fact that is all too clear from the previous discussion of Saudi relations with Gulf and other Arab states. At the same time, Saudi and U.S. interests do coincide in many important ways. This is clear from the analysis of the Saudi economy and petroleum strategy in later chapters, and it is clear when the history of the ups and downs in U.S.-Saudi relations is considered along with current problems and tensions.[170]

The Formative Period: 1933–1953

Saudi Arabia established serious political and economic ties to the United States in the 1930s. King Abd al-Aziz saw the United States as a natural political and economic counterbalance to what was then de facto British dominance of the Gulf, and as a way of obtaining the technology and resources needed to explore the Kingdom's oil resources without the kind of Iranian and Iraqi dependence on British oil companies that threatened their financial and political independence. Saudi Arabia granted its first oil concession to Standard Oil of California on May 29, 1993; the first major oil discovery took place on March 4, 1938; and oil exports began that same year.

This relationship did not develop a security dimension until World War II, and even then the United States saw the Gulf as largely a zone of British strategic influence. King Abd al-Aziz did, however, reject more favorable oil concession offers from Japan and Nazi Germany in the late 1930s, and rejected new German offers after the defeat of Britain and France. This led the Axis to treat Saudi Arabia as a hostile power. It helped force an end of all oil exports in 1943, at a time when the war prevented the Hajj from being a source of income. The result nearly bankrupted Saudi Arabia and led to the start of a Lend-Lease aid program in May 1943 that provided Saudi Arabia with nearly $100 million in aid by 1947.

Saudi Arabia granted the United States the right to build a military air base in Dhahran in early 1943, at a time when Russia still seemed to be losing the war and long before the invasion of Normandy. The United States sent its first military mission to Saudi Arabia in December 1943, and began a military assistance effort that continues today. Prince Faisal and Prince Khalid (both future kings) made the first royal visit to the United States in September 1943, and the growing strength of the allies allowed Saudi oil exports to resume in 1944. The U.S. companies involved in the oil concession—which now included CALTEX and Texaco—formed the Arabian-American Oil Company the same year. The security dimension also strengthened. King Abd al-Aziz met with President Truman at sea, the king declared war on the Axis on March 1, 1945, and Truman awarded Prince Faisal the Legion of Merit in 1946.

Saudi Arabia also began to modernize its forces with U.S. aid in 1946. Until that time, it had no organized army beyond tribal troops using trucks with machine guns and a few token British and U.S. fighters. Progress was slow at best, however. While the king appointed his first minister of defense in 1944, there was no ministry until 1947, when the Ministry of Defense and Aviation (MODA) was formed.

Israel's declaration of independence in 1948 and its U.S. recognition led to the first significant tension in the U.S.-Saudi relationship. Although Saudi Arabia continued to rely on Aramco and the United States for virtually all of its economic aid and development, it turned to Britain for assistance in its first major effort to modernize its army—the creation of a 10,000-man force similar to the Desert Legion of Jordan. The king soon found, however, that this military advisory effort clashed with his efforts to secure favorable borders with the Trucial states, and the British advisors were limited to military training areas near Taif and Jeddah in the south. No further major military modernization effort took place until 1951, although the U.S. Air Force quietly continued to use the air base at Dhahran, which eventually became a secret dispersal and recovery based for nuclear-armed U.S. B-47 bombers. The U.S. Navy made its first major port call to Dammam in 1948.

The armistice in the Arab-Israeli conflict that took place in May 1950 led to more open Saudi-U.S. relations. This improvement in relations occurred at a time when the Kingdom's income from oil and the Hajj was so low that Saudi Arabia teetered on the edge of bankruptcy. As a result, a U.S. Point Four aid mission was sent to the Kingdom in 1951. This mission helped create the Saudi Arabian Monetary agency (SAMA). This helped stabilize the Kingdom's finances, although oil revenues were still limited. While expansion of Saudi production raised annual oil revenues from $56.7 million in 1950 to $234.8 million in 1954 and the United States encouraged heavy investment in education and medical services, little money was available for serious economic development.

The United States also sent a military mission to Saudi Arabia in late 1950 to survey Saudi military needs. This resulted in the first formal U.S.-Saudi military agreement on June 18, 1951—an agreement that took place shortly before a time when Saudi tensions with Britain over Oman and Saudi claims to areas claimed by the other Trucial States led to a virtual breakdown of Saudi-British military relations. By 1952, the U.S. team had helped Saudi Arabia reorganize the MODA as a functioning organization and develop its first serious modernization plan, although the plan only called for the creation of limited numbers of relatively modern ground troops by 1956 and the actual creation of these units took until 1962.

Nasser and Arab Nationalism: 1953–1968

Ironically, the Kingdom's slow movement toward economic and military development helped trigger the second major period of tension in U.S.-Saudi relations. King Abd al-Aziz's death in 1953 brought King Saud to the throne at a time when decolonization, Egypt's Nasser, Pan-Arabism, and various Arab socialist and Marxist movements were creating political and intellectual ferment throughout the Arab world. At the same time, Aramco remained a largely U.S. enclave that did little to help its workers. In May 1953, this led to riots by Aramco's Saudi workers; when the government imprisoned the leaders of the workers in October, some

19,000 workers went on strike and attacked Aramco and U.S. Air Force vehicles in Dhahran.

King Saud responded with a wave of subsidies and paternalism that not only helped end the Aramco protests but began the construction of schools, medical facilities, and more modern government services throughout the Kingdom. He did little, however, to balance the budget or create a stable economy, and outside groups like the Syrian National Socialists began to make serious inroads in the Saudi labor force, military, and schools. This led King Saud to tilt toward Nasser, whom he visited in the Spring of 1954. King Saud also attempted to deal with what he saw as a socialist and Marxist threat by agreeing to create a joint command with Egypt on June 11, 1954. When a minor Marxist mutiny took place in Saudi forces in 1955, King Saud brought in a 200-man Egyptian military mission and began to send significant numbers of Saudi military and other students to Egypt.

King Saud expelled the U.S. Point Four mission on the grounds that $6.4 million in aid was a pointless token compared to the aid the United States was giving Israel. He did, however, maintain the Kingdom's reliance on the U.S. military and refused Soviet offers of modern arms in August 1955. Even so, U.S. supporters of Israel successfully pressured the U.S. government to suspend the sale of modern arms to Saudi Arabia (eighteen medium tanks and a handful of F-86s). President Eisenhower overruled these efforts in February 1956, however, in part because it was already clear that Nasser was more of a threat to Saudi Arabia than Arab socialism.

During 1955, it became clear that some of the labor and military unrest in Saudi Arabia actually had Egyptian backing. Pro-Nasser demonstrations took place in the Aramco labor force, which led Saud bin Jiluwi, the governor of the Eastern Province to arrest 200 workers and flog three to death. A three-day pro-Nasser strike took place in early 1956. Nasser nationalized the Suez Canal in July and pressured King Saud to embargo oil shipments to the West. The first massive political demonstration in Saudi history took place when Nasser visited the Kingdom in September 1956, and it was clear that Nasserism was an active threat to the Saudi regime.

The Saudi reaction was to maintain public ties to Egypt, refuse to join the Baghdad Pact, and sign a ten-year defense pact with Egypt on January 18, 1957. At the same time, Saudi Arabia refused to embargo oil during the Suez conflict of 1956, and continued to renew the U.S. lease on Dhahran on a month-to-month basis when the lease expired. President Eisenhower's pressure on England and France to leave Suez, and the announcement of the Eisenhower Doctrine in January 1957, led King Saud to visit Washington in February 1957. King Saud turned to the United States for a new military agreement in April 1957 and renewed the U. S. lease on Dhahran for five years. This shift was reinforced during 1957 and 1958 by growing Saudi fears of Egypt following the creation of the United Arab Republic with Syria and Yemen, and by more general fears of Pan-Arabism, socialism, and Marxism following the fall of the Hashemite dynasty in Iraq on July 14, 1958.

A growing power struggle between King Saud and Prince Faisal complicated Saudi-U.S. relations, as did the strong pro-Nasserite sympathies of Prince Talal and the so-called "free princes." At the same time, U.S. military interests in Saudi Arabia shifted in 1960 when the U.S. strategic force posture became dependent on ICBMs and long-range bombers and Secretary of Defense Robert McNamara decided to end the lease on Dhahran. USAF operations in Dhahran ended on April 16, 1961. The end result left a major U.S. military mission in the Kingdom, but effectively left Britain as the only Western military presence in the Gulf.

Events in Yemen then created new problems. The imam of Yemen broke with the UAR after Syria withdrew in September 1961, but his now Egyptian-trained military supported Egyptian intervention and staged a coup. Nasser sent in Egyptian forces in October 1962, and a major pro-Nasser civil war and Egyptian military presence developed on Saudi Arabia's southeast border. King Saud proved unable to deal with the complex developments in the Arab world and his efforts at social reform more to disrupt the Kingdom than modernize it.

The end result was a de facto coup by Prince Faisal in October 1962, although the power struggle between Faisal and Saud did not lead to Saud's exile and Faisal becoming king until March 26, 1964. Faisal carried out a systematic purge of all pro-Nasser elements and began to provide large Saudi subsidies and arms shipments to the imam's forces. Nasser countered by putting pressure on the Saudi border area with Yemen and bombing Saudi villages near Najran. This led the Kennedy administration to send F-100s and paratroops to Dhahran as a deterrent to further Egyptian attacks. Faisal also turned to the United States, Britain, and France for a far more serious Saudi military buildup beginning in 1963, largely in response to an Egyptian military presence in Yemen that grew from 36,000 men in 1963 to 80,000 by the mid-1960s.

Faisal did attempt to improve relations with Nasser, however, and made a major effort to peacefully resolve the Yemeni Civil War between 1964 and 1967. He did so in spite of systematic Egyptian efforts to subvert the Saudi military, manipulate the Aramco labor force, and use ex-King Saud and the free princes to overthrow Faisal's government. Faisal responded by turning to the United States for military assistance, only to become involved in a complex three-country deal in which Secretary McNamara effectively brokered a Saudi purchase of British Lightning fighters for a British purchase of F-111s (which eventually turned into a British buy of F-4s.) The United States did, however, sell the Kingdom a large number of Hawk surface-to-air missiles. It is worth noting in passing that the United States manipulated the first really major Saudi purchase of modern arms for its own financial interests. (These agreements totaled less than $150 million.

The first truly massive U.S. arms sales took place in 1973–1975, at a cost of $2.8 billion in new agreements, in spite of the October War and oil embargo.)

King Faisal benefited from a steady rise in oil revenues during 1964–1967 and reformed the country's fiscal management. He developed a far more realistic and effective modernization plan than King Saud and the free princes had advocated, and did so in spite of the fact that Nasser was able to use King Saud, have him claim that Faisal had gained power as part of a CIA plot, and send him to Yemen to publicly support the pro-Nasser government.

Faisal also used the June 1967 Arab-Israel conflict as a political weapon against Nasser. While he was initially forced to support the declaration of an Arab oil embargo and send a brigade to Jordan, the king broke the embargo in July 1967 and Saudi forces never fought in the conflict. In August 1967, Faisal confronted Nasser at the Arab summit in Khartoum and essentially forced him to withdraw from Yemen in return for limited Saudi aid—most of which was never paid.

This diplomatic victory, however, was offset by two developments that still affect U.S.-Saudi relations. First, the Israeli victory, and occupation of Jerusalem, the West Bank, Gaza, and the Golan Heights made the Arab-Israeli conflict a central focus of Arab politics and a continuing problem for Saudi Arabia of a far more serious dimension. Second, Britain's economic crisis led to the announcement on January 17, 1968 that Britain would withdraw all of its forces from the Gulf and Arabia by the end of 1971. On the one hand, U.S. ties to Israel became a far more serious problem for the Kingdom than ever before. On the other hand, it was clear that the Kingdom faced a virtual power vacuum in the Gulf unless the United States provided some kind of presence to check any threat from Iran and Iraq.

One major side effect of all of these complex developments was that the Saudi government became increasingly concerned about the political impact of secular education on the Kingdom's political stability. In the process, the Saudi government became careful to exclude politically active secular foreign teachers, although it allowed teachers with a strong Islamic background into the Kingdom. It put a heavy emphasis on traditional Islamic education and Wahhabi practices in all of the schools as a way of giving priority to the Kingdom's claim to Islamic legitimacy as custodian of the two key Islamic holy places—although it allowed modern educational methods in the sciences, engineering, and medicine and encouraged technical training in the United States and Europe.

While this emphasis on using religious legitimacy to secure the regime was reinforced after the Islamist extremist uprising in the Grand Mosque in 1979, and again to placate Islamists protesting the U.S. presence in the Kingdom during the Gulf War, it is important to note that it had its true genesis in the Nasserite-Pan Arab turmoil of the 1950s. It is also worth noting that some of the princes and Saudis who are loudest in calling for rapid democratization today played a key role in King Saud's failures and destabilizing the Kingdom.

The June 1967 War to the October 1973 War

Several trends dominated U.S.-Saudi relations during the period between the Arab-Israeli conflict in 1967 and the October War in 1973:

- Saudi Arabia experienced considerable internal political stability, although some problems remained with Nasserites, various Arab socialist movements, hard-line Wahhabis, and Shi'ite Islamists. A significant new coup attempt was uncovered in the Saudi military in 1969 and further arrests took place in 1970. This, however, was the last significant sign of unrest in the Saudi military until a Libyan-sponsored coup was uncovered in 1977.

- Saudi forces clashed with Yemeni forces in 1969, and a resulting Saudi air raid on Yemen marked the first time the Kingdom ever used modern forces in combat. While the clash was relatively minor by Western standards and was won by British contract pilots flying Saudi Lightning fighters, it convinced the Saudi royal family that modern military forces were necessary and could be effective.

- The slow Saudisation of Aramco and higher salaries and better living conditions reduced many of the pressures that had radicalized its labor force. A steady rise in the Kingdom's oil export revenues, coupled with better fiscal management, allowed the government to improve education, welfare, and medical services—particularly after 1970 as real oil prices began to rise.

- The near-collapse of Pan-Arabism, socialism, and Marxism; the Nasserite movement; and Ba'athism in both Syria and Iraq removed much of the ideological challenge to al-Saud rule, and Egypt, Syria, and Iraq became much less active in sponsoring opposition groups within Saudi Arabia. After British withdrawal, Iraq did, however, make its first aggressive movements towards Kuwait since 1962–1964. It occupied a Kuwaiti border post in 1973 and made new claims to Kuwaiti islands in the Gulf in 1974 and 1976.

- Britain's withdrawal from the Gulf also created a new potential challenge from the shah of Iran, at least in terms of his search for political power and influence in the Gulf. A major arms race began between Iran and Iraq that inevitably posed a threat to Saudi Arabia. In addition, Iran and Iraq carried out a low-level border war over control of the Shatt al Arab—the main shipping channel between the two countries. Iraq began this conflict after General Hassan al-Bakr came to power in 1968. It lasted until the Algiers Accord of 1975—an agreement forced on Iraq largely because of the shah's sponsorship of Kurdish military resistance in Iraq and his willingness to end this support for the agreement.

- The United States adopted a "twin pillar" policy under Nixon that claimed to see both Iran and Saudi Arabia as key "pillars" supporting moderate and anti-communist positions in the Gulf. In practice, however, the United States clearly relied largely on the shah. The United States did oppose the shah's claims to Bahrain, but did little when the shah seized Abu Musa and the Tunbs from the United States.

- The Kingdom became steadily more dependent on the United States for military equipment, although it continued to import from Britain, France, and other nations. This dependence raised growing issues in the Kingdom, however, as it became clear that Israel had no intention of withdrawing from the territories it occupied in 1967, and in the United States because of the risk that U.S. arms sales might make Saudi Arabia a more serious threat to Israel. These problems were made even more acute by the so-called Canal War between Israel and Egypt in 1970.

- The nationalization of the oil industry in virtually every other Middle Eastern country inevitably pushed Saudi Arabia toward the nationalization of Aramco.

This complex mix of developments did not prevent good U.S.-Saudi relations, but they left America's view of the Kingdom's position in the Gulf uncertain, while external events made the Arab-Israeli conflict an increasingly serious source of controversy.

The October 1973 War to the Fall of the Shah

Saudi Arabia did not play a military role in the October War, although it sent a 1,500-man unit and ten tanks to Jordan. The October War did, however, increase both secular and Islamist resentment of U.S. ties to Israel. The Saudi government reacted sharply to U.S. military resupply of Israel during the war and triggered the first serious Arab oil embargo.

Although it later became clear that this embargo did comparatively little to seriously interrupt the flow of actual oil exports, it resulted in a mass panic in world oil markets that led to a sudden rise in oil prices. It also transformed world oil markets forever. Before the oil embargo, Western control of oil marketing through the major international oil companies—the so-called Seven Sisters—still acted as a near consumer cartel that kept oil prices depressed in market terms. The embargo not only raised prices to well beyond market levels, but made Saudi Arabia far richer in terms of oil export income and laid the groundwork for making the Organization of Petroleum Exporting Countries (OPEC), a cartel that artificially raised prices.

This result of the oil embargo made Saudi Arabia a truly wealthy oil power for the first time. Saudi oil and gas revenues had experienced a major rise between 1969 and 1972, and had risen from 8.1 billion Saudi riyals to 26.3 billion—largely because of the nationalization of oil production in Middle Eastern states. They suddenly rose to 78.4 billion in 1973–1974, however, and 104.7 billion in 1974–1975. They climbed steadily after that time and rose to 131.1 billion riyals in 1978–1979.[171] However, tensions over the embargo and Arab-Israeli conflict led to considerable tension between Saudi Arabia and the United States. Although they did not lead to overt diplomatic clashes, they did lead the United States to go so far as to at least examine contingency plans to seize the Saudi oil fields. It also led Saudi Arabia to deliberately increase the role of European states in the Saudi economy and arms sales, and to try to find ways to reduce its growing dependence on agricultural imports from the West.

The U.S.-led negotiations that brokered ceasefires between Israel and Egypt and Israel and Syria removed much of the Saudi-U.S. tension over the Arab-Israeli conflict. So did the peace between Egypt and Israel, although Saudi Arabia did not openly support the Camp David accords when they were settled in 1978 or signed in March 1979. This led to a renewal of U.S.-Saudi cooperation and major new Saudi arms buys from the United States in spite of sometimes-bitter debates in the U.S. Congress, particularly in 1976.

As would be the case with the Gulf War in 1991, the use of advanced military technology during the October War triggered a major new arms race throughout the Middle East and North Africa that Saudi Arabia inevitably had to join. The end result was that Saudi military forces expanded from 42,500 men, 85 main battle tanks, and 70 combat aircraft in 1974 to 64,500 men, 350 main battle tanks, and 178 combat aircraft in 1979. Nevertheless, Saudi arms imports were only one-fifth to one-third of those of the shah of Iran.[172]

In broad terms, the period between 1974 and 1979 was one of comparatively good Saudi-U.S. relations, but one in which the United States clearly relied on Iran as its main ally in the Gulf. There was little or no strategic pressure on either Saudi Arabia or the United States to have U.S. forces based on Saudi soil, and the "energy crisis" of 1974 quickly proved to have far less impact on Western economies than was initially predicted.

The Fall of the Shah to the Gulf War

Neither the United States nor Saudi Arabia foresaw the fall of the shah in 1979 or the major changes that were to reshape their relations. The United States was suddenly confronted with the loss of the "pillar" that it had relied on to shield the Gulf against the Soviet Union at a time when the Russian movement into Afghanistan seemed likely to give the USSR major new military capabilities in the region. In broad terms, these events produced the following major shifts in Saudi-U.S. relations.

Saudi Arabia suddenly acquired far more strategic importance to the United States, as did the smaller Gulf states. This made the modernization and expansion of Saudi military force far more important than in the past, as well as the ability to find bases, power projection facilities, and prepositioning capabilities in the Gulf region.

Both Saudi Arabia and the United States were confronted by a hostile Khomeini regime in Iran that saw the Saudi royal family as a corrupt tool of the United States, Wahhabi practices as a perversion of Islam, and the Saudi government as persecuting its Shi'ite minority. Although Iran did not focus on the overthrow of the Saudi regime, it treated it as an enemy and used the Hajj repeatedly as an occasion for demonstrations and riots against the Saudi regime and the United States. At least initially, Iran repeated its claims to Bahrain and sought to overthrow other Gulf regimes as part of an effort to create an Islamic nation. The Khomeini regime treated the United States, in turn, as a major enemy and as a power that should be forced out of the Gulf, and Israel as an enemy that should be destroyed. The resulting U.S. embassy hostage crisis shattered U.S.-Iranian relations and led the United States to treat Iran as a major enemy.

It is unclear whether the turmoil surrounding the fall of the Shah and the rise of the new Islamic regime in Iran contributed to the first serious Islamic extremist threat to the Kingdom since the time of the Ikhwan revolts before World War II. However, on November 16, 1979, small groups of Saudi and foreign Islamic extremists began to assemble, and then attacked shrines in Mecca and Medina. The were led by Juhaiman ibn Muhammed ibn Saif al-Otaibi, some of whose relatives had fought against Abd al-Aziz in the battle of Sabillah in 1929; others that had died in the king's suppression of the Ikhwan. They never threatened the regime or aroused much popular support, but held the Mosque for nearly two weeks until the Kingdom could deploy significant forces and obtain French military assistance. The individuals involved were not Wahhabi in any meaningful sense. Indeed, Juhaiman went so far as to proclaim that his brother-in-law was the Mahdi. Nevertheless, the incident, and a rise of religious criticism of the Saudi regime growing out of Saudi Arabia's rapid process of modernization, led the regime to be far more cautious about some aspects of modernization, increase support for the regular Wahhabi Ulema, and crack down on known religious opponents of the regime. It also reinforced the Kingdom's decision—made in the early 1950s—to emphasize the regime's religious legitimacy. This did not lead the regime to keep education Wahhabi and Islamic—a decision it had taken much earlier—but it did make it reluctant to modernize in any way that might increase religious tension.

Khomeini's rise to power led to other religious tensions, as did the persecution of Saudi Shi'ites by an ultraconservative Saudi governor in the Eastern Province. Iranian radio issued its first called call for "death to the criminal and mercenary government of the Saudi family" on January 7, 1980. There were significant arrests of Shi'ites in 1981 and more serious Shi'ite uprisings in 1982 in the area most critical to the Kingdom's oil production. While the riots never threatened Saudi control or even Saudi oil production, they reinforced Saudi hostility to Iran. Moreover, although the king made major efforts to improve the situation for the Shi'ites and put in a far more moderate governor, the problem reinforced the regime's effort to strengthen its legitimacy in Wahhabi eyes and use religious sectarianism as a counterbalance to Iran.

It took time for the new Khomeini regime to consolidate power in Iran. A civil war broke out between the Khomeini government and radical Marxist factions like the People's Mujahideen, while purges led to the near-collapse of the armed forces. Saddam Hussein saw this turmoil in Iran as both an opportunity and a threat and invaded Iran in 1980, with the goal of annexing part of the oil rich areas in Southwest Iraq and avenging the concessions Iraq had made in the Algiers Accords of 1975.[173] The result was the eight-year-long Iran-Iraq War. Although Iraq initially appeared to be defeating Iran, Iran was on the counteroffensive by 1982 and a series of Iranian offensives threatened to defeat Iran from 1984 to the early part of 1988.

All of these pressures interacted with the impact of the Soviet invasion of Afghanistan and the years of war that followed. The United States and the West gradually came to see the Afghan opposition, or Mujahideen, as a key tool in checking Soviet control of Afghanistan and the expansion of the Soviet role in south and southwest Asia. At the same time, Saudi Arabia saw the support of the Afghan opposition as both a holy cause and a way of strengthening its relations with the United States and other Western states. This almost inevitably made Afghanistan a center of Saudi Islamist involvement and led to the training of thousands of young Saudi fighters over the long history of the Afghan War. At the same time, Saudi charities became deeply involved in funding Islamist movements in Pakistan and other countries for both religious reasons and as a check to Marxist movements. In far too many cases these causes were extremist and violent, and both Saudi Arabia and the West paid far too little attention to the longer-term impact of such actions. Once the fighting in Afghanistan was over, Saudi funds continued to flow to Islamist extremist groups. The first Intifada, the fighting in Lebanon, Bosnia, Kosovo, and Chechnya sustained these efforts and involved more young Saudis in fighting and violent movements. The United States turned a blind eye to some of these actions and saw others as providing indirect support for its own foreign-policy objectives. In many ways, the end result was a de facto Saudi-U.S. alliance in promoting Islamic extremism that laid the groundwork for later acts of extremist terrorism in the region and the events of September 11, 2001.

The world oil market panicked for the second time in response to the fall of the shah, the Iran-Iraq War, and Iraq's loss of its oil export facilities in the Gulf and ability to use its oil pipeline through Syria. Saudi oil and gas revenues rose from 131.1 billion riyals in 1978–1979 to 237.2 billion in 1979–1980, 341.0 billion in 1980–1981, and 322.4 billion in 1981–1982, before dropping back to 192.8 billion in 1982–1982 and 143 billion in 1982–1983.[174] The result was initially to create an image of vast oil wealth and raise Saudi military and civil spending to levels that had been unimaginable in the past. This new wealth allowed the Kingdom to fund major new arms purchases and military advisory efforts from the United States as well as a vast paternalistic welfare and subsidy system. However, market forces soon began to operate and economic reality quickly set in. OPEC lost market share as new suppliers entered the market at lower prices, and Saudi efforts to maintain prices collapsed once the drop in Saudi oil revenues grew too serious to endure. To put this into perspective, Saudi oil and gas revenues dropped to 120.3 billion riyals in 1983–1984, 88.3 billion in 1984–1985, 61.3 billion in 1985–1986, and only rose significantly again after 1989. It was only the beginning of the Gulf War in 1990 that drove them back above 100 billion riyals.[175]

Although Saudi Arabia faced continuing problems in obtaining arms from the United States because of the Arab-Israeli conflict, the fall of the shah and the Iran-Iraq War led to closer Saudi-U.S. military cooperation than at any time since the United States had given up its lease on Dhahran. Bitter debates did occur within the United States over the sale of F-15s to Saudi Arabia—in both the early 1980s and during 1985–1986—that forced Saudi Arabia to turn to Britain and France for a massive $7 billion arms purchase called the al-Yamamah package. There was also a bitter debate over the sale of the E-3A AWACS and an Air Defense Enhancement Package in 1981.[176]

This did not, however, affect the mutual need for military cooperation by both countries. U.S. air units returned to Dhahran to provide surveillance of the Gulf, and this cooperation heightened in 1996, when Iran and Iraq stepped up their attacks on tankers, and in early 1997, when Iran began to attack Kuwaiti and Saudi tankers because the two countries were aiding Iraq. In spite of the fact that only seven Kuwaiti flagged tankers had been hit out of 284 attacks on shipping since the beginning of the Iraq-Iraq War, the United States agreed to "reflag" Kuwaiti tankers to protect them from Iran in January 1987.[177] This led to major naval clashes between the United States and Iran in 1987 and 1988, and this "tanker war" lasted until Iraq's military victories reversed the course of the Iran-Iraq War in the summer of 1988 and led to a ceasefire. During this time, Saudi Arabia strongly encouraged the United States to support the reflagging effort and to check any Iranian naval activity in the Gulf while permitting Iraq complete freedom of military action, while quietly providing extensive basing support for the USAF.

Iraq's victory over Iran in August 1988 created a new problem in the Gulf. Rather than consolidate his victory and new prestige, Saddam Hussein demanded that Saudi Arabia and Kuwait forgive the loans they had made to keep Iraq from going bankrupt during the war. In 1989, Iraq demanded Kuwaiti concessions in terms of production from a large oilfield that crossed the Iraq-Kuwait border and a lease on the Kuwaiti islands in the Gulf that affected Iraqi access to the Gulf. When Kuwait did not fully concede, Iraq invaded Kuwait in 1990.

The end result was the formation of a major U.S.-Saudi-led coalition to defend Saudi Arabia and liberate Kuwait that began the Gulf War of 1990–1991. Both Saudi Arabia and the United States had little other choice. Not only had Iraq become the dominant military force in the Gulf, but Saudi Arabia was acutely vulnerable to further Iraqi adventures. The result was a rapid, massive U.S. buildup in the Gulf and what became the deployment of two full U.S. corps, a British corps, and massive amount of U.S., British, and other Western airpower to Saudi Arabia. Even during the Gulf War, however, tensions arose in Saudi-U.S. relations. While many Saudis welcomed the U.S. presence and the fact that the U.S.-Saudi led coalition won a major military victory, many conservative Saudis deeply resented a secular Western presence on Saudi soil, and extremists saw it as a violation of the prohibition of a non-Muslim presence in Arabia.

The Gulf War to the Second Intifada and September 11, 2001

The end of the Gulf War in the spring of 1991 left Saudi-U.S. relations at a seeming high point. In spite of what appeared to be minor tensions, both nations had helped lead a victorious coalition force in what seemed to be a lasting popular victory. As the following chapters show, however, this very real victory was accompanied by other trends.

Saudi hard-line Wahhabis and Islamic extremists were shocked by the presence of a Western force on Saudi soil, which many saw as a violation of a religious prohibition on any overt Christian and Jewish presence in Arabia, rather than Mecca and Medina alone. At the same time, Saudi Shi'ites saw the United States as the firm ally of the Saudi regime, and some pro-Iranian Saudi Shi'ites saw the United States as an enemy.

The United States failed to understand just how serious the Kingdom's cultural and political sensitivities were, and failed to see that its "oil wealth" had declined drastically in real and per capita terms. The United States pushed to preposition U.S. equipment in "sovereign" bases, and to maintain a significant and highly visible U.S. military presence in Saudi Arabia, rather than lower its presence and profile. It sought burden-sharing and Saudi funding of its role in the Gulf War and continued military presence in the region, rather than Saudi internal stability, and gave only limited priority to supporting Saudi economic and social reform. It only backed away from government pressure to sell more arms to Saudi Arabia when the Kingdom experienced a cash flow crisis in 1995, and then episodically still pushed arms or aircraft sales in spite of the Kingdom's problems.

Both the Saudi regime and the U.S. government failed to see a need to explain either Saudi defense policies or the U.S. military role in the Kingdom to the Saudi people. The steady opening of the Kingdom to global media, much higher educational standards, and the pressures of declining oil wealth were ignored. Saudi public resentment of wasteful military expenditures and arms purchases, the inevitable tensions from a U.S. military presence, and the related tensions growing out of the Arab-Israeli conflict were met with little more than silence. Islamic hostility operated in a political vacuum.

There is no fixed point at which Saudi Arabia's rapid population growth can be said to have produced a "youth explosion." Many young Saudi males were unemployed long before 1990, but Saudisation proved to be a dismal failure and job creation lagged far below the number of young Saudis entering the labor force throughout the 1990s—as is almost certain to occur for most of the next decade.

Arguably, Saudi ability to sustain its paternalistic welfare state and maintain high per capita incomes through "oil wealth" disappeared in the early 1980s, at least in terms of per capita income and a balanced budget. However, it was the Saudi government's expenditures on the Gulf War and the low-to-moderate oil export income of the 1980s that began to put serious limits on government spending and what the Saudi economy could provide in terms of opportunities and wealth. As the following chapters show, this put serious pressure on Saudi ability to sustain military and civil spending, as well as compounded the problems Saudi youth faced in terms of unemployment.

Saudi Arabia and the United States both reacted to the end of the Cold War by encouraging Islamist movements in central Asia as a check to any reassertion of Russian power. The United States tolerated Islamist extremist action in the Balkans as a check to Serbia, while Saudi Arabia actively encouraged it. In other regions, Saudi Arabia funded Islamic movements with far too little attention to their real character, while the United States was slow to react to them as a threat and often dealt with them more in terms of human rights issues than as a threat of terrorism.

At the same time, oil became more an economic issue for both countries than a strategic one. In general, this was to the benefit of the United States. Saudi Arabia increasingly needed cash flow and the cost of oil exports was not high enough or uncertain enough to generate serious U.S. policy concern. Neither country developed or implemented a coherent energy policy. Although Saudi Arabia did begin to develop meaningful economic diversification plans in the late 1990s, it did not seriously try to implement them until 2000. The U.S. government largely ignored Saudi efforts and gave only limited priority to such concerns as Saudi membership in the WTO and the creation of an institutionalized exporter and importer dialog and secretariat.

The Oslo Accords and seeming progress in the Arab-Israeli peace process appeared to take the issue off the table as a central focus of Saudi-U.S. relations. Neither side was prepared for its sudden reemergence as a major issue with the beginning of the Second Intifada in September 2000. The Kingdom dealt with the peace issue largely passively and by ignoring it until the Second Intifada exploded into a major crisis. The United States dealt with the issue by relying far too much on the momentum of the Oslo peace process until the Camp David talks in the spring of 2000. The failure of the Clinton initiatives, the initial effort of the Bush administration to distance itself from the issue, and a perceived Bush tilt toward Israel created far broader public hostility in Saudi Arabia than the Islamist extremists had succeeded in creating in decades or past effort, while the Saudi government largely avoid the issue until Crown Prince Abdullah's peace initiative in the spring of 2002.

The very different threats posed by Iran, Iraq, and proliferation were recognized by both Saudi and U.S. policymakers, but no catalyst forced a serious dialogue on any of the three issues—at least in terms of a common recognition to agree on some concerted pattern of action.

It is not fair to say that Saudi-U.S. relations ran largely on momentum during the 1990s, but it is fair to say that neither the Saudi nor the U.S. government understood the cumulative seriousness of the issues that affected their relationship, and that neither government was prepared for the shock of Saudi involvement in the attacks on the World Trade Center and the Pentagon and the steady escalation of the Second Intifada after September 2000.

In retrospect, the bombing of the Saudi National Guard Training Center in Riyadh in 1995, the Al-Khobar bombing in 1996, the attacks on the U.S. embassies in Kenya and Tanzania, and the attacks on the U.S.S. *Cole* should have provided clear strategic warning that that serious problems were developing in Saudi-U.S. relations. The same is true of differences in the Saudi and U.S. policy approaches to Iran, Iraq, and the Second Intifada.

Developments Since September 11

Unfortunately, policymakers rarely find warning to be an effective substitute for compulsion in actually taking action, and relations between the two countries became acutely strained following the events of September 11, 2001. Much of this strain occurred among those who had little direct experience with Saudi Arabia or Saudi-U.S. relations. The American media and U.S. congressmen publicly criticized Saudi Arabia for not taking a more active role in the war against terrorism.[178] The fact that fifteen of the nineteen hijackers were Saudi nationals prompted many Americans to perceive Saudi Arabia as "part of the problem, not part of the solution."[179] Worse, many in the United States who were not familiar with Saudi Arabia virtually demonized the regime, the entire Wahhabi sect of Islam, and came to see Saudi Arabia as an emerging threat in terms of both terrorism and future energy exports.

The Saudi reaction to September 11 was one of shock and denial, as well as resentment of exaggerated U.S. criticism. For months, Saudi Arabia did not publicly acknowledge the role Saudis played, did not explain its own problems with bin Laden, and made no effort to put its problems with Islamic extremism into perspective. When it stepped up intelligence and counterterrorism cooperation with the United States, it kept the details and scope of such cooperation secret. This situation was then made worse by the apparent lack of Saudi support for U.S. military operations in Afghanistan and deep public resentment of U.S. support for Israel as the Second Intifada continued to escalate. While the United States concentrated on terrorism and the "Islamic threat," Saudi Arabia concentrated on Palestinian suffering and the possibility that the Bush administration might launch a new war against Iraq to overthrow Saddam Hussein.

These problems eased somewhat in mid-to-late 2002, as Saudi Arabia took action against its violent Islamic extremists and potential terrorists. It called in or arrested over 4,000 young men and held some 250 extremists indefinitely. Saudi Arabia took the lead in formulating and supporting an Arab peace proposal that offers at least some hope in dealing with the Second Intifada, and refused Iraqi and Iranian calls for a new oil embargo. Saudi Arabia also quietly made its command facilities and air space available for U.S. operations in Afghanistan. U.S. officials, in turn, made it a point to praise Saudi Arabia for it cooperation and to try to counter the more extreme criticism of the Kingdom in the U.S. media.

Important as these developments are, however, Saudi-U.S. relations are certain to remain a problem for the Kingdom and the United States. There is no way to resolve some of the awkward tradeoffs each country must make. Saudi Arabia must deal much more firmly with Islamic extremism, even if this means more internal political tension, but must preserve its Islamic character. The United States must seek to lower its military profile in the Kingdom but must preserve its ability to deter and contain Iran and Iraq and rapidly project power into the Gulf region. Saudi Arabia and the United States must seek to create more stable oil markets and secure oil exports, but must remain competitors in market terms. Both nations must seek an Arab-Israeli peace, but approach the Second Intifada with different biases and perceptions. Both nations must cooperate in trying to enhance the strategic stability of the Gulf, but continue to do so in spite of major differences on issues like Iran and Iraq.

The backlash from both September 11 and the Second Intifada will continue to poison Saudi-U.S. relations, and U.S. and British military action in Iraq could create new problems and challenges. Some of the media, politicians, and intellectuals in each country have reacted by virtually declaring a "clash of civilizations" and focusing on the worst possible interpretation of the other nation's society, politics, and actions. Islamic prejudice against the West has been met with Western prejudice against Islam, and

U.S. critics have made broad charges that Saudi Arabia sponsors terrorism while Saudi critics see the United States as an aggressor and threat to the Kingdom and the Arab world.

Both nations continue to need each other. Unfortunately, one of the lasting ironies of Saudi-U.S. interests is that they are inevitably more complex than the problems the Kingdom faces in dealing with potential threats like Iran and Iraq. The entire history of Saudi-U.S. relations illustrates the fact that common interests are never identical interests, and this seems certain to be as true in the future as in the past.

SAUDI FOREIGN POLICY AT THE BEGINNING OF THE TWENTY-FIRST CENTURY

Like all other countries, Saudi Arabia must continue to search for security and regional stability. This search will continue to be difficult and success will remain uncertain. Nothing the Kingdom does, at least in the near- to mid-term, can remove the potential threat posed by Iran and Iraq and the new threat posed by proliferation. While the Kingdom can—and has— improve its relations with its Southern Gulf allies, they cannot provide regional security arrangements that will meet its needs. Neither can any relationship with other states in the Arab world.

Saudi Arabia can juggle its conflicting interests to play Iran off against Iraq, and to use European and other Arab states to partially reduce its dependence on the United States. The fact remains, however, that the Kingdom must remain dependent on U.S. power projection capabilities as its ultimate guarantee against Iran, Iraq, and any other major threat that may emerge in the near future. As a result, all of the complex problems in Saudi-U.S. relations that have just been chronicled are likely to repeat themselves in new cycles and periods of tension.

A successful Saudi foreign policy can reduce these problems, but cannot eliminate them. At least in the near- to mid-term, the most the Kingdom can do is to pursue the following options:

- Continue its rapprochement with Iran, hoping for a shift in Iranian politics that gives moderates full power, but without any illusions about the fact that Iran is already a serious conventional threat and is a major proliferator.

- Constantly reevaluate its policy toward Iraq in light of the fact that Iraq under Saddam Hussein is certain to be a lasting threat and is far more likely to use CBRN weapons than Iran. Saudi Arabia may be able to live with Saddam as long as UN sanctions still limit his military power and the United States and Britain provide military containment. Saudi Arabia cannot, however, ignore the longer-term risk and the potential need to remove Saddam from power.

- Continue to improve its relations with the smaller Gulf states, avoid petty functions over minor border and prestige issues, strengthen the GCC as much as possible in political and economic terms, and do what it can to transform the GCC into a more effective, mission-oriented, and interoperable military alliance.

- Sustain the effort to improve relations with Yemen and help the states in the Red Sea move toward added political and economic stability.

- Continue to seek friends and allies in other parts of the Arab world without illusions that any form of Pan-Arabism or Islamist solidarity can meet its economic and security needs.

- Pursue Crown Prince Abdullah's Arab-Israeli peace initiative in spite of what may be years of frustration and tension. Crown Prince Abdullah has already shown that the Kingdom does not need to reject Palestinian and Arab causes to serve the cause of peace or reduce the tensions it faces with the United States over Israel. Indeed, there are times when differences with the United States are inevitable. A persistent Saudi search for peace does, however, offer the Kingdom, the Arab cause, and the entire Middle East both the great hope for security and the best hope for the future.

- Look beyond the Arab-Israel peace issue to play a stronger role in helping Jordan develop its economy and maintain political stability.

- Come to grips with the legacy of September 11. Saudi Arabia cannot avoid the complex problems of military dependence on the United States, although they are partially counterbalanced by U.S. dependence on the flow of Saudi oil to the global economy. Saudi Arabia can, however, do much to explain itself better to the United States and the West, and to avoid being trapped into any form of "clash of civilizations." The United States and Saudi Arabia can cooperate in keeping the profile of U.S. forces in Saudi Arabia as low as possible, in strengthening Saudi military capabilities as a substitute for U.S. presence, and in increasinging U.S. power projection capabilities in Saudi Arabia and the entire Southern Gulf region as a substitute for U.S. military presence in the Kingdom.

- Build on the beginning it has made since September 11 to reform the controls it places on the flow of Saudi funds and role of Saudi youths in supporting Islamic extremist and terrorist movements outside the Kingdom. This does not mean abandoning Islamic causes, but does mean firmly rejecting violence and terrorism. This, in turn, means coming to firm grips with the difference between maintaining the Kingdom's core belief in Wahhabi practices and the need for these practices to evolve to deal with the modern world and become more tolerant, while establishing a firm internal dividing line between religion and political extremism in the name of religion.

- Treat Saudi economic reform as a major foreign-policy issue. Translate the Kingdom's reform plans, which are described in detail in Chapters 5 and 6, into an aggressive effort to seek U.S. and other Western investment and support. Give Saudi entry into the WTO, the Saudi call for an official importer-exporter dialogue, and Western investment in the Saudi gas sector a major new priority.

- Sustain a market-oriented energy policy. As is analyzed in detail in Chapter 7, Saudi Arabia's energy policy must primarily serve its domestic development needs, but also interact with many of the foreign policy issues than have just been discussed. The Kingdom has generally been a stable source of oil exports, has used its surplus production capacity to stabilize the market, and has favored long-term market share and price stability. This has reduced or eliminated many of the foreign challenges that would have arisen had it attempted to use its export capacity aggressively as a foreign-policy tool or political weapon. This "silent" dimension of Saudi foreign policy has served the Kingdom well, and Saudi Arabia is certain to benefit from continuing this policy.

Saudi Arabia's problems are scarcely unique. The game of nations never ends. No nation can impose its foreign policy on the world, no success ever prevents future problems, and most successes are limited and temporary. There are, however, two factors that must be considered in evaluating the challenges the Kingdom faces. First, none of the problems appears to fundamentally threaten the Kingdom's security at this point in time. Second, as the following chapters show, the Kingdom's foreign policy and security problems are of secondary importance in comparison with its political, social, economic, and demographic challenges.

This is not a casual point. The Kingdom has often given defense a false priority relative to internal political, social, and economic needs. It has sometimes paid more attention to foreign policy than more pressing internal problems, and it has focused on external threats when internal stability and cohesion is really its best guarantee of security. This is scarcely an argument that Saudi Arabia does not need a strong foreign policy or effective defenses—it does. As will soon become apparent, however, the Kingdom is more threatened from within than without.

NOTES

1. Rosemary Hollis, *Gulf Security: No Consensus* (London: RUSI, 1993).
2. Interview with Prince Khalid bin Sultan, March 1991.
3. Interview with senior Saudi official, November 1993.
4. Eliot A. Cohen *Gulf War Air Power Survey*, Vol. V (Washington: U.S. Air Force/Government Printing Office, 1993), pp. 232, 279–287. Note that these data are not consistent from table to table.
5. Reuters, July 2, 1997; *Washington Post*, July 2, 1997, p. A19; *New York Times*, July 2, 1997, p. A2; *Middle East Economic Digest*, September 19, 1997, p. 26.
6. Ibid.
7. Reuters, July 17, 1997, 0220.
8. *Middle East Economic Digest*, April 4, 1997, April 11, 1997, p. 23, June 13, 1997, p. 23.
9. Reuters, December 9, 1997, 0102.
10. Reuters, February 28, 1998, 0725.
11. Reuters, March 25, 1998, 0815.

12. Reuters, March 30, 1998, 1507; Associated Press, March 25, 1998, 1724EST.

13. Associated Press, April 4, 1998, 1741EST.

14. Reuters, April 20, 1998, 1720.

15. Reuters, May 26, 1998.

16. Reuters, May 27, 1998.

17. Reuters, May 3, 1999.

18. Associated Press, May 2, 1999.

19. Reuters, May 6, 1999; *Washington Post*, April 17, 2001, p. A-14; *Arab News*, April 26, 2001.

20. *Washington Post*, April 17, 2001, p. A-14; *Arab News*, April 26, 2001; Reuters, April 18, 2001 0203; Bloomberg, April 18, 2001, 0926.

21. *Middle East Economic Digest*, November 27, 1998, p. 2.

22. Jane's *Pointer*, May 1997.

23. Reuters, May 12, 2001, 1324.

24. Reuters, May 9, 2001, 1418; *New Yorker*, May 14, 2001, *http://www.newyorker.com*; Bloomberg, May 7, 2001, 1501; Associated Press, May 13, 2001, 1043.

25. Reuters, May 26, 2001, 1127.

26. Associated Press, May 13, 2001, 1043.

27. "The GCC sides with UAE in territory dispute with Iran," *Agence France Press*, December 31, 2000.

28. Associated Press, February 12, 1998, 1231.

29. Reuters, February 16, 1998, 1749.

30. Reuters, February 21, 1998, 1631.

31. Reuters, February 22, 1998, 0348.

32. There have been an almost endless series of such attacks. For typical reports, see Reuters, April 8, 2001, 0416, April 25, 2001, 0531; and Associated Press, March 28, 2001, 1105, May 5, 2001, 1636.

33. Reuters, January 22, 2001, April 8, 2001, 0416; Associated Press, March 28, 2001, 1105; *The Estimate*, April 20, 2001, pp. 2, 79.

34. *Middle East Economic Survey*, January 22, 2001, p. C-1.

35. Reuters, June 4, 2001, 1234.

36. *New York Times*, January 17, 2001, p. A-1; *The Estimate*, February 23, 2001, p. 4.

37. IISS, *The Military Balance, 2001–2002*.

38. Estimate provided by USCENTCOM in June 1996, plus USCENTCOM, *Atlas, 1996* (MacDill Air Force Base: USCENTCOM, 1997), pp. 16–18. Also based on interviews in 2001 and 2002.

39. USCENTCOM briefing by "senior military official," Pentagon, January 28, 1997, pp. 2, 5–8, 10; *Washington Times*, February 1, 1997, p. A-13; Reuters, September 4, 1996, 0911; Jane's *Pointer* (November 1994), p. 2; Associated Press September 9, 1996, 0129; *Washington Times*, January 30, 1997, p. A-3; February 1, 1997, p. A-13; interviews with U.S. experts in March 2002.

40. Ibid.

41. USCENTCOM, *Atlas, 1996*, pp. 16–18, and interviews in the spring of 2001 and 2002.

42. Many different lists exist of the names of such bases. Jane's lists Al Amarah, Al Asad, Al Bakr, Al Basrah—West Maqal, Al Khalid, Al Kut, Al Qayyarah, Al Rashid, Al Taqaddum, Al Walid, Artawi, As Salman, As Samara, As Zubair, Baghdad-Muthenna, Balada, Bashur, Erbil, Jalibah, Karbala, Radif al Khafi, Kirkuk, Mosul, Mudaysis, Nejef, Qal'at Sikar, Qurna, Rumaylah, Safwan, Shibah, Shyaka Mayhar, Sulyamaniya, Tal Afar, Tallil-As Nasiryah, Tammuz, Tikrit, Ubdaydah bin al Jarrah, and Wadi Al Khirr. Many of the bases on this list are of limited size or are largely dispersal facilities. See *Jane's Sentinel: The Gulf States*, "Iraq" (London: Jane's Publishing, 1997), p. 22.

43. IISS, *The Military Balance, 2001–2002.*

44. CIA, *World Factbook 2002.*

45. U.S. Census Bureau, IDB Summary Demographic Data, *http://www.census.gov/ipc/www/idbprint.html*, accessed May 3, 2002.

46. World Bank, *World Population Projections, 1994–1995* (Washington: World Bank, 1995), pp. 512–513; World Bank, *World Development Indicators* (Washington: World Bank, 1999), p. 44; World Bank, *World Atlas, 1997* (Washington: World Bank, 1995), p. 17.

47. CIA *World Factbook 2002*, "Saudi Arabia" and "Yemen." Online edition at *www.cia.gov.*

48. IISS, *The Military Balance, 2001–2002*, "Yemen."

49. *Saudi Arabia*, vol. 13, no. 10 (October 1996), p. 1.

50. *Middle East Economic Digest*, June 30, 1995, p. 9; *Saudi Arabia* (May 1995), p. 7; *Washington Times*, June 7, 1995, p. A-17.

51. *The Estimate*, July 4, 1997, p. 12; Reuters, July 22, 1997, 0825; *Defense News*, April 21, 1997, p. 54; Ramin Seddiq, "Border Disputes on the Arabian Peninsula," *Policywatch*, no. 525, March 15, 2001; Richard N. Schofield, "Border Disputes in the Gulf: Past, Present, and Future," in Gary G. Sick and Lawrence G. Potter, eds., *The Persian Gulf at the Millennium* (New York: St. Martin's Press, 1997), pp. 127–166; and Anthony H. Cordesman, *The Gulf and the Search for Strategic Stability* (Boulder: Westview, 1984), pp. 148–185, 394–475, 568–635, 776–799.

52. Reuters, March 5, 1998, 1445.

53. Reuters, August 4, 1998.

54. *Economist*, July 25, 1998, p. 46.

55. "Saudi Arabia and Yemen Finalize Their Common Land and Marine Borders," *Newsletter of the Royal Embassy of Saudi Arabia* (July 2000); and "Saudi to finance projects worth 300 million in Yemen," *Agence France Press*, February 28, 2001.

56. "More Troops to Withdraw from Saudi Border," *Agence France Press*, February 22, 2001

57. Seddiq, "Border Disputes on the Arabian Peninsula."

58. "Desert Diplomacy: A Tale of Two Yemeni Sheikhs," *The Christian Science Monitor*, March 1, 2001

59. *Middle East Economic Survey*, March 5, 2001, p. B-6.

60. Reuters, May 5, 2001, 0657, May 29, 2001, 1314.

61. World Bank, *World Population Projections, 1994–1995*, pp. 512–513; World Bank, *Trends in Developing Countries* (Washington: World Bank, 1995), pp. 558–561.

62. John Duke Anthony, "Whither Saudi Arabian-Yemeni Relations?: Interest and Implications for U.S. Policies," Issue Briefs No. 3, U.S.-GCC Corporate Co-operation Committee, Inc., Washington, DC, 1999.

63. Reuters, March 9, 1999.

64. *Jane's Defence Weekly*, May 15, 1996, p. 3.

65. Reuters, July 10, 1995, 0552.

66. For maps of the disputed claims, and a controversial but detailed history of the dispute, see J. B. Kelly, *Arabia, The Gulf, and the West* (New York: Basic Books, 1980), pp. 56–57, 65–76. Also see Schofield, "Border Disputes in the Gulf: Past, Present, and Future," pp. 127–166; and Cordesman, *The Gulf and the Search for Strategic Stability*, pp. 148–185, 394–475, 568–635, and 776–799.

67. Kelly, *Arabia, The Gulf, and the West*, pp. 187–188; Helen Chapin Metz, *Persian Gulf States* (Washington: Department of the Army, DA Pam 550-185, January 1993), pp. 191–194; Seddiq, "Border Disputes on the Arabian Peninsula"; Schofield, "Border Disputes in the Gulf: Past, Present, and Future." pp. 127–166; and Cordesman, *The Gulf and the Search for Strategic Stability*, pp. 148–185, 394–475, 568–635, 776–799.

68. Ibid.

69. *Washington Post*, October 1, 1993, p. A-19, October 2, 1992, p. A-41; *Philadelphia Inquirer*, October 3, 1992, p. D-7; *Washington Times*, October 2, 1992, p. A-9.

70. Kelly, *Arabia, the Gulf, and the West*, pp. 56–57; Metz, *Persian Gulf States*, pp. 191–194; Seddiq, "Border Disputes on the Arabian Peninsula"; Schofield, "Border Disputes in the Gulf: Past, Present, and Future," pp. 127–166; and Cordesman, *The Gulf and the Search for Strategic Stability*, pp. 148–185, 394–475, 568–635, 776–799.

71. *Wall Street Journal*, March 21, 1996, p. A-1; *The Estimate*, January 19, 1996, March 1, 1996.

72. Ibid.

73. *Jane's Defence Weekly*, November 13, 1996, p. 22; Reuters, October 27, 1996, 0725.

74. *Middle East Economic Digest*, April 7, 1997, July 11, 1997, p. 13.

75. *The Estimate*, March 23, 2001.

76. *Jane's Defence Weekly*, July 29, 1995, p. 15.

77. *Middle East Economic Survey*, May 15, 2000, July 17, 2000, and February 5, 2001; Seddiq, "Border Disputes on the Arabian Peninsula."

78. Energy Information Agency (EIA), "Saudi Arabia," January 2000, URL: *www.eia.doe.gov/emeu/cabs/saudi.html*.

79. Based on interviews.

80. Bahgat Korany, Paul Noble, and Rex Brynen, eds., *The Many Faces of National Security in the Arab World* (New York: St. Martin's Press, 1993), p. 119.

81. CIA, *World Factbook 2002*.

82. Ibid.

83. Bahrain's unicameral National Assembly was dissolved on August 26, 1975, and legislative powers were assumed by the Cabinet. An appointed Advisory Council was established on December 16,1992.

84. Reuters, October 3, 2000, 1338.

85. *Saudi Arabia: A Country Study*, Area Handbook Series (Washington: American University, 1984), p. 238.

86. *Middle East Economic Survey*, March 5, 2001, p. A12.

87. *The Estimate*, January 3, 1997, March 23, 2001, pp. 5–8, April 6, 2001, pp. 5–8.

88. Seddiq, "Border Disputes on the Arabian Peninsula,"; Schofield, "Border Disputes in the Gulf: Past, Present, and Future," pp. 127–166; and Cordesman, *The Gulf and the Search for Strategic Stability*, pp. 148–185, 394–475, 568–635, 776–799.

89. *The Estimate*, March 23, 2001, p. 2.

90. EIA country analysis of the UAE, September 2000, URL: *www.eia.doe.gov/emeu/cabs/uae.html*.

91. Seddiq, "Border Disputes on the Arabian Peninsula,"; Schofield, "Border Disputes in the Gulf: Past, Present, and Future," pp. 127–166; and Cordesman, *The Gulf and the Search for Strategic Stability*, pp. 148–185, 394–475, 568–635, 776–799.

92. The islands have a number of different names and spellings. The Lesser Tunb is called Tunb as Sughra in Arabic by UAE and Jazireh-ye Tonb-e Kuchek in Persian by Iran; the Greater Tunb is called Tunb al Kubra in Arabic by UAE and Jazireh-ye Tonb-e Bozorg in Persian by Iran. Abu Musa is called Abu Musa in Arabic by UAE and Jazireh-ye Abu Musa in Persian by Iran.

93. This summary was provided as a comment on the draft text by Dr. Christian Koch, Head, Strategic Studies Section, Emirates Center for Strategic Studies and Research, Abu Dhabi, UAE in June, 2000, ckoch@emirates.net.ae.

94. EIA country analysis of the UAE, September 2000, URL: *www.eia.doe.gov/emeu/cabs/uae.html*.

95. Reuters, June 6–8, 1999.

96. Reuters, September, 11, 1999.

97. Mohammed Jaber, "GCC Financial Markets and the Quest for Development," *Middle East Policy*, vol. 7, no. 2 (February 2000), pp. 20015038; *Articles of the Cooperation Council for the Arab States of the Gulf*, 5th ed. (Riyadh: GCC,); Turki al-Hamad, "Imperfect Alliances: Will the Gulf Monarchies Work "Together?" *Middle East Review of International Affairs Journal*, vol. 1, no. 2 (July 1997); David Priess, "The Gulf Cooperation Council, Prospects for Expansion," *Middle East Policy*, vol. 5, no. 4 (January 1998); "The Manama Declaration," *Ain al-Yaqeen* Article 4, January 12, 2001; Anthony H. Cordesman, *The Gulf and the West*, (Boulder: Westview, 1988), pp. 15–48; Cordesman, *The Gulf and the Search for Strategic Stability*, pp. 51–81, 568–635; and Gary G. Sick and Lawrence G. Potter, *The Persian Gulf at the Millennium* (New York, St. Martin's Press, 1997), pp. 31–61, 319–341.

98. These measures are all contained in the Supreme Council's declaration after its meeting in December 2000. See *Ain al-Yaqeen*, January 12, 2001; *Gulf News*, January 29, 2001; *Arabic News*, January 8, 2001, March 10, 2001; Reuters, April 23, 2001, 1616.

99. Jan H. Kalicki, "The U.S. and the Gulf: Commerce Challenges and Opportunities," *Middle East Policy*, vol. 7, no. 1 (October 1999), pp. 72–73. For an excellent practical analysis of the issues involved, see Ibrahim M. Oweiss, *The Arab*

Gulf Economies, Emirates Lecture series 26 (Abu Dhabi: Emirates Center for Strategic Studies and Research, 2000).

100. *Saudi Arabia*, vol. 18, no. 1 (January 2001), pp. 1–3.

101. Ibid.

102. Interviews in Saudi Arabia in 2000 and 2001; *Ain al-Yaqeen*, January 12, 2001; *Jane's Defence Weekly*, January 10, 2001, p. 18; Reuters, May 7, 2001, 1209; *The Estimate*, April 20, 2001. p. 2; *Saudi Arabia*, vol. 18, no. 1 (January 2001), pp. 1–3; *Defence News*, November 27, 2000, p. 3; *Arabia*, December 12, 2000; *Times of India*, February 27, 2001.

103. Reuters, April 8, 2001, 0416; *The Estimate*, April 20, 2001, p. 2.

104. *Defence News*, March 26, 2001, p. 8; Reuters, February 27, 2001, May 7, 2001, 1209; research paper by Michael D. Morgan, "Changes within the Gulf Cooperation Council Over the Last Three Years," Georgetown University, NSSP, May 8, 2001.

105. Reuters, October 1, 1996, 0056.

106. *Middle East Economic Digest*, April 7, 1997, July 11, 1997, p. 13.

107. Reuters, April 9, 1998, 0447.

108. Reuters, March 1, 1999.

109. *Saudi Arabia*, vol. 17, no. 12 (December 2000), p. 1, vol. 18, no.1 (January 2001), p. 3.

110. Reuters, June 6, 2001, 12:53.

111. Abdul Quader Chowdhury, "Saudi Middle East Peace Vision," *The Independent*, March 5, 2002.

112. Saudi Arabian Ministry of Information, "King Fahd orders the opening of al-Quods fund" October 9, 2000, URL: *www.saudinfo.com*.

113. "Arab Leaders to Meet in Saudi Arabia Before Summit," Reuters, October 12, 2000.

114. Royal Embassy of Saudi Arabia, "Kingdom's Aid to Palestinians Nears 10 Billion Riyals," May 2, 2002.URL: *http://www.saudiembassy.net/press_release/02-spa/05-02-aid.htm*. Accessed on May 26, 2002.

115. Ibid.

116. Ibid.

117. Royal Embassy of Saudi Arabia, "Red Crescent Confirms Kingdom's Humanitarian Aid to Palestine," April 10, 2002. URL: *http://www.saudiembassy.net/press_release/02-spa/04-11-mideast.htm*. Accessed on May 26, 2002.

118. Royal Embassy of Saudi Arabia Information Office, "Press Release: The Kingdom of Saudi Arabia Responds to False Israeli Charges," May 6, 2002. URL: *http://www.saudiembassy.net/press_release/releases/02-PR-0506-bandar-mideast.htm*. Accessed on May 26, 2002.

119. Saudi Arabian Ministry of Information, "Prince Saud highlights Saudi initiatives on Palestine" October 23, 2000.

120. Jack Kemp, "Saudi Arabian Peace Plan a Snow Job," *The Seattle Post-Intelligencer*, March 6, 2002, p. B5.

121. Daniel Rubin and Warren P. Strobel, "Saudi Plan Interesting, Sharon tells UN Chief," *The Philadelphia Inquirer*, February 27, 2002.

122. Thomas Friedman, "An Intriguing Signal from the Saudi Crown Prince," *The New York Times*, February 17, 2002, Section 4, page 11.

123. Warren P. Strobel and Daniel Rubin, "Saudis to Seek Arab Support for Their Mideast Plan," *The Miami Herald*, February 28, 2002, Part A, p. 1.

124. Earleen Fisher, "Syria Endorses Saudi Peace Proposal, But Faces Obstacles," *AP Worldstream*, March 6, 2002.

125. Friedman, "An Intriguing Signal from the Saudi Crown Prince."

126. Chowdhury, "Saudi Middle East Peace Vision."

127. Ibid.

128. Scott Macleod, "Anatomy of a Peace Plan," *TIME Europe*, March 26, 2002.

129. Phil Reeves, "Bush Backs Saudi Plan for Peace in the Middle East," *The Independent*, February 27, 202, p. 16.

130. Chowdhury, "Saudi Middle East Peace Vision."

131. Andrew Guthrie, "Saudi Peace Proposal," *World Opinion Roundup*, February 28, 2002, URL: *http://www.globalsecurity.org/military/library/news/2002/02/mil-020228-252e5879.htm*, Accessed on August 21, 2002.

132. "Saudi Peace Proposal Is Public Relations Move to Raise Country's Image in American Eyes," Ascribe Newswire, March 4, 2002.

133. Macleod, "Anatomy of a Peace Plan."

134. Tracey Wilkinson and Michael Slackman, "Unlikely Olive Branch Takes Root; Mideast: Saudi Peace Proposal, Though Vague, Sets the Stage for the Kingdom's Involvement in Possible Talks," *Los Angeles Times*, February 28, 2002, Part A, p. 1.

135. Steve Weizman, "Israeli Prime Minister Said Ready to Meet Saudis on New Mideast Peace Proposal," *Associated Press*, International News Section, February 26, 2002.

136. Daniel Rubin and Warren P. Strobel, "Saudi Plan Interesting, Sharon tells UN Chief," *The Philadelphia Inquirer*, February 27, 2002.

137. Steve Weizman, "Israeli Prime Minister Said Ready to Meet Saudis on New Mideast Peace Proposal," *Associated Press*, International News Section, February 26, 2002.

138. Ibid.

139. Rubin and Strobel, "Saudi Plan Interesting, Sharon tells UN Chief."

140. Associated Press, "Syrian President Backs Saudi Peace Proposal," *The Desert News*, March 6, 2002, p. 4.

141. Fisher, "Syria Endorses Saudi Peace Proposal, But Faces Obstacles."

142. Cameron W. Barr, "Arab Peace Plan Faces First Round," *The Christian Science Monitor*, March 26, 2002, p. 1.

143. Khalid al-Deeb, "Gadhafi calls for Libyan Withdrawal from Arab League, Criticizes Saudi Peace Proposal," *AP Worldstream*, March 2, 2002.

144. Al-Deeb, "Gadhafi calls for Libyan Withdrawal from Arab League, Criticizes Saudi Peace Proposal."

145. Hamza Hendawi, "Saudi Arabia Offers 'Complete Peace' to Israel," *AP Worldstream*, March 10, 2002.

146. Michael Slackman, "Pre-Summit Arab Unity Takes a Hit," *Los Angeles Times*, March 27, 2002, Part A; Part 1; p. 1.

147. Slackman, "Pre-Summit Arab Unity Takes a Hit."

148. Sam F. Ghattas, "Arab Summit Expected to Endorse Saudi Peace Plan," *AP Worldstream*, March 27, 2002.

149. Crown Prince Abdullah, "Speech by Crown Prince Abdullah of Saudi Arabia in the Arab Summit in Beirut," Jerusalem Communication and Media Centre, URL: *http://www.jmcc.org/new/02/mar/saudi.htm*, Accessed on August 27, 2002.

150. Crown Prince Abdullah, "Speech by Crown Prince Abdullah of Saudi Arabia in the Arab Summit in Beirut."

151. Prince Saud al-Faisal, in Yonah Alexander and Edgar H. Brenner, "The Saudi 'Peace' Plan," The *Washington Times*, April 14, 2002.

152. Ghattas, "Arab Summit Expected to Endorse Saudi Peace Plan."

153. CIA, *World Factbook 2002.*, URL: *http://www.cia.gov/cia/publications/factbook/-index.html*, Accessed on August 25, 2002.

154. Susan Sevareid, "Arab Leaders Endorse Peace Proposal," *AP Online*, March 28, 2002.

155. Alexander and Brenner, "The Saudi 'Peace' Plan."

156. *The Arab Peace Initiative*, March 28, 2002, URL: *http://64.77.65.168/arableague/E2801-news1.html*, Accessed on August 27, 2002.

157. Mark Lavie, "Polls Show Israeli, Palestinian Opposition to Saudi Peace Plan," *AP Worldstream*, June 7, 2002.

158. Aaron Lerner, "Polls: Israelis, Palestinians Reject Saudi Plan," *The Jerusalem Post*, June 7, 2002, p. 1A.

159. Lavie, "Polls Show Israeli, Palestinian Opposition to Saudi Peace Plan."

160. Mark Lavie, "Polls Show Israeli, Palestinian Opposition to Saudi Peace Plan," *AP Worldstream*, June 7, 2002.

161. Based on interviews during 1991–1995. For a different description of Egypt's performance during the Gulf War, see Anthony H. Cordesman, *The Gulf War, Lessons of Modern War, Volume IV* (Boulder: Westview, 1996).

162. *Baltimore Sun*, June 15, 1996, p. A-1.

163. *Jane's Defence Weekly*, September 1996, p. 23.

164. *Saudi Arabia: A Country Study*, p. 234.

165. Ibid.

166. *Boston Globe*, August 11, 1996, p. A-23; *Middle East Economic Digest*, August 23, 1996, p. 17.

167. *Saudi Arabia*, vol.16, no.3 (March 1999), p. 1.

168. "Crown Prince Abdullah visits Libya, Syria, Jordan and Egypt," *Monthly Newsletter of the Royal Embassy of Saudi Arabia* (July 1999), p. 1.

169. "Saudi Prince, Ghadafi Plan Joint Projects," *Agence France Presse*, Arabia. On.Line, URL: *http://www.arabia.com*. October 2, 1999.

170. This history is summarized from the author's far more detailed history in *The Gulf and the Search for Strategic Stability*, pp. 85–121, and *The Gulf and the West*, pp. 117–149, 193–211, 269–309, 335–351, 368–441.

171. Saudi Arabian Monetary Agency (SAMA), *Thirty-Sixth Annual Report* (Riyadh: SAMA, 2000), pp. 343–344.

172. Cordesman, *The Gulf and the Search for Strategic Stability*, pp. 157–164.

173. Iraq now denies this. The author reviewed Iraqi government literature in the Iraqi Ministry of Information in 1982 that was never publicly distributed but that explained and justified an annexation that Iraq was never able to execute.

174. SAMA, *Thirty-Sixth Annual Report*, pp. 343–344.

175. Ibid.

176. For more details, see Cordesman, *The Gulf and the West*, pp. 269–387.

177. Ibid., pp. 309–441.

178. "Saudi Prince Accepts Bush Invitation After Snub," Reuters, March 17, 2001.

179. Donna Abu-Nasr, "Shaken by September 11, Saudi-US Relations Appear to Be on the Mend, but Differences Remain over Iraq," The Associated Press, March 16, 2002.

Chapter 3

Politics and Internal Stability

No country is free of political problems and uncertainties. Saudi Arabia faces domestic challenges in terms of the political and religious legitimacy of its royal family and ruling elite, Islamic extremists, problems with its Shi'ites, potential problems with foreign labor, population growth, and the need for social and economic reform. Its political system must adapt to the socioeconomic impact of radical modernization, rapid population growth, and the need to radically restructure its economy. It faces domestic problems because of its de facto alliance with the United States and the resulting hostility from its religious radicals and conservatives, and it cannot ignore the fact that Iran, Iraq, and other states may support internal opposition movements.

At the same time, outside observers have exaggerated Saudi Arabia's political instability for half a century, more often because its closed society is hard for outsiders to understand than because of any clear evidence regarding the actual fragility of the regime. Speculation about tensions within the royal family has become an international, as well as a national, sport among journalists and area experts. The same is true of speculation about the political impact of social and economic change and the potential threat posed by Saudi Arabia's Islamic and reform movements.

It is important to preface any political analysis with the caution that it is far easier to speculate about the Kingdom's domestic stability than it is to find facts on which to base that speculation, and far easier to talk about what might go wrong than to predict the actual path of change. In practice, economic problems, demographic pressures, and the threat from Islamic extremism at the margins of Saudi society, also seem to pose a more serious threat to internal stability than contemporary "politics" and internal opposition movements.

THE MONARCHY, THE MAJLIS AL-SHURA, AND THE ROYAL FAMILY

The al-Saud family currently seems to be in secure control of the country, and to be able to rely more on co-opting opposition rather than repressing it. The monarchy remains the key source of power at every level in the Saudi Arabian government, and the king and senior princes have great authority and considerable freedom of action. However, the Saudi system of government is anything but an absolute monarchy by Western standards.

There is no formal constitution and there are no political parties or elections, but in practice the king's power is limited and consensual. The Saudi political tradition is one of consensus, not authoritarianism, and of pragmatism rather than ideology. As a result, the Saudi government has considerably more popular "legitimacy" than many of its outside critics seem to realize. The king's power is limited by other power centers within the royal family, by religion, by custom, and by the need for a high degree of consensus within Saudi Arabia's key tribes, technocrats, business leaders, and religious figures (Ulema). The al-Saud family may not meet the Western tests of legitimacy in the sense it is elected, but it has long sought to achieve and preserve a broad social and political consensus.

Much of the criticism of the royal family focuses on those princes that are corrupt, venal, and incompetent. Such clear cases exist and do raise political problems inside Saudi Arabia. Members of the royal family sometimes privately criticize such princes themselves, and divisions over such issues are often a major aspect of the family's internal politics. At the same time, such criticism ignores the fact that many other princes are highly educated, focus on careers within government rather than simply acquiring wealth and privileges, and form alliances with technocrats, businessmen, and other influential Saudis.

Almost all major policy decisions require the input of both princes and senior technocrats. Senior technocrats and leading business families have a considerable amount of influence, both as principal advisors to the king and as operational decision makers. As a result, the Saudi monarchy consists more of patriarchal rule by a consensus-driven extended family with large numbers of alliances to other families than rule by an autocrat who acts on his personal desires.

This consensus is not simply a matter of pragmatic politics. Tradition and religion are powerful political forces in Saudi Arabia and within the royal family. The king must observe Islamic law (Shari'a) and other Saudi traditions. In Saudi Arabia, enforcement of the Shari'a is based on Sunni sources and largely on the Hanbali School of Law. Although this school is relatively liberal in terms of commercial practices, it is more conservative and binding in the areas of family law and social systems. The Saudi clergy play a powerful role in ensuring that the Shari'a is fully enforced and limits the pace at which the king and royal family can modernize and still maintain a Saudi social consensus.[1] The royal family has also had to pay close attention to the views of the descendants of Muhammad al-Wahhab, the al-Shaykh family. While the al-Shaykhs have rarely played any open political role, they exert a powerful influence on the actions of the Saudi government.

Saudi monarchs have long recognized that they must maintain the support of senior members of the Saudi royal family, as well as the support of the Ulema, leading technocrats, key businessmen, regional and tribal leaders, and other important elements in Saudi society. As in other Southern Gulf countries, the king and royal family must also be accessible to the people. Saudi Arabia has a long tradition of public access to high officials (usually at a *majlis*, or public audience) and the right to petition such officials directly.

Saudi Arabia also has a long history of consultative decision making, with an emphasis on reaching consensus. King Abd al-Aziz ibn Saud founded a Shura Council of the Hijaz as early as 1927.[2] This council was later expanded to twenty members, and was chaired by the king's son, Prince Faisal bin Abdulaziz al-Saud. The council was expanded to twenty-five members in the early 1950s, under the troubled reign of King Saud ibn Abdulaziz al-Saud, but its functions were then transferred to the Cabinet as King Saud came under political pressure from the other members of the royal family.[3] The Majlis al-Shura was not formally dissolved, however; it merely ceased to operate until King Fahd revived it.[4]

In 1953, the king appointed a Council of Ministers. Since that time, the council has advised on the formulation of general policy and helped to direct the activities of the growing bureaucracy. This council consists of a prime minister, the first and second deputy prime ministers, twenty ministers (of whom the minister of defense is also the second deputy prime minister), two ministers of state, and a small number of advisers and heads of major autonomous organizations. King Fahd also appointed a Board of Grievances (Diwan al-Mazalim) in 1995, although some sources indicate that the Board of Grievances was established under the Office of the Chief Judge during Faisal's reign. This body has judicial powers and investigates and resolves complaints between Saudi citizens and the government.[5]

King Fahd issued decrees in 1997 that expanded the consultative role of the council. Under the new decrees the council will approve loan contracts as well as the national budget, international treaties, and concessions. Ministers on the council cannot hold any other public or private positions and are forbidden to buy, sell, or loan government property. The ministers are also limited to terms of no more than five years unless extended by the king.

Saudi laws are promulgated by a resolution of the Council of Ministers, and are proposed by the king, senior ruling princes, and key ministers. They must be ratified by royal decree and be compatible with the Shari'a, and are increasingly subject to informal debate or review within the Majlis. The Saudi legal system is administered according to the Shari'a by a system of religious courts. The judges in these courts are appointed by the king on the recommendation of the Supreme Judicial Council, which is composed of twelve senior jurists. The Council of Senior Religious Scholars, an autonomous body of fifteen senior religious jurists, including the minister of justice, establishes legal principles for lower courts.[6] Law protects the independence of the judiciary, although the king acts as the highest court of appeal and has the power to pardon and commute death sentences.[7] Saudi Arabia is divided into thirteen provinces, which are governed by princes or close relatives of the royal family; the king appoints these governors.

There has also long been an informal decision making body whose main function is to legitimize royal succession in the form of the *ahl al-aqd wal hal* ("those who tie and unite"). This body lacks any official organizational structure, but consists of about 100 members, most of whom come from the al-Saud family and its allies in the Jilwi, Sudayri, Thunayan, and al-Shaykh families. The remaining elements include influential members of the Ulema, a few influential princes not related by blood to the royal family, and selected influential commoners. These members are selected by "origin, seniority, prestige and leadership qualities" in accordance with previous tribal traditions.[8]

Evolution and Stability

The stability of the Saudi royal family is critical to the security of the Saudi government, which has led to constant speculation over divisions within the royal family and possible conflicts over the succession. This speculation is not simply Western. Rumor-mongering regarding the royal family is a Saudi national sport—although a discreet one—and few educated Saudis seem to feel they lack inside information on the detailed political maneuverings of the major princes. The fact that there appears to be nearly as many different "authoritative" rumors about the politics of the royal family as there are Saudis does little to discourage further speculation. Saudis from the Hijaz region take a particular delight in reporting possible divisions between princes and conflicts over the succession.

Given this background, it is not surprising that the long series of reports of imminent conflict within the al-Saud family that have emerged out of Saudi "royal watching" have rarely proved reliable. There have certainly been many quiet power struggles within the royal family; however, few divisions within the royal family have threatened the government's cohesion.

The one major division between the senior members of the royal family that did lead to open struggle over succession occurred in 1958–1962. Abd al-Aziz was succeeded by his eldest son, Saud, who reigned for eleven years. King Saud proved unable to manage the nation's finances, however, and created serious problems in the Kingdom's foreign affairs. In 1958, this led to a meeting of a powerful and secretive body of senior princes known as the *ahl-aqd wal hal*, which forced King Saud to delegate direct conduct of government affairs to Prince Faisal and make him prime minister.[9] King Saud resisted this arrangement and regained control of the government in 1960–1962, which led to a struggle between members of the family who supported Faisal and those who supported Saud.

King Saud lost this struggle decisively in October 1962. Faisal regained power as prime minister, began to implement a broad reform program that stressed economic development, and was proclaimed king by senior royal family members and religious leaders in 1964. He continued to serve as prime minister, however, and subsequent kings have followed this practice. Faisal also proved to be an extremely competent ruler and dealt effectively with the problems arising from the Six-Day (Arab-Israeli) War of June 1967, the 1973 Arab-Israeli conflict (October War), the subsequent Arab oil boycott, the sudden massive increase in Saudi oil wealth that came out of the oil boycott, and the resulting rise in Saudi political influence. Since that time, the struggle between Saud and Faisal has become more a historical anecdote than any indication of continuing power struggles within the royal family.

After a mentally ill nephew assassinated King Faisal in 1975, the royal family dealt with the succession smoothly, quickly appointing Faisal's half-brother Khalid as king and prime minister. The appointment of the next crown prince was not quite as smooth, but was still resolved without open tension. Prince Fahd, Khalid's half-brother, was in line for appointment as crown prince, but his "Western" lifestyle as a young adult prompted criticism from the traditionalists in the family.

The result was a series of deliberations within the royal family that produced a compromise between the Western-oriented family members, who favored Prince Fahd, and the traditionalists. Fahd was appointed as crown prince and first deputy prime minister, with the expectation that he would conform to a less "Western" lifestyle once in power and with the understanding that the next in line for this position would be another half-brother, the traditionalist Prince Abdullah.[10]

During his reign, King Khalid empowered Prince Fahd to oversee many aspects of the government's international and domestic affairs. This period saw the continuation of rapid economic development within Saudi Arabia, and the Kingdom assumed a more influential role in both regional political and international economic and financial matters. According to some experts, Prince Fahd's growing prominence allowed his six full brothers to begin consolidating their power within the government.[11] According to others, Prince Fahd's growing prominence was not the impetus for his brothers to consolidate their power; six of the seven brothers had already become established as a power bloc at the time of Faisal's reign, and when one dropped out (Turki in 1981), the seventh replaced him.

The next succession took place with equal smoothness. King Khalid died in June 1982. Fahd became king and prime Minister. Prince Abdullah, the commander of the National Guard, was subsequently named crown prince and first deputy prime minister. One of King Fahd's full brothers, Prince Sultan, the minister of defense and aviation, became second deputy prime minister. As a result, Fahd's reign allowed for a further consolidation of power among the al-Fahd. This posed a potential problem for the next succession, but there is little evidence that any serious political struggle took place.[12]

In 1992, King Fahd addressed the issue of succession by decreeing, "Rule passes to the sons of the founding king . . . and to their children's children. The most upright among them is to receive allegiance in accordance with [the principles] of the Holy Qu'ran and the tradition of the Venerable Prophet."[13] Fahd's decree attempted to alleviate concerns over the creation of a perpetual gerontocracy in Saudi Arabia by opening the succession to the grandsons of Abd al-Aziz. However, Saudi officials qualified the statement by indicating that succession would still be according to seniority for the foreseeable future.[14]

Current Prospects for the Succession

These developments scarcely mean that the princes are not rivals, or that they do not participate in competing coalitions. Political rivalry is a constant fact of life at every level in all political systems, and the leading princes are both competitive and jealous of their power. Competition over the succession and senior appointments has been a factor in Saudi royal politics since long before King Abd al-Aziz first met President Franklin Roosevelt. Nevertheless, the al-Saud family has dealt with far more serious problems than exist today.

The ruling elite within the royal family is now broadly divided between the "Sudairi" and other sons of King Abd al-Aziz's (Ibn Saud's) twenty-two wives. There are a total of seven sons by Abd al-Aziz's Sudairi wife, Hassa bin Sudairi; these men have often been called the "al-Fahd"—after the family's eldest brother, Fahd—or the "Sudairi Seven."[15] The key Sudairi leaders now include King Fahd; Prince Sultan, the minister of defense; Prince Nayef, the minister of interior; and Prince Salman, the governor of Riyadh; although some add Abd al-Rahman, the deputy minister of defense. Most analysts see

Prince Sultan and Prince Salman as likely to be the last real candidates for the succession after Abdullah in this generation of Saudi leaders.

Their power is balanced by that of the sons of the other wives of Abd al-Aziz, who have their own alliances. The most important son is Crown Prince and Deputy Prime Minister Abdullah, who now acts as de facto regent and who has commanded the Saudi National Guard since November 1962. Abdullah has six sons, including Prince Mitab, who is being groomed as a potential new commander of the National Guard. Abdullah is also the son of a Bedouin mother, a fact that gives him ties to a number of leading tribes. In Saudi Arabia, however, younger sons do not inherit from their father. Abdullah has no brothers, which means he lacks the kind of broad power base shared by the Sudairis; however, this also means that his rule will not lead to a new "dynasty" within the royal family.

Other influential members within the royal family include Prince Badr bin Abdulaziz, the deputy commander of the National Guard; Prince Turki, the former head of the General Intelligence Directorate; Prince Saud al-Faisal, the foreign minister and son of King Faisal; and a number of other senior princes.

The relations between these senior princes, their competition and alliances, and any frictions between them, make up the most important aspect of royal family politics. These relations, however, often lead to struggles over the allocation of oil reserves, the Saudi budget and actual spending, and ways to use government revenues and jobs for patronage.

The formal succession issue of Crown Prince Abdullah has remained an issue for more than half a decade due to the ill health of King Fahd, who is over seventy-five years old. On November 30, 1995, Fahd was rushed to a hospital emergency room suffering from what most experts believe was a stroke. One month later, he temporarily turned control of the government over to Crown Prince Abdullah, who then attended the summit of GCC leaders in Oman in place of the king. Prince Abdullah ruled in Fahd's absence until he formally reassumed his position as head of the government on February 21, 1996. Since that time, Prince Abdullah has continued to play a key role in ruling the Kingdom, as King Fahd has sometimes been incapable of exercising power and has often been weakened or incapacitated by his physical condition.

It now seems likely that Prince Abdullah will continue to act as a quasi-regent until King Fahd is willing to formally relinquish power or dies. There have been reports that Fahd would formally give up ruling because of his health and retire to a foreign country where he could obtain continuing medical treatment. In July 1999, the king went abroad to Marbella, Spain, for a ten-week vacation. It was his first trip abroad since his stroke and fueled intense speculation that the king had informally turned over rule to the crown prince. However, King Fahd returned to Saudi Arabia on September 29, 1999, and soon after chaired a Cabinet meeting. For a few years, this put an end to rumors that the king was no longer able to assume even titular official duties, but similar rumors surfaced again in 2002 when the king again appeared to have serious medical problems.[16]

There are still occasional rumors of challenges to Abdullah's succession. The most popular of these rumors is the possibility that Prince Sultan, a Sudairi and the minister of defense, might try to seek the throne.[17] Other reports indicate this scenario may have become less probable due to the recent deterioration of Sultan's health, although such rumors never seem to have had much credibility.[18] Other scenarios have speculated that Prince Saud al-Faisal might be promoted to crown prince in place of an aging Abdullah. According to one rumor, this might be accomplished through an alliance with Prince Salman, the governor of Riyadh and one of King Fahd's younger brothers. A variation indicated that King Fahd might make Prince Salman the crown prince, with the succession bypassing both Prince Abdullah and Prince Sultan. A third scenario indicated that Sultan would become the next king, followed by Prince Muhammad bin Fahd bin Abdulaziz, the son of King Fahd and governor of the Eastern Province.[19]

At this point, it is Abdullah's health, rather than any rivalry, that seems to be the only real issue. Prince Abdullah is seventy-five, although his health seems relatively good, and it is impossible to totally dismiss such speculation. Prince Abdullah has steadily consolidated his authority and is a popular ruler. Although Prince Sultan remains one of the most influential centers of power in the Kingdom, Prince Abdullah is a formidable figure and his succession to the throne now seems all but assured. He has signed joint communiqués with King Fahd since the king's return to power, including the Eid al-Fitr statement in February 1997. He has also been able to command the support of the other senior princes, and has a strong power base of his own. He continues to command the National Guard and maintains support from the large Bedouin tribes of the Najd, from which the Guard is drawn. Abdullah also has a Shammari link, as his mother was from the Bani Shammar, a powerful tribe that drove the al-Saud family into exile in the nineteenth century, but which King Abd al-Aziz then defeated before bringing into the royal family through marriage.

If Abdullah does formally become king, it will be something of an anticlimax. He has already shown through over more than a half decade of de facto rule that he will bring an interesting combination of tradition, continuity, and reform to the throne. Abdullah is a strong Arab nationalist who has criticized the West's close association with Israel in the past—criticism that has gained him support among traditionalist and conservative Saudis.

Abdullah maintains close ties to many Arab leaders, but at the same time he has already shown that there are good reasons to challenge reports that he is in any way less friendly to the United States. Abdullah faces serious political problems because of the growing backlash from the "Second Intifada" and U.S. ties to Israel, and because of the opposition of some

Islamists to a U.S. presence in the Kingdom. Some other senior princes have already criticized him for being too aggressive in making a new Arab-Israeli peace proposal in 2002, and then for meeting with President George W. Bush without getting a U.S. commitment to put more pressure on Israel. Abdullah has shown, however, that he fully recognizes both Saudi Arabia's vulnerability and its need for ties to the United States. He has long relied on the United States to train and equip the National Guard, and is credited with playing a major role in Saudi Arabia's decision to allow the United States to base forces in Saudi Arabia after the Iraqi invasion of Kuwait, as well as allowing the United States to use several Saudi facilities during the Afghan conflict. Many Saudis and outside experts feel that Abdullah is better able to balance the conflicting needs of Saudi military ties to the West, military development, the economy, the problems created by the Second Intifada, and the need to deal with radical Islamists than either King Fahd or Prince Sultan.

Prince Abdullah has already given the Kingdom added stability. He is widely viewed as a more traditional leader than King Fahd, and one who gives more weight to religion and Arab causes than some other leading princes. More important, he is seen as having a high degree of integrity and as actively attempting to curb the excesses and extravagances of some members of the royal family.[20] He has banned influential relatives from taking lucrative government contracts without competitive bidding, and tried—albeit with limited success—to tighten control over national spending and keep such spending within the limits imposed by the budget.[21] He opposes the kind of massive showpiece purchases and projects that waste government funds and the kind of fees and corruption that affect many government purchases and contracts. U.S. military experts, including those in USCENTCOM, hope that he will be even more cautious about Saudi Arabia's military purchases, limit its tendency to overspend on flashy showpiece projects, and emphasize training, sustainability, and military effectiveness over arms purchases once he becomes king.

The prince has shown that his ties to traditional elites and "conservatism" do not prevent him from understanding Saudi Arabia's needs for economic reform and the need to provide jobs for the Kingdom's rapidly growing population. He has good relations with many of the younger and more progressive princes and technocrats. He has spoken out openly and consistently about the country's economic difficulties, stating that "the days of the [Saudi] oil boom are over."[22] Prince Abdullah's "conservatism" has not hindered his vision of modernization in the Kingdom; he is a firm believer in economic reforms that will enable the Kingdom to be competitive in the twenty-first century. The Arab-Israeli conflict is a constant "wild card" in U.S.-Saudi affairs, as are relations with Iraq and Iran. Barring some new crisis, however, Abdullah's succession seems more likely to change the personal style of the monarchy while moving Saudi Arabia forward in the direction where it needs to go. It will be outside forces, not Crown Prince Abdullah, that lead to major changes in Saudi Arabia's relations with the West and the United States.[23]

In short, Abdullah's tenure as defacto ruler has shown there is little evidence that current rivalries will lead to any conflict between the top members of the royal family. Barring health problems, it seems equally likely that Prince Sultan will be content to take over the title of Crown Prince, once Abdullah becomes king.[24]

There are no certainties, however, because Prince Abdullah was born in 1921 and even the youngest of Abd al-Aziz's sons is now a relatively old man. Nevertheless, evidence suggests that the succession is likely to continue to be determined peacefully and quietly by internal consultation among the *ahl-aqd wal hal* or other senior members of the royal family at least until Prince Abdullah and Prince Sultan are deceased. If Prince Sultan does become king, he may well not be the last prince in this generational line of succession. There are still a number of other surviving sons of Ibn Saud, and it seems likely that Prince Salman may be appointed crown prince if Sultan becomes king.

There are some in the Kingdom, however, who raise questions about whether Sultan has shown the capability to lead the Kingdom toward reform while preserving its character and political cohesion. One of Crown Prince Abdullah's great strengths is that he has been able to maintain close ties to Saudi Arabia's tribes, build a reputation for honesty, and forge alliances with Saudi Arabia's technocrats and reformers. His ties to the al-Faisal branch of the royal family have helped in this regard. Prince Sultan does not command the same degree of respect. He does have ties to Saudi traditionalists, but there is little respect for his leadership of the Ministry of Defense and Aviation since the early 1990s, he has a reputation for careless spending and for ignoring financial and budget issues, and does not have Crown Prince Abdullah's reputation for integrity. Some senior Saudis question whether he will be able to show the leadership the Kingdom needs and make a suitable alliance with the princes and technocrats who are seeking to reform Saudi Arabia's economy.

There is also the possibility that Prince Sultan's weaknesses might interact with those of another prince who is not considered part of the succession. The minister of the interior, Prince Nayef bin Abdulaziz al-Saud, has not shown that he can adapt to the changes in the internal threats to the Kingdom and the need to shape and operate a modern intelligence system. The problems in the Saudi intelligence and internal security system are described in detail in the companion volume in this series, and they include the need to adapt Saudi internal security efforts to the growth of public opinion as a major force and to deal effectively with the threat of Islamic extremism. It is not clear that Prince Nayef has the flexibility to make these changes. The problem of age and leadership capability goes far beyond the problem of succession, and the Ministry of the Interior is a particularly critical case.

Prince Salman is highly respected, and at least some senior Saudis feel he has the strengths that Prince Sultan lacks. It should be noted, however, that interviews scarcely produce any transparency into the affairs of the senior members of the royal family, and there is a tendency among Saudi royal watchers to exaggerate their differences. It is more likely that Crown Prince Abdullah, Prince Sultan, and Prince Salman share a broad agreement over the need for economic reform and social evolution than differ in any radical way over the future path the Kingdom should take. Certainly, aside from rumors and journalistic reports that the Sudairi are in alliance with Islamic extremists and that Abdullah and the sons of Faisal are pro-Western reformers are just as silly and unfounded as earlier reports that Crown Prince Abdullah was anti-Western.

Moreover, there are some indications that the royal family may take a more structured approach in an attempt to ease any future intrafamily disputes and debates over the succession question. In June 2000, King Fahd set up a family council chaired by the crown prince and eighteen other princes, marking a break from the traditionally informal nature of intraroyal affairs. The council deals with issues pertaining to the royal family, and having excluded Prince Nayef and Foreign Minister Prince Sa'ud al-Faisal is unlikely to influence the day-to-day running of the Kingdom.

The Need for Change in the Next Generation

In any case, the need for continuing change and reform is the real challenge to the Saudi royal family and the regime. The al-Saud family already faces serious internal challenges, and at some point not to far in the future, a basic generational change must occur within it. The king and senior ministers must then be selected from the large number of junior princes that will compete for power once the sons of Ibn Saud are gone.

There is no consensus over how many such "princes" there now are or how many have the status to compete for power. It is almost certain, however, that there are over 5,000 males who can claim some kind of title as a "prince" in the Saudi royal family, and well over 80 younger princes who have significant status as ranking members of the "next generation" and thus have some claim to power. Some estimate the total number of "princes" goes over 10,000; the figure could easily reach 20,000 by 2020, although only a fraction are descendants. There are obvious limits as to what the Kingdom can or should pay members of the al-Saud family as these numbers increase, particularly because so many adult princes have shown they can make no claim to public funds except by accident of birth.

The more influential younger princes are reported to already be forming informal alliances that they can use once a "new generation" of leaders has to be selected, although their status and ties to today's senior princes remains the more immediate issue. More will be involved in the resulting jockeying for power or influence than a place in the government. Approximately 2,000 princes already play an active role in the economy. Many play a substantive role in government or business, but some demand special privileges and/or use their influence corruptly and violate Saudi law.[25]

This mix of royal political and economic power has caused a substantial amount of jealousy and political friction within Saudi society. Saudi Arabia's economy and political stability has suffered from a failure to demarcate clearly the powers and rights of members of the royal family. The corrupt minority of princes has also sometimes seriously abused its political power to dominate major military and civil deals and developments, and at least some of the worst abuses attributed to senior princes have actually been committed by their younger sons.

There have been royal abuses of government funds, property rights, and contracts. Royal influence has also abused civil and criminal justice procedures, both against Saudis and foreign businessmen. Various princes have used their influence to obtain shares of private businesses and the profits from oil sales and state-financed corporations. They have interfered or profiteered in contract awards, the allocation of money from oil sales, offset programs, and contracts for the delivery of arms imports and military services. In some cases, they have seized the property of others or have been sufficiently corrupt to damage the reputation of the royal family.

These problems have steadily increased with the size of the royal family, the decline in Saudi Arabia's relative oil wealth, and the growing complexity of the Saudi economy. While a royal role in business is a traditional aspect of Saudi society, and major abuses have been relatively limited, there have been enough problems in the royal family to cause growing resentment in all levels of Saudi society. Furthermore, not all of the princes involved in commercial and business abuses and corruption are outside the power structure at the top of the royal family. Some of the sons of Saudi Arabia's most senior figures have been deeply involved. In June 2002, the royal family council set up by King Fahd began examining the behavior and competency of the politically active members of the al-Saud family.

The need to redefine the role princes play in Saudi government, politics, and business extends to the military command level, where divisions between members of the royal family sometimes lead to poor selection of commanders or effective unity of command. This discord discourages the appointment of younger and more competent officers from outside the royal family who might be competitive and demanding if given high ranks. Some princes in senior positions in the regular military have had to be shunted aside for corruption. Some have had undeserved promotions and a few junior princes have insisted on keeping their titles rather than leaving out their royal title and using only their military rank.

The politics of the ruling elite has, however, sometimes limited the careers of very competent princes. For example, Prince Fahd Abdullah, widely recognized as one of the most outstanding officers in the Royal Saudi Air Force (RSAF), was not promoted to a top command position. Prince Khalid bin Sultan, who successfully led the Arab forces in the Gulf War, was passed over for promotion to the post of military chief of staff and resigned in September 1991—although he returned to become assistant minister of defense in 2000.[26]

It is becoming all too clear that demographics are a major problem in the royal family as well as within the Saudi population as a whole. The high birth rate within the royal family means the number of "princes" now doubles every twenty-two to twenty-six years and that there are about 70% more "royal" males under the age of eighteen than there are above it. This same growth affects the al-Shaykh and other leading families. At some point in the near- to mid-term, the Kingdom simply will not be able to afford subsidizing either its expanding royal family or the descendants of other leading families.

The exponential growth of the size and potential cost of the Saudi royal family is scarcely a unique problem in the Southern Gulf, but it reinforces the need to limit payments and subsidies, to place clear limits on eligibility for state funds and support, and particularly to put a firm end to the favoritism and corruption of its middle and junior princes. Saudi Arabia also needs to reduce most of the subsidies and cut down on large numbers of special accounts and commissions given various senior princes. While many members of the royal family do provide active public service or engage in legitimate business, there are many who are little more than parasites and whose abuse of public funds threatens Saudi Arabia's political cohesion and popular support for the members of the ruling members of the royal family.

At the same time, the need for such reforms and generational change hardly means Saudi Arabia cannot maintain its stability while being ruled by a monarchy. Many princes are highly respected and play a major role in public service. There is little evidence of popular opposition to the monarchy, and most opposition movements that do exist are from conservative Islamists rather than the liberal reform-minded Saudis.

The challenge is evolutionary. Saudi Arabia has time to find a stable answer to the problem of who will rule once the direct sons of Ibn Saud no longer participate in the succession, to add a steadily increasing degree of pluralism and a stronger rule of law, to lead the modernization of the economy, to deal with the challenge of extremism, and to redefine the role of the royal family in ways that sharply reduce state subsidies as well as the abuse of royal status. The royal family must ensure that commoners can count on promotion for merit, and that the Saudi people do not believe members of the royal family abuse the courts and legal system.

Western-style democracy may not be a critical aspect of Saudi Arabia's political and social development, but broad social and economic change is vital and the rule of law is essential. Difficult decisions have to be made about the reallocation of power at some point in the near future or the growth and cost of the al-Saud family will become a much more serious destabilizing factor in Saudi politics.

The Saudi Cabinet or Council of Ministers

The Saudi Cabinet is of considerable practical importance and its composition reflects the distribution of power within the senior ranks of the royal family and Saudi Arabia's technocrats. The Cabinet is a large body headed by the king, with more than twenty members, including six ministers of state. There are twenty-two separate ministries, with the king acting as prime minister. Prince Abdullah is first deputy prime minister and head of the National Guard. Prince Sultan is second deputy prime minister and minister of defense and aviation. Prince Saud al-Faisal is foreign minister, Prince Nayef is minister of the interior, and Prince Mutib is minister of public works and housing.[27] These appointments give the senior members of the royal family control over the government, defense, internal security, the budget and oil revenues, and other key areas of patronage.

The Cabinet also includes and is supported by a wide range of technocrats who head well-organized and relatively modern ministries. The following list of Saudi ministers and key officials make this clear. Only a limited number are members of the royal family—those highlighted in bold. Italics denote the small additional number who are direct descendants of Muhammad ibn Abd al-Wahhab. The rest are technocrats, many of whom are "new men" without ties to other dominant Saudi families or tribal leaders. This point is often ignored in discussions of Saudi government. Much of the planning and management of the Kingdom is conducted by Western-educated experts, who are supported by roughly 250 other senior appointments and a network of approximately 700 senior civil servants. Only about one-third of these appointments come from traditional leading families. The rest are also "new men," a few of whom are one generation away from nomadic tribesmen.

- King: Fahd bin Abdulaziz al-Saud
- Prime Minister: Fahd bin Abdulaziz al-Saud
- First Deputy Prime Minister: Abdullah bin Abdulaziz al-Saud
- Second Deputy Prime Minister: Sultan bin Abdulaziz al-Saud
- Minister of Agriculture and Water: Abdullah bin Abdulaziz al-Mu'ammar
- Minister of Civil Service: Muhammad bin Ali al-Fayez
- Minister of Commerce: Osama bin Jafar bin Ibrahim Faqih

- Minister of Communications: Dr. Nasir bin Muhammad al-Salloum
- Minister of Defense and Aviation: Sultan bin Abdulaziz al-Saud
- Minister of Education: Dr. Muhammad bin Ahmed al-Rasheed
- Minister of Finance and National Economy: Ibrahim bin Abdulaziz bin Abdullah al-Assaf
- Minister of Foreign Affairs: Saud al-Faisal bin Abdulaziz al-Saud
- Minister of Health: Dr. Osama bin Abdulmajeed Shobokshi
- Minister of Higher Education: Dr. Khalid al-Angary
- Minister of Housing and Public Works: Meteeb bin Abdulaziz al-Saud
- Minister of Industry and Electricity: Dr. Hashim bin Abdullah bin Hashim al-Yamani
- Minister of Information: Dr. Fouad bin Abdulsalaam bin Muhammad al-Farsi
- Minister of the Interior: Nayef bin Abdulaziz al-Saud
- Minister of Islamic Affairs, Endowments, Call, and Guidance: Shaikh Saleh bin Abdulaziz al-Ashaikh
- Minister of Justice: Abdullah bin Muhammad bin Ibrahim al-Ashaikh
- Minister of Labor and Social Affairs: Dr. Ali bin Ibrahim al-Namlah
- Minister of Municipal and Rural Affairs: Dr. Muhammad bin Ibrahim al-Jarallah
- Minister of Petroleum and Mineral Resources: Ali bin Ibrahim al-Naim
- Minster of Pilgrimage: Iyad bin Ameen Madani
- Minister of Planning: Khalid bin Muhammad Qusaibi
- Minister of Posts, Telegraphs, and Telephones (Acting): Khalid bin Muhammad Qusaibi
- Minister of Water: Dr. Ghazi bin Abdulrahman al-Qusaibi
- Ministers of State: Abdulaziz bin Fahd bin Abdulaziz, Madani bin Abdulgadir Alagi, Dr. Muhammad bin Abdulaziz al-Shaiki, Dr. Musaid bin Muhammad al-Eiban, Dr. Abdulaziz bin Abdullah al-Khuwaeitir, Dr. Abdulaziz bin Ibrahim al-Manie, Dr. Muttlab bin Abdullah al-Nafissa

In the past, these technocrats and senior officials usually served in the same position for much of their professional life. Many appointments lasted fifteen to twenty-five years. As a result, Saudi technocrats were slow to adapt to changing circumstances and many ministries developed an institutional resistance to change. This problem became clear during the Gulf War, when many civil ministries had severe difficulties in meeting the sudden, new requirements necessary to support the Saudi military and foreign troops. As a result, King Fahd issued a decree in 1992 declaring that Cabinet ministers could not remain in their posts for more than five years without a special royal decree. This decree, however, did not lead to rapid turnover within the Cabinet and senior ranks.

Between 1993 and 1995 Saudi Arabia experienced a growing economic crisis, partly as a result of Gulf War expenditures. It again became apparent that many ministries were slow to adapt to Saudi Arabia's growing debt, income, and cash flow problems. Many ministries were slow to control expenses; they continued to advocate very large and grandiose projects and failed to give priority to social and political needs. At the same time, Saudi Arabia experienced growing problems with Islamic extremists.

By the spring of 1995, King Fahd and the royal family took dramatic action. Significant shifts occurred in appointments within the Saudi bureaucracy affecting around 160 of 250 top posts. At the same time, changes were made in appointments to senior religious and educational positions. These changes reached a scale close to a "generational change" in the senior ranks of the Saudi government.[28] In late July 1995, King Fahd replaced 157 of Saudi Arabia's senior officials. On August 2, 1995, he made the first sweeping changes in the Saudi Cabinet in twenty years and replaced six members of the Majlis al-Shura. While the role of senior members of the royal family did not change, sixteen of twenty-eight Cabinet members were replaced and two ministers swapped jobs.

These changes in the Cabinet affected high-profile ministries like the Ministry of Petroleum and Mineral Resources and the Ministry of Information. Hisham M. Nazer, the minister of petroleum and mineral resources, was replaced by Ali bin Ibrahim al-Naimi, a "new man" who was chairman of ARAMCO. Mohammed A. Aba al-Khayl, who had been minister of finance for twenty-five years, was replaced by Sulaym al-Sulaym, the minister of commerce.[29] Other key ministries relating to the economy and social welfare services were replaced, including the ministers of telecommunications and electricity. These changes resulted in a Cabinet that included fifteen members with postgraduate degrees from Western universities.[30]

It is impossible for an outsider to determine the purpose or exact scale of these changes—many of which went far beyond the Cabinet—or the meaning of most of the changes that have taken place since that time. It seems clear, however, that they reflected growing concern with the problems of dealing with Islamic extremism and finding jobs for Saudi Arabia's young population. They reflected a concern over the age and lack of flexibility of many ministers and other officials and their failure to control costs and expenditures, scale back projects, emphasize privatization, and be far more demanding in planning governmental investments.

One factor that almost certainly influenced the king's action was Saudi Arabia's 1995 budget deficit, which rose well above the planned $4 billion, although oil revenues were nearly $2.3 billion higher than forecast during the first five months of the year. King Fahd asked ministers to propose new cost-cutting measures on July 9, 1995.[31]

Another Cabinet shuffle took place on June 16, 1999, once again following a time when Saudi Arabia had serious economic problems. There had been some speculation that Petroleum Minister Ali bin Ibrahim al-Naimi would be discharged. Al-Naimi was widely blamed for the 1997 Jakarta agreement, which led to record low oil prices and insufficient oil revenues to fund Defense Minister Prince Sultan's defense budget.[32] However, al-Naimi's central role in securing OPEC cutbacks and boosting oil prices enabled him to keep his post, presumably for another four-year term.[33]

Instead, the most drastic changes came in the area of labor and social affairs, where action was needed to stem the rise in Saudi unemployment, and "Islamic guidance," where a new appointee had clearly been chosen to allay conservative fears about social change. In all, four ministries changed hands and a new one was created to supervise civil service affairs.[34] The new ministers appointed included Labor and Social Affairs Minister Dr. Ali bin Ibrahim al-Namlah, Islamic Affairs Minister Shaikh Saleh bin Abdulaziz al-Ashaikh, Planning Minister Khalid bin Muhammad al-Qusaibi, and Iyad bin Ameen Madani as minister of pilgrimage.[35]

Saudi political appointments have tended to become somewhat younger and seem to be shifting toward the grooming of a younger generation for senior positions. Crown Prince Abdullah seems to favor such changes and is likely to continue them once he becomes king. Saudi Arabia still, however, has a tendency to allow officials to serve too long, without proper regard to current performance. The appointments made since 1995 also have included important new officials who deal with key issues like private investment and the creation of important new councils to deal with the economy and energy. However, there still seems to be a need for more rapid turnover to allow a steady process of promotion at all levels and to create a structure of government where top-level positions depend on success in reform and effective government rather than seniority.

The Creation of the Majlis al-Shura

There have already been some important movements toward increased pluralism. The issue of how to create some kind of majlis first became a subject of serious concern during the time of Nasser. The flood of oil wealth into the Kingdom after 1973 deferred much of the public pressure for change, however, and although Fahd wanted to establish some form of majlis as early as 1982, he faced opposition from puritanical Islamists who felt that Shari'a should be the only basis for law-making. It was the complex mix of social and economic pressures that arose during the Gulf War that finally led King Fahd to reorganize his Cabinet on August 5, 1990, and announce a series of reforms on March 17, 1991. These reforms included the formation of a Council of Saudi Citizens (Majlis al-Shura), the introduction of a basic body of governing laws, and increased autonomy for the provinces.[36]

King Fahd's announcement of his intent to form a Majlis al-Shura was a reaction to the demands of both traditional fundamentalists and modernizing reformers for greater participation in the government. His announcement was followed by further speeches by the king; by senior religious figures like Sheikh Ibn Baz, who denounced religious extremism; and by senior political figures like Prince Turki Faisal, who gave a rare speech in a mosque condemning those who used Islamic extremism to attack Saudi society.

The king announced on March 2, 1992, that the Majlis al-Shura would have sixty-one members, including the speaker of the consultative council. The Majlis would have a four-year term of office, and its responsibilities included examining plans for economic and social development, questioning Cabinet members, examining annual plans submitted by each ministry, and proposing new laws or amendments. He announced that similar ten-man councils would be set up in each of the fourteen provinces, and that the provincial governors would have added power and autonomy.[37]

The king issued a long written list of decrees setting forth the basic rules of the government, the first codification of these laws since the founding of Saudi Arabia sixty years earlier. The code included the following provisions: making the king the commander-in-chief of the armed forces; calling for the succession to pass to the most qualified member of the royal family, rather than according to the order of succession; establishing an independent judiciary; guaranteeing the privacy of the home, mail, and phone; and prohibiting arbitrary arrest.

On September 23, 1992, the sixtieth anniversary of the founding of the monarchy, King Fahd appointed Muhammad bin Jubair as speaker of the Majlis al-Shura. At the same time, the king delayed appointing the council, stating, "The democratic systems prevailing in the world are systems which, in their structure, do not suit this region and our people. . . . The system of free elections is not part of Islamic theology."[38]

On August 21, 1993, the king appointed the members of the council. King Fahd read a decree over state television that again made it clear that the role of the Majlis was purely advisory. He also stated that he was retaining the power of the monarchy, and that Saudi Arabia would remain an Islamic state and would not become a Western democracy.[39] The creation of the council drew on the formal Islamic concept of Shura to institutionalize the method by which political participation in Saudi Arabia was conducted: the consultation of people of knowledge and expertise in order to legitimize public policy.

The king appointed all sixty members of the Majlis al-Shura, including one Shi'ite, to a four-year term. Among the first appointees to the council were businessmen, technocrats, diplomats, journalists, Islamic scholars, and professional soldiers representing all regions of the country. Most were young by Saudi standards and had exposure outside of the country.

The Majlis met first in 1994. Its initial meetings focused on procedures and regulations and the establishment of various technical and administrative committees, such as those on foreign affairs and defense. According to Saudi reports, the council met twenty-nine times in 1994, discussed forty-five issues, and presented twenty-five recommendations. The council's General Authority held twenty-one meetings and reached twenty-three decisions, and the various committees of the Council held more than 260 meetings and submitted more than fifty studies and reports. There were no public reports of any debates or issues the Majlis al-Shura raised during its first year, or any indications of differences with the royal family.[40]

The council began the first session of its second year on January 8, 1995. This was the first time that King Fahd presented a national budget to the council. Although this did not lead to any open debate by Western standards, the Majlis expanded its coverage to include social and policy issues during the course of the 1995 and 1996 sessions, and increased its advisory role. It also started having weekly meetings that sometimes lasted several days at a time, rather than meeting for a one-day, biweekly session. While little was published on the substance of the council's work, the Saudi government reported that the full council had held 103 meetings by the end of its first four-year session in mid-1997, and that it had passed resolutions on 133 topics while studying another forty-nine. Its eight subcommittees had held 727 meetings to discuss 143 subjects and issued 133 resolutions. It had also begun to regularly send delegations to other countries.[41]

King Fahd expanded the Majlis al-Shura from sixty to ninety members at the beginning of its second four-year session on July 20, 1997. He held a high-profile swearing-in ceremony, with Prince Abdullah and Prince Sultan present. King Fahd's speech mixed a traditional emphasis on the importance of Shari'a and the Sunnah (the sayings and teachings of the Prophet) in shaping the council's work, the need for higher education and scientific and engineering training, and for more reliance on the private sector. Muhammad bin Jubair, the chairman of the Majlis, stressed the increasing activity of the council and announced the formation of eight ad hoc committees to meet twice a week. These committees had eight to sixteen members each, and included the:[42]

- Organization and Administration Committee
- Education, Information, and Cultural Affairs Committee
- Islamic Affairs Committee
- Services and Public Utilities Committee
- Health and Social Affairs Committee

- Foreign Affairs Committee
- Economic and Financial Affairs Committee, and a
- Security Affairs Committee, chaired by a retired major general.

Further changes were announced in the Majlis al-Shura at the beginning of the third year of its second term in July 1999. At that time, four new members were added to the council and the number of ad hoc committees was increased from eight to eleven as a result of the division of some of the current committees.[43] Among these were the Economic Affairs Committee and the Financial Affairs Committee, which were originally combined into a committee that dealt with both issues. The Education, Information, and Cultural Affairs Committee was divided into two committees: the Educational Affairs Committee and the Cultural and Media Affairs Committee. In addition, the Services and Utilities Committee expanded its role to become the Services, Utilities, Communications, and Transport Committee.[44]

A study of the membership of the second Majlis al-Shura indicated that it was relatively young for a Saudi government council, with an average age of fifty-two, (members ranged from as young as thirty-four to as old as sixty-nine). Although only 17% of the members were over sixty, 30% were between the ages of thirty and forty, and 53% were in their fifties. The membership was broadly based in terms of occupation, although members of the bureaucracy and the business sector were underrepresented. Roughly 23% were modernizing academics, 7% were traditional religious academics, 3% were journalists, 19% were full-time bureaucrats, 24.3% were bureaucrats with other roles such as academic or judge, 4.4% were from the police, 3.3% were from the military, and 7.8% were from the business sector.

Overall educational levels were high: approximately 64% had doctoral degrees, 14.4% had master's degrees, and 21.2% held bachelor's degrees. About 80% of the members with doctoral and master's degrees had been educated in the West. Historically, only about 17% to 19% of the first two Majlis al-Shuras consisted of members who could be classified as Islamists. The Majlis was heavily weighted in favor of members from the Najd, who made up 44% of the council. Roughly 29% came from the Hijaz, 90% from the Eastern Province, and 18% from the other regions of the Kingdom.[45]

King Fahd swore in the third Majlis al-Shura in Jeddah on June 4, 2001. He expanded the Council from 90 to 120 members, and expanded the role of the Shura's committees, which cover issues such as finance, the five-year plan, Islamic and social affairs, and education. The members were nominated—along with the name of one substitute for each position—by the provincial governors from among the leading doctors, lawyers, military, businessmen and financial experts, academics, scientists, and lawyers. Each nomination was then vetted by the royal court, and nominees were asked to confirm their willingness to serve before the king formally announced their selection.

The expanded body still had very high educational levels. All members had college degrees and extensive experience, and more than 60% had Ph.Ds. Sheikh Muhammad bin Jubair, an Islamist and former justice minister, remained chairman of the council, and roughly half of the members of the previous Majlis were retained. Jubair died in January 2002. (In theory, half of the Majlis serve only one four-year term while half are retained in order to provide both a suitable turnover and new ideas, but the steady expansion of the Majlis has forced Saudi Arabia to alter these policies. New appointments are also made immediately if a member dies or cannot perform his duties.)[46]

In 2002, the expanded Majlis had twelve major committees with eleven members each. These committees operated along democratic lines with each member having one vote, as did the council as a whole. The decree creating the Majlis specifies that voting shall be on a majority basis, and that issues that do not result in a majority shall only be sent to the king after an effort is made to create a majority in the next session.

By 2002, the Majlis had also established its the right to ask any member of the Cabinet or Council of Ministers to appear and answer questions. It still did not play a direct role in shaping security and defense policy and reviewing the draft budget, but it did review and approve the Seventh Development Plan. Both the Majlis as a body and its committees analyzed and discussed the five-year plan in some detail. Members of the Majlis also indicated that they could indirectly review the budget as part of their review of the annual reports issued by each ministry, and that giving the Majlis direct review of the budget was under consideration. The review of the annual reports and the actions of each ministry is the subject to detailed review by the committees of the council, which develop evaluations and recommendations for review by the Majlis as a whole.

There is one staff for each two members of the Majlis, plus separate staffs for key committees and for analyzing whether the recommendations of the Majlis are carried out. There is also a department for handling petitions; any Saudi citizen may petition the Majlis. Committee review is generally on an article-by-article basis and the committees sometimes hold extensive hearings. For example, the Finance Committee did this when reviewing a new tax law, and held follow-on hearings after several key articles were referred back to the committee by the Majlis as a whole.

The Majlis and its committees hold oversight hearings and seek outside views and criticism of the behavior and effectiveness of given ministries. In several cases, these hearings have allowed the Saudi business community to force significant changes in the efficiency or structure of government operations. The Majlis reviews major foreign-policy decisions and holds hearings that include questioning of the foreign minister. The king or crown prince attends some sessions of the Majlis, and the king is supposed to make an annual address to the Majlis that sets out his program for the year, health permitting.

According to members, debate is often heated by Saudi standards, criticism of the government is common, and differences do occur with the Council of Ministers. The Majlis does, however, emphasize consensus rather than divided recommendations and adversarial positions, and an effort is made to avoid confronting the king with unresolved debates or recommendations that might force him to cast a veto. Members estimated that this meant the king upheld the decisions of the Majlis in "99.7%" of all cases.

The law of the Majlis al-Shura states that its role shall be defined by royal order, and recognizes the king's paramount role under the Saudi interpretation of Shari'a. At the same time, the Koran does call on the king to consult with his advisors, and there is a potential precedent in Shari'a that the king should not overrule any recommendation where both the Majlis and Council of Ministers agree.[47] In fact, some members of the Majlis complained that Crown Prince Abdullah had bypassed the Majlis when he unilaterally abolished a separate department for women's education in 2002. It should also be noted that the Majlis is bound by Shari'a and must defer to the judiciary on Islamic law. The Islamic Committee of the Majlis reviews its actions to ensure that they comply with Shari'a. The Council of Ministers must also review any action by the Majlis if the Islamic Committee does not reach a consensus, as was a case in its review of drafts of a new insurance law.

The Majlis is due to expand to 150 members in 2004. This slow expansion of the role of the Majlis al-Shura scarcely marks a shift toward a Western-style representative democracy. Nevertheless, it does denote a significant move toward a structured, formal broadening the saudi power base. Members of the Majlis take their role very seriously, and some members of the royal family indicate that the Majlis and the Council of Ministers may be made equal branches of government. It is also important to stress that Saudi society avoids open confrontation wherever possible, and that the slow development of a technocratic body that develops precedents that take on some of the character of an unwritten constitution is an important evolutionary step.

The Changing Saudi Political System

The Kingdom has made other reforms, including expanding the role of the thirteen provincial assemblies that were created when the Majlis al-Shura was revived.[48] At the same time that Saudi Arabia established the Majlis al-Shura, it established thirteen Regional Councils, each made up of fifteen to twenty members. Membership is by appointment and members are chosen for their extensive experience in public service or business and reflect sections of Saudi society from academia to clergy. Opinions from the regional council are submitted, when appropriate, for consideration to the Majlis al-Shura. These councils play an important country-wide role in allowing expression of local opinion, although their role in the Kingdom's movement toward political reform is unclear.

Another example of efforts at evolutionary reform is illustrated by the attendance of Saudi women at a council session for the first time on October 4, 1999. Although they did not partake in the session, approximately twenty Saudi women followed the proceedings from a balcony overlooking the meeting hall. This event occurred a day after comments by Sheikh Muhammad bin Jubair, the chairman of the Majlis, indicated that there was no prohibition on women attending meetings of the Shura Council and that even though they could not serve as members, their experience and opinions would be valuable and useful to the council's discussions.[49] At the same time, the regime's need to carefully stage-manage this event is indicative of the difficulties associated with increasing the measure of political expression allowed by the Shura, and in increasing pluralism, especially in relation to widening the opportunities available to women in the country. Nevertheless, the Kingdom has moved further even in religiously sensitive areas. For example, women—who hold 50% of the shares in the guide's organizations in Makkah and Medina—were allowed to cast proxy votes in electing the boards of directors for the organizations providing pilgrim services for the first time in 2002.[50]

The U.S. State Department assessed the structure of the Saudi government and the role of these bodies as follows in its human rights reporting in 2002,[51]

Saudi Arabia is a monarchy without elected representative institutions or political parties. It is ruled by King Fahd bin Abd Al-Aziz Al Saud, a son of King Abd Al-Aziz Al Saud, who unified the country in the early 20th century. Since the death of King Abd Al-Aziz, the King and Crown Prince have been chosen from among his sons, who themselves have had preponderant influence in the choice. A 1992 royal decree reserves for the King exclusive power to name the Crown Prince. Crown Prince Abdullah has played an increasing role in governance since King Fahd suffered a stroke in 1995. The Government has declared the Islamic holy book the Koran and the Sunna (tradition) of the Prophet Muhammad to be the country's Constitution. The Government bases its legitimacy on governance according to the precepts of a rigorously conservative form of Islam. Neither the Government nor the society in general accepts the concept of separation of religion and state. The Government prohibits the establishment of political parties and suppresses opposition views. In 1992 King Fahd appointed a Consultative Council, or Majlis Ash-Shura, and similar provincial assemblies. The Majlis, a strictly advisory body, began holding sessions in 1993 and was expanded first in 1997 and again in May. The judiciary is subject to influence by the executive branch and members of the royal family.

. . . The King is also the Prime Minister, and the Crown Prince serves as Deputy Prime Minister. The King appoints all other ministers, who in turn appoint subordinate officials with cabinet concurrence. In 1992 the King appointed 60 members to a Consultative Council, or Majlis al-Shura. This strictly advisory body began to hold sessions in 1993. In 1997 and again in May the King expanded the membership of the Council; it has 120 members plus its chairman. There are plans to expand the Majlis al-Shura again in 2005. There are two Shi'as on the Council. The Council engages in debates that, while closed to the general public, provide advice and views occasionally contrary to the Government's proposed policy or recommended course of action. The Government usually incorporates the Majlis' advice into its final policy announcements or tries to convince it why the Government's policy is correct.

The Council of Senior Islamic Scholars (ulema) is another advisory body to the King and the Cabinet. It reviews the Government's public policies for compliance with Shari'a. The Government views the Council as an important source of religious legitimacy and takes the Council's opinions into account when promulgating legislation.

Communication between citizens and the Government usually is expressed through client-patron relationships and by affinity groups such as tribes, families, and professional hierarchies. In theory any male citizen or foreign national may express an opinion or a grievance at a majlis, an open-door meeting held by the King, a prince, or an important national or local official. However, as governmental functions have become more complex, time-consuming, and centralized, public access to senior officials has become more restricted. Since the assassination of King Faisal in 1975, Saudi kings have reduced the frequency of their personal contacts with the public. However, during the year, Crown Prince Abdullah held a variety of meetings with citizens throughout the country. Ministers and district governors more readily grant audiences at a majlis.

Typical topics raised in a majlis include complaints about bureaucratic delay or insensitivity, requests for personal redress or assistance, and criticism of particular acts of government affecting family welfare. Broader "political" concerns—social, economic, or foreign policy—rarely are raised. Complaints about royal abuses of power are not entertained. In general journalists, academics, and businessmen believe that institutionalized avenues of domestic criticism of the regime are closed. Feedback is filtered through private personal channels and has affected various policy issues, including the Middle East peace process, unemployment of young Saudi men, and the construction of new infrastructure.

Any analysis of Saudi efforts to broaden and restructure its political system must take account of the fact that Saudi Arabia a consensus-driven society that must recognize efforts to preserve the nation's character as a Wahhabi Islamic state and the need to adapt religious and social custom to modern social and economic needs. It is easy to talk about "democratization," but it is far from clear that any popular vote today would lead

Saudi Arabia to modernize and reform its economy at anything like the rate its current government is seeking. A nation without well-established moderate political parties, and where the only serious opposition now consists of Islamic activists, is almost a model of the risk that a rush toward instant democracy would only result in "one man, one vote, one time" and then the creation of some form of traditionalist authoritarianism. As a result, the creation of an advisory Majlis, a focus on political consensus, a written code of law, and other limited reforms may well mark the present limits of how far the Saudi government can now go without increasing internal instability rather than reducing it.

Given this background, it is a steady process of change—and occasional delay and compromise—that is most likely to serve Saudi interests and protect the human rights of all Saudis. Any sudden efforts to make broad and more sweeping reforms might do little more than lead to open confrontation between Saudi Arabia's advocates of modern reform, its traditionalists and fundamentalists, and its militant Islamists.

At the same time, even some reform-oriented members of the royal family have long called for more rapid political change. One well-known example is Prince Talal bin Abdulaziz al-Saud, half-brother of King Fahd and father of billionaire mega-investor Prince al-Waleed bin Talal. He has called for more democracy for many years and repeated this point on March 4, 1998, when he urged the Kingdom and other Arab states to eventually hold "real" elections.

Talal is one of the "free princes" of the 1960s and was speaking outside the country during a visit to attend a UNESCO conference on higher education in Beirut. Nevertheless, he did make similar statements after the attack on the World Trade Center and the Pentagon on September 11, 2001, and his words provide possible indication of how Saudi Arabia may modernize the Shura and expand its role in the future:[52]

Are we more backwards than other countries to hold elections that are cosmetic? What is required now is the development of the Shura Council until we reach a stage in which the Kingdom of Saudi Arabia can hold real and authentic elections. . . . This plan [expanding the role of the Shura], in my opinion, if the situation continues, it will lead to elections. I prefer them later rather than now. Now is not the time. I don't believe we are ready. The Arab countries that have elections, do you think they have real parliaments? . . . Some countries have elections. But the elections are cosmetic. They amount to decorations for the outside world. Do you want these kinds of elections? . . . The majority in Saudi Arabia, like the majority in other Arab countries, prefer gradual steps towards a democratic life. If the citizen can express an opinion and take part in decisions in one way or another, that is what is important. . . . The structure of the Saudi system is different than the outside world. . . . These are customs and customs are stronger than laws. . . . The small man respects the big man. And the big man listens to the little man. We are moving in this way. There are differences of opinion and this is healthy.

POLITICAL REFORM AND OPPOSITION

Evolution is not stasis. Saudi Arabia does need broadly based political, social, and economic reform. Western critics need to understand, however, that such reform must evolve in a Saudi way and on Saudi terms. It is easy to say that Saudi Arabia must mimic the West. In practice, however, any such effort would ignore the religious, cultural, tribal, and regional character of the Kingdom. It would be destabilizing and impractical; a narrow focus on rapid "democratization" would result in political divisiveness, factionalism, "service politics," and the politization of Islam rather than progressive social change. Saudi Arabia's complex mixture of Wahhabi Islam, population and economic problems, regional divisions, and a centralized government by monarchy supported by modern technocracy is anything but easy to change. Most important, peaceful change requires the evolution of a uniquely Saudi form of government.

The following chapters show that the Saudi government has begun a process of political economic and social reform that should help deal with these internal political problems as well as serious social, demographic, and economic pressures. At the same time, the regime's present approach to change is faltering and often more regressive than evolutionary. The Saudi royal family sometimes seems to be in a state of denial when it deals with internal security problems, or moves so slowly that the problem grows faster than the implementation of the solution. To be specific, a proper approach to internal security requires the government and royal family to concentrate on many of the same reforms it must make to deal with the pressures of economic and demographic change:

- *The leadership of the royal family needs to set clear limits to the future benefits family members receive from the state and phase out those special privileges and commissions that limit the competitiveness and efficiency of the Saudi economy and private sector.* It needs to transfer all revenues from oil and gas to the state budget, and to ensure that princes obey the rule of law and are not seen as "corrupt" or abusing the powers of the state. At some point, most members of the royal family will also have to earn a living on their own. It does not take much vision to see that the Saudi monarchy cannot give 15,000 princes the same money, rights, and privileges it once gave several thousand.

- *The Majlis al-Shura needs to be steadily expanded in influence and decision-making, and in regional and sectarian representation, to provide a more representative form of government.* The Majlis has made a good beginning, but it needs younger members, more members that are moderate critics of the royal family, and some Shi'ites that are permitted to speak for their ethnic group.

It needs to play a more direct role in reviewing the Saudi budget, and its debates need to be more open and receive better coverage in the media. It may be some years before Saudi Arabia is ready for a fully elected Majlis or National Assembly, but it is time to begin open elections at lower levels. The Saudi government needs to be more open, and some body other than the royal family needs to be seen as playing a major role in decision-making. The present closed, overcentralized process of government breeds extremist opposition.

- *Saudi Arabia must come to grips with the need to reform and adapt its religious doctrines so it can forge a path of modernization and competitiveness that will drive the Kingdom into the twenty-first century.* Although Saudi Arabia does not need to change its Wahhabi character, its religious practices must become more flexible. Some reforms have already begun in areas dealing with the sciences, modern media, education, investment and insurance, legal and social practices, and even in difficult issues like reinterpreting pre-Islamic history and archeology. Saudi religious modernists have already shown that that the Kingdom can move forward in changing its economy, education, and social structure without losing any of its Islamic character. Qatar is showing that a Wahhabi society can develop more pluralism and political flexibility.

- *There is an equal need to evolve interpretations of legal procedures and the required punishments that are as humane as possible and to find ways to encourage peaceful opposition on Saudi terms and deal with opposition by responding with reform and effective governance.* It is unrealistic and impractical for Saudi Arabia to attempt to adopt Western standards of human rights. The West needs to be careful not to become trapped into supporting the efforts of Islamic extremists who claim to advocate human rights and democracy as a way of attacking the Saudi regime. It also needs to understand that Saudi law is an expression of Islam and Shari'a, rather than Western or more secular interpretations of law; deeming every religious practice that differs from the West a human rights abuse means demanding that Saudi Arabia abandon its religion and culture.

- *Saudi Arabia must accept the need to give Saudi Shi'ites a special religious status and proper economic rights, emphasize the protections of the individual already granted under Saudi law, and sharply rein in the growing abuses of the religious police.* The government must reestablish public faith in the legal process and the rule of law.

Saudis often quite correctly criticize Western analysts for demanding that Saudi Arabia become a mirror image of the West. This particular form of globalism implies convergence on a kind of Western secularism that is the antithesis of multiculturalism, and that attempts to emphasize the strengths of the Western approach with little regard to its weaknesses. Saudi culture and legal and political practices have strengths of their own, in addition to the weaknesses some Western critics focus on. These strengths include social cohesion, firm control of crime, tightly knitted and supportive extended families, and a patriarchal sense of the government's obligation to the people. These are not values that any practical observer can easily dismiss.

At the same time, it seems valid to criticize the current political structure of the Saudi royal family and government for being too slow to react to the seriousness of some of the Kingdom's problems and for recognizing the lessons from other Arab regimes that were too slow to change and evolve. The Saudi monarchy and Saudi society may not want to adopt Western democracy and cultural and legal processes, but Saudis should pay close attention to the mistakes that have helped cause the fall of other monarchies and that have produced political, social, and economic instability in so many Arab states—regardless of the nature of their regimes. The Saudi government must recognize that legitimate criticism can only be disarmed by recognizing its legitimacy and acting to make the necessary changes. Saudi Arabia must find a new "golden mean" between preserving its conservative Islamic character and meeting the need for change.

NOTES

1. David E. Long, *The Kingdom of Saudi Arabia* (Gainesville: University Press of Florida, 1997), pp. 46–51.

2. Long, *The Kingdom of Saudi Arabia*, pp. 41–42.

3. R. Hrair Dekmejian, "Saudi Arabia's Consultative Council," *Middle East Journal*, vol. 52, no. 2 (Spring 1998), pp. 204–218; Rahshe Aba-Namay, "Constitutional Reforms: A Systemization of Saudi Politics," *Journal of South Asian and Middle Eastern Studies*, vol. 16, no. 3 (Spring 1998), pp. 44–48.

4. Drawn from St. John Armitage's comments.

5. Long, *The Kingdom of Saudi Arabia*, pp. 41–42.

6. *U.S. State Department Human Rights Report, 1998* (Washington: GPO, 1999); and *2001 Country Reports on Human Rights Practices*, U.S. Department of State, March 4, 2002, URL: *http://www.state.gov/g/drl/rls/hrrpt/2001/nea/8296.html*.

7. Ibid.

8. Mai Yamani, *Changed Identities: The Challenge of the New Generation in Saudi Arabia* (London: Royal Institute of International Affairs: 2000), p. 20.

9. Robert Cullen, "Uneasy Lies the Head That Wears a Crown," *Nuclear Energy* (Third Quarter 1995), p. 24.

10. *The Estimate*, January 5, 1996, p. 11.

11. Cullen, "Uneasy Lies the Head," p. 24.

12. *The Estimate*, January 5, 1996, p. 11.

13. *Baltimore Sun*, January 4, 1996, p. 2A.

14. Long, *The Kingdom of Saudi Arabia*, pp. 54-57; *New York Times*, January 2, 1996, p. A-3.

15. Long, *The Kingdom of Saudi Arabia*, p. 54.

16. Reuters, September 29, 1999; Saudi Press Agency Information Release, October 18, 1999.

17. *New York Times*, January 2, 1996, p. A-3; *Washington Post*, January 2, 1996, p. A-20. *Washington Times*, January 3, 1996, p. A-10; Executive News Service, February 22, 1996, 1858. For typical press report on possible problems within

the royal family see *The Economist*, March 18, 1995, pp. 21–27; and James Bruce, "Fundamentalist unrest threatens stability in the Gulf," *Washington Times*, April 9, 1995, p. A-9.

18. The Economist Intelligence Unit, July 15, 1999.

19. *Washington Times*, January 3, 1996, p. A-10; *Middle East Economic Digest*, June 13, 1997, p. 24.

20. Drawn from interviews.

21. Dean Fischer and Scott MacLeod, *Time*, vol. 152, no. 15 (October 12, 1998), p. 44.

22. Joseph A. Kechichian, *Succession in Saudi Arabia* (New York: Palgrave, 2001), pp. 60–62.

23. *New York Times*, January 2, 1996, p. A-3; *The Estimate*, January 5, 1996, p. 11;
Washington Times, January 3, 1996, p. A-10.

24. The Economist Intelligence Unit, September 1, 2000.

25. Estimates range from 2,000 to 7,000 princes. The higher figure represents many sons with little or no influence who are descended from collateral branches of the family. The 2,000 figure is a rough estimate of the number who have any real influence. The main power is concentrated in first- and second-generation sons descended directly from Abdul Aziz. The high end of such estimates is 4,000 princes in the main lines of succession and a total of 30,000 including children.

26. This dismissal was partly the result of the fact that Khalid had used U.S. Green Berets during the buildup for Desert Storm to help reorganize Saudi forces and remove some of their bureaucratic rigidities. This caused considerable resentment and made Khalid's promotion more difficult, although it significantly improved Saudi performance during the Gulf War. *New York Times*, October 15, 1991, p. 1; *Washington Post*, March 15, 1992, p. A-35.

27. Reuters, August 2, 1995, 1133; *Middle East Economic Digest*, April 5, 1996, pp. 28–30.

28. Reuters, August 2, 1995, 1133, 1421, August 3, 1995, 0800, August 4, 1995, 1013; *Los Angeles Times*, August 3, 1995, p. A-8; *New York Times*, August 3, 1998, p. A-8; *Washington Post*, p. A-5, B-5; ASI-AFP-IR99 08-02 0588; RTR0494 OVER 50, August 2, 1995, 1936; *The Estimate*, July 21–August 3, 1995, pp. 2–4.

29. Sulayman al-Sulayman was later replaced by Ibrahim al-Assaf.

30. Reuters, August 2, 1995, 1133, 1421, August 3, 1995, 0800, August 4, 1995, 1013; *Los Angeles Times*, August 3, 1995, p. A-8; *New York Times*, August 3, 1998, p. A-8; *Wall Street Journal*, pp. A-5, B-5; ASI-AFP-IR99 08-02 0588; RTR0494 OVER 50 August 2, 1995, 1936; *The Estimate*, July 21–August 3, 1995, pp. 2–4; *Middle East Economic Digest*, August 18, 1995, pp. 2–3.

31. Reuters, July 7, 1995, 1513.

32. *The Estimate*, June 4, 1999, p. 9.

33. The survival of al-Naimi was due to the influence of Abdullah and the creation of a Supreme Oil Council chaired by Prince Saud al-Faisal, who formerly served as a deputy minister of oil. This neutralized the demand, stemming from King Faisal's reign, that a member of the royal family should be oil minister.

34. The Economist Intelligence Unit, August 9, 1999, "Saudi Arabia."

35. *The Estimate*, June 18, 1999, p. 2.

36. Saudi Arabia feels the Koran is the constitution under Islamic law. The Basic Laws, however, perform much the same function as constitutional guarantees in the West. The Majlis al-Shura was never formally dissolved, but merely ceased to operate until King Fahd revived it in 1991.

37. Dekmejian, "Saudi Arabia's Consultative Council," pp. 204–218; Aba-Namay, "Constitutional Reforms: A Systemization of Saudi Politics," pp. 44–48.

38. *New York Times*, August 6, 1991, p. A-5, November 18, 1991, p. A-3, December 31, 1991, p. A-1, March 30, 1992, p. A-6; *Washington Post*, December 31, 1991, p. A-10, March 2, 1992, p. A-1, March 6, 1992, p. A-16, September 18, 1992, p. A-31; *Boston Globe*, September 18, 1992, p. 6; *Chicago Tribune*, September 18, 1992, p. I-4; *Philadelphia Inquirer*, September 18, 1992, p. B-22; *Newsweek*, March 16, 1992, p. 45.

39. *Washington Post*, August 22, 1993, p. A-24; *Washington Times*, August 22, 1993, p. A-9; U.S. State Department, *Country Report on Human Rights Practices for 1994* (Washington: GPO, February, 1995), pp. 1165–1173; and *2001 Country Reports on Human Rights Practices*, U.S. Department of State, March 4, 2002, URL: *http://www.state.gov/g/drl/rls/hrrpt/2001/nea/8296.html*.

40. Dekmejian, "Saudi Arabia's Consultative Council," pp. 204–218; Aba-Namay, "Constitutional Reforms: A Systemization of Saudi Politics," pp. 44–48.

41. *Saudi Arabia*, vol. 12, no. 2 (February 1995), pp. 1–2, (August 1997), pp. 1–2.

42. Interview with Saudi official, August, 1997; *Saudi Arabia*, vol. 12, no. 2 (February 1995), pp. 1–2; (August 1997), pp. 1–2.

43. *Monthly Newsletter of Royal Embassy of Saudi Arabia*, "Inauguration of New Session of Consultative Council" (August 1999), p. 1.

44. "Saudi Speaker on Shura Council Role," *Al-Sharq Al-Awsat*, October, 17, 1999, accessed through World News Connection on October 25, 1999.

45. Dekmejian, "Saudi Arabia's Consultative Council," pp. 204–218; Aba-Namay, "Constitutional Reforms: A Systemization of Saudi Politics," pp. 44–48.

46. Reuters, May 24, 2001, 1038; June 4, 2001, 1432.

47. *The Law of the Majlis ash-Shura*, 3rd ed. (Riyahd: 1999).

48. Reuters, May 24, 2001, 1038; June 4, 2001, 1432.

49. "Saudi women attend council meeting for first time," Reuters, October 4, 1999.

50. *Arab News*, September 25, 2002, p. 1.

51. U.S. Department of State, Bureau of Democracy, Human Rights, and Labor, *1999 Country Reports on Human Rights Practices*, February 25, 2000, URL: *http://www.state.gov/www/global/human_rights/1999_hrp_report/saudiara.html*; and U.S. Department of State, *2001 Country Reports on Human Rights Practices*, March 4, 2002, *http://www.state.gov/g/drl/rls/hrrpt/2001/nea/8296.html*.

52. Reuters, March 4, 1998, 1606.

Chapter 4

Opposition and Islamic Extremism

Saudi Arabia does not face major political challenges from the mix of progressives, democratic reformers, human rights advocates, Arab socialists, Marxists or other secular political movements that shape the political debate in many other Arab countries. Saudi Arabia has political advocates in all of these areas, and some are quite active as individuals. There are many progressive Saudi businessmen, academics, journalists, and technocrats who actively seek evolutionary reform. Nevertheless, Saudi Arabia is one of the few countries in the world where the vast majority of politically conscious adult citizens are more conservative than a conservative regime.

Saudi politics still center around religious legitimacy, and the commitment of the al-Sauds to the teachings of Mohamed ibn Abd al-Wahhab and to preserving the regime's religious legitimacy is as important today as during the first rise of the al-Sauds to power. Much of Saudi political stability is shaped by popular perceptions of the aspect of the regime's commitment to Islam rather than the elections and pluralism that shape legitimacy by Western standards. Even the most reform-minded technocrats, businessmen, and members of the royal family normally make Islamic values part of all their decision-making, speeches, laws, decrees, and public life.

Although the Saudi regime did face serious "popular" challenges from Nasser and Arab socialism in the past, there is little evidence that such movements retain any political strength today. Modern Saudi society is focused on the values of puritanical Islamic beliefs. While there are elements of Arab nationalism in this Saudi belief structure, they are bound by the traditions ingrained in Saudi society. As a result, most advocates of reform must work through the Saudi royal family, the government, and the Kingdom's technocrats. In fact, it is this elite that has led virtually all of the Kingdom's efforts to modernize and reform Saudi politics and society.

As one experienced observer, who served as a senior U.S. diplomat in Saudi Arabia, puts it,

> Challenges to Saudi Arabia's rulers come . . . from an Islamic environment that the rulers themselves have created, shaped, and maintained. It is a remarkable Saudi phenomenon that a regime unrivalled across the Islamic world in its conservatism presides over a body politic that for the most part is even more conservative.
>
> Saudi society today is, and has been for several hundred years, built on the values of what we in the West call "Wahhabi" Islam. Relative to Islamic cultures elsewhere, that of the Saudi Kingdom is strict, even harsh, in its insistence on public observance of fundamental principles of Islam. Our own history has a weak parallel, the age of the Puritans, but the extent of Puritan control never matched that of "Wahhabi" Islam in Saudi Arabia. Within the Saudi environment—and while seeking to keep it intact—Saudi royals and western-educated elites and technocrats lead efforts to reform and modernize their society, politics, education and the infrastructure of modern global development.
>
> Within this environment too, there exists a culture that is inward-looking, traditional and insular, a culture itself challenged by world and regional events it cannot control or adequately understand. This is an environment that gives rise to shaykhs and men of religion who rebuke their leaders on Islamic grounds, and who assess the shortcomings of alien cultures by a peculiarly high standard of Islamic principle. It is an environment where young men who are true believers strain to see threats from outside through the lens of a strict Islam, and then dare to fight accordingly, even while violating precepts observed by Muslims everywhere.

WORKING WITHIN THE SYSTEM: THE ROLE OF SAUDI "MODERNIZERS"

Saudi Arabia does have its "modernizers." Many Saudi princes, educators, technocrats, businessmen, Western-educated citizens, and more progressive Islamists have favored more rapid social change than has been possible in the face of opposition from Saudi Islamic extremists and conservatives who can influence large elements of Saudi society and have often delayed progress. Such elements in Saudi society differ significantly over their vision of Saudi Arabia's future, but most reject an ultraconservative or radical interpretation of Islam. They support educational and economic reform and Saudi Arabia's opening to the outside world—both Arab and

Western spheres. Many favor the creation of a more representative and active majlis and the eventual creation of an elected assembly. Many complain about nepotism and the abuse of power and legal rights by members of the royal family, other leading families, and officials.

Many also support the liberalization of current religious restraints on subjects such as commerce, the role of women, and social practices. For example, modernists and reformers petitioned the king at the time of the Gulf War, and Saudi women have carried out protests for women's rights by driving their own cars.

Yet most Saudi "modernizers"—who include significant numbers of deeply religious Saudis—recognize that Saudi religious practices and traditions can only evolve slowly over time. A few businessmen, technocrats, and Western-educated professionals have been arrested, or have had difficulties with the authorities, for such activities. However, such incidents are relatively rare. Most "modernizers" understand that the royal family and Saudi technocrats offer a far more practical evolutionary road toward change than opposition to the regime. Intelligent "modernizers" understand they are in a minority and must work within the system.

THE CHARACTER AND IMPACT OF SAUDI PURITANISM

The Islamic practices of the vast majority of Saudis are puritanical, involve a conservative form of Hanbali jurisprudence, and are bound by conservative tribal social customs. The Saudi interpretation of Islam and the actions Saudi clergy reflect the teaching of Muhammad ibn Abd al-Wahhab, a conservative and fundamentalist reformer who reshaped the worship and social practices of virtually all elements of Sunni society in the mid-1700s. Saudis generally regard Muhammad ibn Abd al-Wahhab as a *Mujaddid*, a kind of key reformer called for in Islamic Hadith (tradition). The Mujaddid is a voice that God sends at the beginning of each century to call on Muslims to return to the true revelations of the Koran and bring moral restoration to the Umma (Muslim community).

Abd al-Wahhab's descendents—the al-Shaykh—still have great influence in the clergy as well as in managing the pilgrimage (Hajj) and pious endowments (Awqaf). They have also sometimes played a role in shaping the policies of key ministries including education and justice. Abd al-Wahhab's teachings about Islamic practices and legal interpretations dominate the legal system and must be considered in shaping virtually every major public policy decision. Although Saudis generally do not use the name of a religious teacher or individual like Muhammad ibn Abd al-Wahhab to describe such religious practices—in fact al-Wahhab is one of the ninety-nine names of Allah—this has led outsiders to use the term Wahhabi Islam or "Wahhabism."[1]

Putting Saudi Wahhabi and Salafi Beliefs into Perspective

Saudi Muslims think of themselves as "Muwahiddun" or "Unitarians," Muslims who believe Allah is the one and only god and is the only legitimate derivation of correct Islamic beliefs. This consensus has been a basic part of Saudi society and culture since the founding of the first al-Saud state. Mainstream Wahhabi practices act as a binding force that holds Saudi Arabia together. Saudi Arabia is generally a remarkably nonviolent and polite society, where hospitality and good manners are the rule in dealing with foreigners as well as fellow Saudis. Mainstream Wahhabi preaching and thought rarely advocates the use of violence or terrorism in the name of politicoreligious disputes. The only major exception has been Saudi support for the Palestinian cause in the Second Intifada.

Even mainstream "Wahhabi" religious practices limit critical aspects of the Kingdom's progress, such as modernizing the financial services sector, improving the quality of education, and expanding the role of women in the Saudi economy. Religious practices affect human rights and the modernization of the legal system as well. While there are progressive Wahhabi thinkers, there are others who find it difficult to think beyond the concerns of the Islam and Arab world, or accommodate the realities of modern science and technology. The Saudi inability to come to grips with population growth and birth rates is also at least partly a result religious conservatism.

More significantly, there are darker undercurrents in Saudi religious practices that advocate religious hatred and help encourage terrorism. Some Saudi sermons preach hatred and xenophobia, and some Saudi textbooks and religious books attack Christians and Jews and the practices of other Muslims. The fact that they rarely motivate the ordinary Saudi reader into action is no excuse for their existence—any more than there is an excuse for the similarly bigoted forms of Judaism or Christianity.

A minority of Saudi religious hard-liners and extremists go beyond words and either carry out terrorist and violent acts or support and fund them. Most such extremists not only are hostile to the outside world and nonbelievers, they oppose the al-Saud regime and virtually all efforts by Saudi technocrats and businessmen to modernize the Kingdom. They perceive the Saudi royal family as corrupt in religious as well as political and social terms, and as being hypocritical in its professed religious beliefs and claims of being the guardian of the Islamic holy places. They see Saudi technocrats and the more cosmopolitan members of the Saudi business community as near apostates from Islam and as being driven by Western or non-Islamic values. In fact, this minority of violent religious extremists currently poses the only serious political challenge to Saudi stability.

Many such extremists are strongly anti-Shi'ite, condemn many of the practices of Sunnis in other Islamic countries, and fear that there are vast Judeo-Christian conspiracies against Islam. For them, Western society is fundamentally corrupt and degrading, and leads Saudi society away from the true faith of Islam. It has spawned equally corrupt Arab secular political beliefs, all of which are betrayals of Islam regardless of whether they are right- or left-wing. To such extremists, the United States is a co-conspirator with a Zionist enemy that has seized the third-most important Islamic holy place—the Temple Mount or Haram al-Sharif. These extremists also believe the United States military is not securing Saudi Arabia but rather occupying it.

A number of different influences have helped politicize virtually all Saudi extremists and give them a potential broader base of public support. These influences include the Arab-Israeli conflict, the social costs of changes like hyper-urbanization, the educational system, the failure of Arab socialism, and nationalism. They also include the long history of militancy that helped make the Ikwan such a potent military force under Ibn Saud as well as the kind of marginal movement that led to the attack on the Grand Mosque in Mecca.

Other influences include outside groups like the Muslim Brotherhood, and the example of Khomeini and the Iranian revolution. More recently, they include the constant images in Arab media of Palestinian suffering as a result of the Second Intifada and the continuing U.S. and British military presence in Saudi Arabia since the Gulf War and Liberation of Kuwait.

As has been the case in many other Islamic countries, the Saudi regime has inadvertently helped support such extremism even while it has made efforts to suppress it. The continuing need of the Saudi monarchy to maintain its political legitimacy by stressing its role as an "Islamic government" has led the royal family to try to prove itself to be a worthy inheritor of the Wahhabi legacy by fostering religious education and by funding Islamic charities and Arab causes. Far too often, it has done so while paying little attention to what such educators, charities and causes are actually doing.

Fortunately for Saudi Arabia, most Saudi extremists have had little unity, although some have formed loose organizational links and a few have created formal organizations and even serious terrorist bodies like al-Qaeda. Most leading extremist Ulema do little more than give sermons that attack the royal family and Saudi government, often by indirection. Extremist believers circulate cassettes, faxes, or sermons and other writings, or communicate through the Internet. However, while such extremists often test the limits of government tolerance, only a few have even gone on to plan or commit acts of violence.

It is difficult to define the goals of Saudi Islamic extremists in terms of the practical changes they wish to make in the Saudi government, society, and economy. There are many diverse voices, and most focus on what they oppose rather than what they want. However, many extremists do believe that the nation's wealth should be shared more broadly and that religious charities and taxes should be a key factor shaping Saudi society. Most claim that a true return to a "pure" faith requires laws and social standards that are far more stringent and demanding than are now the practice in Saudi society.

Saudi extremists also divide over how to deal with the West. Some openly reject the West. Others are willing to exploit Western concerns for human rights and "democracy" in seeking their own freedom of action without showing any concern for the rights of their opposition. The end result is more a matrix of critical ultraconservative voices, whose key members are known to each other and to most religious Saudis, than a coherent movement.

Charity and Extremism: The Flow of Money

Osama bin Laden has shown all too clearly that the impact of Saudi religious thought can lead to extremism and violence outside Saudi Arabia as well as within it. However, once again, there is a need for perspective. The poorly controlled flow of Saudi money outside the Kingdom has probably done more to influence Islamic extremism outside Saudi Arabia than has Saudi religious thinking and missionary efforts. A clear distinction must also be made between the deliberate Saudi support of Islamic extremism and violence and the fact that many Saudis have contributed to what appeared to be Islamic charities or gave money to what they felt were legitimate Islamic causes—such as the struggles in Afghanistan, Bosnia, and Kosovo—without knowing the true character of the groups involved or where their money ultimately went.

One of the strengths of Saudi culture also proved to be a weakness. Saudi Arabia has a long tradition of public and private charity, much of which is given informally on a personal basis. Those Muslims that can afford it have a religious obligation to charity called "Zakat," which is a nominal 2.5% of their income-producing assets, but their actual contribution is often far higher and sometimes closer to 10%. In the case of public figures, charity is combined with patronage, and those in need or seeking funding for good causes make constant personal requests. In many cases, the money is given with minimal investigation, if any. Virtually any type of personal contact, petition, or reference is often enough. In the case of senior princes and wealthy businessmen, major contributions are often made to religious organizations outside Saudi Arabia, and the Kingdom has long been seen as the key source of Islamic charity, particularly to conservative Islamic causes. These customs have aided many Saudis and legitimate causes outside the Kingdom. At the same time, they have made it easy to exploit the situation, and Saudi giving to charities, and freedom fighters in Afghanistan, Bosnia, Kosovo, and the Second Intifada has blurred the often uncertain distinction between freedom fighter and terrorist.

Very senior Saudis privately admit that the Ministry of the Interior, Foreign Ministry, and Saudi intelligence community failed to properly characterize many of the "Islamic" causes that have received Saudi money. Even funds transferred to very reputable causes like the Saudi Red Crescent seem to have been misused in some cases. The Muslim World League is a heavily funded group whose missionary efforts are reported to have moved money to elements of al-Qaeda and different extremists groups like Gamiat Islamiya and the Islamic Jihad in Egypt, and Abu Sayyaf in the Philippines. Money also went to causes with hard-line or extremist elements like the Muslim brotherhood in Egypt and Jordan or Hamas in the Gaza.

Even though the Saudi government put strict controls on Osama bin Laden's overt sources of funding after 1994, senior Saudi officials admit that money from members of the royal family and senior Saudi businessmen went to charities and causes that were extremist in character. The Saudi government did not begin to properly analyze and control the flow of funds to movements like the Taliban and extremist groups in South Asia, central Asia, and the rest of the world until 1998. Even after 1988, the flow of Islamic charity and funds, even from royal offices like those of King Fahd, was allocated with remarkable carelessness to what was really being funded—not only in terms of extremism, but in terms of whether the money was properly being spent and managed and actually served the claimed purpose.

At the same time, at least some Saudi businessmen did fund such organizations knowing they were extremist or violent in character. The problem of controlling such funds was made still worse by the fact that so much Saudi private capital is held and invested outside Saudi Arabia and is beyond the government's control.

Most Islamic Puritanism and Extremism Is Not "Wahhabism"

The West, however, has shown signs of its own form of extremism in reacting to the situation. Some Western writing since September 11, 2001, has blamed Saudi Arabia for most of the region's Islamic fundamentalism, and has used the term Wahhabi carelessly to describe all such movements. In fact, most such extremism is not based on Saudi Islamic beliefs. It is based on a much broader stream of thought in Islam, known as the Salafi interpretation—which literally means a return to Islam's original state—and by a long tradition of movements in Islam that call for islah (reform) and tajdid (renewal).

Blaming Saudi beliefs or "Wahhabism" for the views and actions of most of today's Salafi extremists is a little like blaming Calvin for today's Christian extremists or Elijah for today's Jewish extremists. In practice, it is more modern Islamist thinkers like the Egyptians Sayyid Qutb and

Hassam al-Banna (the founder of the Moslem Brotherhood) who laid the foundation of modern Islamic puritanical politics and who called for Jihad (struggle) to achieve their goals. Other figures like Aiman al-Zawahiri and Muhammad al-Farag helped create movements like the Egyptian Islamic Jihad and fostered an approach to violence that helped shape Islamic extremism in Afghanistan—although some Saudi clerics like Sheikh Abdulaziz bin Baz played a role.

No one can ignore the fact that Osama bin Laden is a Saudi and al-Qaeda has Saudi roots. Nevertheless, outside Islamists like Sheikh Abdullah Azzam—a Jordanian-born Palestinian and a bitter, violent critic of the Saudi regime—did more to shape the beliefs of men like Osama bin Laden than mainstream Wahhabi thinking. So did figures like Sheikh Omar Abdul-Rahman, who founded the Egyptian Islamic Group and helped transform modern Salafi beliefs into Islamic terrorism.[2]

The use of the word "Wahhabi" to describe Islamic extremist movements in other countries is equally misleading. The Deobandi seminary movement in Pakistan, and parties like the Jamiat-ul-Ulema-e-Islam (Party of Religious Scholarship) did more to shape Islamic extremism in Afghanistan and Pakistan than Wahhabi missionaries. While Saudi and U.S. money made much of the Afghan resistance possible, the Pakistani ISI controlled the flow of much of this money and helped fund Afghan extremists like Gulbuddin Hekmatyar and his Hizb-e-Islami. Pakistani intelligence then provided direct Pakistani support to the Taliban, although the initial rise of the movement led by Mullah Muhammad Omar Akhund seems to have been a largely Afghan phenomena with little ties to any outside Salafi movements.

Other Salafi movements with few ties to Saudi Wahhabi beliefs and practices have arisen in Yemen. These have included the Islamic Army of Aden, led by Zein Abu Bakr al-Mihdar (Abu Hassan). There have been Kurdish Salafi groups like the Jund al-Islam (Ansar al-Islam). The Syrian Muslim Brothers have been a significant political force in Syria in the past and are still active. Sunni Palestinian religious groups are equally independent of Saudi influence, as are most Sudanese and Somali groups and key figures like Hassan al-Turabi and the Sudanese Islamic People's Congress.

Iran's various hard-line Shi'ite groups have backed Saudi Shi'ites in carrying out terrorist acts in Saudi Arabia, but such movements have no ties to Saudi Sunni extremism. The most violent Islamic extremist groups in the world—Algeria's Armed Islamic Group (AIG) and Salafist Group for Call and Combat (GSPC)—are homegrown products of Algeria's corrupt military junta and violent domestic political traditions. Virtually every country in central Asia has its own Salafi movements and extremists, and while many have benefited from Saudi Arabia's careless funding of Islamic causes and charities, none are Wahhabi in any meaningful sense of being tied to Saudi teaching and tradition; virtually all of the Madrassas in South and central Asia teach interpretations and practices that differ from mainstream

Wahhabi teaching. Lumping all of these diverse elements together is like calling all Protestants Baptists.

Similarly, the fact some Saudi money has gone to Islamic extremists—both indirectly and directly—scarcely means that Saudi Arabia is the only or even principal source of such funding. The other Southern Gulf states have been equally careless in managing their charitable efforts in foreign countries and the flow of funds to "charitable" causes. A great deal of money from Muslims around the world that was intended to aid Muslims in Kosovo and Bosnia ended up in the hands of bin Laden and other terrorist/extremist groups. Most of the extremist groups in North Africa are largely self-financing, and drug money and Iranian and Pakistani government funds and arms have played a major role in supporting Islamic violence in Afghanistan and central and south Asia. The flow of money to the Palestinian cause since the beginning of the Second Intifada also presents the problem that for most Arabs and Muslims the Palestinian cause is legitimate, as are violent Palestinian tactics, while Israel is seen as a violent occupying power that attacks Palestinian civilians. This inevitably means that most Muslims and Arabs—including Saudis—do not see movements like Hamas, the Palestinian Islamic Jihad, or the Fatah Hawks as terrorists but rather as freedom fighters.

Islamic Extremism and Saudi Youth

It is difficult to discuss the level of support that Islamic extremists have achieved among Saudi youth without resorting to speculation and stereotypes. For example, it is possible to divide Saudi youth into groups like those who enjoy the favors and the success of elder generations and young Saudis who lack such opportunities, but it is far from clear that those who become Islamic extremists do so because of their lack of access to advancement and opportunities in society. One must also be careful about confusing words with actions. Talk is far more common than action among Saudi youth and some degree of verbal support for extremism is almost inevitable given the challenges and frustrations facing a new generation that is seeking to forge its own identity.

Figures like Osama bin Laden have shown, however, that some Saudi youths are influenced by the current lack of any compelling secular ideological and political alternatives in an Arab world where Nasserism, socialism and Marxism have been such conspicuous failures, and where Western democracy and capitalism seem to deal with the Arab world largely in terms of self-interest and material values. Another is the feeling of frustration and impotence caused by an ongoing Arab-Israeli conflict. It is also evident that for a growing number of Saudi youths, "traditional" Islam is the only ideological answer that society offers to a lack of clear career opportunities, the alienation produced by social change, and the search for a cultural identity—although it is far from clear that they agree on what "traditional" Islam really means or that what they want is really "traditional."

As the following chapters show, the Saudi "patriarchal bargain" is slowly breaking down in the face of declining oil wealth. There is also little doubt that a growing number of Saudi youths perceive the royal family to be over-privileged, lacking in social conscience, and corrupt. These attitudes are symbolized by the comments of one Saudi youth, who stated, "There is no consistency in the law, and penalties that are set should be respected. The satellite [dish] is illegal but the king has the biggest satellite [dish] in Mecca." Another youth commented, "They [the government] should have more fear of God. On the one hand they pray but in the other they pick up the bottle."[3]

Education and mass communications are transforming public opinion and turning it into a growing force. Resentment of the Second Intifada, Israel, U.S. support of Israel, and the perceived U.S. indifference to the suffering of the Iraqi people are serious popular issues in Saudi Arabia. Since the spring of 2002, they have led to student-led boycotts of U.S. products. There also have been scattered popular demonstrations that the Ministry of Interior has been forced to tolerate because of the depth of popular feeling.

At the same time, Crown Prince Abdullah is seen as a leader in the ef-fort to halt Palestinian suffering, and these issues do not necessarily make Saudis anti-regime or even broadly anti-American. It is far from clear that any significant percentage of Saudi youth is so deeply alienated that they see violent and extreme political forms of Islam as offering answers to their economic problems. Surveys of Saudi public opinion have uncertain cred-ibility, particularly when the questions do not distinguish clearly between Islamic extremism and hostility to U.S. foreign policy. The failure of the American press to understand this point has contributed to at least some of the journalism that grossly exaggerates Saudi popular hostility to the United States and sympathy for terrorist actions. This tendency is reinforced by a peculiar brand of Israeli right-wing and U.S. neoconservative scholar-ship that seems dedicated to finding the worst examples of Saudi extrem-ism and turning them into portrayals of mainstream Saudi thought—a form of analysis that often acts as if the Second Intifada did not exist and did not influence Saudi opinion.

Zogby International conducted what seems to be a highly credible sur-vey of some 700 Saudis in the spring of 2002—with good distribution in terms of age and background—and did so at a time when the impact of both the backlash from the Second Intifada and U.S. treatment of Saudi Arabia after September 11 were having a major impact. The poll found that 71% were still favorable to U.S. science and technology, 58% were favor-able to U.S. education, 53% were favorable to U.S. products, 52% were favorable to U.S. freedom and democracy, and 54% were favorable to U.S.

movies and television. It also found that although a majority (51%) of the Saudis had hostile feelings toward the American people, only 23% supported the U.S.-led effort to liberate Kuwait, and only 30% supported the U.S. war on terrorism.

Some 69% of the Saudis polled did state that the Palestinian issue was the most important issue to them (with little or no change by age group), and 79% of those polled indicated they would be more favorable to the United States if it were to apply pressure for the creation of an independent Palestinian state (with a clear emphasis on a peace settlement over Israel's destruction).

These figures did not, however, reflect any polarization in favor of Islamic extremism or against the West among younger Saudis. The poll found that 54% of the Saudis in the age group of eighteen to twenty-nine were still favorable toward the American people, versus 45% in the age group from thirty to forty-nine, and only 35% in the age group from fifty to sixty-four. Some 54% of the Saudis in the age group of eighteen to twenty-nine indicated that they would be favorable toward the United States if it consistently applied its stated foreign policy values versus 39% in the age group from thirty to forty-nine, and 38% in the age group from fifty to sixty-four. Furthermore, 37% of the Saudis in the age group of eighteen to twenty-nine were favorable to the United States' war on terrorism, versus 29% in the age group from thirty to forty-nine and only 14% in the age group from fifty to sixty-four.[4] This is scarcely evidence of strong Islamist tendencies or a youth that is more alienated than its parents.

An organization called NFO Middle East and Africa made another credible survey of media and market priorities of 3,150 Saudis in thirteen cities in March and April 2002 that reflected an evolving Saudi society with a similar focus on domestic concerns. It found that virtually all urban Saudis had access to satellite TV and that 31% said they had online access to the Internet, but that only 12% watched highly polarized channels like Al-Jazeera; the figures for those who thought of themselves as modernists were 8%, while those who thought of themselves as disaffected were 8%. Some 76% felt that "adhering to religious values was central to their personal beliefs and ways of living," but this did not mean alignment with Islamic extremism. Out of the 24% of the population that were youths, half indicated they were happy and comfortable living with their families, while most of those who called themselves disaffected were concerned with fights with their father, a lack of freedom for women, and issues like education and marriage.[5]

Those polled indicated that they still strongly supported Saudi rather than Western values and morality. They did so by 60% to 40%—although 64% are worried about Saudi youth turning to Western values. Only 33% of all Saudis who regarded themselves as "disaffected" felt that religious observance was as important as it was fifty years ago, versus 42% of all Saudis,

56% of whom thought of themselves as conservatives, and 69% who viewed themselves as "conformists." Some 38% indicated they had shifted purchasing patterns away from U.S. products, but almost all did so because of the Second Intifada. Somewhat ironically, 98% of self-described "feminists"(12% of those sampled) indicated they always listened to and respected their fathers' opinions, and 77% felt their father or husband should be the head of the family and make important decisions, although only 12% felt a woman's place was in the home with her family, versus 74% of all Saudis. If these polls are representative, they portray a Saudi population that is far less polarized and divided than that in many Western countries, rather than a population deeply concerned with most political issues or a youth deeply concerned with Islamic extremism.

Nevertheless, it is all too clear that Saudi religious extremists have gathered significant support among a large enough minority of younger Saudis to create a serious extremist and terrorist problem. Some experts feel this is particularly true in the areas around Buraida and Riyadh, although there is little hard data to support this. Other experts feel such support is greater among Saudis who had only recently become urbanized, who lived in the Najd, and/or lived outside the mainstream economy. Yet, still other experts note that many extremists are descendants of established families, come from urban areas like Riyadh, are well educated, and/or are educated in secular rather than religious subjects.

It is also clear that the Saudi government long underestimated the seriousness of extremist feelings among Saudi youth, and was slow to address the broader educational, social, and economic problems created by its "youth explosion." If anything, the government made the gap between Islam and modernism worse by encouraging a type of Islamic education that did little to prepare youth for economic reality and that allowed the teaching of relatively radical and hard-line views of Islam.

It is hardly surprising, therefore, that there have been an increasing number of alienated youth and student organizations since the early 1990s. Many circulate literature and poems that are far more critical of the government and royal family than all but the most extreme religious figures. Some have organized informal cells and have received paramilitary or terrorist training in Afghanistan, Iran, Lebanon, and elsewhere.

At the time, the numbers of true Saudi extremists seems small. Senior Saudi intelligence officials made an estimate following the Al-Khobar bombing, however, that at least 12,000 young Saudi men had spent some time training or serving as paramilitary extremists or "Afghani," and estimated that the number associated with such activities might have gone as high as 25,000. A few of these youth groups have received funding from wealthy and sympathetic Saudi businessmen. Osama bin Laden is the most obvious case in point, although his family has disowned him due to his extremism.

Trying to Co-opt Islamic Extremism: The Rising at the Grand Mosque

Islamic extremism at the margins of Saudi society is scarcely a new problem. The al-Saud family rose to power by exploiting extremism against the Turks, and then against rival families in what became Saudi Arabia. King Abd al-Aziz carried out most of his conquests with a religiously inspired paramilitary force of Bedouin called the Ikhwan, and then had to actively suppress extremist factions that turned against him. Abd al-Aziz carefully controlled the Saudi clergy throughout his reign. His successors have had to place a number of religious figures under arrest over the years and suppress several small extremist movements.

The most dramatic postwar example of Saudi problems with extremists before the rise of Osama bin Laden was the "uprising" at the Grand Mosque in Mecca that took place in November 1979. Armed Islamists seized the mosque and forced the Saudi government to respond in ways that resulted in weeks of fighting and a siege of the Mosque that cost 177 rebel and 127 government lives. Nearly all of the 500-odd insurgents came from clandestine groups formed within the most puritanical Wahhabi tribes, such as the Otaibas and Qahtani, but the uprising also had support from individuals who had earlier shown sympathy for Nasser or radical Arab socialist movements.[6]

The insurgents were led by Juhaiman ibn Muhammed ibn Saif al-Otaiba, a would-be Mahdi. Al-Otaiba's grandfather was an Ikhwan warrior who fought against King Abd al-Aziz and what he perceived the king stood for. Al-Otaiba accused King Fahd of corruption and reliance on the West, and attempted to challenge the royal family by forcibly overtaking the sacred mosque in Mecca.[7] Al-Otaiba, however, was scarcely a true "Wahhabi," and the vast majority of conservative tribesmen and clergy immediately opposed him. He failed to win substantial popular support, partly because he chose to occupy such a holy site, and also because he had no credible goals and sought to give himself an absurd religious status he had not earned through any form of preaching or scholarship. If anything, the Saudi government had to prevent traditional Wahhabis from carrying out their own attacks to free the mosque.

Nevertheless, the incident led the government to give more power to Saudi Islamists and to emphasize its commitment to Islamic education and the enforcement of strict Wahhabi social practices. The government did not change the Saudi curriculum and teaching practices to make them more Islamic and conservative, but it did fail to continue to modernize them. It also kept women's education segregated and allowed lower teaching standards at the primary and secondary level. It gave the religious authorities more money, and there was "greater religious surveillance over the population, more power was granted to the Mutawwa'in [the Saudi "police" of public virtue], new constraints were placed on mobility and freedom of and on the process of reform."[8]

Islamic Extremism and the Failure of Co-option in the 1980s and 1990s

Islamic extremism remained a problem throughout the 1980s, despite the government's efforts to co-opt Saudi Islamists and the powerful distractions provided by oil wealth. Saudi involvement in the war in Afghanistan had a powerful impact, as did the revolution in Iran. Although the revolution was Shi'ite, and led by clergy whose beliefs and practices differed sharply from those of Saudi Arabia, the revolution did show that a religious minority could seize power. The Arab-Israeli conflict provided another source of continuing tension.

The dissolution of the Soviet Union discredited the already-weak socialist and Marxist movements in Saudi Arabia. While the failures of secular Arab nationalism throughout the Arab world made it steadily less attractive since Nasser's defeat in 1967, groups such as the Arabian Peninsula People's Union and Voice of the Vanguard had never been a particularly important force in Saudi politics. However, the combined impact of the defeat of Saddam Hussein, the collapse of most Marxist governments, and Egyptian-Syrian cooperation with the United States left few places for oppositionists besides Islamic extremism.

The visible presence of Western forces in Saudi Arabia during and after the Gulf War gave Islamic extremists new reason to attack the "corrupt" Western influence over the Saudi government. After the Gulf War, low oil revenues and massive payments to other nations for the cost of the war reduced the government's ability to make welfare payments and the Saudi economy's ability to create new jobs.

Broadening the base of education, combined with population growth and declining per capita income, meant that younger Saudis with better overall levels of education had to accept progressively less-prestigious and well-paid positions. Furthermore, the conflict between the modernists and traditionalists was fueled by the spread of nearly 1 million satellite TV receivers, some 20 million VCRs, and growing use of the Internet. Censorship and government control over the media became far less effective, and new Arab media appeared that constantly attacked the West and Israel while the growing availability of Western media led to growing religious and conservative protests. These forces led various Islamic extremists to heighten their demands that Saudi Arabia conform to their particular definition of "Islam." At the same time, they made the Saudi royal family and traditional and mainstream religious leaders, political, social, and economic forces that were changing Saudi society.

The Saudi government again responded by trying to defuse the rise of Islamic extremism in reaction to these events by increasing official and popular adherence to strict religious law and custom and by strengthening the role of the religious police. Like the government's longstanding failure to address the problems in the educational systems, such actions sometimes helped give the government some temporary support—but each new accommodation of extremist demands ultimately tended to strengthen the hands of extremists.

The Saudi government made things worse in the process by turning a blind eye to the increasingly violent and rigid actions of the religious police (Mutawaa'in) and related actions by the civil police. The Mutawaa'in have always been a problem—often going beyond religious custom and enforcing arbitrary interpretations of religious law. After the Gulf War, however, they increasingly were allowed to abuse women and foreigners and detain and sometimes beat and torture Saudi men. There were many sudden raids of private homes on the basis of suspicion alone, and use was made of "fallaqa," or beating the soles of the feet, as well as the systematic beating of the body.

Although the situation improved somewhat after 1996, the Mutawaa'in continued to detain suspects for more than the legal maximum of twenty-four hours for violations of behavior standards. There were reports of sleep deprivation and torture. While Saudi legal procedures required that a police officer accompany the Mutawaa'in before the latter made an arrest, this requirement was often ignored. The Saudi government tolerated abuses by the volunteer auxiliaries of the Mutawaa'in and sometimes encouraged interpretations of Shari'a—or Islamic law—in civil cases that were designed to appease religious extremists rather than enforce the traditions of Islam.

The Saudi government did show, however, that it could get the support of key clerics in dealing with extremists when it really needed such support. One example was the statement of Sheik Abdulaziz bin Abdallah Abd al-Shaykh, the grand mufti of Saudi Arabia, on April 21, 2001, that Islam prohibits suicide terrorist attacks. The Saudi government clearly encouraged him to make this statement, and he issued it despite the fact that it provoked considerable opposition in the Arab world.[9] Some senior Saudi clerics—such as Sheikh Abdulaziz bin Baz and Muhammad Bin'Uthaimin—had blessed Palestinian suicide operations in the past and had defended such actions as an act of martyrdom permitted by jihad (istishhad).[10] Their rationale was the assumption that all non-Muslims are infidels and Israel is a foreign entity in Muslim lands.

EDUCATION AS A SELF-INFLICTED WOUND

In retrospect, the most serious failure that resulted from the government's efforts at co-option throughout the 1980s and 1990s was its failure to set proper educational standards and carry out effective educational reform. In the process, co-option became a self-inflicted wound.

Many aspects of the Saudi curriculum were not fully modernized after the 1960s. Some Saudi textbooks taught Islamic tolerance while others condemned Jews and Christians. Anti-Christian and anti-Jewish passages remained in grade school textbooks that use rhetoric that was little more than hate literature. The same was true of more sophisticated books issued by the Saudi Ministry of Islamic Practices. Even the English-language Korans available in the hotels in the Kingdom added parenthetical passages condemning Christians and Jews that did not appear in any English-language editions of the Koran outside Saudi Arabia.[11] The wound such co-option inflicted on Saudi Arabia was made worse by the fact that it had the practical impact of encouraging students to pursue patterns of education for which there were no real jobs. It also perpetuated the illusion that schools that emphasized religious instruction, low quality rote learning, a poor curriculum and teaching materials, and poor instruction could use faith to substitute for economic realities. Inadequate education added to the problems in attracting investment and modernizing the economy that I describe in the following chapters. It also made it more difficult for the Saudi government to reduce the Saudi birth rate, make fully productive use of female labor, reduce dependence on foreign labor, encourage labor mobility among the natives of the GCC, and integrate the economy of the Southern Gulf.

The resulting problem with Islamists interacted with other forces such as pressures on the Saudi budget. Until the events of September 11, 2001, forced the government to face these problems, the government neglected the quality of education and focused on "quantity" and the need to deal with massive increases in the number of students. The need to rapidly increase the number and size of schools also led to a decline in the quality of the facilities involved, particularly for female students. Far too much teaching was left to relatively low-quality instructors; and underqualified or over-ideological young Saudis were hired as teachers in an effort to create jobs. At the same time, the system continued to focus on Islam without proper concern for developing career-related skills and training the labor-force to work. The Ulema were allowed to increase their influence over the curriculum, and to encourage more and more students to pursue Islamic studies of a kind that offered few real-world career opportunities.

The Saudi domestic educational system not only relied on dated teaching materials, but also relied on dated methods, and particularly on memorization and rote learning through the completion of high school. The focus of learning is on memorizing the Koran and Hadith (the sayings and examples of the Prophet), and not on problem solving or creative thought. Approximately one-third of the curriculum is religious, one-third is Arabic, and one-third covers other subjects—often paying limited attention to the sciences and business. As a result, much of the teaching at Saudi universities has to be remedial, and some universities even fail to put proper emphasis on independent reasoning and problem solving.

These problems are not apparent from Saudi Arabia's favorable educational statistics or budget, or from contacts with Saudi Arabia's sophisticated, Western-educated technocrats, academics, businessmen, journalists, and princes. Saudi Arabia spends roughly 7% of its GDP on education, or roughly the same percentage as the world's high-income countries. It also claims a pupil to teacher ratio of 14:1 in its primary schools, one of the lowest ratios in the world.[12] Nevertheless, Saudi education lags in quality and relevance, and does so at the secondary-school and university level, as well as at the primary level.

There has been some change since September 2000. The Ministry of Education has been given responsibility for educating both women and men, and has begun to emphasize educational quality and to reform and restructure Saudi education accordingly. The fact remains, however, that much of Saudi Arabia's leadership elite is willing to admit that Saudi education is failing to meet the country's needs, but is unwilling to take the required action.

A royal study group that was formed after September 11 described some 5% of Saudi teaching material as clearly having such content, and at least another 10% as "suspect." It also found that many teachers were of uncertain quality and taught their own hard-line views. It found that many aspects of Saudi teaching materials and methods did encourage extremism and it also found that even many Saudis with Ph.D.s from Saudi universities received a relatively low-grade Islamic education.

Nevertheless, the Kingdom is still failing to create a native-educated elite that is competitive in skills with the output of secondary schools and universities in East Asia and other leading developing countries. Far too few students receive the kind of education that trains them to play a leading role in Saudi Arabia's economy. The futility of such education is exemplified by a glut of graduates in Islamic studies whose degrees are not taken seriously by Islamic scholars in other Arab countries and who have often become the opponents of the government that has educated them.[13]

MAKING WOMEN PART OF THE PROBLEM, RATHER THAN PART OF THE SOLUTION

The impact of Saudi Islamic practices and social customs on the role of women presents another problem for internal stability and development. The role of women in Saudi society does not present the same problems as dealing with young males in terms of Islamic extremism and political unrest. However, there is a growing gap between the ongoing education of women and the effort to provide a more meaningful role for women in the Saudi economy. Women have the right to own property and are entitled to financial support from their husbands or male relatives. They account for roughly 20% to 25% of the commercial registrations in the Kingdom and they inherit a large portion of the nation's private wealth. They also have access to free education through the university level, although teaching is always segregated from that of men.

As noted earlier, women make up 58% of all university graduates in a male-dominated society, although they are excluded from studying such subjects as engineering, journalism, and architecture. Men are freely able to study overseas. In theory, women may do so only if accompanied by a spouse or an immediate male relative, although some young women in Western-educated families are simply escorted to the West and then study on their own.

The U.S. State Department's report on human rights indicates that women are subject to discrimination in Islamic law, which stipulates that daughters receive only half the amount of inheritance awarded to their brothers. In a Shari'a court, a woman's testimony does not carry the same weight as that of a man. Also, in a Shari'a court, the testimony of one man equals that of two women. Although Islamic law permits polygamy, it is becoming less common. Islamic law enjoins a man to treat each wife equally, but in practice such equality is left to the discretion of the husband. Some women participate in al-Mesyar (or "short daytime visit") marriages, where the women relinquish their legal rights to financial support and nighttime cohabitation. Additionally, the husband is not required to inform his other wives of the marriage, and the children have no inheritance rights. The government places greater restrictions on women than on men regarding marriage to non-Saudis and non-Muslims.

Women must demonstrate legally specified grounds for divorce, while men may divorce without giving cause. If divorced or widowed, a woman normally may keep her children until they become a specified age: seven years for boys, nine years for girls. Children over these ages are awarded to the divorced husband or the deceased husband's family. Foreign women are often prevented by their former husbands from visiting their children after divorce.

There are no active women's rights groups. Women, including foreigners, may not legally drive motor vehicles and are restricted in their use of public facilities when they are not accompanied by a mahram (relative with whom marriage is prohibited). Thus, women risk arrest by the Mutawaa'in for riding in a vehicle driven by a male who is not an employee or a close male relative. In addition, women may not be admitted to a hospital for medical treatment without the consent of their male relative. By law and custom, women may not undertake domestic and foreign travel alone. The U.S. State Department has issued reports that women are no longer being issued business licenses for work in fields that might require them to supervise foreign workers, interact with male clients, or deal on a regular basis with government officials.

Despite these limitations, women do find ways to widen their role outside the home. In addition to separate businesses for women, women have made use of the Internet to manage and run their own businesses, and more than 20% of all commercial registrations are by women.[14] The Majlis al-

Shura has spent considerable time debating and studying the role of women, and now allows women to attend Shura Council meetings.[15] Women actually inherit more of the nation's wealth through matrilineal lines than Saudi law might indicate and hold a substantial amount of Saudi Arabia's private capital. Women are free to inherit and manage property, and women's banks play a growing role in handling assets, but they must do so through specialized financial institutions if they intend to keep their capital in Saudi Arabia.

Female participation in the labor force is still very low, even by Middle Eastern standards. Women earn less than men, and often do not get jobs that match their qualifications. However, the Saudi government has made efforts to create more jobs for women, and Crown Prince Abdullah has supported the expansion of women's rights in Saudi Arabia in spite of pressure from conservatives not to do so.[16]

All officially recognized workplaces are segregated, however, and women can only accept jobs in rural areas if they live with their families. Contact with male supervisors or clients is only allowed by telephone or fax machine and the level of segregation is growing worse as the level of female education improves. The end result is a series of cultural barriers that limit the productivity of what is becoming the best educated half of the Saudi workforce.

Regardless of how one feels about women's rights and feminism, it is far from clear that Saudi Arabia can afford to continue this sacrifice. There is no reason why Saudi society should treat women in exactly the same way as the West, but current Saudi restrictions on women have serious economic as well as social consequences. According to U.S. State Department estimates, women now make up only 5% of the workforce.[17] They do not receive the same salary and other benefits as men, and their primary goal in working is often simply to find some job or position in the private or public sector. Most employment opportunities for women are in education and health care, with lesser opportunity in business, philanthropy, banking, retail sales, and the media.[18]

RELIGIOUS EXTREMISM AND ACTIVE POLITICAL OPPOSITION

The government's problems with co-option have never meant that it has ignored the threat posed by active extremists. The ability of Saudi-based religious groups to threaten the Saudi regime has been sharply constrained by the actions the government has taken to repress their movements. Many have been arrested in the past and all such groups face future arrests if the government chooses to act. At the same time, the government has rarely overreacted with violence or imprisonment, and has preferred bribes, co-option, and "divide and conquer" tactics to repression. The regime recognizes that arrest and imprisonment often make martyrs of otherwise-weak opposition figures. If criticism is not highly provocative, the government does continue to monitor such figures but rarely takes stronger action.

The end result is that no individual religious figure or group has yet exhibited enough power inside Saudi Arabia to directly challenge the government, although there have been scattered acts of low-level violence and terrorism. Nevertheless, the overall mix of different Islamic extremist advocates and groups inside the Kingdom does pose a serious cumulative problem in terms of the Kingdom's foreign relations and internal security, and it is likely that new leaders and figures will emerge if Saudi Arabia's economic, social, and demographic problems are not dealt with by serious reform efforts.

Only tenuous data are available on the background, character, and number of Saudi Islamic oppositionists and extremists, and they differ sharply by individual and movement. The forces at work can be illustrated, however, by examining the case histories of several of the key Islamic opposition leaders and movements. These include both peaceful oppositionists and political movements such as the Committee for the Defense of Legitimate Rights (CDLR). They also include more serious threats like bin Laden and al-Qaeda. In both cases, external bases allowed such movements to act outside the range of Saudi control.

The CDLR was able to influence foreign relations between outside countries and Saudi Arabia by operating on foreign soil and using modern communications media. The CDLR also showed that it could exploit the West's concerns for human rights as a political tool. While it did not overtly support violence, it indirectly encouraged violence by showing its public "understanding" of terrorist incidents. It also found that it could simultaneously use extreme religious rhetoric and conduct political attacks on democracy and human rights in Arabic while hiding behind a shield of English rhetoric about its concern for democracy and human rights.

Osama bin Laden and al-Qaeda, showed all too clearly that they could use external bases and sanctuaries to create a serious threat both inside and outside the Kingdom. The damage done to the Saudi regime by attacks on the U.S. embassies in Kenya and Tanzania and the U.S.S. *Cole* had a powerful impact long before September 11. Each major incident of terrorism placed political pressure on the Saudi government and deeply embarrassed it.

These case studies also show that far more is involved than just Saudi security. The events of September 11, 2001, showed that terrorist attacks outside Saudi Arabia could exploit serious fault lines between Saudi Arabia and the United States, and between Saudi modernizers and traditionalists. Targeting U.S. and Western facilities, or facilities in which there is a joint Saudi and Western presence, allows extremists to use Western targets as a non-Islamic, non-Arab proxy for their ultimate target—the Saudi regime. The same is true of less violent attacks on Saudi modernization and reform that charge necessary change is non-Islamic or an affront to Saudi and Arab traditions. Attacking the West as an alien and foreign presence, exploiting the political backlash from the U.S. alliance with Israel, and claiming that the regime has become a U.S. tool that threatens the royal family's cultural and religious legitimacy. Such tactics offer extreme oppositionists their best hope for isolating the regime from the Saudi people.

Moderate Opposition: Religious Fundamentalism

Any examination of Saudi Islamist movements must recognize that religious opposition to the Saudi government can be loosely categorized into three major groups: intellectual nonviolent criticism, nonviolent political activism, and those individuals and groups that use violence to achieve their ends. Each group presents a different level of threat to the Saudi regime. Some forms of Saudi religious and fundamentalist dissent are clearly peaceful and legitimate. While the government (and the West) may not like them, opposition by nonviolent fundamentalists has the same legitimacy as any other form of peaceful opposition.

The "Memorandum of Advice" that 107 leading clerics circulated in 1992 symbolizes such opposition. The Memorandum called for the strict enforcement of Islamic law, the severing of relations with all non-Islamic countries and the West, and the punishment of all who gained wealth through illegal means, "whoever they are and without any exception of rank." It called for a Majlis al-Shura that was certain to be dominated by religious figures, a separate review body of Ulema to review every state regulation and edict to ensure compliance with the Shari'a, the creation of a religious supreme court with the power to invalidate any law or treaty found to be in conflict with the Shari'a, and making the Ulema a separate and co-equal branch of government with its own budget and sources of revenue.

The Saudi government quickly showed it could deal with such criticism, although scarcely using methods based on freedom of speech and pluralism. It responded to the memorandum by forcing other senior members of the Ulema to condemn it and by stepping up surveillance of the Ulema by the security forces. In December 1992, King Fahd dismissed seven elderly religious leaders from the Supreme Authority of Senior Scholars, the most senior clerical body in the country. He did so because they would not join the other ten members of the council in denouncing the "Memorandum of Advice."

King Fahd gave a speech the same month that attacked the use of mosques for political proselytizing. He stated, "The pulpit was only made for certain limited things." He then went on to attack the role of Iran and Islamic fundamentalists from other countries in supporting Islamic extremism:

> Two years ago, we started seeing things unfamiliar to us that were nonexistent here. . . . Do we accept that somebody comes to us from outside our country and directs us? No. . . . Has it come to the point where we depend on criticism and cassette tapes that do us no good? . . . We should not follow the path of foreign currents, foreign to our country.[19]

The Saudi government went on to follow a series of actions designed to handicap opposition movements and took additional measures to deal with extremist organizations. The first of these involved an effort to impose limits on the funding of Islamic extremist movements outside Saudi Arabia. Long before September 11, 2001, the government recognized that while private and public Saudi money had played a key role in supporting the Afghan freedom fighters in their struggle with the Soviet Union and in aiding the Muslims in Bosnia, it was now contributing to hard-line movements that opposed the Saudi regime and to violent Islamic extremist movements in Algeria, Egypt, Jordan, Tunisia, and the Sudan.

In April 1993, the Interior Ministry required Islamic civic and religious groups to obtain government authorization before soliciting funds. The ministry actively started to prevent the flow of funds to groups that may have used Islam as their rationale, but who sought political power—sometimes with Iranian and Sudanese support.[20] This effort had some success, but it focused on those who directly challenged the Saudi regime and other Arab governments, ignored other Arab movements, and was only lightly enforced.

In addition, the Saudi government made systematic arrests of individuals suspected of supporting terrorists and extremists.[21] For example, the government arrested Sheikh Salman al-Audah and Safr al-Hawali, two radical clerics, in 1994. It did so even though their detention incited a rare instance of open civil unrest in the northern city of Buraida and resulted in a large number of additional arrests. Many others were pressured, taken in for questioning, or briefly held in custody.

The government did find, however, that such measures had their limits. Hard-line religious opposition movements kept growing despite these measures, and the government could not control the flow of private money to elements of the Islamic opposition outside Saudi Arabia without far more drastic action than it was then willing to take. Many of the Saudis involved proved to have large foreign investments or handle large flows of transfers as part of their business. The government did not make the level of effort necessary to clearly identify which movements were legitimate religious efforts and which were cover organizations for more radical movements. It also failed to create the necessary intelligence effort or financial controls.[22]

Hard-line Peaceful Opposition: Sheikh Safar al-Hawali

A focus on well-known Saudi Islamists has its disadvantages. The situation in Saudi Arabia is fluid and constantly changing, and it is probably the Islamists no one has yet heard of that will emerge as the most significant future threat. Any abbreviated case study also tends to oversimplify the views and actions of those involved, as well as the religious and cultural issues being debated in the Kingdom. Nevertheless, Sheikh Safar bin Abd al-Rahman al-Hawali does provide a useful example of the challenges the government faces in dealing with peaceful opposition. Hawali was born in 1950 in the al-Baha region, south of Taif and comes from a minor, but reputable tribe. This, along with his credentials as an Islamic scholar, makes him the most mainstream of all critics of the Saudi regime. He is a graduate of prominent Islamic universities in Mecca and Medina.

Many of Hawali's lectures and writings reveal his belief that modernism and reform are a Western way of undermining Islamic society from within. According to Hawali, the most serious threat facing Saudi Arabia has been "the imposition of Israeli and American hegemony over the whole area." The Arab world is unprepared to meet this threat due to their political disunity and military and economic dependency on the West. Arabs and Muslims must unite in one Islamic cause to combat the Western threat, withdraw all assets from Western financial institutions and reinvest in Islamic countries, and more strictly control media and communications to prevent the weakening of Arab and Islamic culture by Western secularism. Hawali has been deeply distrustful of the policies and influence of the United States in the Arab world. He has stated his belief that the Gulf War was merely a means for the United States to subdue any regional power that opposed the West and to bind the region into a security arrangement based on dependency.

Hawali's ultraconservative views led to his arrest in 1994, although his views were shared by many other Islamic figures in the Gulf region and elsewhere in the Arab world. Many Saudis resented the fact that U.S. forces remained in Saudi Arabia, did not understand why America continued sanctions that hurt the Iraqi people, and were confused by the cat-and-mouse game between Washington and Baghdad. To many, America's role in the Middle East and support of Israel and secular Arab rulers corroborated Hawali's view of the West.

At the same time, Hawali and his supporters are more representative of Saudi religious nationalism than Islamic extremism. Their main grievances have not been based on direct criticism of the Saudi government and the royal family, but rather on external issues such as Western domination and neocolonialism. Hawali did not question the political or religious authority of the Saudi state, but criticized its subordination to "its enemy," the United States. In his view, Saudi Arabia did not do enough to propagate

Islamic faith or preserve it from the onslaught of Western secularism and the kind of reform and modernism opposed by Saudi Arabia's religious traditionalists. Such ideas had support among many Saudis after 1991 and were echoed in newspapers all over the Middle East. His imprisonment was more the reaction of a government unaccustomed to public criticism than a response to a direct threat.[23]

Nonviolent Islamist Opposition: Salman al-Auda

Sheikh Salman al-Auda (Awda) is another case example of the ideas that shape nonviolent Islamic opposition in Saudi Arabia. He was born in the province of Qasim, a poor, conservative, agricultural area that has long been a fertile ground for religious discourse. His worldview is linked to the area's social, economic, and political problems. In his early taped sermons, his criticisms of the government were general and included no direct mention of the royal family. Al-Auda rose to prominence during the Gulf War and like many similar Islamists, his sermons became more hostile toward the government. He used the Gulf War and the media's focus on Saudi Arabia to popularize his criticisms of the government and society at large.

Al-Auda preached that the political violence transpiring in Egypt and Algeria was the result of secular dictatorship and the muffling of opposing opinions and voices of religious dissent. According to al-Auda, any government that is not based on justice and the Shari'a will eventually be overthrown. At the same time, his message was scarcely extremist. He also advocated a return to the original contract and alliance between the state and religious forces on which the foundation of the modern Saudi state was based. Although al-Auda echoed other Islamists in disapproving of modern education and financial extravagance, he also mentioned the need for economic restructuring and privatization. He urged Saudi Arabia to speed the process of reform and dialogue, lest the country descend into violence.

He did, however, advance claims to racial superiority that had few serious precedents in Saudi revivalist thought. He claimed that the Saudi people were strong in physique and mental abilities because of environmental conditions, and that being part of an Arab nation was inherently superior due to that superior nature of the language, its approach to reasoning, and emphasis on the ability to memorize.

Al-Auda was arrested in 1994 because he was considered to be one of the harshest open critics of the government, but he remained as much a Saudi nationalist as an Islamist. His views hovered between extremes. At one level, he believed that Saudi Arabia was heading toward much political violence and strife. At another level, he represented Saudi Arabia as a nation of peace, full of invincible people, willed by God to be unshakable. While he criticized the government, he also held the nation, as a whole, responsible for Saudi Arabia's problems.

Al-Auda was released from house arrest in 1999. Like some other Saudi Islamists in similar positions, he has since criticized the acts of terrorism that Osama bin Laden and al-Qaeda committed on September 11, 2001, as a "deviant understanding" of Islam and a "deviant application of legitimate teachings."

Nonviolent Islamic Opposition: Sheikh 'Ayd al-Qarni

Sheikh 'Ayd al-Qarni is another example of an Islamist who reemerged as a "moderate" after September 11. The Saudi government had not allowed al-Qarni to conduct religious services and proselytizing activities for some time before the attacks on the World Trade Center and the Pentagon. Afterwards, he was allowed to do so, almost certainly because he stated that he shared the view of the Saudi government that Saudis had to "unite ranks, unify Muslim discourse, call to God and avoid exaggeration" in religion.

He publicly criticized the rush to jihadist activities among Muslim youth, warned against actions that threatened national unity, and reminded Saudis of their obligation of loyalty to their rulers. It is obvious that the Saudi government played a behind-the-scenes role in both cases, but such Islamists probably would not have spoken in this way simply because of government pressure. They are typical of powerful oppositionist preachers who gained considerable public support after the Gulf War, but they are also examples of the kind of fundamentalism that involves reasoned arguments rather than relying on subversion or force.[24]

"Quasi-Violent" Islamist Opposition: The Committee for the Defense of Legitimate Rights (CDLR) and Muhammad al-Mas'ari

Other opposition figures have organized more formal opposition movements and have obtained foreign as well as domestic support in making more direct challenges to the government. Some of these oppositionists have also come very close to crossing the line between nonviolence and violence—and many have actually crossed it.

The Committee for the Defense of Legitimate Rights (CDLR) is a good example of what happens when Islamic opposition transcends intellectual criticism to become an organized movement. Six Saudi citizens established the CDLR in 1993. Their mission was to struggle for the elimination of injustices, the restoration of legitimate rights, and the guarantee of people's right to express their opinions freely and to live in honor and dignity in an environment of equality and justice.[25] They were headed by Muhammad al-Mas'ari, a former physics professor whose interviews and writings indicate support for both fundamentalism and the far left, with little regard for human rights or democracy except as a rhetorical device to help achieve his goal of overthrowing the Saudi government.[26]

Although the CDLR claimed to the West that it was formed for the purpose of supporting human rights and democracy in Saudi Arabia, it supported a strict interpretation of the Shari'a and Islamic custom, opposed most rights for women, made strong anti-Shi'ite statements, opposed the Arab-Israeli peace process, and denied Israel's right to exist. It has never supported the need to protect the kind of human rights recognized in the West, and takes a rigidly Islamic fundamentalist approach in its Arabic writings and propaganda. [27]

The initial success of the CDLR was another consequence of Gulf War. Once again, the presence of approximately 500,000 non-Muslim soldiers in Saudi Arabia, the Kingdom's perceived lack of capability to defend itself, and the systematic assault on Iraq raised serious questions among nationalist Saudis.[28]

The CDLR began to be treated as a serious opposition group after it openly criticized the Saudi government in the international press in 1993. The security forces detained thirty-eight of its members, including al-Mas'ari, confiscated their passports, and forbade them to travel or speak publicly. Al-Mas'ari was released in November 1993, after spending six months in detention. The security forces subsequently released the rest of the detainees, but only after they signed statements promising not to discuss the government's policies or communicate with anyone outside the country by telephone or fax machine. The authorities also dismissed several founding members of the CDLR from their government jobs.[29]

In 1994, al-Mas'ari secretly fled to the United Kingdom, where he sought political asylum and established an overseas branch of the CDLR. He continued to disseminate tracts critical of the Saudi government from the UK. He was particularly critical of King Fahd, Interior Minister Prince Naif, and the governor of Riyadh, Prince Salman. He continued to express opposition to peace with Israel and to Saudi support for the peace process. At least some of the CDLR's tracts had considerable impact, although perhaps as much for the novelty of such criticism and of an organized opposition movement as for their content.

After al-Mas'ari fled to England, the Saudi security forces arrested fifteen to twenty of his relatives and supporters. The government released several of these detainees in late 1994, including Dr. Fouad Dahlawi; al-Mas'ari's brother, Lu'ay al-Mas'ari; and al-Mas'ari's brothers-in-law, Rashad and Nabil al-Mudarris. However, the government did not publicly acknowledge its detention of CDLR supporters until 1995.

The CDLR responded during 1995–1996 by making repeated claims that more than 300 clerics were being detained for political reasons. Detentions on such a scale are impossible to confirm although the Saudi authorities did continue to detain Salman al-Auda and Safar al-Hawali for criticizing the government. The government also continued to detain 27 men out of the 157 persons it had arrested for antigovernment activities in October 1994. While the Saudi government released thousands of prisoners and detainees as part of the annual Ramadan amnesties in 1994–1996, these did not seem to include major political dissidents. The U.S. State Department reported in 1998, however, that the total number of political detainees could not be accurately determined but was probably less than fifty.[30]

Supporters of the CDLR responded by making occasional use of violence. The Saudi government announced in August 1995 that it had executed Abdullah bin Abd al-Rahman al-Hidaif for assaulting a security official with acid. At the same time, however, the government applied severe penalties for more peaceful opposition. It sentenced one Saudi man to five years in prison simply for possessing leaflets and posters mentioning the CDLR, and another to three years in prison for attending meetings in support of the group and its exiled spokesman, Mohammad al-Mas'ari. Both were associates of Abdullah bin Abd al-Rahman al-Hidaif.[31]

These government actions led the CDLR to focus largely on activity outside Saudi Arabia. From 1994 onward, al-Mas'ari issued a flood of faxes and press releases attacking the royal family and government from his new headquarters in Britain. He also did his best to make the CDLR appear like a Western-style democratic and human rights movement in order to win Western support. He down-played the CDLR's Islamic extremism, and in the process the fact that "legitimate" in its title referred to religious legitimacy in Arabic.

Yet, during this same period, al-Mas'ari expressed the CDLR's "understanding" of two fatal terrorist bombings of the U.S. Air Force housing compound at Al-Khobar and sympathy for the perpetrators—although the CDLR did say it played no role in such actions. These activities caused the Saudi government to put intense pressure on Britain to deport al-Mas'ari. The Conservative Party government of then–prime minister John Major responded by trying to expel al-Mas'ari to Dominica, but al-Mas'ari appealed the decision in court and was eventually granted permission to remain in the United Kingdom for four years, with the option of applying for permanent residency at the end of that period.[32]

As a result, the CDLR continued to criticize the Saudi government, using computers and facsimile transmissions to send newsletters back to Saudi Arabia. This led to a serious confrontation between Saudi Arabia and Britain in April 1996. The Saudi ambassador to the United Kingdom stated that his government would withdraw from its large arms contracts for British weapons unless the United Kingdom expelled al-Mas'ari. No Saudi government retribution actually took place against the British government, but this may be because Saudi intelligence found other ways to deal with al-Mas'ari and the CDLR. Al-Mas'ari was successful in avoiding deportation, but he could not afford the legal fees involved. As a result, he became

£10,000 in debt. A London high court declared him bankrupt on January 8, 1997, and the resulting judgment meant that donations to al-Mas'ari were assigned to his creditors rather than to the CDLR.[33]

According to the U.S. State Department report on human rights, the CDLR also suffered from internal problems that resulted in a major split. In March 1996, these internal tensions led some of the supporters of the CDLR to create a rival faction called the Islamic Reform Movement (IRM) or Movement for Islamic Reform in Saudi Arabia (MIRA). This faction was headed by Sa'ad al-Faqih, who was able to persuade most of the CDLR's major backers to support MIRA. As a result, the CDLR lost much of its funding.

By the end of 1996, the CDLR's activities had come to a virtual halt. The IRM did, however, continue at a much lower level of activity and it also implicitly condoned the two terrorist attacks in Saudi Arabia—arguing that they were a natural outgrowth of a political system that does not tolerate peaceful dissent.[34] The IRM's mission statement, however, is more peaceful. It says that the movement seeks major reforms in Arabia; in particular, freedom of expression, freedom of assembly, and the abolition of the secret police units subverting political movements and activity. It says these reforms are a precondition for the political, judicial, economic, and social reforms that need to take place, and it has said in other statements that it will use all peaceful legitimate means including information, communication, and political pressure to achieve these aims.[35]

Violent Islamic Opposition: The Saudi National Guard Bombing

The threat from more violent militant Islamists has been far more serious, sometimes murderous, and provides case examples of a very different kind. The first major act of post–Gulf War violence took place on November 13, 1995. A 150 to 225 pound bomb, placed in a pickup truck, exploded outside the building housing the headquarters of the U.S. Army Materiel Command's Office of the Program Manager (OPM) for the Saudi National Guard. The OPM is the U.S. program that provides training support to the National Guard.

The bomb was detonated at 11:30 A.M. when most Saudis would be at prayer and off the streets.[36] The blast killed seven people, including five Americans and two Indians, and wounded sixty others, of which thirty-seven were American. The timing of the bomb indicated that it might have been directed primarily at Americans. In fact, none of the sixty-seven casualties were Saudi citizens. The bombing was the first such attack on Western military forces in Saudi Arabia since 1991, when two Americans were wounded in an attack on a shuttle bus in Jeddah, and clearly shocked both American and Saudi officials.[37]

There still are some questions as to who was responsible. An extremist group called Movement for Islamic Change in the Arabian Peninsula—Jihad Wing claimed responsibility, as did two previously unknown groups calling themselves the Tigers of the Gulf and the Combatant Partisans of God. All demanded the immediate withdrawal of U.S. troops from Saudi Arabia. The Combatant Partisans of God also demanded the release of Sheikh Omar Abd al-Rahman and Mousa Abu Marzouk from U.S. custody. The CDLR indicated that it had never heard of these groups and officially condemned the attack, but it was al-Mas'ari's equivocation in condemning the bombing that prompted the British government to order his expulsion and led to the deportation proceedings mentioned earlier.[38]

Although Western and Saudi sources had no information concerning these groups, the third group, the Movement for Islamic Change, had faxed two previous warnings to the U.S. embassy in Riyadh in April and June 1995. The statements demanded a withdrawal of all U.S. forces from the Kingdom by July 1995. U.S. Ambassador Raymond E. Mabus indicated that the earlier faxes were not taken seriously enough because, "of all the places in the world, [Saudi Arabia] was deemed one of the safest."[39] A U.S. review of the faxes revealed phrases that suggested that the group adhered to mainstream Sunni beliefs and was likely to be indigenous to Saudi Arabia.

The Saudi government was initially unwilling to publicly acknowledge the possible involvement of indigenous opposition groups. The Saudi ambassador to the United States, Bandar bin Sultan bin Abdulaziz, declared, "Dissidents did not cause the car bombing."[40] These public denials were partly the result of a Saudi belief that acts this violent had to have been conducted by foreign groups, and partly the result of an effort to discourage indigenous groups from copycat incidents. They also were affected by U.S. intelligence reports that Iranian agents had carried out increased surveillance of U.S. installations prior to the attack.[41]

At the same time, the investigation by the Ministry of the Interior focused on both foreign and indigenous opponents of the regime and on Saudis operating both outside and inside the country. The Saudi authorities sorted through the files of some 15,000 known Saudi "Afghanis" and Islamic extremists. Shortly after the blast, the Saudis released a sketch of one suspect, and the Saudi and U.S. governments offered a $3 million reward for information regarding those responsible. The United States assisted by providing technical expertise, and dispatched nineteen FBI investigators and two State Department security officials to the site of the bombing within days after it occurred.

The first arrests indicated that Saudis outside Saudi Arabia might be involved. On February 1, 1995, Pakistan extradited an individual believed to match the sketch, a Saudi national named Hassan as-Suraihi, at the request of the Saudi government. As-Suraihi was known to have fought with

Islamic groups in Afghanistan in the early 1990s and to have supported Islamic militants in India's Kashmir region. However, as-Suraihi was not charged with the attack. Instead, the Saudi government arrested four Saudis living in Saudi Arabia and broadcast their confessions on April 22, 1996.

The four men were Abdulaziz Fah Nasser, Riyadh Harji, Muslih Shamrani, and Khalid Ahmed Said. The Interior Ministry announced that three of the four men were Saudi Islamic extremists that had joined the Mujahideen forces fighting in Afghanistan in the late 1980s, and the fourth had fought in Bosnia. They had smuggled in the explosives from Yemen, and had at least some ties to the Islamic group in Egypt. Shamrani was an ex-solider who had fought in Afghanistan and Bosnia, and was the son of an army officer. However, all four were part of the large class of Saudi young men with no real career prospects, family wealth, or connections. The four men said they had planned a much more extensive series of kidnappings and assassinations, but had given up their plans because they feared they would be caught as a result of the massive increase in security measures following the bombing.[42]

The Interior Ministry did not indicate that any of the four men were part of the three groups that had originally claimed responsibility for the attack. It also issued press releases that vaguely linked the four men to a foreign power or foreign group. According to some Saudi sources, the men were an independent cell that was influenced by clerical extremists linked to the Islamic radical Hizb al-Tahrir, or Liberation Party, which draws on the thinking from clerics based in Jordan. Other Saudi sources indicate, however, that al-Mas'ari and Osama bin Laden may have influenced them, and that the Saudi government may have suppressed the details of their involvement in other groups. All four were beheaded on May 31, 1996.[43]

Militant Islamist Opposition: The Al-Khobar Tragedy

The next major case study in Islamic violence illustrates how diverse the problem of Islamic extremism can be even in a country dominated by one Islamic sect. This time the attack was committed by Saudi Shi'ites that may have had ties to Iran. The attack did not occur without warning. The successful bombing of the National Guard Training Center had demonstrated the vulnerability of targets within the Kingdom to terrorist attacks. The end result was a series of intelligence indicators that further bombings were being planned and a major new attack on U.S. facilities in Saudi Arabia was likely. These warnings were taken very seriously because there were approximately 30,000 Americans living in Saudi Arabia, many of whom were easy targets for terrorists.

In December 1995, the U.S. embassy released a statement in which it stated that the United States had "unconfirmed information that additional bombings may be planned against Western interests in Saudi Arabia, including facilities and commercial centers occupied and/or frequented by Americans." A similar statement was released by the State Department on January 31, 1995, a week prior to a scheduled visit by Secretary of State Warren Christopher to Saudi Arabia. The visit was then canceled, ostensibly because of scheduling conflicts, but actually because of the terrorist threats.

On March 29, 1996, Saudi border guards intercepted a new shipment of explosives at the Jordanian border. The possibility of additional attacks had also prompted concern by corporate contractors in Saudi Arabia as to the safety of their employees and dependents. New anonymous threats were made against Americans in May 1996, prompting the U.S. embassy to ask Americans living in Saudi Arabia to keep a "low profile."

On June 25, 1996, threats turned into a major tragedy. A truck bomb exploded outside a U.S. military housing complex located in Khobar Towers, which was located in Al-Khobar—a town near the Saudi air base at Dhahran, where the United States had a significant combat presence. While the U.S. base commander had planned defenses against bombs up to several hundred pounds, the bomb weighed closer to 5,000 and some estimates put it in the 10,000- to 25,000-pound category. It was placed in a large fuel tanker parked about thirty-five yards from the perimeter of the base, and was so large that the explosion could be felt in Bahrain. It toppled one of the apartment towers at the complex, and the crater was approximately eighty-five feet across and thirty-five feet deep. The attack killed 19 U.S. servicemen and injured 373 others. It was the worst terrorist disaster affecting the United States since 241 Marines and sailors were killed in the bombing of a U.S. barracks in Beirut on October 23, 1983.

In fact, the incident was so serious that the United States responded by relocating most of the several thousand USAF personnel stationed in Saudi Arabia to an isolated Saudi air base at Al-Kharj, some sixty miles southeast of Riyadh, at a cost to the United States and Saudi Arabia of several hundred million dollars. Unlike the Al-Khobar area, the Al-Kharj area was virtually unoccupied and could be made almost completely secure, to the point where the United States even operated services like trash handling. The United States restricted temporary duty in Saudi Arabia to Al-Kharj and other sealed, secured areas, and rushed in extensive new perimeter-defense equipment, including advanced thermal imaging equipment for vehicles and fixed surveillance, and strengthened Force Protection Groups from the USAF. It also removed most of the USAF presence from the joint command center in the Saudi Air Force headquarters in Riyadh.

The Initial Course of the Al-Khobar Investigation

The Al-Khobar attack is one of the few case studies in which considerable detail is available on what happened, but little information on the identity of the bombers after the initial investigation. Large-scale arrests produced few results—in part because Saudi Arabia rushed to arrest the "usual suspects" before it carried out a serious investigation. Saudi and U.S. investigations of al-Mas'ari and bin Laden produced little indication they had direct responsibility. Both the United States and Saudi Arabia offered massive rewards, but no solid informer came forward (like the Yemeni truck driver who had informed on those involved in the National Guard bombing).

By November 1996, however, there was growing evidence that the bombers were a different kind of threat from the Wahhabi extremists discussed earlier, and might be Saudi Shi'ites affiliated with a movement known as the Saudi Hezbollah. This group had made earlier claims for responsibility for the bombing, but its claims only became convincing after its ties to the Hezbollah in Lebanon and to training facilities in Iran emerged. It also became clear that the bombers might be linked to a series of much-lower-level Shi'ite attacks on the oil facilities and other targets in Saudi Arabia's Eastern Province.

The Saudis arrested Shi'ite religious figures like Abdul Karim Hubail and Sheik Jaffer Mubarak, and conducted other arrests that indicated that the Saudi Hezbollah might have as many as 1,000 members, with a core of up to 250. There were indications that some members operated out of Syria or Lebanon, and that Iranian officials had been involved in the Al-Khobar bombing. Iranian Foreign Minister Velayati formally denied Iranian involvement as early as December 12, 1996. He stated that such bombings were an internal Saudi matter and that, "We deny any involvement directly or indirectly. We are against any kind of terrorist actions against any country. . . . There are some opposition groups in Saudi that have admitted they are involved in different blastings there. We don't want to support this kind of activity."[44]

Unfortunately, at this point, the investigation was slowed by Saudi Arabia's policy of avoiding any public disclosure of its internal problems, as well as by tensions between Saudi and U.S. investigators and a "clash of intelligence and law enforcement cultures." The Saudis have always treated internal unrest as a virtual state secret, and had no desire for any American "help" that would directly interfere in their investigation or give the United States access to Saudi Arabia's internal problems. The Saudi security forces have also focused largely on domestic human intelligence, networks of local informers, wire tappings and communications intercepts, and large-scale arrests of possible suspects who were held for long periods. They conduct direct, often forcible interrogation with limited regard to Western concepts of human rights. As a result, the Saudis were not used to working with foreigners or relying on technical data, forensics, and intelligence. They had little experience in conducting complex technical law enforcement investigations with demanding chains of evidence of the kind common in the West.

The FBI approached the Al-Khobar investigation in a very different way. It rushed in teams of Americans with limited Arabic and little regional political background, who were trained largely in forensics and highly technical methods of investigation. The FBI investigators gave the Saudis the impression that they were trying to take over the investigation without really knowing anything about the various factions or movements they were dealing with or the political consequences of their actions. Things were then made even worse on the U.S. side by poor interagency coordination. Some FBI agents also alienated U.S. intelligence and State Department personnel as thoroughly as they alienated the Saudis. While professional counterterrorists and U.S. and Saudi intelligence experts worked relatively well together, the U.S. effort involved several other agencies that sometimes did little more than hold meetings, generate new rumors, and issue more requests for data from the field.

U.S.-Saudi coordination was often poor. The Saudi investigators often seemed unable to open their mouths, while the FBI investigators seemed unable to keep them shut and avoid posturing for the press and Congress. Cooperation was minimal, with both sides trading countercharges and making little progress. Prince Nayef, the minister of the interior, who was in charge of the Saudi side of the investigation, made it publicly clear that he resented some of the actions taken by the FBI. The FBI in turn, "leaked" complaints about the Saudis.

The politics of a possible Iranian role in the Al-Khobar bombing made Saudi-U.S. cooperation worse. Some U.S. officials leaped ahead of the evidence to condemn Iran. The Saudis, however, were seeking a broader political rapprochement with Iran, and could not firmly decide if it was better to openly blame the Iranians for Saudi Arabia's internal problems with its Shi'ites, or to minimize any publicity about possible Iranian involvement to avoid a crisis with Iran. The evidence also remained ambiguous. It did become clear that the Saudi Hezbollah had ambiguous relations with Iran, and with the Hezbollah in Lebanon, but the seeming involvement of a few Iranian officials could not be linked to direct orders for such an attack or to any direct involvement by the Iranian government. This made it difficult to separate Iran's role of encouraging such movements ideologically, and with training or funding, from a direct involvement or sponsorship of terrorism acts like the bombing.

In March 1997, the investigation reached the point of tragicomedy. The media was already filled with rumors about Iran and possible U.S. reprisals when a Saudi named Hani Abdel Rahim al-Sayegh was arrested in Canada on charges that he had driven one of the vehicles involved in the Al-Khobar attack. In the months that followed, al-Sayegh was reported to have identified Iranian Brigadier General Ahmad Sherifi as having directly encouraged him to commit attacks on U.S. personnel in Saudi Arabia.

It then slowly became clear, however, that al-Sayegh was primarily concerned with avoiding possible deportation to Saudi Arabia. While he made an agreement to talk if he was deported to the United States, this turned out to be little more than opportunism. Once al-Sayegh arrived in the United States, he appealed his status in the U.S. court system. He stated that his previous confessions were false, made under duress, and without due process of law. He also reiterated an earlier claim that he was in Syria during the actual bombing. He also used the U.S. press and courts to publicize the problems of Saudi Arabia's Shi'ites.

In September 1997 the Justice Department moved to drop the charges against al-Sayegh, citing their inability to develop the requisite evidence. Al-Sayegh went on to seek immigration relief under the Convention Against Torture, but his appeal was denied in September 1999. He was deported to Saudi Arabia a week later, where the Saudi government initiated legal proceedings against him.

Serious Progress in the Al-Khobar Investigation After May 1997

Tensions between Saudi Arabia and the United States eased in May 1997, when U.S. officials—including the secretary of state, secretary of defense, and chairman of the joint chiefs—made it clear that they had no evidence of foreign involvement or sponsorship by Iran. There were also new reports that a Saudi Sunni group now claimed responsibility for the bombing.

At the same time, it was far from clear that Iran was innocent. Al-Sayegh does seem to have tried to organize attacks against U.S. citizens in Saudi Arabia during 1994 and 1995, and to organize such attacks after visits to Qum in Iran and a Hezbollah camp in Lebanon. Another Saudi Shi'ite who might have been involved in the bombing—Ahmed Ibrahim Ahmad Mughassil—was reported to have fled to Syria after the attack. Mughassil was then said to have crossed into Iran—although Iran denied it had given Mughassil shelter. Mughassil was particularly important because Saudi Arabia listed him as a leader of the Saudi Hezbollah and as a key conspirator.

Similarly, a Saudi Shi'ite named Jaafer Chueikhat was also reported to have been involved in the bombing. Chueikhat was trained by the Hezbollah in Lebanon before the bombing, and then committed "suicide" in prison in Syria under conditions that made it look like his death might have been politically convenient to both Syria and Iran. Three of the twelve suspects in the Al-Khobar bombing who the Saudis identified by August 1997 had clear ties to Iranian-connected organizations, and several others were believed to be in Hezbollah camps in Lebanon.

Saudi and U.S. differences over how to conduct the investigation also continued to surface. In late March 1998, Prince Nayef announced in Mecca that Saudi Arabia had finished the investigation and would announce the findings when the time was right, "All the facts of the crime are with us and our intelligence exerted huge efforts to discover everything about the incident and we will leave the announcement for its time." In contrast, State

Department Spokesman James P. Rubin stated, "As far as we're concerned the investigation is still wide open. We do not believe it's over. We are continuing to pursue it and believe that at the end of the day those responsible will need to pay a price."

Both sides appeared to reach a compromise a few days later, but the result did little to clarify the situation. Rubin issued a statement that Saudi Arabia was still investigating details of the unsolved bombing. He said, "We are continuing to have exchanges with the Saudi government and have had repeated and very high-level assurances of cooperation from them." He also said that "it was not all that clear" that the minister meant the Saudis had closed the investigation.

> On the contrary, [the Saudi minister] appeared to be saying that . . . there's nothing new and nothing new to find, but they're working on the details. . . . Well, most investigations focus on the details, and from that, one can build out into understanding what might have happened. . . . Let me say this. From the perspective of the United States, the Al-Khobar bombing investigation remains wide open.

Despite these problems, the Saudi-U.S. investigation continued to make slow progress and aspects of Saudi-U.S. cooperation improved. The FBI and Saudi intelligence and security services, despite different cultural approaches to criminal and security investigations and different political goals, gradually learned to work together more closely. Saudi Arabia and the United States jointly identified twelve Saudi Arabians and one Lebanese as suspects in the bombing. FBI experts indicated in November 1999 that they had some degree of evidence of indirect Iranian involvement from Saudi and other sources.

At the same time, the nature of the organization or organizations involved remained unclear, as did their strength inside Saudi Arabia. The issue of Iranian involvement also remained open. Reports surfaced that Ahmad Sherrif, a senior official in the Iranian Revolutionary Guard, was involved in the planning of the Al-Khobar bombing. Ahmad Sherrif has been associated with covert Iranian special operations, and was identified in 1996 as an Iranian intelligence officer in the June 1996 trial of fifteen Shi'a dissidents in Bahrain who were convicted of bombing several hotels and restaurants in the Emirate. Six of the sixteen Bahrainis confessed that Sherrif had recruited them in 1993 in a madrassa in Qom. Intelligence sources suspect that Sherrif may have first contacted al-Sayegh during the Saudi dissident's stay in Qom.[45] A major London-based Saudi newspaper, *al-Hayat*, claimed that two Saudis and one Lebanese, believed to have planned the bombing, were thought to have initially fled to Iran although later investigation indicated they were not there.

These reports presented growing problems for Saudi Arabia as it solidified its rapprochement with the Khatami government of Iran. It was doing so at a time when the United States continued to impose sanctions on Iran and call it a terrorist nation. In 1999, Saudi Arabia quietly asked Iran to provide background data on some aspects of the investigation. In 2001, however, Saudi officials publicly denied that the Al-Khobar issue was a subject of formal discussions with Iran. The Saudi government never formally denied that Iran might be connected to the Al-Khobar bombing, but it increasingly sought to avoid public debate over the issue. When a *New York Times* article that linked Iran with the bombing appeared, Foreign Minister Saud al-Faisal stated that it "is not a good thing to launch accusations here and there, reporting a matter on which the investigation has not been completed." The testimonies of two Saudis arrested for the bombing, Hani al-Sayegh and Muhammad Qassab, were never made public.

The United States Issues an Indictment

All of those issues took on new importance on June 21, 2001, when a federal grand jury in Alexandria, Virginia, indicted thirteen Saudi militants and a Lebanese chemist for the attack on the Al-Khobar Towers. U.S. Attorney General John Ashcroft announced the indictment at an afternoon press conference, and stated that the fourteen suspected terrorists were charged with murder, attempted murder of federal employees, conspiracy to commit murder, and conspiracy to use a weapon of mass destruction in the bombing. Ashcroft explained that the indictment was issued because many of the charges might have become impossible to file under the statute of limitations after the fifth anniversary of the attack, which was June 25, 2001.

Nevertheless, the United States put all U.S. military forces in the Persian Gulf on the highest state of alert—"Threat Condition Delta"—on June 22. It ordered ships from the 5th Fleet in Bahrain to go to sea, and withdrew U.S. Marines from an exercise in Kuwait. It linked this action to increased terrorist threats from Osama bin Laden and his organization al-Qaeda, but U.S. officials privately made it clear that the United States was equally concerned about Iran. Edmund J. Hull, the U.S. ambassador to the Republic of Yemen and former U.S. Department of State acting coordinator for counterterrorism, stated on April 30, 2001, "We have a very long memory and we have as long an arm as possible."[46]

It is striking, in retrospect, that indictment made no mention of the threat of Sunni extremism, Osama bin Laden, or Iraq. Instead, the defendants included Abdel Karim Nasser, the leader of the Saudi Hezbollah terrorist organization; Ahmed Mughassil, the head of the group's military wing; and members of terrorist cells in Saudi Arabia who planned and carried out the attack. Hani al-Sayegh was identified as the driver of the vehicle used to scout the bombing site. The Saudi Hezbollah responded by issuing a statement denying its involvement in the bombing in November 1996.

The Role of the Saudi Hezbollah

The name "Hezbollah" is used by a number of Shi'ite extremist groups, principally the Lebanese Hezbollah. It is taken from the Koran and literally means "Party of God." It refers to active defenders of Islam. All of the various Hezbollah groups are linked by interpretations of Islam that make it legitimate to lie and conceal in the defense of the faith. The organizational ties between various Hezbollah groups are uncertain, although many train or meet together and have some ties to Iranian and Syrian intelligence and Iranian and/or Syrian sponsored training centers in Lebanon, Syria, and Iran. The Lebanese Hezbollah, for example, has repeatedly denied that it had ties to the Saudi Hezbollah since the Al-Khobar bombing, but was named in the U.S. indictment.

Saudi Shi'ites in the Eastern Province founded Saudi Hezbollah in the 1980s as a reaction to the harshness of Saudi treatment of what many Wahhabis regarded as a suspect branch of Islam. The organization sought support from Iran, which trained many of the Saudi Shi'ite clerics and provided money and military training.

Although the Saudi Hezbollah has focused primarily on attacking the Saudi regime, it is also strongly anti-American. It attacked the Saudi government for allowing U.S. troops to remain in the Kingdom after the end of the Gulf War. Nevertheless, some reports indicate that the Saudi government allowed approximately 200 Saudi Shi'ites to return to Saudi Arabia in 1993, some of who may have included members of the Saudi Hezbollah.

The text of the indictment described the Hezbollah, the role of the attackers in the Hezbollah, and the role of Iran and other outside organizations as follows:

- Hezbollah, or "Party of God," was the name used by a number of related terrorist organizations operating in Saudi Arabia, Lebanon, Kuwait, and Bahrain, among other places. These Hezbollah organizations were inspired, supported, and directed by elements of the Iranian government.
- Saudi Hezbollah, also known as Hezbollah Al-Hijaz, was a terrorist organization that operated primarily in the Kingdom of Saudi Arabia and that promoted, among other things, the use of violence against nationals and property of the United States located in Saudi Arabia. Because Saudi Hezbollah was an outlaw organization in the Kingdom of Saudi Arabia, its members frequently met and trained in Lebanon, Syria, or Iran.

The indictment stated that the "regular gathering place for members of Saudi Hezbollah was the Sayyeda Zeinab shrine in Damascus, Syria, which was an important religious site for adherents of the Shi'ite branch of Islam."[47] It also stated that the

> Saudi Hezbollah drew its members primarily from among young men of the Shi'ite faith who resided in the Eastern Province of Saudi Arabia, near the Persian Gulf. Those young men would frequently have their first contact with Saudi Hezbollah during religious pilgrimages to the Sayyeda Zeinab shrine. They would then be approached by Saudi Hezbollah members to gauge their loyalty to Iran and dislike for the government of Saudi Arabia. Young men who wished to join Saudi Hezbollah then would be transported to Hezbollah-controlled areas in Lebanon for military training and indoctrination.[48]

The indictment indicated that the Saudi Hezbollah was organized in departments, or "wings," headed by a Hezbollah member. Each department head reported to the leader of Saudi Hezbollah. At the time of the Al-Khobar bombings, the leader was Abdelkarim Hussein Muhammad al-Nasser. The indictment went on to describe the role of the Hezbollah and the members who participated in the attack as follows:

- The "military wing" of Saudi Hezbollah was headed at all relevant times by Ahmed Al-Mughassil, aka "Abu Omran," a native of Qatif, in the Eastern Province of Saudi Arabia. In his role as military commander, Al-Mughassil was in charge of directing terrorist attacks against American interests in Saudi Arabia. Al-Mughassil was actively involved in recruiting young Saudi Shi'ite men to join the ranks of Hezbollah; arranging for those men to undergo military training at Hezbollah camps in Lebanon and Iran; directing those men in surveillance of potential targets for attack by Hezbollah; and planning and supervising terrorist attacks.

- Ali Al-Houri was a member of Saudi Hezbollah who served as a major recruiter for the Hezbollah party; scheduled party functions; and transported explosives for the party. He also acted as a liaison for the party with the Iranian embassy in Damascus, Syria, which was an important source of logistics and support for Saudi Hezbollah members traveling to and from Lebanon. Al-Houri was a close associate of Al-Mughassil and participated directly in surveillance, planning, and execution of terrorist attacks.

- Hani Al-Sayegh was a prominent member of Saudi Hezbollah. He was actively involved in recruiting young Saudi Shi'ite men to join the ranks of Hezbollah; arranging for those men to undergo military training at Hezbollah camps in Lebanon and Iran; assisting in the surveillance of potential targets for attack by Hezbollah; and carrying out terrorist attacks. Al-Sayegh also spoke fluent Farsi and enjoyed an unusually close association with certain military elements of the Iranian government.

- Ibrahim Al-Yacoub was a prominent member of Saudi Hezbollah, actively involved in recruiting young Saudi Shi'ite men to join Hezbollah, and in planning and carrying out terrorist attacks. He also served as a liaison between Saudi Hezbollah and the Lebanese and Iranian Hezbollah organizations.

- Mustafa Al-Qassab was a Shi'ite Muslim from Qatif, Saudi Arabia. He joined Saudi Hezbollah in the late 1980s after traveling from Saudi Arabia to Iran and meeting Al-Mughassil and others. Over time, Al-Qassab came to play an important role in the military affairs of Saudi Hezbollah.

- Sa'ed Al-Bahar was a Qatif native who first became associated with Hezbollah in 1988, when Al-Yacoub arranged for him to travel to Iran for religious study. He also spent time with Al-Yacoub in Damascus. In Damascus, he met and became close friends with Al-Sayegh, who introduced him both to Hezbollah and to elements of the Iranian government. In Qom, Iran during 1989 or 1990, he also met Al-Houri, who accompanied him to military training sponsored by the Iranian government in southern Iran.

- Abdallah Al-Jarash was recruited into Hezbollah at the Sayyeda Zeinab shrine in Damascus. At the time of his recruitment, Al-Jarash met Al Mughassil, Al-Houri, Al-Yacoub, and Al-Sayegh, all of whom were important party members.

- Al-Jarash learned that, as a member of Hezbollah, he would need to be loyal to the party and to Iran; he also learned that the goal of the party was to target foreign interests, American in particular, in Saudi Arabia and elsewhere. In about 1989, Al-Jarash was sent to Lebanon in a Mercedes supplied by the Iranian embassy in Damascus for military training provided by Lebanese Hezbollah members. After being trained, he was assigned to recruit others who felt a strong connection to Iran.

- Hussein Al-Mughis was a native of Qatif, Saudi Arabia who came into contact with Hezbollah in about 1990, when he traveled to the Sayyeda Zeinab shrine in Damascus and met Al-Mughassil, Al-Houri, and Al-Sayegh, among others. With Al-Mughassil's support, Al-Mughis underwent religious training in Qom, Iran, where he met Al-Yacoub. Then, in about 1992, Al-Mughassil arranged for Al-Mughis to spend two weeks in Lebanon receiving weapons and explosives training. At that time, he filled out a Hezbollah membership form provided by Al-Mughassil and learned that Hezbollah Hijaz and Lebanese Hezbollah were both part of Iranian Hezbollah. After this training, Al-Mughassil directed Al-Mughis to secretly recruit others for Hezbollah.

- Ali Al-Marhoun was another Shi'ite Muslim from the town of Qatif in Eastern Saudi Arabia. His first contact with the organization came in about 1991, when he met Al-Yacoub at the Sayyeda Zeinab shrine in Damascus. After Al-Marhoun discovered that both he and Al-Yacoub wished to be martyrs for Islam, Al-Yacoub introduced Al-Marhoun to Al-Mughassil, who arranged for Al-Marhoun to travel to Lebanon for Hezbollah training and indoctrination.

- Saleh Ramadan and Mustafa Mu'alem were recruited into Saudi Hezbollah in approximately 1992 by Al-Marhoun, whom they knew from their common hometown of Qatif, Saudi Arabia. Ramadan was chosen because he was very religious and a great admirer of Ayatollah Khomeini, the former Supreme Leader of Iran. Both Ramadan and Al-Mu'alem agreed to join Hezbollah and form a "cell" under Al-Marhoun. After being recruited by Al-Marhoun, Ramadan and Al-Mu'alem traveled to Lebanon for military training, where they met Al-Mughassil, who had them fill out written applications for

Hezbollah membership. Fadel Al-Alawe was a Qatif native who joined Hezbollah in about 1992 at the Sayyeda Zeinab shrine in Damascus. He was recruited by Al-Qassab, who introduced him to Al-Mughassil. Shortly thereafter, Al-Mughassil arranged for Al-Alawe to undergo military training in Lebanon.

- John Doe was a member of Lebanese Hezbollah who assisted Saudi Hezbollah with the construction of the tanker truck bomb used to attack the American military residences at Khobar Towers. He is described as a Lebanese male, approximately 175 cm tall, with fair skin, fair hair, and green eyes.

The Detailed History of the Attack

Other parts of the indictment provided additional details on the attack. It stated that the terrorist activities leading to the 1996 Al-Khobar blast began as early as 1993. At this time, Ahmed Ibrahim al-Mughassil, who was identified as the Hezbollah leader in charge of attacks against Americans in Saudi Arabia, ordered three of the other defendants to look for possible targets in Saudi Arabia, while other members of Saudi Hezbollah began "extensive surveillance to find American targets in Saudi Arabia." These reports were sent to Mughassil and Iranian officials, and described possible targets like the American embassy in Riyadh and locations in the eastern province of Saudi Arabia, including Khobar Towers apartment complex.

The indictment stated that an Iranian military officer directed several of the other defendants to search for alternative potential terrorism sites along the coast of the Red Sea in 1995. It also says that Mughassil told another defendant that he sustained ties with Iranian officials and that they provided financial support for Hezbollah. It maintains that Mughassil decided in the fall of 1995 that Khobar Towers would be the site of the attack, which would serve Iran by driving Americans from the Persian Gulf region.

Mughassil then instructed another defendant to transport explosives by car from an unidentified member of Lebanese Hezbollah in Beirut to hiding places in eastern Saudi Arabia in the vicinity of Khobar Towers in early 1996. The conspirators then bought a tanker truck and converted it into the truck bomb used in the attack. The resulting bomb was larger than the one that destroyed the Oklahoma City federal building in 1995 and more than twice as powerful as the one used at the Marine barracks in Beirut in 1983.

The indictment gave the following detailed history of the attack:

- In about 1993, Al-Mughassil instructed Al-Qassab, Al-Yacoub, and Al-Houri to begin surveillance of Americans in Saudi Arabia. As a result, Al-Qassab and Al-Yacoub spent three months in Riyadh conducting surveillance of American targets. Al-Sayegh joined them during this operation. They produced reports, which were passed to Al-Mughassil, then on to Saudi Hezbollah chief Al-Nasser, and to officials in Iran. At the end of their mission, Al-Mughassil came in person to meet with them and review their work. Also in about 1993,

Al-Yacoub assigned Al-Jarash to conduct surveillance of the United States Embassy in Riyadh, Saudi Arabia and to determine where Americans went and where they lived. Also at Al-Yacoub's direction, Al-Jarash and Al-Marhoun conducted surveillance of a fish market frequented by Americans, located near the United States Embassy in Riyadh. They reported the results of their surveillance to Al-Yacoub. In early 1994, Al-Qassab began conducting surveillance, focusing on American and other foreign sites in the Eastern Province of Saudi Arabia, an area that includes Khobar. He prepared written reports, which were passed to Al-Nasser and Iranian officials.

- In about Fall 1994, Al-Marhoun, Ramadan, and Al-Mu'alem began watching American sites in Eastern Saudi Arabia at Al-Mughassil's direction. They passed their reports to Al-Mughassil, who was then spending most of his time in Beirut, Lebanon. At about the same time, Al-Bahar began conducting surveillance in Saudi Arabia at the direction of an Iranian military officer. Khobar Towers was a housing complex in Dhahran, Saudi Arabia, which the United States, among other countries, used to house military personnel assigned to Saudi Arabia. Building #131 was an eight-story structure within the Khobar Towers complex that United States Air Force personnel, among others, used as their place of residence while serving in Saudi Arabia.

- In late 1994, after extensive surveillance in Eastern Saudi Arabia, Al-Marhoun, Ramadan, and Al-Mu'alem recognized and confirmed Khobar Towers as an important American military location and communicated that fact to Al-Mughassil. Shortly thereafter, Al-Mughassil gave Ramadan money to find a storage site in the Eastern Province for explosives. During the course of the cell's surveillance, Al-Mughassil reported to Al-Marhoun that he had received a phone call from a high Iranian government official inquiring about the progress of their surveillance activity.

- In 1995, Al-Bahar and Al-Sayegh conducted surveillance at the direction of an Iranian military officer from the area of Jizan, Saudi Arabia, located on the Red Sea near Yemen; they also surveyed American sites in the Eastern Province. Their goal was to gather information to support future attacks against Americans. Al-Sayegh took their surveillance reports and passed them to the Iranian officer.

- In about April or May 1995, Al-Marhoun attended four days of live-fire drills sponsored by Hezbollah in Lebanon. While he was there, he met with Al-Mughassil at his Beirut apartment. During that meeting, Al-Mughassil explained to Al-Marhoun that Hezbollah's goal was to expel the Americans from Saudi Arabia. Al-Mughassil also explained that he had close ties to Iranian officials, who supplied him with money and gave him directions for the party. Al-Mughassil then gave Al-Marhoun $2000 in $100 United States bills to support Al-Marhoun's cell in their surveillance activity in Saudi Arabia. Al-Marhoun used the money to finance a trip to Riyadh with Ramadan to look for American sites.

- In about June 1995, the Hezbollah cell composed of Al-Marhoun, Ramadan, and Al-Mu'alem began regular surveillance of Khobar Towers at Al-Mughassil direction. Shortly thereafter, Ramadan traveled to Beirut to brief Al-Mughassil, who instructed the cell to continue surveillance. At about the same time in

1995 that Ramadan went to Beirut to update Al-Mughassil on surveillance activities, Al-Alawi was summoned to Beirut by Al-Mughassil. Although Al-Alawe did not see Ramadan, he noticed surveillance reports from Ramadan on Al-Mughassil's desk. During their meeting, Al-Mughassil explained to Al-Alawe that explosives were going to be used against Americans in Saudi Arabia and he instructed Al-Alawe to drive a vehicle he said contained explosives from Lebanon to Saudi Arabia. Al-Alawe did so, only to discover that the car held no explosives; Al-Mughassil explained that he had only been testing him.

- In about October 1995, an unknown man visited Al-Alawe at his home in Eastern Saudi Arabia and delivered a map of Khobar, saying Al-Mughassil wanted Al-Alawe to check its accuracy. A short time later, the same man retrieved the map and left a package weighing about one kilogram. Al-Alawe kept the package until Al-Mughassil called and told him to deliver it to another man unknown to him. Al-Alawe did as instructed and did not look inside the package.

- In the late fall of 1995, Ramadan brought more surveillance reports to Al-Mughassil in Beirut. It was then that Ramadan, Al-Marhoun, and Al-Mu'alem learned from Al-Mughassil that Hezbollah would attack Khobar Towers, using a tanker truck loaded with a mixture of explosives and gasoline. At the end of 1995 or the beginning of 1996, Ramadan again returned to Beirut, where he and Al-Mughassil again discussed the planned tanker truck attack on Khobar Towers and the fact that Ramadan, Al-Marhoun, and Al-Mu'alem would each have a role in the attack. Al-Mughassil said they would need enough explosives to destroy a row of buildings and that the attack was to serve Iran by driving the Americans out of the Gulf region. In January or February 1996, Al-Mughassil traveled to Qatif, in the Eastern Province, and instructed Al-Marhoun to find places to hide explosives. In about February, at Al-Mughassil's direction, Ramadan met Al-Mughassil in Beirut and drove back to Saudi Arabia with a car loaded with hidden explosives. He delivered the car to a man in Qatif who wore a veil over his face.

- In March 1996, Al-Mughassil summoned Al-Alawe to Beirut and again outfitted him with a car that was to contain explosives. Al-Alawe drove the car from Lebanon, through Syria and Jordan, to the Al-Haditha border crossing in northern Saudi Arabia. There, on March 28, 1996, Saudi border guards discovered 38 kilograms of plastic explosives hidden in the car and arrested Al-Alawe. Saudi investigators then arrested Al-Marhoun, Al-Mu'alem, and Ramadan on April 6, 7, and 8, 1996, respectively.

- After the arrests of Al-Alawe and the Al-Marhoun cell, Al-Mughassil went back to Saudi Arabia in April or May 1996 to continue the planning for the Khobar attack. On or about May 1, 1996, Al-Mughassil appeared unannounced at Al-Jarash's home in Qatif, explaining that he had come as part of a pilgrimage and was traveling on a false passport. Al-Mughassil told Al-Jarash of the plot to bomb Khobar Towers, gave him a forged Iranian passport, and asked for his help. He told Al-Jarash that Al-Alawe and Al-Marhoun had been arrested. He also showed him a map of Khobar and described a plan in which Al-Houri and Al-Qassab would be involved; he told Al-Jarash to be ready for a call to action at any time.

- Three days later, on about May 4, 1996, Al-Mughassil showed up unannounced at Al-Mughis' home in Qatif to tell him of a plan to attack an American housing complex. Al-Mughassil explained that Al-Jarash, Al-Houri, Al-Sayegh and a Lebanese Hezbollah member would help. Al-Mughassil then gave Al-Mughis a timing device to hide at his home.

- Also during the first half of 1996, Al-Houri arrived at Al-Mughis' home on at least two occasions and enlisted Al-Mughis' help in hiding large amounts of explosives. They buried 50-kilo bags and paint cans filled with explosives at various sites around Qatif, near Khobar.

- In early June 1996, Al-Mughassil and the Lebanese Hezbollah member, John Doe, started staying at Al-Mughis's home in Qatif. Also in early June, a conspirator purchased a tanker truck from a car dealership in Saudi Arabia, using stolen identification. The conspirator paid about 75,000 Saudi riyals for the truck. Over the next two weeks, the conspirators worked at a farm in the Qatif area to convert the tanker truck into a large truck bomb. Present at the farm were Al-Mughassil, Al-Houri, Al-Sayegh, Al-Qassab, and John Doe. Al-Mughis assisted by returning the timing device and retrieving hidden explosives, while Al-Jarash supplied tools and wire to the group. During the bomb construction, Al-Mughassil also discussed plans to bomb the United States Consulate in Dhahran, Saudi Arabia.

- Between June 7 and June 17, 1996, key members of the conspiracy attended a meeting at the Sayyeda Zeinab shrine in Damascus. Present were Al-Nasser, Al-Mughassil, Al-Houri, Al-Yacoub, Al-Sayegh, Al-Qassab, and other high-ranking Saudi Hezbollah leaders. At that meeting, Al-Nasser, the head of Saudi Hezbollah, discussed the bombing with, among others, Al-Mughassil, Al-Houri, Al-Yacoub, Al-Sayegh, and Al-Qassab; Al-Nasser also confirmed that Al-Mughassil was in charge of the Khobar attack.

- On the evening of June 25, 1996, Al-Mughassil, Al-Houri, Al-Sayegh, Al-Qassab, Al-Jarash, and Al-Mughis met at the farm in Qatif to review final preparations for the attack that evening. The group then executed the bombing plan. Shortly before 10:00 P.M. on the evening of June 25, 1996, Al-Sayegh drove a Datsun with Al-Jarash as his passenger. The Datsun entered the parking lot adjoining Khobar Towers building #131 as a scout vehicle and parked in the far corner. Next to enter the parking lot was the getaway car, a white four-door Chevrolet Caprice that Al-Mughis had borrowed from an acquaintance. The Datsun containing Al-Sayegh and Al-Jarash signaled that all was clear by blinking its lights. With that, the bomb truck, driven by Al-Mughassil, with Al-Houri as passenger, entered the lot and backed against a fence just in front of Al-Khobar Towers building #131.

- After parking the truck, Al-Mughassil and Al-Houri quickly exited and entered the back seat of the white Caprice, which drove away from the lot, followed by the Datsun from the corner. Within minutes, the truck bomb exploded, devastating the north side of building #131, which was occupied by American military personnel. The explosion killed nineteen members of the United States Air Force and wounded 372 other Americans.

- As planned, the attack leaders immediately left the Khobar area and Saudi Arabia using a variety of false passports. Only Al-Jarash and Al-Mughis remained behind in their hometown of Qatif. Al-Sayegh reached Canada in August 1996, where he remained until his arrest by Canadian authorities in March 1997.

- In May 1997, Al-Sayegh met with American investigators at his request. Among other things, Al-Sayegh falsely denied knowledge of the Khobar Towers attack and falsely described a purported estrangement between Saudi Hezbollah and elements of the Iranian government. After he was transported to the United States in June 1997 on his promise to assist American investigators, Al-Sayegh reneged on that promise and unsuccessfully sought political asylum in the United States.

The Role of Iran and the Threat of an American Follow-up

Attorney General Ashcroft went on to publicly link the Al-Khobar bombing to Iranian government officials. He attested that

> the indictment explains that elements of the Iranian government inspired, supported and supervised members of Saudi Hezbollah. In particular, the indictment alleges that the charged defendants reported their surveillance activities to Iranian officials and were supported and directed in those activities by Iranian officials.[49]

While the indictment did not name any Iranians as criminal defendants, Ashcroft did note that the case brought against the fourteen defendants was limited to those dependents because "as with any criminal case, [this] is what we believe we can prove in a court of law."[50] He also stated that the United States would pursue further indictments. The text of the indictment also stated that members of the Iranian Revolutionary Guard Corps and the Ministry of Intelligence and Security "continued to be involved in the planning and execution of terrorist acts and continued to support a variety of groups that use terrorism to pursue their goals."[51]

President Bush stated,

> For the last five years, the Department of Justice and the Federal Bureau of Investigation have conducted an intensive investigation of this deplorable act of terrorism. . . . I applaud the work of the Department of Justice and the FBI who have spent countless hours pursuing this case. And I want to thank the Kingdom of Saudi Arabia for their assistance in this investigation.[52]

Acting U.S. Attorney Kenneth Melson, who prosecuted the case, gave a press interview stating that he was looking forward "to working with our Saudi partners and law enforcement around the world to apprehend the fugitives and to bring all these defendants to justice."[53]

Shortly thereafter, however, FBI Director Louis Freeh gave a press conference that was far more controversial. He was careful to praise Saudi

Arabia for its help and thank the Saudis involved, but he also stated that the investigation would remain open and the FBI would pursue it "to ensure that all those responsible are ultimately brought to justice." Freeh commented that some of the Saudis indicted that day were in jail in Saudi Arabia. While the United States did not have an extradition treaty with Saudi Arabia, efforts were made to bring the defendants to the United States. When Freeh was asked if the Saudis had agreed to extradite the suspects, he said only, "I am very confident that they will be brought to justice, and hopefully in the United States, some of them, at some point."[54] He refused to comment on why no charges were brought against Iranian officials, but stated,

> [E]veryone who could be charged based on the sufficiency of the evidence has been charged. That does not mean, however, that our investigation is over or that this indictment can't be amended or superseded if we reach the threshold of evidence which would be required to address additional subjects.[55]

The Saudis React with Denials

These events pushed the Saudis into the position of having to deal with the public exposure of internal dissent within Saudi Arabia, the problem of preserving their rapprochement with Iran, and with the fact the United States was indicting a group that was largely Saudi for crimes inside Saudi Arabia. The Saudi interior minister, Prince Nayef, gave a statement indicating that the United States had not consulted with Saudi Arabia before issuing the indictment, and asserted Saudi Arabia's jurisdiction over the issue. According to Prince Nayef, "The trials must take place before Saudi judicial authorities and our position on this question will not change. . . . No other entity has the right to try or investigate any crimes occurring on Saudi lands." Nayef went further and denied the very existence of the "Saudi Hezbollah."[56]

Saudi Minister of Defense Prince Sultan publicly agreed with Prince Nayef in that the United States should not have interfered in Saudi affairs. According to Prince Sultan, it was an issue that should only concern Saudi Arabia.

> The American side should send all the documents, complete proof and a list of names of the accused to us, because Saudi authorities alone are concerned with this case. We are glad to know of any country that has any background or information about any person who has a clue or was involved in [the bombing] and we will cooperate.

At the same time, Iran's state radio accused the United States of trying to undermine Iranian-Saudi rapprochement by implicating Tehran in the bombing. Iran quickly responded by denying any involvement. It stated that the U.S. indictments were an act of interference in Saudi internal affairs and would stir "more hatred in the Arab world" against the U. S. military presence in the Gulf. According to Iranian Foreign Ministry spokesman Hamid-Reza Assefi, "The U.S. judiciary has leveled charges against Iran which have no legal and judicial basis. The charges are only supplemental to the ceaseless efforts of the United States to pressure the Islamic Republic."[57] Assefi claimed that the U.S. charges were the result of the "the Zionist lobby and its influence."[58]

SUNNI VERSUS SHI'ITE

These events illustrate weaknesses in the Saudi approach to terrorism, as well as in the U.S. approach to dealing with Saudi Arabia, which were apparent long before September 11, 2001. At the same time, they show that serious terrorist threats exist that have nothing to do with Sunni extremism or bin Laden. Saudi Arabia must continue to deal with another type of religious extremist threat, with regional friction between traditionalists in the coastal cities and conservative traditionalist "Wahhabis" in the Najd, and with the Shafii and Shi'ite immigrants in the Hijaz. In addition, it may have to deal with vestigial tensions between the followers of Ibn Saud in the Najd and the North and the citizens of the Hijaz around Mecca and Medina, which date back to the time King Abd al-Aziz drove the Hashemites into exile.[59] There are also many longstanding tribal resentments and feuds, some of which predate the rise of King Abd al-Aziz.

The divisions between Sunni and Shi'ite are more serious, however, and affect both Saudi internal security and the region with most of Saudi Arabia's oil reserves. The Shi'ites make up about 5% to 6% of Saudi Arabia's total population, and something under 10% of its native population, although some estimates go as high as 15%. They probably number between 400,000 and 700,000, although one estimate goes as high as 2 million. They clearly make up a substantial part of the native population of the oil-rich Eastern Province—possibly as much as 40%.[60] Saudi Shi'ites have some current and historical ties to the Farsi-speaking Shi'ites of Iran, but they are traditional Arabs who have occupied the coastal area and towns like Qatif, and the inland oasis of Al-Hasa and its city of Hofuf, for centuries. They are the original town-dwellers and farmers in the Eastern Province; the nomadic Bedouin were Sunni.

The tension between Saudi Shi'ite and Sunni is especially intense because Saudi "Wahhabis" actively reject all veneration of a man, even the prophet. At one point they even attempted to destroy Muhammad's tomb in Medina. In contrast, the Saudi Shi'ites are "Twelvers," a branch of Shi'ite Islam that venerates the Prophet's son-in-law Ali, and believes that the leadership of Islam must pass through Ali's line. They venerate each of the past imams, and make pilgrimages to their tombs. Their religious practices included self-flagellation and a high degree of mysticism. All of these practices are abhorrent to Wahhabis.

As a result, the Shi'ites have long been largely excluded from any political role in Sunni-ruled areas and have been treated as second-class Saudi citizens. There has been little intermarriage or social contact between Shi'ite and Sunni, and Shi'ite economic opportunities have been severely restricted. These Wahhabi pressures on Saudi Shi'ites diminished during the Turkish interregnum from the 1870s to 1913, but Abd al-Aziz's reconquest of Arabia again made them a reality from the 1920s onward.

Ironically, this discrimination was a factor that led many Saudi Shi'ites to go to work for Aramco once oil was discovered in Saudi Arabia. For the most part, they had few other major opportunities even though they were a more stable and better-educated workforce than most Sunni Bedouin. The Shi'ites also showed more interest in secondary and technical education than did most Bedouin. As a result, Shi'ites made up 30% to 40% of the Aramco workforce from the 1950s to late 1970s, often rising to relatively senior positions. Most of Aramco's security personnel were Shi'ite until the mid-to-late 1970s, and many of the residents of key "oil cities" like Abqaiq, Dammam, Dhahran, and Ras Tanura areas were Shi'ite.

Saudi Shi'ites exhibited little separate political identity until after World War II, although the Shi'ite clergy were relatively well organized by Saudi standards and the Shi'ite elders did furnish a traditional political framework at the local level. The main points of political friction occurred between the Shi'ite community leaders and the leaders of the Jiluwi tribe, which provided the governors and senior officials of the Eastern Province from the 1920s to the late 1970s. The Jiluwis ruthlessly suppressed any dissent, and prevented demonstrations or efforts at political organization beyond the local level.

Things began to change, however, in the late 1940s. Aramco and higher education exposed local workers to union labor, in part because of the wave of anti-colonial, "anti-imperial" rhetoric sweeping the developing world, and in part due to Pan-Arabism and Nasser. At the same time the increases in Shi'ite education and wealth encouraged Shi'ite political development. A short-lived Shi'ite uprising—led by Muhammad ibn Hussein al-Harraj—took place in Qatif in 1948 and was followed by growing unrest in the region. Much of this labor unrest was more pro-Nasser and pro-labor than sectarian, but the Shi'ites did begin to organize more effectively at the community level.

Shi'ite resentment of the Jiluwi governors, the occasional Wahhabi crackdowns on Shi'ite religious ceremonies, and the economic and educational discrimination practiced by the Saudi government increased steadily during the 1950s and 1960s. The Jiluwis did little to develop Qatif and Hofuf, and a series of governors continued to be harsh and repressive. Abdullah Jiluwi and his son Saud were particularly disliked, although Abd-al-Mushin

Jiluwi attempted to ease tensions when he became governor in the 1970s.[61] The Saudi government did appoint a Shi'ite minister of agriculture and a Shi'ite director-general of the Royal Commission at Jubail, but this tokenism did not help develop career opportunities in the Eastern Province and new economic problems began to emerge.

Shi'ites began to be excluded or removed from jobs in Aramco, or denied promotion. They were also excluded from student offices at the University of Petroleum and Minerals in Dhahran although they comprised more than half of the student body. The Jiluwis arrested any Shi'ite who threatened to organize other workers or strike and increased their surveillance over Shi'ite religious leaders. In 1970, riots occurred in Qatif that were so serious that the town had to be sealed off for a month. Severe riots again occurred in 1978 and were followed by fifty arrests and several executions.

The situation exploded on December 3–5, 1979, shortly after the Ayatollah Khomeini rose to power in Iran. The excuse was the Ashura, or 10th of Muharram, which is the anniversary of the martyrdom of Hussein, the prophet Muhammad's grandson. This is the holiest day in the Shi'ite calendar, and the fall of the Shah meant that Iranian Shi'ites could openly celebrate the day with self-flagellation for the first time in decades. Saudi Shi'ites reacted to Khomeini's victory by organizing protests and demonstrations in Qatif and in Khafji, calling for a more equitable sharing of the nation's wealth and for the al-Saud family to support the Iranian revolution. The government sent in the National Guard, a key Guard commander panicked, and at least five demonstrators were killed and several hundred were arrested.

The Saudi crackdown that followed was severe, partly because the governor and National Guard greatly exaggerated the seriousness of the riots that occurred shortly after the uprising at the Grand Mosque. The government feared the loss of oil production and the destruction of oil facilities. In addition, Ayatollah Khomeini denounced the Saudi royal family and called for its overthrow and death.

As time went on, however, it became apparent to the leaders of the royal family that neglect, discrimination, and the Jiluwis had been responsible for much of what had happened. As a result, the royal family shifted to a policy of conciliation. Development funds were poured into Qatif and Hofuf, and new schools, hospitals, and housing developments were announced and rushed into construction. Political prisoners were freed. Prince Ahmad, Prince Nayef's younger brother and deputy minister of interior, toured the area in early 1980 and promised reforms. This visit was followed by a series of "flying Majilises" in the Shi'ite towns and cities, and by a speech by Crown Prince Fahd that called for Islam without discrimination. The king made a ten-day visit in November 1980. The Jiluwi governors were bypassed and replaced by Muhammad bin Fahd, a son of the king, in 1983.

The government of the Eastern Province was then modernized and fully integrated with that of the rest of Saudi Arabia.

These steps helped but scarcely ended the problem. Although there were few public incidents, a number of Shi'ites remained in exile. In addition, several loosely organized Shi'ite groups and cells were set up to oppose the government—some with Iranian support. A major new wave of arrests took place in 1981, and a long series of incidents of petty sabotage followed. Shi'ites were slowly excluded from Aramco's security forces and from many sensitive jobs. There were few incidents involving real violence, but there were recurrent arrests of students and workers and some arrests of Shi'ite religious figures. Saudi officials also indicated that there was some cooperation between Saudi Shi'ite extremists and Iranian pilgrims throughout some of the Iranian protests during the Hajj.

Prior to 1990, the government continued to prohibit Shi'ite public processions during the Islamic month of Muharram and restricted other processions and congregations to designated areas in the major Shi'ite cities. The authorities have since permitted marches on the Shi'a holiday of Ashura, provided the marchers do not display banners or engage in self-flagellation. Commemorations of the Ashura have gone on peacefully in the Eastern Province since that time. However, the government still left religious problems for the Shi'ites. For example, it seldom permits the private construction of Shi'ite mosques. Yet the Shi'ites decline government offers to build state-supported mosques because Shi'ite motifs would be prohibited in them.

Religious tensions then interacted with the decline in Saudi Arabia's oil wealth during the late 1980s and early-to-mid-1990s. Shi'ite towns received less investment, less money went to Shi'ite areas after 1990, and housing loans became harder to get. Shi'ites increasingly complained about discrimination in admission to advanced education, job hiring, and even medical treatment. This led to new political problems. New Shi'ite protests took place, and some Shi'ite groups began to publicly attack the U.S. military presence in the Eastern Province as a mercenary force that was aiding Saudi royal family in occupying the area, which controlled it on behalf of the Sunnis, and which was supporting Zionism and preparing to attack Iran.

The Saudi government tried to deal with these problems by improving economic and educational opportunities and by co-opting Shi'ite leaders rather than repressing them. It allowed a number of Shi'ite leaders to return from exile in 1993, and promised them additional benefits and government projects. However, the government no longer had the money or job opportunities to buy its way out of its problem. It also could not compromise too much or too publicly with the Shi'ites without creating additional problems with its Sunni Islamic extremists.

The revival of Sunni Islamic fundamentalism after the Gulf War, in turn, convinced many Shi'ites that they could only be second-rate citizens in their own country. The fact that the government increasingly restricted the jobs open to Shi'ites in an effort to reduce any Shi'ite threat to key petroleum and economic facilities did not help.

Even so, extremist Shi'ite movements like the Saudi Hezbollah probably have less than 1,000 members of any kind and less than 250 hard-core members. Most Saudi Shi'ites still are not militant, and even most Shi'ites in exile advocate peaceful change.[62] The al-Khoei Foundation and Shi'ite Reform Movement are two examples of such Shi'ite groups. The Shi'ite population of Saudi Arabia is also too small to succeed in any kind of uprising or separatism. It is, however, large enough to present a significant source of social tension in the world's most important oil producing area. This has been demonstrated by the fact there have been recurrent, minor incidents of sabotage of oil facilities.

The Saudi security services cannot deal with this problem beyond suppressing individual movements like the Saudi Hezbollah. It is unlikely that repression can ever be a workable solution. There are still cells of radical Shi'ites in the Eastern Province that have obtained some support from Iran, and the improving relations between Saudi Arabia and Iran do not mean that young Saudi Shi'ites do not continue to train in Iran and Lebanon. There continue to be occasional incidents between Shi'ite groups and the government, while the arrest of younger Shi'ite clerics like Abdul Karim Hubaillast and Sheikh Jaffar Mubarak still continue.[63]

MILITANT SAUDI EXTREMISTS:
OSAMA BIN LADEN AND AL-QAEDA

Osama bin Laden was Saudi Arabia's best-known violent militant long before September 11, 2001, and had sponsored or supported major acts of terrorism like the attacks on the U.S. embassies in Kenya and Tanzania and the U.S.S. *Cole*. Bin Laden had already emerged as the one Saudi extremist competent and charismatic enough to have a major influence outside Saudi Arabia. Since September 11, bin Laden has become so well known that there is little reason to repeat his history in depth. It is important to note, however, that bin Laden became a problem for the Saudi government long before he became a threat to the United States, that his beliefs and ideology were shaped by forces from outside Saudi Arabia as well as within it, and that his organization—al-Qaeda—is far more transnational than Saudi.

In brief, bin Laden joined the Afghan resistance almost immediately after the Soviet invasion in December 1979. He did so as a "secular" Saudi trained in engineering and without formal religious education. According to Saudi and U.S. experts, he played a significant role in financing, recruiting, transporting, and training Arab nationals who volunteered to fight in Afghanistan. During the Afghan war, bin Ladin founded al-Qaeda (the Base) to serve as an operational hub for like-minded extremists, and to train and organize his own terrorist and military groups. He initially used this network not only to "track friends and fellow mujahadeen fighters," but also to be able to "give answers to families with missing loved ones and friends who were out of touch."[64]

Soon after Iraq invaded Kuwait, bin Laden began expressing his dismay that Saudi Arabia sought the help of western governments, particularly the United States, during the Gulf War. Bin Laden was so enraged that he decided to leave the Kingdom and move to Pakistan. Not long after he arrived in Pakistan, bin Laden moved back to Afghanistan and struggled to bring the opposing factions together while also soliciting support for a new "Jihad."[65] After his attempts failed and several assassination attempts were made on his life, he fled to the Sudan.[66]

In 1993 the Saudi government froze all of bin Laden's financial assets and in 1994 the government publicly revoked his citizenship. Soon thereafter, bin Laden's family officially disowned him. It has been speculated that while bin Laden was living in the Sudan, the Saudi government went so far as to make several failed assassination attempts on his life, and Saudi intelligence officials have claimed they tried to have him forced over to the United States.[67] International pressure on the Sudanese government then forced him to move back to Afghanistan in 1996.[68]

On his return to Afghanistan, bin Laden issued several public statements, including a Declaration of Jihad, and several "fatwas" calling for all Muslims "to kill Americans and their allies, civilian and military, [as] an individual duty."[69] In addition, he helped set up training camps in Afghanistan where members could be trained in various military and terrorist skills, including those necessary to conduct a "Jihad" against the United States.[70]

Bin Laden became progressively more openly anti–Saudi government after he was made to leave the Kingdom. His main public grievances against the Saudi regime included a "lack of commitment to the teachings of Sunni Islam, the state's inability to conduct a viable defense policy, the mismanagement of public funds and squandering of oil money, and the state's dependence on non-Muslims for protection."

Bin Laden and al-Qaeda played a major role in the bombings of the U.S. embassies in Nairobi, Kenya, and in Dar es Salaam, Tanzania, on August 7, 1998. Bin Laden had made a series of public threats to drive the United States and its allies out of Islamic countries before the attacks, and issued a "fatwa" on February 23, 1998, under the name "World Islamic Front for Jihad Against the Jews and Crusaders." This kind of "fatwa" is personal, and has no religious legitimacy according to Wahhabi religious practices. Neither does its assertion that it is a religious duty for all Muslims to wage war against U.S. citizens, both military and civilian, anywhere in the world.

In December 1998, bin Laden gave a series of interviews in which he denied direct involvement in the East Africa bombings but said that he

"instigated" them by calling for attacks on U.S. citizens worldwide in re-
taliation for the strikes against Iraq. The United States has blamed bin
Laden and al-Qaeda for these attacks, and for playing a major role in the
attack on the U.S.S. *Cole* in October 2000. Several Saudi nationals, including Muhammad Omar al-Harazi, have been arrested in connection with
these attacks. Al-Harazi was identified by Jamal al-Badawi as a chief fin-
ancier of the U.S.S. *Cole* attack,[71] while other sources have identified him
as the "operations leader" of the attack.[72] Al-Harazi established the first
al-Qaeda cell in Saudi Arabia, and was involved in a failed attack in January 2000 on the United States warship, the U.S.S. *The Sullivans.*[73]

The tragic events of September 11 are now too well known to merit
detailed discussion, but it is important to note that bin Laden and al-Qaeda
continue to pose a threat to Saudi stability as well as to the United States
and other Western states. While their primary target has been U.S. and
Western influence in the Arab world, they have consistently called for the
overthrow of the Saudi royal family and government as part of a broader
effort to destroy what it deems corrupt—Western-oriented governments in
predominantly Muslim countries. In the process, they have also posed a
challenge to Saudi Arabia's traditional religious practices, its Ulema, social
and educational reforms, and economic modernization.

As discussed earlier, bin Laden has no formal religious training or status in Saudi religious terms, and al-Qaeda is scarcely a purely "Saudi"
organization, although fifteen of the nineteen attackers on the World Trade
Center and Pentagon had Saudi passports and many of al-Qaeda's members are Saudi. Most of al-Qaeda's senior leaders have been North African
and non-Saudi. Moreover, many—if not most—of al-Qaeda members in
other terrorist attempts and attacks have been non-Saudi. For example, the
suspects identified after the bombings of the U.S. embassies in Kenya and
Tanzania included Egyptians, one Comoran, one Palestinian, one Saudi, and
U.S. citizens.[74]

Bin Laden has established serious liaisons with a wide range of other
groups including many whose version of Islamic extremism has little to do
with Wahhabi practices and teachings. He uses money he has inherited and
obtained from business interests and contributions from sympathizers in
various countries. He has obtained support from allies such as the Egyptian and South Asian groups that have signed his "fatwa." He funds, trains,
and offers logistic help to extremists not directly affiliated with his organization. Al-Qaeda has sent trainers to Tajikistan, Bosnia, Chechnya,
Somalia, Sudan, and Yemen as well as to Afghanistan. It has trained fighters from numerous other countries, including the Philippines, Egypt, Libya,
Pakistan, Eritrea, and the Occupied Territories in Gaza and the West Bank.

Al-Qaeda has, however, sought to set social and political goals for Saudi
Arabia as well as for the Gulf and the entire Islamic world. It has four major
aims: to eliminate the United States and Western presence from the region,

to eradicate all forms of non-Islamic rule and apply the Islamic teachings to all aspects of life, to achieve true Islamic justice and eradicate all forms of injustice; to reform the political system and purify it from corruption and to "revive" a system to make it possible for citizens to bring charges against state officials. At the same time, al-Qaeda believes that all means to bring about an Islamic state are legitimate as long as they conform to Islamic teachings. Essentially, this viewpoint contends that violence is legitimate whenever deemed necessary.

Bin Laden lacks many of the personal qualities that are normally necessary for credibility and importance within Saudi society. He is the seventeenth son of a wealthy businessman whose family has become a leading force in the Saudi construction business, but which has a marginal status in terms of tribal genealogy and place of birth. Although he was born in Riyadh, his family comes from the Hadhramaut region of Yemen. In spite of his family's wealth, he is still considered a non-Saudi and is looked down upon by many in the intensely tribal Najdi heartland. He issues personal "fatwas" despite a lack of any Saudi religious credentials or right to do so. In addition, his criticism of royal corruption seems somewhat hypocritical because most of bin Laden's money has come from his family's connections to the royal family. When bin Laden was declared an opposition figure, his family chose to disown him rather than let their relationship with the royal family suffer. Bin Laden, however, has never disowned its money.

There is no way to predict exactly how much of al-Qaeda's organization and affiliates the United States will destroy as a result of its war on terrorism, whether bin Laden will be imprisoned or killed, and how many supporters of al-Qaeda will emerge in new movements or continue to be violent opponents of the Saudi regime. It is all too clear, however, that other "new men" like bin Laden can and will suddenly emerge as serious threats to the Saudi regime and its ties to the other states. It is equally clear that nothing the Saudi government does can control the flow of funding to extremist movements, as long as so much Saudi capital is held outside of the Kingdom. Even if the world does hear the last of bin Laden, it seems doubtful that he will be the last violent Sunni extremist to come out of Saudi Arabia.

MILITANT SAUDI EXTREMISTS: OTHER THREATS

There may already be emerging cadres of such extremists. The Saudi government rarely reports publicly on internal security problems, and when they do become public, it tries to deal with them as criminal rather than political activity. While it has arrested as many as 300 men involved in religious extremism since September 2001, a significant number of whom do not have ties to bin Laden or al-Qaeda, it has done so as quietly as possible. When it does have to deal with internal security problems publicly, it usually focuses on foreign suspects and does not mention or downplays the role of Saudis. It also tries to avoid public reporting on internal violence that does not involve foreign targets.

There were scattered indications of violence against foreigners long before September 11, 2001. The Saudi government has arrested a Briton, Canadian, and Belgian, among others, for what it claims were criminal attacks related to the smuggling of alcohol and drugs. These include bombings on November 17 and 22, 2000 that killed one British man and injured five other foreigners. Another bombing took place on December 15, 2000. The Saudi government did not publicize any details of this conspiracy when it announced the arrests on February 4, 2001. On May 2, 2001, a parcel bomb injured Gary Hatch, an American physiotherapist at Saad Medical Center, and on October 6, 2001 Ayman bin Muhammad abu Zinad, a Palestinian dentist at a private clinic in Riyadh, injured four expatriate workers and killed himself and an American citizen when he set off a bomb. On September 29, 2002, a German man was killed by a car bomb.[75]

According to Prince Nayef, the minister of the interior, none of these attacks had political motives. However, U.S. and other experts believe that they may well have had such motives and that a number of small Saudi extremist attacks on Saudis and Saudi targets, both by Sunni extremists and Saudi Shi'ites, continue to go unreported. Most such attacks seem associated with small Islamic splinter groups and do not seem to pose a serious threat. However, there was a significant attempt to attack U.S. military aircraft in 2002, and there have been unconfirmed reports of serious terrorist attempts on Saudi targets.[76]

It may be possible to defeat a man or an organization, but it is unlikely that the Saudi government can defeat an idea or ideology that will inevitably attract a minority of Saudis. It only takes a comparative handful of Saudis to create both internal and external problems, and only minor financial resources are involved. As long as a combination of social turmoil, demographic pressure, Islamic extremism, and the backlash from the Second Intifada continue to put pressure on Saudi society, new violent extremists will continue to emerge.

OPPOSITION, EXTREMISM, TERRORISM AND SAUDI COUNTERTERRORISM

Nevertheless, Islam is still far more of a stabilizing force in Saudi Arabia than a threat to the al-Saud regime. Conservative practices do constrain Saudi Arabia's social and economic development, but the Kingdom has so far managed to modernize many aspects of its society and economy in evolutionary ways that have avoided social conflict. This progress is slower than in many parts of the Arab world, but it has generally been fast enough to meet Saudi needs. The two exceptions are education and the role women play in the Saudi economy, and these areas are where faster evolution is needed although some change is already underway.

Saudi Islamic extremism is both an internal and external threat. Of the two, the internal threat seems least important. Terrorists do exist, as well as religious bigots that threaten Saudi relations with the outside world. There will almost certainly be more attacks on Saudi government facilities and Westerners inside the Kingdom. In broad terms, however, there is little evidence of a broad political consciousness that is hostile to the regime, and less evidence of major popular support for Islamic extremism. There is little evidence that support for violence goes beyond a small minority. The emerging forces of public opinion seem more focused on domestic issues like jobs, education, and health care than political causes. The one exception is broad popular support for the Palestinian cause, and Saudi public opinion does see the Palestinians as "freedom fighters" and the Israelis as "terrorists." This has already created broad popular resentment of the United States, and has been made worse by the mutual mistrust and misunderstanding that has developed since September 11, 2001. Although Islamic extremists have tried to capitalize on the issue, however, they seem to have had limited success. The same may well be true of the new tensions that arise over the U.S. confrontation with Iraq.

The role Saudi Arabia has played in exporting Islamic extremism, and funding terrorist actions has had more serious effects. The legacy of Saudi funding for the Afghan Mujahideen in their struggle with the FSU, for Islamic fighters in Bosnia and Kosovo, and for the Palestinian Islamic movements has been to aid extremist and terrorist movements that cannot be described as freedom fighters. Saudi charitable funding has been very poorly controlled, and Saudi Arabia has often provided money to Islamic movements and schools in other countries that are not "puritan" or "Unitarian" in any legitimate sense, but rather highly politicized forms of Islam or political movements that have cloaked themselves in Islam. The end effect has been serious destabilization in south and central Asia and has indirectly aided movements like al-Qaeda in a number of Middle Eastern, Western, and Southeast Asian nations. The fact that this has little to do with Wahhabi movements in any classic sense, and has been more careless than deliberate, does not mean that the Kingdom does not need to take blame when blame is due and take the necessary action to put an end to such practices.

Fortunately, Saudi Arabia has taken a much stronger stand toward all forms of Islamic extremism since September 11. While Saudi senior officials initially dealt with the attack on the World Trade Center and the Pentagon with an awkward mix of sympathy and denial, they have since taken a more realistic approach. They have stepped up intelligence cooperation with the United States, arrested a wide number of suspects, and systematically tightened control over the flow of money to domestic and foreign extremist groups from within the Kingdom.[77]

Saudi officials have reported that the Kingdom has taken a wide range of new counterterrorism measures designed to control Islamic extremism and terrorism since September 11, 2001. U.S. intelligence experts have informally confirmed the existence of these measures, and by November 2002, they involved a wide range of actions in several key areas.[78]

International Cooperation

Saudi Arabia has stepped up its support of many international and regional efforts through multilateral and bilateral agreements in the fight against terrorism and has begun to work more closely with the U.S., European, and Asian governments and the United Nations to ensure that information is shared more quickly and effectively. This has included the following specific actions:

- Maintaining a counterterrorism committee with the United States comprised of intelligence and law enforcement personnel who meet regularly to share information and resources and to develop action plans to root out terrorist networks. Saudi Arabia has sought to strengthen cooperation between the Kingdom and the United States through reciprocal visits.

- Encouraging Saudi government departments and banks to participate in international seminars, conferences and symposia on combating terrorist financing activities. Saudi Arabia has hosted seminars, conferences and symposia on combating terrorism and is a member of the GCC Financial Action Task Force (FATF).

- Completing and submitting the Self-Assessment Questionnaire regarding the forty recommendations of the FATF. Saudi Arabia has also submitted the Self-Assessment Questionnaire regarding the eight Special Recommendations of the FATF.

- Having the Saudi Arabian Monetary Authority (SAMA) exchange information on money laundering related activities with other banking supervisory authorities and with law enforcement agencies. SAMA has created a committee to carry out a self-assessment for compliance with the recommendations of the FATF, and these self-assessment questionnaires have been submitted. Saudi Arabia has invited the FATF to conduct a mutual evaluation in April 2003.

Arrests and Questioning of Suspects

Saudi intelligence and law enforcement authorities have been working closely with the United States, Interpol, and other countries to identify, question, and when appropriate, arrest suspects. It has taken the following actions:

- Saudi Arabia has questioned over 2,000 individuals. Many of these people fought in Afghanistan during the Soviet invasion as well as in Bosnia and Chechnya.

- Saudi intelligence and law enforcement agencies identified and arrested a cell composed of seven individuals linked to al-Qaeda who were planning to carry out terrorist attacks against vital sites in the Kingdom. The cell leader was extradited from the Sudan. This cell was responsible for the attempt to shoot down American military planes at Prince Sultan Airbase using a shoulder-launched surface-to-air missile.

- Detaining about 200 suspects for questioning and interrogation.

- Successfully negotiating with Iran for the extradition of sixteen suspected al-Qaeda members. These individuals are now in Saudi custody and are being questioned. The Iranian authorities handed over the al-Qaeda fugitives, all Saudis, knowing that whatever intelligence was obtained from them during interrogation in Saudi Arabia would be passed on to the United States for use in the war against terrorism.

- Asking Interpol to arrest 750 people, many of whom are suspected of money laundering, drug trafficking, and terror-related activities. This figure includes 214 Saudis whose names appear in Interpol's database and expatriates who fled Saudi Arabia.

- Helping to identify a network of more than fifty shell companies that Osama bin Laden used to move money around the world. The companies were located in the Middle East, Europe, Asia, and the Caribbean. A sophisticated financial network that weaved through more than twenty-five nations was uncovered and virtually shut down.

Legal and Regulatory Actions, Freezing Terrorist Assets, and Combating Money Laundering

The Kingdom has taken the following specific actions to prevent the financing of terrorism, which include a wide range of legal and regulatory measures:

- Signing and joining the UN Convention against Illicit Trafficking of Narcotics and Psychotropic Substances in 1988.

- Freezing assets of Osama bin Laden in 1994.

- Establishing anti–money laundering units at the Ministry of Interior, SAMA, and commercial banks in 1995.

- Having SAMA issue "Guidelines for Prevention and Control of Money Laundering Activities" to Saudi banks to implement "Know Your Customer Rules," maintain records of suspicious transactions, and report then to law enforcement officials in SAMA in 1995.

- Identifying and freezing all Saudi bank assets relating to terrorist suspects and entities per the list issued by the U.S. government on September 23, 2001. Saudi banks have complied with the freeze requirements and have initiated investigation of transaction that suspects linked to al-Qaeda may have undertaken in the past.

- Investigating bank accounts suspected to have been linked to terrorism. Saudi Arabia froze thirty-eight accounts belonging to four individuals that totaled about $3,722,180.00.

- Establishing a special committee with personnel from the Ministry of Interior, Ministry of Foreign Affairs, the Intelligence Agency, and SAMA to deal with requests from international bodies and countries with regards to combating terrorist financing.

- Reorienting the activities of the GCC FATF to deal with terrorism and creating a committee to carry out a self-assessment for compliance with the recommendations of the FATF.

- Joining finance ministers and central bank governors of the G-20 in order to develop an aggressive action plan directed at the routing out and freezing of terrorist assets worldwide.

- Having SAMA instruct Saudi banks to promptly establish a supervisory committee to closely monitor the threat posed by terrorism and to coordinate all efforts to freeze the assets of potential terrorists. The committee is composed of senior officers from banks responsible for risk control, audit, money-laundering units, legal, and operations. The committee meets regularly in the presence of SAMA officials.

- Requiring Saudi banks to put in place mechanisms to respond to all relevant inquiries, both domestically and internationally, at the level of their chief executive officers, as well as at the level of the supervisory committee. To ensure proper coordination and effective response, all Saudi banks route their responses and relevant information via SAMA.

- Having the Ministry of Commerce issue Regulation #1312 aimed at preventing and combating money laundering in the nonfinancial sector. These regulations are aimed at manufacturing and trading sectors and also cover professional services such as accounting, legal, and consultancy services.

- Creating an institutional framework for combating money laundering, including the establishment of anti–money laundering units, with a trained and dedicated specialist staff. These units work with SAMA and law enforcement agencies. The government has also encouraged banks to bring money laundering–related experiences to the notice of various bank committees (chief operations officers, managing directors, fraud committee, etc.) for exchange of information and joint actions.

- Creating specialized Financial Intelligence Unit (FIU) in the Security and Drug Control Department of the Ministry of Interior. This unit is specially tasked with handling money-laundering cases. A new liaison group dealing with terrorist finances has been established between SAMA and the Ministry of the Interior.

- Carrying out regular inspection of banks to ensure compliance with laws and regulations. Any violation or non-compliance is cause for serious actions and is referred to a bank's senior management and the board. Furthermore, the government has created a permanent committee of banks' compliance officers to review regulations and guidelines and recommend improvements, and to ensure all implementation issues are resolved.

- Freezing bank accounts suspected of links to terrorists.
- Supporting UN resolutions, such as UN Security Council Resolution 1368 to limit the financing of terrorist activities.
- Working with the United States and other countries to block more than $70 million in possible terrorist assets in Saudi Arabia and other countries.
- Providing data on suspect private Saudi accounts in Switzerland, Liechtenstein, Luxembourg, Denmark, and Sweden.
- Directing SAMA to issue rules "Governing the Opening of Bank Accounts" and "General Operational Guidelines" in order to protect banks against money laundering activities in May 2002. For instance, Saudi banks are not permitted to open bank accounts for nonresident individuals without specific approval from SAMA. Banks are required to apply strict rules, and any noncustomer business has to be fully documented.
- Carrying out regular inspection of banks to ensure compliance with laws and regulations. Any violation or noncompliance is cause for serious actions and is referred to a bank's senior management and the board. Creating a permanent committee of banks' compliance officers to review regulation and guidelines and recommend improvements, and to ensure all implementation issues are resolved.
- Making significant new efforts to train staff in financial institutions and the Security and Investigation departments in the Ministry of Interior as well as others involved in compliance and law. Special training programs have been developed for bankers, prosecutors, judges, customs officers and other officials from government departments and agencies. Furthermore, training programs are offered by the Prince Nayef Security Academy, King Fahd Security Faculty and Public Security Training City.
- Establishing a permanent committee of representatives of seven ministries and government agencies to manage all legal and other issues related to money laundering activities.
- Directing SAMA to organize a conference with the Riyadh Interpol for the First Asian Regional meeting in cooperation with law enforcement agencies and financial institutions on January 28–30, 2002.
- Having the Council of Saudi Chambers of Commerce and Industry, in cooperation with SAMA, conduct an International Conference on Prevention and Detection of Fraud, Economic Crimes and Money Laundering on May 13–14, 2002.
- Directing Saudi banks and SAMA to computerize reported cases to identify trends in money laundering activities to assist in policymaking and other initiatives.

Actions Taken in Regard to Charitable Organizations

Since September 11, Saudi Arabia has conducted a thorough review of its charitable organizations and has taken a number of steps to limit the use of funds for terrorism:

- Working with the U.S. Treasury Department to block the accounts of the Somalia and Bosnia branches of the Saudi Arabia–based al-Haramain Islamic Foundation in March 2002. While the Saudi headquarters for this private charitable entity is dedicated to helping those in need, the United States and Saudi Arabia determined that the Somalia and Bosnia branches of al-Haramain Islamic Foundation engaged in supporting terrorist activities and terrorist organizations such as al-Qaeda, AIAI (al-Itihaad al-Islamiya), and others.
- Taking joint action with the United States to freeze the assets of a close bin Laden aide, Wa'el Hamza Julaidan, a Saudi fugitive who is believed to have funneled money to al-Qaeda. Julaidan served as the director of the Rabita Trust and other organizations.
- Establishing a high commission for oversights of all charities, contributions and donations and setting up operational procedures to manage contributions and donations to and from the charities.
- Auditing all charitable groups to ensure there are no links to suspected organizations since September 11, 2001.
- Issuing new guidelines and regulations, including financial control mechanisms to make sure terrorist and extremist organizations cannot take advantage of legitimate charities.
- Requiring that charitable activities outside Saudi Arabia be reported to the foreign ministry.
- Setting up the Higher Saudi Association for Relief and Charity to oversee the distribution of donations and guarantee they are channeled to the needy.
- Strengthening the role of the Saudi–U.S. counterterrorism committee comprised of intelligence and law enforcement personnel who meet regularly to share information and resources on the misuse of charities and charitable funds and develop plans of action to root out terrorist networks.
- Requiring that charitable activities that extend outside Saudi Arabia be reported to the Saudi government and are routinely monitored.
- Freezing bank accounts involving the flow of charitable funds that are suspected of being linked to terrorism.

Other Initiatives Related to Fighting Terrorism

Saudi Arabia has publicly improved its cooperation with various international efforts to combat terrorism. These include:

- Signing a multilateral agreement under the auspices of the Arab League to fight terrorism.
- Participating in G-20 meetings and signing various bilateral agreements with non-Arab countries.
- Preparing and submitting a report on the initiatives and actions taken by the Kingdom, with respect to the fight against terrorism, to the UN Security Council Committees every ninety days.

- Establishing communication points between the Ministry of Foreign Affairs and the Permanent Representative to the United Nations.
- Supporting and meeting the requirements of various UN resolutions related to combating terrorism.
- Freezing funds and other financial assets of the Taliban regime based on UN Security Resolution 1267.
- Freezing funds of listed individuals based on UN Security Council Resolution 1333.
- Signing the International Convention for Suppression and Financing of Terrorism based on UN Security Council Resolution 1373 on reporting to the UN Security Council's committee regarding the implementation of the Rules and Procedures pertaining to 1373.
- Reporting to the UN Security Council the implementation of Resolution 1390.

It has also made new efforts to reform the educational system. Key religious officials like Tawfeeq al-Sediry, the deputy minister of Islamic affairs, have made it clear that Saudi mosques and religious teaching must be reformed to remove anti-Jewish and anti-Christian references, and that the ministry is, "concerned about hiring moderate preachers who have a moderate outlook that represents the true Muslim path."[79]

LOOKING TOWARD THE FUTURE

Many Saudi actions have come too late, however, and much still needs to be done. The companion volume to this book deals with Saudi national security addresses the strength and weaknesses of the Saudi internal security system in depth; this is still a system that clearly needs further major improvement. The Kingdom cannot deal with Islamic extremism and terrorism without a more effective internal security effort, and must act accordingly.

Even with such efforts, it is nearly certain that Americans and Westerners will continue to be targets at some level of activity. Attacking U.S. citizens—particularly the U.S. military—allows Saudi extremists to attack proxies that are non-Islamic, and to obtain foreign sanctuary, if not foreign support. Attacking non-Saudi targets defuses some of the resentment that follows attacks on Saudi citizens. It also furnishes a way in which extremists can indirectly attack the al-Saud family by attacking its strongest ally. Such proxy attacks are hardly safe, but they do not provoke the kind of extreme action that would follow an attack on a prince. It is scarcely surprising, that the U.S. embassy has issued a steady stream of alerts since the Al-Khobar bombing and September 11, and further attacks and bombings seem almost inevitable.[80]

It is equally unlikely that the Saudi government can shut down all of the flow of funding to extremist and terrorist movements outside Saudi Arabia.

- First, there is a fundamental difference of perspective between Saudis and other Arabs and Americans and many others in the West over the nature of the Israeli-Palestinian struggle. Saudis see Israel's methods and tactics as being extremist and terrorist in character, which inevitably means a flow of money to Hamas and other Palestinian causes.

- Second, the royal family can police its own funding activities and the Saudi government can control the flow of money within the Kingdom and across its borders, but there are many financial instruments in the Arab world that bypass the banking systems. Moving funds to other Gulf countries is easy.

- Third, the bulk of private Saudi capital is still held outside the Kingdom in Europe and other countries where the government cannot monitor or control the flow of such funding; and

- Finally, Saudi charity is still highly personal and informal. Controls can be improved, but many will still give without checking the exact nature of the person or the cause they give to, and extremism and terrorism are relatively cheap. The Saudi government already fully understands this, as do most Western counterterrorism experts. It is far less clear that Western politicians, reporters, and experts outside of government are equally aware of what is and is not possible.

Repression is clearly not an effective answer to the challenges the Kingdom faces. The pattern of arrests following September 11 has been very similar to the kind of "rounding up the usual suspects" that the Saudi security services have used since the time of Nasser. It is similar in some ways to the arrests of religious figures, academics, and staff members at King Saud University in the early and mid-1980s—arrests that probably did just as much to alienate many of those involved as it did to suppress them.[81] Counterterrorism means focusing on real terrorists, not a convenient list of suspects.

The danger also exists that the United States will ignore the broader causes of terrorism and extremism in Saudi Arabia and push the Kingdom to focus on counterterrorism without regard for the need for broader forms of reform. The United States and some other Western countries have already grossly exaggerated the level of Islamic extremism in Saudi Arabia, while their politicians and much of their media have exaggerated Saudi Arabia's role in supporting and funding terrorism and extremism outside the Kingdom. The political problems in cooperating on counterterrorism are bad enough at the best of times and the West does not help by making broadly based attacks on every aspect of Saudi society, the regime, and Saudi practices; neither, however, do those Saudis that deny the seriousness of the Kingdom's problems rather than try to solve them.

Both Saudi officials and outside governments must recognize that the key to any lasting Saudi success in dealing with Islamic extremists and terrorists must be political, economic, and social reform. The Saudi government still needs to do more to modernize Saudi society and the role of Islam within it. In spite of its progress to date, the Saudi government still needs to fundamentally reevaluate its educational policy. It needs to firmly tie its educational policies to its economic policies. It also needs to face the fact that it has allowed "Islamic" education to become a societal dead end that encourages further unrest. As later chapters help document, the failure to address these realities is particularly troubling because the Saudi economy already is failing to absorb the more than 170,000 males that enter the labor force each year, and has no clear policy for dealing with the roughly similar number of educated women.

Reform also means more successful governance. The Saudi government must put an end to corruption and the abuses of the royal family and officials, successfully manage and reform the economy and the distribution of wealth, respect the core values of Islam, demonstrate that Saudi military efforts are cost-effective, and show that Saudi security ties to the United States and the West serve the national interest.

Finally, the Saudi government must make the teaching of tolerance a major goal. The following statement by Crown Prince Abdullah stresses exactly the right priorities:

> Ours is a tolerant and temperate faith and we must conduct ourselves accordingly. There is no room for extremism or compulsion in Islam. In fact, it violates the tenants of our faith and the traditions of our prophet. . . . [W]isdom and reason must guide your statements and actions; you must not let your emotions sway you. It is your responsibility, when you return to your nations, to counsel people to employ wisdom, patience and reason in dealing with issues.[82]

NOTES

1. The reader should be aware that much of this analysis draws heavily on work by Jeffery D. Leary, who helped research and edit this book and who has done extensive additional research on Salafi extremism.

2. For a good summary of bin Laden and al-Qaeda's history, and tensions with the Saudi regime, see Daniel Benjamin and Steven Simon, *The Age of Sacred Terror* (New York: Random House, 2002), particularly pp. 95–219; for good field research in this area, see Peter L. Bergen, *Holy War, Inc.* (New York: The Free Press, 2001).

3. Mai Yamani,. *Changed Identities: The Challenge of the New Generation in Saudi Arabia* (London: Royal Institute of International Affairs, 2000), p. 39.

4. "The Ten Nations Impressions of America Poll," Zogby International, April 11, 2002, p. 14, 15.

5. The full survey does not seem to be publicly available, but a summary is available the Review Section of the *Arab News*, vol. 9, no. 11 (September 26, 2002).

6. See Anthony H. Cordesman, *The Gulf and the Search for Strategic Stability* (Boulder: Westview, 1984), pp. 228–243.

7. Gwenn Okruhlik, "Networks of Dissent: Islamism and Reform in Saudi Arabia," Social Science Research Council Website, URL: *http://www.ssrc.org/sept11/essays/okruhlik.htm*, accessed on August 26, 2002.

8. Ibid.

9. The International Policy Institute For Counter-Terrorism, "The Saudi Fatwah against Suicide Terrorism," Reuven Paz, May 2, 2001.

10. Reuven Paz, "The Saudi Fatwa Against Suicide Terrorism," Peacewatch, No. 323 (May 2, 2001); Agence France Presse, May 9, 2001, 0651; Bloomberg, May 9, 2001, Cairo.

11. The author found these passages in a Koran in the Riyadh Marriot in October 2002. The passages in textbooks and religious books referred to are based on the research of Jeffery D. Leary.

12. World Bank, *World Development Indicators, 1997* (Washington: World Bank, 1996), pp. 60, 68; UNESCO, *Statistical Yearbook, 1996*.

13. For more background, see Milton Viorst, "The Storm and the Citadel," *Foreign Affairs* January/February 1996), pp. 98–99; F. Gregory Gause, *Oil Monarchies: Domestic and Security Challenges in the Arab Gulf States* (New York: Council on Foreign Relations, 1994); Augustus R. Norton, "The Future of Civil Society in the Middle East," *Middle East Journal* (Spring 1993); Mary Tetrault, "Gulf Winds," *Current History* (January 1996); and Michael Collins Dunn, "Is the Sky Falling?" *Middle East Policy*, 3ol. 3, no. 4 (1995).

14. *Economist* (Internet version) "How Women Beat the Rules," October 2–8, 1999, URL: *http://www.economist.com*.

15. Reuters, October 4, 1999.

16. *Petroleum Economist,* "Playing It by Ear on Western Upstream Investment in Oil," July 29, 1999. Accessed through Lexis-Nexis.

17. U.S. State Department, *Country Report on Human Rights, 2001*, Internet edition, URL: *http://www.state.gov/g/drl/rls/hrrpt/2001/nea/8296.htm*, accessed May 3, 2002.

18. Ibid.

19. *New York Times*, December 22, 1992, p. A-10.

20. *New York Times*, May 1, 1993, p. A-4; U.S. State Department, *Country Report on Human Rights Practices for 1994* (Washington: GPO, February, 1995), pp. 1165–1173, Internet version for 1995 downloaded April 5, 1996, and Internet version for 1996 downloaded August 11, 1997.

21. *Los Angeles Times*, November 14, 1995, p. A-6; U.S. State Department, *Country Report on Human Rights Practices for 1994*, pp. 1165–1173, Internet version for 1995 downloaded April 5, 1996, and Internet version for 1996 downloaded August 11, 1997; and U.S. State Department, *2001 Country Reports on Human Rights Practices*, URL: *http://www.state.gov/g/drl/rls/hrrpt/2001/nea/8296.html*, accessed March 4, 2002.

22. *Los Angeles Times*, November 14, 1995, p. A-6.

23. Mamoun Fandy, *Saudi Arabia and the Politics of Dissent* (New York: St. Martin's Press, 1999).

24. This section draws heavily on Fandy's *Saudi Arabia and the Politics of Dissent*. It also draws on the work of F. Gregory Gause III, the Director of the Middle East Institute and Associate Professor of Political Science at the University of Vermont.

25. "Communique Number 3," *CDLR Yearbook*, 1994–1995, pp. 9–10

26. For example, see the report on Mas'ari in the *Independent*, May 23, 1995.

27. *Los Angeles Times*, November 14, 1995, p. A-6; *Washington Post*, November 14, 1995, p. A-1.

28. Joseph Kechichian, *Succession in Saudi Arabia*(New York: Palgrave, 2001), pp. 109–110.

29. U.S. State Department, *Country Report on Human Rights Practices for 1994*, pp. 1165–1173, Internet version for 1995 downloaded April 5, 1996, and Internet version for 1996 downloaded August 11, 1997; and U.S. Department of State, *2001 Country Reports on Human Rights Practices*.

30. Ibid.

31. Ibid. l.

32. *Washington Post*, April 19, 1996, p. A-31.

33. Jane's *Pointer*, August, 1996, p. 2; March 1997, p. 5;

34. U.S. State Department, *Country Report on Human Rights Practices, 1997*; and U.S. Department of State, *2001 Country Reports on Human Rights Practices*.

35. The Movement for Islamic Reform in Arabia, URL: *www.miraserve.com*, July 9, 2001.

36. *Los Angeles Times*, November 15, 1995, p. A-7; *Washington Times*, November 15, 1995, p. B-11.

37. *Los Angeles Times*, November 14, 1995, p. A-1.

38. *Boston Globe*, November 15, 1995, p. 2; *Jane's Defence Weekly*, November 25, 1995, p. 5; Jane's *Pointer*, January 1996, p. 6; *New York Times*, January 11, 199, p. A-8; *New York Times*, November 15, 1995, p. A-7; *Washington Post*, November 14, 1995, p. A-15.

39. *Washington Times*, November 16, 1995, p. A-13.

40. *Wall Street Journal*, December 26, 1995, p. A-7.

41. *Philadelphia Inquirer*, November 16, 1995, p. A-11.

42. *New York Times*, April 26, 1996, p. A-13;

43. *Washington Post*, April 23, 1996, p. A-13; *Chicago Tribune*, November 15, 1995, p. I-3; *Jane's Defence Weekly*, November 25, 1995, p. 23; *New York Times*, January 11, 1996, p. A-8; *Washington Post*, February 5, 1996, p. A-22, June 1, 1996, p. A-19; *Los Angeles Times*, April 23, 1996, p. A-2; *Boston Globe*, April 23, 1996, p. 2.

44. Reuter News Service, "Latest Denial from the Iranian Ministry of Defense," posted on *iran-news@rostam.neda.com*, December 12, 1996.

45. *Jane's Intelligence Review* (June 2001), pp. 34–35.

46. U.S. Department of State, Phillip T. Reeker, Acting Spokesman;Edmund J. Hull, Acting Coordinator for Counterterrorism, Briefing Upon the Release of the Report "Patterns of Global Terrorism 2000," Washington, DC, April 30, 2001, Full text available from URL: *http://www.state.gov/s/ct/rls/rm/2001/2571pf.htm*, Accessed on December 18, 2002.

47. U.S. District Court Eastern District of Virginia, Alexandria Division, "Indictment: June 2001 Term at Alexandria," Full text available fromURL: *http://www.fbi.gov/pressrel/pressrel/khobar.htm*, Accessed on September 3, 2002.

48. Ibid.

49. Attorney General John Ashcroft statement, June 21, 2001, Available from URL: *http://www.usdoj.gov/opa/pr-/2001/June/275ag.htm*, Accessed on September 5, 2002.

50. Ibid.

51. U.S. House of Representatives, Eric Cantor, Chairman, "Task Force on Terrorism and Unconventional Warfare," October 16, 2001, Available from URL: *http://cantor.house.gov/terrorism/terrorism-2htm*, Accessed on September 5, 2002.

52. U.S. Office of the Press Secretary, Statement by the President, President George W. Bush, June 21, 2001, Available from URL: *http://www.whitehouse.gov/news/releases/2001/06/20010621.htm*, Accessed on September 5, 2002.

53. U.S. Department of Justice, Press Release, June 21, 2001, Available from URL: *http://www.fbi.gov/pressrel/pressrel01/khobar.htm*, Accessed on September 5, 2002.

54 CNN correspondent, "Khobar Towers Indictments Returned," June 22, 2001, Available from URL: *http://europe.cnn.com/2001/LAW/06/21/khobar.indictments/*, Accessed on September 5, 2002.

55. Ibid.

56. Adnan Malik, "Last of U.S. Troops in Jordan Leave as U.S. Military on Alert," *North County Times*, June 24, 2001, Available from URL: *http://nctimes.net/new/2001/20010624/62953.html*, Accessed on September 5, 2002.

57. John Ward Anderson, "Iran Rejects Allegations of Bombing Role," June 23, 2001, Section A, p. 22.

58. Ibid.

59. The reader should be aware that this often leads to exaggerated reports of tension and corruption. Anyone who has lived in Saudi Arabia becomes aware that royal family rumors, and rumors of internal conflicts, are almost a national sport. The Hijazi are masters of this sport, although sometimes surpassed by whatever businessman has just suffered in a deal with one of the princes. It is far harder for a Westerner to understand the pressures building up within the Islamic fundamentalists, but the movement does affect a significant number of Saudi youths, and often has intense support at the university level. Cassettes are circulated nationally, and many very well educated Saudis, as well as many traditionalists, support fundamentalism.

60. These estimates are based on interviews with U.S. and Saudi exports, work by Michael Dunn summarized in *The Estimate*, and Cordesman, *The Gulf and the Search for Strategic Stability*, pp. 228–243. Figures referring to 60% to 70% Shi'ite do not seem to be correct. See U.S. State Department, *Country Report on Human Rights Practices for 1994*, pp. 1165–1173, on-line edition for 1999; and U.S. Department of State, *2001 Country Reports on Human Rights Practices*.

61. Cordesman, *The Gulf and the Search for Strategic Stability*, pp. 228–243.

62. *Washington Post*, November 4, 1996, March 29, 1997, p. A-12.

63. *Washington Times*, September 11, 1996, p. A-13; Reuters, July 1, 1997, 2045; *Chicago Tribune*, July 11, 1997, p. I-5; *Washington Post*, November 4, 1996, February 26, 1997, p. A-7; *Philadelphia Inquirer*, November 3, 1996, p. A4; *New York Times*, July 10 1997, p. A-14.

64. Yonah Alexander and Michael S. Swetnam, *Usama Bin Laden's al-Qaida: Profile of a Terrorist Network* (New York: Transnational Publishers, Inc., 2001).

65. Ibid.

66. Ibid.

67. Ibid.

68. The analysis of bin Laden's recent role in terrorism and violence draws heavily on the U.S. State Department's *Report on Global Patterns in Terrorism, 1999*, URL: *http://www.state.gov/www/global/terrorism/1999report/mideast.html#Arabia*, April 2001. Also see Associated Press, May 5, 2001, 1803.

69. U.S. Department of State, "Fact Sheet: The Charges Against," Alexander and Swetnam, *Usama Bin Laden's al-Qaida: Profile of a Terrorist Network*.

70. Alexander and Swetnam, *Usama Bin Laden's al-Qaida: Profile of a Terrorist Network*.

71. *Al-Bab.com*, "Attack on the United States Ship *Cole*," Yemen Gateway, December 12, 2001, Available from URL: *http://www.al-bab.com/yemen/cole7.htm*, Accessed on August 26, 2002.

72. Alexander and Swetnam, *Usama Bin Laden's al-Qaida: Profile of a Terrorist Network*, p. 19.

73. Ibid.

74. Reuters, May 29, 2001, 1508.

75. *The Times*, May 3, 2001, p. 17.

76. Dow Jones, October 15, 2002, 0029.

77. See Maurice R. Greenberg, William F. Webster, and Less S. Wolosky, *Terrorist Financing* (New York: Council on Foreign Relations, October 17, 2002); PR Newswire October 17, 2002.

78. This list was prepared with the help of U.S. and Saudi officials in October and November 2002. It draws on the Kingdom of Saudi Arabia's *Summary Report on Initiatives and Actions in the Fight Against Terrorism*, August 2002, URL: *www.saudiembassy.net*; PR Newswire October 17, 2002; Reuters, October 22, 2002, 1605, and additional materials provided to the author.

79. Associated Press, October 14. 2002, 0725; *Arabnews.com*, October 14. 2002.

80. For typical reporting, see *Philadelphia Inquirer*, November 3, 1996, p. A4; *New York Times*, July 10 1997, p. A-14.

81. The author has encountered many of these attitudes during his visits to Saudi Arabia. For typical U.S. reporting see the *Baltimore Sun*, July 28, 1991, p. 11-A; *Security Intelligence*, February 10, 1992, p. 8; *New York Times*, January 30, 1992, p. 3 and March 1, 1992, p. 8; *Amnesty International 1994*, pp. 254–256; U.S. State Department, *Country Report on Human Rights Practices for 1994*, pp. 1165–1173; and U.S. Department of State, *2001 Country Reports on Human Rights Practices*.

82. Royal Embassy of Saudi Arabia, "Crown Prince Abdullah Urges Muslims to Shun Extremism in Islam," Press Release, November 2, 2002.

Chapter 5

Economic, Demographic, and Social Challenges

Saudi Arabia faces structural economic, demographic, and social problems that may well be far more significant than foreign threats, the politics of its royal family, its speed of "democratization," and its Islamic and sectarian problems. It must transform and diversify its economy over the next decade to catch up with population growth and fund continuing social change.

Oil wealth will still underpin the Saudi economy, but there is no way that the petroleum sector can provide enough revenue to meet Saudi Arabia's future needs or employ all of the large number of young Saudis flooding into the labor market. Diversification is also needed to repatriate much of the vast amount of private capital that is now invested abroad, to attract foreign direct investment, and to create a more efficient economy that offers meaningful jobs centered around a globally competitive, knowledge-based financial system.

THE DYNAMICS OF RECENT DEMOGRAPHIC CHANGE

There is no way to be sure of the true size of the Kingdom's demographic challenge. Saudi Arabia uses advanced sampling techniques to obtain some base population data, and there is rough agreement on the total population and the number of native and foreign residents. However, there are no precise estimates of Saudi Arabia's past or current population, and there has been no comprehensive census. Consequently, much of the information needed to understand Saudi Arabia's future labor problems is missing or contradictory.

The Saudi Ministry of Planning issued estimates in the Seventh Development Plan in 2000 that put the total population of the Kingdom at 21.4 million in 1999—with 15.7 million native Saudis and 5.7 million non-Saudis—using techniques developed for the 1992 population census. It estimated that the total population of the Kingdom would grow to 29.7 million in 2020, a rise of 89.2 %, and that the annual growth in the Saudi population of working age would remain high, ranging between 3.5% and 4.1% during 2000–2020.[1]

Trends in Total Population

The Saudi Central Department of Statistics calculated in 2001 that the Kingdom's total population was 22.01 million in 2000, that population growth was 3.6% in 1995 and 3.2% in 2000, and that the average rate of growth was 2.9% during 1992–1999. It estimated that Saudis accounted for 16.2 million, or roughly 75% of the population, whereas non-Saudis accounted for 5.8 million or roughly 25.1%. It also estimated that native Saudi population increased at an average annual rate of 3.5% during 1995–2000, and from 13.59 to 16.21 million persons (73.4% of the total Saudi population). Although the fertility rate of Saudi women had declined from 1980s levels of over 6%, it was still 5.5 infants per woman in 2000. This compared with a global average of 2.7 and a Middle East and North Africa (MENA) average of 3.5. At the same time, the population was increasing in size due to the positive effects of improved health care, which increased the life expectancy of the average Saudi to seventy-two years.[2]

The same Saudi estimates indicate that the size of the foreign population increased at an average annual rate of 2.1% during 1995–2000—from 5.21 to 5.80 million, or 26.4% of the total. The Makkah region was home to 25.2% of the population, Riyadh had 22.5%, and the Eastern Province had 14.5%. As of 2000, some 73% of the population was twenty-nine years of age or younger. These estimates of population growth differ from those of other government ministries, however, which often estimate average population growth rates of well over 3.0%. Additionally, these estimates may also undercount illegal foreign residents.[3]

Some more recent Saudi estimates produce slightly slower growth rates for the 1990s. The Saudi Central Department of Statistics has recalculated some demographic data for the mid-1990s, which it issued in June and September 2002. Chart 5.1 provides graphs showing the differences between the 2001 and 2002 estimates. Regardless of which figures are correct, they do not materially affect the demographic trends and projections discussed in this chapter.

Outside estimates differ somewhat from Saudi estimates. U.S. State Department estimates indicate that Saudi Arabia had a total population of only

Chart 5.1

Comparative Projection of the Trends in the Saudi GDP Per Capita in Current Dollars and Population: The View of the Saudi American Bank (Population in Millions)

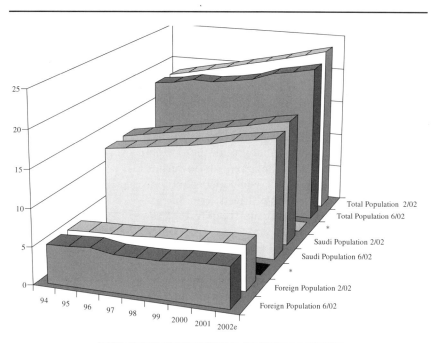

	94	95	96	97	98	99	2000	2001	2002e
■ Foreign Population 6/02	5.2	5.3	5.5	5	5	5	5.3	5.4	5.5
□ Foreign Population 2/02	5.1	5.2	5.3	5.4	5.6	5.7	5.8	6	6.1
■ *									
□ Saudi Population 6/02	12.8	13.2	13.6	14	14.4	14.9	15.6	16	16.5
■ Saudi Population 2/02	13.1	13.6	14.1	14.6	15.1	15.7	16.2	16.8	17.3
□ *									
■ Total Population 6/02	18.2	18.5	19.1	19	19.4	19.9	20.9	21.4	22
□ Total Population 2/02	18.2	18.8	19.4	20	20.7	21.3	22	22.7	23.4

Sources: Adapted by Anthony H. Cordesman from data in Brad Bourland's *The Saudi Economy in 2002* (Riyadh: Saudi American Bank, February 2002) and *The Saudi Economy in Mid-Year 2002* (Riyadh: Saudi American Bank, August 2002). The data show the difference resulting from a recalculation of basic economic and population data, driven in part by increasing the estimate of the role of the private sector, made by the Saudi Central Statistics Bureau in June 2002.

4.8 million people at the time of the June 1967 Arab-Israeli conflict. This population reached 5.4 million people by 1970, 6.2 million people by 1975, and 9.4 million people by 1980. It was 13.2 million people in 1990, 18.6 million by 1995, and more than 21.7 million in 2000.[4] U.S. Census Bureau statistics indicate that Saudi Arabia had a total population of 3.86 million in 1950, 4.72 million in 1960, 6.11 million in 1970, 9.95 million in 1980, 15.85 million in 1990, 18.63 million in 1995, and 22.02 million in 2000.[5]

World Bank estimates issued in 2001 and 2002 indicate that Saudi Arabia had a population of 9.4 million people in 1980 and 20.7 million in 2000, and that the population would increase to 32.1 million in 2015 and 46 million in 2030.[6] These trends are compared to those in other Gulf states in Chart 5.2.

Trends Toward Urbanization

Regardless of the differences between estimates, it is clear that extremely rapid population growth has taken place. This growth was accompanied by massive social changes. What was once a rural and isolated Saudi society, divided into regional and tribal groups, has become a society that is largely urbanized, although tribal links remain powerful. It is a society that is exposed to a wide range of electronic media and one that has become dependent on a modern, petroleum-driven economy.

According to the World Bank, roughly 49% of the total population was urbanized as early as 1970, and 12% of the population was living in cities with a population of 1 million or more. By 1980, 66% of the total population was urbanized, and 19% of the population was living in cities with a population of 1 million or more. The percentage of the population living in cities reached 79% by 1995, when the total population had reached a total of roughly 14.9 million people, and 21% of Saudi Arabia's population lived in cities of over 1 million by 1995. Urbanization reached 86% in 2000, with 25% in cities of over 1 million.[7]

The number of people living in Riyadh—Saudi Arabia's largest city—rose from 16% of the population to 19% in 2000. By 2015, the percentage of Saudis living in cities with a population over one million may reach 30%.[8] In the process, the number of Saudi males employed in agriculture dropped from roughly 45% as late as 1980 to under 7% in 1998.[9]

Trends Toward Education

The increase in urbanization has been matched by a major increase in the level of education, although much still needs to be done if Saudi Arabia is to compete in skill and knowledge levels on a global basis. CIA and World Bank statistics indicate virtually all children now receive education through the secondary-school level. The CIA estimated in 2002 that Saudi Arabia's once largely illiterate population had reached an overall literacy rate of 84.2% for males and 69.5% for women. The World Bank indicates that the illiteracy rate for adult males dropped from 33% in 1980 to 17% in 2000, and from 67% to 33% for adult women. During that same period, the expected years of schooling for men increased from seven to nine years for men, and nearly doubled from five to nine years for women.[10]

Chart 5.2

Living in a Crowded Desert: Saudi Population Growth Compared to Trends in Other Gulf Countries (Population in Millions)

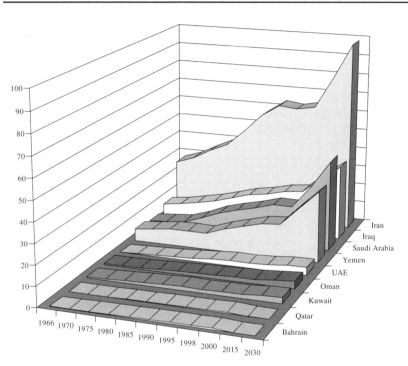

	1966	1970	1975	1980	1985	1990	1995	1998	2000	2015	2030
☐ Bahrain	0.18	0.22	0.3	0.4	0.4	0.5	0.6	0.6	0.6	NA	NA
☐ Qatar	0.07	0.09	0.14	0.3	0.3	0.4	0.5	0.6	0.7	NA	NA
▨ Kuwait	0.5	0.8	1	1.4	1.7	2.1	1.7	1.9	2	2.7	3
▨ Oman	0.6	0.7	0.8	1.1	1.5	1.8	2	2.3	2.4	3.3	4
☐ UAE	0.2	0.3	0.7	1	1.6	2.3	2.8	2.7	2.9	3.8	4
☐ Yemen	6.1	7.2	8.3	8.5	8.4	11.6	14.1	16.6	17.5	27	36
▨ Saudi Arabia	4.8	5.4	6.2	9.4	13.2	15.9	18	20.7	20.7	32.1	46
☐ Iraq	8.2	9.4	11.1	13	15.7	18.4	19.9	22.3	23.3	31.2	38
☐ Iran	26.8	30.1	34.9	39.1	47.6	56.9	63.1	61.9	63.7	80.4	98

Sources: Adapted by Anthony H. Cordesman from data provided by the U.S. State Department, the World Bank database for *World Development Indicators, 2000*, pp. 40, 44, and the World Bank, *World Development Indicators, 2002*, pp. 48–50. The World Bank does not report on Bahrain and Qatar. World Bank figures are otherwise used for 1980, 1998, 2000, and 20015.

As has been discussed earlier, the Saudi government reports that the number of males graduating annually from secondary school rose from 2,437 in 1970 to 68,643 in 1999, while the number of female graduates rose from 369 to 98,145. The number of males graduating annually from university rose from 795 in 1970 to 21,229 in 1999, while the number of female graduates rose from 13 to 21,721—ending in a total that slightly exceeded the number of male graduates.[11]

The number of Saudi women graduating from university has grown at an average rate 2.5 times that of male graduates during the last decade, and these trends in education reflect a general pattern in education in the Gulf.[12] Social and professional restrictions on women are leading them to stay in school longer than men and to qualify for more advanced degrees. This obviously has a specific impact in Saudi Arabia, because although it needs highly educated "person power," it continues to impose exceptionally serious de facto limits in terms of numbers and types of jobs for women.

Population Exposure to Media

The growth in the Saudi population and education rates has been accompanied by radical changes in the flow of information. Saudi Arabia ceased to be a closed, rural-tribal society even before the oil boom began in 1974. Education outside the Kingdom, large numbers of foreign teachers, and the widespread availability of transistor radios had already led to the widespread circulation of Nasserite ideas and propaganda by the late 1950s; Saudi Arabia has since leapfrogged into the electronic age. It had over 260 television sets per 1,000 people in 2000, and over 95% of the Saudi people had exposure to radio.[13]

According to CIA analysts, the Kingdom had 117 television stations by 1997, establishing virtually universal coverage in its populated areas, and one television set for every three people in the Kingdom. Satellite dishes are common, as are short-wave radios, fax machines, and access to the Internet. In fact, the Saudi government estimates that the average Saudi spent 50% to 100% more time watching television in 2000 than his or her U.S. or European counterpart. This almost certainly is caused partly by religious practices that limit the availability of other social activities.

These changes continue to accelerate. Radio has provided widespread access to outside news media for decades, and Saudi censorship has never been particularly effective in blocking the flow of foreign publications. However, the recent increases in satellite receivers, TV and radio broadcasts by neighboring states, and access to the Internet, have sharply increased the number of Saudis with personal direct access to outside news over the last decade. A majority of native Saudis probably had access to such sources of information by 2002. As a result, outside media and news reach a large percentage of Saudis in ways that are beyond the government and clergy's control. These developments are putting an end to effective censorship, and their impact continues to grow despite occasional efforts to control the Internet, satellites, or inflow of foreign publications and faxes.

THE FUTURE PACE OF DEMOGRAPHIC CHANGE

Even if the Saudi birthrate declines slowly in future years, the pace of demographic change will continues to accelerate. There is no way to accurately estimate how quickly Saudi Arabia's population will grow in the future. Chart 5.1 provides one estimate, and it is important to note that these increases are likely to take place even though the World Bank estimates shown in Chart 5.3 assume that Saudi population growth will drop from an annual average growth rate of 4.0% during 1980–1999 to only 2.9% during the time period from 2000–2015.[14]

Chart 5.3

World Bank versus Census Bureau Estimates of Saudi Population and Population Growth (Population in Millions)

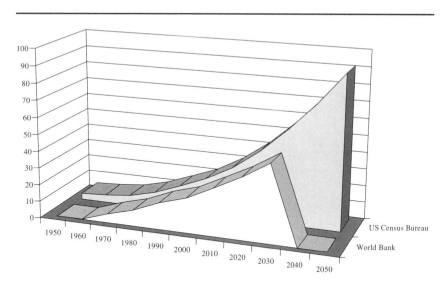

	1950	1960	1970	1980	1990	2000	2010	2020	2030	2040	2050
☐ World Bank	NA	NA	5.4	9.4	15.9	20.7	28.3	36.4	46	NA	NA
☐ US Census Bureau	3.8	4.7	6.1	9.9	15.8	22	30.5	41.9	55.8	72.3	91.1

Sources: Adapted by Anthony H. Cordesman from data provided by the U.S. State Department, the World Bank database for *World Development Indicators, 2000*, pp. 40, 44, the World Bank, *World Development Indicators, 2002*, p. 50, and U.S. Census Bureau IDB summary demographic database (URL: *http://www.census.gov/cgi-bin/ipc/idbsum?cty*), accessed March 28, 2002.

Population momentum ensures, however, that the labor force will grow faster than the total population because the Saudi population is so young. The World Bank estimates that the Saudi labor force will grow from 3 million in 1980 to 7 million in 2000, and 10 million in 2010, with an average growth of 4.5% from 1980 to 2000, and 3.4% during the time period 2000–2010. Social change has also meant major changes in the role of women. The female portion of the total labor force grew from 7.6% in 1980 to 16.1% in 2000.[15]

The U.S. Census Bureau provides another source of detailed estimates of Saudi Arabia's population, which should be compared to the World Bank estimate in Chart 5.2. Chart 5.4 shows the assumptions behind the Census Bureau estimate of future Saudi population growth; this estimate is dependent on a shift in Saudi family size and social behavior that cuts the rate of population growth from a peak of 4.9% during 1970–1980, and today's

Chart 5.4
Estimated Trends in Saudi Population Growth: 1950–2050 (Annual Growth Rate per Country in Percent)

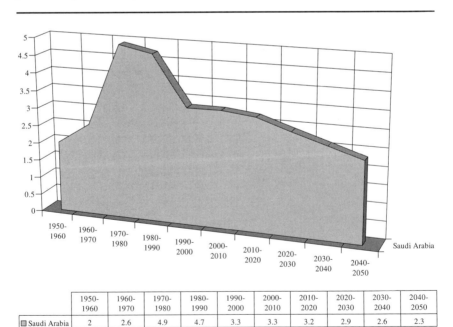

	1950-1960	1960-1970	1970-1980	1980-1990	1990-2000	2000-2010	2010-2020	2020-2030	2030-2040	2040-2050
▢ Saudi Arabia	2	2.6	4.9	4.7	3.3	3.3	3.2	2.9	2.6	2.3

Sources: Adapted by Anthony H. Cordesman from World Bank, *World Development Indicators, 2000*, pp. 38–40, and U.S. Census Bureau IDB summary demographic database (URL: *http://www.census.gov/cgi-bin/ipc/idbsum?cty*), accessed March 28, 2002.

rate of 3.3%, to 2.3% after 2040. Even if Saudi Arabia's population growth rate is cut back to a much more moderate annual average of 2%, its total population will exceed 25 million in 2010 and 31 million in 2020.[16]

Demographic shifts toward a lower birth rate are common in developing states, particularly as urbanization increases, women enter the labor force, and economic pressures lead to smaller families. So far, however, the impact of such shifts on Saudi Arabia has been limited. In fact, Saudi demographers in the Ministry of Planning raised their estimates of the current annual population growth rate from 3.2% to 3.4% in February 2001.

Several sources also show that the Saudi growth rate is not steadily decreasing with time. The CIA estimates that the Saudi growth rate rose to 3.45% in 1995 and 3.6% in 1996, declined to 3.32% in 1997, rose to 3.41% in 1998, and declined to 3.39% in 1999, 3.28% in 2000, and 3.27% in 2001 and 2002.[17] The U.S. Census Bureau projects that population growth will only decline from 3.1 % in 2000 to 2.9% in 2025.[18] Chart 5.5 shows how estimates of Saudi population growth compare to those of estimates of the population in similar states; it is clear that Saudi growth rates are exceptionally high.

Saudi figures provide additional insight into these trends. The estimates for the Seventh Development Plan (2000–2004) indicate that the native Saudi population will increase from 16.2 million in 2000 to 29.7 million in 2020, a rise of 89.2%, with an average annual growth rate of 3%. Other Saudi government agencies estimate that the total population will increase from 22.0 million in 2000 to 33.4 million in 2020, an increase of 51.4%, with an average annual increase of 2.1%. This would mean that the non-Saudi population would be 3.7 million in 2020, or 11.1% of the Kingdom's total population.[19]

These Saudi estimates of population growth do not offer a notably easier future than the estimates of the World Bank and CIA. Although any such judgments are speculative, the Kingdom will need to reduce its native population growth to figures much closer to 2% than 3% in order to ensure economic reform, the expansion of infrastructure and education, and funding for social services in relation to the probable rate of development in the Saudi economy.[20]

All of these estimates show that the extent to which the rate of Saudi population growth does or does not drop after 2000 will have an immense impact on the Kingdom's stability, its political future, and its economic wealth and development. It will determine the size of the labor force, the scale of the problems created by Saudisation and unemployment, the burden in maintaining subsidies and welfare payments, and the size of the investment needed in infrastructure and education. Like compound interest, even small shifts can have a massive cumulative impact.

Chart 5.5
Saudi Arabia and Comparative Birth Rates in the Gulf (Average Percent of Annual Growth)

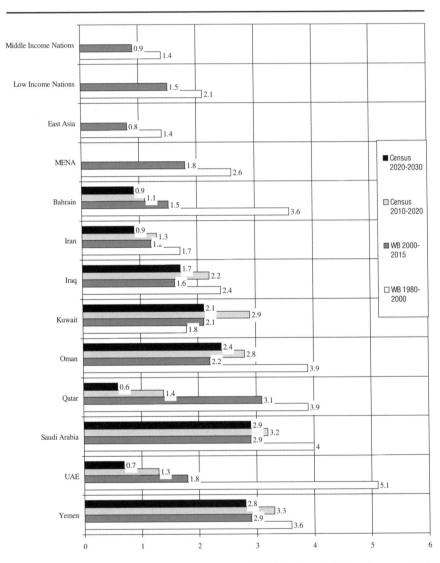

Sources: Adapted by Anthony H. Cordesman from World Bank, *World Development Indicators, 2002*, pp. 48–50, and U.S. Census Bureau IDB summary demographic database (URL: *http://www.census.gov/cgi-bin/ipc/idbsum?cty*), accessed March 28, 2002.

DEMOGRAPHICS, PER CAPITA INCOME, AND CONSUMPTION

Demographics interact with economics to determine relative wealth and per capita income. The economic impact of explosive Saudi population growth has already been shown in Chart 5.2, and it is clear that population growth has already had a major impact on the relative wealth of the Saudi people. So have the trends in economic growth, which have failed to match the increase in population.

This mix of demographic and economic trends is not easy to analyze. There are a wide range of conflicting data on the Saudi gross national product (GNP), gross domestic product (GDP), and population. Conversions into constant Saudi riyals or U.S. dollars often use different deflators and standards of conversion. Effort to add estimates of the nonmarket value of economic activity to the GNP and GDP (the so-called purchasing power parity or PPP estimate) use such diverse and undefined methods that the value of any PPP data is extremely uncertain. The PPP method of calculating GNP and GDP also tends to level out the rise and fall of market activity by estimating economic "growth" in response to a growing population. As a result, the total PPP, GNP, and GDP, and per capita income figures almost certainly sharply understate the Kingdom's true economic and demographic problems.

Furthermore, Saudi Arabia revised some of its economic reporting for the 1990s in June 2002 in ways that produced notably more favorable figures in terms of GNP, growth, and per capita income for the Kingdom. The Central Department of Statistics added some 60 billion Saudi riyals ($16.2 billion) to the size of the economy for 1996–2001 by reestimating the role of the non-oil sector in previous years. It also suddenly cut its population estimates.

The resulting figures are shown in Table 5.1, and may be compared with earlier projections in Chart 5.1. They have not yet been incorporated in the data issued by the Ministry of Planning and other Saudi reporting available as of October 2002, and they are somewhat questionable. There are indications that Saudi Arabia did undervalue its private sector during the 1990, but the revisions may be partly the result of politics of economics rather than more accurate methods of reporting.[21]

Historical Patterns of Inadequate Real Economic Growth

Even so, some common trends do emerge out of the mix of conflicting sources. The Saudi Ministry of Planning provides detailed historical data on the growth of the Saudi GDP in constant 1994 prices for both the oil and non-oil sectors. These data indicated that the Saudi economy grew by 14.5% in real terms between 1969 and 1974, and by 8.0% between 1974

Table 5.1
A Saudi Estimate of Trends in the Saudi GDP, Budget, Per Capita Income, and Oil Income, 1994–2002

	1994	1995	1996	1997	1998	1999	2000	2001	2002e
Nominal GDP									
In SR Billions	450.0	478.6	590.8	617.9	546.6	603.6	706.7	698.4	685.5
In $US Billions	120.0	127.6	157.5	164.8	145.8	161.0	188.4	186.2	182.8
% of Annual Change	1.4	6.4	n/a	4.6	-11.5	10.4	17.1	-1.2	-1.8
Real GDP (% of Annual Change)									
Total	0.10	0.00	1.40	2.60	2.80	-0.80	4.90	1.20	0.20
Oil Sector	0.20	0.27	2.10	-1.40	3.20	-7.50	6.90	-1.20	-5.80
Non-Oil Private Sector	0.70	0.30	1.10	4.60	2.60	4.20	4.30	3.50	4.20
Government	0.00	-0.30	1.30	6.10	1.90	0.90	3.20	1.70	1.00
Budget									
Revenues ($US billions)	34.4	39.1	47.8	54.8	38.1	39.2	66.1	61.3	58.7
Expenditures ($US Billions)	43.7	46.4	52.8	59.0	50.4	48.3	54.1	68.0	63.7
% of Surplus/Deficit	-9.28	-7.31	-5.07	-4.21	-12.27	-9.07	12.00	-6.70	-5.06
Budget Balance as % of GDP	-7.7	-5.7	-3.2	-2.6	-8.4	-5.6	6.45	-3.6	-2.8

Impact of Oil Revenues

Average Production in MMBD	—	8.02	8.10	8.01	8.28	7.65	8.09	8.02	—
Average Price of Saudi Light									
Crude/BBL ($US)	14.50	16.73	19.85	18.80	12.24	17.40	26.81	24.70	21.75
Average of all Saudi Oil	—	15.65	19.00	18.25	11.50	17.45	27.00	21.50	21.75
Oil Export Value ($US billions)	—	43.4	54.1	53.2	32.5	44.7	72.1	—	—
Oil Revenue Contribution to Saudi									
Budget ($US billions)	—	28.19	36.26	42.66	21.33	27.86	57.17	49.33	—
Population (Millions)									
Total	18.2	18.5	19.1	19.0	19.4	19.9	20.9	21.4	22.0
Saudi	12.8	13.2	13.6	14.0	14.4	14.9	15.6	16.0	16.5
Non-Saudi	5.2	5.3	5.5	5.0	5.0	5.02	5.26	5.40	5.5
Per Capita Income ($US)									
GDP	6,060	6,896	8,244	8,663	7,502	8,092	9,038	8,691	8,309
Unemployment									
% of Saudi Native Labor Force	—	—	—	—	—	—	14.0	15.0	15.0
Cost of Living (% Change)	0.6	4.8	1.3	0.0	-0.2	-1.2	-1.0	-0.8	-0.5

Source: Adapted from Brad Bourland, *The Saudi Economy at Mid Year 2002* (Riyadh: Saudi American Bank, August 2002; URL: *www.samba.com.sa*), pp. 2, 32, 37.

and 1979, but then dropped to −1.8%% between 1979 and 1984. There was virtually no real growth between 1985 and 1989. The sudden rise in Saudi oil revenues caused by the Gulf War led to a 9.5% rise in 1990 and a 10.3% rise in 1991—although the economic impact of the rise in oil revenues was largely offset by the outflow of Saudi expenditures on the war.

Real growth then dropped to 2.0% in 1992 and averaged less than 1% annually between 1993 and 1995. It rose to 1.3% in 1996, 1.6% in 1997, and 1.8% in 1998. It then dropped by 0.9% in 1999 because of low prices, only to rise by 4.7% in 2000 as a result of a sudden peak in oil revenues.[22] GNP growth is estimated to fall well below population growth for the decade between 1992 and 2001, which is scarcely good performance for any developing country. Sustained real development generally requires economic growth rates that are at least 2% above the population growth rate, and the Saudi population growth rate was well over 3%.

The Saudi Seventh Development Plan projects average annual real growth of 3.16% during 2001–2005, including 5.04% in the non-oil sector.[23] These goals seem optimistic in view of past trends, but even if they are achieved, they would still produce a small decline in real Saudi per capita or leave per capita income static, given current projections of population growth.

Outside estimates of the trends in the Saudi GNP are less favorable. World Bank estimates of Saudi economic growth are shown in Chart 5.2, which includes Iran as a point of comparison. They indicate that Saudi Arabia's population rose by over 110% during 1980–1995, but that its GDP dropped from $156.5 billion in 1980 to $125.5 billion in 1995. This is a drop of nearly 20% in current dollars and well over 30% in constant dollars. U.S. estimates indicate that the Saudi GNP dropped by over 35% during the same period. More recent World Bank data show better results, but they still show zero growth in the Saudi GDP during the period from 1980 to 1990, and only 1.5% growth from 1990 to 2000—only about half the rate of population growth during the same period.[24] More recent World Bank estimates show an average annual growth in GNP of only 2.3% during 1998–1999, despite rising oil revenues.[25]

The World Bank fails to provide the estimates of future economic growth for Saudi Arabia that it usually includes for other countries, for reasons it does not explain in its reports.[26] The World Bank does, however, forecast that economic growth for oil exporting states, in the long run, will average 2.7%, in comparison to growth for nations with a more diversified slate of exports, whose economies are expected to grow at an annual average rate of 4.3%.[27] Additionally, the International Monetary Fund, in its December 2001 *World Economic Outlook*, predicted that as a result of slowing sales of oil post–September 11, Saudi Arabia will see GDP growth of 1.6% in 2002, compared to a growth rate of 2.3% in 2000.[28]

Population, Per Capita Income, and Relative Wealth

Saudi Arabia does not analyze per capita income in its financial reports or project it in its five-year plans. This is a major—perhaps critical—defect in Saudi reporting and planning. It is compounded by issuing what sometimes seem to be politicized figures designed to make the Saudi economy appear more favorable, and by a tendency to adopt "input goals" in almost all of Saudi Arabia's reports on its budgets, five-year plans, and development rather than measures of the extent to which per capita income or employment will increase or decrease, or whether given actions and trends will meet the projected need.

The Kingdom only reports data on its achievements, like the number of schools built, jobs created, or hospital beds produced. It does not analyze how the facilities and services provided meet the trends in demand and the growth of the Saudi population. As a result, virtually every benchmark and spending figure publicly reported by the Saudi government is useless in determining how well it meets the needs of the Saudi people or deals with the steady increase in Saudi Arabia's population. Unfortunately, this same attitude seems to affect Saudi leaders and technocrats. They rarely analyze "outputs" in terms of per capita benefits, income distribution, or other measures of actual achievement in human or social need. They quote figures on gross progress without regard to benchmarks in meeting requirements.

There also are no figures on the distribution of income within Saudi Arabia, and no meaningful data on unemployment. The Saudi Central Department of Statistics issued its first estimates ever of Saudi unemployment data in September 2002. These data reported the situation at end-1999 and showed a native unemployment figure of 8.1%, with 6.8% for males and 15.8% for women. The unemployed rate for non-Saudi labor was put at 0.83%. These figures are extremely suspect, however, and assume that only 19% of the population, and 35.3% of the population of working age, actually participates in the labor force. This 19% compares with 33% in the rest of the Middle East, 41% in Latin America, 45% in Europe, 50% in the United States, and 56% in east Asia. Taken at face value, it implies that sheer lack of Saudi participation in labor force amounts to a socio-economic disaster and is a far worse problem than unemployment per se.

Other estimates indicate, however, that direct Saudi unemployment among native males is 11.7% rather than 6.8%. Rough estimates by outside experts of the combined impact of direct and disguised unemployment (unemployment plus make-work jobs with no meaning or productive output) put the figure at least 17% and at levels that could reach 20% to 30%.[29]

The failure to look at income distribution makes per capita income data of dubious value in a highly oligarchical monarchy where the rich seem to be getting richer, while the middle class seems to be declining in per capita income, and poorer Saudis seem to be getting poorer in relative terms.

This unwillingness to develop realistic unemployment data seems to be a deliberate failure to come to grips with some of the critical problems in Saudi demographics, and is compounded by an unwillingness to analysis disguised unemployment and employment in terms of productivity gain. This hides major problems in employing native Saudis in government and private sector jobs that are little more than make-work for political and family reasons, the problems in Saudisation, and the problems in making productive use of women. Furthermore, the Kingdom has no meaningful data on job retention and training, which makes its estimates of Saudisation uncertain to say the least, and has no regional or sectoral data to track employment, Saudisation, and per capita income trends in detail. These are crippling deficiencies from the viewpoint of development planning and compound the problems created by a recent tendency to politicize other aspects of econometric data.

Western analyses of the Saudi economy suffer from different problems. There is no agreement among various sources, and even the various agencies of the U.S. government are unable to decide how to properly define and measure the Saudi GDP and GNP. Estimates in "constant" dollars are not fully explained, and the various contradictory methods the West uses to correct estimates of the Saudi GDP and GNP to add nonmarket value and come up with a purchasing power parity or PPP number, range from mathematical "black boxes" to black magic. Both Saudi and Western estimates also seem to exclude much of the large private income Saudis earn from overseas investments. As a result, the true income of Saudis is often understated.

Nevertheless, Western estimates of Saudi per capita income do seem to provide broadly accurate insights into the key trends in the Saudi economy in terms of relative wealth. Both World Bank and U.S. estimates indicate that Saudi Arabia's per capita income has declined to less than 40% of its peak at the height of the oil boom in the late 1970s and early 1980s, although the resulting figure is still high by the standards of most developing countries. The World Bank estimates that Saudi Arabia's per capita income totaled $7,230 in 2000. This compares with $34,100 for the United States, but with $2,090 for MENA as a whole, and $1,080 for east Asia (a fact that must always be kept in mind in comparing Saudi growth rates to those of Asia). From the perspective of other Gulf states, it compares to $570 in Iran, $1,680 in Iraq, $1,803 in Kuwait, and $370 in Yemen (Bahrain, Oman, Qatar, and the UAE are not reported).[30]

The Saudi American Bank estimates that the Saudi participation GDP was $18,000 in 1981, roughly equal to that of the United States. Between 1981 and 2001, however, the Saudi per capita income dropped to lows of $7,000. If one accepts a Saudi recomputation of the GDP and population in June 2002, it then rose from $6,660 in 1994 to $8,309 in 2002, in current dollars. By the same method of calculation, however, U.S. per capita income rose to over $35,000.[31] Using a period of peak oil revenues and lower population like 1980 as a standard of reference may set an artificial benchmark, and many Saudi economists argue that the more recent trends shown in Table 5.1 provide a more realistic standard of reference. However, the years of peak oil wealth are still a standard that many Saudis see as the "proper" level of oil wealth that should be used in assessing Saudi economic progress. This is a reality that is very unlikely to ever again be the case.

Furthermore, even if one looks at trends that do not involve preferences toward peak oil revenues, any comparison of Saudi economic growth and population growth still creates concern, although scarcely a near-term risk of economic crisis:

- The data in Table 5.1 and Chart 5.1, estimated by the Saudi American Bank, show a relatively high per capita income in current dollars during 1994–2002. These data also show a nominal growth in current dollars 1991 and 2001. However, this means little real growth in constant dollars occurred, and other estimates by the Saudi American Bank indicate that the "boom and bust" cycle in oil prices also reduced per capita income in current dollars by 14% between 1996 and 1998, and then raised it by 27% between 1998 and 2000. Such volatility is scarcely desirable, either socially or as a means of encouraging stable government and private sector investment.

- Chart 5.6 shows the trends noted by the World Bank. In other reporting, the World Bank estimates that Saudi Arabia's per capita income dropped by an annual average of 2.9% during 1970–1995, and by a total of nearly 20% during 1985–1995. More recent World Bank estimates show an annual average growth in GNP per capita of only 0.5% in the period from 1965 to 1998, and a decline of –1.0 % during 1998–1999, despite rising oil revenues.[32] According to other U.S. estimates, the Saudi GDP per capita dropped from over $20,000 in 1981 to under $6,800 in 1994 (in constant 1994 $US).[33] Although Saudi per capita income rose back to well over $7,000 in 1995–1997, this scarcely marked a "recovery"; it dropped again during 1988–1997, until oil prices rose again in mid-1999.

- Chart 5.7 uses U.S. State Department data to provide a broad indication of such trends and shows just how quickly the Saudi population has grown since the sudden rise in oil revenues following the Arab oil embargo in 1974. It also shows that population growth has since interacted with a decline in real oil revenues to affect per capita income.

Population growth, entitlements, and changing living standards have also interacted with fluctuations in oil export earnings to affect the relative portions of the GDP/GNP that go to Saudi consumption and investment. Saudi Arabian private consumption rose from $34.5 billion to $52.0 billion during 1980–1995. This growth in consumption reflected both the impact of population growth and a growing social dependence on imports

Chart 5.6
Saudi Annual Growth in GDP and GNP Per Capita, 1966–1999 (in Percent)

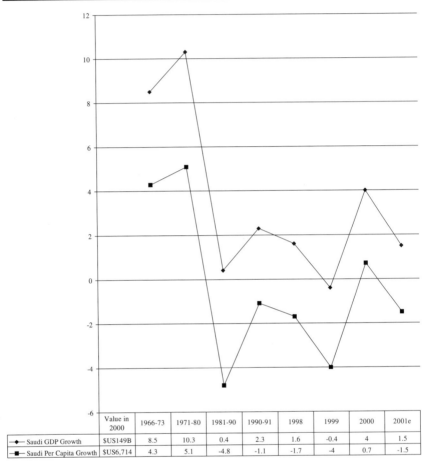

	Value in 2000	1966-73	1971-80	1981-90	1990-91	1998	1999	2000	2001e
◆ Saudi GDP Growth	$US149B	8.5	10.3	0.4	2.3	1.6	-0.4	4	1.5
■ Saudi Per Capita Growth	$US6,714	4.3	5.1	-4.8	-1.1	-1.7	-4	0.7	-1.5

Sources: Adapted by Anthony H. Cordesman from World Bank, *Global Economic Prospects: 2000* (Washington: World Bank, 2000), pp. 152—153, and *Global Economic Prospects: 2002* (Washington: World Bank, 2002), pp. 230–234.

and commercial services. Private consumption rose from 22% of the GDP in 1980 to 35% in 1997 and 41% in 1998, decreasing to 33% of GDP in 2000. Government consumption rose from 16% in 1980 to 30% in 1997, and then 32% in 1998, decreasing to 27% in 2000. At the same time, gross domestic investment dropped slightly from 22% in 1980 to 20% in 1997. Gross domestic savings dropped precipitously from 62% of GDP in 1980 to 35% in 1997, 25% in 1998, and 16% in 2000.[34]

Chart 5.7

Boom and Bust in Per Capita Wealth: Saudi Arabia: Population Growth in Millions and Per Capita Income (Population in Millions; Per Capita Income in Thousands of Constant 1997 $US)

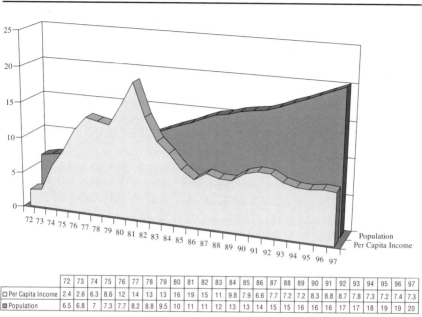

	72	73	74	75	76	77	78	79	80	81	82	83	84	85	86	87	88	89	90	91	92	93	94	95	96	97
☐ Per Capita Income	2.4	2.6	6.3	8.6	12	14	13	13	16	19	15	11	9.8	7.9	6.6	7.7	7.2	7.2	8.3	8.8	8.7	7.8	7.3	7.2	7.4	7.3
▣ Population	6.5	6.8	7	7.3	7.7	8.2	8.8	9.5	10	11	11	12	13	13	14	15	15	16	16	16	17	17	18	19	19	20

Source: Adapted by Anthony H. Cordesman from data in various editions of *World Military Expenditures and Arms Transfers* (Washington: U.S. Department of State).

REDEFINING "OIL WEALTH" IN MACROECONOMIC AND HUMAN TERMS

The importance of the ratio of total population to total oil and gas earnings is as important as the ratio of total population to GDP/GNP because of the special character of the Saudi economy. Saudi Arabia's economy is still shaped largely by its earnings from oil and gas exports. It is easy to call for economic diversification and privatization, and the Kingdom has made increasingly serious efforts along these lines. At the same time, though, there are limits to what market forces and any economic reform program can hope to accomplish, particularly as long as the native labor force is not globally competitive in terms of education, skills, work ethic, productivity, and cost.

Saudi Arabia does have iron, gold, zinc, and copper resources, and its Seventh Development Plan calls for the development of eight projects in these areas, but its resources are relatively marginal in terms of projected

Saudi income needs and the world market. Saudi Arabia also has major bauxite, magnesite, and phosphate resources, and its Seventh Development Plan calls for one major project in each area, including the Al-Jalamid project at what Saudi Arabia claims is the largest phosphate deposit in the world.[35]

The cost-effectiveness of such mining at competitive returns on investment is uncertain, however, and long-needed reforms in mining laws have still not been implemented. A new rail system is needed to mine most such resources, and Saudi estimates of the cost-benefits of such mining seem over-optimistic.[36] The Kingdom has made progress by creating the Saudi Arabian Mining Company (Ma'aden), a state-owned autonomous joint stock company, in 1997, although it has as yet been more exploratory than productive. It continues to review a new mining code and it created a new railroad executive program in June 2002. It will be well over a decade, however, before it is clear whether mining can supplement oil and gas production with any major macroeconomic benefits.[37]

As is analyzed later, agriculture is already heavily influenced by subsidies and entitlements, and there is little room for added productive diversification. Only about 2% of Saudi land is arable. Although some pasturage is available in 56% of Saudi territory, most is desert and of very marginal value. Only 6% of the Saudi GNP comes from agriculture.[38] Much of this revenue comes only at the cost of subsidies that distort the Saudi economy and increase the Kingdom's water problems. Agriculture's share of the GNP would be much lower if the agricultural sector had to operate on competitive terms.

There also are serious near-to-mid-term limits on the potential growth of the industrial, trade, and service sectors. The growth in Saudi manufactures and industry is closely tied to the petroleum sector and the value of downstream products. While Saudi figures estimate that the contribution the petroleum sector makes to the GDP dropped from 56.1% in 1969 and 65.3% in 1974 to 35% to 36% from 1990 to 1999, these numbers present an mirage of diversification. About 17% to 18% of the non-oil sector portion of the GDP actually consists of government services financed by oil revenues, and another 6.3% to 6.5% comes from highly subsidized agriculture.

Although a precise estimate of the component parts of Saudi GDP is impossible, about another 18% comes from service industries, transportation, and activities that are actually dependent on petroleum-related revenues and investment. The manufacturing sector only contributes about 5% of the GDP and exhibited no real growth from 1985 to 1999, with the amount of value added to GDP increasing from 8% in 1990 to only 10% in 2000. The only other major market-related activity is construction—

which includes a significant amount of petroleum-related activity. This activity declined from around 15% of the GDP in the mid-1980s to around 11% in the late 1990s.[39]

Saudi Arabia is still heavily dependent on petroleum exports, which is greater than some Saudi figures imply. The Saudi Arabian Monetary Agency (SAMA) reports that "mineral products" (oil and gas) accounted for 88% of all Saudi exports in 1997—a figure that is typical for the late 1990s. These figures, however, understate the true role of oil and gas in the economy because they do not include another 2.5% in plastics exports and 4.9% in chemical products. As a result, petroleum actually accounts for something approaching 95% of all exports.[40] Estimates by the Ministry of Planning indicate that crude oil accounted for 74.2% of all exports in 2000, and petroleum products for 17.1%, bringing the total to 91.3%.[41]

All of these factors limit the Kingdom's actual "oil wealth." Saudi Arabia is only "wealthy" in oil and gas terms to the extent its export revenues preserve a high ratio of oil and gas income per capita. While no precise statistics are available, this ratio seems to have dropped by more than 65% between the peak of the oil boom in the early 1980s and the worst point in the "oil crash" of 1998. Chart 5.8 provides a comparison of Saudi estimates of the trends in the value of both the GDP and petroleum production in constant 1994 riyals relative to the trend in population. There are data problems in oil petroleum export earnings that, combined with the previous uncertainties in population data, make it impossible to provide an accurate picture of oil income per capita; however, it is all too clear that the population is rising significantly faster than oil revenues. Estimates by the U.S. Department of Energy, for example, indicate that a combination of higher population and lower oil prices cut the value of Saudi per capita oil export revenues from $23,820 in 1980 to $2,563 in 2001, as measured in constant 2000 U.S. dollars.

The importance of such trends is also indicated by what happened during the sudden drop in oil prices during late 1997 to 1998. As has been touched on earlier, the Saudi economy was severely hit. GDP fell by 11% to 12.3%, the budget deficit rose to $12.3 billion, and the current account recorded a $13.1 billion deficit—the first in three years.[42] Real GDP grew only about 0.4%, less than one-eighth the rate of population growth. Saudi Arabia is not a poor country, and its per capita income is scarcely low even if it is only a fraction of its peak level. It may be well able to solve its problems through economic reform and privatization, but it must come to grips with demographics. The Economist Intelligence Unit forecasts that economic growth in current dollars will be 2.5% in 2002, and 2.0% in 2003—well below the rate of population growth.[43] The Saudi American Bank estimated real growth at only 1.5% in 2001, and 2.0% in 2002.

Chart 5.8
Boom and Bust in Per Capita Oil Wealth: Saudi Arabia: Population Growth in Millions
versus Total Petroleum Income and GDP (Population in Millions × 10; Economic Data
in Billions of Constant 1994 Saudi Riyals)

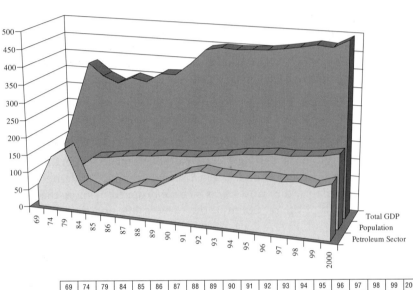

	69	74	79	84	85	86	87	88	89	90	91	92	93	94	95	96	97	98	99	2000
☐ Petroleum Sector	61.5	147.8	175.1	76.3	59.5	89.7	77	93.8	93	116.8	142.4	152.5	146.7	146	147	150.8	147.2	152.2	142.5	156.3
☐ Population	52	70	95	128	134	141	148	151	156	159	161	167	174	182	185	191	190	194	199	209
☐ Total GDP	132.8	256.6	379.2	346.7	328	347.8	338.1	364.4	365.7	400	441.3	450	448	450	452.7	458.8	466.3	474.7	470.5	492.9

Sources: Adapted by Anthony H. Cordesman from data in Kingdom of Saudi Arabia, Ministry
of Planning, *Achievements of the Development Plans 1970-2001, Facts and Figures* (Riyadh:
Ministry of Planning, 2001), 19th Issue, p. 200, and population estimates taken from data
provided by the U.S. State Department and Saudi Central Bureau of Statistics.

DEMOGRAPHIC PRESSURES ON SAUDI SOCIETY AND THE SAUDI LABOR FORCE

Population pressures have already put a heavy pressure on the Saudi
budget and the Saudi economy, and have interacted with other forces for
social change. For example, the Saudi budget allocated 18% of its resources
to education in 1996. This percentage grew to over 25% in 1999.[44] These
same population pressures require a steady expansion of the Saudi labor
force, although estimates of the labor force and future job needs are contradictory and uncertain. The government estimates that the labor force will
grow at an annual rate of at least 3.2% between 1998–2015.[45]

The estimates of the changes in the Saudi labor force made for the Seventh Development Plan are shown in Table 5.2. They indicate that the total Saudi labor force was 7.17 million in 1999 (out of an eligible base of 9.7 million), and estimate that it would reach 10.76 million in 2020. The number of native Saudi workers would increase from 3.17 million to 8.26 million between 1999 and 2020—growing at an average annual rate of 4.7%. The number of foreign workers would decline from 4.0 million to about 2.5 million, at an average annual rate of 2.57% during the Seventh Development Plan (2000–2004) and by 2.25% during 2000–2020. There would be 9.6 million workers in the private sector in 2020, or 89.7% of the total. The remaining workforce would involve 1 million workers in the government sector (9.1%) and 100,000 workers in the oil and gas sectors (1.2%).[46]

Estimating Future Job Needs

Saudi labor statistics are sometimes contradictory—a major problem in a country where accurate labor statistics are absolutely critical to effective Saudisation and economic and educational planning, and where far more detailed government projections are needed of the relationship between job creation and the number of young Saudis entering the labor force.

For example, the Saudi Central Department of Statistics reported government civilian employment at 916,000 in 1999, while the Ministry of Civil Service reported it at 668,000 in 1998. Nevertheless, the Saudi Central Department of Statistics seems to be a reliable source, and Saudi perceptions of the Kingdom's labor problems and its estimates track in very rough terms with those of the World Bank. The Saudi Central Department of Statistics estimated in 2001 that the Saudi native labor force was 3.3 million in 2000, and would rise to 8.3 million in 2020.[47]

It reported in September 2002, however, that the Saudi labor force at the end of 1999—defined as males fifteen years of age or older who were job holders or job seekers—was only 2.82 million, and that the foreign labor force was only 3.02 million out of 5.02 million. These figures seem to have a strong political bias toward underreporting unemployment—a problem common even in sophisticated Western countries like Germany—but they do illustrate how hard it is to get meaningful Saudi data.[48]

The Saudi American Bank has made similar estimates, and its numbers differ in virtually every category. The Saudi Central Department of Statistics bases its estimates of a 6.77% rate of unemployment among Saudi males at the end of 1999 on a male labor force of 2,41,006, of which 2,247,720 are employed and 163,286 are unemployed. The Saudi American Bank estimated a Saudi male direct unemployment rate of 11.93% in 2002 based on a total native Saudi male labor force of 2,422,720, with 2,422,720 employed and 328,286 unemployed. The unemployment rate is driven by

Table 5.2
The Labor Force Numbers and Qualification Estimates Used in the Seventh Development Plan (Manpower Numbers in 1,000s)

Projections of Total Native Saudi Population and Labor Force

Category	Number in 1999	Number in 2004	Change 1999–2000	Average Annual Growth Rate (%)
Population below Working Age	5999.2	6814.8	818.6	2.6
Working Age Population	9662.2	11705.5	2043.3	3.9
Total population	15658.4	18520.3	2861.9	3.4
Population in Work Force	3172.9	3990.2	817.3	4.7
Dependency Ratio (%)	62.1	58.2	—	3.8
Aggregate Labor Force Participation Rate (%)	32.8	34.1	—	1.2

Manpower Supply and Demand Projections

Category	1999	2004	2020	Average Annual Growth Rate 2000–2020	
Supply					
Total Saudi Population	15658.4	18520.3	29717.0	3.41	3.10
Total Saudi Labor Force	3172.9	3990.2	8263.0	4.69	4.66
Demand					
Government Services	916.2	932.3	984.0	0.35	0.34
Crude oil and gas	98.9	100.4	127.0	0.30	1.20
Private Sector	616.2	6427.2	9635.0	0.99	2.15
Total	7176.3	7504.9	10746.0	0.90	1.94
Supply/Demand Balance					
Non-Saudi Labor Force	4003.4	3514.7	2483.0	−2.57	−2.25

continued

Table 5.2 Continued

Qualifications of New Native Saudi Entrants During 2000–2004

Category	Number	Share (%)
Tertiary Level		
Universities	178.6	21.9
Teacher Training Institutes	36.7	4.5
Intermediate Technical Colleges	16.7	2.0
Subtotal	232.0	28.4
Secondary Level		
Secondary (General)	213.9	26.2
Technical and Vocational	78.7	9.6
Subtotal	292.6	35.8
Primary Level		
Intermediate	143.1	17.5
Elementary	92.3	11.3
Subtotal	235.4	28.8
Total Educated Entrants	760.0	93.0
Other Entrants	57.3	7.0
Total New Entrants	817.3	100.0

Source: English-language version of the *Seventh Development Plan 1420/21–1424/25 AH (2000–2004 AD)* (Riyadh: Ministry of Planning, 2001), pp. 77–78, 162–164.

the estimate that 340,000 Saudi males enter the labor force each year, but that only 175,000 jobs are created.[49]

Chart 5.9 provides another estimate of the possible growth in the Saudi labor force between 2000 and 2025, using U.S. Census Bureau estimates. As has been touched on earlier, the World Bank estimates that the Saudi labor force has already grown from 3 million in 1980 to 7 million in 2000,

Chart 5.9
The Challenge to Come: Growth in the Saudi Labor Force, 2000 versus 2025 (in Thousands in Prime Working Age)

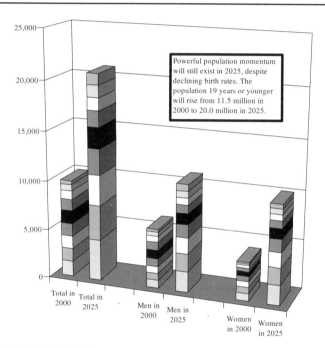

Powerful population momentum will still exist in 2025, despite declining birth rates. The population 19 years or younger will rise from 11.5 million in 2000 to 20.0 million in 2025.

	Total in 2000	Total in 2025		Men in 2000	Men in 2025		Women in 2000	Women in 2025
Age 60-64	415	1,143		265	683		151	460
Age 55-59	616	1,220		421	677		195	543
Age 50-54	888	1,291		621	688		266	603
Age 45-49	1,165	1,597		802	839		363	758
Age 40-44	1,332	2,139		874	1102		457	1038
Age 35-39	1,308	2,643		796	1346		511	1297
Age 30-34	1,309	3,100		728	1590		581	1511
Age 25-29	1,318	3,543		692	1809		626	1733
Age 20-24	1,588	4,153		818	2119		771	2034

Source: Adapted by Anthony H. Cordesman from U.S. Census Bureau online demographic data for Saudi Arabia, accessed May, 2001.

and that it must grow to 10 million by 2010. This comes out as an average annual growth rate of 4.5% during 1980–2000, and is based on a projected growth rate of 3.4% during 2000–2010.[50]

This projection, however, falls far short of the steady increase in the number of male and female Saudis entering the labor force during this period and does not seem to allow for significant increases in the percentage of women employed. The World Bank estimate also differs from Saudi estimates in that more Saudi women are excluded from the labor force: the number for Saudi women grew from 7.6% in 1980 to 16.1% in 2000, a lower percentage than in Saudi estimates.[51]

The Labor Force Implications of the Seventh Development Plan

The Seventh Development Plan provides a more structured estimate of the future Saudi job market, although one drawing on data generated in 1999. Table 5.2 shows that it calls for the creation of 328,000 new job opportunities to raise total employment from 7,176,3000 in 1999 to 7,504,900 by 2004. Virtually all of these jobs are to come from the private sector, which is projected to create 311,000 out of the 328,000 jobs, with only 16,100 new jobs in the government sector (4.9% of the new jobs). This would cut government employment from 12.8% of all jobs in 1999 to 12.4% in 2004.

A significant number of the projected new jobs are in areas in which Saudis have been reluctant to take jobs in the past. These include 81,400 new jobs in construction, 72,000 in manufacturing, and 24,400 in agriculture. Some 9,000 jobs are estimated to arise in attractive service sector jobs like management and administration, and an additional 15,500 jobs in professional and technical positions. However, 93,100 jobs are estimated to come from less attractive areas of the service sector like sales, services, and clerical. Accordingly, even if all of the new jobs called for in the plan were created, they would require significant social shifts in employment of a kind that seem unlikely to occur at the required rate. In contrast, agriculture is estimate to grow three times more quickly (0.9%).[52]

The planned rate of job creation in the Seventh Development Plan raises the most serious issue—the average annual rate of job creation in 0.9% versus a population growth rate that has averaged well over 3.0% and over 3.5% in recent years. The plan organization puts the average annual growth rate in the working population at 3.9%, and says the rate below working age has dropped to 2.6%, which seems unrealistically low. It can only guess at employment for women, but estimates that they will increase from 32.8% of the labor force in1999 to 34.1% by 2004.

The Seventh Development Plan projects negligible absolute growth in employment in traditional areas. The oil sector is estimated to have a growth rate of 0.3% in government services, 0.3% in the oil and gas sector, and 0.3% in oil refining. Only 700 new jobs are projected in petrochemicals. Private manufacturing (2.4% average annual growth), construction (1.5%), and finance and real estate (2.3%) are the fields that will dominate job growth—all areas largely outside the control of the government and involving only limited direct government investment in the plan.

Job creation is also far easier to call for than achieve. Foreign Minister Saud al-Faisal has suggested that each billion dollars invested in new energy projects should produce 10,000–16,000 jobs. The Saudi American Bank estimates that $5,000 million has been invested over the last twenty-five years in foreign direct investments and has created 54,000 jobs, while joint venture projects by the Kingdom created a further 21,000. As a result, only after a major restructuring of the Saudi labor force (to eliminate foreign labor from existing jobs) can significant improvements be made. It is also clear that the government still lacks a viable national manpower strategy that can actually achieve the goal of replacing 60% of the foreign labor force with Saudi nationals.[53] Saudi Arabia's declining real per capita income, persistent budget deficits, and overdependency on oil revenues will not be easy to change.

Moreover, the estimates in the Seventh Development Plan indicate that the vast majority of employment opportunities must come from either Saudisation or the retirement of existing workers. The plan estimates that there will be 817,300 new employees but only 328,000 new jobs. Furthermore, the number of new employees happens to coincide exactly with the plan's new estimate of total entrants to the labor market during 2000–2004. As Table 5.2 shows, this is made possible by estimating a continued high dependency rate to limit the number of job applicants and a low participation rate in the labor forces.

Skill Levels and the Saudi Labor Force

All Saudi estimates ignore the fact that much of the projected employment has occurred at the cost of serious disguised unemployment of Saudis in nonproductive jobs in the state sector, petroleum sector, and private sector. This disguised unemployment is both the result of past government policy and an extended family and social safety net that creates large numbers of unnecessary, unproductive jobs.

Although it is impossible to do more than make sophisticated guesstimates, Chart 5.10 provides a rough indication of the fact that Saudi Arabia must have very high level of disguised unemployment in the form of jobs that do not contribute much—if any—productive output to the economy. While there has been progress in terms of absolute numbers, the growth of Saudi-held jobs in the private sector has been very slow relative to the number of Saudis entering the labor force, and the number of foreigners in the private sector actually increased through 1998. Accordingly, while

Chart 5.10

Overdependence on Nonproductive Government Jobs Has a Cost: A Rough Estimate of Comparative Direct and Disguised Unemployment Rates in the Middle East (Rate Measured in Percent)

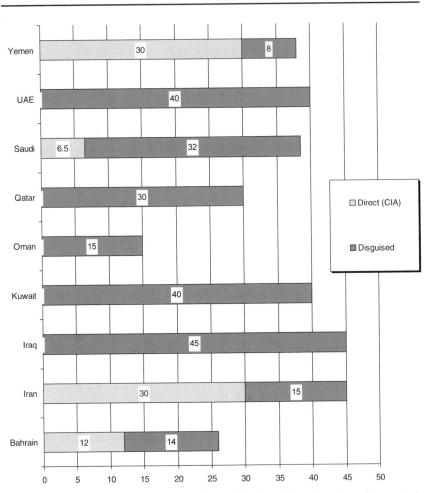

Source: Rough estimate by Anthony H. Cordesman based on informal estimates by experts in the U.S. government and an international financial organization for 2002. Disguised includes public sector, civil service, and private sector jobs with no use economic output.

Saudi government officials privately estimated native Saudi male unemployment at 15% to 18% in April 2002, the real figure could be anywhere between 25% and 35%.

Chart 5.11 shows that virtually all of this workforce must find non-traditional jobs in urban areas. Traditional rural and agricultural jobs are

Chart 5.11

Massive Ongoing Pressures for Social Change: Massive Urbanization and the Sharp Decline in the Role of Agriculture (Labor in Agriculture in Percentages of Labor Force and Urbanization as Percent of Total Population)

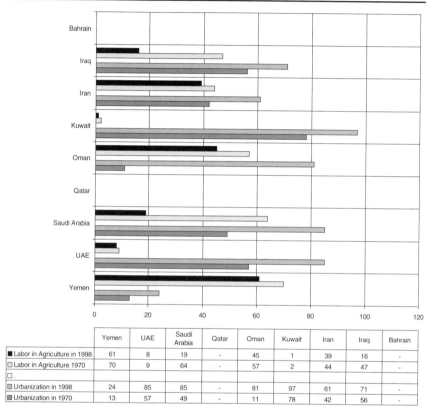

	Yemen	UAE	Saudi Arabia	Qatar	Oman	Kuwait	Iran	Iraq	Bahrain
■ Labor in Agriculture in 1998	61	8	19	-	45	1	39	16	-
□ Labor in Agriculture 1970	70	9	64	-	57	2	44	47	-
□ .									
▨ Urbanization in 1998	24	85	85	-	81	97	61	71	-
▨ Urbanization in 1970	13	57	49	-	11	78	42	56	-

Source: Adapted by Anthony H. Cordesman from the World Bank's *World Development Indicators, 2000*, pp. 26–28.

vanishing from the economy as a percentage of the workforce, and although agricultural jobs are now subsidized, they will continue to shrink steadily as a percentage of the labor force even if subsidies continue.

The government clearly recognizes the need to expand the native labor force and to ensure that younger Saudis have the education and motivation necessary to become globally competitive. Senior Saudi officials talk about a knowledge-based economy as the key to giving young Saudis not only employment, but jobs that are globally competitive enough to ensure that they receive relatively high salaries. It makes both creating new jobs and increasing education levels a high priority.

Saudi labor statistics show that the labor force already has substantial skills, although Saudi statistics do exaggerate the technical skills of the present labor force. Saudi figures show that the Kingdom had 1.1 million scientific and technical jobs in 1999 (15.6% of the entire labor force). The rest of the labor force was divided to include 534,000 in clerical jobs (7.4%), 134,000 in administrative and business jobs (1.9%), 507,000 salesmen (7.1%), 551,000 in agriculture and fishing (7.8%), and 2.2 million in construction and production works (30.5%). Some 916,000 workers were in government services;[54] another 98,900 of 7.176 million worked in the oil and gas sector, plus 21,500 in oil refining and 9,400 in petrochemicals. This compares with the 557,900 still working in agriculture.

The problem with these figures, however, is that they imply that Saudis are working productively in skilled or white-collar jobs, although the reality may be limited skills or disguised unemployment. Moreover, 2.217 million out of the total labor force worked in finance and real estate, while 1.037 million worked in trade. These are job categories where the extended family often creates jobs regardless of whether they are needed or not. [55]

Other data show that the Saudi government is making real progress in raising the educational standards of new entrants to the labor force. The level of education and qualification for the new entrants to the labor force estimated in Table 5.2 is impressive. It does not track in detail with other Saudi demographic data, however, and is subject to all of the problems in Saudi education that have already been discussed. It also shows that 290,000 out of the 817,300 entrants will have limited or poor education. Nevertheless, the Saudi totals in Table 5.2 are still very good for a developing country. Saudi Arabia will have a higher percentage of well-educated entrants than a number of Asian countries and many countries in the Middle East with a much longer history of modern education.

There is no one solution to these interactions between demographic, economic, and social problems. Saudi Arabia clearly needs to encourage smaller families and engage in efforts to reduce population growth. There are few prospects, however, that Saudi Arabia can prevent major future population growth. Its population is so young that its "demographic momentum" will produce major future growth even if the birth rate drops. In fact, Saudi Arabia has a population momentum ratio of 1:6, which is one of the highest in the world—about 45% higher than that of high-income countries. As a result, Saudi Arabia must privatize and diversify its economy far more rapidly than in the past, expand oil export capacity as quickly as possible, develop far more comprehensive infrastructure and water supply plans, and take more aggressive steps to eliminate most of its foreign labor.

THE "YOUTH EXPLOSION," FOREIGN LABOR, AND SAUDISATION

Saudi Arabia already faces the equivalent of a "youth explosion"—one that inevitably creates pressures to create massive numbers of new jobs for Saudi men and women and to reduce the numbers of foreigners employed in the Kingdom. The World Bank has estimated that the total number of young Saudi men reaching job age (fifteen to nineteen years) will rise from 789,000 in 1990 and 1.0 million in 1995 to 1.3 million in 2000, 1.5 million in 2010, 1.8 million in 2015, and 2.1 million in 2020.[56] Chart 5.12 provides a comparative estimate of the number of youths entering the labor market in various Gulf countries; the CIA estimates that 221,000 native Saudi male citizens reached the age where they should enter the work force in 2000, and 223,400 in 2002. If women are included, the total number of potential annual entrants to the workforce in 2000–2002 exceeded 440,000.[57]

The U.S. Census Bureau does not estimate the size of the Saudi labor force per se, but does estimate the total number of young Saudis in the fifteen-to-nineteen age group. This will increase from 2,125,000 (1,076,000 males) in 2000 to 3,120,747 (1,599,000 males) in 2010; 4,169,000 (2,130 males) in 2020; 5,815,000 (2,968,000 males) in 2030; 7,472,000 (3,816,000 males) in 2040; and 9,032,000 (5,019,000 males) in 2050. If one calculates the annual average by dividing the five years in the fifteen-to-nineteen age group by five, this means that 425,000 men and women reached job age each year, beginning in 2000, and 624,000 will reach job age beginning in 2010, 834,000 beginning in 2020, 1.16 million in 2030, 1.49 million in 2040, and 1.8 million in 2050. This averaging method obviously understates the real number slightly.[58]

These trends—as well as the previous figures on job creation—explain why the Saudi government puts so much emphasis on Saudisation, although scarcely without limits. For example, the Saudi Ministry of Labor issued an announcement in May 2001 that it intended to cut foreign jobs by 85% over the next thirty years, from 7.2 million to 1 million. At the same time, it still projected that foreigners would make up 10 million out of a projected 39 million people in 2030.[59]

It is far from clear, however, that the government can meet any of the various goals it has set. While Saudi Arabia has actively pushed for Saudisation since its Fourth Development Plan, Chart 5.13 shows that it has so far had little real success, except in the government sector—an area where more efficient organization and methods could easily, if not massively, lead to significant reductions in total employment. Anyone who visits Saudi Arabia and goes on tours of "Saudiized" plants and facilities also finds that many of these tours reveal that many—if not all—of the Saudis involved have already left these jobs, that job training is often wasted, and that Saudi

Chart 5.12
The Search for Jobs: CIA Estimate of the Number of Young Males Entering the Labor Market Each Year

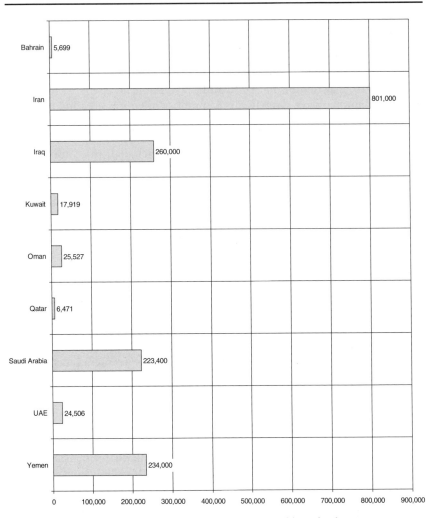

Source: Adapted by Anthony H. Cordesman from CIA, *World Factbook, 2002*.

workers not only will not stay in low prestige jobs but even refuse long commutes, much less relocation, away from their extended families. Although such cases are anecdotal, it is clear that the government is only tracking input to Saudisation, not the end result in terms of performance and retention.

Chart 5.13
Recent Trends in the Saudi Labor Force: Saudisation Is Failing in the Private Sector (in Thousands)

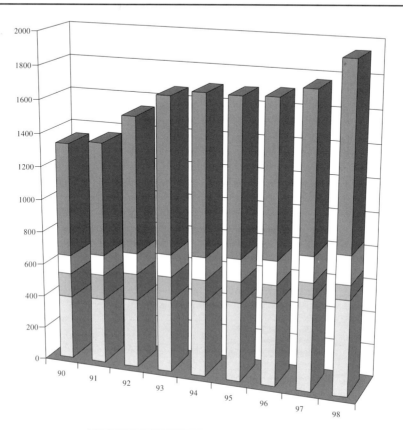

	90	91	92	93	94	95	96	97	98
▣ Foreigners in Private Sector	686.2	686	822.2	938.1	964.4	945	940.8	949.6	1097.8
▢ Saudis in Private Sector	114.2	122.2	128.9	136	137.1	137.6	142.7	155.3	173.6
▣ Foreigners in Government	147.9	151.6	159.6	144.9	133	128.7	109.7	96	89
▢ Saudis in Government	386.8	396.9	420.7	444.4	460.8	480.3	506.6	560.7	579.4

Sources: Adapted by Anthony H. Cordesman from data in Saudi Arabian Monetary Agency, *Thirty-Sixth Annual Report, 1421H (2000G)* (Riyadh: SAMA, 2000), Tables 4 and 5, and population estimates taken from data provided by the U.S. State Department.

Saudisation also involves gender issues. Estimates of female employment in Saudi Arabia is a statistical morass, complicated by a failure to distinguish between native and foreign labor and to develop effective methods for defining employment and the number of native women who want to enter the labor force versus those estimated to actually be seeking jobs.

Chart 5.14 shows that the employment rate for Saudi women is well below the potential requirement if the percentage of women employed is to
approach the percentage of other Arab and developing countries.[60]

The new data the Saudi Central Department of Statistics issued in September 2002 date back to the end of 1999 and have serious problems, but
also illustrate this point. The department estimated a total of 2.82 million
job holders and job seekers: 2.41 million were male and only 413,000 were
female, and Saudi males earn about twice as much as Saudi females with
the same level of education. A total of 2.60 million Saudis were actually
employed: 2.25 million males and 347,000 females. This put the unemployment rate for males at 6.8% and 15.8% for females.

Chart 5.14
Women as a Percent of the Labor Force: The Pace of Social Change

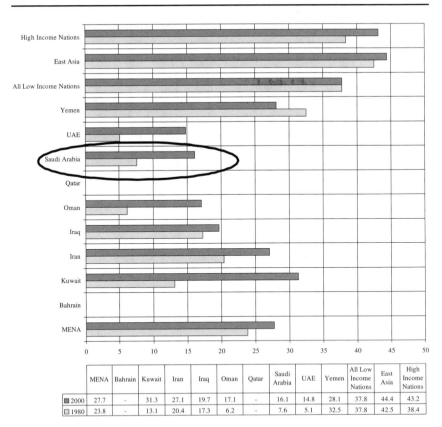

	MENA	Bahrain	Kuwait	Iran	Iraq	Oman	Qatar	Saudi Arabia	UAE	Yemen	All Low Income Nations	East Asia	High Income Nations
■ 2000	27.7	-	31.3	27.1	19.7	17.1	-	16.1	14.8	28.1	37.8	44.4	43.2
□ 1980	23.8	-	13.1	20.4	17.3	6.2	-	7.6	5.1	32.5	37.8	42.5	38.4

Sources: Adapted by Anthony H. Cordesman from the World Bank's *World Development
Indicators, 2000*, pp. 46–48; and *World Development Indicators, 2002*, pp. 52–54.

Even these figures, however, only assume a 6% female participation rate as a percent of the total participation versus 32% for males. This labor participation rate for males is bad enough. It compares with 49% for the rest of the Middle East, 51% for sub-Saharan Africa, 55% for Latin America, 61% for East Asia, 72% for Europe, and 77% for the United States. Even allowing for Saudi Arabia's young population, it implies that Saudis are some of the least production people in the world.

The 6% for Saudi women, however, compare with 17% labor participation for the Middle East as a whole. It compares with 27% for Latin America, 37% for sub-Saharan Africa, and 51% for East Asia—where female productivity has been a key driving force in development. The figures are 18% for Europe and 23% for the United States, but these numbers are skewed by a rapidly aging population and large numbers of elderly female dependents. The labor participation rate among young females is much higher.

These Saudi data may well sharply underreport female participation. At the same time, they are probably broadly accurate in reflecting a level of discrimination and religious and cultural barriers to female employment that creates a productivity crisis in the Saudi labor force, where massive rapid changes are needed to take advantage of the comparatively high educational standards of young Saudi women. The failure of Saudi economic planners to address this ignores a critical priority in Saudi economic reform.[61]

The problem of analyzing present and future Saudisation for women is further complicated by the Saudi employment patterns for foreign women shown in Chart 5.15. Most of the women shown in Chart 5.15 work as servants or menials, as do a significant number of the men, and the data in Chart 5.15 understate the problem because they only include jobs reported by the government. Most Saudis are not willing to work at such jobs, and rightly so. The goal for both Saudi men and women must be to secure jobs that are fully competitive in market terms, deliver real productivity gains, and match the education and skills of new generations of Saudis. Saudisation that menializes the native Saudi workforce is the last thing the Kingdom needs.

Charts 5.16 and 5.17 show the distribution of both the total current Saudi population by age and sex, and of the native population. Chart 5.18 shows how the total population divides between the native and foreign population by age. The number of foreigners is much larger in the older age groups, and most foreign women give up working in the Kingdom— where they are employed largely as servants—by their early thirties. Even so, the Census Bureau estimates that 43% of the Saudi population was fourteen years of age or younger in 2000.[62]

Chart 5.19 shows that the CIA makes similar estimates. It reports that over 42% of the population was under fifteen years of age in 2000, and more than 58% of the Kingdom's population was under the age of

Chart 5.15
The Challenge of Saudisation Is Greater than It Appears: Far Too Many Current Jobs are Now Held by Foreign Women, Many as Servants

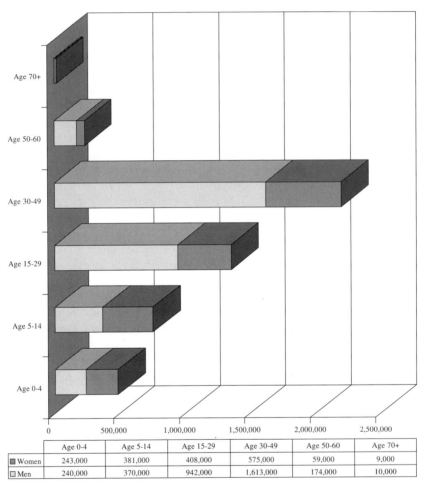

	Age 0-4	Age 5-14	Age 15-29	Age 30-49	Age 50-60	Age 70+
▣ Women	243,000	381,000	408,000	575,000	59,000	9,000
▢ Men	240,000	370,000	942,000	1,613,000	174,000	10,000

Source: Adapted by Anthony H. Cordesman from data in Saudi Arabian Monetary Agency, *Thirty-Sixth Annual Report, 1421H (2000G)*, Table 16.3.

seventeen. Even allowing for the fact that some men and a larger number of women never enter the labor force, these CIA estimates indicate that the creation of over 440,000 jobs a year is already required to fully employ young Saudis. This must take place in a country where the CIA estimates the total labor force is only 7 million, 35% of the population in the age group from fifteen to sixty-four is foreign, and the maximum number of

Chart 5.16
The "Youthening" of Saudi Arabia—Part One: U.S. Census Bureau Estimate of
the Distribution of the Total Native and Foreign Population by Age and Sex in
2000 (in Thousands)

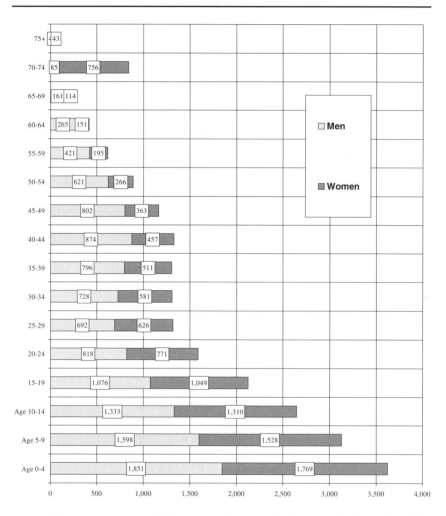

Source: U.S. Census Bureau, IDB Summary Demographic Data for Saudi Arabia (URL:
www.census.gov/cgi-bin/ipc/idbsum?cty=SA), May 2001.

Saudis employed in that labor force is only 4.6 million.[63] It also is quite
clear from Charts 5.16, 5.17, and 5.18 that this requirement for new jobs
can easily double in the next decade.

Saudi statistics make these points even more clearly. It is clear from
Chart 5.18 just how young the Saudi native population really is. It is

Chart 5.17

The "Youthening" of Saudi Arabia—Part Two: Saudi Central Department of
Statistics Estimate of the Distribution of the Total Native and Foreign Population
by Age and Sex in 2000 (in Thousands)

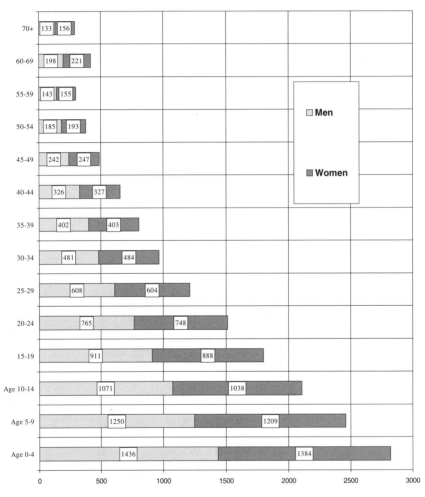

Source: Adapted from SAMA, *37th Annual Report* (Riyadh: SAMA, 2001), pp. 268–269.

equally clear just how heavily Saudi Arabia now relies on its foreign population for labor. According to Saudi data, the foreign population made
up 5.02 million out of a total population of 19.90 million in 1999
(roughly 25% of the total). If one looks at the key age groups that contributed to the labor force, however, the non-Saudi population totaled
3.53 million while the native Saudi population totaled 6.60 million.[64]

Chart 5.18
The "Youthening" of Saudi Arabia—Part Three: Saudi Estimate of the Distribution
of the Total Native and Foreign Population by Age and Sex in 1999 (in Percent of
Total Population)

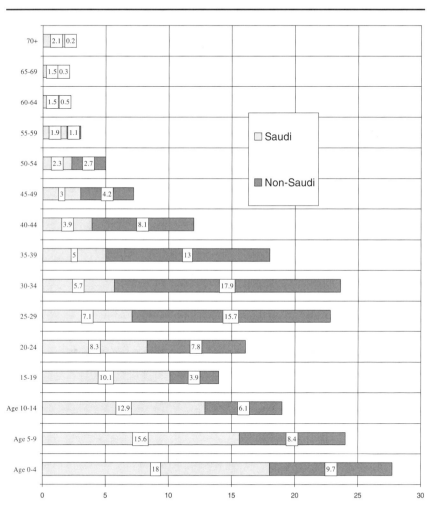

Sources: Adapted by Anthony H. Cordesman from Saudi Arabian Monetary Agency, *Thirty-Sixth Annual Report, 1421H (2000G)*, pp. 250–257; SAMA, *Thirty-Seventh Annual Report, 1422H (2001G)*, p. 268. Figures do not total 100% because they had to be extrapolated by the author from graphic data.

Chart 5.19
Population Momentum and Pressure on the Job Market: The CIA's Comparative Estimate of the "Youth Rate" (Percentage of the Population Aged Fourteen Years or Less in 2002)

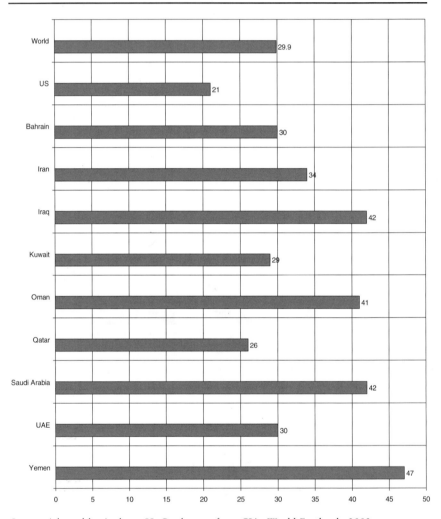

Source: Adapted by Anthony H. Cordesman from CIA, *World Factbook, 2002*.

These figures are somewhat speculative because there are still significant numbers of illegal foreign workers.

A study by the Saudi American Bank issued in February 2002, using data from the Saudi Central Department of Statistics, summarizes the Kingdom's demographic challenges as follows:[65]

- 45.6% of the population is fourteen years of age or younger.
- 73.9% of the population is twenty-nine years of age or younger.
- 38% of the 16.75 million Saudi nationals alive in 2001 were born after Iraq's invasion of Kuwait in 1990.
- The fertility rate of native Saudi women was 5.5 infants per woman in 2000, compared with a world average fertility rate of 2.7 and a Middle East average of 3.5.
- Although 210,000 Saudis graduated from secondary school in 2001, 402,000 entered elementary school.
- The population of Saudi nationals is projected to almost double by 2020, expanding the Saudi labor force from 3.3 million in 2000 to 8.3 million in 2020.
- The Riyadh region had 4.49 million people in 1999, and the Mecca region, including Jeddah, had 5.2 million.

The Blessings and Curses of Saudisation

The possible "blessing" inherent in Saudi Arabia's present dependence on legal and illegal foreign labor is that expelling most of the foreign population could, in theory, create large numbers of job openings for young Saudis as they mature and enter the labor force. However, the "curse" of the present level of dependence on foreign labor is that many of the non-Saudis are working in jobs that young Saudis do not prefer, that often have little or no social value, and where the productivity is often so low that the jobs would not exist in their present form if the employer had to pay Saudi natives. Turning Saudisation theory into practice means restructuring much of the present labor market to create the new types of knowledge-based jobs that young Saudis want and expelling and replacing roughly 2 million foreign workers over the next decade.

Fortunately, a large part of the foreign work force is highly skilled and now occupies jobs that Saudis may well accept in an era of more realistic expectations. Saudi statistics show there are nearly as many foreign university graduates in Saudi Arabia as native Saudi university graduates (536,000 versus 594,000). There are some 232,000 more foreigners with diplomas. There are 565,000 who completed secondary school, and 598,000 with an intermediate education. This is a total of 1.9 million educated foreigners, or nearly half of the 4.1 million foreigners of adult age.[66]

However, the bottom of the foreign workforce will never be Saudiized and never should be. There were some 1.7 million foreign females in the Kingdom in 1999; nearly 1 million were in the fifteen to forty-nine age group, and a very large number worked as servants. These jobs are not going to be replaced by Saudi men or women. Similarly, Saudi officials estimate that something like 800,000 foreign males out of a total of 3.3 million worked in menial or low-status jobs.[67]

Data issued by Saudi Central Department of Statistics in September 2002 also shows that native Saudis earn about two to three times as much as non-Saudis, even in low quality jobs. The average Saudi earned 84,516 riyals ($22,538) a year. The average non-Saudi earned 37,860 riyals ($10,096) a year. If one looks at monthly compensation in 2000 in Saudi riyals, an illiterate Saudi earned 3,155 riyals versus 1,136 for a non-Saudi. The comparisons for employees with basic literacy were 3,450 versus 1,260 riyals. Primary-school graduates earned 4,600 versus 1,378, secondary school graduates earned 7,200 versus 2,580; intermediate college graduates earned 6,810 versus 2,880; and university graduates earned 10,893 versus 5,581. The average for native Saudis was 7,043 riyals versus 2,354. It is obvious that the Saudi economy cannot afford to replace current non-Saudi jobs at twice their present cost, much less three times the present cost. Even if Saudis wanted jobs at the bottom of the labor market, Saudization could not possibly occur at anything remotely approaching a one-for-one basis.[68]

Foreign jobs have other negative economic consequences. Most foreigners expatriate capital to their home countries and almost none invest their savings in Saudi Arabia. Foreign workers also face major barriers in any kind of entrepreneurial activity. The Kingdom must organize its infrastructure and many of its social services to support foreign labor, as significant numbers of foreign workers become de facto permanent residents —both legally and illegally.

Saudi government estimates of the outflow of capital due to foreign workers seem to be based purely on formal transactions and sharply undercount the real total, but it is well in excess of $5 billion a year and some estimates go well over $10 billion. There are no meaningful estimates of the related costs of infrastructure and social services, but even though foreign workers generally receive a lower share of services than natives, they still account for at least 15% of Saudi expenditures.[69]

Real-World Progress in Saudisation

The problems in Saudisation also become clearer when history is compared with rhetoric. The Saudi government has been actively pursuing Saudisation policies for more than a decade, and the previous charts have already shown how much of Saudi Arabia's total population remains foreign. To put the numbers in these charts in further perspective, the 1993 Saudi census calculated that Saudi Arabia had 4.6 million foreign residents out of a total population of 14.6 million. Saudi government estimates put the number of foreign workers at 4.9 million in 1999 and the number of Saudi workers at 2.5 million.[70] These estimates suggested that foreign workers constituted 65% of a workforce numbering 7.2 million.

The International Institute for Strategic Studies (IISS) estimates that roughly 73% of Saudi Arabia's population was native in 2000, of which

Bedouin make up 10%. The other 27%, or 4.6 million people, is foreign: 8% other Arab, 21% Asian, 2% African, and less than 1% European and American.[71] The CIA estimates that roughly 4.2 million foreign workers were employed in the government or the service sector in 2000. It estimates that as much as 60% of Saudi Arabia's labor force, and 26% of its total population, were still foreign. The Saudi government has issued estimates that suggest the presence of up to 6 million expatriate workers, including over 1 million Egyptians, 800,000 Indians, and 600,000 Filipinos.[72]

The CIA estimates that 40% of the total labor force worked in government in 2000, 30% worked in services, 5% in agriculture, and 25% in industry, construction, and oil. Other estimates indicate that 85% of Saudi Arabia's foreign workers worked in the private sector—50% in industrial and related jobs. Roughly six out of every seven jobs in the Saudi service sector were held by foreign workers. As a result, foreign workers repatriated between $13 and $15 billion a year. This figure adds up to roughly 10% of the Saudi GDP, and compares with total repatriation payments of around $8 billion a year in the early 1980s—when the Saudi GDP per capita was much higher.[73]

The practical problem is to go from recognizing the problem to actually solving it. Good intentions and plans are a meaningless, if not destructive, substitute for effective action. The Saudi Fourth Development Plan (1985–1990) attempted to reduce these problems by seeking a 600,000-man reduction in the Saudi labor force by 1990. In fact, the foreign labor force increased by 200,000, despite the hiring of large numbers of native Saudis by creating significant numbers of unproductive and unneeded jobs in the state sector. No progress on Saudisation took place under the Saudi Fifth Development Plan (1991–1995), and the number of foreign workers employed in the Kingdom actually increased by a rate of 8% to 10% per year during 1993–1994. As a result, foreign workers in Saudi Arabia sent home $15.25 billion in 1994 and an estimated $17.6 billion in 1995—an increase of 40% over total remittances in 1989.

About 500,000 more work visas were issued in 1995 than in 1994, and the total number of expatriate workers and their families living in Saudi Arabia rose to 6.2 million.[74] This led the Kingdom to raise the cost of work permits for foreign laborers, increasing the fee from 1,000 riyals to 2,000 riyals ($533). The London-based Saudi paper *Al-Hayat* reported that the Kingdom expected to make 80 million riyals ($21.3 million) from the work permit fees.[75]

King Fahd recognized the failure of Saudisation as a key Saudi problem when he reorganized his cabinet in 1995. He called for increased privatization to aid Saudisation and provided guidance for review of the Kingdom's development, or five-year, plan.[76] In July 1995, Prince Nayef, the minister of the interior, made a statement calling for major reductions in foreign labor, and on July 20, 1995, the Saudi government announced new measures to reduce foreign labor.[77] Following this announcement, the Saudi government issued major new directives calling for increased Saudisation in October 1995. For example, these directives required hotels to increase the Saudi portion of their labor force by 5% per year. They also established penalties for firms that did not "Saudiise," including denying subsidies and loans, refusing new applications to import foreign labor, and barring them from competing for government contracts.

The Sixth Development Plan (1995–1999), which was issued in July 1995, again called for accelerated Saudisation. It set a goal of creating 191,700 new jobs, filling 148,700 vacancies as a result of turnover, and generating 319,500 jobs by replacing non-Saudis with Saudis. It also called for the creation of 660,000 new jobs in the private sector.[78] Saudi words, however, remained stronger than Saudi actions.

This, however, changed when the oil crash that began in 1997 created a crisis in Saudi revenues and led Saudi Arabia to take still stronger measures. In 1997, the Saudi government stepped up its efforts in dealing with the problem of foreign labor. It offered an amnesty, which expired in October, under which foreign laborers in Saudi Arabia illegally were to volunteer for deportation; in exchange, the Saudi government waived the penalty to which they were subject. Under this amnesty, more than 500,000 illegal foreign workers left the country. Following the expiration of the amnesty, Saudi police began rounding up thousands of illegal workers. Reports surfaced that Saudi police surrounded entire neighborhoods in Jeddah to search for expatriates, and that the police had arrested almost 2,500 illegal immigrants from Africa and Asia. Additionally, the government also increased recruitment fees for many positions, including housemaids.

The government took further measures in 1999, including denying visas to foreigners applying for certain job categories. The government also ordered all state departments and agencies to have their foreign consultants in management contracts set up training programs for Saudi nationals. Another Saudisation measure restricted fruit and vegetable market traders' jobs for nationals only. According to one Saudi estimate, the net effect was to cut total remittance outflows of $1 billion a year to $14,060 million in 1999. Additional steps were taken in 2000: The Saudi government declared that all private firms employing more than twenty people must increase their Saudi-born staff by 25% by October 1, 2001, and set an objective to replace 60% of the total foreign-national workforce.[79]

The Current Level of Progress and Nonprogress in Saudisation

These figures make it clear that the government has never fully enforced many of the measures it took to reduce Saudi dependence on foreign labor.[80] The U.S. State Department issued the following assessment of the progress and problems with Saudisation in February 2000:[81]

Saudisation is the Government's attempt to decrease the number of foreigners working in certain occupations and to replace them with Saudi workers. To accomplish this goal, the Government has taken several long-term steps, most notably limiting employment in certain fields to citizens, prohibiting renewal of existing contracts, and requiring that 5 percent of the work force in private sector companies be filled by citizen workers. The Government also requires firms to increase the proportion of citizen workers by 5 per cent each year. There are a limited number of persons, both influential and otherwise, who attempted to circumvent the requirements of the law. For example, employers have altered job descriptions or hired foreigners for nominally low-level positions but in fact had them fill positions reserved for citizens. Influential persons effectively may circumvent the law because the Ministry of Labor is simply unwilling to confront them.

The ongoing campaign to remove illegal immigrants from the country has done little to Saudiize the economy because illegal immigrants largely work in low-income positions, which most Saudis consider unsuitable. However, the campaign did improve overall working conditions for legally employed immigrants in low-income positions. The Government is carrying out the campaign by widely publicizing its enforcement of existing laws against illegal immigrants and Saudis employing or sponsoring illegal immigrants.

In addition to deportation for illegal workers and jail terms and fines for Saudis hiring illegal workers, the Government announced in 1998 that houses rented to illegal aliens would be ordered closed. In 1997 the Government offered an amnesty of several months duration, which allowed illegal immigrants and their employers or sponsors to avoid the possibility of prosecution by voluntarily seeking expeditious repatriation. As of September, as many as 1.1 million persons departed the country under terms of the amnesty or were deported for violating residence and labor laws in the past 3 years.

During this process, the Government bowed to domestic pressure and granted grace periods and exemptions to certain categories of illegal immigrants (such as servants, drivers, and shepherds), thereby allowing many illegal immigrants to legalize their status without leaving the country. The effect of the expeditious repatriation of some illegal immigrants and the legalization of others has been to improve overall working conditions for legally employed foreigners. Illegal immigrants generally are willing to accept lower salaries and fewer benefits than legally employed immigrants. Their departure or legalization reduced the competition for certain jobs and thereby reduced the incentive for legal immigrants to accept lower wages and fewer benefits as a means of competing with illegal immigrants. Furthermore, their departure or legalization removed a large portion of the class of persons most vulnerable to abuse and exploitation because of their illegal status.

The government has not yet succeeded in addressing the fact that its proposed salary scales, welfare charges, and regulations requiring the firing of Saudi employees create a major deterrent to hiring native labor. For example, the salary scales proposed for unskilled laborers in 1997 called for a salary of 600 to 800 riyals for expatriates and 1,500 to 2,000 for nationals. The scale for skilled laborers was 1,500 to 2,000 riyals for ex-patriates and 3,000 to 4,000 for nationals. The scale for experienced employees was 3,500 to 4,000 riyals for expatriates and 5,000 to 7,000 for nationals, and the scale for engineers was 3,000 to 4,000 riyals for ex-patriates and 6,000 to 8,000 for nationals.

The government has also failed to come to grips with the fact that a viable Saudi economy cannot be created by creating or sustaining unneeded government jobs or unproductive jobs in the private sector, particularly when the Kingdom must be competitive on a global basis. Given the low work ethic and productivity of many Saudis, the main incentive to hire a Saudi national has often been either that a prospective employee was a relative or son of a friend, or to meet some quota. The main success of the Saudisation program has also been in government jobs—which often are awarded without demanding the proper qualifications and performance—and white-collar jobs like the banking sector, where local workers account for 75% of the staff. Significantly, however, the gap between the salary paid to the expatriate and the salary paid to the average local worker is narrow, with the former earning a monthly average of $1,746 versus $1,762.

In those cases where salaries are higher, the lack of experience and skills in domestic staff has proved a serious obstacle. Saudisation also often prevents efficient restructuring and downsizing. For instance, the new Saudi Electric Company chairman, Suleiman Alkadi, wants to restructure and downsize the system, laying off 5,000 staff members. This move will run into tremendous opposition, as it would require firing some native employees. In those cases where salaries are higher, Saudis feel that much of the work done by foreign labor is beneath them. One Saudi woman comments, "Even if a Saudi woman is starving, she would not work for anyone else [in a housekeeping capacity]. . . . [W]e do need the Indians to do the menial work. These are jobs difficult for the Saudi to do." This sense of pride in being Saudi creates a mindset that undermines the underlying philosophy of Saudisation.[82]

Saudisation and Native Saudi Unemployment

An analysis by the Saudi American Bank paints a somewhat different picture of how Saudisation relates to the native Saudi workforce and how to estimate the current levels of direct unemployment of native Saudis. Using data from the Saudi Central Department of Statistics, it estimates that there were 659,900 entrants to the Saudi labor market between 1995 and 1999—although the basis for distinguishing "entrant" from the larger total for those in the age group is unclear. The Ministry of Civil Service reports that 118,570 Saudis were added to already swollen government payrolls during 1995–1998, an annual average of 30,000 a year. This gives a projected total of 148,570 additional jobs for 1995–1999. A large portion—if not

most—of this job creation consisted of introducing additional unproductive jobs or added productive jobs, without eliminating existing unproductive government jobs. In practice, much of this job creation total effectively
consists of disguised unemployment. (Chart 5.20 compares Saudi Arabia's
direct and disguised unemployment rates with those in other Middle Eastern

Chart 5.20
**A Rough Estimate of the Comparative Direct and Disguised Unemployment Rate
in the Middle East in 2001 (Rate Measured in Percent)**

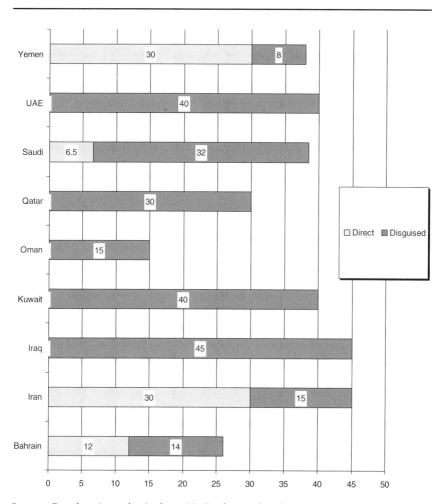

Sources: Rough estimate by Anthony H. Cordesman based on CIA and World Bank staff
working estimates. Disguised includes public sector, civil service, and private sector jobs
with no use economic output.

countries.) Nevertheless, Saudi plans called for creating roughly 30,000 more government jobs a year in 2000 and 2001.

The private sector added 220,000 jobs to the labor force from 1995 to 1999 in firms with twenty or more employees and the Saudi American Bank estimates another 50,000 were added to smaller firms—in all, a total of 270,000 new jobs. Saudi figures, however, underestimate the number of new hires that leave the labor force, and make no attempt to calculate unproductive jobs created for the sons of family members and friends or disguised unemployment. They also assume a largely male labor force, ignoring the fact that Saudi women not only are a critical potential part of the labor force, but are now better educated than Saudi men.

If one ignores disguised unemployment and productivity outside the petroleum sector—where productivity is high because extremely intense capital investment and automation occurs with little job creation—the number of persons now unemployed would total 241,330 according to the Saudi American Bank, versus 418,570 new jobs out of 659,900. Combined with an existing base of 95,000 persons unemployed, according to 1994 Saudi estimates, this would produce 337,330 unemployed Saudis at the end of 1999, creating an unemployment level of around 12%.

Here, however, population momentum and the "youth explosion" may account for much of the difference. The problems in the unemployment data the Saudi Central Department of Statistics issued in September 2002 have already been mentioned; these data show an unemployment rate of 6.8% at the end of 1999, when the real rate is likely to have been at least 11.7%. Nevertheless, they still show major employment problems for young Saudis. Unemployment for Saudis between ages twenty to twenty-four was still 28%, and it was 9.8% for Saudis between twenty-five and twenty-nine. The rate for Saudis over thirty was only 0.9%. These figures also show very little employment for Saudis fifteen to nineteen years old (only 67,113), although the Seventh Development Plan says that about 28% of the new entrants to the labor force (some 50,000) are dropouts from high school or below. These data not only dramatize the impact of the youth explosion, but also indicate that the Saudi government is in a state of near-denial in facing the full scope of the problem.[83]

The Saudi American Bank estimates that 817,000 Saudis will enter the labor market between 2000 and 2004, or an average of 163,000 a year. It also assumed an average of 30,000 new public-sector and 50,000 new private-sector jobs a year. This means 80,000 annual hires out of the 163,000 annual new entrants, leaving an additional 83,000 unemployed per year. This would add a total of 166,000 unemployed in 2000–2001 and raise the total unemployed to 503,330, which would constitute 15.3% of the estimated total labor force of 3.3 million Saudis in 2001. This unemployment level would only be 7% if all foreign labor were eliminated, although it should be noted that far more Saudi youths come of age each year and that the number of unemployed relative to employed will increase sharply each year unless job creation increases equally sharply. Further, the impact of even perfect Saudisation on native Saudi unemployment will drop sharply over time because the number of foreign jobs will remain relatively constant while the pool of potential entrants to the native Saudi labor force is rising.[84]

The Impact of the Seventh Development Plan

The Seventh Development Plan (2001–2005) makes an interesting contrast to the Sixth Development Plan. As has been shown in the data in Table 5.2, it calls for accelerated Saudisation. The Seventh Development Plan

> places special emphasis on the development of human resources and provision of adequate job opportunities. This is attributed to the plan's keenness to enhance the participation of national manpower, raise their efficiency to meet the requirements of the national economy, and replace non-Saudi manpower with Saudis.

It calls for the creation of an additional 488,600 jobs, in contrast to 319,500 in the Sixth Development Plan, by replacing non-Saudis with Saudis. Additionally, it calls for rationalization of the recruitment of the non-Saudi labor force, while limiting jobs in some occupations and sectors to native Saudis only.[85]

The Ministry of Planning states that,[86]

> The Seventh Development Plan expects the provision of 328,600 job opportunities to meet the development needs of the labor force, thereby increasing total employment from 7,170,000 workers in the base year 1419/1420 (1999) to 7,500,000 in 1424/25 (2004). Employment in the non-oil private sector is expected to increase from 6,160,000 in the base year 1419/1420 (1999) to 6,470,000 by the end of the plan 1424/25 (2004). Thus, the total number of job opportunities available in the private sector will be 311,000, or about 94.6% of the total job opportunities available during the period.[87]

These are good intentions, but such intentions are not particularly reassuring ones. The Ministry of Planning figures are not consistent from section to section and raise more statistical questions than they answer. Like almost all Ministry of Planning figures, they do not really show how the goal is to meet the need, and they do not attempt to estimate either the percentage of young Saudis entering the labor forces that will get jobs or the overall level of real and disguised employment that will result. It is unclear how they address Saudis in the military and National Guard, and there is no attempt to address the issue of the employment of women. The Ministry of Planning data imply a freeze on the creation of government jobs and severe limits on the turnover of jobs in government held by foreigners or retiring Saudis, but the reports on the plan do not explicitly address these issues.

Most important, if these figures are taken at face value, they imply a steady and serious deterioration in the economic situation. Job creations relative to the number of young Saudis would steadily decline to below 50% of the total demographic need, even for males. Moreover, virtually all meaningful Saudisation and job creation in the plan now must come from the private sector. There already are about half a million young Saudis that do not even have a token job and over 150,000 males already enter the labor force each year, of which a large number do not have more than secondary education. As a result, the Seventh Development Plan provides little evidence that the Saudi job market will keep up with the growth in its population, create the labor force needed for a globally competitive information-based economy, or reach anywhere near the progress in Saudisation the Kingdom actually needs.

SAUDI ECONOMIC DEVELOPMENT VERSUS SAUDI EDUCATION

The Saudi government faces equally serious and directly related challenges in providing the proper level of education, and it faces additional challenges in its efforts to restructure Saudi education to properly train young Saudis for jobs. Table 5.2 has already provided the favorable estimate developed by the Saudi Ministry of Planning. However, studies by the ILO and World Bank in the late 1990s indicated that the Saudi educational system was failing to adequately educate either male or female students for future jobs and that it was also steadily deteriorating in quality and economic relevance. Analysts claimed that only 17% of the 600,000 Saudis entering the labor force between 1995 and 1999 had college degrees. Furthermore, there were only 10,000 engineering graduates out of 114,000, compared with 48,000 in social sciences and literature.[88]

A Mixed Picture of Strengths and Weaknesses

Saudi figures provide a mixed picture of overall developments in education. They indicate that there were 3,999,778 students in general education in 1998–1999, with slightly more men than women, but do not report on percentages in school versus total numbers in the population. The Ministry of Planning does report that the number of number of Saudi students in elementary and intermediate education lagged slightly behind population growth from 1995 to 2000 and that the construction of new schools fell behind need.[89] At the same time, the number of actual graduates from general education rose from 309,000 in 1994 to 452,000 in 1999.[90]

Enrollment in secondary education increased at an average annual rate of well over 10% during 1999–2000, substantially faster than the population in the age group. The Saudi government reports that only 452,000 students enrolled in secondary education programs in 1995.[91] There were 704,566 students in secondary school in 1999 and the ratio of students to teachers was a relatively low 12:1.[92] The annual number of graduates increased from 87,000 in 1994 to 167,000, in 1999.[93]

The average annual rate of increase in higher education was in excess of 15% during 1995 to 2000, although most of this increase took place in colleges and technical schools rather than universities.[94] In 1995, Saudi Arabia had some 306,548 male and female students enrolled at the Kingdom's seven universities, seventy colleges, and seventy-eight institutes of higher learning. These included 297,830 undergraduates, 7,288 postgraduates, and 1,466 students studying for doctorates. Saudi Arabia had nine universities and seventy-six university departments or colleges in 1999. Additionally, Saudi Arabia had 186,650 students enrolled at a university and a teaching staff of 10,018—a student-to-teacher ratio of 19:1, but still acceptable.

Women made up almost exactly 30% of the student body at universities, 18% of the faculty, and 27% of new entrants. Saudi Arabia also had six more colleges of education and technical colleges in 1999, and at total of some 138 other teaching centers or colleges. If the number of students in these schools were added to the total for the universities, the total number would be 371,552 students.[95] This is a significant increase over 1995, but it does not seem sufficient to keep up with the growth in Saudi population.

Although the figures for universities alone show a low ratio of women, a total of 120,666 new students enrolled in universities and specialized colleges in 1999, 54% of whom were women. The disparity is partially explained by the fact that some 145,000 Saudi women were enrolled in women-only colleges and 146,000 were enrolled in other educational agencies, versus 3,890 males enrolled in similar all-male institutions. (Only males are enrolled in the technical colleges and industrial colleges in Jubail and Yanbu.)[96]

Progress in the Sixth Development Plan

The government is trying to correct some of these problems. The Sixth Development Plan emphasized redirecting education toward job opportunities by expanding technical and vocational training and limiting college scholarships to those fields that will enhance Saudi manpower.[97] As a result, several Saudi chambers of commerce and industry created major training programs focused on realistic job opportunities. The Ministry of the Interior has set up a manpower council that meets regularly to discuss training needs for the country as a whole. Nevertheless, effort still fell far short of the need and Saudi Arabia continued to expand Islamic education more quickly then taking action to make native Saudis more employable.[98]

The Saudi government reports that technical and vocational school enrollment rose twenty-nine-fold between 1970 and 1996.[99] However, the total registration still amounted to only 28,972 students at technical schools and 9,653 at vocational institutes in 1996. In the same year, there were a total of around 62,534 students if one includes all the students training at Saudi Arabia's six colleges of technology, eight industrial institutes, and numerous vocational centers.[100] The total number of males enrolled at the institutions for technical education and vocational education totaled only 46,058 in 1999, and only 11,666 graduated that year. Less than half of these received training related to non–white collar jobs in the private sector.

The data on women's education also indicate that they are being trained largely for teaching and clerical jobs, severely restricting their access to the labor market.[101] In general, these figures reveal a very limited total output of Saudis relative to both the total labor force and the total number of young men and women entering the labor force each year. Saudi and Western businessmen also indicate that the output of vocational schools was often poorly trained in the skills needed for real-world jobs.

On paper, Saudi Arabia can draw on some 114,700 post-secondary graduates produced during 1995–1999. However, the areas of specialization among these graduates illustrate the severity of some of the problems in the structure of Saudi education. Roughly 8.8% graduated in engineering (10,100); 13.5% in the natural sciences (15,500); 7.1% in medical sciences and health (8,100); 14.7% in commerce, mathematics, and computer science (2,900); 2.9% in agriculture, zoology, and nutritional science (2,900); and 10.9% in teacher training (12,500). Some Saudi educators note, however, that many of these graduates do not have the equivalent of a Western junior college education, and that even at the post-secondary level, far too few teachers insist on the proper performance level or are willing to fail Saudi students. They are particularly concerned with the low quality of teacher training and a tendency to emphasize Islam at the expense of teaching skills in core areas. This is particularly disturbing because the Saudi government attempted to create 86,000 Saudi teacher jobs to reduce unemployment in the 2002 budget.

A total of 42.2 % of 114,700 post-secondary graduates produced from 1995 to 1999 are also graduates of "social sciences and Islamic studies," a category that largely includes students with no meaningful job skills. Given the reality that Saudi Arabia had 659,900 male job entrants in 1995 to 1999—many of whom graduated from heavily Islamic programs—the fact that 48,400 of the 114,700 post-secondary school graduates came from such low-grade programs is not reassuring.

The Impact of September 11

There is nothing wrong with Islamic education, provided that it sets the proper overall standards. The reality, however, is that the quality of Saudi education has been sacrificed for quantity. Long before September 11, however, many Saudi educators felt that the Kingdom set inadequate standards for teacher qualification and performance, and that a focus on Islam led far too much of Saudi education to forego the proper educational standards and depth in other areas. Some also noted that some of the religious materials had an anti-Christian and anti-Semitic character.

Since that time, Saudi Arabia has had good cause to reflect on the costs of supporting Islamic studies while failing to properly educate Saudi youth. Although both the government and many Saudi educators have tended to publicly deny such failures, the attacks on the World Trade Center and the Pentagon have led to a great deal of quiet examination. As a result, many members of the Saudi political and religious elite—including some senior members of the al-Saud and al-Sheikh families—privately admit that the Kingdom made serious mistakes that may take a decade to repair.[102]

Very senior Saudi officials found serious problems when they surveyed the content of Saudi teaching materials and schools following September 11. One of Saudi Arabia's most senior ruling princes stated privately that the government found a great deal of content that attacked Islamic practices in other Muslim countries and was anti-Semitic and anti-Christian. He stated that "five percent of this content was horrible, 10% was suspect, and the other 85% was alright." He also stated that the review also revealed the emphasis on rote learning discussed earlier, the lack of emphasis on problem-solving skills, and a lack of quality in technical and language skills.

Experts in the Ministry of Education were more optimistic about the quality of Saudi education, but also admitted that some of the course content was dated and biased. They noted that the ministry was considering measures to constantly reevaluate the performance of teachers and schools and provide more standardized and competitive forms of examination.

These numbers disguise other problems. Saudi sources indicate that one reason Crown Prince Abdullah abolished a separate management structure for women's education in 2001, following a tragic school fire where a number of young women died, was the discovery of poor physical plant facilities and poor overall management. The rush to create new schools has not always created good, or even competent, ones.

Saudi experts privately indicate that the educational standards in Saudi institutions are much lower than comparable foreign institutions, and only 1,500 Saudi students graduated from foreign universities in 1999 versus 41,450 from local universities.[103] As a result, a "generation gap" is growing between today's graduates and older, foreign-educated Saudis. Far too few current students are trained to enter business or are studying the technical or specialized areas needed by the government and private sector. Some Saudi professors feel that King Saud University is now the only Saudi institution of higher education that is really competitive in global terms. This university has a total enrollment of 7,938, all of whom are males. At the same time, the events of September 11 have made it harder for Saudis to study in the United States and have created a backlash against studying in countries with anti-Saudi and anti-Arab prejudices.

The problems in education also interact with Saudi prejudices against many types of jobs, a lack of a work ethic, and a lack of experience with globally competitive and merit-based hiring and promotion present further problems. As has been noted earlier, much of the native Saudi labor force now works in government and in the service sectors, and much of it does not work at real jobs.

A total of 34% of the entire labor force worked for the government in 2000 and 22% more worked in services; 28% of the labor force worked in industry and oil and 16% in agriculture. Many of theses industrial jobs were in state-related positions that were overstaffed or not really needed, and many of the agricultural jobs were made possible by state subsidies for agriculture. As a result, the distribution of the native Saudi workforce represented a serious lack of productive employment within the private sector. Saudi officials are the first to admit that government and government-related jobs often employ three to four Saudis for every real job but hire a foreigner to do the actual work. Some estimate that as many as half of the Saudis now employed do not perform any real economic function. At the same time, there are social barriers to productive labor. Many Saudis still feel that work in the private sector has less status than work in government, and that government employees have better or more secure jobs. The end result is that many young Saudi males seek a job or non-job in government, rather than risk losing social status or reducing their marriage prospects by seeking something truly productive.[104]

Progress Planned in the Seventh Development Plan

That said, the Saudi government did seek to make major improvements in the quality of Saudi education long before September 11. The government steadily increased funding for education, and was already examining the problem of quality in the government's current teaching staff and in Saudi secondary and higher education. Technocrats and businessmen were both pushing hard for more demanding and practical education programs, and some Saudi firms were pursuing a policy of only hiring on a competitive basis and pursuing merit-based promotion.

The Seventh Development Plan (2000–2004) called for higher educational standards for the new Saudi entrants to the labor market it estimates will leave school during this period. It not only projected that 28.4% would be college or university graduates and that 35.8% would be secondary school graduates, but it projected that only 28.8% would have dropped out of secondary school before graduating. This compares with 31.3% dropouts during the previous five-year period.

The Seventh Development Plan set ambitious goals for improving educational quality, such as:[105]

- Providing educational opportunities to all eligible Saudis, upgrading special education, opening more technical secondary education institutions, and giving more attention to women's technical education and vocational training.

- Improving educational standards by updating educational programs and curricula in line with labor market needs.

- Expanding the private sector's participation in financing educational programs.

- Expanding on-the-job training programs.

- Expanding technical education at every level and providing training in all regions of the Kingdom.

- Improving training in advanced technology.

- Developing academic research and postgraduate studies programs oriented to meet the needs of the private sector.

- Reconsidering the size of employment in the government sectors and weighing the possibility of directing surplus manpower in the government sector toward work in the private sector.

- Increasing the absorptive capacity of universities, technical schools, and vocational training institutions in the specializations required by the national economy, as well as directing admission policies in the higher-education institutions to meet the needs of the labor market.

- Ensuring the participation of the private sector in the continuous review of curricula and the proposal of new academic trends that are commensurate with the actual needs of the labor market.

- Developing a manpower information system and establishing a unified information network for all labor offices in the Kingdom that would ensure regular provision of labor market–related information to manpower, employers, students, and education and training institutions for utilization in the selection of jobs and occupations.

- Improving the productivity of the national labor force, upgrading skills, and preparing it to keep up with technical developments.

- Increasing job opportunities for Saudi women and enhancing their share in the labor market in conformation with Islamic Shari'a.

- Developing a national plan for the use of information technology as well as the use of information sources, developing databases for use by the public and private sectors, and establishing a national integration information system with regional sub-networks.

There are still serious problems, however, in both the goals set forth in the Seventh Development Plan and in the numbers it uses. The Ministry of Planning uses somewhat different statistics in its plan based on its report on achievements, but states that the total number of students entering the general education system will increase from 4.40 million in 1419–1420 AH to 4.52 million in 1424–1425 AH. This is only a 2.7% increase over five years and does not make sense in terms of population growth or school expansion plans. The total number of annual general-education graduates should increase from 3.16 million to 4.53 million over the same five-year period. This is an increase of 43%, which tracks much better with population growth and the Kingdom's needs.

The number of students in higher education is also supposed to increase from 263,000 to 480,000, an 83% increase. This not only would do much to keep up with population growth, but would help correct for much of the existing shortfall. Interestingly enough, the total annual number of males graduating from higher education will increase from 69,000 to 127,000, while females will increase from 85,000 to 146,000. This again illustrates a massive shift in Saudi society, where more females continue to graduate from higher education than males, and where the number of highly educated females potentially entering the job market rises by 72% over five years. This will make it even more critical that the Saudi economy make full competitive use of female labor.

The total number of students in the technical education system will only increase from 33,000 to 55,000, and those in vocational training from 12,000 to 17,000. These are reasonable percentage increases, but the absolute numbers do not come close to providing an adequate training base for diversification of the economy and projected growth of the private sector.

The statistics shown in other parts of the Seventh Development Plan are summarized in Table 5.3, and it is all too clear why the Kingdom faces major challenges in the short term in expanding both the quality and quantify of its education that will continue well beyond 2030. Saudi plans for higher education alone during 2000–2004 require a 1.4% average annual rise in students, a 13.6% rise in new entrants, a 16.8% rise in graduates, and a 19.5% rise in Saudi staff (with a 6.5% annual cut in foreign staff).[106]

Looking Toward the Future

Saudi Arabia has set the right general priorities in education, but its goals and means are not yet adequate to solving the problem. A serious mismatch will remain between educational output, quality and the expansion of the job market, even if the Kingdom meets all its goals. Saudi educators are also among the first to admit that the Kingdom has yet to demonstrate that it will purge and update its curriculum, raise standards for teachers to the

Table 5.3
Male and Female Graduates in Saudi Education During the Seventh Development Plan (in Thousands)

Stage	1999	2000	2001	2002	2003	2004
Graduates (Male)						
Elementary	180	190	200	211	222	235
Intermediate	128	130	136	138	142	146
Secondary	80	86	92	97	102	107
Teacher's Colleges (4 years)	3.2	2.5	2.6	2.8	2.9	3.1
Graduates (Female)						
Elementary	166	168	173	178	182	188
Intermediate	138	143	146	149	154	163
Secondary	95	107	118	130	144	159
Teacher's Colleges (2 years)	6.8	7.1	7.4	7.7	8.0	8.2

Source: Kingdom of Saudi Arabia, Ministry of Planning, *Seventh Development Plan* (Riyadh: Ministry of Planning, 2000), p. 259.

proper level and evaluate their performance, properly evaluate school performance, and set realistic national competitive standards for educational qualifications. Above all, it has not shown that it will abolish reliance on rote learning and place the proper emphasis on creative learning and problem solving.

As is discussed in the following chapters, it is also far from clear that the Kingdom is giving realistic attention to the need to create "job pull" in the private sector, as distinguished from "education push." Educators sometimes live in a fantasy world where education alone is felt to create job opportunities, and educators feel they can somehow predict the needs of the job market without systematic surveys and constant efforts to tailor and update the curriculum.

The reality has been very different. Education per se does not increase jobs, and government officials and academics have demonstrated on a global basis that they are not competent to predict the educational needs of business. Coupled with problems with work ethic, job status, and hiring women, it is far from clear that the Saudi private sector will really get the "person power" it needs, or that young Saudis will really get the opportunities they deserve. Things should get slightly better, but it is obvious that any real solution to these aspects of the Kingdom's internal stability problems will have to come after the Seventh Development Plan and will require a radical new degree of self-honesty and decisive action to deal with critical problems in the sectors most critical to the Kingdom's stability and future.

SAUDI ENTITLEMENTS, INFRASTRUCTURE, AND DIVERSIFICATION PROBLEMS

Population pressure puts increasing strain on the Saudi national budget. It makes its subsidy and entitlement programs increasingly less affordable and also puts a burden on Saudi Arabia's existing infrastructure while creating a growing demand for rapid and continuing expansion. Saudi government sources do not always report on the relevant trends and various Saudi sources report in ways that make it very difficult to track trends and estimate total costs; nevertheless, the scale and importance of the problem is clear.

Unlike most Middle Eastern countries, Saudi Arabia provides a wide range of detailed information about its budget. This reporting is not always consistent or transparent, particularly in the national security sector, and it is sometimes impossible to separate government operating expenses, spending on investment and economic development, and spending on entitlements. Chart 5.21, however, provides what seems to be a relatively accurate picture of how the total budget is currently divided.

Several aspects of the data in Chart 5.21 are important. There are no rules as to how given nations divide out their budgets. It is clear, however, that Saudi Arabia gives human services, welfare, and entitlements a high priority. Its direct spending on development and infrastructure is relatively low, but the public administration sector includes substantial investment expenditures, as well as spending on government operations and human services.

The data in Chart 5.21 only cover two years of spending and reflect a period of relatively high oil revenues. The year 2000 had particularly high revenues and produced a significant increase in human services, welfare, and entitlements. Chart 5.22, however, shows contrary economic trends; it uses different reporting categories to show the cuts in both investment and entitlement expenditures that have to be made in a period of low oil revenues. A review of a wide range of Saudi budget data shows that the budget is comparatively inelastic in the short term: Cuts in revenue force cuts in outlays, even in human services and entitlements. At the same time, the Saudi budget is less rigid in areas like social security, subsidies, and health, for example, than the U.S. budget.

Somewhat similar patterns emerge in social security and social insurance expenditures, although these expenditures have cumulatively increased over time. All social security assistance averaged about 1.3 to 1.5 billion riyals during the late 1980s to early 1990s. It rose to 2.5 to 3.0 billion in the late 1990s due to an increase in regular versus relief assistance in the mid-1990s.[107] The same is true of medical services and facilities, which did not grow in proportion to the population during the 1990s—although a very young population normally does not require high levels of medical services

Chart 5.21

Pressures on the Saudi Budget—Part One: How the Budget was Spent, 1999–2000 (in Billions of Riyals)

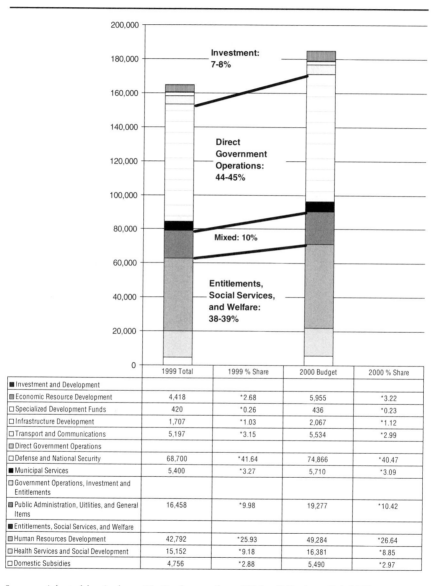

	1999 Total	1999 % Share	2000 Budget	2000 % Share
■ Investment and Development				
▣ Economic Resource Development	4,418	*2.68	5,955	*3.22
☐ Specialized Development Funds	420	*0.26	436	*0.23
☐ Infrastructure Development	1,707	*1.03	2,067	*1.12
☐ Transport and Communications	5,197	*3.15	5,534	*2.99
▣ Direct Government Operations				
☐ Defense and National Security	68,700	*41.64	74,866	*40.47
■ Municipal Services	5,400	*3.27	5,710	*3.09
☐ Government Operations, Investment and Entitlements				
▣ Public Administration, Uitlities, and General Items	16,458	*9.98	19,277	*10.42
■ Entitlements, Social Services, and Welfare				
▣ Human Resources Development	42,792	*25.93	49,284	*26.64
☐ Health Services and Social Development	15,152	*9.18	16,381	*8.85
☐ Domestic Subsidies	4,756	*2.88	5,490	*2.97

Sources: Adapted by Anthony H. Cordesman from *US-Saudi Business Brief* (Winter 1998), p. 1; and Reuters, December 28, 1998, 1728.

Chart 5.22

Pressures on the Saudi Budget—Part Two: The Downtrend Following the Crash in Oil Prices in Late 1997 (in Billions of Riyals)

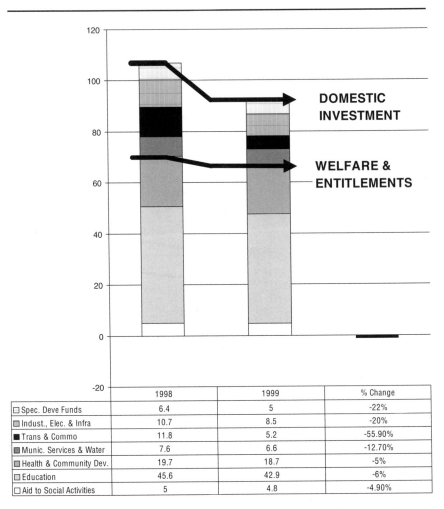

	1998	1999	% Change
☐ Spec. Deve Funds	6.4	5	-22%
▥ Indust., Elec. & Infra	10.7	8.5	-20%
■ Trans & Commo	11.8	5.2	-55.90%
▨ Munic. Services & Water	7.6	6.6	-12.70%
▨ Health & Community Dev.	19.7	18.7	-5%
☐ Education	45.6	42.9	-6%
☐ Aid to Social Activities	5	4.8	-4.90%

Sources: Adapted by Anthony H. Cordesman from *US-Saudi Business Brief* (Winter 1998), p. 1, and Reuters, December 28, 1998, 1728.

and such growth may not have been necessary.[108] As a result, there is only a rough correlation between some aspects of budget expenditures and population growth.

In broad terms, the Saudi government must increase its "Human Resource Development" spending as fast as young Saudis require such services. Young people can only compete for skilled jobs if such expenditures keep pace with the need for better education, medical services, and other important areas. Because Saudi Arabia must also continue to provide better services for its existing population, this probably means an average real increase in spending on services of at least 5% to 7% will be needed for the next ten to fifteen years. This is not an inconsiderable pressure on the Saudi budget, since such expenditures already consume more than 25% of the total. Such expenditures will also have to rise at levels that will be far more costly than any savings the Kingdom can make in subsidies and pure welfare.[109]

Similar patterns are likely to affect medical services, which will have to be expanded at a significantly faster rate by the late 2000s as today's youth begins to age and require significant medical care. The Seventh Development Plan attempts to address some of these issues by improving preventive health services and enhancing the role of the private sector. It also calls for substantial increases in many medical facilities, such as building 61 new hospitals and rehabilitation centers, 80 emergency centers, and 500 primary health centers, as well as adding 4,530 new hospital beds and opening 60 recently built emergency centers.[110] Other Saudi data, however, indicates that such developments will at best cope with a backlog in improvements that were underfunded in the 1990s.

Infrastructure, transportation, water, sewers, and power are other costly areas where the Kingdom must spend in proportion to its increasing population. This spending must take into account the fact that much of the infrastructure bought before 1986 is now undersized or requires refurbishment. Further compounding the infrastructure problem is the Kingdom's recent underspending in some areas over the last decade. As a result, the Kingdom will face steadily growing pressures on its budget over the next decade unless it changes its revenues to include significantly higher levels of taxation or makes major cuts in defense spending.

THE CHALLENGE OF SUBSIDIES

Entitlements are only part of the problem. The oil wealth that Saudi Arabia obtained in 1974 led it to establish many subsidies that still affect its budget.[111] Chart 5.23 shows the fluctuation over time in the cost of direct subsidies. A slightly more recent assessment puts the peak cost of subsidies at 12.1 billion in 1984, and then estimates that subsidies declined to 5.3 riyals in 2000.[112] The Saudi government reports that cuts have taken place in social security, foodstuffs, and electricity, and that farm subsidies have been limited.

These figures, however, sharply understate the actual level of subsidies in many areas; pricing of gas and electricity well below the cost of investment and maintenance; under pricing of domestic petroleum products; and indirect subsidies like agricultural loans and pricing water at roughly 5%

Chart 5.23

Pressures on the Saudi Budget—Part Three: The Subsidy Problem Does Not Increase with Population But Is Still Significant (in Millions of Riyals)

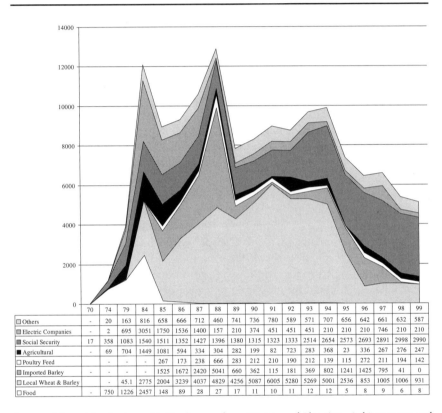

	70	74	79	84	85	86	87	88	89	90	91	92	93	94	95	96	97	98	99
☐ Others	-	20	163	816	658	666	712	460	741	736	780	589	571	707	656	642	661	632	587
☷ Electric Companies	-	2	695	3051	1750	1536	1400	157	210	374	451	451	451	210	210	210	746	210	210
■ Social Security	17	358	1083	1540	1511	1352	1427	1396	1380	1315	1323	1333	2514	2654	2573	2693	2891	2998	2990
■ Agricultural	-	69	704	1449	1081	594	334	304	282	199	82	723	283	368	23	336	267	276	247
☐ Poultry Feed	-	-	-	-	267	173	238	666	283	212	210	190	212	139	115	272	211	194	142
☷ Imported Barley	-	-	-	-	1525	1672	2420	5041	660	362	115	181	369	802	1241	1425	795	41	0
☐ Local Wheat & Barley		-	45.1	2775	2004	3239	4037	4829	4256	5087	6005	5280	5269	5001	2536	853	1005	1006	931
☐ Food	-	750	1226	2457	148	89	28	27	17	11	10	11	12	12	5	8	9	6	8

Source: Adapted by Anthony H. Cordesman from Ministry of Planning, *Achievements and Development Plans, 1390–1420 (1970–2000)* (Riyadh: Ministry of Planning, 2001), Table 26.

of its cost.[113] They also disguise the fact that the government limited some costs by not paying its bills until a sharp rise in oil revenues in 2000 allowed it to reduce some of its arrears by paying contractors and agricultural debts through a budget supplemental. Moreover, previously suspended subsidies were reintroduced when oil revenues once again rose. For example, the government reintroduced the barley subsidies in mid-2000 that it had suspended in 1998, at a cost of around 4 billion riyals ($1.1 billion) a year.[114]

The Kingdom has long subsidized low-cost utilities, low-cost fuel, telecommunications, and airfares. It has also provided highly subsidized or free housing, education, and medical services. It has created direct and indirect subsidies for many forms of Saudi businesses through offsets, tariffs, and investment and partnership arrangements. The subsidies for electricity, fuel, and petroleum products alone cost the government an estimated $2.7 billion in 1997 in world market prices. Diesel fuel, for example, sold for 8.59 cents per gallon in Saudi Arabia, although it costs 12 cents per gallon to produce.[115]

The Saudi government has taken some steps to reduce the burden of such expenses. It cut loans by government development agencies to agricultural, industrial, and real estate projects by one third in 1994. Direct subsidies for electricity, which rose from 2 million Saudi riyals in 1974 to 3.1 billion in 1984, have averaged around 210 million since 1994—although these figures do not reflect massive indirect subsidies by underpricing electricity.[116] The Kingdom raised fuel prices two to four times in January 1995; the price of premium gasoline was increased by 82%, kerosene went up by 150%, diesel fuel went up by 250%, and gas oil went up 353%. The price of fuel oil and natural gas, however, remained at a small fraction of the normal world market price.[117] In January 1995, the Saudi government doubled gasoline prices to 50 cents per gallon. This increase generated up to $2 billion in revenues a year.[118] In an attempt to generate more revenue, the Saudi government increased the price of natural gas by 50%.

Unfortunately, the rise in oil revenues in 1995 and 1996 brought a temporary halt to these measures. Like many governments, the Saudis failed to persist the moment the problem eased, and actually increased some subsidies for education and health. It ignored advice from the IMF and United States, and reverted to its boom and bust budgeting policies.[119]

It took the oil crash of 1997 to force the Saudi government to consider further measures, such as raising service fees, cutting other subsidies, and privatizing some state sector firms, such as SABIC. In late 1998, the cabinet approved the unification of four regional power companies and six smaller subsidiaries into the Saudi Electricity Company (SEC).[120] This is expected to begin a larger process that will restructure and privatize basic industries.[121] The government also capped some government expenditures and began reducing others. It introduced a massive rise in the visa fees for foreign labor and attempted to enforce foreign labor restrictions more seriously.[122] Saudi Arabia is also attempting to increase revenues by reducing state subsidies on gasoline, diesel fuel, water, electricity, and air travel.

The Saudi government also discussed other cost-cutting measures, including the institution of a three-tiered system for public utility billing. This system offered the electricity and water-generation sectors the potential ability to break even by charging high-end users substantially higher rates. As will be discussed shortly, such a reform is critical not only because of its revenue impact, but because of the challenges the Kingdom faces in expanding and modernizing its infrastructure.[123]

In practice, however, oil export revenues rose sharply in 2000, before the Kingdom took decisive action to reform prices and subsidies. As of April 2002, water was left at about 5% of market cost to most consumers, electricity was left sharply underpriced, a rise in gasoline prices was rolled back, and natural gas continued to be sold at about 75 cents per million BTUs—about half the $1.25 to $1.40 cost in other Southern Gulf countries.

PRESSURE ON INFRASTRUCTURE

The same demographic and economic factors affect infrastructure. While no precise figures are available, it is clear that since 1990, Saudi Arabia has also underinvested in infrastructure. Indeed, it has built up a substantial investment backlog in meeting its future needs for water, electricity, roads, housing, medical facilities, education, and every other aspect of the economic and social setup of the Kingdom.

Electricity as a Case in Point

Saudi figures indicate that electricity demand increased by 35% in the period from 1990 to 1995. Annual per capita consumption increased by roughly 1% a year, and the number of customers increased from 2,815,500 in 1994 to 3,432,000 in 1999. The peak load increased from 17,373 megawatts to 21,927 megawatts during the same period. Total consumption multiplied at an annual rate of 4.2% during 1994-1998, while the peak load grew by an annual average of 2.7%.[124]

Population and economic growth will increase future demand at least as sharply. The World Energy Council forecasts an electricity demand increase from 22 gigawatts in 2000 to 58 gigawatts by 2020. The Seventh Development Plan estimated that total demand for electric power would grow at an average rate of 5.2% through 2004, and 4.5% per year through 2020. It also estimated that 793,000 new customers would be created between 2000 and 2004, and that the peak load would increase from 22 gigawatts in 1999 to 28 gigawatts in 2004. It projected that the Kingdom would have to meet the needs of well over 7 million new households by 2020.[125]

Charts 5.24 and 5.25 show some of its implications for Saudi Arabia. Meeting the rise in demand will be very expensive. According to some Saudi estimates, the economy must fund an increase in the total average need for electric power to over 60,000 megawatts in 2023. Saudi Arabia also must provide a substantial additional capacity to meet the needs of peak periods, largely for air conditioning. This means an estimated need for up to 69,500 megawatts of total capacity. Put differently, this is an average increase of 1,500 to 2,000 megawatts, or at least one massive new generation facility, per year. Many studies also indicate that Saudi Arabia will need

Chart 5.24
The Infrastructure Challenge During the Coming Decades: Electric Power as a Case
Example

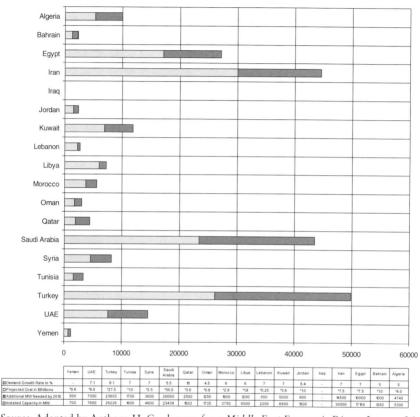

	Yemen	UAE	Turkey	Tunisia	Syria	Saudi Arabia	Qatar	Oman	Morocco	Libya	Lebanon	Kuwait	Jordan	Iraq	Iran	Egypt	Bahrain	Algeria
□ Demand Growth Rate in %	-	7.1	8.1	7	7	5.5	10	4.5	6	6	7	7	6.4	-	7	7	5	5
□ Projected Cost in $Billions	*0.6	*8.0	*27.5	*10	*2.5	*30.0	*3.0	*0.8	*2.9	*18	*0.25	*3.6	*10	-	*7.5	*7.5	*10	*4.0
■ Additional MW Needed by 2010	500	7000	23603	1700	3600	20000	2500	1250	1900	1200	500	5000	900	-	14500	10000	1000	4740
□ Installed Capacity in MW	700	7600	26226	1600	4600	23438	1933	1735	3750	6000	2200	6900	1500	-	30000	17150	1260	5300

Source: Adapted by Anthony H. Cordesman from *Middle East Economic Digest*, January 26, 2001, p. 24.

a natural gas supply grid to meet the needs of its additional power stations and consumer demand for thermal energy.[126]

Saudi figures indicate that meeting this need for power could require an investment of $115 billion by 2020, with $63.2 billion for generation, $33.6 billion for new transmission capacity, and $20 billion for upgrading the existing transmission system. The Saudi Ministry of Industry and Electricity has stated that an investment of $117 billion is required over the next twenty-four years, averaging $4.9 billion a year. According to some estimates 8% to 10 % of Saudi investments will have to be diverted to develop Saudi power generation capacity.[127]

Chart 5.25
Saudi Arabia's Massive Needs for Infrastructure Investment: Electric Power as a Test Case ·

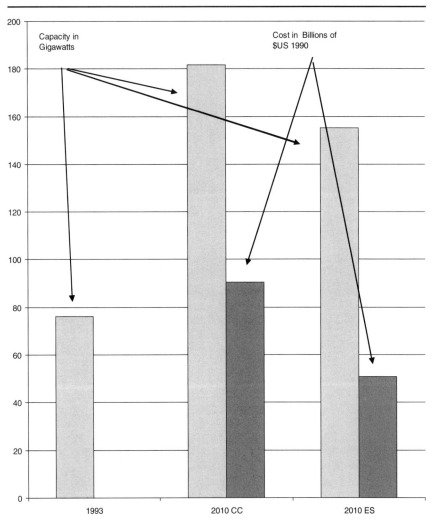

CC = capacity constrained, or maximum production; ES = energy savings, or reduced energy use.

Source: Adapted by Anthony H. Cordesman from IEA, *World Energy Outlook, 1996,* pp. 189–191.

The government will face problems in self-financing such an effort, even though it is only one of the infrastructure problems the Kingdom faces. Others—like water—are easily as important.

This has led the government to employ financing mechanisms that are new to Saudi Arabia's electric power sector. For example, the PP9 power station in Riyadh is being funded with extra revenues generated by a special tariff imposed on heavy users since January 1995. Expansion of another power plant, Ghazlan, is being financed by an internationally syndicated commercial loan. Greater private-sector involvement is planned for a 1,750-megawatt Shuaiba power station project. In addition, the Royal Commission for Jubail and Yanbu is launching a joint venture company to develop power and water utilities in Saudi Arabia's flagship industrial zones.[128] An estimate of the potential cost of this effort is shown in Chart 5.24.

A Swiss company, Asea Brown Boveri (ABB), has finalized an $835 million contract to build the 1,750-megawatt steam-powered Shuaiba power station. The contract involves the supply and installation of three 370-megawatt oil-fired generating units, with an option to build two more. The other two will become operational eight and fourteen months after construction.[129] The power station is expected to increase the western region's capacity by 25%, and eventually to 50%.[130] A U.S. firm, CMS Energy Corporation, is also reported to be the preferred bidder on a 320-megawatt privately owned power plant planned for Jubail.[131]

The Saudi government faces a dilemma: it is impossible to properly privatize a power, water, or gas industry that sells its output below cost. It is also impossible to convince foreign firms to invest, without guarantees that power will either be sold at market prices or that the government can fund the resulting deficit. The government, therefore, not only faces the consequences of excessive population growth, but also of a growth in demand based on years of subsidies and inefficient and wasteful use of power. It also faces the legacy of having treated the nation's infrastructure as welfare rather than as part of its economy, and of years of ignoring the need to create a strong private sector that the nation can rely on.

The Broader Infrastructure Problem

Electricity is only one of the more dramatic aspects of the Saudi infrastructure problem. Saudi Arabia must finance similar investments in areas such as its ports, roads, oil production and distribution, housing, education, and its physical plant to meet its social needs, and do so at a time when much of its earlier investment in infrastructure no longer meets current needs or requires major renovation and modernization One estimate indicates that Saudi Arabia will need 4.5 million additional housing units at a cost of $261 billion, plus 22,500 new primary schools, 6,000 institutes of higher education, 5,400 clinics, and 360 hospitals.[132]

The effort to meet these goals and needs will again interact with the problems inherent in a declining real per capita income. Unless Saudi Arabia reduces both its population growth and dependence on foreign labor, current projections indicate that petroleum wealth per capita could drop by another 10% to 20% by the year 2010. Even though Saudi Arabia will probably receive much higher total oil revenues in the future, a combination of increased population and increased development and production costs will outstrip that growth.

The Seventh Development Plan stresses

achieving continuous expansion of infrastructure facilities in a manner than conforms with growing demand for them arising from the steady population growth, and contributes towards preparing a conducive environment for the growth of all sectors of the national economy. The plan also gives attention to the maintenance of the existing infrastructure to upgrade the operational efficiency of the productive assets in addition to boosting the role of both preventive and normal maintenance in elongating the operational life of these assets.[133]

With regard to infrastructure, the plan sets the following main objectives:

• Preserve and maintain transport facilities.
• Achieve equilibrium between an adequate expansion of the domestic and international transportation network and expected demand and trends in traffic flow, taking into account safety aspects as well as the reduction of adverse impacts on the environment.
• Asphalt 1,600 kilometers of main municipal roads and 11,000 kilometers of secondary municipal and rural roads.
• Provide a modern telecommunications infrastructure within an integrated digital network for fixed and mobile services as a basis for the provision of all domestic and international services.
• Exert ongoing efforts to improve the productivity as well as the economic and financial performance of the telecommunication and postal services.
• Encourage private-sector investments in telecommunications services and the establishment and operation of networks.
• Improve the operational efficiency of municipal facilities, infrastructure, and services and ensure optimal utilization.
• Provide and develop residential lands in suitable locations. Provide about 110 million square meters of residential land to meet the demand for housing at a rate of 22 million square meters a year.
• Provide 57,000 loans for construction of 70,000 housing units at a total cost of 15.7 billion riyals.

- Finalize feasibility studies of new projects and expansion of the railroads.
- Link more cities and villages to the main road network.
- Increase telephone service coverage to reach at least twenty-two to twenty-five lines per hundred people. Reduce waiting lists and eliminate disparities in the rate of coverage and service between urban and rural areas.

In broad terms, however, the Seventh Development Plan provides no real details as to how it will achieve its objectives, no real cost estimates, and no estimates of performance relative to need. It often shifts much of the burden to the private sector without indicating whether market forces create the necessary incentives or what level of economic reform is necessary to both incentivize and allow the private sector to act. In general, it does a far better job of describing how well the Kingdom met the goals of the Sixth Development Plan than describing what the Kingdom needs to accomplish during 2000–2004, and it provides no long-term view for the future. As is the case with most other aspects of the plan, goals and actions for 2000–2004 are never put in the context of long-term needs and costs and overall efficiency in meeting both short- and mid-term goals.

The plan's goals are good ones, but the proposed scale of effort seems likely to lag behind the growth of the population and demand in many areas. There is often a tacit emphasis on privatization to provide expanded services without addressing the practical details or noting how this would affect the cost of now-subsidized services. There is no analysis of the level of investment required or whether Saudi revenues and budgets can realistically provide the necessary money.

THE INTERACTION BETWEEN DEMOGRAPHICS, WATER, AND AGRICULTURE

For the Saudis, water is both an economic problem that inevitably grows with population and a major strategic vulnerability. Saudi Arabia's annual rainfall is less than 100 millimeters in most areas. It has only about 2.33 million cubic kilometers of internal renewable water resources. These water resources provide only minimal amounts of water even for Saudi Arabia's current population. They total about 156 cubic meters per person—less than one-seventh the total for a citizen of the United States.

About 82% of Saudi Arabia's total present water use consists of non-renewable, or "fossil," water obtained from deep wells; 14% is surface and shallow ground water; 4% is obtained from desalination; and less than 1% is reclaimed or treated water.[134] At least some Saudi aquifers are already increasing in saline content. Saudi Arabia steadily increasing its number of dams and has some twenty-two ongoing dam projects (plus plans to build sixty-two more), but these have limited value in a country with no major rivers and limited rainfall. Saudi Arabia also produces some 1.5 million cubic meters of wastewater a day, but only 340,000 cubic meters is used for agricultural purposes—around 23%.[135]

The Seventh Development Plan, however, projects a continuing massive increase in Saudi Arabia's water needs:[136]

- The total demand for water is projected to increase from 21.1 billion cubic meters in 2000 to 22.5 in 2004 and 27.8 in 2020. Water demand is estimated to increase by an annual average of 1.3% during 2000–2004 and 1.4% during 2000–2020.

- Domestic demand for water is projected to increase from 1.8 billion cubic meters in 2000 to 2.0 in 2004 and 3.10 in 2020. Water demand is estimated to increase by an annual average of 2.4% during 2000–2004 and 2.8% during 2000–2020.

- Industrial demand for water is projected to increase from 0.47 billion cubic meters in 2000 to 0.60 in 2004 and 1.66 in 2020. Water demand is estimated to increase by an annual average of 5.0% during 2000–2004 and 6.5% during 2000–2020.

- Agricultural demand for water is projected to increase from 18.8 billion cubic meters in 2000 to 19.9 in 2004 and 23.0 in 2020. Water demand is estimated to increase by an annual average of 1.1% during 2000–2004 and 1.0% during 2000–2020.

Saudi Arabia's rapid increase in population is causing its natural water resources to drop sharply. The World Resources Institute and the World Bank estimate that Saudi natural per capita water resources dropped from 537 cubic meters in 1960 to 156 cubic meters in 1990 and project that they will drop to 49 cubic meters in 2025. The government has raised water prices in recent years, but Saudi Arabia still wastes nearly 90% of its natural water on agriculture, versus 6% for domestic needs and 2% for industry, due to government subsidies.[137] Agriculture used a total of 18.3 billion cubic meters of water in 1999, with about 8 billion cubic meters coming from renewable and surface water sources and 0.1 billion cubic meters coming from sewage water. The remaining 88% of total consumption came from nonrenewable groundwater sources.[138]

Saudi Arabia must depend on an extensive system of desalinization plants for its drinking water. The production of such desalinated water increased from only 4.4 million gallons per day in 1970 to 491.6 million gallons per day in 2000. Saudi production accounted for 30.2% of all world production from such plants in 2000, and the Kingdom's growing dependence on the plants has made them potentially lucrative military targets whose importance will increase with time.[139]

A separate agency called the Saline Water Conversion Corporation (SWCC) operated some twenty-seven plants in 2000 that produced 827 million cubic meters a year. There were four major plants along the eastern coast at Jubail and Al-Khobar that produced a total of 441.8 million cubic meters in 2000, and twenty-three plants along the western coast that produced 385.4 million cubic meters. (The Red Sea plants include two facilities to service Jubail and Madinah; plus facilities to serve at Jeddah, Makkah, Tair and the Assir; as well as other smaller facilities for Wajh, Duba, Khafji, Umluj, Firsan, Hagl, Rabigh, and Bark.)

The growth of the Saudi population, economy, and agriculture, has led to the almost-constant construction of new plants and pipelines; output increased by over 29 billion cubic meters between 1998 and 1999. There were three major projects under construction in 2000.[140] Saudi near-term plans call for a total of thirty plants, with twenty-four on the Red Sea Coast and six on the Gulf Coast. They will produce 2.9 million cubic meters of water a day and 3,400 megawatts of electricity.

The pipeline network needed to distribute such water will grow to well over 4,000 kilometers, with 29 pumping stations, 10 blending stations, and 164 storage tanks with a capacity of over 9 million cubic meters.[141] Some key pipelines—such as Jubail to Riyadh—are over 400 kilometers long and are already beginning to show their age.[142] The partial failure of one pipeline caused serious water problems in Riyadh in 2001, and similar problems could occur in Jeddah. Sewer construction has also lagged behind in some areas, which presents an additional problem. The SWCC also recognizes that the majority of existing water facilities will reach an age at which capacity begins to drop by 2050.

At the same time, some 75% of the water in the central and eastern regions still comes from nonrenewable underground lakes. These reserves will be exhausted within eighty years at present rates of water usage—if not substantially sooner. The Kingdom is very reluctant to talk about increasing problems with the salinisation of its aquifers.[143] This depletion of natural water will eventually confront Saudi Arabia with far more serious problems than it faces today.[144]

The Kingdom's problems have been made much worse by creating a level of demand for water that in no way reflects its cost. Saudi Arabia has long priced water as if were virtually free. In 1998, it officially sold for about 0.3 riyals ($0.08) per thirty-five cubic feet. This was less than 50% of the price of recovering all production, distribution, and maintenance costs; many homes and businesses were never billed at all. In 2001, water rates still ranged from 0.1 riyal per square meter ($0.26) to 6.0 riyals per square meter ($0.26) where water consumption exceeded 300 square meters a month—although the higher rate was rarely charged and most industries paid different rates. As a result, water use is extraordinarily high for a nation with Saudi Arabia's overall level of economic development. Many experts feel it averages about ninety gallons per person per day—about twice the international average.

Water and the Goals of the Seventh Development Plan

The Seventh Development Plan places particular emphasis on the water sector, but does not address key issues like allocation and cost. It sets the following objectives:

- Continue to supply potable water in sufficient quantities and good quality.
- Make water a basic factor and significant criterion in assessing the economic efficiency of public and private projects.
- Preserve water resources and rationalize water consumption.
- Enhance the private sector's contribution in the management, operation, and maintenance of water facilities.

The plan calls for the constructing 2,500 kilometers of new water networks, replacing 2,000 kilometers, and implementing 130,000 domestic water connections. It also calls for the construction of sixty-two large, medium, and small dams; completing construction of twenty-two dams; and renovating twenty-five dams. It would establish twelve new desalination plants with a total design capacity of 2.1 million meters of water and 2,502 megawatts of electricity. The plan gives a new priority to the use of wastewater and would construct 2,800 kilometers of wastewater networks, implementing 170,000 domestic wastewater connections and building treatment plants with a capacity of 450,000 cubic meters a day. Special attention is given to Riyadh, which has limited surplus capacity and has had water problems. A new transmission system would be created to provide 360,000 cubic meters of water a day from Al Hani.

Some estimates indicate that the total capital cost of meeting 50% of individual demand for water (300 liters per day, per person) through desalination will total 46.5 billion riyals ($12.4 billion) through 2020. The average expenditure will be around 2.3 billion riyals a year, or $620 million.[145] These estimates seem low. The SWCC estimates the total cost of meeting the Kingdom's growing demand for desalinated water alone at $54 billion by 2020.

A Saudi briefing issued in April 2002—based on Ministry of Agricultural and Water figures—indicated that Saudi water consumption would rise from 7 million cubic meters per day in 2002 to 11.3 million in 2022. This was based on estimated population growth from 23.4 million in 2002 to 38 to 48 million in 2022, with a nominal estimate of 43.0 million. The cost was estimated to total 180 billion riyals from 2002 to 2022, including funds for the construction of new desalination plants and rehabilitating old ones, costs for operations, and maintenance fees. This effort, however, would only be part of the story. Preserving natural (brackish) water supplies and wellhead supplies will cost another 70 billion riyals, increasing distribution will cost 40 billion riyals, and providing modern sewage and wastewater recovery capability with cost 130 billion riyals. The total price of future water related projects will be 400 billion riyals.[146]

The Impact of Agriculture

Desalination is only part of the water problem—there is a clear interaction between the misallocation of water and a poorly managed Saudi agricultural policy. A great deal of Saudi Arabia's total water supply still goes to subsidized agriculture because Saudi concerns over the Kingdom's growing dependence on Western food led to a policy of self-sufficiency in the 1970s that it has pursued ever since.[147] Agriculture uses about 18,000 million cubic meters of water a year, but renewable underground water can only meet about 40% of Saudi needs.[148]

This policy led Saudi Arabia to pay massive subsidies for advanced modern farms at a time when most Bedouin and rural small farmers were finding other forms of work. Between 1970 and 1997, subsidies to agriculture made up about 55% of total government subsidies.[149] Although the total percentage of the workforce devoted to agriculture dropped by over 60% from 1970 to 1995, the amount of cultivated land rose from only 0.5 million hectares to 1.6 million, the milling capacity of Saudi flour mills rose to 1.35 million tons, and Saudi Arabia invested in enough grain silos to store 2.38 million tons.[150] Saudi estimates indicate that between the years 1985 and 1990, agricultural production grew by an average of 13.4% a year.

Although Saudi Arabia claimed it had become self-sufficient in wheat as early as 1984, this did not stop the expansion of production. Saudi grain production rose from 258,000 tons in 1980 to a peak of 5.3 million tons in 1993—and the cost of direct agricultural subsidies rose to more than $2 billion a year.[151] This increase took place even when the government cut its subsidy in half in 1984; it was so high that farmers invested in increased productivity and raised their yields from 2.12 tons a hectare in 1980 to 4.7 tons in 1988.[152]

Government aid also encouraged the excessive use of water by providing virtually free deep wells and low-cost diesel fuel for pumps. These subsidies supposedly were reduced in 1995, but costs remained so far below free market prices that farmers had little reason to be efficient. Total water use increased from 643 billion cubic feet in 1994 to 653 billion cubic feet a year in 1996. This produced so much wheat that Saudi Arabia was exporting 600,000 tons by 1988 which peaked at 2.4 million tons in 1992. With every ton exported the Saudi government lost $300.[153]

The government reacted by sharply restricting its wheat subsidy and setting limits on what it would purchase from each farmer. As a result, wheat cultivation dropped from 907,000 hectares in 1992 to a low of 268,000 in 1996, and output decreased from a peak of 4.07 million tons to 1.2 million. This, however, brought the total below the 1.8 million limit that Saudi Arabia had set for self-sufficiency. It also shifted production to crops that were still subsidized, like barley and alfalfa. The government left the price of barley at 267 riyals per ton, and production rose from 73,000 hectares during 1991 to 317,000 hectares in 1994.

This shift increased water demand—because barley used more water than wheat—and forced the government to make the same kind of cutbacks in barley purchasing in 1995 that it had previously made for wheat. By 1997, both wheat and barley production was rising again, and farmers were also increasing output for animal forage—which used more water per hectare than either wheat or barley.[154]

The government did cut subsidies in 1998 due to the "oil crash," but restored them in 2000 after a major rise in oil revenues. Ironically, the low price of water and other agricultural subsidies led some farmers back into wheat. While the number of wheat farmers shrank from a peak of around 32,300 in 1994 to 14,200 in 1998, deliveries to the Saudi Grain Silos and Flour Mills Organization rose back to 1.7 million tons in 1998.[155]

Moreover, the Sixth Development Plan called for still further increases in agricultural output during 1996–2000. The output of the agriculture sector was supposed to increase at an average rate of 3.1% per year, and its value from 31.9 billion riyals to 39.5 billion. This represented a cumulative increase of 24%.[156] This somewhat-quixotic quest continues in the Seventh Development Plan, with the goal of increasing agricultural output by 3%.[157] The Saudi Agricultural Bank alone paid some 6.6 billion Saudi riyals for agricultural loans and subsidies in the 1999, most of which were short-term loans to finance operating expenses. This brought the total loans dispersed to a value of over 31 billion riyals. By 1999, the government had also distributed some 2.9 billion hectares of fallow land. The fact that this distribution went to over 90,000 individuals and 18,800 agro-businesses also created a growing constituency for agricultural and water subsidies.

Ironically, Saudi dependence on food imports has continued to rise due to the steady increase in population and a shift toward a more varied diet. Food imports rose in value from around $3.5 billion in the early 1990s to around $7 billion in 1997. According to the Ministry of Agriculture and Water, Saudi Arabia claims it is self-sufficient in wheat, dates, and eggs, and has high rates of sufficiency in many other areas. However, many of Saudi Arabia's claims of self-sufficiency in specific crops have a touch of absurdity. For example, Saudi Arabia has stated it is nearly self-sufficient in lamb, chicken, eggs, and milk. This "self-sufficiency" was dependent on oil exports, which the government subsidized at least 65% to 75% of the total cost.[158] Furthermore, virtually all of the feed for Saudi Arabia's "self-sufficient" chickens is imported.[159]

Sustaining a National Water Problem

The end result is a set of policies that mix the need for the constant expansion of desalination facilities with failed agricultural policies and massive and unnecessary problems in water use. The Kingdom remains largely in denial, however, about both the cost of treating water as a human right without seeking efficiency and recoupment of costs and pursuing agricultural policies that are almost as silly in their own way as the very different kind of subsidies provided in the United States and European Union.

Saudi experts believe that the Kingdom can continue meet future demand for water but question the efficiency of several important aspects of the Saudi effort:

- Whether water, pipeline, and sewer development and renovation projects will start and finish on time.
- Whether serious action will be taken to make water use and costs a basic criterion in assessing the economic efficiency of public and private projects.
- Whether the Kingdom can ever bring its water and agricultural policies into a cost-effective balance.
- Whether water will ever be priced in ways that both make use efficient and ensure that suitable facilities can be funded without increasing the burden on the public.

Saudi Arabia recognizes that it has not properly funded the maintenance and expansion of its pipeline system and understands that it faces a major future challenge both in funding such plants and in creating an effective management structure to ensure reliable service. As a result, it took water out of the functions of the Ministry of Agriculture in July 2001, and created a new Ministry of Water. This Ministry is responsible for oversight of water facilities, research of water resources, the establishment of water and sewer networks throughout the country, distribution of water resources, and regulation of water supplies. It is tasked with creating a new administrative structure for water tariffs and collecting fees.[160]

It also is responsible for financing, implementation, operation, and maintenance of water projects by the private sector. It will issue licenses for new construction of water projects, and will encourage a shift to public-private partnerships to fund, undertake, and operate water projects. For example, the Kindasa Company has become the Kingdom's first fully private water utility company with its own desalination plant. It sells over 10,000 cubic meters a day of water to private industry, with plans to expand to 60,000 cubic meters a day. The Jeddah Holding Corporation has requested a $6 billion concession to expand water and sewerage services in Jeddah through 2020, and proposals have been forwarded to the Saudi Privatization

Committee. Potential international investments could come from firms like Sumitomo, Ondeo, Vivendi, and Doosan Heavy Industries.

Far more cost-effective approaches to water may be possible if the government acts decisively. The actual appointment of a water minister, however, took until September 2002, and the man chosen was the ambassador to the United Kingdom, Ghazi al-Gosaibi, who had come under political fire for publishing a poem praising Palestinian suicide bombers. He will also chair the SWCC, which raises questions about how serious the Kingdom is about the kind of hard choices it needs to make about water policy and prices.[161]

MEETING THE KINGDOM'S ECONOMIC, DEMOGRAPHIC, AND SOCIAL CHALLENGES

Saudi Arabia has set some of the right goals, but it largely ignores the problems caused by its birth rate, has failed to come to grips with the true nature of its demographic challenges, and faces a daunting cumulative set of challenges. As the next chapter shows, there also is little prospect that oil prices will rise to the point where crude oil and product exports will allow Saudi Arabia to meet the economic expectations of much of its youth or to sustain the present living standards of many families.[162] The problems must therefore be solved by limiting net population growth, achieving substantial growth in other sectors of the economy, and creating more jobs for native Saudis by shifting from a largely foreign labor force to one that is largely domestic.

As Crown Prince Abdullah and most senior Saudi princes and technocrats recognize, the key to meeting the Kingdom's demographic and social challenges is the reform and diversification of the Saudi economy discussed in the following chapters. The previous analysis suggests, however, that economic growth and reform will not be enough. Saudis need to begin a serious debate to define the kind of society the Kingdom wants to create in the twenty-first century.

- *The Saudi royal family, the government, and the Kingdom's society as a whole need to face the fact that Saudi oil wealth is limited and that Saudi Arabia faces a potential demographic crisis.* Strong leadership is needed to persuade the Wahhabi Ulema that voluntary population control is necessary and convince Saudi families that they should limit their number of children. There needs to be a firm, rational understanding that even the best economic development plan cannot maintain the present standard of real per capita wealth in Saudi Arabia without a much sharper decline in the birthrate, and that population growth is a major factor affecting political stability.

- *Job creation and Saudisation require more than good intentions.* Saudi Arabia is quite unlikely to meet the goals it sets forth in its Seventh Development Plan. It must, however, truly enforce its Saudisation policies if it is to approach those goals. It also needs to give the private sector clear priority in economic development and accelerate every measure that will aid the private sector in job creation.

- *Education and the development of a suitable mix of work ethic, job skills, and educational standards still need serious improvement and should be Saudi Arabia's highest priority.* The Saudi education system is not expanding quickly enough on a number of levels and needs to improve in quality and focus. This does not mean that education should not be Islamic; it does mean, however, that Islamic education must do a far, far better job of training young men and women to be truly competitive in the real world and that it must be purged of Islamic extremism.

- *Existing population momentum will place massive pressure on the Saudi budget, and suitable infrastructure and services will probably require better sources of revenue, such as a real income tax, reductions in entitlements, and prices much closer to market levels.* Saudi Arabia simply cannot afford a patriarchical solution to its youth explosion or the cumulative underfunding of key services and infrastructure.

- *Saudi economic planning is too disconnected from the responsibility for action, is based on a weak analytic structure, and lacks a clear vision for the future.* The previous analysis, as well as the analysis in the next chapter, shows that Saudi planning is based on a very weak data base for human resources that lacks meaningful statistics on unemployment, Saudisation, and many areas of economics. The failure to provide proper cost estimates and to tie broad goals to specific methods of implementation and a clear picture of whether they meet estimated need is equally serious. So is the lack of any tie between the analysis of the period in the five-year plan to longer-term needs and objectives—a critical failure in a nation with so much momentum in its population growth. There are also indications that the Ministry of Planning has become too decoupled from the ministries that must actually implement economic development and reform. A stronger Ministry of Economics, incorporating a more operational planning organization and activity, might be more effective.

Saudi stability requires the nation to look far more deeply into the implications of its current demographics, the analysis of labor trends and unemployment, investment needs, and social change. The royal family and government, as well as all educated Saudis, need to ask existential questions about the future of the Kingdom's society and the role of young Saudis in that society. Far too many educated Saudi women now face a dead end at the completion of their education, and most Saudi young men graduate into purposeless government and service-sector jobs that offer little real future or productive value to the economy. Islamic values and tradition cannot be allowed to drift into Islamic extremism or resistance to legitimate reform and change. There is no conceivable way that Saudi society can retreat into the past, but defining a truly viable Saudi future means looking beyond statistics and determining broader goals based on the modernization of Saudi values in ways that can actually work in a nation that must compete and survive in a global economy.

Both the Saudi ruling elite and the West need to recognize that Saudi Arabia's key security challenge is not external threats or internal extremism, but the need to come firmly to grips with demographics, education, social change, and popular economic needs. The key economic challenge the Kingdom faces is not a matter of macroeconomics or budget deficits, but the creation of a form of capitalism that suits Saudi social custom, that is run and staffed by Saudis, that creates a knowledge-based labor force that is globally competitive, and that steadily expands the productive sector beyond oil and gas exports and large-scale downstream operations.

NOTES

1. Kingdom of Saudi Arabia, Ministry of Planning, *Seventh Development Plan, 1420/1421–1424/1425 AH (2000–2004 AD)* (Riyadh: Ministry of Planning, 2001), English edition, pp. 77–78.

2. Saudi Arabian Monetary Agency (SAMA), *Thirty-Sixth Annual Report, 1421H (2000G)*, (Riyadh: SAMA, 2000), p. 45; *Thirty-Seventh Annual Report, 1422H (2001G)* (Riyadh: SAMA, 2001), p. 265.

3. Ibid.

4. These figures are taken from the database developed by the State Department for *World Military Expenditures and Arms Transfers*, with updates for 2000 provided informally to the author.

5. U.S. Census Bureau, March 23, 2002, URL: *www.census.gov/cgi-bin/ipc/idbsum?cty=SA*.

6. World Bank, *World Development Indicators, 2000* (Washington: World Bank, 2000), pp. 40, 44; *World Development Indicators, 2001* (Washington: World Bank, 2001), p. 46; *World Development Indicators, 2002* (Washington: World Bank, 2002), p. 50.

7. Based on various editions of World Bank, *World Development Indicators*. The latest figures are taken from the 2002 edition, p. 172.

8. World Bank, *World Development Indicators, 1997* (Washington: World Bank, 1997), pp. 12, 68, 116, 286; CIA, *World Factbook, 2000, 2001, and 2002* (Washington: GPO), "Saudi Arabia"; The World Bank, *World Bank Atlas, 1999* (Washington: World Bank, 1999), pp. 36–37; World Bank, *World Development Indicators, 2000*, pp. 40, 44; *World Development Indicators, 2001*, p. 30; *World Development Indicators, 2002*, p. 172.

9. Author's estimate based on data in World Bank, *World Development Indicators, 2000*, Table 2.4 and CIA *World Factbook, 2000*; *World Development Indicators, 2001*, pp. 30, 164.

10. CIA, *World Factbook, 2000, 2001, and 2002*, "Saudi Arabia"; and *World Factbook, 2000*, Figure 2.12. World Bank, *World Development Indicators, 2002*, p. 100. Further statistical and analytic background is taken from material provided by the World Bank, including "Will Arab Workers Prosper or Be Left Out in the Twenty-First Century?" (August 1995); "Forging a Partnership for Environmental

Action" (December 1994); and "A Population Perspective on Development: The Middle East and North Africa" (August 1994).

11. Kingdom of Saudi Arabia, Ministry of Planning, *Achievements of the Development Plans 1970–2000, Facts and Figures* (Riyadh: Ministry of Planning, 2000), Figure 44 and supporting text; and Kingdom of Saudi Arabia, Ministry of Planning, *Achievements of the Development Plans 1970–2001, Facts and Figures* (Riyadh: Ministry of Planning, 2002), 19th Issue.

12. Ibid.

13. *World Development Indicators, 1999; World Development Indicators, 2002*, p. 318. CIA, *World Factbook, 1996*, CD ROM, "Saudi Arabia," and CIA, *World Factbook, 2000, 2001,* and *2002*, "Saudi Arabia"; World Bank, *World Bank Atlas, 1997*, pp. 36–37; and *World Bank Atlas, 2001*.

14. *World Development Indicators, 2001*, p. 46; *World Development Indicators, 2002*, p. 50.

15. World Bank, *World Development Indicators, 2002*, p. 54.

16. Brad Bourland, *The Saudi Economy in 2002* (Riyadh: Saudi Arabian Bank, February 2002), p. 20.

17. World Bank, *World Development Indicators, 1997*, pp. 12, 68, 116, 286; and various editions of the CIA *World Factbook*. Note that the CIA method of estimation means that the annual growth rates shown could be attributed to the previous calendar year with equal validity.

18. U.S. Census Bureau, March 23, 2002, *www.census.gov/cgi-bin/ipc/idbsum?cty=SA*, accessed March 28, 2002.

19. SAMA, *Thirty-Seventh Annual Report, 1422H (2001G)*, p. 270.

20. SAMA, *Thirty-Sixth Annual Report, 1421H (2000G)*, p. 250.

21. Brad Bourland, *The Saudi Economy in Mid-Year 2002* (Riyadh, Saudi Arabian Bank, August 2002), pp. 5, 7.

22. Saudi Arabian Ministry of Planning, *Achievements of the Developments Plans, 1390–1420H (1970–2000)* (Riyadh: Ministry of Planning, 2000), Tables 5–8; and Kingdom of Saudi Arabia, Ministry of Planning, *Achievements of the Development Plans 1970–2001, Facts and Figures*, p. 201.

23. Mimi Mann, "Saudi Arabia: New Development Plan-Development Plan: Saudi American Bank Say's Plan's Goals Are Achievable," *Middle East Executive Reports* (April 2000).

24. World Bank, *World Development Indicators, 1997*, pp. 12, 68, 116, 286; CIA, *World Factbook, 2000*, CD ROM, "Saudi Arabia"; World Bank, *World Bank Atlas, 1999*, pp. 36–37; World Bank, *World Development Indicators, 2000*, pp. 184, World Bank, *World Development Indicators, 2002*, p. 206.

25. World Bank, *World Development Indicators, 2000*, p. 12.

26. See the blank spaces in World Bank, *Global Economic Prospects, 2000*, pp. 151–152.

27. World Bank, *Global Economic Prospects, 2002*, pp. 208–209.

28. *Middle East Economic Survey*, 45:5, 4 February 2002, Vol. 45, No. 5, p. B-8.

29. Brad Bourland, *Saudi Arabia's Employment Profile* (Riyadh: Saudi American Bank, October 6, 2002). The estimates on disguised unemployment were provided informally by analysts in the U.S. government and international financial institutions.

30. World Bank, *World Development Indicators, 2002,* pp. Sections 1.1 and 1.4.

31. Bourland, *The Saudi Economy in 2002.*

32. World Bank, *World Development Indicators, 2000,* pp. 12, 24.

33. Bureau of Arms Control (formerly ACDA), U.S. State Department, computerized database for *World Military Expenditures and Arms Transfers,* Table I.

34. World Bank, *World Development Indicators, 1997,* pp. 12, 68, 116, 286 and *World Development Indicators, 1999;* CIA, *World Factbook, 1996,* CD ROM, "Saudi Arabia," and CIA, *World Factbook, 2000, 2001,* and *2002,* "Saudi Arabia"; World Bank, *World Bank Atlas, 1997,* pp. 36–37, and *World Bank Atlas, 1999;* World Bank, *World Development Indicators, 2002,* p. 238.

35. Kingdom of Saudi Arabia, Ministry of Planning, *Seventh Development Plan,* pp. 203–205.

36. Briefing by Saudi experts, April 17, 2002.

37. Kingdom of Saudi Arabia, Ministry of Planning, *Achievements of the Development Plans 1970–2001, Facts and Figures,* pp. 129–133.

38. *CIA World Factbook, 2002,* "Saudi Arabia."

39. Saudi Arabian Ministry of Planning, *Achievements of the Developments Plans, 1390–1420H (1970–2000),* Tables 11–14; World Bank, *World Development Indicators, 2002,* 2002, pp. 210; and Kingdom of Saudi Arabia, Ministry of Planning, *Achievements of the Development Plans 1970–2001, Facts and Figures.*

40. SAMA, *Thirty-Sixth Annual Report, 1421H (2000G),* pp. 360–361.

41. Kingdom of Saudi Arabia, *Ministry of Planning, Achievements of the Development Plans 1970–2001, Facts and Figures,* p. 57.

42. Bourland, *The Saudi Economy in Mid-Year 2002,* p. 2.

43. *Saudi Arabia,* Vol. 17. No. 12, p. 1; Economist Intelligence Unit (EIU), URL: *www.eiu.com,* March 2, 2001, 1143.

44. *Saudi Commerce and Economic Review,* No. 22 (February 1996), p. 6; World Bank, *World Development Indicators, 1997,* p. 40 and *World Development Indicators, 1999;* *U.S.-Saudi Business Brief,* Vol. 4, No.1, 1999, p. 2.

45. Briefing by Saudi government expert, April 16, 2002.

46. SAMA, *Thirty-Seventh Annual Report, 1422H (2001G),* p. 270; Kingdom of Saudi Arabia, Ministry of Planning, *Seventh Development Plan, 1420/1421–1424/1425 AH (200–2004 AD),* pp. 75–79.

47. Bourland, *The Saudi Economy in 2002,* pp. 1, 20–24; SAMA, *Thirty-Seventh Annual Report, 1422H (2001G),* pp. 271–275.

48. Bourland, *Saudi Arabia's Employment Profile.* The estimates on disguised unemployment were provided informally by analyst in the U.S. government and international financial institutions.

49. Ibid.

50. World Bank, *World Development Indicators, 2001,* p. 50; World Bank, *World Development Indicators, 2002,* p. 54.

51. World Bank, *World Development Indicators, 2000,* p. 48; World Bank, *World Development Indicators, 2002,* 2002, p. 54.

52. The figures in this analysis are based on briefings by the Ministry of Planning and on the English-language version of the *Seventh Development Plan 1420/21–1424/25 AH (2000–2004 AD),* especially pp. 158–167.

53. *Middle East Economic Digest,* June 30, 2000, pp. 22–37.

54. SAMA, *Thirty-Seventh Annual Report, 1422H (2001G)*, pp. 276, 279.

55. SAMA, *Thirty-Seventh Annual Report, 1422H (2001G)*, Riyadh, SAMA, 2001, pp. 276, 279.

56. World Bank, *World Population Projections, 1996*, and *World Development Indicators, 1999; Middle East Economic Digest*, July 28, 1995, p. 11; CIA *World Factbook, 1996*, "Saudi Arabia"; and CIA, *World Factbook, 2000, 2001*, and *2002*, "Saudi Arabia."

57. CIA, *World Factbook, 2000, 2001*, and *2002*, "Saudi Arabia."

58. U.S. Census Bureau IDB summary demographic database on *http://www.census.gov/cgi-bin/ipc/idbsum?cty*, accessed March 28, 2002.

59. Bloomberg, May 9, 2001, 1737; Associated Press, May 9, 2001, 1435.

60. Interviews in Saudi Arabia in February 2001.

61. Bourland, *Saudi Arabia's Employment Profile*; and World Bank, *Social Indicators of Development, 2001*.

62. U.S. Census Bureau IDB summary demographic database.

63. CIA, *World Factbook, 2000, 2001*, and *2002*, "Saudi Arabia."

64. SAMA, *Thirty-Sixth Annual Report, 1421H (2000G)*, pp. 250–257.

65. Bourland, *The Saudi Economy in 2002*.

66. SAMA, *Thirty-Sixth Annual Report, 1421H (2000G)*, p. 258.

67. SAMA, *Thirty-Sixth Annual Report, 1421H (2000G)*, p. 258.

68. Bourland, *Saudi Arabia's Employment Profile*. The estimates on disguised unemployment were provided informally by analyst in the US government and international financial institutions.

69. Interviews with Saudi officials in Saudi Arabia in 2000 and 2001.

70. The most recent figures reported in *Middle East Economic Survey* by the Riyadh-based Consulting Center for Finance and Investment (CCFI) gave the number of expatriate workers in Saudi Arabia for 1998–1999 as 4,698,000 and Saudi workers as 2,456,000.

71. Executive News Service, October 11, 1995, 1631; UPI, October 11, 1995, 1631.

72. Executive News Service, July 20, 1995, 0306; Reuters, June 16, 1997, 0906; *Christian Science Monitor*, October 23, 1996, p. 2; CIA, *World Factbook, 1997*, "Saudi Arabia"; CIA, *World Factbook, 2000, 2001*, and *2002*, "Saudi Arabia"; IISS, *Military Balance, 1996–1997* and *1999–2000*.

73. Executive News Service, October 11, 1995, 1631; UPI, October 11, 1995, 1631; *Wall Street Journal*, September 12, 1996, p. A-1; CIA, *World Factbook, 1997*, "Saudi Arabia"; CIA, *World Factbook, 2000, 2001*, and *2002*, "Saudi Arabia"; IISS, *Military Balance, 1996–1997* and *1999–2000*.

74. *Middle East Economic Digest*, April 5, 1996, pp. 54–57.

75. Reuters, May 6, 1999.

76. Executive News Service, September 18, 1995, 1631; *Wall Street Journal*, "Saudi Arabia," September 22, 1995.

77. Executive News Service, July 20, 1995, 0306.

78. Saudi Ministry of Information, October 1995; Executive News Service, September 18, 1995, 1631; *Wall Street Journal*, "Saudi Arabia," September 22, 1995, and May 27, 1997, special section.

79. Reuters, "Saudi Says Nationals Must Make 25 Percent of Staff at Firms" September 27, 2000.

80. *Saudi Arabia*, Vol. 13, No. 1, January 1996, p. 3; *Middle East Economic Digest*, April 5, 1996, pp. 30–43.

81. Bureau of Democracy, Human Rights, and Labor, *1999 Country Reports on Human Rights Practices*, U.S. Department of State, February 25, 2000, URL: *http://www.state.gov/www/global/human_rights/ 1999_hrp_report/saudiara.html*; and *2001 Country Reports on Human Rights Practices*, U.S. Department of State, March 4, 2002, URL: *http://www.state.gov/g/drl/rls/hrrpt/2001/nea/8296.html*.

82. Mai Yamani, *Changed Identities: The Challenge of the New Generation in Saudi Arabia* (London: Royal Institute of International Affairs, 2000), p. 81.

83. Bourland, *Saudi Arabia's Employment Profile*. The estimates on disguised unemployment were provided informally by analyst in the U.S. government and international financial institutions.

84. Bourland, *The Saudi Economy in 2002*, pp. 7, 21, 22.

85. Saudi Ministry of Information, October 1995; Executive News Service, September 18, 1995, 1631; *Wall Street Journal*, "Saudi Arabia," September 22, 1995, and May 27, 1997, special section.

86. Saudi Arabian Ministry of Planning, *Statement of the Ministry of Planning on the Seventh Development Plan, 1420–1425* (Riyadh: Ministry of Planning, October 2000); Saudi Arabian Ministry of Planning, *Seventh Development Plan, 1420–1425* (Riyadh: Minister of Planning, 2001 [English version]).

87. Ibid.

88. *Middle East Economic Digest*, June 30, 2000, pp. 22–37.

89. Saudi Arabian Ministry of Planning, *Achievements of the Development Plans, 1390–1420 (1970–2000)*, Table 87; and Kingdom of Saudi Arabia, Ministry of Planning, *Achievements of the Development Plans 1970–2001, Facts and Figures*.

90. Ibid.

91. Saudi Arabian Ministry of Planning, *Achievements of the Development Plans, 1390–1420 (1070–2000)*, Table 90.

92. SAMA, *Thirty-Sixth Annual Report, 1421H (2000G)*, pp. 235–241.

93. Saudi Arabian Ministry of Planning, *Achievements of the Development Plans, 1390–1420 (1070–2000)*, Table 90; and Kingdom of Saudi Arabia, Ministry of Planning, *Achievements of the Development Plans 1970–2001, Facts and Figures*.

94. Ibid.

95. SAMA, *Thirty-Sixth Annual Report, 1421H (2000G)*, pp. 235–241.

96. Ibid.

97. Saudi Ministry of Information, "General Objectives and Strategic Bases of the Sixth Development Plan."

98. Saudi Ministry of Information, October 1995; Executive News Service, September 18, 1995, 1631; *Wall Street Journal*, "Saudi Arabia," September 22, 1995.

99. *Saudi Arabia* (Spring 1997), pp. 13–17.

100. SAMA, *Thirty-Sixth Annual Report, 1421H (2000G)*, pp. 235–241.

101. Ibid.

102. Bourland, *The Saudi Economy in 2002*, pp. 21–23.

103. Saudi Arabian Ministry of Planning, *Achievements of the Development Plans, 1390–1420 (1070–2000)*, Table 98; and Kingdom of Saudi Arabia, Ministry of Planning, *Achievements of the Development Plans 1970–2001, Facts and Figures*.

104. Interviews in Saudi Arabia.

105. Saudi Arabian Ministry of Planning, *Statement of the Ministry of Planning on the Seventh Development Plan, 1420–1425*; Saudi Arabian Ministry of Planning, *Seventh Development Plan, 1420–1425*.

106. Saudi Arabian Ministry of Planning, *Seventh Development Plan, 1420–1425*, p. 260.

107. Saudi Arabian Ministry of Planning, *Achievements of the Development Plans, 1390–1420 (1070–2000)*, Tables 116–117; and Kingdom of Saudi Arabia, Ministry of Planning, *Achievements of the Development Plans 1970–2001, Facts and Figures*, p. 328.

108. Saudi Arabian Ministry of Planning, *Achievements of the Development Plans, 1390–1420 (1070–2000)*, Tables 108–109; and Kingdom of Saudi Arabia, Ministry of Planning, *Achievements of the Development Plans 1970–2001, Facts and Figures*.

109. These patterns become clear from even a cursory review on such data as provided in Kingdom of Saudi Arabia, Ministry of Planning, *Achievements of the Development Plans 1970–2001, Facts and Figures*, pp. 39, 328, 329, etc.

110. Saudi Arabian Ministry of Planning, *Statement of the Ministry of Planning on the Seventh Development Plan, 1420–1425*; Saudi Arabian Ministry of Planning, *Seventh Development Plan, 1420–1425*.

111. D. F. Hepburn, Bahrain Petroleum Company, USCENTCOM SWA Symposium, May 17, 1994.

112. Kingdom of Saudi Arabia, Ministry of Planning, *Achievements of the Development Plans 1970–2001, Facts and Figures*, p. 39.

113. Saudi Arabian Ministry of Planning, *Achievements of the Development Plans, 1390–1420 (1070–2000)*, Table 76.

114. Brad Bourland, *The Saudi Economy: 2000 Performance, 2001 Forecast* (Riyadh: Saudi American Bank, February 2001), pp. 7–88.

115. *Middle East Economic Digest*, April 21, 1995, pp. 32–33.

116. Kingdom of Saudi Arabia, Ministry of Planning, *Achievements of the Development Plans 1970–2001, Facts and Figures*, p. 40.

117. IEA, *Middle East Oil and Gas* (Paris: OECD/IEA, 1995), p. 200.

118. DOE/EIA Online database, analysis section, country section. Accessed July 25, 1995.

119. Ibid.

120. Agence France-Presse "Saudi plans to merge regional electricity firms," *Arabia.On.Line*. URL: *http://www.arabia.com*, November 11, 1999.

121. *Middle East Economic Digest*, December 11, 1998, pp. 6, 17.

122. *Middle East Economic Digest*, April 21, 1995, pp. 32–33; *Middle East Economic Digest*, "Special Report: Saudi Arabia," March 10, 1995, pp. 28–30.

123. *Middle East Economic Digest*, April 18, 1997, p. 3.

124. Kingdom of Saudi Arabia, Ministry of Planning, *Seventh Development Plan*, p. 222.

125. Ibid., p. 226.

126. *Middle East Economic Digest*, June 13, 1997, p. 37; Bloomberg, April 25, 2001, 0319.

127. *Middle East Economic Survey*, March 6, 2000; Bloomberg, April 25, 2001, 0319.

128. EIA, Online data base on Saudi Arabia, accessed August 26, 1997.

129. *Middle East Economic Digest*, December 4, 1998, p. 22.

130. *Middle East Economic Survey*, Vol. 42, No.10, March 8, 1999, p. B2.

131. *Middle East Economic Digest*, April 27, 2001, p. 16; Bloomberg, April 25, 2001, 0319.

132. *Middle East Economic Digest*, January 31, 1997, pp. 10–15, June 13, 1997, p. 37, July 11, 1997, pp. 2–3; *Wall Street Journal*, September 23, 1996, B-10D.

133. Saudi Arabian Ministry of Planning, *Statement of the Ministry of Planning on the Seventh Development Plan, 1420–1425*; Saudi Arabian Ministry of Planning, *Seventh Development Plan, 1420–1425*.

134. See SAMA, *Thirty-Seventhth Annual Report 1422H (2001G)*, p. 229.

135. Saudi Arabian Ministry of Planning, *Seventh Development Plan, 1420–1425*, pp. 95–99.

136. Ibid., pp. 96–97.

137. *Los Angeles Times*, January 28, 1992, p. C-1; working papers from the Royal Institute of International Affairs (RIAA) conference on Saudi society, economy, and security, October 4–5, 1993; working data provided by World Bank, February 1997; *Baltimore Sun*, August 3, 1997, p. 22A.

138. SAMA, *Thirty-Sixth Annual Report, 1421H (2000G)*, pp. 224–227.

139. For further background, see SAMA, *Thirty-Seventh Annual Report 1422H (2001G)*, pp. 229–233.

140. Ibid.

141. Ibid., p. 233.

142. SAMA, *Thirty-Sixth Annual Report, 1421H (2000G)*, pp. 224–227.

143. *Los Angeles Times*, January 28, 1992, p. C-1; working papers from the Royal Institute of International Affairs (RIAA) conference on Saudi society, economy, and security, October 4–5, 1993.

144. SAMA, *Thirty-Sixth Annual Report, 1421H (2000G)*, pp. 224–227.

145. Bourland, *The Saudi Economy: 2000 Performance, 2001 Forecast*, p. 11.

146. Briefing by Saudi official, April 17, 2002.

147. *Middle East Economic Digest*, July 19, 1996, pp. 2–3

148. SAMA, *Thirty-Seventh Annual Report, 1422H (2001G)*, p. 229.

149. *Middle East Economic Survey*, August 2, 1999. Data cited from Consulting Center for Finance and Investment.

150. *Saudi Arabia* (March 19970, p. 3; *Middle East Economic Digest*, July 19, 1996, pp. 2–3, June 13, 1997, pp. 41–45.

151. Ibid.

152. *Middle East Economic Digest*, June 13, 1997, pp. 41–45.

153. Ibid.

154. Ibid.

155. SAMA, *Thirty-Sixth Annual Report, 1421H (2000G)*, pp. 217–224.

156. *Saudi Commerce and Economic Review* (February 1966), pp. 12, 15.

157. Ministry of Planning "Statement on the Seventh Development Plan 1420–1425"; Saudi Arabian Ministry of Planning, *Seventh Development Plan, 1420–1425*.

158. For more detail on Saudi agricultural production and its costs, see SAMA, *Thirty-Seventh Annual Report 1422H (2001G)*, pp. 223–230.

159. CIA, *World Factbook,* "Saudi Arabia," various editions. Further statistical and analytic background is taken from material provided by the World Bank, including "Will Arab Workers Prosper or Be Left Out in the Twenty-First Century?," "Forging a Partnership for Environmental Action," and "A Population Perspective on Development: The Middle East and North Africa."

160. *Middle East Economic Digest*, November 9, 2001, p. 22, September 20, 2002, p. 20; *Global Water Intelligence* (August 2001), URL: *www.globalwaterintel.com*; Saudi government press release, July 18, 2002.

161. *Trade Arabia*, September 30, 2002; IPR Strategic Business Information Database, September 18, 2002; Agence France Presse, September 17, 2002; *Middle East Economic Digest*, September 20, 2002, p. 20.

162. CIA, *World Factbook, 1997*, "Saudi Arabia."

Chapter 6

Building True Wealth versus Overdependence on Petroleum and the State

If Saudi Arabia is to cope with its political, demographic, and social challenges, it must move away from a largely patriarchical, state-driven economy that is dependent on oil wealth and create a much more diversified economy that is heavily dependent on its private sector for success. There are no near- or mid-term prospects that Saudi Arabia can eliminate a heavy dependence on petroleum or the state sector of its economy, but the time when Saudi Arabia could rely on oil wealth alone is over, and its current overdependence on the petroleum sector is creating growing economic, political, and military risks. The Kingdom must move to diversify its economy, strengthen its private sector, and encourage foreign and domestic investment as aggressively as possible.

Some Saudis do still act as if the Kingdom's past level of oil wealth will recur. In spite of a series of major price shocks since 1986, they still see the oil booms of the mid-1970s and early-1980s as the eventual norm, rather than the "temporary" exception. They regard low-to-moderate oil prices as an aberration in what they view as a natural long-term movement toward higher prices, and they feel the Kingdom's current economic problems will be solved by the wealth inherent in Saudi Arabia's vast oil reserves. This view of Saudi economics assumes that time and oil wealth will ultimately remedy the situation, that new expenditures will eventually be affordable, and that little discipline is needed to restructure the Saudi economy and Saudi government spending. This view of the future also generally reflects a tacit faith in the state as a planner and manager, although most

Saudis who hold this view give lip service to the importance of the private sector and efforts to diversify the economy.

There are other Saudis that have no real vision of the future. They feel that the Kingdom should continue to spend largely on the basis of historical momentum or that maintaining welfare and entitlement spending is more important than economic reform. The impact of this "muddle through" approach to Saudi Arabia's future is reflected in the fact that Saudi Arabia has often maintained higher levels of public spending than its revenues justify. The Kingdom has sustained its spending on domestic and public services and military forces at the cost of budget deficits. It has done so even though the rapid increase in Saudi Arabia's population has meant a steady reduction in its per capita GDP and oil exports and has imposed growing limits on the Kingdom's capacity to spend on subsidies and its social "safety net."

Fortunately, most informed Saudis—including the Crown Prince and the vast majority of senior princes, technocrats, and businessmen—understand that Saudi Arabia must make major structural economic reforms. These "modernists" often are as Islamic as every other element of Saudi society, but they are supported by most well-educated Saudis and by a generational shift in favor of reform. They realize that Saudi Arabia must cap or reduce its funding of social services and must focus on a pattern of economic development that will ensure that all national groups receive a share of the nation's oil wealth. They recognize that reform must take place within a "safety net" that defuses or reduces social protest. At the same time, they understand that "oil wealth" is as relative as any other form of wealth, and that it is steadily declining in terms of per capita income. They see the need to diversify and privatize the economy and to create a competitive economic environment dependent on Saudi labor.

THE SAUDI ECONOMY AT THE EDGE OF THE TWENTY-FIRST CENTURY

There is no way to calculate the precise scale and pace of reform that is needed. As has been discussed in earlier chapters, there are many different estimates of the trends in the Saudi economy and of how they interact with demographic and social pressures, and they differ significantly in portraying the level of the future problems Saudi Arabia faces.[1]

The previous chapters have shown there is no consistency of the trends and pressures within the Saudi economy, even within the U.S. government. For example, CIA estimates indicate that Saudi Arabia's GDP had a purchasing power equivalent of $173.1 billion in 1994 current dollars, $189.3 billion in 1995, $205.6 billion in 1996, $206.5 billion in 1997, and $191 billion in 1999. The CIA estimated per capita income at $10,100 in 1995,

$10,600 in 1996, $10,300 in 1997, $9,000 in 1998 and $9,000 in 1999.[2] In contrast, World Bank estimates indicate that Saudi Arabia's GDP had a value of $133 billion in 1995 and $143 billion in 1998, using the Atlas method, and that its per capita income was worth $7,040 in 1995, $7,150 in 1997, and $7,230 in 2000.[3]

Saudi data differ between ministries and have many inconsistencies. There are serious problems in estimating even basic data like the size of the GNP and per capita income. For example, one Saudi government source reported a GDP of $136 billion for 1996, but did not report a per capita income.[4] The Saudi finance minister used an entirely different definition of GDP in summarizing the Sixth Development Plan. He called for an increase from a GDP of $101.5 billion (380.8 billion riyals [SR]) in 1995 to a GDP of $122.3 billion (SR 458.6 billion) by 2000.[5] Several years later, the Saudi Finance Ministry reported that Saudi Arabia's GDP totaled $125.1 billion (SR 469 billion) in 1995, $136 billion (SR 510 billion) in 1996, and $145.8 billion (SR 547 billion) in 1997.[6]

There are no certainties in forecasting for any country at any time, regardless of the quality of the data. As is the case with most economies, experts, estimates, and projections have a long history of being wrong. Data from both Saudi and international institutions, like the World Bank, tend to be overoptimistic in estimating current and future performance. This often gives the impression that problems are actually being solved, when the reality is that the forecaster is picking the most favorable assumptions and trends. At the same time, other outside experts have been predicting critical economic crises for decades, and other international institutions like the IMF have tended to err of the side of pessimism.

Yet, for all of those uncertainties, a number of trends seem clear. As discussed in the previous chapter, the Saudi economy is already under severe demographic pressure. Table 6.1 provides World Bank and Saudi estimates of the trends in the Saudi economy. While virtually every source of such data provides slightly different figures, there is enough consensus between estimates to show that the estimates in Table 6.1 are typical in showing the overdependence of the Saudi GDP and budget on petroleum revenues, the lack of economic diversification, and the existence of chronic budget deficits.

Virtually all of the data available also indicate that Saudi Arabia still has time in which to act, and the data in Table 6.1 reflect a number of positive trends. The Kingdom has kept inflation low, limited its budget deficits, preserved a positive trade balance, and managed significant capital formation except in years when oil revenues were exceptionally low. As might be expected from the previous chapters, the macroeconomic data in Table 6.1 portray an economy under growing stress, but not one in crisis.

Table 6.1
Recent Trends in the Saudi Economy (Costs in Billions of Current Saudi Riyals Unless Otherwise Stated)

	1990	1991	1992	1993	1994	1995	1996	1997	1998	1999	2000
GDP (Purchaser's Values)	392.0	442.0	461.4	443.8	450.0	478.7	529.3	548.4	481.2	535.0	649.3
Real GDP (1994 constant prices)											
(% Change)											
Oil	9.4	10.3	2.0	-0.4	0.5	0.6	1.3	1.6	1.8	-0.9	4.7
Non-Oil Private	25.5	21.9	7.1	-3.8	0.2	0.5	2.1	-2.4	3.4	-6.4	9.7
Government	3.0	2.9	1.9	0.7	0.7	0.0	1.1	3.8	1.1	1.7	3.1
	6.3	13.3	-7.2	2.9	0.5	0.6	0.9	3.4	0.5	2.0	1.5
Total Budget Revenues	154.7	161.9	165.4	141.4	129	146.5	179.1	205.5	141.6	147.5	258.0
Petroleum Revenues	118.1	*118.1	127.1	106.0	95.5	105.7	136.0	160.0	80.0	104.5	214.4
Other Revenues	36.6	*36.6	38.3	35.5	33.5	40.8	43.1	45.5	61.6	43.0	43.6
Total Budget Expenditures	476.8	*476.8	232.5	205.5	163.8	173.9	198.1	221.3	190	183.8	225.3.
Budget Deficit	-160.2	*-160.2	-67.2	-64.1	-34.8	-27.4	-19.0	-15.8	-48.5	-36.3	+22.7
Budget Deficit as % of GDP	19.2%	19.2%	14.6%	14.4%	7.7%	5.7%	3.2%	2.6%	8.4%	5.6%	-6.4%

Exports	166.3	178.6	188.3	158.8	159.6	187.4	227.4	227.4	145.4	190.1	295.8
Crude Petroleum	123.3	139.8	148.3	119.9	117.2	133.0	163.3	163.0	97.2	136.3	219.5
Petroleum Products	27.0	23.5	25.9	24.7	25.6	30.1	40.0	36.8	24.7	29.9	51.5
Other	16.1	15.3	14.1	14.1	16.8	24.3	24.2	27.7	23.4	21.9	24.8
Imports	90.1	108.9	124.5	105.6	87.4	105.2	104.0	107.6	112.4	105.0	113.2
Unemployment	—	—	—	—	—	—	—	—	—	—	14%
Current Account											
Receipts	212.1	222.1	228.9	194.3	187.2	219.1	257.0	265.0	184.9	232.0	321.0
Disbursements	227.7	325.6	295.4	259.0	226.5	239.1	254.5	263.8	234.1	230.5	267.3
Balance	-15.5	-103.5	-66.4	-64.7	-39.3	-19.9	2.5	1.1	-49.2	1.5	53.7
As % of GDP	—	—	—	—	-8.83	-4.29	0.45	0.21	-10.18	—	—
Government Domestic											
Debt	—	—	—	—	336	384	422	468	566	—	—
As % of GDP	—	—	—	—	76	83	84	87	116	—	—

*Saudi Arabia changed its annual budget cycle in 1991, so it reports 1990 and 1991 as one year.

Sources: Adapted by Anthony H. Cordesman from material provided by SAMA; Ministry of Planning, Kingdom of Saudi Arabia: Achievements of the Development Plans 1390–1418 (1970–1998), Facts and Figures, 16th Issue (Riyadh: Ministry of Planning, 1999); Kingdom of Saudi Arabia, Ministry of Planning, Achievements of the Development Plans 1970–2001, Facts and Figures (Riyadh: Ministry of Planning, 2001); and Brad Bourland, The Saudi Economy: 2000 Performance; 2001 Forecast (Riyadh: Saudi American Bank, February 2001).

The Key Challenges the Economic Reform Must Meet

If the good news is that the Kingdom has both the resources and time in which to react to the demographic and social pressures discussed in Chapter 5, the bad news is that Saudi economy faces the following additional challenges.

- A wide range of external forces shape the value of the Kingdom's petroleum revenues in ways that it cannot control. These include normal market forces (which are global because oil is a global commodity), politics, and war. This can lead to massive unpredictable swings in oil revenues, although the value of Saudi petroleum exports dropped in absolute terms from the early 1980s to the late 1980s, and total Saudi exports have experienced only limited peaks and growth since that time. As shown in Chapter 1—and discussed in more detail in this chapter—oil revenues have been erratic and real oil revenues have not come close to meeting Saudi Arabia's economic and budget needs.

- Saudi Arabia has faced serious problems in planning its budget and five-year plans because it has had no way to predict its cash flow. Its petroleum revenues have been highly erratic, and its economy and budget are dependent on these revenues. For example, Saudi Arabia put intense pressure on OPEC in late November 1997 to increase its production quotas, believing that rising demand would give it major increases in revenue without cutting oil prices. The decision turned out to be disastrous. The Asian economy collapsed shortly thereafter, a rise in Atlantic production provided alternative sources of oil, and a mild winter caused by El Niño reduced demand outside Asia. The end result was a massive glut and an "oil crash" resulting in the lowest oil prices in a quarter of a century. Saudi Arabia was forced to cut production back twice in the spring of 1998, and still had no way to plan its estimated revenue for its budget and five-year plan or its investment in future oil and petrochemical production. Within a little more than a year, however, oil prices had risen to $30 a barrel, Saudi oil revenues swelled sharply, and the Kingdom was increasing production to bring oil prices back into balance. The end result was a new set of budgeting problems involving overspending and the inability to predict how long high oil prices would last.

- Structural change has slowed sharply over the last fifteen years, and many of the sectoral changes in the Saudi economy are more productive on paper than they are in practice. Saudi Arabia has expanded its private sector to the point where it now generates a nominal 35% of the GNP, but its diversification efforts have had limited productive impact, have not generated the necessary jobs or "knowledge-based" economy, and have taken place largely in the service and construction sectors. The nonpetroleum sector accounted for 76.1% of the economy in 1985 and 64.7% in 1990. It was less than 63% from 1991 to 1999, with no increase during this period. The Kingdom has not always succeeded in diversifying the industrial output of its economy in ways that exceed the investment cost of its diversification attempts or in making increases in real jobs at anything approaching the rate of its population growth.

- The expansion of the service sector has often had the net impact of increasing dependence on imports and reliance on foreign labor.

- Saudi Arabia's productivity remains low. The Kingdom is not competitive and needs to open up its markets to join the World Trade Organization (WTO) and ensure matching access to foreign markets for its exports. Saudi Arabia became an observer at the WTO in 1998 and is seeking to become a full member. To become a member Saudi Arabia must make its private industry significantly more competitive and reduces its tariffs and barriers to foreign investment.[7]

- Saudi educational standards remain too low, and far too many Saudis received secondary and advanced education in an Islamic curriculum that does not train them for real-world careers or in programs that do not enforce the proper standards.

- Saudi foreign investment income is about half of what it was in the mid-1980s, and increases in payments mean that net income is about one-third of the former level.[8]

- Total Saudi savings and foreign investments have dropped significantly as a result of the end of the oil boom and the cost of the Gulf War, although estimates differ sharply as to how much.

- Saudi government expenditures have normally exceeded revenues for more than a decade. The budget for 2000—a year of peak oil revenues—is the only recent exception. The government has only repaid its foreign debt by borrowing extensively from its banks and is still is unable to pay all its domestic debts.

It is to the credit of the Saudi government that it has recognized most of these problems and is seeking to address them. Crown Prince Abdullah has warned that a period of austerity lies ahead, and that the "boom period" for Saudi Arabia and other Gulf oil-producing countries is over. The Saudi government has accepted the need to sharply reduce state involvement in the economy and increase the role of the private sector—including foreign investment in the economy. It has taken near-term steps to expedite such changes and has included them in its five-years plans.

The Kingdom is still moving slowly, partly because of the fear of job losses for Saudi citizens, and partly because of resistance within the Saudi bureaucracy, the traditional sections of society, part of the private sector, and by some members of the royal family.[9] Saudi Arabia has been slow to cut government subsidies and reduce government expenditures. It has been equally slow to create major new incentives for foreign and domestic investment, increase taxes, and reform the financial sector.

Tangible Steps Toward Economic Reform

Any analysis of the Kingdom's future economic challenges must be made in the context of ongoing efforts at reform. The reform cabinet appointed in 1995 was much more oriented toward the private sector than its predecessor, many of whose members emphasized state-controlled projects and central planning.[10] The Sixth Development Plan called for the private nonoil sector to grow by an annual average of 4.3% during the period from 1996 to 2000, and from a value added of SR 169.5 billion in 1995 to SR 209.3 billion in 2000—a cumulative growth of 23%.[11] Total private-sector investment was planned to reach SR 212.7 billion, 45% of the total of SR 472 billion to be invested during the Sixth Development Plan.

While many of these efforts faltered or were poorly executed through the mid-1990s, the "oil crash" in the late 1990s led the government to become more serious about encouraging the private sector. Crown Prince Abdullah stated that privatization should be a "strategic choice," began to reform government spending, and introduced a series of reform measures.

The Seventh Development Plan (2000–2004) clearly recognized the need for fundamental economic reform and diversification, although not without many caveats:[12]

Although nonoil revenues have increased over the course of previous development plans, such improvements are not yet sufficient. Because of the multiple and interlinked economic and social dimensions of this issue, careful study is needed to develop the best policies. Hence, the Seventh Plan will develop the following policies:

- To reconsider the existing tax system with the aim of upgrading it and improving collection efficiency while avoiding any adverse social impact.
- To review the rules and regulations concerning the collection of customs duties with the aim of simplifying them, improving the efficiency of concerned agencies, and increasing government customs revenues without affecting its regional and international commitments.
- To adjust the current charges and fees for government services to ensure they are commensurate with their costs and to improve the efficiency of agencies responsible for collection.
- To review foreign labor recruitment fees in order to support Saudisation projects.
- To move the balance of payments into surplus in the future, while continuing public and private sector efforts to develop nonoil resources.
- To encourage private investment (both national and foreign) in the exploration and utilization of untapped mineral resources.

Most important, the Saudi government has shown that it is becoming far more serious in taking action. It has instituted a long series of reforms and is contemplating a long list of others. Since the late 1990s, it has taken the following major steps:[13]

- Corporatization of the Saudi Telecommunications Company (1998);
- Establishment of the Supreme Economic Council (SEC; August 1999);

- Opening of the stock market to foreign investment in mutual funds (November 1999);
- Royal decree outlining the restructuring and corporatization of the electricity sector (December 1999);
- Establishment of the Supreme Council for Petroleum and Mineral Affairs (SCPMA; oil policy decision-making, Gas Initiative negotiations, oversight of Aramco; January 2000);
- Foreign Investment Law and creation of the Saudi Arabian General Investment Authority (SAGIA; April 2000);
- Real Estate Law allowing foreigners to own real estate, except in Mecca and Medina (October 2000);
- Creation of Human Resource Development Fund to train Saudis in job skills (November 2000);
- Creation of the Supreme Tourist Authority for maximizing growth of tourism in Saudi Arabia (November 2000);
- Transfer for responsibility for privatization to the Supreme Economic Council, and requirement that the SEC establish a plan and timetable for privatization (February 2001);
- Guidelines for transparency of economic and fiscal data (May 2001);
- Reductions in tariffs from 12% to 5% (May 2001);
- Establishment of the Saudi Telecommunications Authority as a telecommunications regulator (May 2001);
- Creation of a separate Water Ministry (June 2001)
- Creation of the Electricity Services Regulatory Authority as an electric power regulator (November 2001);
- Acceleration of harmonization in GCC tariffs (at 5%) from March 2005 to January 2003 (December 2001);
- New health services law (June 2002);
- Issuing of a new government privatization strategy (June 2002);
- Creation of a railroad executive program (June 2002);
- Privatization regulations for water desalination (June 2002); and
- First steps in privatizing the post office (June 2002).

Other recent measures include the creation of an Industrial Cities Development Authority, the restructuring of the electrical sector, an antidumping law, new social insurance and social security laws, new visa procedures for foreign businessmen, and new incentives for family businesses and small–medium business incubators. The Kingdom has allowed the creation of privately funded colleges as business enterprises, the licensing of water desalination to the private sector, and the creation of labor committees and labor representation on company committees. In areas outside the economy, the Kingdom has issued a new law of governance, and new laws on regions, litigation, criminal procedures, the role of advocates, the authority of the attorney general, and press and publications.

In creating these reforms, Saudi Arabia focused on enlarging its private sector and the eventual creation of a structured system of utilities based on real market prices. It also focused on creating a climate where Saudis would have a major incentive to repatriate their private capital and investment in Saudi Arabia, where a globally competitive economy with high-value ("knowledge-based") jobs could develop, and where foreign capital could replace much of the burden on government expenditures to provide the capital need for investment. Such measures were a critical step in increasing government revenues and in releasing capital to fund other development projects. Foreign private investment had only amounted to $4 billion between 1984 and 1997, of which only 20% went to the Saudi private sector.[14]

The Supreme Economic Council

The establishment of the Supreme Economic Council (SEC), or Higher Economic Council, on August 28,1999, is a key example of the steps being taken to strengthen the private sector.[15] The eleven-member body has been set up with the goal of devising and implementing the country's economic policy. The council is chaired by Crown Prince and First Deputy Premier Prince Abdullah, with Second Deputy Premier Prince Sultan bin Abdulaziz as deputy chairman. Other members include the chairman of the General Committee of the Council of Ministers, and the governor of the Saudi Arabian Monetary Agency (SAMA). It also includes the ministers of finance and national economy, planning, labor and social affairs, petroleum and mineral resources, commerce, and two ministers of state.

The SEC assumes the responsibilities of the Council of Ministers in terms of economic issues. It has a permanent committee called the Economic Consultative Commission that includes a number of ministers, and there is also an advisory committee for economic affairs. The SEC is responsible for studying the general framework of the development plans, financial policies and bases for preparing budget drafts and priorities for expenditure, commercial policies at the domestic and international levels, industrial and agricultural policies, economic and commercial agreements, and relevant economic studies prepared for it by consultative committees.[16] It also reviews reports, monetary policies, and information presented by SAMA.

A decision by the Council of Ministers on February 5, 2001, gave the SEC responsibility for supervising the privatization program and the implementation and coordination of all related activities with other government ministries. It also charged the SEC with formulating a strategic plan and timetable to ensure that such activity took place. The SEC decides the scope of the activity of organizations to be privatized and reviews and approves the programs proposed by feasibility studies.[17] The council was reformed on September 23, 2001, and given a revised membership that included leading and highly educated technocrats. It meets regularly under the chairmanship of the crown prince and covers a wide range of issues from conventional economic policy to the environment.[18]

While the SEC is relatively new, it has already contributed to the approval of a new foreign investment law and drafted the organizational structure of a new General Investment Authority (SAGIA), regulations permitting ownership and investment in real estate by non-Saudis, the establishment of a Human Resources Development Fund, new regulations for employers with expatriate labor, the Seventh Development Plan, and review of the state budget. It has also reviewed new limits on corporate taxes and allowable corporate losses, reduced customs duties, regulations to help privatize Saudi telecommunications, and new standards for transparency and dissemination of economic and financial data. It also reviews educational stipends and some aspects of educational quality.[19]

The Economic Consultative Commission (ECC)

The SEC has a sixteen-member affiliate body called the Economic Consultative Commission (ECC), which was also formed in September 1999.[20] The ECC is made up of nongovernmental experts and provides the chairman of the SEC with advice. It meets at least once a week.[21] Combined with the SEC, the ECC serves as an answer to calls for allowing greater participation of citizens in policy making, especially in economic issues.

These councils were created by Crown Prince Abdullah to encourage Saudi businessmen to invest more money into the Saudi economy, rather than keep their capital overseas.[22] The councils, however, are only beginning to have a significant impact, and the ECC has been criticized for not involving more experienced members of the Saudi business community.[23] According to Dr. Abdulaziz Muhammad al-Dukhail, president of the Saudi-based Consulting Center for Finance and Investment, "Privatization is one of the slowest moving areas in Saudi Arabia. Maybe the [newly established] Supreme Economic Council (SEC) can speed it up, but so far it is not taking the role it should and it is not a very active stream of change."[24]

The Supreme Council for Petroleum and Minerals (SCPM)

Saudi Arabia has taken a number of steps to try to improve the management of its petroleum and minerals programs. It first established Supreme Consultative Council in 1992, and then strengthened the new organization in 1996. It announced the creation of an eleven-member Supreme Council for Petroleum and Minerals Affairs (SCPM) on January 4, 2000.

The members include the king as chairman and the crown prince as deputy chairman, with the second vice premier as second deputy chairman. Its membership includes six ministers and the president of Saudi Aramco.

The creation of the SCPM created a body in charge of all matters related to petroleum, gas, and other hydrocarbon affairs in onshore and offshore areas. It has the mission of developing and managing a long-term strategy for the development of both petroleum and minerals, and reviews international draft agreements. It is responsible for the general policy of Saudi Aramco, including five-year plans, crude oil production and exploration, the five-year capital investment program, and the company's capital position.

While the primary responsibility of the SCPM is the petroleum sector, which is described in Chapter 7, it also is pushing for the development of the mining industry. Its mission statement also includes helping to support Saudi Arabia's effort to restructure its economy and accelerate private sector involvement in the country's energy sector.

This council approved a major initiative in January 2000 to open up part of Saudi Arabia's gas industry to foreign investment, which led to the new pattern of foreign investment in the gas sector described in the next chapter.[25] It quickly issued invitations to international oil companies (IOC) to resume talks on investment proposals for the energy sector. This move was made to overcome the resistance of anti-privatization forces, and in response to the rejection by the technical committee, consisting of Saudi Aramco staff, of initial proposals made by IOCs in September 1998. To catalyze the process, Foreign Affairs Minister Prince Saud al-Faisal was appointed to head the ministerial committee to report on the investment proposals. The council has proved instrumental in rapidly pushing through measures to reform foreign investment laws.[26]

The SCPM has approved a detailed petroleum strategy for the Kingdom that will be reviewed every two years. Additionally, it has made significant progress in other areas:

- In the spring of 2000, Prince Saud announced increased opportunities for foreign investment in the gas sector:
  - "For areas where Saudi Aramco, the national oil company, is currently producing natural gas, foreign companies would be given opportunities for investment in the in the post-production phases."
  - "For areas where gas has been discovered, but not yet exploited, foreign companies will be allowed to contribute in its development as well as participate in post-production."
  - "For areas where gas has not yet been discovered, foreign companies will have the chance to invest in exploration, in addition to development, production and post-production."[27]

- In November 2000, the council approved individual foreign company participation in three core upstream gas projects.

- In June 2000, the Kingdom selected three foreign companies for the upstream gas projects, although completion of the actual deals was still pending in October 2002.

A Saudi government press release on an SCPM meeting in August 2000 exaggerates some aspects of how the council operates, but does give a clearer picture of its functions and the kind of strategic decisions it reviews:

Custodian of the Two Holy Mosques King Fahd bin Abdulaziz, who is also President of the Supreme Council for Petroleum and Minerals (SCPM), today chaired a meeting of the council, which reiterated the continuing Saudi policy on oil that aims at realizing a balance in global markets in a way that preserves the interests of petroleum-exporting countries, ensures continued international economic growth, and stabilizes supplies and prices at reasonable levels in line with the June 2000 agreement reached by the member states of the Organization of Petroleum Exporting Countries (OPEC).

Minister of Petroleum and Mineral Resources Ali bin Ibrahim Al-Naimi was urged to continue to work for realization of these goals through collaboration with OPEC member states for a suitable increase in production in a way that restores balance to the oil market and stabilizes prices. He was also urged to review suitable mechanisms for realizing this stability while continuing coordination with other oil-producing countries, both OPEC and non-OPEC.

The council welcomed the upcoming Second OPEC Summit in Caracas, Venezuela, and hoped that the conference would culminate in success as regards evaluation of its experiences and readiness to deal with future developments.

In his report, SCPM Secretary-General Dr. Mutlab Al-Nafeesa said the council had discussed the following topics:

First: The Kingdom's oil strategy as prepared by the Ministry of Petroleum and Mineral Resources and revised by the ministerial committee. This strategy stems from the strategic goals of the development plans, which have focused on developing human resources, improving the standard of living, diversifying the base of the national economy, enhancing infrastructure, and broadening the role of the private sector.

The strategy covers the Kingdom's distinguished role in the oil market and its continued cooperation with various countries both inside and outside OPEC for stabilization of that market, guaranteeing oil supplies to consuming countries and building an integrated petroleum industry that contributes positively to the process of economic development. The strategy aims at safeguarding the share of petroleum in global energy consumption, and at safeguarding the Kingdom's share in the world oil market.

The strategy, on the other hand, encourages research aimed at diversification of petroleum usage, improvement of its products, and their conformity with environmental standards.

The strategy appreciates the pioneering role of Saudi Aramco in exploring oil reserves throughout the Kingdom and in developing the sectors of refining and local marketing, and its participation in joint projects in petroleum operations both with the Saudi private sector and with international oil companies. The strategy focuses on enabling the private sector to contribute to the development of services and supporting industries.

The strategy underscores the importance of cooperation with the concerned state authorities for realization of optimum energy use in addition to continued training and rehabilitation of Saudi cadres in the technologies of the oil industry and its marketing.

Second: The working plan for Saudi Aramco 2000–2004, which includes: Application of a great many new technologies for increasing its productive capacity and reducing its costs; Continued evaluation of the company's selection of suitable grades of oil, whose prices are reflected by market conditions; Increase of supplies of natural gas for boosting industrial development in the Kingdom; Preservation of reasonable levels of productive capacity so as to enable the Kingdom to meet world demand and confront any adverse impact on the situation of the petroleum market; Production and marketing of profitable crude oil, and making lead-free gasoline available in the local market by 2001; Development of security and safety measures and preservation of the environment; Continued development of the skills of Saudi employees so as to enable them to occupy posts at all levels, with the percentage of nationals in the work force expected to reach 87 percent by 2005.

Third: The Saudi Aramco Annual Report for 1999, which included the following achievements:

- Inauguration of the Al-Shaybah field in the Empty Quarter, by Crown Prince Abdullah bin Abdulaziz, Deputy Prime Minister and Commander of the National Guard;

- Development of Ras-Tanura refinery, and the pipeline for transportation of petroleum products from Dhahran to Riyadh and Qassim;

- Expansion projects for the gas laboratory at Al-Juaymah and for the treatment utilities at the gas laboratories at Al-Othmaniya and Beiri, and commencement of setting up the gas laboratory at Al-Hawiyya.

Dr. Al-Nafisa went on to say that the council adopted a number of decisions, including the following:

- Approval of the Kingdom's oil strategy;

- Approval of the working plan for Saudi Aramco for 2000 to 2004, and for the work of the preparatory committee to continue with study of comments concerning the plan;

- Approval of the annual report of the company for 1999; and

- Approval of the general budget of the company.

Formation of a committee comprised of representatives from the Ministries of Petroleum and Mineral Resources, Finance and National Economy,

Industry and Electricity, and Agriculture and Water, the executive official of the assigned team for negotiations with international petroleum companies, and a representative from the experts commission at the cabinet for consideration of ways to supervise gas supplies and their prices. The committee will consult the concerned persons and specialists in both government and non-government sectors and then submit its recommendations to the SCPM within a period not exceeding 90 days.

It is obvious that the primary function of the council is to review and coordinate the plans prepared by Saudi technocrats. However, a review of reports of its meetings through April 2002 reveals that it has continued to focus on energy strategy, major energy investments, OPEC issues and quotas, and the possible role of private foreign and domestic firms and capital in developing the energy sector.

This included approval of the eight international firms that the Kingdom announced were selected to invest in the Saudi gas sector on May 18, 2001. A Saudi press release on that date stated that Prince Saud had headed a national team that had been negotiating with the international oil companies, together with Minister of Petroleum and Minerals Ali al-Naimi, Minister of Industry and Electricity Dr. Hashim al-Yamani, Minister of Finance and National Economy Dr. Ibrahim al-Assaf, and Minister of Planning Khalid Qusaibi. It stated that the SCPM had approved the selection of Exxon-Mobil, Royal Dutch Shell, British Petroleum, Phillips, Enron, Occidental, TotalFinaElf and Conoco. Dr. Abdulrahman al-Tuwaijri was the secretary general.[28]

The Saudi Arabian General Investment Authority (SAGIA)

The Council of Ministers established the Saudi Arabian General Investment Authority (SAGIA) on April 10, 2000. The creation of the SAGIA followed several previous steps toward reform:

- In 1998, the government corporatized the telecommunications component of the Ministry of Posts, Telephones, and Telegraphs, and established the Saudi Telecommunications Company (STC).
- In November 1999, the government initiated a program to encourage foreign investment by permitting foreign investors permitted to invest in local shares through established open-ended mutual funds.
- In November 1999, the government announced it would implement the unification of GCC customs tariffs by March 2005.
- In December 1999, Saudi Arabia issued a budget for 2000 that called for only a 2% increase in government spending, that had conservative assumptions about oil revenues, and that required a Ministerial Committee to approve a new privatization strategy.

The creation of the SAGIA provided a centralized body to create new incentives for foreign investment and an incentive for the indirect repatriation of part of $600 to $850 billion in Saudi private investment outside Saudi Arabia.[29] The Council of Ministers gave the SAGIA the task of preparing and submitting government policies in development and increasing foreign investment for submission to the SEC, preparing executive plans and rules for investment, making decisions on investment applications and their cancellation, proposing lists of activities to be excluded from foreign investment, preparing studies on investment opportunities and their promotion, coordinating these activities with other government authorities, establishing suitable domestic and foreign conferences, and creating suitable databases and statistics.[30]

SAGIA was also charged with establishing a "one-stop-shop" for foreign investors. This had representatives from sixteen government agencies. The goal was to reduce red tape by making a single agency responsible for approving and overseeing each foreign investment project. The mission of the SAGIA also included facilitating and shortening government approval procedures, seeking to reduce the time for approval to thirty days, providing information to foreign companies and investors, and creating service centers at the chambers of commerce and industry in Riyadh, Jeddah, and Dammam.[31]

The SAGIA is headed by Prince Abdullah bin Faisal bin Turki, a younger prince who worked his way to the leadership of the Royal Commission in Jubail and Yanbu—one of Saudi Arabia's largest single efforts at economic development—and who is highly regarded by both Saudi technocrats and foreign businessmen. Prince Abdullah is a good example of the kind of new leadership needed to make Saudi economic reform work. He was born in 1951, making him part of a new generation of royal technocrats. He studied engineering in Saudi Arabia and the United Kingdom, and joined the Royal Commission in Jubail and Yanbu in 1975, shortly after its creation. He coordinated many of the development studies for the two cities and later became responsible for industrial safety. He was made acting secretary general of the commission in 1985, and became the permanent secretary general in 1987. In 1991, he became the chief executive officer and chairman of the board of directors. On his appointment to SAGIA, he was given ministerial rank.

Unlike some aspects of Saudi reform efforts, SAGIA has been aggressive in performing its mission and granting investment licenses, and is now a major force in both reducing the barriers to foreign and domestic investment and in expediting individual projects. It works closely with U.S., European, and other potential investors, and Prince Abdallah has become one of Saudi Arabia's most effective spokesmen in promoting the Kingdom.

Nevertheless—as is discussed in more detail in Chapter 7—progress has been slow. The events of September 11, 2001, have had a serious impact on the global economy that has interacted with the collapse of the technology sector and stock boom in the West. Outsiders have been more reluctant to invest in the Kingdom, while Saudis have taken private capital out of the United States without repatriating it to the Kingdom or repatriating it in ways that involve productive investment. Regulatory and bureaucratic barriers have proven hard to reduce at the rate required. Lead projects like foreign investment in Saudi Arabia's gas production sector have been delayed by politics and disputes over issues like the size of the reserves involved and return on investment (ROI).

A New Foreign Direct Investment Code and Other Measures

Saudi Arabia has implemented a new foreign investment code that gives foreign investors the same benefits, incentives, and guarantees offered to Saudi Arabians and companies. The law allows foreigners to own property either independently or with a Saudi partner. It allows investors to remit funds abroad and reduces taxes by 15% for foreign companies with an annual profit in excess of SR 100,000 ($26,700).[32]

The Provisions of the New Foreign Investment Law

Minister for Finance and National Economy Ibrahim al-Assaf announced the new Foreign Direct Investment Code on April 10, 2000. It contained the following changes:[33]

- It calls for rapid decisions—SAGIA must make decisions within thirty days after receiving the required documents. If no decision is otherwise taken, SAGIA should approve the request. It must provide reasons for any rejection and provide a method for appeal.
- A foreign investor may obtain more than one license for various activities, and licensed investments may be both joint ventures or fully owned enterprises. A licensed project enjoys all benefits, incentives, and guarantees enjoyed by a national project.
- A foreign investor may freely transfer the proceeds of a sale of its share, profits, and benefits from liquidation.
- A licensed enterprise may own the necessary premises and real estate.
- Sponsorship of the foreign investor and non-Saudi personnel will be by the licensed enterprise.
- No investment may be sequestered except by a legal award, and a foreign investor may appeal such an award to the Grievance Bureau.
- Amendments to the country's tax rates on foreign business profits to not exceed 30% from the previous ceiling of 45%.
- Changes in legislation allow foreign companies 100% ownership of projects and property ownership, compared to the previous limit of 49% stake in joint ventures requiring a Saudi sponsor.

- The Saudi Industrial Development Fund (SIDF) is understood to have confirmed that foreign businesses now qualify for SIDF soft loans, even if the corporation is 100% foreign owned.

Reductions in Taxes

The Council of Minister issued a resolution on April 10, 2000, saying the state would bear 15% of taxes on corporate profits over SR 100,000 per year. The tax for profits of SR 100,001 to SR 500,000 was reduced from 35% to 20%. It was also reduced from 40% to 25% for profits of SR 5001,000 to SR 1,000,000, and from 45% to 30% for profits above SR 1 million.[34]

In a speech on April 15, 2001, Ibrahim al-Assaf stated that that a new regulation was under consideration by the Supreme Economic Council that would cap the tax rate at 30% of the net profits of foreign companies and foreign partners in joint ventures. This move was consistent with efforts to make the system more competitive, and followed the revocation in the New Investment Law of the ten-year and five-year tax exemptions. He explained that the government was assuming liability for fifteen percentage points of net profits above SR 100,000 as a transitional measure, which would in effect limit the tax burden to a maximum of 30% of net profits as compared with the current rates. These were 25% up to SR 100,000; 35% from SR 100,000 to SR 500,000; 40% from SR 500,000 to SR 1 million; and 45% over SR 1 million.

In addition, he said that losses would be permitted to be carried over from year to year for an indefinite period of time, instead of being limited to one year. Dr. al-Assaf further explained that the provisions of this decree, which took effect on April 10, 2000, would apply to all foreign taxpayers in Saudi Arabia. Current investors who enjoy tax exemptions granted under the old investment law will, however, continue to do so until such exemptions expire.[35]

Foreign Ownership of Real Estate

On July 10, 2000, the Council of Ministers amended the real estate laws to allow foreigners to own real estate for their enterprises although investments above SR 30 million require approval by the Council of Ministers. Foreigners may own their house of residence with clearance from the Ministry of the Interior. Property in Mecca and Medina is exempted, but non-Saudi Muslims may rent land for up to two years.[36]

Fund for the Development of Human Resources

On July 31, 2000, the Council of Ministers established a Fund for the Development of Human Resources under the chairmanship of the minister of the interior. The purpose of the fund was to facilitate the employment and training of Saudi citizens for work in the private sector. This fund can be used to extend subsidies for qualification and training, share in the cost of qualification and training, pay a percentage of salaries for up to two years, support and finance field programs, loan funds for training, and conduct suitable research to set goals for such activities.

"Negative List" of Areas Excluded from Foreign Investment

These were all important steps in improving the climate for foreign investment, but the SEC did retain a long "negative list" of areas where foreign investors could not invest in the Kingdom. This list included:

- Oil exploration, drilling, and production, except the services related to the mining sector listed in international industrial classification codes.
- Manufacturing of military equipment, devices, and uniforms.
- Manufacturing of civilian explosives.
- Catering to military sectors.
- Security and detective services.
- Insurance services.
- Real estate investment in Mecca and Medina.
- Tourist orientation and guidance services related to the Hajj and Umrah.
- Recruitment and employment services including local recruitment offices.
- Real estate brokerage.
- Printing and publishing.
- Distribution services, wholesale and retail trade (including medical retail services such as private pharmacies), and commercial agencies, except franchise rights listed by international industrial classifications, with foreign ownership not exceeding (49%), and the granting of one franchise to each area.
- Audiovisual and media services.
- Primary, secondary, and adult education.
- Telecommunications services.
- Land and air transportation.
- Transmission and distribution of electrical power.
- Satellite transmission services.
- Pipeline services.
- Services rendered by midwives, nurses, natural therapists, and paramedics listed at 93191 by international classification codes.
- Fisheries.
- Blood banks, poison centers, and quarantines.

More generally, the foreign community has repeatedly warned the Saudi government that the investment law will not have its desired effect until the Saudi courts operate with a more consistent approach toward commercial law, and until the government actually enforces the decisions of the courts. This is scarcely an unusual problem in developing countries, where policy-level investment incentive programs and reforms are often paralyzed, in practice, by a combination of bureaucratic and permitting delays and by the government's failure to develop and enforce anything approaching an effective uniform commercial code. The fact remains, however, that Saudi Arabia only began to solve its many permitting and bureaucratic delay problems by creating SAGIA and still had failed to create a working legal system for steps as basic as debt collection and contract enforcement as of the spring of 2002.

A Saudi proposal to tax the income of foreign workers earning more than $800 (SR 3,500) a month at 2.5%, which was issued in early 2002, also produced some hostile reaction. The tax potentially affects some 1.7 million foreign businessmen, out of roughly 6 million "legal" foreign workers, many of who already paid some form of tax abroad. On the other hand, the resulting rate was far lower than the level of taxation in many other countries. The Saudis paid a 2.5% religious tax, or *zakat*, and the Saudi government was still earning a little under 5% of nonoil government revenues.[37]

It is hard to put Saudi Arabia's needs and current levels of investment in perspective. Saudi data shows that the average annual growth of private fixed capital formation grew by 4.7% between 1969 and 2000, but such growth effectively peaked relative to demand in 1985, at SR 65.1 billion, as measured in 1994 constant riyals. Saudi Arabia did not exceed this total until 2000, and the estimate of SR 67.0 billion for 2000 is uncertain. Some growth did take place during the 1990s, but it was erratic between 1992 and 1999, and the figure ranged from SR 55.5 to 63.3 billion. This is very limited compared to the types of needs projected in the Saudi development plans, although the plan sets no investment goals as specific numbers.[38]

Another way to look at the issue is growth in factory capital and size. Data are not available in constant riyals, but other Saudi data show substantial growth in operating capital up to 1993, and little real growth after that time:[39]

- Saudi Arabia had 199 factories in 1970, with a total operating capital of 2.8 billion current Saudi riyals and total manpower of 13,865.

- Saudi Arabia had 734 factories in 1975, with a total operating capital of 6.3 billion current Saudi riyals and total manpower of 27,978.

- Saudi Arabia had 1,196 factories in 1980, with a total operating capital of 21.1 billion current Saudi riyals and total manpower of 75,334.

- Saudi Arabia had 1,298 factories in 1985, with a total operating capital of 96.5 billion current Saudi riyals and total manpower of 145,299.

- Saudi Arabia had 1,800 factories in 1975, with a total operating capital of 150.1 billion current Saudi riyals and total manpower of 183,011.

- Saudi Arabia had 2,647 factories in 1994, with a total operating capital of 215.8 billion current Saudi riyals, and total manpower of 213,039.

- By the year 2000, however, Saudi Arabia had 3,207 factories, with a total manpower of 293,971, but total operating capital was still only SR 231.9 billion.

There has been considerable foreign investment activity in Saudi Arabia despite these problems, and foreign investors do participate in a significant number of joint ventures. The bad news is that the number of foreign companies remains very limited and the growth of joint ventures lags far behind the levels the Kingdom needs. There is a clear need for reform if Saudi Arabia is to get the level of investment it needs, both from outside and inside the Kingdom:[40]

- Saudi Arabia had 923 operating companies in 1972, the first year for which data are available, with a total operating capital of 1.3 billion current Saudi riyals. Roughly thirty-four of these companies were foreign with capital investments of SR 0.13 billion. There were 108 joint ventures with a capital of SR 0.26 billion.

- By 1985, Saudi Arabia had 6,268 operating companies, with a total operating capital of 78.7 billion current Saudi riyals. Only fourteen of these companies were foreign, with capital investments of SR 0.05 billion. However, there were 1,260 joint ventures with a capital of SR 15.3 billion.

- By 1990, Saudi Arabia had 6,621 operating companies, with a total operating capital of 94.9 billion current Saudi riyals. Only twenty-one of these companies were foreign, with capital investments of SR 0.12 billion. There were 1,093 joint ventures with a capital of SR 17.2 billion.

- By 1995, Saudi Arabia had 8,319 operating companies, with a total operating capital of 142.5 billion current Saudi riyals. By this timer, 109 of these companies were foreign, with capital investments of SR 1.0 billion. There 1,062 joint ventures with a capital of SR 23.1 billion.

- In 2000, Saudi Arabia had 10,179 operating companies, with a total operating capital of 162.9 billion current Saudi riyals. A total of 144 of companies were foreign, with capital investments of SR 1.1 billion. This was a token increase in foreign companies as a percentage of total companies in 1972, and their capital investments in the Kingdom had experienced only limited real growth since 1994. There were 1,219 joint ventures with a capital of SR 30.4 billion—still very limited.

Saudi Efforts to Join the WTO

Saudi Arabia's efforts to join the World Trade Organization (WTO) are another important attempt at reform. The Kingdom first applied to join the forerunner of the WTO, the General Agreement on Tariffs and Trade (GATT), in 1993. In November 1999, King Fahd stated that "the world is heading for . . . globalization" and that "it is no longer possible for [Saudi Arabia] to make slow progress."

The Saudi effort to join the WTO is designed to attract foreign investment (up to $200 billion over the next twenty years, according to Foreign Minister Prince Saud; this would include over $100 billion in the power sector alone, plus billions more in petrochemicals and telecommunications). Another goal of Saudi WTO membership is to ensure markets for the country's petrochemical industry and to create new markets in the future.

As part of Saudi Arabia's effort to accede to the WTO, the government has indicated that it will take a phased approach toward:

- Establishing new trademark and intellectual property laws.
- Removing technical barriers to trade by easing travel visa requirements.
- Signing the Information Technology Agreement and phase-in tariff-free trade in information technology equipment.
- Phasing in the Basic Telecommunications Agreement to allow competition in telecommunications services.
- Changing competition laws to provide anti-trust protections and consumer protection in accordance with WTO rules.

The Kingdom reduced most tariffs from 12% to 5% in May 2001. The GCC summit meeting then agreed, in December 2001, that tariffs would be harmonized at 5% throughout the GCC in January 2003, two years earlier than originally planned.[41]

However, progress again has been slower than the Saudi government hoped. Osama Jaffar Faqih, the minister of commerce, noted in an interview in April 2001 that Saudi Arabia was now the only member of the GCC that had not yet joined the WTO, but was the world's sixteenth-largest exporter in 2000 (SR 190 billion), and the twenty-third-largest importer (SR 112.5 billion). He noted that the Kingdom had been pursuing membership in the WTO for four years because

> Saudi Arabia's accession would help ensure its integration into the multilateral trading system and maintain the momentum for economic development. It would allow greater transparency and more open policies. Membership of the WTO would lock in the ambitious economic reform program that Saudi Arabia is undertaking. It is a reassurance that this process is irreversible. The further opening up of the Saudi market to foreign goods and services will speed up privatization and make Saudi Arabia more attractive for foreign investment.[42]

He blamed the delay in Saudi Arabia's entry on the lack of clear WTO rules, but said that membership was crucial for the Kingdom's economic development.

> Since the beginning of this year, substantial progress has been made toward bringing the negotiations to a successful conclusion. . . . The accession of the Kingdom has moved to an advanced stage and strong momentum has been generated. . . . Intensive negotiations are taking place to arrive at a package of rights and obligations which is balanced and beneficial for the current and future economic needs of Saudi Arabia.

He said that while the WTO's rules were more balanced than those of the GATT, they did not provide the needed flexibility for developing nations.

> The WTO, while priding itself on providing a rule-based system for the conduct of world trade, inter alia the principles of transparency, predictability and mutual advantages, it does not always follow them in practice. . . . In fact, the WTO does not have clear rules and guidance on accession. . . . [T]he accession process is hampered and prolonged by the absence of such rules and criteria.[43]

Saudi Arabia originally hoped to be admitted to the WTO by the end of 2000, but entry was delayed by a variety of issues, including Saudi willingness to increase market access to its banking, finance, and upstream oil sectors and the failure to issue new anti-trust regulations. Until 2001, Saudi officials continued to meet with various negotiators, including those from the European Union.[44] The Kingdom also sought negotiate and finalize the Working Party Report and the Protocol of Accession, and some Saudi officials still hope the Kingdom could be admitted to the WTO by the end of 2002.[45]

In practice, however, other nations felt Saudi Arabia sought unrealistic concessions and attempted to disguise efforts to limit compliance by making claims that such concessions are necessary for cultural and religious regions. As a result no Working Party meetings were held in 2001 or through August 2002.[46]

If Saudi Arabia does enter the WTO, this should help increase Saudi Arabia's volume of trade, but it does present several negotiating, cultural-religious, and economic problems. While Saudi officials tend to blame the WTO for being insensitive to Saudi restrictions on non-Islamic imports (like alcohol) and religious problems in dealing with interest and insurance, WTO negotiators indicate that the Kingdom has not yet been willing to show that it will grant the required access to its banking, finance, and upstream oil sectors. The negotiators called for better copyright laws; tribunals to rule on trade disputes; and new legislation on technical trade barriers, customs evaluation, and food health regulations. Additionally, they called for the Kingdom to limit tariffs to 15% and to agree to several sectoral initiatives, including an Information Technology Agreement, chemical harmonization, a government procurement agreement, and agreements on textiles, pharmaceuticals, medical and construction equipment, and publishing services.

WTO membership also threatens some local businesses. Some Saudi firms are designed to function in a secure environment protected by high tariffs and monopoly agency agreements. A number of manufacturing enterprises fall under this category, and their managers are deeply worried that having to operate in a WTO environment would put them out of business.[47] Opening up the economy to foreign multinationals and imports will threaten their profit margins and the commercial agencies' monopoly.

The Supreme Commission for Tourism

The Kingdom created a Supreme Commission for Tourism, chaired by Prince Sultan bin Salman, on April 17, 2000. The Supreme Commission for Tourism was given a board of directors and secretariat and made responsible for surveying all existing tourist activity by region, promoting tourism, planning regional tourist infrastructure, removing barriers to tourist activities, extending incentives to investors, creation a comprehensive plan to encourage tourism, creating a central information center, and coordinating government and private sector efforts.[48]

As part of the Kingdom's efforts, visas for pilgrims have been extended from fifteen to thirty days, and pilgrims are now allowed to visit other parts of the Kingdom besides Mecca and Medina.[49] In addition, Saudia Airlines and other Saudi tourism organizations were allowed to create package tours for non-Muslims, and the government made a deliberate effort to open pre-Islamic sites to foreign tourists.

The potential importance of this Saudi initiative is demonstrated by the fact the government estimated that Saudis spent some $15 billion a year on travel outside the Kingdom, and that internal tourism was one of the most job-intensive single areas where the government could encourage investment. It is far from clear that the government can meet its goal of reducing Saudi tourism spending abroad by 10% to 25% during the initial phases of its national tourism plan or come close to raising the tourism sector to 7.3% of the GDP or 6.5% of total employment opportunities— particularly if government subsidized activity related to the Hajj is excluded.

The Supreme Commission for Tourism's estimates that the Kingdom has some 10,000 tourist spots, including places of historic and cultural importance, is also almost certainly exaggerated. Nevertheless, the Kingdom does have many real potential tourist attractions, particularly for Islamic tourists, and can benefit from linking tourism throughout the Kingdom to the greater and lesser Hajj. Some pre-Islamic sites are of interest to Western tourists, and the Kingdom unquestionably has some of the best scuba diving areas in the world on its Red Sea coast. Tourism revenues may never give the Kingdom the level of revenue it is seeking from this sector, but they did increase from SR 3.8 billion in 1992, to SR 6.1 billion in 1999 and SR 6.75 billion in 2000.[50]

Saudi Efforts to Use the GCC to Strengthen the Saudi and Gulf Economies

Saudi Arabia has sought to strengthen regional trade and create a customs union among the Gulf Cooperation Council (GCC) countries. Currently, goods from GCC countries are exempt from all Saudi import duties as long as 40% of their value has been added within the GCC and the producing company is owned by at least 51% by GCC citizens. The Kingdom acted to establish free trade zones in the ports of Jeddah and Dammam, which were to gradually evolve from being used for re-export and warehousing to become full free trade ports.[51]

In November 1999, King Fahd called for improved regional unity among Gulf States—economically, politically, and militarily. In December 1999, the GCC agreed on a customs union. This customs union is expected to come into force by 2005, adopting a unified import tariff. In May 2001, Saudi Arabia began to move toward the customs union by announcing new regulations to ease the import of goods from other GCC states under preferential tariffs. These regulations dropped a requirement that imports were only eligible if they were made by firms owned by Gulf citizens. Instead, all goods were made eligible with 40% value added in the other GCC states.

These steps moved the Kingdom toward a GCC-wide goal of a tariff union limited to 5.5% to 7.5% tariffs by 2005.[52] They also affected a trade balance that ranged from SR 8 to SR 10 billion annually in Saudi imports from other GCC states, and around SR 7 billion in exports. This represented around 8% to 10% of total Saudi imports (although many were essentially reexports), and 3% to 5% of Saudi exports.[53] In addition to improving the potential for trade and private enterprise activity on a GCC-wide bases, they were designed to help move the Kingdom and other GCC states toward a free trade agreement with the European Union and help ease the Kingdom's entry to the WTO.[54] Moreover, in December 2001, the GCC accelerated the date for such a union from March 2005 to January 2003.[55] If such a union actually increases productive intra-GCC trade and helps reduce dependence on non-GCC labor, the GCC may be able to move on to goals like the creation of a common currency and productive trade agreements with other blocs like the EU.

Future Reforms Now Under Consideration

Useful as some of Saudi Arabia's recent efforts have been, both Saudi and foreign experts agree that the Kingdom still has a long way to go before the government both fully implements the reforms it has already begun and implements other steps that are critical to creating the broader climate needed to restructure and diversify its economy. The government has announced, however, that it does have a number of further reforms in preparation. As of the fall of 2002, these reforms included:[56]

- The effort to accede to the WTO described earlier, plus the drafting of suitable anti-trust regulations.
- Reforming the company law to modernize it and existing regulations. This law is in draft and would modernize the regulations for establishing business entities.
- Improving the capital markets and stock market law by establishing a stock exchange supervisory commission, regulating fixed income markets, and developing a bond market.
- A major gas initiative, allowing foreign companies to develop natural gas production facilities and domestic uses for the gas, and potentially the single largest investment initiative in the Kingdom since the creation of the infrastructure for oil production.
- Privatization at various levels and phases of telecommunications, electric power, the national airline, postal services, railways, port services, and many other smaller state-owned assets.
- Reforming the agency law to reduce the requirements for local agents.
- Reviewing the tax law.
- Developing new laws for e-commerce.
- Creating an arbitration center.
- Changing the sponsorship law to allow companies to be their own sponsors, and liberalize the sponsorship requirements for foreign workers.
- Altering the mining law to make domestic and foreign private sector investment in minerals easier.
- Changing competition laws to provide anti-trust protections and consumer protection in accordance with WTO rules.
- Revising labor laws to rationalize employment procedures and increase labor mobility.
- Modernizing the mortgage law.
- Issuing a law allowing toll roads.
- Establishing a new cooperative health insurance law. The current draft of the law will require the 5 to 6 million expatriate workers to have private health insurance, replacing the existing system where employers are responsible for the medical costs and expatriates have some access to free medical care. The new law is intended to aid private hospitals to become revenue earners.

- Increasing market regulation in the insurance sector, as it wants to broaden the coverage of existing private health insurance. (Out of the eighty active local firms, only the state-owned National Company for Co-operative Insurance is licensed to operate.)[57]
- Moving toward a GCC customs union in 2003 and a common currency in 2010.

There is no question that the Kingdom is making progress, and it is clearly setting many of the right priorities and goals. The practical problem for the Kingdom is the need to match the pace of reform to the pace of demographic need, and to compensate for the underfunding of investment in infrastructure and government services during the 1990s. This is still possible, but the Kingdom's progress continues to lag behind requirement. Like reform in virtually all other countries—including those in the West—the Kingdom also is finding that it is one thing to issue decrees and legislation and another to actually change bureaucratic procedures, see reform translated into action, and remove a host of minor barriers in terms of paper work, permits, and fees.

PUTTING CURRENT SAUDI EFFORTS IN PERSPECTIVE: PLANS AND GOALS VERSUS ACTIONS AND ACHIEVEMENTS

Saudi Arabia has some of the most sophisticated development planning of any nation in the developing world, and certainly in the Middle East. As is the case with its economic reforms, however, good intentions and good plans are never enough. Anyone who studies the past performance of Saudi five-year development plans, and the reforms called for in these plans, discovers that that reform efforts have never before had the necessary continuing support to ensure they are implemented, particularly if the economy benefits from relatively high world oil prices.

Saudi leaders have often set the right priorities in times of economic pressure, or when the issue was writing a plan versus taking difficult and unpopular action. They have then failed to act or eased the pace of reforms whenever they have created political difficulties or in periods when as petroleum revenues rise and the signs of prosperity return. As is the case with every government in the world, it is all too easy to delay the political and economic cost of reforms when money is available. It takes real courage to persevere consistently over a broad front and over time.

The History of Saudi Planning: The First through Fourth Development Plans

A review of Saudi development planning provides a clearer picture of the Kingdom's ability to restructure its economy as well as explains the key priorities in its current development plans. Saudi Arabia has a long history of systematic development planning, and has issued seven five-year plans over a period of three decades. Its First Development Plan was prepared in 1970 (1390/1391), and each of the plans since that time has had a social and institutional dimension as well as an economic dimension.

In broad terms, Saudi Arabia has defined the same major strategic objectives for each of its seven plans:

- To safeguard Islamic values and confirm Allah's Shari'a.
- To defend the Faith and the Nation; to uphold security and social stability; and to deepen the values of national loyalty and belonging.
- To improve the standard and quality of life.
- To develop human resources, increase productivity, and replace non-Saudi manpower with qualified Saudis.
- To realize balanced growth throughout all the regions of the Kingdom.
- To diversify the economic base and to reduce dependence on the production and export of crude oil through development of other natural resources and promotion of other economic activities.
- To provide a favorable environment for the activities of the private sector, and to encourage it to play a leading role in the development process.
- To enhance the Kingdom's position within the global economy, promote economic integration among the GCC countries, and strengthen economic cooperation with other Arab and Islamic countries.

As Table 6.2 shows, the First Development Plan (1970–1974) involved expenditures of SR 34.1 billion and emphasized the Kingdom's rapid transformation into a more advanced nation by focusing on providing a modern infrastructure and basic government services such as water supply and electricity generation, as well as expanding social services and developing human resources. Some 41.4% of total expenditure went to infrastructure versus 27.7% for economic resources, 20.6% for human resources, and 10.3% for social and health development.

The Second Development Plan (1975–1979) came after the explosive rise in oil prices following the oil embargo in 1973 and involved total expenditures of SR 347.2 billion—more than ten times the total expenditures of the first. Some 49.3% of total expenditure went to infrastructure versus 28.0% for economic resources, 14.7% for human resources, and 8.0% for social and health development. As in the First Plan, the development of an integrate infrastructure was designed to accelerate socioeconomic development and was given top priority. The Second Development Plan differed sharply from the First Plan, however, in the fact it could be executed in a period where there were far fewer financial constraints The Second Development Plan focused on four major directions:

Table 6.2
Expenditures During the Saudi Development Plans

Expenditures	Economic Resources Development SR Billion	(%)	Human Resources Development SR Billion	(%)	Social and Health Development SR Billion	(%)	Infrastructure Development SR Billion	(%)	Total SR Billion	(%)
First Development Plan: 1970–1974 (Actual)	9.5	27.7	7.0	20.6	3.5	10.3	14.1	41.4	34.1	100
Second Development Plan: 1975–1979 (Actual)	97.3	28.0	51.0	14.7	27.6	8.0	171.3	49.3	347.2	100
Third Development Plan: 1980-1984 (Actual)	192.2	30.7	115.0	18.4	61.2	9.8	256.8	41.1	635.2	100
Fourth Development Plan: 1985–1989 (Actual)	71.2	20.4	115.1	33.0	61.9	17.7	100.7	28.9	348.9	100
Fifth Development Plan: 1990–1994 (Actual)	34.1	10.0	164.6	48.0	68.0	20.0	74.2	22.0	340.9	100
Sixth Development Plan: 1995–1999 (Actual)	48.2	11.5	216.6	51.5	87.5	20.8	68.1	16.2	420.4	100.0
Seventh Development Plan: 2000–2004 (Planned)	41.7	8.5	276.9	56.7	95.8	19.6	73.8	15.2	488.2	100.0

Source: Saudi Ministry of Planning, September 2002.

- The first was expansion of transport, electricity, water and housing infrastructure.

- The second was conservation of hydrocarbon resources, encouragement of energy-intensive industries, and export of high value added products. This direction was supported by the establishment of the Royal Commission for Jubail and Yanbu, in order to create the infrastructure for hydrocarbon industries.

- Third, the plan placed "particular emphasis on the development of financial and administrative policies and regulations in conformity with development requirements and the progress of the national economy, as well as facilitating cooperation between the public and private growth sectors in order to realize higher growth rates." As a result, the plan made a number of proposals to give the Kingdom a modern administrative structure.

- The fourth direction concentrated on supporting and encouraging the private sector, and established specialized credit funds and policies and measures to support private sector activity.

The Third Development Plan (1980–1984) came during a period when oil revenues continued to increase, and involved total expenditures of SR 625.2 billion—nearly twice the total in the Second Plan. Some 41.1% of total expenditure still went to infrastructure versus 30.7% for economic resources, 18.4% for human resources, and 9.8% for social and health development. The preparation of the Third Development Plan occurred during a period when Saudi Arabia had become the largest oil exporter in the world and a major financial power. It also covered a period when the infrastructure and development expenditures of the earlier plans were beginning to have a substantial effect and it was clear that the Kingdom had to make more efficient use of foreign labor. As a result, it focused on making structural changes in the economy by defining oil and gas production levels in ways that would maintain national resources, continuing to build hydrocarbon industries and completing infrastructure projects. The plan also sought to expand growth and development in all regions of the Kingdom, along with efforts to improve administrative organization and government procedures and enhance economic and management efficiency.

The Fourth Development Plan (1985–1989) involved major changes in both the focus and methodology of the plan. The focus shifted away from new investment in infrastructure to operations and maintenance, restructuring the economy to allow the private sector to play a substantial role in the development process and diversifying the production base. This was necessary in part because a major reduction in oil revenues forced total spending in the Fourth Plan to be cut to SR 348.9 billion—a little more than half the total for the Third Plan. At the same time, population growth, a maturing infrastructure base, and the need to deal with a steady rise in the number of Saudi youths shifted spending so that 33% of the Fourth

Plan was spent on human resources development versus 18.4% in the Third Plan, and spending on social and health development rose from 9.8% to 17.7%. Capital investment–heavy activity like infrastructure dropped from 41.1% of total spending to 28.9% and economic resources development dropped from 30.7% to 20.4%. As part of the focus on strengthening the private sector, the methodology of the plan shifted from a central planning and projects-based approach to a program planning method that also gave government agencies more flexibility.

The Fifth Development Plan and the Gulf War

The Fifth Development Plan (1990–1994) was heavily influenced by the Gulf War and by an increasing understanding that the world oil market was highly volatile and that the Kingdom could not count on high oil revenues. It did even more to encourage the private sector to participate in development and sought to encourage the private sector to provide services in areas where the government had traditionally provided services. It placed a high priority on increasing the technology base. In practice, however, low oil revenues forced a number of downward adjustments in government spending and the government had to give priority to human services and shift resources away from development and infrastructure.

The total value of expenditures under the plan was SR 340.9 billion in current riyals, and human resources development rose to 48.0% of the total and social and health development rose to 20.0%. Capital investment–heavy activity like infrastructure dropped to 22% (about half the percentage in the First Plan) and economic resources development dropped to only 10%. While roughly 70% of the First Plan was capital investment–intensive in development, the percentage for the Fifth Plan was closer to 30%.

The Fifth Development Plan is also a case example of good intentions and weak implementation. It was a well-structured plan that set many of the right priorities for development, expansion of the private sector, diversification, and Saudisation. In practice, however, the high cost of Saudi expenditures on the Gulf War during 1990–1991 made the content of the Fifth Plan largely moot and had a powerful impact on the Sixth Development Plan that followed. It also left the country with an estimated $55 billion debt.

The average rate of annual real growth (in constant 1989 prices) in the government petroleum sector during 1990–1994 was sharply affected by a boom in oil revenues during the peak of the Gulf War followed by nearly zero growth during the later part of the plan: It was 25.2% in 1990, 20.4% in 1991, 6.3% in 1992, –3.8% in 1993, and 0.2% in 1994. The Gulf War was so expensive, however, that it more than offset any benefits the Kingdom obtained from high oil revenues. Saudi Arabia sustained large current account deficits in the early 1990s, and official reserves fell from $23 billion in 1987 to only $7.4 billion in December 1994. Saudi Arabia's deficit on account totaled $27.6 billion during the peak war year of 1991, and was still $8.7 billion in 1995. The Kingdom had a surplus of $200 million in 1996, but the deficit totaled more than $3.4 billion in 1997.

Annual average real growth in the nonpetroleum government sector consisted largely of defense expenditures for the Gulf War, followed by growth rates of 0.8% from 1992 to 1994. Growth in the private sector averaged only 1.3% over the entire period of the Fifth Plan. The shifts in both private and public capital expenditure fluctuated sharply by year, depending largely on oil revenues. Gross fixed capital formation had to be war-oriented in many areas, although the average increase in expenditures in the petroleum sector was relatively high except in 1991.[58]

Even so, real economic growth was higher during the Fifth Plan than during the Sixth Development Plan that followed. The total private and government nonoil sectors grew from SR 220.5 billion in 1990 to SR 237.0 billion in 1994 (+7.5%), measured in constant 1989 prices. The oil sector grew from SR 113.6 billion to SR 140.5 billion (+24%), and the entire GDP in purchaser's values grew from SR 341.0 billion to SR 377.4 billion (+11%)[59]

Studies by the World Bank indicate that Saudi Arabia's GDP per capita dropped by an average of 3.3% per year in current dollars during the time period from 1980 to 1992.[60] The World Bank also estimates that Saudi Arabia's GDP experienced an average annual decline of 1.9% from 1985 to 1995, and rose by only 1.9% from 1996 to 1997, when oil prices were relatively high. Even then, demographic pressures cut the Saudi GNP per capita by 1.4%.[61] Furthermore, Saudi Arabia experienced budget deficits in every year but two of the last twenty years.[62]

GDP is an uncertain measure of economic performance in Saudi Arabia, since increases in services subsidized activity, welfare payments and government deficit spending are included, regardless of the fact they scarcely benefit the economy. Even if these problems are ignored, however, Saudi Arabia's performance was not particularly impressive. SAMA reports that the total GDP rose by 1.4% during 1994, 4.3% during 1995, 8.6% during 1996, and 7.1% in 1997, but these figures are much more optimistic than the estimates of the IMF. Like the CIA, the IMF estimates that no real growth took place in 1995, while 1996 saw a growth of 2.5%, and GDP rose 2.0% in 1997.[63] In contrast the EIU estimates 0.5% growth in 1995, 5 % in 1996 and 2.5% in 1997.

The Sixth Development Plan

The Sixth Development Plan eventually involved total expenditures of SR 420.4 billion, nearly SR 80 billion more than the Fifth Plan. Like the Fifth Plan, however, the Sixth Development Plan emphasized human resources and services over investment in development and infrastructure. Human resources development rose to 51.5% of the total and social and health development rose to 20.8%. Capital investment–heavy activity like infrastructure dropped to 16.2% and economic resources development only totaled 11.5%.

The Sixth Development Plan, adopted the following macroeconomic strategy:[64]

- "Real" average growth of 3.9% in the nonoil sector's contribution to the GDP, compared to 3.2% growth during the period of the Fifth Plan.[65]
- Total investment growth of 8.5% per year, amounting to more than 18% of the GDP.
- An average annual growth of nonoil exports of 12% in current prices.
- Increased domestic nonoil revenues for the government.
- Progressive elimination of the budget deficit and balance of payments deficit on current accounts.
- Balanced government budget by the end of the Sixth Development Plan, and rationalization of government expenditure.
- Shift in government expenditures from consumption and current operating expenditures to investment.
- Steady increase in opportunities for the private sector through the gradual and selective use of alternative financing and privatization initiatives.
- Mobilization of the private sector's financial assets by broadening the domestic capital market.
- Reductions in the number of low-skilled foreign workers and increased capability of the Saudi workforce in order to improve productivity.

The Sixth Development Plan sought to increase the Saudi GDP from SR 380.8 billion in 1995 to SR 458.6 billion in 2000, while maintaining an average annual growth rate of 3.8%. Additionally, it called for the nonoil sector to grow from SR 235.9 billion in 1995 to SR 285.1 billion in 2000, while maintaining an average annual growth rate of 3.9%.

The private sector portion of the nonoil sector was planned to grow from SR 169.5 billion Saudi to 209.3 billion, with an average annual growth rate of 4.3%. The oil sector was planned to grow from SR 142.8 billion to SR 172.5 billion, and by an average annual growth rate of 3.8%. In contrast, the government services portion of the nonoil sector was only planned to grow from SR 66.4 billion to SR 75.8 billion, an average annual growth rate of 2.7%.[66] It called for the oil and gas sector to increase from 27% of the GDP in 1990 and 32.9% in 1995, to 33.8% in 2000.[67]

The Sixth Development Plan also called for an average level of 4.2% growth in the producing sectors and 4.4% growth in the service sectors. Meeting these goals required a 3.4% annual increase in private sector investment and a 5.5% annual growth in government investment. Annual private investment was to rise from SR 126.5 billion in 1995 to SR 176.9 billion in 2000; government investment was to rise from SR 273.5 billion in 1995 to SR 335.5 billion in 2000.[68] The government services share of total investment was planned to rise from 18.1% in 1995 to 25.0% in 2000, with much of the producing sector investment in manufacturing to go toward government-run petroleum refining and petrochemical activity. Even if it had been successful, this shift in investment scarcely represented rapid "privatization" and was highly dependent on improved oil revenues. It did not meet the plan's stated goal of increasing the role of the private nonoil sector, which remains at almost exactly the same 10% share of the economy today as it had in 1990.[69]

If one looks at the achievements of the Sixth Development Plan, however, the planned level of real growth and reform did not take place in either the government or private sector. If one accepts Saudi figures, the government calculates that the average rate of annual real growth (in constant 1989 prices) was 0.6% in the government petroleum sector during 1995–1999, 1.8% in the non-petroleum government sector, and 1.3% in the private sector. The shifts in both private and public capital expenditure fluctuated sharply by year, depending largely on oil revenues. The annual rate of government gross fixed capital formation varied from −5.8% to +14.1%. The rate in the oil sector varied from −43/4% to +6.5%, and the rate in the private sector varied from −10.4% to +26.2%.[70]

The total value of private and government nonoil sectors grew from SR 237.9 billion in 1995 to SR 255.7 billion in 1999 (+7.5%), measured in constant 1989 prices. The oil sector grew from SR 140.5 billion to SR 144.5 billion (+2.8%), and the entire GDP in purchaser's values grew from SR 387.3 billion to SR 409.4 billion (+5.7%)[71] Total growth over the period of the Sixth Development Plan was only about half the rate achieved during the Fifth Plan, and well under one-third the rate of population growth.

There were other areas where the Sixth Development Plan failed to set a meaningful course for the nation's future. It required reductions in the past level of subsidies to water-intensive agriculture, but still called for a 3.1% increase in output and for agriculture to increase from 36.9% of the nonoil GDP in 1990 and 38.3% in 1995, to 40.2% in 2000. It is difficult to see how this growth could ever have been achieved without the massive subsidies, as water and fuel are sold far below cost and market prices. The planned growth in the service sector was also highly dependent on import-related income and left the share of government services in 2000 (24.0%) at a level very close to that in 1990 (25.8%).[72] In practice, however, oil revenues and budget problems made many of these issues moot.

In any case, progress fell far short of Saudi goals and the government failed to make most of the reforms necessary for the plan to work. As has been noted, the Gulf War and limited oil revenues still had a lingering impact in the mid-1990s. The crash in oil prices that began in late 1997 then led to a new deficit of US$ 12.9 billion in 1998 and US$ 9.1 billion in 1999.[73] Once again, the Sixth Development Plan demonstrated that good intentions did not pave the road to major progress.

LOOKING AT THE FUTURE: THE SEVENTH DEVELOPMENT PLAN

The goals and policies of the Seventh Development Plan (2000–2004)—which was released in August 1999—again set all of the right priorities, and its expenditure and implementation plans again present the same basic problems. The plan calls for total expenditures of 488.2 billion in current Saudi riyals. This is a nearly SR 60 billion increase over actual expenditures in the Sixth Development Plan, but still means that the Kingdom will spend roughly 60% of the peak expenditures it made in the Third Plan as measured in constant riyals.

As was the case in the Fifth and Sixth Plans, the Seventh Development Plan also emphasizes the need to solve the Kingdom's increasingly urgent human resources problems over investment in development and infrastructure. Human resources development is planned to rise to 56.7% of the total and social and health development is nearly constant at 19.6%. Capital investment–heavy activity like infrastructure is planned to drop to 15.2%—in spite of expanding demand and underinvestment in the maintenance of some key systems like water—and economic resources development is only planned to total 8.5%.[74]

The Macroeconomic Implications of the Seventh Development Plan

Some aspects of the Seventh Development Plan have already been discussed in the previous chapter, but its major macroeconomic goals are:

- Achieve an annual GDP growth of 3.16%, with annual growth in the private sector of 5.04%. Achieve average annual growth rate of 3.44% in the service sector, 3.05% in agriculture, 8.34% in non-mining, and 5.14% in the industrial sector.

- Diversify the economy by attaining a nonoil sector growth of 4.01% per year, expanding the role of the nonoil sector from 68.4% to 71.6% by 2004. Much of this growth should be targeted toward the manufacturing sector, rather than in the service sector.

- Achieve an average annual growth rate of 8.29% in petrochemicals and 7.16% in other manufacturing.

- Increase gas production to develop reserves and domestic use in order to serve development objectives and contribute to the diversification of income sources.

- Enhance the private sector's participation in petroleum industries.
- Consolidate efficiency in production, refining, and distribution.
- Achieve average annual real growth rate of 6.85% in investment; increase investment from 22.7% of GDP in 2000 to 25.4% in 2004, with 71.2% of the total investment in the economy coming from private sector sources.
- Reduce the state budget deficit as a percentage of GDP, from –10.8% in 1999 to zero percent by 2004 through measures such as increasing government nonoil revenues, and rationalizing government expenditures.
- Improve the current account balance, and go from a deficit equal to 3% of GDP in 1999 to a surplus of 6.9% in 2004.
- Increase the role that the Saudi Credit Bank plays in investing in small business.
- Increase the size of the electricity, gas, and water sector by an average annual rate of 4.62% and increase construction on related projects by 6.17%.
- Increase the share of national manpower in total employment from 44.2% to 53.2% and replace 488,600 foreign workers with Saudi nationals.
- Develop human resources and the value of Saudi nationals through programs that expand higher and vocational education, with an increased emphasis on on-the-job training, by increasing technical school enrollment from 33,000 to 55,000.
- Develop a national manpower database to match individuals with appropriate jobs for their level of qualifications.
- Increase the effectiveness of the Saudi health care system, achieving a 95% immunization rate for children and adding 4630 beds to hospitals, including the construction of forty-four new hospitals, each with fifty-bed capacities.
- Increase the amount of transportation infrastructure including roads, highways, and water networks.

The broad macroeconomic goals of the Seventh Development Plan are summarized in Table 6.3. The plan calls for an average annual GDP growth of 3.16%, although even if this goal was achieved it would lag Saudi population growth. The plan only calls for annual average growth in the oil and gas sector of 1.21%. It leaves the burden of growth to the nonoil sectors, which must grow at an average annual rate of 4.10%, so that the nonoil sectors of the GDP must grow from 68.4% in 1999 to 71.6% in 2004. It is important to note that oil refining and petrochemicals are defined as parts of the nonoil sector. Even if they are added to the oil and gas sector, however, they still only account for 35.5% of the GDP in 1999 and 32.7% in 2004.[75]

The other producing sectors must grow at an annual average rate of 5.04%, and the service sector must grow at 3.44%. The bulk of growth is meant to occur in the private sector—with the non-government service sector growing at 5.03% versus 1.21% for the government services sector.

Table 6.3
Macroeconomic Goals of the Seventh Development Plan (in 1414/1415 [1994] Millions of Saudi Riyals)

Sector	Value Added (SR Million)		Share in GDP (%)		Average Annual Growth Rate (%)
	1999	2004	1999	2004	
Crude Oil and Natural Gas	147791	156934	31.0	28.2	1.21
Non-Oil Sectors	325393	397728	68.4	71.6	4.10
Producing Sectors	130505	166901	27.4	30.0	5.04
Agriculture	34666	40282	7.3	7.2	3.05
Non-Oil Mining	2207	3295	0.5	0.6	8.35
Industry	45313	58206	9.5	10.5.	5.14
Oil refining	17146	18064	3.6	3.3	1.05
Petrochemicals	4475	6665	0.9	1.2	8.29
Other manufacturing	23692	33479	5.0	6.0	7.16
Electricity, Gas, and Water	765	959	0.2	0.2	4.62
Construction	47553	64158	10.0	11.6	6.17
Services Sector					
Nongovernment Services	110366	141070	23.2	25.4	5.03
Trade	35899	44117	7.5	7.9	4.21
Transport and Communications	32473	39029	6.8	7.0	3.75
Finance and Real Estate Services	29054	42053	6.1	7.5	7.68
Real-Estate Services	7728	9633	1.6	1.7	4.51
Finance and Business Services	21326	32420	4.5	5.8	8.74
Community and Personal Services	12940	32420	4.5	5.8	8.74
Government Services	84522	89758	17.8	16.3	1.21
Import Duties Less Imputed Bank Services Charge	2489	1038	0.6	0.2	−16.00
Total GDP	475673	555701	100.0	100.0	3.16

Source: English-language version of the *Seventh Development Plan 1420/21–1424/25 AH (2000–2004 AD* (Riyadh: Ministry of Planning, 2001), p. 131.

Nonoil (private sector) mining is planned to grow by an average of 8.29%, petrochemicals by 8.29%, other nonoil manufacturing by 7.16%, and finance and business services by 7.68%. In broader macroeconomic terms, the growth in other manufacturing (less refining and petrochemicals), construction, nongovernment services, nonoil trade, real estate, and finance business services is planned to make up for a lack of growth in all petroleum-related activity and a decline in government services as a share of GDP (17.8% to 16.3%).

Table 6.4 provides an additional perspective by showing the Seventh Development Plan's estimate of capital formation and investment. It shows that gross capital formation is expected to reach SR 671.73 billion during the life of the plan in constant 1994 riyals, and that the nonoil private sector is expected to implement SR 478.48 billion of this total, or 71.2%. The non–oil producing sectors are projected to account for 32.2% of planned investments, and the finance, insurance, real estate, and business sectors to account for 11.8%. The nonoil government services sector will account for 33.41%

Like previous plans, the Seventh Development Plan stresses the importance of a continued drive toward privatization, with the goal of achieving "lower costs, improved [economic] performance, and providing jobs for citizens."[76] Tables 6.3 and 6.4 show, however, that the Seventh Development Plan differs from other plans in the government's sharply growing need for a level of private sector and foreign investment that can alleviate much of its capital budget deficit. It is also clear from the plan that this be accomplished largely by reforms that remove the barriers to foreign and private investment, rather than by direct financial incentives or government-funded programs to encourage investment. At the same time, all of the expenditures and investment proposals in the Seventh Development Plan are increasingly evaluated in terms of their potential effect on the job market and the need to emphasis social and entitlement expenditures, operations, and maintenance—even at the cost of necessary government investment.

Saudi Arabia will continue to make progress under the Seventh Development Plan. In fact, the data in the previous tables and charts show it already has done so. It is doubtful, however, that the Kingdom will meet its goals in replacing government with private and foreign investment, lead to the required growth in the private sector, create the necessary jobs, and make the Seventh Development Plan any more successful than the Fifth or Sixth.

As has been noted earlier, the Saudi investment climate has been sharply affected by the instability in the region, the regional turmoil coming from the Second Intifada, the backlash from the events of September 11, and the uncertainties regarding a U.S.-British attack on Iraq. At the same time, many key elements of government's plans for economic reform legislation already

Table 6.4
Structure of Investment in the Seventh Development Plan (in 1414/1415 [1994] Millions of Saudi Riyals)

Sector	Values in Billions of SR	Share in Total (%)
Crude Oil and Natural Gas	33.41	5.0
Non-Oil Sectors	638.32	95.0
Producing Sectors	222.69	33.2
Agriculture	17.5	2.6
Non-Oil Mining	3.51	0.5
Industry	104.82	15.6
Oil refining	4.93	0.7
Petrochemicals	35.00	5.2
Other manufacturing	64.89	9.7
Electricity, Gas, and Water	79.00	11.8
Construction	17.86	2.7
Services Sector	169.11	25.2
Trade	36.24	5.4
Transport and Communications	33.99	5.1
Finance and Real Estate Services	78.81	11.8
Real-Estate Services	38.81	5.8
Finance and Business Services	40.03	6.0
Community and Personal Services	20.07	3.0
Total Non-Oil Private Sector	478.48	71.2
Government Services	159.83	23.8
Total Investment	671.73	100.0

Source: English-language version of the Seventh Development Plan 1420/21–1424/25 AH (2000–2004 AD) (Riyadh: Ministry of Planning, 2001), p. 140.

lag by one or two years, and the government cannot now come close to meeting many of its goals for privatization and foreign investment in areas like gas. The growth of the producing sectors still calls for excessive growth and investment in agriculture. The other producing sectors, with the exception of construction, are lagging and many activities in the services sector continue to expand demand for imports rather than produce balanced growth.

The Labor Force Implications of the Seventh Development Plan

All of these factors interact with the fact that the Seventh Development Plan reflects all of the demographic, job creation, and educational problems discussed in the pervious chapter (summarized in Table 5.2). The planned rate of job creation in the Seventh Development Plan, however, raises truly serious issues. The average annual rate of job creation is 0.9%, versus a population growth rate that has averaged well over 3.0% and reached over 3.5% in recent years. The plan organization puts the average annual growth rate in the working population at 3.9% (and says the rate below working age has dropped to 2.6%, which seems unrealistically low). It can only guess at employment for women, but estimates that they will increase from 32.8% of the labor force in1999 to 34.1% by 2004.

As has been discussed in the previous chapter, job creation is far easier to call for than to achieve. Foreign Minister Saud al-Faisal has suggested that each billion dollars invested in new energy projects should produce 10,000 to 16,000 jobs. The Saudi American Bank estimates that $5,000 million has been invested over the last twenty-five years in foreign direct investments and has created 54,000 jobs while joint venture projects by the Kingdom created a further 21,000. As a result, significant improvements can be made only after a major restructuring of the Saudi labor force to eliminate foreign labor from existing jobs. It is also clear that the government still lacks a viable national manpower strategy that can actually achieve the goal of replacing 60% of the foreign labor force with Saudi nationals.[77] Saudi Arabia's declining real per capita income, persistent budget deficits, and overdependency on oil revenues will not be easy to change.

THE CHALLENGE OF DEPENDENCE ON PETROLEUM EXPORTS AND REVENUES

All of Saudi Arabia's economic reform efforts and development plans center around the fact that its economy is oil-driven, with the resulting strengths and weaknesses. The Saudi petroleum sector accounted for over 39% of the Saudi GDP in 2000, by Saudi estimates. The Energy Information Agency (EIA) of the U.S. Department of Energy (DOE) estimates that petroleum and petroleum-related exports accounted for around 90% to 95% of total Saudi export earnings in 2000, as well as for 70% of state revenues, and 35% to 40% of the country's GDP.[78] More than 55% of Saudi capital investment still goes to oil and petrochemicals.

Chart 6.1 shows a Saudi estimate of the Kingdom's dependence on the main elements of the petroleum sector in constant prices. As discussed in Chapter 3, it is clear that Saudi Arabia is less dependent on the petroleum sector than it was at the start of the oil boom or in the early 1990s, but its dependence did not vary in the 1990s except according to the forces exerted by world demand for petroleum and the resulting revenues.

SAMA data show that the total value of crude oil, natural gas, and petroleum refining was $51.7 billion in 1992, out of a GDP of $123.0 billion (42%). It was $48.2 billion out of $127.6 billion in 1995 (39.0%),

Chart 6.1

Oil and Petroleum as a Share of the Saudi GDP, 1970–2000 (Million Riyals at producers' values at constant prices: 1970 = 100)

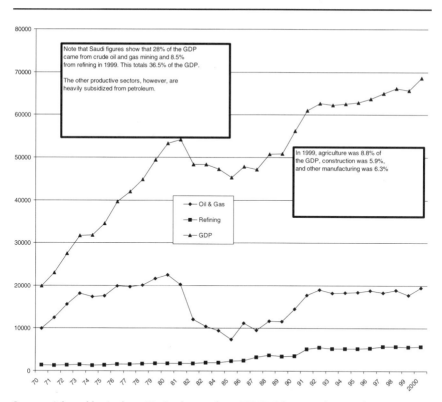

Sources: Adapted by Anthony H. Cordesman from SAMA, *Thirty-Sixth Annual Report (2000)* (Riyadh: SAMA Research and Statistics Department, 2000), pp. 346–348; and *Thirty-Seventh Annual Report (2001)* (Riyadh: SAMA Research and Statistics Department, 2001), pp. 356–358.

$39.1 billion out of $128.76 billion in 1995 (30%), and $77.6 billion out of $173.1 billion in 2000 (44.8%). Saudi Arabia did not diversify—it simply won or lost at a global economic lottery.

Charts 6.2 and 6.3 illustrate the continuing importance of the petroleum sector to the Saudi economy in simpler terms. They show that that in 2000, an average annual change of even $1 in the price of a barrel of oil can cut or raise the Saudi GDP by $2.5 billion.[79]

Chart 6.2
The Impact of Major Changes in Oil Prices on the Saudi Economy (in Current $US Thousands)

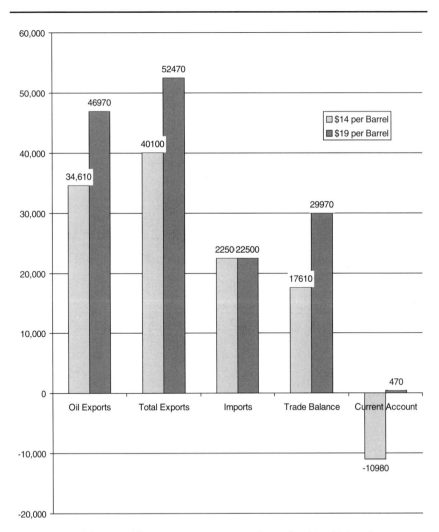

Source: Adapted from *Middle East Economic Digest*, September 27, 1996, p. 5.

Chart 6.3
The Impact of Changes in Oil Prices on the Saudi Economy in 2000 (in Current
$US Thousands)

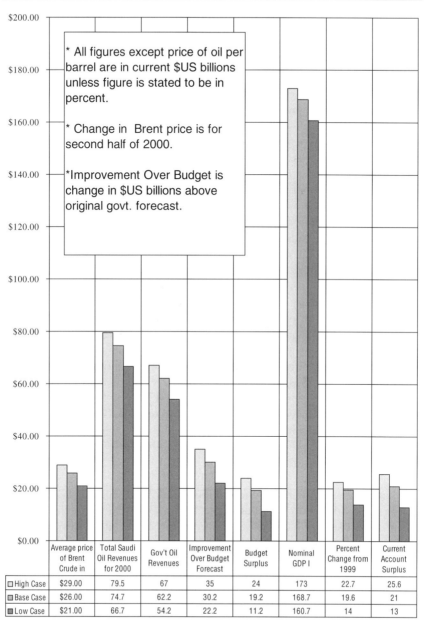

	Average price of Brent Crude in	Total Saudi Oil Revenues for 2000	Gov't Oil Revenues	Improvement Over Budget Forecast	Budget Surplus	Nominal GDP I	Percent Change from 1999	Current Account Surplus
☐ High Case	$29.00	79.5	67	35	24	173	22.7	25.6
☐ Base Case	$26.00	74.7	62.2	30.2	19.2	168.7	19.6	21
■ Low Case	$21.00	66.7	54.2	22.2	11.2	160.7	14	13

* All figures except price of oil per barrel are in current $US billions unless figure is stated to be in percent.

* Change in Brent price is for second half of 2000.

*Improvement Over Budget is change in $US billions above original govt. forecast.

Source: Adapted from Brad C. Bourland, *The Saudi Economy: Mid-2000 Update* (Riyadh: Saudi American Bank, August, 2000), pp. 4–8.

Chart 6.4 shows that the rate of diversification in the Saudi economy slowed sharply in the 1990s, and that much of the decline in the relative size of the petroleum sector has been the product of massive government spending, rather than an increase productive activity. It also shows that a combination of state-owned petroleum activity and other government activity accounts for over 60% of the total economy, and that there has been no meaningful change in the relative importance of petroleum, other government, and private sectors on the Saudi economy for a decade.

In fact, the total value of all nonpetroleum sectors in constant 1994 prices declined from a peak of 80.8% of the total GDP in 1985 (a year of extremely low oil revenues) and 72.5% in 1989, to levels well below 70% through all of the 1990s. There was no meaningful growth in share through 2000, when the nonpetroleum sector totaled 66.2% of the GDP. The situation was more impressive in terms of absolute growth. The private sector did add 11% in terms of value in constant 1994 riyals between 1994 and 2000, but this is less than 2% per year. Expenditures in the government sector also increased by 9.2%, or virtually the same amount. The growth outside the petroleum sector is even less impressive in reality because the way in which the Saudi government measures the value of petroleum sector understates Saudi Arabia's true dependence on oil and gas. Saudi data normally includes most petroleum-related construction as construction activity in the other government and private sectors, and the Saudi data only counts refining activity under the petroleum sector and not activities like the manufacturing of petrochemicals and fertilizers.[80]

The data in these charts also shows the limited impact the Saudi downstream activity has so far had on the economy. While some reporting on individual ventures emphasizes Saudi efforts to expand downstream operations like refining, most of the growth in the value of refining activity in the petroleum sector took place from the mid-1980s to 1990. Measured in constant 1994 Saudi riyals, refining activity rose from 5.8 billion in 1970 to 10.9 billion in 1985, and then to 12.5 billion in 1990 and 16.3 billion in 1991. It dropped below SR 16 billion annually in 1993–1996. Since that time, the value of refining activity has ranged between SR 16 and SR 17 billion, peaking at SR 16.97 billion in 2002—a year of very high oil prices.[81] (The value of refining in current dollars was $5.0 billion in 1992, $5.3 billion in a year of solid oil earnings like 1997, $3.9 billion in a year of low oil earnings like 1997, and $5.8 billion in a year of high oil earnings like 2000.)[82]

Charts 6.5 and 6.6 show how the Saudi economy has shifted by activity, as measured in both producers' values in constant 1989 prices and in current dollars, using two different Saudi sources. This analysis again illustrates the dangers of relying too much on any single source, or the precision of the data now available. Econometrics is at best an art form, and one where the analysis of multiple sources, their origin, and their definition

Chart 6.4
Saudi Oil Production, Government Expenditures, and Other Economic Activity as a Percent of GDP at Constant 1994 Purchaser's Prices

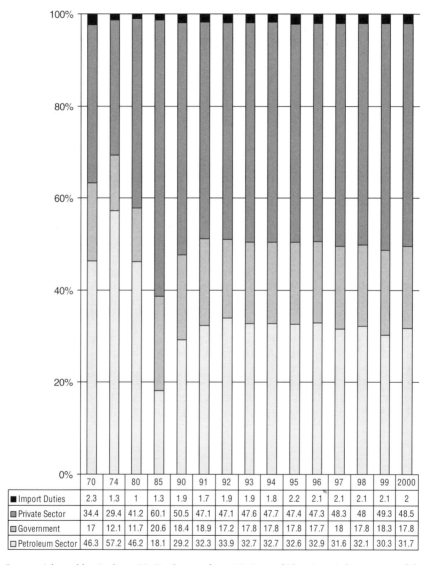

	70	74	80	85	90	91	92	93	94	95	96	97	98	99	2000
■ Import Duties	2.3	1.3	1	1.3	1.9	1.7	1.9	1.9	1.8	2.2	2.1	2.1	2.1	2.1	2
▦ Private Sector	34.4	29.4	41.2	60.1	50.5	47.1	47.1	47.6	47.7	47.4	47.3	48.3	48	49.3	48.5
▨ Government	17	12.1	11.7	20.6	18.4	18.9	17.2	17.8	17.8	17.8	17.7	18	17.8	18.3	17.8
□ Petroleum Sector	46.3	57.2	46.2	18.1	29.2	32.3	33.9	32.7	32.7	32.6	32.9	31.6	32.1	30.3	31.7

Source: Adapted by Anthony H. Cordesman from Ministry of Planning, *Achievements of the Development Plans, 1390–1420 (1970–2001), Facts and Figures* (Riyadh: Ministry of Planning, 19th Edition, 2002), Tables 9 and 10.

Chart 6.5
The Composition of the Saudi Economy by Sector in Billions of Constant 1994 Riyals in Producers Values

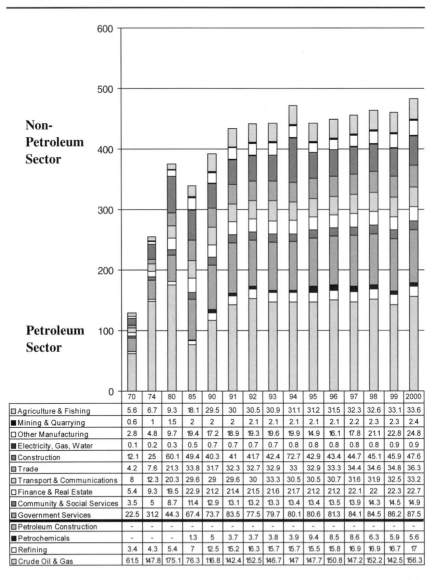

	70	74	80	85	90	91	92	93	94	95	96	97	98	99	2000
☐ Agriculture & Fishing	5.6	6.7	9.3	18.1	29.5	30	30.5	30.9	31.1	31.2	31.5	32.3	32.6	33.1	33.6
■ Mining & Quarrying	0.6	1	1.5	2	2	2	2.1	2.1	2.1	2.1	2.1	2.2	2.3	2.3	2.4
☐ Other Manufacturing	2.8	4.8	9.7	19.4	17.2	18.9	19.3	19.6	19.9	14.9	16.1	17.8	21.1	22.8	24.8
■ Electricity, Gas, Water	0.1	0.2	0.3	0.5	0.7	0.7	0.7	0.7	0.8	0.8	0.8	0.8	0.8	0.9	0.9
☐ Construction	12.1	25	60.1	49.4	40.3	41	41.7	42.4	72.7	42.9	43.4	44.7	45.1	45.9	47.6
☐ Trade	4.2	7.6	21.3	33.8	31.7	32.3	32.7	32.9	33	32.9	33.3	34.4	34.6	34.8	36.3
☐ Transport & Communications	8	12.3	20.3	29.6	29	29.6	30	33.3	30.5	30.5	30.7	31.6	31.9	32.5	33.2
☐ Finance & Real Estate	5.4	9.3	19.5	22.9	21.2	21.4	21.5	21.6	21.7	21.2	21.2	22.1	22	22.3	22.7
■ Community & Social Services	3.5	5	8.7	11.4	12.9	13.1	13.2	13.3	13.4	13.4	13.5	13.9	14.3	14.5	14.9
☐ Government Services	22.5	31.2	44.3	67.4	73.7	83.5	77.5	79.7	80.1	80.6	81.3	84.1	84.5	86.2	87.5
☐ Petroleum Construction	-	-	-	-	-	-	-	-	-	-	-	-	-	-	-
■ Petrochemicals	-	-	-	1.3	5	3.7	3.7	3.8	3.9	9.4	8.5	8.6	6.3	5.9	5.6
☐ Refining	3.4	4.3	5.4	7	12.5	15.2	16.3	15.7	15.7	15.5	15.8	16.9	16.9	16.7	17
☐ Crude Oil & Gas	61.5	147.8	175.1	76.3	116.8	142.4	152.5	146.7	147	147.7	150.8	147.2	152.2	142.5	156.3

Source: Adapted by Anthony H. Cordesman from Ministry of Planning, *Achievements of the Development Plans, 1390–1421 (1970–2001), Facts and Figures* (Riyadh: Ministry of Planning, 19th Edition, 2002), Tables 11 and 12.

Chart 6.6
The Composition of the Saudi Economy by Sector in Current $US Billions

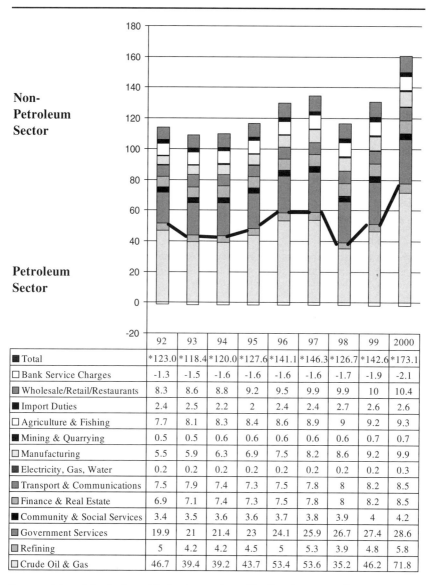

Non-Petroleum Sector

Petroleum Sector

	92	93	94	95	96	97	98	99	2000
■ Total	*123.0	*118.4	*120.0	*127.6	*141.1	*146.3	*126.7	*142.6	*173.1
□ Bank Service Charges	-1.3	-1.5	-1.6	-1.6	-1.6	-1.6	-1.7	-1.9	-2.1
▨ Wholesale/Retail/Restaurants	8.3	8.6	8.8	9.2	9.5	9.9	9.9	10	10.4
■ Import Duties	2.4	2.5	2.2	2	2.4	2.4	2.7	2.6	2.6
□ Agriculture & Fishing	7.7	8.1	8.3	8.4	8.6	8.9	9	9.2	9.3
■ Mining & Quarrying	0.5	0.5	0.6	0.6	0.6	0.6	0.6	0.7	0.7
□ Manufacturing	5.5	5.9	6.3	6.9	7.5	8.2	8.6	9.2	9.9
▨ Electricity, Gas, Water	0.2	0.2	0.2	0.2	0.2	0.2	0.2	0.2	0.3
▨ Transport & Communications	7.5	7.9	7.4	7.3	7.5	7.8	8	8.2	8.5
▨ Finance & Real Estate	6.9	7.1	7.4	7.3	7.5	7.8	8	8.2	8.5
■ Community & Social Services	3.4	3.5	3.6	3.6	3.7	3.8	3.9	4	4.2
▨ Government Services	19.9	21	21.4	23	24.1	25.9	26.7	27.4	28.6
▨ Refining	5	4.2	4.2	4.5	5	5.3	3.9	4.8	5.8
□ Crude Oil & Gas	46.7	39.4	39.2	43.7	53.4	53.6	35.2	46.2	71.8

Sources: Adapted by Anthony H. Cordesman from SAMA, *Thirty-Seventh Annual Report* (Riyadh: SAMA, November 2001); and Brad Bourland, *The Saudi Economy in 2002* (Riyadh: Saudi American Bank, February 2002), p. 34.

363

is critical to making even broad judgments. Nevertheless, both sets of data show the same overdependence on oil as analysis by sector and a lack of serious momentum behind diversification.

If anything, both sets of data understate Saudi dependence on the petroleum sector because it is impossible to break out petroleum-related construction, government activity, and manufacturing—such as plastics— with any consistency. Nevertheless, some recent trends seem fairly clear:

- The Saudi construction sector is one of the few areas outside the petroleum and government sectors that has long had a major impact on the Saudi economy. This sector, however, has scarcely been an engine for recent growth and diversification. It accounted for around 11% of the GDP in 1985, but was 8.5% in 1992, 8.4% in 1995, 9.9% in 1998, and 7.9% in 2000. It too has grown relatively slowly since the end of the Gulf War, and at an average real rate of less than 1% since 1992. [83]

- The data in Chart 6.6 reflect a significant sales sector in wholesale, retail, and restaurant activity, which has grown from around $8 billion in 1992 to $10 billion in 2000. This activity, however, consists largely of the marketing of imported goods, and growth is virtually inevitable given Saudi demographics.

- The growth of the transportation and communication sector has been significant, but the value of the sector still declined from 8.7% of the GDP in 1985 to 6.4% in 1990. The growth of the finance, insurance, real estate, and business services sector was also relatively static, and shrank from 7.4% of the economy in 1985 to around 5.0% in the late 1990s. It was only 4.9% in 2000, although its share was inevitably higher in years with low oil revenues. [84]

- The total share of government services in the economy has been relatively static and has not declined over time. It was 16% of the GDP in 1992, 18% in 1995, 18% in 1997, and 17% in 2000. The community, social, and personal services sector and the electricity and water sector have grown more steadily, but have still lagged population growth and have not grown in ways that have contributed more to the economy than they have consumed. [85]

- While agriculture accounts for over 6% of the GDP, it only does so because of government subsidies, the waste of irreplaceable "fossil" well water, and the underpricing of desalinated water. [86] Even with such subsidies, agriculture averaged less than 2% real growth during the 1990s, and it might well have shown no growth, or a decline, without subsidies. [87] The trade sector shrank from 10.2% of the GDP in 1985 to 7.7% in 1990, 6.4% in 1995, and then rose to around 7% in the late 1990s. [88] The average rate of annual growth was less than 1% after 1992, however, and employment per dollar shrank slightly while the ratio of imports per trade dollar increased slightly. [89]

- The two sectors where there has been positive growth that actually have benefited the economy have been mining and quarrying and manufacturing. Mining and quarrying had a low real growth rate of less than 2.0% during most of the 1990s, but this rose to around 3% during 1997–1999. This at least approached the population growth rate. Unfortunately, mining and quarrying remains a sharply undeveloped aspect of the Kingdom's economic activity in spite of substantial resources, and accounted for only about 0.5% of the GDP in 2000. SAMA estimates the net value of the nonpetroleum-related mining and quarrying sector only rose from $0.5 billion in current dollars in 1992 to $0.7 billion in 2000, while the total GDP rose from $123.0 to 173.1 billion.

- Nonpetroleum-related manufacturing had a low real growth rate of less than 2.0% during most of the 1990s, but this rose to around 5% during 1997–1999. Its value rose from $5.5 billion in 1992 to $9.9 billion in 2000. Manufacturing accounted for around 4% to 6% of the GDP in 2000, but this was roughly the same share of the Saudi GDP as in the mid-1980s. As a result, the absolute expansion in the value of nonpetroleum-related manufacturing between 1992 and 2000 had little effect in further diversifying the composition of the Saudi GDP over the last decade.[90]

The Other Impacts of Petroleum Dependence

While most estimates indicate that some 35% to 40% of the Saudi GDP now comes from the private sector, much of this output comes from activity that consists of selling imports and services funded through oil exports. This contributes to Saudi Arabia's heavy trade deficit in services, which has consistently averaged around $15 billion a year since the end of the massive service payments made for the Gulf War.[91] In other words, the apparent growing diversity of the Saudi economy is often more a function of how it reports its statistics rather than the kind of restructuring and growth that makes the Kingdom less dependent on oil revenues and exports.

Chart 6.7 reinforces this point. It shows that Saudi government expenditures have been financed largely by oil exports and that the government's share of the GDP has been funded largely by oil. The figures in Chart 6.7 do, however, actually understate the importance of the petroleum sector because they do not include revenues from areas like plastics and petrochemicals in oil revenues. At the same time, it is clear from this chart that the government has not succeeded in making major reductions in its dependence on the petroleum sector since the mid-1980s. The fluctuations in the share of petroleum revenues in Chart 6.8 from mid-1985 onward is more a matter of oil prices and the volume of oil sales in any given year than the result of the structural diversification of government revenues.

Chart 6.9 shows that virtually all of Saudi Arabia's exports are petroleum-related and that Saudi Arabia is only making moderate progress in moving into downstream operations. This is particularly important because Saudi Arabia has few natural resources other than oil and gas, and once again the Kingdom has not made significant improvements in the diversification of its exports for more than a decade. Chart 6.9 illustrates the resulting problem in a critical recent case. Nonoil exports did virtually nothing to ease the impact of the massive "crash" in oil prices that began in late 1997.

Chart 6.7

Saudi Oil Exports as a Percent of Total Government Revenues, 1974–1999 (in Current Billions of Riyals)

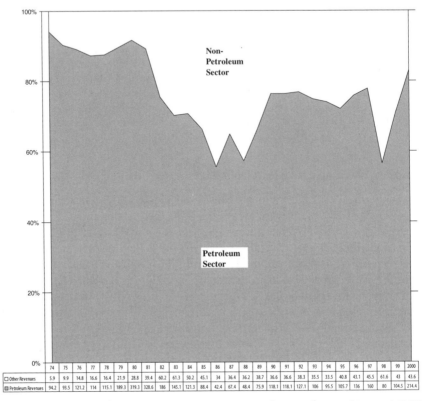

	74	75	76	77	78	79	80	81	82	83	84	85	86	87	88	89	90	91	92	93	94	95	96	97	98	99	2000
☐ Other Revenues	5.9	9.9	14.8	16.6	16.4	21.9	28.8	39.4	60.2	61.3	50.2	45.1	34	36.4	36.2	38.7	36.6	36.6	38.3	35.5	33.5	40.8	43.1	45.5	61.6	43	43.6
▨ Petroleum Revenues	94.2	93.5	121.2	114	115.1	189.3	319.3	328.6	186	145.1	121.3	88.4	42.4	67.4	48.4	75.9	118.1	118.1	127.1	106	95.5	105.7	136	160	80	104.5	214.4

Sources: Adapted by Anthony H. Cordesman from SAMA, *Thirty-Sixth Annual Report 1421H (2000G)* (Riyadh: SAMA, 2000), pp. 360–361; *Thirty-Seventh Annual Report 1422H (2001G)* (Riyadh: SAMA, 2001), pp. 372–373, and Ministry of Planning, *Achievements of the Development Plans, 1390–1421 (1970–2001), Facts and Figures* (Riyadh: Ministry of Planning, 19th Edition, 2002), Tables 1 and 4.

More recent data on Saudi exports indicate that Saudi Arabia's nonoil exports increased by only 2.4% to SR 25.4 billion in 2001 compared to SR 24.8 billion in 2000, although this occurred in spite of a global economic slowdown. They were estimated to account for about 11% of total exports and 3.8% of nominal GDP. However, nonoil exports financed through commercial banks constituted only 46% of total nonoil exports last year compared to 53% in 2000 and 48% in 1999. The value of nonoil private sector exports financed through commercial banks fell substantially by 11.4% to SR 11.63 billion in 2001 compared to a six-year peak of SR 13.13 billion the year before.

Chart 6.8
Saudi Petroleum Exports Relative to Total Exports (in Current Billions of Riyals)

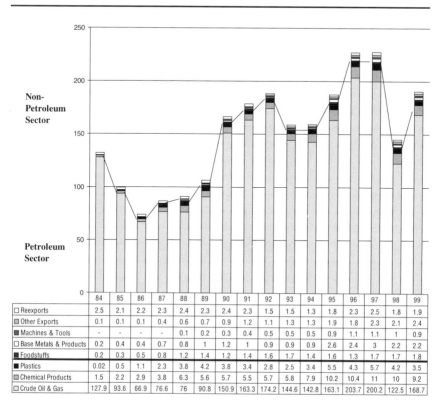

	84	85	86	87	88	89	90	91	92	93	94	95	96	97	98	99
☐ Reexports	2.5	2.1	2.2	2.3	2.4	2.3	2.4	2.3	1.5	1.5	1.3	1.8	2.3	2.5	1.8	1.9
▨ Other Exports	0.1	0.1	0.1	0.4	0.6	0.7	0.9	1.2	1.1	1.3	1.3	1.9	1.8	2.3	2.1	2.4
■ Machines & Tools	-	-	-	-	0.1	0.2	0.3	0.4	0.5	0.5	0.5	0.9	1.1	1.1	1	0.9
☐ Base Metals & Products	0.2	0.4	0.4	0.7	0.8	1	1.2	1	0.9	0.9	0.9	2.6	2.4	3	2.2	2.2
■ Foodstuffs	0.2	0.3	0.5	0.8	1.2	1.4	1.2	1.4	1.6	1.7	1.4	1.6	1.3	1.7	1.7	1.8
■ Plastics	0.02	0.5	1.1	2.3	3.8	4.2	3.8	3.4	2.8	2.5	3.4	5.5	4.3	5.7	4.2	3.5
▨ Chemical Products	1.5	2.2	2.9	3.8	6.3	5.6	5.7	5.5	5.7	5.8	7.9	10.2	10.4	11	10	9.2
☐ Crude Oil & Gas	127.9	93.6	66.9	76.6	76	90.8	150.9	163.3	174.2	144.6	142.8	163.1	203.7	200.2	122.5	168.7

Source: Adapted by Anthony H. Cordesman from SAMA, *Thirty-Sixth Annual Report 1421H (2000G)* (Riyadh: SAMA, 2000), pp. 360–361.

"Nonoil exports" are also a misleading title because they have a very large component of petroleum-related content, most of which comes from very capital-intensive and low labor-intensive industry. The petroleum market-driven Saudi Basic Industries Corporation (SABIC), which does not obtain funds through commercial loans, accounts for one-third of all industrial production in Saudi Arabia, and around 70% of its total production is destined for the export market. Its net profits fell by more than 50% to SR 1.78 billion in 2001 compared to SR 3.63 billion in 2000. In contrast, the Saudi cement industry increased its exports by 3.7% to 2.88 million tons in 2001, mostly to countries in the region, including Jordan, Syria, and Egypt.

SAMA classifies those nonoil exports that are financed through local banks into three major categories: chemicals and plastics, agriculture and

Chart 6.9
Saudi Oil versus Nonoil Exports During the "Oil Crash" in 1996–2000 (Value in Millions of Riyals)

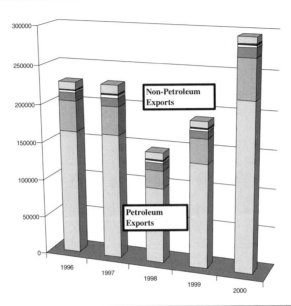

	1996	1997	1998	1999	2000
☐ Others	9443	11385	9055	8099	8268
■ Agriculture/Food	1339	1660	1663	1768	1700
☐ Construction Materials	2964	3593	2737	2808	2712
■ Petrochemicals	10435	11036	9961	9189	12125
▨ Refined	39965	36755	23133	31977	51480
☐ Crude Oil	163282	163016	98839	136321	219470

Source: Adapted by Anthony H. Cordesman from SAMA, *Thirty-Sixth Annual Report 1421H (2000G)* (Riyadh: SAMA, 2000), pp. 360–361; and *Thirty-Seventh Annual Report 1422H (2001G)* (Riyadh: SAMA, 2001), pp. 157–158.

animal products, and other products. Chemicals and plastics exports are also closely tied to the conditions in the petroleum market, and financing of chemicals and plastics dropped sharply by 16.7% in 2001 to SR 3.19 billion, compared to SR 3.83 billion in 2000. However, chemicals and plastics exports still accounted for 27.4% of Saudi Commercial Bank's financing in 2001, compared to 29.2% in the previous year.

Agriculture and animal products, the smallest category of nonoil exports financing accounted for only 1.2% of total bank financing, and its value was nearly halved to SR 136 million in 2001. This continued decline reflects the noncompetitive nature of the Kingdom's agricultural industry, where most products are backed by direct and indirect subsidies.

The third major component of Saudi nonoil exports and export financing is "other industrial goods." It includes numerous manufacturing goods such as base metals, building materials, paper products, textiles, machinery, and electrical appliances, and represents a substantial 71.4% of total bank financing. Export financing of this category decreased by 8.1% to SR8.31 billion in 2001 after reaching a six-year peak of SR 9.04 billion in 2000. Again, the fall of this category was largely attributed to lower demand for Saudi industrial products on the international market, due to the U.S.-led global recession. The decrease of total export financing was also reflected by falling international commodity prices. According to the IMF, the market price indices for metals and agricultural raw materials dropped by 9.5% and 7.2%, respectively, in 2001.

One positive trend that has occurred in recent years is a growth in regional trade, although this does not affect the level of diversification in the Saudi economy or as yet generate added growth. The GCC's share of bank-financed Saudi nonoil exports has risen because of the favorable custom treatment among GCC countries affecting domestically produced goods with at least 40% local value added and 51% GCC ownership. They are exempted from tariffs, and export financing of Saudi products through local banks to GCC countries amounted to SR 5.0 billion last year, up 1.3% from SR 4.93 billion in 2000. Other Arab countries constituted the second-largest market for Saudi exports financed through local banks with a 15.5% share, but remained relatively flat. Elsewhere, the shares of such Saudi exports financed by local banks to Western Europe and the United States remained small at 5.5% (SR 637 million) and 4.6% (SR 537 million), respectively.[92]

Once again, it must be stressed that there are no macroeconomic rules about economic dependence on petroleum or that determine the level of diversification required. Nevertheless, Charts 6.10 and 6.11 put Saudi dependence on the oil sector in a broader perspective, one that is often ignored in discussions of the Gulf. They demonstrate that the oil economies in the Middle East have shown relatively slow sustained growth since the oil boom following the fall of the Shah in 1979, and the first two years of the Iran-Iraq War in 1980–1981. In contrast, diversified economies have had higher average growth over time than oil economies in the Middle East, and much higher growth in the developing world as a whole.

Political and Military Risks of Saudi Overdependence on Petroleum

The risks inherent in Saudi Arabia's structural dependence on the petroleum and petroleum-related industries and exports are increased by a number of exogenous factors. Petroleum is a global economy commodity whose price is dictated by factors outside Saudi Arabia's control. These include

Chart 6.10

GDP Growth of Saudi Arabia versus the Other Gulf and MENA States, East Asia, and Middle-Income States, During the 1980s and 1990s (Percent of Real Annual Change during 1980–2000)

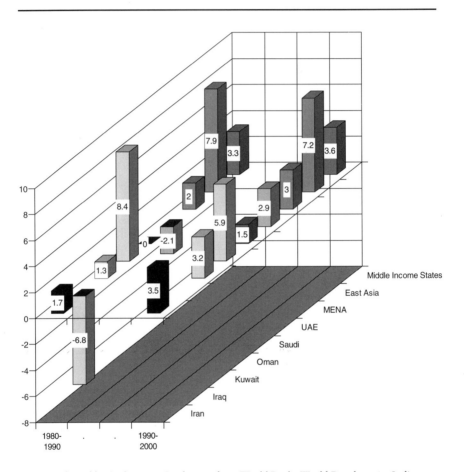

Source: Adapted by Anthony H. Cordesman from World Bank, *World Development Indicators, 2002* (Washington: World Bank, 2002), pp. 204–206.

weather, the health of the economies of importing states, and the taxes, regulations, and environmental policies of importing states. External events such as wars and political crises can also lead to major fluctuations in the price of oil. The Arab-Israeli conflict in 1973, the fall of the Shah in 1979, the outbreak of the Iran-Iraq War in 1980, the Iranian hostage crisis and U.S. sanctions against Iran, the bombing of Pan Am 103 and UN sanctions against Libya, and Iraq's invasion of Kuwait, the Gulf War, and more than

Chart 6.11
GDP Growth of the MENA Oil Exporters versus Diversified Exporters, 1981–1995
(Percent of GDP Growth)

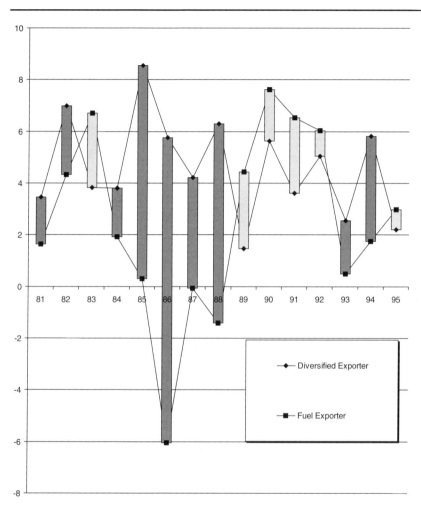

Diversified exporter = Egypt, Israel, Jordan, Morocco, Syria, and Tunisia; Fuel exporter = Algeria, Bahrain, Iran, Kuwait, Oman, Qatar, Saudi Arabia, and the UAE.
Source: Adapted by Anthony H. Cordesman from IMF, *World Economic Outlook* (Washington: IMF, May 1996), pp. 98–105.

a decade of UN sanctions against Iraq, are all examples of such political and military events.

Charts 6.12, 6.13, and 6.14 show the combined impacts of market forces and military and political events on oil prices, the total oil revenues of

Chart 6.12
Politics, War, and the Trends in the Price of Saudi Arabia Light Crude, 1970–1999 ($US Current and $US 1997 Constant)

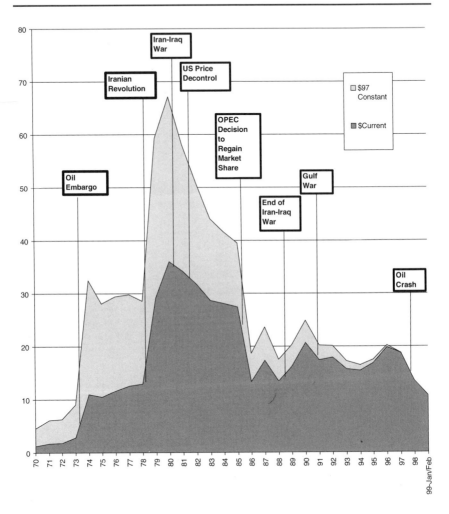

Total ME
OPEC	13/31	18/87	17/91	9/53	15/19	14.77	15.99	16.75	16.84	16.99	17.18	18.30
Total ME	13.95	19.57	18.40	10.25	16.49	16.19	17.43	18.34	18.59	18.84	19.08	20.16

Source: Adapted by Anthony H. Cordesman from Cambridge Energy Research Associates, *World Oil Trends, 1998* (Cambridge, MA: CERA, 1998), pp. 26–27.

Chart 6.13
The Combined Impact of War, Politics, and Global Market Forces on Gulf Oil
Revenues, 1970–2000 ($US Current Billions)

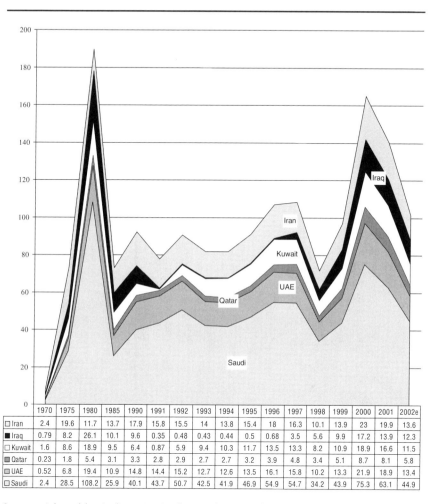

	1970	1975	1980	1985	1990	1991	1992	1993	1994	1995	1996	1997	1998	1999	2000	2001	2002e
☐ Iran	2.4	19.6	11.7	13.7	17.9	15.8	15.5	14	13.8	15.4	18	16.3	10.1	13.9	23	19.9	13.6
■ Iraq	0.79	8.2	26.1	10.1	9.6	0.35	0.48	0.43	0.44	0.5	0.68	3.5	5.6	9.9	17.2	13.9	12.3
☐ Kuwait	1.6	8.6	18.9	9.5	6.4	0.87	5.9	9.4	10.3	11.7	13.5	13.3	8.2	10.9	18.9	16.6	11.5
▨ Qatar	0.23	1.8	5.4	3.1	3.3	2.8	2.9	2.7	2.7	3.2	3.9	4.8	3.4	5.1	8.7	8.1	5.8
☐ UAE	0.52	6.8	19.4	10.9	14.8	14.4	15.2	12.7	12.6	13.5	16.1	15.8	10.2	13.3	21.9	18.9	13.4
☐ Saudi	2.4	28.5	108.2	25.9	40.1	43.7	50.7	42.5	41.9	46.9	54.9	54.7	34.2	43.9	75.3	63.1	44.9

Sources: Adapted by Anthony H. Cordesman from Cambridge Energy Research Associates,
World Oil Trends, 1998 (Cambridge, MA: CERA, 1998), pp. 26–27; Cambridge Energy
Research Associates, "OPEC Tilts to Market Share," *World Oil Watch* (Winter 2002), p.
28; and from projections by the EIA based on various editions of the "OPEC Revenues
Fact Sheet," URL: *www.eia.doe.gov/emeu/cabs/opecrev2.ntml.*

OPEC, and Saudi oil revenues in particular. These swings are particularly
great if they are measured in constant dollars, which reflect their real economic impact. As Chart 6.14 shows, Saudi Arabia earned $223.2 billion
from crude oil exports in 1980, measured in constant 2000 dollars. It earned

Chart 6.14

The Swings in Saudi Oil Export Revenues, 1972–2001: Even the Boom in 2000 Was No Boom By Past Standards (in $US Current and 2000 Constant Billions)

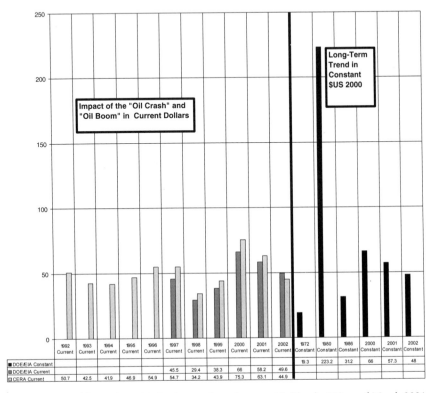

	1992 Current	1993 Current	1994 Current	1995 Current	1996 Current	1997 Current	1998 Current	1999 Current	2000 Current	2001 Current	2002 Current	1972 Constant	1980 Constant	1986 Constant	2000 Constant	2001 Constant	2002 Constant
■ DOE/EIA Constant												19.3	223.2	31.2	66	57.3	48
▣ DOE/EIA Current						45.5	29.4	38.3	66	58.2	49.6						
□ CERA Current	50.7	42.5	41.9	46.9	54.9	54.7	34.2	43.9	75.3	63.1	44.9						

Sources: Adapted by Anthony H. Cordesman from data provided by the EIA as of March 2001 and December 2001 (URL: *www.eia.gov/emeu/cabs/opecrev2.html*); and in Cambridge Energy Research Associates, "OPEC Tilts to Market Share," *World Oil Watch* (Winter 2002), p. 28.

only $66 billion in 2000, a year with exceptionally high oil revenues by the standards of the 1990s.

If one looks at the swings in current dollars, which are far smaller than the differences in constant dollars, the Saudi oil revenues in Chart 6.13, the revenues reached a peak of $133 billion a year in 1981, and dropped to $46 billion in 1983. As Chart 6.13 shows, the swings in Saudi oil revenues were particularly acute at the end of the 1980s. Saudi oil revenues only averaged around $19 billion to $25 billion from 1984 to 1988, about one fifth of their 1981 level, and Saudi financial reserves dropped to as little as one-third of their 1981 level of $190 billion. Oil revenues were under $24 billion in 1988.[93]

The Gulf War changed this situation as prices firmed and Saudi oil production rose to compensate for the embargo of Iraq. Total Saudi merchandise exports from $28.3 billion in 1989 to $44.4 billion in 1990, and then to $47.8 billion in 1991 and $50.3 billion in 1992. This new burst of oil wealth was, however, more than consumed by the cost of the Gulf War and aid to the United States and other Saudi allies. Further, oil prices and oil revenues dropped sharply in 1993 and remained low in 1994, and total merchandise exports dropped to $42.4 billion and $42.6 billion respectively.

Rises in oil prices again increased the value of Saudi exports in 1995. Total merchandise exports rose to $49.90 billion, $60.6 billion in 1996 and $60.6 billion 1997.[94] As a result of low oil prices, they dropped to $38.8 billion in 1998 and were still only $50.5 billion in 1999. They rose with oil prices to $80.7 billion in 2002. This total, however, scarcely has the economic impact of about $111 billion in real dollars from roughly 9 MMBD of exports in 1981, and $73 billion from exports of only 5.6 MMBD in 1992. The Saudi economy also showed no growth even in current dollars in other exports during 1992–2000. Such exports fluctuated from $5.8 billion to $7.4 billion during the 1990s, but they were $6.5 billion in 1992 and were still only $6.6 billion in 2000.[95]

Moreover, Saudi Arabia received less from its foreign investments, in part because it had to pay for the Gulf War. During the late 1980s, Saudi Arabia received a net balance of well over $9 billion a year from investment income. This income dropped to less than $7 billion in 1991, reached a low of $1.4 billion in 1994, and averaged from $2.8 to $3.8 billion a year during the mid 1990s.[96] Saudi official foreign assets did begin to rise again in the late 1990s: they rose from $67.9 billion in 1995 to $78.0 billion in 1996 and $86.0 billion in 1997. However, the drastic cut in oil revenues that began that year forced Saudi Arabia to cut them to $78.3 billion in 1998 and 68.34 billion in 1999. They rose back to $73.5 billion in 2000 as a result of the shift from "oil bust" to "oil boom," and to $82.6 billion in 2001.[97] They were expected to reach $78.5 billion in 2002. These shifts are measured in current dollars, however, and are too small to have much macroeconomic impact. In any case, the days in which the Kingdom could accumulate official assets approaching $200 billion in constant 2001 dollars seem to be long over.

These swings in oil prices and oil revenues have an inevitable impact on the Kingdom's trade balances. During the late 1980s, the Kingdom's deficits on current account ranged from $4.1 billion to $9.8 billion. This figure increased dramatically from $4.2 billion in 1990 to $27.6 billion in 1991. Since that time, the deficit has dropped to $17.8 billion in 1992, $17.3 billion in 1993, $9.1 billion in 1994, and $5.3 billion in 1995. There was a positive balance of $0.7 billion in 1996, and $0.3 billion in 1997, but the oil crash in 1998 led to a deficit of $13.8 billion, which could only be financed through capital payments provided by the oil and private sectors.[98]

The rise in oil revenue during 1999 changed current account balance to a positive $0.4 billion in 1999, produced a surplus of $15.6 billion in 2000, and is expected to produce surplus of $3 billion in 2001.[99] It obvious from these figures that the Kingdom wins as well as loses, but it is equally obvious that it cannot shape the outcome of such trends, predict them, and plan for them as long as it is so dependent on the petroleum sector.

"OIL BUST" AND "OIL BOOM": THE INTERACTION BETWEEN OPEC AND MARKET FORCES

Saudi Arabia must also cope with the interaction between market forces and the politics of OPEC. Saudi Arabia has often acted independently of OPEC and in ways that have greatly benefited the global economy by stabilizing the world's oil supplies and keeping prices relatively moderate. At the same time, the politics of OPEC can impose limits on the Kingdom's production, and Saudi Arabia does come under political pressure from other OPEC states to reduce its production in times of low oil prices or when other states feel this may serve Arab political causes. For example, the Kingdom came under such pressure in April 2002, when Iraq cut off oil exports to countries that supported Israel against the Palestinians as a result of the Second Intifada and when Iran also called for a boycott. Instead, the Kingdom raised production to compensate for Iraq's cuts and stated that it would not use oil as a weapon, but would rather push forward with Crown Prince Abdullah's peace initiative.[100]

As is discussed in depth in the next chapter, Saudi Arabia's vast oil reserves give it a strong long-term strategic interest in maintaining an increasing level of oil exports at comparatively moderate prices. For all of Saudi Arabia's short-term economic problems, it must think ahead to the market conditions of 2010 and beyond, and it is under far less pressure to maximize oil revenues than states like Iran, Iraq, Algeria, and Nigeria. As a result, Saudi Arabia is also often under pressure to reduce its exports more sharply than those of other OPEC states. Nevertheless, Chart 6.15 shows that the interaction between OPEC and market forces does add another set of uncertainties to Saudi oil revenues and creates another reason that Saudi Arabia must seek to diversify and reform its economy.

OPEC, Mild Winter, and Asian Recession: The Oil Crash of 1997

These risks, and the massive swings in oil revenues that can result, are illustrated by both the sudden oil crash that took place the late 1990s and the boom that followed. In late 1997, Saudi Arabia pushed OPEC into giving the Kingdom its highest oil output quota in more than fifteen years. The Kingdom secured a new quota of 8.76 million barrels per day (bpd)

Chart 6.15

The OPEC Game Adds Another Uncertainty: Saudi and Other OPEC Member Production Targets and Actual Output, 1999–2002 (in MMBD)

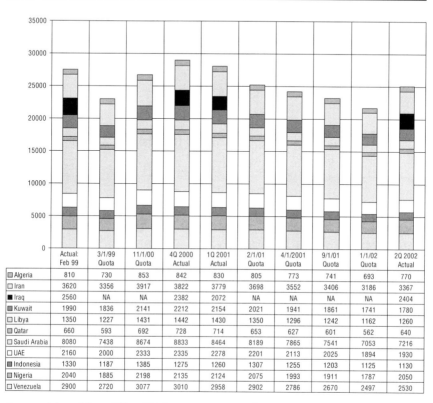

	Actual: Feb 99	3/1/99 Quota	11/1/00 Quota	4Q 2000 Actual	1Q 2001 Actual	2/1/01 Quota	4/1/2001 Quota	9/1/01 Quota	1/1/02 Quota	2Q 2002 Actual
▨ Algeria	810	730	853	842	830	805	773	741	693	770
☐ Iran	3620	3356	3917	3822	3779	3698	3552	3406	3186	3367
■ Iraq	2560	NA	NA	2382	2072	NA	NA	NA	NA	2404
▨ Kuwait	1990	1836	2141	2212	2154	2021	1941	1861	1741	1780
☐ Libya	1350	1227	1431	1442	1430	1350	1296	1242	1162	1260
▨ Qatar	660	593	692	728	714	653	627	601	562	640
☐ Saudi Arabia	8080	7438	8674	8833	8464	8189	7865	7541	7053	7216
☐ UAE	2160	2000	2333	2335	2278	2201	2113	2025	1894	1930
▨ Indonesia	1330	1187	1385	1275	1260	1307	1255	1203	1125	1130
▨ Nigeria	2040	1885	2198	2135	2124	2075	1993	1911	1787	2050
☐ Venezuela	2900	2720	3077	3010	2958	2902	2786	2670	2497	2530

Sources: Adapted from EIA, "OPEC," URL: *www.eia.doe.gov/emeu/cabs/opec2.html*, various editions; *Middle East Economic Digest*, March 26, 1999, p. 5; EIA, *Monthly Energy Review*, various editions, and *www.eia.doe.gov/emeu/cabs/opec2.html*.

at OPEC's ministerial meeting in Jakarta. This quota was 760,000 bpd higher than the quota it had held over the last four years, although Saudi Arabia had been pumping between 8.2 million bpd and 8.3 million bpd in the months leading up to the agreement.

Saudi Arabia took this action despite the fact that OPEC's overall production ceiling rose from 25.03 million bpd to 27.5 million bpd and the concern of other states in the eleven-member group that oil prices would fall because of increased supplies. Saudi experts felt that demand and prices were firm enough that the benchmark price of Brent crude would average $20 a barrel even with the new OPEC ceilings. Brent was then trading at $19 a barrel, equivalent to around $17.50 for a typical Saudi export barrel.

Saudi motives in seeking higher production were clear. Saudi officials stated that the rise in quota was necessary to increase the Kingdom's cash flow and funding for its 1998 budget and five-year plan and reduce or eradicate its $4.5 billion budget deficit. The Saudis also sought to clear contractual debt, some of which stretched back to 1991, and eliminate any difficulties in marking loan repayments such as the $4.3 billion loan Saudi Arabia took out in November 1997 to pay for new aircraft for the country's national airline, Saudia. Finally, Saudi Arabia sought funding to pay for new infrastructure projects and military equipment, such as replacements for some 100 aging US F-5 warplanes.

The end result was an oil crash that led to a major cut in oil prices and revenues—the impacts of which still cannot be estimated. An estimate of this decline in Saudi and other Gulf oil revenues is shown in Charts 6.14 and 6.16. Chart 6.15 shows the EIA estimate of the value of crude oil exports, while Chart 6.17 shows the trend in total petroleum-related exports.[101]

Several factors helped cause this oil crash. Asia was Saudi Arabia's largest crude export market, accounting for 60% of sales, with its main buyers in Japan and South Korea. Asia was already in an economic downturn and slid into a major recession even before the new quota went into effect on January 1, 1998. A mild winter and low demand for heating fuel and uncertainty over the volume of Iraqi crude exports under the United Nations' oil-for-food deal then made things much worse.

Rises in Iraqi production also had an impact. While OPEC output fell by nearly 1 million bpd, Iraqi output rose by more than 400,000 bpd, thus effectively reducing the OPEC cutback to only 500,000 bpd.[102] Iraq also stepped up its verbal attacks against the Kingdom and its oil policy, accusing Saudi Arabia of flooding oil markets with its production, "pursuing a U.S. policy aimed to reduce oil prices to suit its interest in the Middle East and in Iraq in particular."[103] Iraqi oil minister Amir Muhammad Rasheed blamed Saudi Arabia for the deterioration in world oil prices, saying Arab countries had lost $929 billion between 1997 and 1998 because of the Saudi oil policy.[104]

Oil prices dropped sharply from around $23 a barrel in October 1997 and reached a nine-year low of $12.80 a barrel on the New York Mercantile Exchange in March 1998 and $14.61 for the most active futures contracts. Prices rose briefly to $16.50 a barrel when Saudi Arabia, Mexico, and Venezuela agreed to a joint cutback of 1.325 million barrels per day (MMBD). Nevertheless, prices then dropped again. The OPEC "basket" price (a weighted average of Algeria's Saharan Blend, Indonesia's Minas, Nigeria's Bonny Light, Saudi Arabia's Arabian Light, Dubai, Venezuela's Tia Juana, and Mexico's Isthmus) fell to a low of under $10 per barrel in December 1998.

Chart 6.16
Oil Crash to Oil Boom in 1996–2001: The Cumulative Impact on Saudi and OPEC
Revenues (in $US Current Billions)

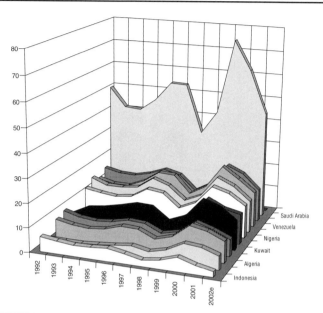

	1992	1993	1994	1995	1996	1997	1998	1999	2000	2001	2002e
☐ Indonesia	6.1	5.2	4.6	4.8	5.4	4.2	2.7	3.7	5.9	3.8	2.3
☐ Qatar	2.9	2.7	2.7	3.2	3.9	4.8	3.4	5.1	8.7	8.1	5.8
▨ Algeria	8.4	7	6.4	7.1	9.2	8.9	5.9	7.9	13.4	12	8.9
▨ Libya	9.6	7.7	7.1	7.7	9.3	8.9	5.7	7.3	12.3	10.1	7.1
■ Kuwait	5.9	9.4	10.3	11.7	13.5	13.3	8.2	10.9	18.9	16.6	11.5
▨ Iraq	0.5	0.4	0.4	0.5	0.7	3.5	5.6	9.9	17.2	13.9	12.3
☐ Nigeria	12.7	11.5	10.6	11.5	15.7	14.8	9.1	12.4	20.1	18	13.5
☐ UAE	15.2	12.7	12.6	13.5	18.1	15.8	10.2	13.3	21.9	18.9	13.4
▨ Venezuela	12.8	11.2	11.2	14	18.7	18.3	11.1	15	24.5	19.8	14.8
▨ Iran	15.5	14	13.8	15.4	18	16.3	10.1	13.9	23	19.9	13.6
☐ Saudi Arabia	50.7	42.5	41.9	46.9	54.9	54.7	34.2	43.9	75.3	63.1	44.9
■ TOTAL	*140.4	*124.3	*121.4	*136.3	*165.5	*163.5	*106.2	*143.2	*241.2	*204.2	*148.1

Sources: Adapted by Anthony H. Cordesman from projections by the EIA in various editions
of its "OPEC Revenues Sheet," and from Cambridge Energy Research Associates, "OPEC
Tilts to Market Share," *World Oil Watch* (Winter 2002), p. 28.

Prior to the OPEC meeting of June 1998, Saudi Arabia, Venezuela, and
Mexico agreed to cut production by 450,000 barrels per day as of July 1.
This cut failed, and even further OPEC cuts of 2.6 MMBD during 1998
only helped to halt a further fall in oil prices and did not produce a recovery.[105] Real-world oil prices during 1998 and early 1999 were at the lowest levels since 1973, prior to the Arab Oil Embargo late that year, and since
1986, following the oil price collapse of late 1985/early 1986.

Chart 6.17

U.S. Projections of Saudi Oil Production Capacity and Implied Oil Export Earnings (EIA Reference Case in MMBD)

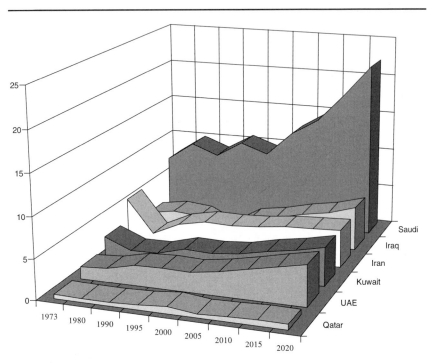

	1973	1980	1990	1995	2000	2005	2010	2015	2020
☐ Qatar	0.57	0.472	0.5	0.6	0.9	0.5	0.6	0.7	0.7
▦ UAE	1.533	1.709	2.5	2.6	2.5	3	3.7	4.4	5.1
■ Kuwait	3.02	1.656	1.7	2.6	2.5	2.8	3.5	4.1	4.8
☐ Iran	5.8	1.662	3.2	3.9	3.8	4	4.4	4.5	4.7
☐ Iraq	2.018	2.514	2.2	0.6	2.6	3.1	3.9	4.5	5.5
■ Saudi	7.596	9.9	8.6	10.6	9.4	12.5	14.6	18.2	22.1

Total Gulf	—	18.7	—	21.7	25.9	30.7	36.4	42.9	
Saudi Arabia as % of Total	—	45.95	—	43.35	48.2	47.6	50.0	51.53	
Total OPEC	—	27.2	—	31.4	38.4	44.8	52.0	60.2	
Total World	—	69.4	—	77.4	88.0	98.4	109.8	121.3	
Saudi Arabia as % of Total	—	12.4	—	12.1	14.25	14.8	16.6	18.21	

Sources: Adapted by Anthony H. Cordesman from U.S. Department of Energy, *International Energy Outlook, 1997* (Washington: Energy Information Agency, April 1997), pp. 157–160, and U.S. Department of Energy, *International Energy Outlook, 2002* (Washington: Energy Information Agency, March 2002), Table D1.

OPEC revenue had peaked in 1980, at $439 billion in constant 1990 U.S. dollars. In contrast, 1998 was OPEC's worst revenue year in constant dollar terms since the early 1970s ($77 billion in 1972), when revenues reached only $80 billion (in constant US$ 1990). The previous low revenue year had been 1986 ($83 billion in earnings), which followed the oil price collapse of late 1985/early 1986.[106] As a result, the Saudi domestic debt rose from SR 336 billion in 1994 to SR 612 billion in 1999, and from 76 to 115% of the GDP. The government could only stabilize its budget through domestic borrowing (as an alternative to foreign borrowing) and by making a steady increase in the percentage of net expenditure on operating expenses and entitlements at the cost of investment. [107]

In March 1999, major OPEC members reached a preliminary agreement to cut world oil production by more than 2 MMBD beginning on April 1. Special emphasis was placed on resolving the dispute over Iran's adherence to this and previous output cut agreements. Iran had maintained that its 300,000 bpd reduction should be taken from a baseline of 3.9 MMBD, whereas other OPEC states said it should have been 3.6 MMBD. The issue was resolved when Saudi Arabia, Kuwait, and the UAE agreed to absorb the missing Iranian cut and Iran accepted the benchmark of 3.6 million bpd for all future cutbacks in return. All other OPEC states accepted production cuts below the July 1998 quotas, and all OPEC members except Iraq then agreed to the cuts. The agreement of March 1999 brought Saudi Arabia's production to 7.438 MMBD, substantially below the level of 8 MMBD that it had tried to defend for the past several years.[108]

The Wheel Turns: The Oil Crash Turns into an Oil Boom

In the late spring of 1999, this situation reversed itself. An unexpectedly rapid Asian recovery and high economic growth in the developed world began to drive demand back up. As a result, oil prices rebounded following OPEC's March 23, 1999, agreement to cut oil production by 1.7 MMBD and West Texas Intermediate and other major crude prices approximately tripled in less than a year.

The increase in oil prices was caused by several other factors: OPEC's March 1999, 1.7-million bbl/d quota cut agreement, in addition to over 2.5 million bbl/d in two output cutbacks agreed to earlier; high levels of OPEC compliance to its quota agreement; and strong world oil demand, including the rebounding Asian economies and the surging U.S. economy. As a result, the EIA's data and forecast information indicated that OPEC oil export revenues for 2000 were 59% higher than 1999, and 113% higher than it 1998.

Saudi oil prices increased sharply following OPEC's March 23, 1999, cutback agreement. They reached a ten-year high of $30 per barrel in early

March 2000, and averaged $25 to $30 per barrel during late 1999 and early 2000. The Hague and Amsterdam production agreements successfully cut global production by 420,000 barrels in June 1999. Total production averaged 76.48 million bpd and Brent crude prices edged above $31 in the first quarter of 2000. The average price of Brent in 1999 averaged $17.90 a barrel, up from $12.70 a barrel in 1998. As a result, Saudi revenues from crude oil exports rose to $38 billion in 1999.[109]

Oil prices continued to rise in 2000, reaching a new ten-year high of $37 a barrel in the third quarter of 2000, a price not seen since the Gulf War. This rise in oil prices led to an improvement in Saudi finances and the Kingdom's economic situation, as oil prices continued to rise to the point where they were 52% higher in early 2000 than in 1999. By Saudi calculations, the value of oil exports, which had dropped from $52.2 billion in 1997 to $32.5 billion in 1998, rose back to $44.7 billion in 1999, and then leaped to $72.1 billion in 2000.

The Saudi budget deficit, which had increased from 2.9% in 1997 to 9.6% in 1998, dropped to 6.4% in 1999, and there was a budget surplus of 3.5% in 2000. The Saudi deficit on current account went from +0.21% of the GDP in 1997 to –10.21% in 1998, but rose to +0.28% in 1999 and +9.01% in 2000. The government domestic debt as a percentage of GDP, which had averaged 76% to 87% in 1994–1997, risen to 116% to 119% in 1998 and 1999, dropped to 95% in 2000.[110]

This one-year oil boom helped to improve the overall financial stability of the Kingdom, but scarcely solved any of the Kingdom's structural problems. Even in a year like 2000, the real growth in the GDP at most only marginally exceeded population growth The oil boom of 2000 also did not allow the government to make major increases in its official foreign assets, even though it allocated some of its year-2000 budget surplus to such spending. These had climbed back from levels near or below $60 billion during the Gulf War to a peak of around $86 billion in 1997. The oil crash forced the Kingdom to cut them to $74 billion by the beginning of 2000, and they were still around $79.0 billion in early 2001.[111]

Moreover, petroleum revenues dropped again in 2001. The average price of Saudi crude dropped from $27.00 in 2000 to $21.80. The real value of the oil sector of the Saudi GDP, which had increased by 8.5% in 2000, dropped by 3.6% in 2001. GDP growth was at most well under half the population growth.[112] The budget surplus, which was 3.5% of the GDP in 2000, dropped to a deficit equal to 3.9% of the GDP in 2001. In short, Saudi Arabia certainly benefited from the increases in oil revenues in 1999–2001. It has no way to plan as if it could count on them in the future, however, and the fact such booms follow busts without warning means it cannot even plan how to use such unexpected windfalls efficiently.

OIL WEALTH AND DEMOGRAPHICS:
UNDERSTANDING THE FUTURE LIMITS

There is no way to accurately model any aspect of Saudi Arabia's economic future. In fact, virtually every part of the preceding economic analysis has documented major unpredictable swings in some aspect of Saudi Arabia's economy. At the same time, no discussion of the limits of oil wealth can be complete without examining possible future trends.

History has shown that this is anything but easy. Oil prices are anything but stable, and the average price of a barrel of Saudi light crude oil went from $18.80 in 1997 to $12.24 in 1998 (–45%), only to rise to $17.40 in 1999 (+42%), $26.81 in 2000 (+54%), and go down to $24.70 in 2001 (–8%). Put differently, the price of oil nearly doubled between 1999 and 2000, although it fell back in the first half of 2001.[113]

The broader economic impact of these changes is illustrated by the fact the Saudi per capita income in current U.S. dollars fell from $7,313 in 1997 to $6,208 in 1998 (–15%), only to rise to $7,863 in 2000 (+27%). The fact that the previous charts reflect similar massive swings that occurred in oil revenues and the Saudi economy in 1973–1975, 1979–1982, 1986, and 1991–1992, is a warning that any effort to predict future trends borders on hubris.[114]

There are, however, practical limits to how far Saudi Arabia's oil revenues can swing as long as the world remains dependent on oil for much of its energy. This is a dependence that would require a massive shift in energy technology, and both the IEA and the EIA of the U.S. Department of Energy currently project a steady increase in world demand for oil through at least 2020—even under the scenarios that make the most favorable assumptions about increases in alternative energy resources.

Demand is scarcely likely to be stable, but world economic growth is virtually certain to steadily increase demand over time.[115] Some things simply do not happen. Oil prices do not reach sustained levels that cause the global economy to collapse. Oil prices do not drop to sustained levels below the cost of production. A nation like Saudi Arabia—with more than some eighty years of proven reserves, even at export levels in excess of 8 million barrels of oil—does not run out of oil. Beyond these limits, however, any estimate must be more illustrative than predictive.

Even so, it is interesting to examine what happens when relatively favorable assumptions are made about the increase in world demand and oil prices, and the resulting Saudi oil revenues, and then look at how these would affect Saudi Arabia's future per capita income. The data in Charts 6.17 to 6.22 portray a complex set of numbers, but they also portray a relatively straightforward way of illustrating the best real-world case that Saudi Arabia is likely to encounter in terms of oil revenues and oil wealth over the coming two decades:

- Chart 6.17 illustrates the EIA's projection of the increase in Saudi and other Gulf state oil production capacity through 2020. These estimates are based on the EIA's reference case, which sees Saudi Arabia as the key swing state in increasing world oil supply. It should be noted that Saudi production capacity is estimated to rise from 9.4 million barrels per day (MMBD) in 2000 to 22.1 MMBD in 2020. This is an increase of well over 100%, and senior Saudi officials seriously doubt that the Kingdom will actually reach 20.0 MMBD by 2020. As such, it makes very optimistic assumptions about Saudi production capacity.

- Chart 6.18 provides a similar EIA projection of total actual Gulf exports. This projection does not break out the level of actual Gulf production by country, but it too indicates an increase in production of more than 100% by 2020. At the same time, it shows that total exports are projected to be much lower than total production capacity—both because of increases in domestic demand and diversion to the production of petroleum products. The EIA projects that total Gulf production capacity in 2020 will be 42.9 MMBD, but that actual exports will only be 33.5 MMBD, or 78% percent of total capacity.

- Chart 6.19 examines the possible revenues Saudi Arabia can earn from its oil production under a wide range of prices. The first set of figures show the EIA estimate of total production capacity under different market conditions. The second set of figures show the average landed cost of an imported barrel of oil to the United States. These price estimates are significantly higher than price estimates based on average refiner acquisition cost or Brent crude prices which are, in turn, are higher than the average price of Saudi crude The chart then examines three sets of scenarios for Saudi oil revenues. The first set of revenue calculations is based on the total potential value of all oil sales if Saudi Arabia produced and exported at 100% of capacity under the low, reference, and high demand cases. The second set of revenue estimates is more realistic in that it assumes that Saudi Arabia can export a stable average of about 80% of its total production capacity. This too seems to be a favorable assumption for Saudi Arabia.

- The estimates in Chart 6.19 project a major increase in real Saudi oil revenues between 2000 and 2020, and show that Saudi oil revenues could increase from some $66 billion in 2000 to $145.55 to $161.26 billion by 2020. At the same time, it is important to note that even under the most favorable case, Saudi Arabia would only earn 78% of its peak real oil earnings in 1980, and would only earn 68% in the reference case. Put simply, these figures warn that Saudi Arabia is unlikely to ever earn the same real oil export revenues it earned in 1980.

- Charts 6.20 and 6.21 add another parameter to the model. They show the range of per capita Saudi oil earnings using the population growth estimates made by the World Bank and Census Bureau. As discussed in Chapter 4, such estimates have much the same range of uncertainty as oil production and oil revenue, but the results are striking. Population growth has already had a massive impact on Saudi oil wealth. Oil wealth per capita peaked in 1980 at $22,596 per person. Population growth and drops in oil revenue had driven

Chart 6.18
U.S. Projections of Actual Saudi Exports, 2000 versus 2020 (in MMBD)

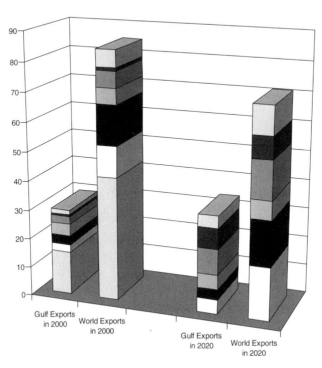

	Gulf Exports in 2000	World Exports in 2000		Gulf Exports in 2020	World Exports in 2020
☐ Rest of World	1.5	5.9		4.3	9.9
■ China	0.7	1.1		7.1	7.6
▨ Pacific Rim	2.7	5.6		8.7	13.1
▨ Industrial Asia	4.1	5.4		5	6.5
■ Western Europe	3.2	13.7		3.5	15.6
☐ North America	2.6	10.7		4.9	18.2
☐ TOTAL	14.8	42.4		*33.5	*70.9

Gulf as % of World   34.9%   47.2%

Source: Adapted by Anthony H. Cordesman from U.S. Department of Energy, *International Energy Outlook, 2002* (Washington: Energy Information Agency, March 2002), Table 13, p. 38.

it down to $3,041 in 2000, even though this was a very favorable year for oil revenues.

• Chart 6.22 simply portrays the range of the per capita oil export income figures shown in Charts 6.20 and 6.21 in a form that shows the range of uncertainty involved. It shows that oil revenues per capita in 2020 can range

Chart 6.19
Even Extremely Favorable Estimates of Future Saudi Oil Revenues Do Not Bring Them Back to the 1980 Peak

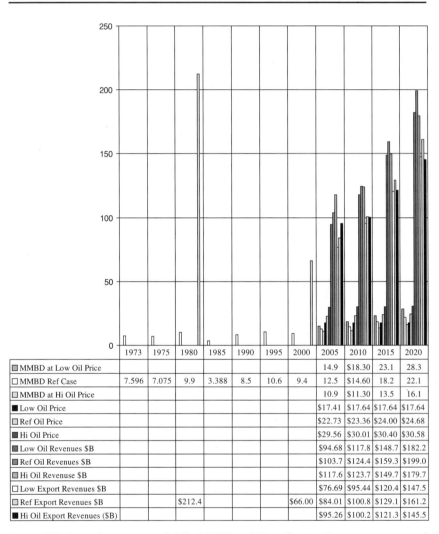

	1973	1975	1980	1985	1990	1995	2000	2005	2010	2015	2020
▣ MMBD at Low Oil Price								14.9	$18.30	23.1	28.3
☐ MMBD Ref Case	7.596	7.075	9.9	3.388	8.5	10.6	9.4	12.5	$14.60	18.2	22.1
☐ MMBD at Hi Oil Price								10.9	$11.30	13.5	16.1
■ Low Oil Price								$17.41	$17.64	$17.64	$17.64
☐ Ref Oil Price								$22.73	$23.36	$24.00	$24.68
■ Hi Oil Price								$29.56	$30.01	$30.40	$30.58
■ Low Oil Revenues $B								$94.68	$117.8	$148.7	$182.2
■ Ref Oil Revenues $B								$103.7	$124.4	$159.3	$199.0
☐ Hi Oil Revenuse $B								$117.6	$123.7	$149.7	$179.7
☐ Low Export Revenues $B								$76.69	$95.44	$120.4	$147.5
☐ Ref Export Revenues $B			$212.4				$66.00	$84.01	$100.8	$129.1	$161.2
■ Hi Oil Export Revenues ($B)								$95.26	$100.2	$121.3	$145.5

Notes: EIA Cases. Revenues equal daily MMBD × 365 × oil price. Export revenues equal 0.81 × total revenues. Prices in constant 2000 $US.

Source: Adapted by Anthony H. Cordesman from U.S. Department of Energy, *International Energy Outlook, 2002* (Washington: Energy Information Agency, March 2002), Table 12, p. 39 and Appendix D, pp. 239–241.

Chart 6.20
Rough Estimates of Future Saudi Oil Revenues, Population, and Exports Per Capita: World Bank Population Data

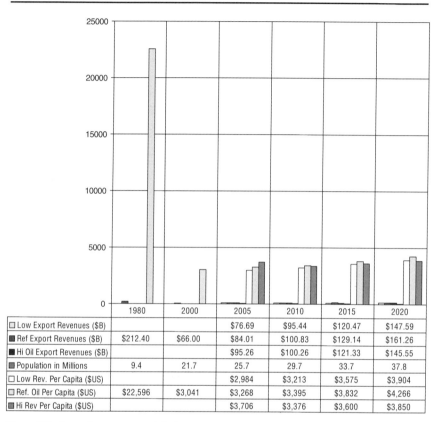

	1980	2000	2005	2010	2015	2020
☐ Low Export Revenues ($B)			$76.69	$95.44	$120.47	$147.59
■ Ref Export Revenues ($B)	$212.40	$66.00	$84.01	$100.83	$129.14	$161.26
■ Hi Oil Export Revenues ($B)			$95.26	$100.26	$121.33	$145.55
■ Population in Millions	9.4	21.7	25.7	29.7	33.7	37.8
☐ Low Rev. Per Capita ($US)			$2,984	$3,213	$3,575	$3,904
☐ Ref. Oil Per Capita ($US)	$22,596	$3,041	$3,268	$3,395	$3,832	$4,266
■ Hi Rev Per Capita ($US)			$3,706	$3,376	$3,600	$3,850

Notes: EIA Cases. Revenues equal daily MMBD × 365 × oil price. Export revenues equal 0.81 × total revenues. Prices in constant 2000 $US. Revenues per capita are total export revenues divided by population.

from $3,199 to $4,266. It should again be stressed, however, that these estimates are made under very favorable assumptions for Saudi Arabia, and that in the real world, it is very unlikely that actual per capita oil revenues will significantly exceed $3,000.

Uncertain as such a modeling effort is, it does show that even very favorable assumptions still indicate that Saudi Arabia cannot rely on oil wealth in the future, and that the historical problems over dependence on oil has created for Saudi Arabia will be just as valid in the future, even if Saudi Arabia is able to more than double its gross real oil exports over the

Chart 6.21
Rough Estimates of Future Saudi Oil Revenues, Population, and Exports Per Capita: U.S. Census Bureau Population Data

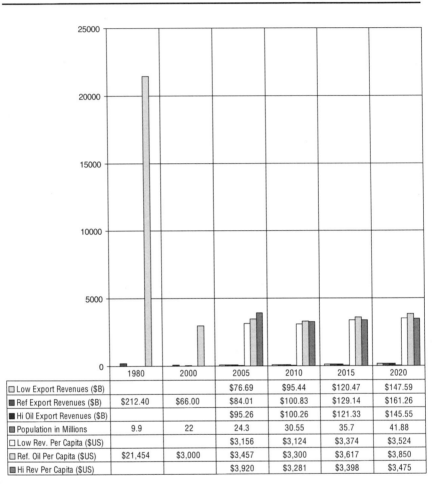

	1980	2000	2005	2010	2015	2020
☐ Low Export Revenues ($B)			$76.69	$95.44	$120.47	$147.59
■ Ref Export Revenues ($B)	$212.40	$66.00	$84.01	$100.83	$129.14	$161.26
■ Hi Oil Export Revenues ($B)			$95.26	$100.26	$121.33	$145.55
■ Population in Millions	9.9	22	24.3	30.55	35.7	41.88
☐ Low Rev. Per Capita ($US)			$3,156	$3,124	$3,374	$3,524
☐ Ref. Oil Per Capita ($US)	$21,454	$3,000	$3,457	$3,300	$3,617	$3,850
■ Hi Rev Per Capita ($US)			$3,920	$3,281	$3,398	$3,475

Notes: EIA Cases. Revenues Equal Daily MMBD × 365 × oil price. Export revenues equal 0.81 × total revenues. Prices in constant 2000 $US. Revenues per capita are total export revenues divided by population.

next two decades. This is not a warning that Saudi Arabia will be poor, nor does it mean that oil will not be of immense value to the Kingdom. It is, however, a clear indication that Saudi Arabia's emphasis on economic reform, diversification, and expanding its private sector is absolutely critical to both Saudi Arabia's welfare as a nation and its future stability.

Chart 6.22
Oil "Wealth" Equals Oil "Adequacy" or Oil "Poverty": Future Saudi Oil Exports Per Capita, 2000–2020

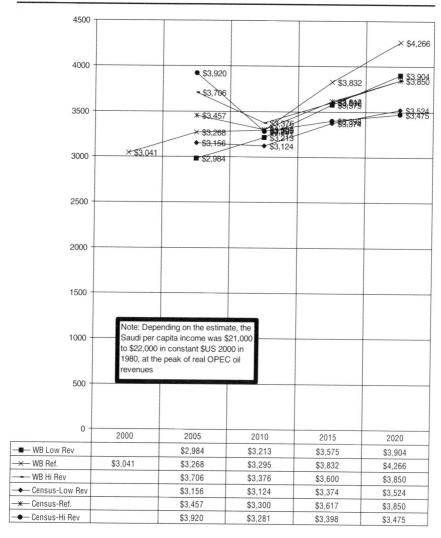

	2000	2005	2010	2015	2020
─■─ WB Low Rev		$2,984	$3,213	$3,575	$3,904
─✕─ WB Ref.	$3,041	$3,268	$3,295	$3,832	$4,266
─■─ WB Hi Rev		$3,706	$3,376	$3,600	$3,850
─◆─ Census-Low Rev		$3,156	$3,124	$3,374	$3,524
─✻─ Census-Ref.		$3,457	$3,300	$3,617	$3,850
─●─ Census-Hi Rev		$3,920	$3,281	$3,398	$3,475

Notes: EIA Cases. Revenues Equal Daily MMBD × 365 × oil price. Export revenues equal 0.81 × total revenues. Prices in constant 2000 $US. Revenues per capita are total export revenues divided by population. Cordesman case is 75% of reference case.

THE CHALLENGE OF REDUCING THE GOVERNMENT SECTOR

Political and military factors also increase problems Saudi Arabia has in reducing government spending and the role of government in its economy. Chart 6.23 shows that Saudi Arabia has an exceptionally high rate of state spending even in a region where the state dominates most economies. Furthermore, the Kingdom's actual level of "statism" is higher than the data in Chart 6.23 indicate. Much of the "private sector" activity in Saudi Arabia consists of service industries, state-subsidized private industries, and activities that add little value to imports. The funding of such activity is ultimately dependent on petroleum-related export income and deficit spending.

Chart 6.23 also shows how military expenditures and arms imports impact on this situation. Saudi Arabia has good reasons for many of its military expenditures. Nevertheless, they do put a massive burden on the Saudi economy, the Saudi budget, and discretionary government spending. The trend data in Chart 6.23 provide a U.S. estimate of the long-term trends in the Saudi GDP, central government spending, Saudi military spending, and arms imports. These data are measured in constant 1999 dollars, and they reflect many of the broader macroeconomic problems that have already been discussed. Chart 6.24 shows that the total cost of military expenditures and arms imports have averaged well over $20 billion a year for nearly two decades, that they have ranged from 13% to 29% of the GNP depending on the political and military conditions in the Gulf, and that they have ranged from 37% to over 70% of central government expenditures (CGE).[116]

National security is not an idle luxury. Nevertheless, the data in Chart 6.24 clearly illustrates the tragedy of arms in the Gulf, and the cost to Saudi Arabia of dealing with the threats discussed in Chapter 2. Unfortunately, there is little near-to-mid-term prospect that the Kingdom can substantially reduce these expenditures and use them for economic reform and economic development.

MANAGING AND RESTRUCTURING THE SAUDI BUDGET

All of these issues increase the challenges that Saudi Arabia faces in managing its national budget. Revenue shortfalls and budget deficits are not new problems for Saudi Arabia. Demographics, excessive subsidies and welfare payments, overdependence on petroleum, politics, and the cost of war began to put serious pressure on the Saudi budget nearly a decade before the Gulf War. Chart 6.25 shows the macroeconomic trends involved in shaping the history of Saudi Arabia's budget deficits, and Chart 6.26 and Table 6.5 show that major budget deficits were the rule, rather than the exception, during the 1990s. The only time Saudi Arabia was able to avoid

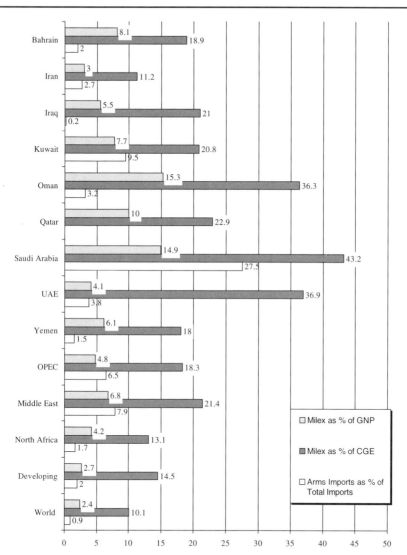

Note: Military spending as a percent of central government expenditures (CGE) and gross
national product (GNP), and arms imports as a percent of total.

Source: Adapted by Anthony H. Cordesman from U.S. State Department, *World Military
Expenditures and Arms Transfers, 1999–2000* (Washington: Bureau of Verification, 2002),
Tables I and II.

Chart 6.24
Saudi Gross National Product, Central Government Expenditures, Military Expenditures, Total Exports, Total Imports, and Arms Import Deliveries, 1984–1999 (Constant $99 millions)

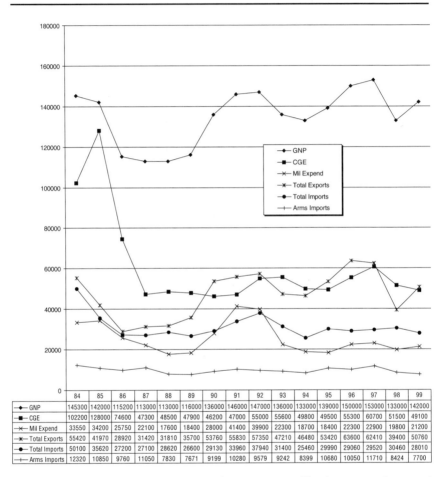

	84	85	86	87	88	89	90	91	92	93	94	95	96	97	98	99
◆ GNP	145300	142000	115200	113000	113000	116000	136000	146000	147000	136000	133000	139000	150000	153000	133000	142000
■ CGE	102200	128000	74600	47300	48500	47900	46200	47000	55000	55600	49800	49500	55300	60700	51500	49100
✕ Mil Expend	33550	34200	25750	22100	17600	18400	28000	41400	39900	22300	18700	18400	22300	22900	19800	21200
✳ Total Exports	55420	41970	28920	31420	31810	35700	53760	55830	57350	47210	46480	53420	63600	62410	39400	50760
● Total Imports	50100	35620	27200	27100	28620	26600	29130	33960	37940	31400	25460	29990	29060	29520	30460	28010
＋ Arms Imports	12320	10850	9760	11050	7830	7671	9199	10280	9579	9242	8399	10680	10050	11710	8424	7700

Sources: Adapted by Anthony H. Cordesman from ACDA, *World Military Expenditures and Arms Transfers, 1995* (Washington: ACDA/GPO, 1996); U.S. State Department, *World Military Expenditures and Arms Transfers, 1998* (Washington: Bureau of Verification and Compliance, 2000); and *World Military Expenditures and Arms Transfers, 1999–2000* (Washington: Bureau of Verification and Compliance, 2002).

such deficits was during a period of peak oil revenues in 2000, and it retuned to deficit spending in 2001 in spite of a projected surplus and exceptionally high oil revenues.

The Kingdom's financial problems became truly serious after the first oil crash in 1986. Saudi Arabia's FY1988 budget was projected at SR 141.2

Chart 6.25

Saudi Arabian Government Oil and Total Revenue versus Total Expenditures and Surplus/Deficit

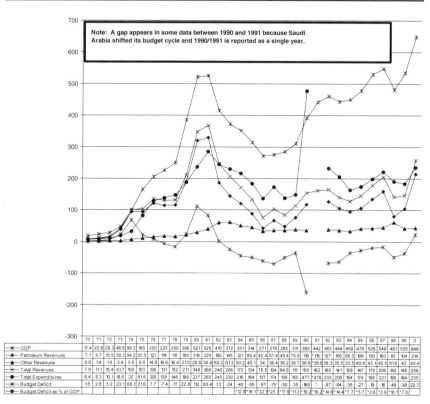

Note: A gap appears in some data between 1990 and 1991 because Saudi Arabia shifted its budget cycle and 1990/1991 is reported as a single year.

	70	71	72	73	74	75	76	77	78	79	80	81	82	83	84	85	86	87	88	89	90	91	92	93	94	95	96	97	98	99	0
GDP	17.4	22.8	28.3	46.6	99.3	165	205	225	250	386	521	525	415	372	351	314	271	276	285	311	392	442	461	444	450	479	529	549	481	535	649
Petroleum Revenues	7.1	9.7	13.5	39.3	94.2	93.5	121	114	115	189	319	329	186	145	121	88.4	42.4	67.4	48.4	75.9	118	*118.1	127	106	95.5	106	136	160	80	104	214
Other Revenues	0.8	1.4	1.9	2.4	5.9	9.9	14.8	16.6	16.4	21.9	28.8	39.4	60.2	61.3	50.2	45.1	34	36.4	36.2	38.7	36.6	*36.6	38.3	35.5	33.5	40.8	43.1	45.5	61.6	43	43.6
Total Revenues	7.9	11.1	15.4	41.7	100	103	136	131	132	211	348	368	246	206	172	134	76.5	104	84.6	115	155	162	165	141	129	147	179	206	142	148	258
Total Expenditures	6.4	8.3	10.1	18.6	32	81.8	128	138	148	188	237	285	245	230	216	184	137	174	139	150	477	*476	233	206	164	174	198	221	190	184	235
Budget Deficit	1.5	2.8	5.2	23.1	68.1	21.6	7.7	-7.4	-17	22.8	112	83.4	1.3	-24	-45	-50	-61	-70	-50	-35	-160	*.	-67	-64	-35	-27	-19	-16	-49	-36	22.7
Budget Deficit as % of GDP															*12.8	*16.1	*22.5	*25.3	*17.6	*11.2	*19.2		*14.6	*14.4	*7.7	*5.7	*3.6	*2.9	*10.1	*7.0	

Sources: Adapted by Anthony H. Cordesman from SAMA, *Thirty-Sixth Annual Report 1421H (2000G)* (Riyadh: SAMA, 2001), pp. 343–346, 360–361, 393–395, and *Thirty-Seventh Annual Report 1422H (2001G)* (Riyadh: SAMA, 2001), pp. 354–355, 406.

billion ($37.7 billion), down 17% from the 1987 level of SR 170 billion. Oil revenues were unofficially projected at SR 65.2 billion. The 1988 deficit was projected at SR 35.9 billion ($9.57 billion) versus deficits of about SR 50 billion in each of the previous four years.

Saudi Arabia sought to reduce this deficit by imposing 12% to 20% import duties and local borrowing in the form of some $8 billion in bonds.[117] If it had not been for Iraq's invasion of Kuwait, these measures might have helped to reduce Saudi Arabia's budget deficits, but the cost of the Gulf War made the Saudi situation much worse. Although Saudi oil

Chart 6.26
Saudi Arabian Government Oil and Total Revenue versus Total Expenditures

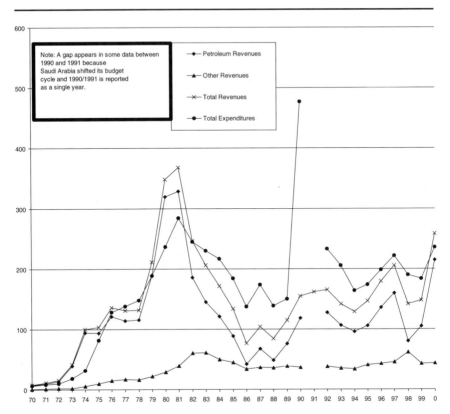

Note: A gap appears in some data between 1990 and 1991 because Saudi Arabia shifted its budget cycle and 1990/1991 is reported as a single year.

—◆— Petroleum Revenues

—▲— Other Revenues

—✕— Total Revenues

—●— Total Expenditures

Source: Adapted by Anthony H. Cordesman from SAMA, *Thirty-Sixth Annual Report 1421H (2000G)* (Riyadh: SAMA, 2001), pp. 343–346, 360–361, 393–395.

revenues rose sharply during the war, Saudi Arabia had to make unplanned expenditures costing billions of dollars, ranging from payments to members of the UN Coalition to expenses for the Saudi military and refugee housing. Estimates of these costs differ, but the IMF puts them at around $65 billion, of which $12.8 billion was paid to the United States.[118]

Saudi Budgets in the Early- to Mid-1990s

The Saudi budget deficit grew from 6.4% of GDP in 1990 to 11% of the GDP in 1993, forcing the government to make significant cuts in its expenditures. This resulted in a 1994 budget plan calling for a 19% cut in government spending from $52.5 billion in 1993 to $42.7 billion. This was

Table 6.5
Saudi Arabia's Annual Budgets, 1990–2002

Fiscal Year	Revenues		Expenditures		Deficit		Balance as
	B Riyals	B $US	B Riyals	B $US	B Riyals	B $US	% of GNP
1990	118	31.5	143	38.1	-25	-6.7	—
1991*	118	31.5	143	38.1	-25	-6.7	—
1992	151	40.3	181	48.3	-30	-8.0	—
1993	169	45.1	197	52.5	-27.8	-7.4	—
1994	120	32.0	160	42.7	-40	-10.7	-7.7
1995	135	36.0	150	40.0	-15	-4.0	-5.7
1996 (Original Draft)	131.5	35.07	150	40.0	-18.5	-4.9	
1996 (Actual)	177	47.2	194	51.73.	-17.0	-4.53	-3.6
1997	204	54.40	210	56.00	-6.0	-1.60	-2.9
1998 (Estimate) 12/97	178	47.5	196	53.3	-18.0	-4.80	
1998 (Actual)	143	38.13	189.0	50.40	-46.0	-12.26	-9.6
1999	147.0	39.20	181.1	48.27	-33.7	-9.07	-6.4
2000	—	66.82	—	62.76	45.0	6.06	3.5
2001 (Estimate)	215.0	57.33	215.0	57.33	0	0	-3.9
2001 (Actual)	230	61.3	255	68.0	25	6.7	
2002 (Estimate Jan. 02)	157.0	41.90	202.0	53.90	45.0	-12.0	-7.3
2002 (Estimate Aug. 02)	220.0	58.67	239.0	63.73	-5.1	-2.8	

Notes: 3.75 Saudi riyals = $1; *Major off-budget expenditures to finance Gulf War.

Sources: Data for 1990–1995 are adapted from data provided in the monthly newsletter of the Information Office, Royal Embassy of Saudi Arabia, Vol. 12, No. 2 (February 1995), p. 3. Data for 1996–1998 have been adapted from IMF Article IV report 1994, *Saudi Arabia,* Vol. 14, No. 2 (February 1997), p. 3; *Saudi Arabia,* Vol. 18, No. 1 (January 2001), p. 2; and Brad Bourland, *The Saudi Economy in 2002* (Riyadh: Saudi American Bank, February 2002), p. 2 and *The Saudi Economy in Mid-Year 2002* (Riyadh: Saudi American Bank, August 2002), p. 12.

followed by the 1995 budget plan, which (based on an underlying oil price assumption of $14.00–$14.50 per barrel) called for an additional cut of 6.25% in spending. A combination of austerity measures and unexpectedly high oil revenues reduced Saudi Arabia's deficit to 8% of the GDP in 1994 and 6% in 1995.[119]

By the mid-1990s, Saudi Arabia had paid for the Gulf War but still faced serious budget problems. Additional increases in oil prices gave the government total revenues of SR 177 billion in 1996, instead of projected revenues of SR 131.5 billion. This additional income could have given Saudi Arabia a slight budget surplus for the first time in recent history. In practice, however, Saudi spending leaped from a projected level of SR 150 billion to an actual level of SR 194 billion—following a pattern that the Saudi budget always expands to consume every increase in oil revenues. As a result, the official estimate of the 1996 deficit reached SR 17 billion, close to the SR 18.5 billion that had originally been projected.

The government also increasingly dealt with its budget problems by raising its domestic civil debt as a substitute for foreign loans. Foreign debt was reduced to low levels by the late 1990s, but only at the cost of increasing central government domestic debt.[120] In fact, Saudi Arabia was unable to make significant reductions its domestic debt, despite high oil revenues in 1999 and 2000. Domestic debt rose each year from 1994 to 2000. It rose from SR 336 billion and 76% of the GDP in 1994 to SR 625 billion and 119% of the GDP in 1999. It was still SR 616 billion and 95% of the GDP in 2000 and rose back to SR 630 billion and 99% of the GDP in 2001. It was projected to be SR 675 billion and 109% of the GDP in 2002.[121]

These trends in Saudi Arabia's budgets are shown in more detail in Table 6.5 and Chart 6.26, although the data in these charts omit a portion of Saudi Arabia's extraordinary expenditures on the Gulf War. If these additional expenditures are included, the Saudi fiscal deficit might have reached $37 billion during 1990–1991, and $10 billion during 1992. In fact, the war made Saudi financial management so uncertain that Saudi Arabia was forced to adopt a working budget for 1991 because it could not keep track of its expenditures. It then had to raise its estimated 1992 expenditures by 27% over the 1990 budget to allow for unanticipated costs.[122]

Charts 6.27 and 6.28 show that Saudi Arabia also experienced a drastic drop in liquidity due to both the low oil revenues and its expenditures for the Gulf War. Saudi Arabia has never provided a full accounting of its budget expenditures during the Gulf War, but U.S. estimates indicate that central government expenditures rose from $38.5 billion in 1989, in constant 1999 dollars, to $60.6 billion in 1990 and 72.5 billion in 1991, and then returned to $40.1 billion in 1992 and $37.6 billion in 1993. This total budget increase is partly explained by a rise in military spending from $18.4 billion in 1989 to $28 billion in 1990, $44.4 billion in 1991, and $39.9 billion in 1992, before dropping to $22.3 billion in 1992 and $18.7

Chart 6.27

Saudi Arabia: Government Foreign Assets and Liquidity—Part One: Liquidity in Billions of U.S. Dollars, 1960–1994

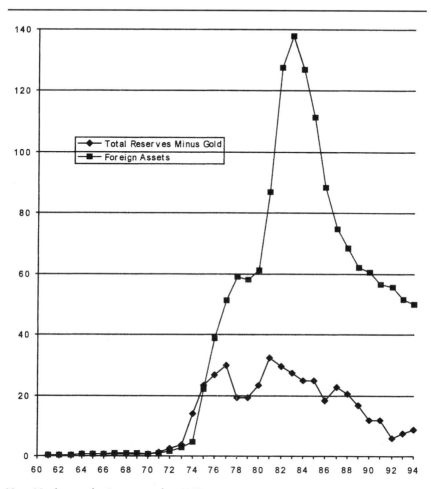

Note: No data on foreign assets after 1992.

Sources: Adapted by Anthony H. Cordesman from IEA, *Middle East Oil and Gas* (Paris: IEA, 1995), pp. 305–309, and based on IMF, *International Financial Statistics*.

billion in 1993. These trends not only show the total burden of Gulf War spending, but that Saudi Arabia had to cut back in some areas of domestic spending to limit its total budget costs.[123]

Under these conditions, it is hardly surprising that the Kingdom had to borrow some $7 billion ($4.5 billion from internationally syndicated loans and $2.5 billion from local banks). This need to borrow while paying

Chart 6.28
Saudi Arabia: Government Foreign Assets and Liquidity—Part Two: Official
Foreign Assets, 1994–2002

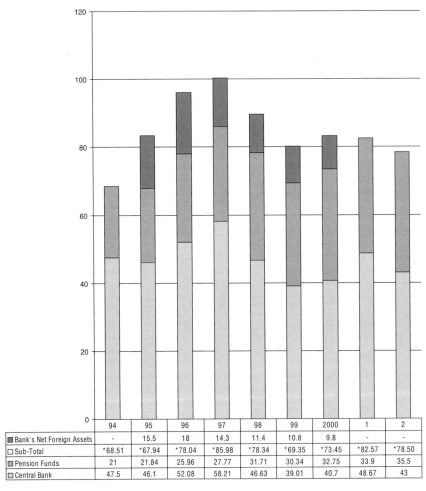

	94	95	96	97	98	99	2000	1	2
■ Bank's Net Foreign Assets	-	15.5	18	14.3	11.4	10.8	9.8	-	-
□ Sub-Total	*68.51	*67.94	*78.04	*85.98	*78.34	*69.35	*73.45	*82.57	*78.50
■ Pension Funds	21	21.84	25.96	27.77	31.71	30.34	32.75	33.9	35.5
□ Central Bank	47.5	46.1	52.08	58.21	46.63	39.01	40.7	48.67	43

Source: Adapted by Anthony H. Cordesman from Brad Bourland, *The Saudi Economy in 2002*
(Riyadh: Saudi American Bank, February 2002), p. 2.

interest created new tensions with Saudi Arabia's Islamic fundamentalists,
who believe that interest is forbidden by the Koran.[124] Central bank reserves
dropped from more than $100 billion to around $35 to $40 billion, and
official foreign assets from well over $100 billion in 1989 to roughly $68.5
billion in 1994.[125] By 1995, Saudi Arabia had to cut some defense expen-

ditures, including the delaying and canceling certain arms purchases.[126] Saudi Arabia made the last payment on its $4.5 billion debt in June 1995, but continued to run a budget deficit. This deficit reached $7.4 billion in 1993 and rose to $10.7 billion in 1994 (some estimates show $9.28 billion)—a rise that finally triggered more decisive action by the Saudi government.

Budgets and the Sixth Development Plan

Saudi Arabia has been seeking to break out of its pattern of budget deficits ever since the Gulf War. The Sixth Development Plan (1996–2000) sought to eliminate all deficits by the year 2000. Even at the time the plan was issued, however, it was recognized that this goal was based on unrealistically optimistic assumptions about both oil revenues and total spending.

The IMF's Article 5 report for 1995 took a more realistic view of Saudi finances and estimated that the Saudi budget deficit might well return to a level equaling 10% of the GDP by the year 2000—unless the Saudi government made further cuts in expenditures and increases in nonoil revenues.[127] The IMF report also indicated that Saudi Arabia might run a net deficit on current account of $8 billion to $10 billion by the year 2000, and that domestic debt might rise from 77% of GDP in 1994 to 110% in the year 2000.

These problems explain why many Saudi experts felt that the IMF was correct in calling for major reforms that went far beyond the steps the Saudi Arabia set forth in its Sixth Development Plan.[128] The proposed IMF reforms included:[129]

- Freezing total government expenditures at their 1995 level;
- A consumption tax of 5%; an excise duty of 10% on goods like jewelry, clothes, and vehicles; a 2% turnover tax for local and foreign companies;
- A 20% increase in gasoline and diesel fuel prices in 1996 and subsequent price rises to match inflation;
- An annual wage cut of 1% in government wages in 1996–1997 and a 2% cut in 1998–2000;
- Market prices for gasoline and diesel fuel, and
- Further reductions in all subsidies to the minimal level necessary to preserve the social safety net.

In any event, some aspects of the IMF projections proved to be overly pessimistic. The IMF failed to account for the reduction of imports and subsidies by the Saudi government in 1995, unexpected rises in oil prices during 1995–1997, and record profits by Saudi Arabia's downstream and industrial operations—like those of the Saudi Basic Industries Corporation

(SABIC). These developments led the Saudi government to estimate a deficit of just under $4 billion for 1995, or 4.1% of GDP, while IMF experts believed that the Saudi government might not be able to reduce its annual deficits to less than 4% of its GDP in 1995 and 1996. In fact, some IMF experts estimated that the Saudi deficit would be closer to $5.5 billion instead of $4.0 billion.[130]

The actual situation was different. There was a considerable reduction in Saudi Arabia's actual and estimated deficits. Saudi deficit predictions for 1996 originally totaled $4.9 billion in current dollars, and would have created a deficit of around SR 15 billion or 3% to 4.1% of the Saudi GDP.[131] However, a surge in oil prices brought Saudi Arabia some $8 billion more in oil revenues in 1996 than it had originally projected. This extra revenue produced a nominal growth rate of around 8.7% of the GDP, or twice the 4.3% growth rate Saudi Arabia had projected in 1995. In fact, Saudi Arabia might have been able to eliminate most of its deficit if the government had not proved unwilling to pursue the additional spending cuts and revenue increases required to meet the country's fiscal needs.

At the same time, the IMF was right about the need for continued reform even if its near-term forecasts were wrong. Once Saudi planners felt they could safely forecast increased oil revenues they cut back on many of the plans to control government spending they had begun to implement in 1995. They allowed the deficit in the 1996 budget to reach $5.07 billion.

Budget Deficits, the Oil Crash, and the Oil Boom

Saudi Arabia's 1997 budget called for total expenditures of $48.3 billion dollars (SR 181 billion), revenues of $43.7 billion dollars (SR 164 billion), and a deficit of $4.53 billion dollars (SR 17 billion). Saudi Arabia originally estimated that this spending would produce a deficit equal to about 3% to 3.5% of its GDP. A rise in oil prices during 1997 provided Saudi Arabia with substantial additional funds.[132] However, spending also increased in 1997 to $54.8 billion (SR 204 billion) creating a deficit of $4.21 billion. Moreover, Saudi Arabia planned its 1998 budget on the assumption it would have even higher oil revenues. Its 1998 budget originally called for revenues of $47.46 billion (SR 178 billion), expenditures of $52.26 billion (SR 196 billion) and a deficit of $4.8 billion (SR 18 billion).

The oil crash in late 1997 had a serious adverse effect on these projections. Saudi Arabia had to announce on December 28, 1998, that its actual 1998 budget deficit had soared to SR 46 billion ($12.27 billion) versus a corrected deficit estimate of SR 18 billion in mid-1998. This occurred even though actual spending in 1998 was only SR 189 billion, rather than the original projection of SR 196 billion. The problem was that revenues were only SR 143 billion, rather than the forecast SR 178 billion.[133]

The inability to predict rises in oil prices created other problems, and

Saudi Arabia faced another serious financial squeeze in drafting its 1999 budget. On December 28, 1998, Saudi Arabia announced its budget for 1999. The draft budget projected revenues of $32.3 billion (SR 121 billion) and expenditures of $44 billion (SR 165 billion), resulting in a projected deficit of $11.7 billion (SR 44 billion)—about 9% of the GDP. This was nearly equal to the deficit in 1998, which stood at $12.26 billion (SR 46 billion), although the total budget for 1999 was 13% lower than the budget for 1998.[134]

Saudi Arabia cut back significantly on domestic investment in public service and infrastructure programs to minimize the reduction in annual services, welfare, and entitlements.[135] The most significant cuts were made in transportation and communications, social affairs and subsidies, and unallocated funds, which are estimated to include the areas of defense, civil aviation, security, foreign affairs, and government agencies.[136]

The Kingdom continued to focus on temporary spending cuts rather than true economic reform. It did not introduce serious price reform, or introduce major new taxes and take other measures to boost revenues. The most it did in 1998 was to reduce subsidies to the national airline by raising business and first class fares on domestic routes and to introduce a departure fee for international flights. In December 1999, the government announced plans to levy a highway toll as part of an attempt to raise state revenues.[137] Even the extra revenue from the reduction in airline subsidies did not reduce state funding, because Saudia Airlines needed to finance a massive plane purchase program if it was to keep up with domestic demand.[138]

The government did announce somewhat more realistic electricity prices for major consumers but deferred actual implementation until the expected merger of regional power companies in 1999. The government raised the price of gasoline by 50 cents in early May of 1999 and doubled the cost of work permits for foreigners. Sales of premium gasoline were intended to generate an extra $100 million a year at the new rate, but the price remained at levels comparable to the lowest prices paid at the pump in the United States, and regular gas prices remained sharply underpriced.[139] It did not announce rises in water prices and did not raise the prices for visas, permits, other petroleum products, and telephone services as it did in 1995.[140]

Fortunately for the Saudi government, oil prices began to rise following OPEC production cuts of March 1999. This produced an increase in oil revenues that reduced the Kingdom's budget deficit at the end of 1999 to $9.1 billion (SR 34 billion), versus the $11.7 billion previously predicted. Nevertheless, the government still faced the risk it would encounter its seventeenth year of budget deficits in 2000. This led it to try to cut spending despite the increase in oil revenues. The state budget for FY2000 has projected expenditure to $49.33 billion with estimated revenue of $41.87 billion. This gap between revenue and spending, despite the current oil

Chart 6.29
Saudi Government Budget Plans—Part One: Expenditures, Revenues, and Planned versus Actual Deficits (in Current $US Billions)

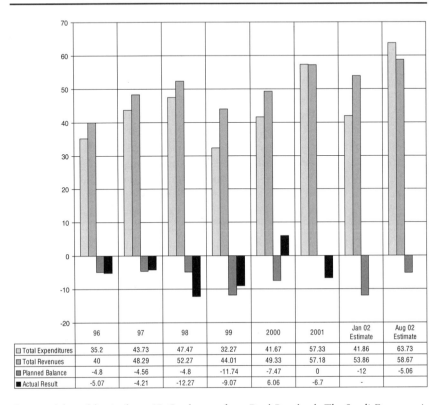

	96	97	98	99	2000	2001	Jan 02 Estimate	Aug 02 Estimate
☐ Total Expenditures	35.2	43.73	47.47	32.27	41.67	57.33	41.86	63.73
☐ Total Revenues	40	48.29	52.27	44.01	49.33	57.18	53.86	58.67
▨ Planned Balance	-4.8	-4.56	-4.8	-11.74	-7.47	0	-12	-5.06
■ Actual Result	-5.07	-4.21	-12.27	-9.07	6.06	-6.7	-	

Sources: Adapted by Anthony H. Cordesman from Brad Bourland, *The Saudi Economy in 2002* (Riyadh: Saudi American Bank, February 2002), p. 36, and *The Saudi Economy at Mid-Year 2002* (Riyadh: Saudi American Bank, August 2002), p. 36.

boom, was largely the result of loan repayment—amounting to 17% of budget spending in 1999—mainly to Kuwait and UAE.[141]

The broad trends in recent Saudi budget plans are shown in Charts 6.29 and 6.30. At the time the budget for 2000 was formulated, there were many different estimates of how much the Saudi economy and budget have or have not benefited from high oil revenues:

- An economist at the National Commercial Bank estimated that government expenditure was expected to increase between 8% to 10%, partly offsetting the decrease in the deficit.[142] According to SAMBA, the actual result at the end of 1999 was SR 181 billion worth of spending and a 34 billion riyal or $9 billion deficit.[143]

Chart 6.30

Saudi Government Budget Plans—Part Two: Spending by Major Sector (in Current $US Billions)

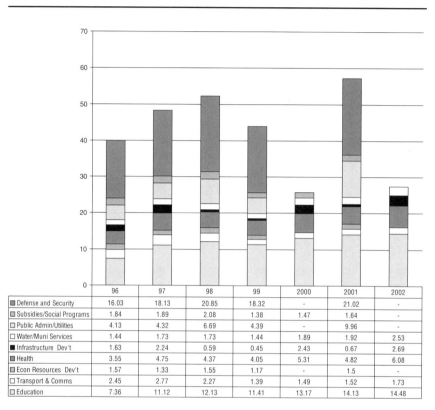

	96	97	98	99	2000	2001	2002
▣ Defense and Security	16.03	18.13	20.85	18.32	-	21.02	-
▣ Subsidies/Social Programs	1.84	1.89	2.08	1.38	1.47	1.64	-
☐ Public Admin/Utilities	4.13	4.32	6.69	4.39	-	9.96	-
☐ Water/Muni Services	1.44	1.73	1.73	1.44	1.89	1.92	2.53
■ Infrastructure Dev't	1.63	2.24	0.59	0.45	2.43	0.67	2.69
▣ Health	3.55	4.75	4.37	4.05	5.31	4.82	6.08
▣ Econ Resources Dev't	1.57	1.33	1.55	1.17	-	1.5	-
☐ Transport & Comms	2.45	2.77	2.27	1.39	1.49	1.52	1.73
☐ Education	7.36	11.12	12.13	11.41	13.17	14.13	14.48

Source: Adapted by Anthony H. Cordesman from Brad Bourland, *The Saudi Economy in 2002* (Riyadh: Saudi American Bank, February 2002), p. 36.

- SAMBA indicated that the government had budgeted $49 billion, or SR 185 billion for 2000, which would only be SR 4 billion above 1999. The budget anticipated $41.87 billion (SR 157 billion) in revenues. As a result, the deficit would be $7.47 billion (SR 28 billion). This estimate was based on an average price of around $18 per barrel for Saudi oil.[144] SAMBA also estimated that the nominal growth in the Saudi GDP was 8.4% in 1999, and would be 6% in 2000 (2% real growth.).[145]

In practice, oil prices rose as sharply in 2000 as they had dropped in 1998. Oil prices rose to extremely high levels due a global economic boom and weather conditions. This allowed the Saudi government to develop a revised budget with revenues of SR 248 billion ($66.13 billion) in 2000, and expenditures of SR 203 billion ($48.27 billion), resulting in a projected surplus of SR 45 billion($12 billion). Revenues were projected to be some 60% higher than the original budget projection of SR 157 billion ($41.9 billion). At the same time, expenditures were still projected at levels 10% higher than the government had originally planned.

It is notable that the rise in planned expenditures was limited relative to the rise in revenues, and that some of the rise in expenditures would have occurred regardless of the rise in revenues. Saudi Arabia has an obligation to pay a thirteenth month of wages every three years because the Saudi lunar Hijri year is shorter than the Gregorian year; this obligation is not included in the Saudi budget. It accounted for SR 8 billion out of the SR 18 billion rise. An additional SR 10 billion was also paid to farmers and contractors for work done in previous years. This reduced the government's arrears from a peak of around $30 billion in the mid-1990s to around $3 billion at end-2000. The government did not add to its debt and seems to have put much of the unexpected surplus in revenues into foreign government investments.[146] Nevertheless, actual revenues were $68.82 billion in 2000 and expenditures still rose to $62.76 billion, creating a surplus of only $6.06 billion.[147] Despite the planners' efforts, actual spending still exceeded the budget by 27%.[148]

Saudi Arabia showed similar restraint in planning its 2001 budget— a restraint that proved wise because of dropping oil prices and an unstable global economy. Saudi Arabia projected revenues of SR 215 billion ($57.33 billion) and expenditures of SR 215 billion ($57.33 billion), resulting in a balanced budget.[149] This involved an increase over 2000's driven largely by the kind of entitlement and welfare costs discussed in Chapter 4. There was an 8.15% increase in human resource development, a 4.81% increase in transport and communications, a 10.1% increase in health services and human development, a 6% increase in infrastructure expenditures, and a 23% increase in municipal services.[150]

When the Council of Ministers announced its estimate of the actual expenditures in the 2001 budget on December 8, 2001, however, government spending had risen to SR 255 billion ($68 billion), and revenues were SR 230 billion ($61.3 billion) for a deficit of SR 25 billion ($6.7 billion). Revenues were 7% higher than forecast, but spending was 16.6% overbudget. Saudi Arabia was clearly consistently underestimating expenditures by at least 10%.

As Charts 6.29 and 6.30 show, it is far from clear that the situation will change in 2002, although the Saudi budget plan was down by 20% relative to 2001. Spending was projected to be SR 202 billion ($53.9 billion) and revenues to be SR 157 billion ($41.9 billion), creating a deficit of SR 45 billion ($12 billion). By mid-2002, however, the situation seemed more favorable. Average annual oil prices per year estimated at $21.75 per barrel in July 2002, versus $18.00 in January 2002. The projected GDP was estimated at SR 685.5 billion in July 2002, versus 616.16 in January, and real growth was projected to rise from –2.0% to +0.2%.

The impact of these changes was so great that government budget deficit was estimated to drop from $12.0 billion to $5.06 billion (from 7.3% of GDP to 2.8%). The GDP per capita was estimated to $8,309 instead of $7,039, the current account balance was estimated to be $10.5 billion versus –$7.9 billion, and the government debt was estimated to drop from 109% of GDP to 95%. These favorable trends, however, were purely the result of world oil prices, driven up largely by fear of war with Iraq. They were little more than a further example of the impact of Saudi dependence on oil export income, and the future remained as uncertain as ever.[151]

The Seventh Development Plan sets broad financial objectives that—if properly implemented—would ease the Saudi government's problems. It does not, however, set clear goals for achieving such objectives nor provide any clear plan for future revenues and expenditures.[152]

- Increase nonoil government revenues;
- Reduce budget deficit to lowest possible level;
- Finance the deficit (if any) through issuing development bonds;
- Use surpluses of government oil revenues to reduce the public debt; and
- Maintain strict adherence to approved expenditure limits, ensuring that the limits set are not exceeded during the fiscal year.

There is no way to know exactly how the Saudi deficit in investment spending compares with the overall budget deficit. The Saudi budget does not provide a detailed enough breakout of operating costs versus investment costs by sector to track the extent to which given expenditures keep up with the rise in demand imposed by increase in population. Saudi experts do feel, however, that there has been a growing backlog in many areas of investment in infrastructure and social services.

Spending on municipal services has not kept pace with need; there has been underinvestment in urban water and sewer infrastructure. Moreover, Chart 6.30 shows that some of the activities most impacted by population growth—health, infrastructure, and water/municipal services—have been funded at relatively low levels in recent years. The estimated rise in the planned 2002 budget seems to be an attempt to compensate in part for past underfunding but it can scarcely compensate for a near-decade of low funding, and the planned rise cannot be accomplished within the total shown without underfunding other high-priority areas.

One thing is all too clear from these figures: As long as the Saudi government is dependent on crude oil and petroleum exports for 75% to 85% of its revenues, even peak oil revenue years like 2000 will not allow Saudi Arabia to reach even a temporary solution to the government's spending problems. This is particularly true because the growth of the nonpetroleum sector of the economy has not affected government dependence on oil revenues.

Oil revenues were 90.4% of total government revenues in 1975, 91.7% in 1980, 66.2% in 195, 77.8% in 1990 and 1991. They ranged from 74.0% to 77.9% during 1992–1997. They dropped to 56.5% in 1998, a year of exceptionally low oil revenues, and rose back to 83.1% in 2000, a year of high oil revenues. The official Saudi figures indicate that nonoil revenues have averaged SR 42 billion a year and were 26% of the budget over the last eleven years, with a low of 16.9% in 2000—a year of high oil revenues— and a high of 43.5% in 1998—a year of low oil revenues.[153] They totaled SR 40.9 billion in 1992 and SR 43.6 billion in 2000, an increase of only 6.6% in current riyals over eight years and no increase in constant riyals.[154]

There is no current prospect that future oil revenues will ever again provide anything like the immense surplus wealth the Kingdom obtained in the 1980s. The government will face steadily increasing difficulties in capping spending at moderate levels due to population growth and the need to fund economic diversification.

The Need for Budget Reforms

There is no precise way to estimate either the size of future Saudi budgets or what level of future state spending the Kingdom actually requires. Past trends clearly show that the budget is under pressure, but they do not reflect any kind of structural crisis in either the economy or the budget. Most developing countries, and many developed ones, would count themselves fortunate if their problems were only as severe as the *current* problems of the Saudi government.

At the same time, Saudi Arabia faces growing problems in managing its state budget and ones that only major reforms can address:

- *There is a lack of overall transparency coupled with a lack of clear benchmarks in measuring the adequacy of government efforts to meet the needs of both the Saudi public and Saudi economic development.* While Saudi Arabia has improved the transparency of its financial reporting and budget data in recent years, the limited data it provides on the impact of the budget only reports on things to be bought or built, and on not performance relative to demand or public need. Effective planning and public discussion require a budget than not only is transparent, but also provides meaningful output measures. It also requires both the use of foreign official investments and the level of both foreign and domestic debt to be addressed in detail. At some point, the budget must also account in much more detail for the impact of state industries on the budget, the full range of subsidies, payments to the Saudi royal family, and the division of the budget into investment, operating, and entitlements expenditures.

- *This transparency needs to be applied to military and national security expenditures, which should be subject to the same cost-benefit review and debate as civil expenditures.* These expenditures account for over 40% of the national budget, and were reported to total SR 68.7 billion ($18.3 billion) in 1999 and SR 74.9 billion ($21.0 billion) in 2000.[155] In practice, Saudi Arabia's public reporting of its budget also conceals additional off-budget expenditures like military costs financed through the transfer of oil and purchases paid through royal accounts.[156] Even this level of transparency, however, is new. Past Saudi budgets did not specifically identify military spending, but lumped it together with various programs into an "other spending" category, which accounted for 54% of the 1996 budget; this percentage still seems to have understated the true cash flow for arms imports.[157] This helped raise the final cost of the deficit to $5.9 billion in 1996. If payments for past arrears are included, then this figure ignored an additional $1.3 to $2.7 billion in arrears from previous years.[158]

- *A combination of Saudi Arabia's economic problems, budget deficit, and growing population have increased the burden of military spending per capita relative to GNP per capita.* These trends are shown in Chart 6.31, although it should be noted that the rate of military spending per capita peaked in the early 1990s because of the Gulf War. As a result, military spending per capita is significantly lower than in the early 1990s. Nevertheless, military expenditures per capita remain relatively high, and consume around 13% to 15% of all per capita income. The annual defense budget still amounts to 16% of the GNP and imposes a strain on both the budget and Saudi capability to meet domestic, economic, and social needs, and financing Saudi military expenditures is likely to be a steadily growing problem.

- *It is increasingly uncertain that Saudi Arabia can increase the share of the budget that goes into investment to the levels it will require.* Even if Saudi Arabia controls military expenditures and receives higher oil revenues, many of the bills for Saudi Arabia's rapid population growth are coming due. In fact, this trend has already begun. Education rose from a level of around SR 27 billion during 1995–1996 to SR 41.7 billion in 1997 and SR 45.6 billion in 1998. While Saudi Arabia probably underspent on education and vocational training during the half-decade following the Gulf War, this still brought the cost of education to 23% of the 1997 budget ($11.1 billion) with the percentage remaining constant for the 1998 budget. Furthermore, Saudi Arabia has not increased most public sector and government salaries since the 1980s. Even in a country with relatively low inflation, this creates a major potential demand for added government spending.[159]

- *Saudi Arabia's real welfare, social, and entitlements program is rising in cost relative to investment even if it is not sustaining the past level of expenditure per capita.* The rise between 2000 and 2001 has already been discussed. Similar increases also took place during the oil crash. The 1997 budget allocated SR 17.3 billion ($4.73 billion) for health and social development and SR 7.1 billion ($1.9 billion) for domestic subsidies. It also allocated SR 6.5 billion ($1.72 billion) for municipal services and water, SR 6.7 billion ($1.78 billion) for transportation and communications, and SR 8.3 billion ($2.2 billion) for

Chart 6.31
Saudi GNP Per Capita versus Military Expenditures Per Capita, 1983–1999
(Constant 1999 $US)

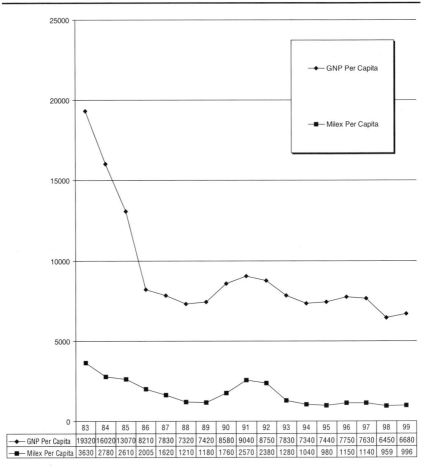

	83	84	85	86	87	88	89	90	91	92	93	94	95	96	97	98	99
◆ GNP Per Capita	19320	16020	13070	8210	7830	7320	7420	8580	9040	8750	7830	7340	7440	7750	7630	6450	6680
■ Milex Per Capita	3630	2780	2610	2005	1620	1210	1180	1760	2570	2380	1280	1040	980	1150	1140	959	996

Source: Adapted by Anthony H. Cordesman from ACDA, *World Military Expenditures and Arms Transfers, 1995* (Washington: ACDA/GPO, 1996); U.S. State Department, *World Military Expenditures and Arms Transfers, 1998* (Washington: Bureau of Arms Control, 1999); and *World Military Expenditures and Arms Transfers, 1999–2000* (Washington: Bureau of Verification and Compliance, 2002).

infrastructure, industry, and water.[160] Despite drastic cuts in revenues, the 1998 budget allocated SR 19.9 billion ($5.3 billion) for health services and social development, SR 7.5 billion ($2 billion) for municipal services and water, SR 17.3 billion ($11.6 billion) for transportation and communication and SR 10.5 billion ($2.8 billion) for infrastructure, industry, and electricity. A review of spending on autonomous governmental institutions indicates major increases were also made in subsidy-related spending on, among other things, flour mills, power, desalination, railways, and ports.[161]

- *As discussed in Chapter 4, a large amount of current expenditures for municipal services, water, transportation, communications, and infrastructure still go to pay for subsidies while the Kingdom underinvests in the maintenance, upgrading, and expansion of capacity.* Saudi Arabia cannot sustain such subsidies when its own estimates indicate that it needs so much investment in new capacity. As discussed earlier, Saudi estimates indicate a requirement for at least 4.5 million new housing units by 2020, at an estimated cost in excess of $260 billion (SR 980 billion). They also include 22,500 new primary schools, 6,000 new institutes of higher education, 5,400 clinics, and 360 hospitals.[162]

- *Saudi revenue streams are still far too dependent on the petroleum sector and duties.* The Kingdom needs to implement new tax laws and strengthen the collection of existing taxes and duties. The previous budget data has shown that income taxes and taxes on domestic businesses account for only token amounts of Saudi revenues. Wealthy Saudis have hundreds of billions of dollars in domestic assets and additional hundred of billions of dollars in private foreign investments. It may make sense to have tax laws that encourage domestic investment and the repatriation of capital, but it makes no sense to subsidize the wealthy for nonproductive consumption with the government equivalent of a free lunch.

- *Civil service reform is needed just as much as the Saudisation of government jobs.* As discussed in Chapter 4, the Kingdom cannot solve its problems in Saudisation by hiring more Saudis to work in already overstaffed government jobs. The number of Saudis employed in government rose at roughly twice the rate of population growth during the 1990s and now seems to be in excess of 600,000.[163] Most of these jobs contribute nothing to economic productivity and many ministries and state firms are badly overstaffed. This is a major drain on the budget.

- *Privatization and the development of the private sector are both necessary, but shaping government activity around market prices is even more important.* The previous analysis has already stressed the importance of diversification and expansion of the private sector. Privatization is equally desirable, particularly as a way of reducing investment burden in the state budget. At the same time, one needs to be careful about ideological statements that the Kingdom should privatize for the sake of privatization. Many of Saudi Arabia's state companies are relatively efficient, and it is not always clear that private Saudi or foreign companies and consortia would really improve the situation. The merits of privatization are a matter of the economics and efficiency of individual ventures and not economic theory. However, if Western experts tend to push privatization for the sake of privatization, Saudi government officials tend to push privatization as a means of dumping burdens on the private sector. The basic problem in many Saudi government services is that their present cost does not include either fair return on investment or recoupment of operating and maintenance costs. Private ventures cannot operate except on the basis of market prices that include both all expenses and a fair profit. Subsidizing private ventures simply disguises subsidies and does not solve any of the Kingdom's problems, although it can sometimes be politically manipulated to disguise the nature of price increases.

FOREIGN AND DOMESTIC STATE DEBT

Debt is another factor that affects the Kingdom's future ability to develop its economy, carry out reform, and meet the goals of its five-year plan. As the previous discussion has noted, a combination of the decline in oil wealth and security problems like the Gulf War forced Saudi Arabia to liquidate a substantial amount of its official foreign investment in the early 1990s, although these investment levels have since recovered. It also forced Saudi Arabia to become a significant borrower. Estimates indicate Saudi state foreign investments dropped to levels below $30 billion in the early 1990s.[164] Foreign debt rose from practically zero to 2% of GDP in 1990–1991 and then to 4% in 1992–1993, although the debt dropped to 1% in 1994.[165] The Saudis were forced to acquire their first sovereign loan since the Gulf War in the amount of $433 million dollars to finance an aircraft purchase from Boeing.

The Saudi debt has not been high by regional standards. Nevertheless, Saudi Arabia's net outstanding domestic debt increased from about 23% to 24% of GDP in 1989–1991 to 53% in 1992, 63% in 1993 70% in 1994, 87% in 1997, 116% in 1998, 119% in 1999, 95% in 2000, and 99% in 2001; it is estimated to be 95% in 2002.[166] This is a rise from SR 342 billion in 1994 to SR 630 billion in 2001; the only year it dropped was in 2000, and even then it still totaled SR 616 billion. The debt was estimated to total SR 630 billion ($171 billion) in mid-year 2002, and projected to rise to 649 billion ($176.1 billion) by the end of 2002.[167]

The Limited Impact of the Present Debt Burden

Domestic borrowing equal to, or greater than, 55% of GDP is normally an indication of serious economic problems, but the linkage between these borrowing requirements and the payment of wartime costs, and the fact that Saudi Arabia does not raise revenue from income tax, makes it difficult to apply such standards to Saudi Arabia.[168] Some economists argue that this level of debt is sustainable because of the limited exposure of banks to government debt and their healthy position in terms of foreign assets.[169] Some 75% to 80% of Saudi domestic debt is held by two government pension funds (which do not report in any detail on their investment holdings), and less than 15% to 20% by commercial banks. Less than 5% is held by private companies and individuals in the form of bonds given in lieu of various payments and subsidies in past years. The fact the government essentially owes most of the debt to itself allows it to manipulate it, and indeed shift funds to more productive foreign investments rather than repay domestic debt. This was the course the government followed during the boom year of 2000.[170]

Past History and Future Risk

Nevertheless, the recent history of Saudi borrowing illustrates that debt can be a serious problem in years of low oil revenues and will become a much more serious problem if the Kingdom does not succeed in economic reform.

During the early 1990s, Saudi Arabia dealt with the foreign debt problem it incurred during the Gulf War by paying off foreign debt at the cost of increasing domestic borrowing, by delaying payments to foreign contractors, and using the windfalls it obtained from unexpectedly high oil prices to reduce its domestic debt. Public borrowing allowed Saudi Arabia to finance major foreign purchases during the 1990s like the purchase of some $6 billion worth of Boeing and McDonnell-Douglas air liners although this was a key factor that raised the Saudi domestic debt to creditors to $94 billion by March 1995, and pushed debt to over 80% of the GDP.

These measures allowed Saudi Arabia to largely retire its Gulf War foreign debt by May 1995. However, the growing domestic debt had a negative impact on the Saudi private sector, whose growth is one of the most important priorities for reforming the Saudi economy. Increased public borrowing created a substantial government public debt that affected banking and investment capabilities. It also created a backlog in payments to foreign companies that some sources estimate reached several billion dollars in 1995.[171]

The Saudi government only avoided further massive increases in domestic borrowing during 1993–1995 by delaying or defaulting on countless domestic contracts. Saudi Arabia owed its farmers nearly $3 billion in subsidy payments in early 1996. While it has since "paid" them much of the money, nearly $2.5 billion of the payment consisted of non–interest bearing certificates that are little more than IOUs that defer actual cash transfers.[172] The government provided interest-bearing bonds worth more than SR 5.200 million ($1.387 billion) to pay off its overdue debts more than 120 major contractors, and asked other contractors to forgive the government's debt due to past profits.[173]

While the Saudi government repeatedly denied that it was delaying and defaulting on its payments, virtually every Saudi and foreign businessman operating in Saudi Arabia had practical evidence that these denials were false.[174] These delays and defaults raised still further questions about how long the Kingdom could continue its rate of domestic borrowing and how much such borrowing might conflict with its efforts to privatize and diversify its economy.

Saudi Arabia was able to deal with some of these problems in 1996. Unexpectedly high oil revenues allowed it to pay some $5.9 billion (SR 22 billion) to its domestic creditors. However, it still remained at least $1.3 billion to $2.7 billion in arrears.[175] The Saudi Ministry of Health remained notorious for its failure to pay its bills. The government also created potential future problems by initiating more new projects than it was clear it could afford.[176] Estimates of the domestic debt varied, but some felt it could have been as high as $120 billion, about 80% of the GDP.[177]

The government was successful in rescheduling its military debt, but only at the cost of increasing the total cost of the debt, including interest. By 1994, its arms purchases during and after the Gulf War had raised its total foreign military sales (FMS) debt to the United States to $23 billion. Saudi Arabia had additional military debts to Europe and to U.S. firms that had sold to Saudi Arabia through commercial sales. This military debt interacted with Saudi civil debts and forced Saudi Arabia to reschedule its FMS debt. This rescheduling took place in November 1994, and did little more than create an extended payment schedule. Saudi Arabia did, however, reduce the number of end items it bought and reduced spending on munitions, military construction, and sustainment. It also eliminated orders to deal with worst-case contingencies.

King Fahd also issued five major guidelines: no new programs, reduce the total FMS debt to $10 billion, stretch out all military program payments where possible, pay all bills on time, and avoid new starts. These guidelines had a significant impact and helped cut Saudi Arabia's total FMS debt from $23 billion in FY1994 to $18 billion in FY1995, $14 billion in FY1996, and $10 billion in FY1997.

Saudi Arabia did not follow these guidelines with sufficient firmness, however, and did not reduce its new military purchases to the level required. A new rise in oil prices and revenues in 1995 and 1996 led Saudi Arabia to increase its new arms orders as part of what one senior advisor called an "insatiable appetite for new hardware." Prince Sultan, the minister of defense, rejected U.S. advice to limit further major arms purchases and stay strictly within the $10 billion limit agreed to in 1994, and threatened to buy from other countries if the United States did not sell. As a result, Saudi Arabia faced a new payments problem following the oil crash of 1997 and could not make all of its military payments to U.S. contractors and other countries on time.

Saudi policies made some international banks reluctant to approve loans for major projects even before the oil crash began to sharply reduce Saudi oil revenues in late 1997. In January 1996, Saudi Consolidated Electric Company for the Eastern Province (Sceco-East) sought a $500 million loan as part of a $1.4 billion project to boost capacity at its Ghazlan power-generating plant. The uncertain political climate, the distortion of cash-flow assumptions by Saudi subsidies, and Sceco's debt to another government entity, Saudi Aramco, all raised doubts in the minds of international financial institutions as to the government's future repayment ability. Some banks were unwilling to invest in a venture with government-subsidized companies, such as Sceco, believing them not to be commercially viable risks. This reaction from financial institutions underscores the need for faster privatization.[178]

As analyzed earlier, the oil crash that began in late 1997 increased the Saudi deficit from $13 to $15 billion and put serious strain on the Saudi budget. As a result, Saudi Arabia had to borrow up to $5 billion from Abu Dhabi as an emergency bridge loan. Saudi Finance Minister Ibrahim al-Assaf denied these reports, but it was clear that the Kingdom did have to borrow from its neighbors and had scarcely solved its structural debt problems.[179]

Bank claims on the government and quasigovernment agencies rose to 28.5% of the total assets of Saudi commercial banks in late 1998. Saudi commercial banks still held enough foreign investments to have a $7.3 billion foreign interbank surplus, plus foreign investments of nearly the same value. According to some estimates, this gave Saudi banks the capability to raise up to $11 billion to help the government in 1999, although only at the cost of a massive short-term draw-down in foreign assets. According to some estimates, the government also took some $5 billion in Aramco assets and income in 1998, and another major draw-down in 1999.[180] Total domestic and foreign debt reached $120 billion by March 1998, or about 80.1% of the GDP.[181]

According to SAMBA, the government's domestic debt rose to $160 billion or SR 600 billion in 1999. This was 115% of Saudi Arabia's GDP for 1999, as calculated by SAMBA. Other sources show an increase in domestic borrowing by the government from commercial banks in 1999 through bond purchases.[182] This level reached $120 billion by March 1998, or about 80.1% of the GDP.[183] Despite its prior efforts, the Kingdom still has some foreign debt—which stood at $10 billion in 1999—raising the total foreign and domestic debt to 120% of GDP.[184]

The issue of how much the Kingdom borrows in the future, however, is only one part of the story. There is also the issue of why it's borrowing money. If the money is used for productive investment to support economic reform, diversification, and the private sector—and is counterbalanced through effective private and foreign investment—it will help meet the Kingdom's needs. If it is used to deal with budget deficits, operating expenses and entitlements—or to fund showpiece arms and aircraft purchases—it will add an unnecessary burden to the economy that could well become steadily worse as demographic pressures increase over time. Misuse of domestic borrowing will also act to limit both foreign investment and the repatriation of private Saudi capital.

It is striking that debt issues are not seriously addressed in the SAMA 2000 and 2001 annual reports or in the public literature on the Seventh

Development Plan. Debt strategy is a key part of the Kingdom's overall effort to achieve economic reform, and it needs to be as well managed and transparent as any other major economic activity. There is a clear need to combine the strategy for domestic and foreign borrowing with the strategy for investing in Central Bank and government pension fund official foreign assets, and to link this to clear plans for government domestic investment in both the government and private sectors. Saudi government fiscal reporting on past expenditures is quite good in some of these areas, but there is no public evidence of a coherent plan for the future.

PRIVATIZATION AND THE PRIVATE SECTOR: INTENTIONS VERSUS IMPLEMENTATION

There is a broad consensus within the ruling elite, technocrats and educators, and businessmen and professionals that the nation needs to diversify its economy, to reduce dependence on the petroleum sector, to solve the problems in managing and financing the budget, and find ways of limiting the government's foreign and domestic debt. There is a consensus that the Kingdom truly needs to make economic reform work, and it can only do so by strengthening the private sector, finding other sources of investment, and encouraging repatriation of capital.

Once again, Saudi Arabia's problem is not a lack of good intentions, or of setting the proper priorities, but rather that there is no matching consensus as to how much action is needed and how quickly and when it should act. While Saudi Arabia has already made progress in many areas, the measures that the government has taken so far have lacked the scale and speed needed to restructure the economy at the rate required. It is also clear that the Seventh Development Plan does not provide an adequate map for future progress.

While it is impossible to assign precise priorities and values to the level of additional effort required, it is clear that success will depends on far more rapid progress being made in four areas:

- Strengthening the private sector,
- Privatization,
- Obtaining increased foreign investment, and
- Persuading Saudis to repatriate their foreign investments and invest in the Kingdom.

It is also important to understand that success in each area will require major macroeconomic change. It is not enough to have some progress in each of these areas; there must be structural change in the entire economy and it must occur during the next decade. In the real world, however, all societies and economies have tremendous inertia. The trends shown earlier have shown this, and the growth of the government share of the nonoil sectors of the economy consistently outpaced the growth of the private sector during 1990–1997. In fact, this trend accelerated during 1995–1997, a period in which government policy was supposed to strongly favor the private sector. Saudi government and SAMA figures indicate that the private sector accounted for 35.3% of the GDP in 1997, which compares with 36.0% in 1990. In contrast, government activity in the nonoil sector rose from 25.9% of the GDP in 1990 to 28.5% in 1997. This growth fully offset the decline of the oil sector's share of the economy from 38.0% to 36.2%, and the government share of the total GDP rose slightly from 63.9% to 64.7%.[185]

Chart 6.32 shows just how static the share of the private sector and government nonoil sector have been since the end of the Fifth Development Plan. Similarly, Chart 6.33 shows that the Ministry of Planning reports that real growth in the nonoil sector of the economy has been far too low to meet the country's needs except in construction and government-related areas. Chart 6.34 shows that SAMA reports there was virtually no meaningful growth in the nonoil sector under the Sixth Development Plan. The only major change shown in Chart 6.34 is a substantial drop in the value of the manufacturing sector, driven almost solely by an oil price–related cut in the value of refining in 1998.

Chart 6.35 focuses on the impact of two key sectors on the GDP. It shows the value of the industrial sector from 1989 to 1999 and its impact on the economy. It reflects an increase in the value of the industrial sector in current prices and supplements the data provided earlier on the growth of Saudi companies and factories and private investment. At the same time, the increase shown in Chart 6.35 would be much lower in constant riyals, and industry only grew from around 8% of the GDP in 1989 to 10% in 1999—scarcely the rate of change needed by the economy. The heavily government-subsidized agricultural sector has also grown in current riyals and occupies much the same share of the GDP it did in 1989.

SAMA data on the Saudi GDP following the end of the expenditures for the Gulf War by type of economic activity—as measured in producers' values in constant prices—seem to sharply understate some aspects of government-sector activity in the petroleum sector. Nevertheless, these data also indicate that the growth of the private sector had only limited macroeconomic impact during the period from 1993 to 2000:[186]

- The heavily subsidized agriculture, forestry, and fishing sector had limited growth during the 1990s, rising erratically from SR 5.466 million in 1993 to SR 5.932 million in 2000 (+8.5% over eight years).

Chart 6.32
Private versus Public Sector Share of the Saudi Economy (in Billions of Riyals at Constant 1970 Prices)

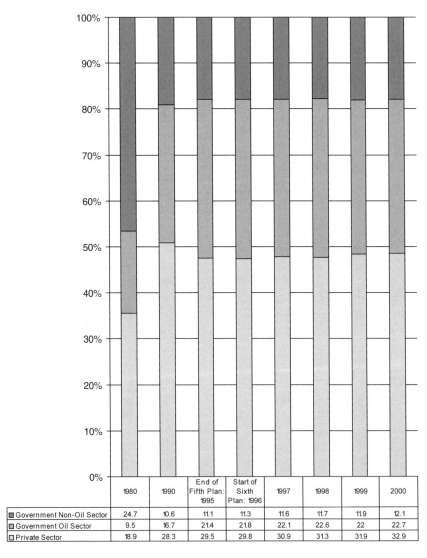

	1980	1990	End of Fifth Plan: 1995	Start of Sixth Plan: 1996	1997	1998	1999	2000
■ Government Non-Oil Sector	24.7	10.6	11.1	11.3	11.6	11.7	11.9	12.1
▨ Government Oil Sector	9.5	16.7	21.4	21.8	22.1	22.6	22	22.7
☐ Private Sector	18.9	28.3	29.5	29.8	30.9	31.3	31.9	32.9

Sources: Adapted by Anthony H. Cordesman from SAMA, *Thirty-Sixth Annual Report, 1421H (2000G)* (Riyadh: SAMA, 2001), pp. 190–192; *Thirty-Seventh Annual Report, 1422H (2001G)* (Riyadh: SAMA, 2001), pp. 354–355, 406.

Chart 6.33
Ministry of Planning Estimate of Nonpetroleum Activity in the Saudi Economy by
Sector (in Billions of Constant 1994 Riyals in Producers Values)

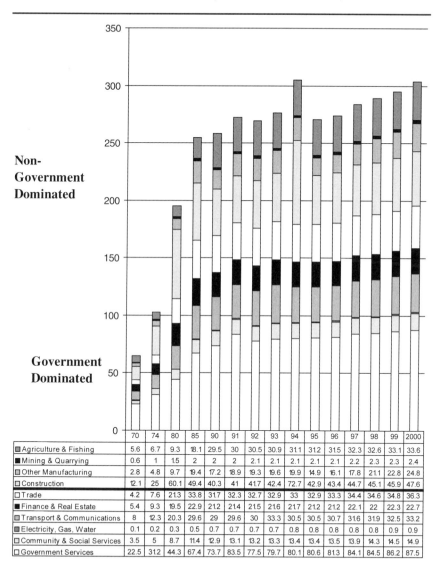

Non-Government Dominated

Government Dominated

	70	74	80	85	90	91	92	93	94	95	96	97	98	99	2000
Agriculture & Fishing	5.6	6.7	9.3	18.1	29.5	30	30.5	30.9	31.1	31.2	31.5	32.3	32.6	33.1	33.6
Mining & Quarrying	0.6	1	1.5	2	2	2	2.1	2.1	2.1	2.1	2.1	2.2	2.3	2.3	2.4
Other Manufacturing	2.8	4.8	9.7	19.4	17.2	18.9	19.3	19.6	19.9	14.9	16.1	17.8	21.1	22.8	24.8
Construction	12.1	25	60.1	49.4	40.3	41	41.7	42.4	72.7	42.9	43.4	44.7	45.1	45.9	47.6
Trade	4.2	7.6	21.3	33.8	31.7	32.3	32.7	32.9	33	32.9	33.3	34.4	34.6	34.8	36.3
Finance & Real Estate	5.4	9.3	19.5	22.9	21.2	21.4	21.5	21.6	21.7	21.2	21.2	22.1	22	22.3	22.7
Transport & Communications	8	12.3	20.3	29.6	29	29.6	30	33.3	30.5	30.5	30.7	31.6	31.9	32.5	33.2
Electricity, Gas, Water	0.1	0.2	0.3	0.5	0.7	0.7	0.7	0.7	0.8	0.8	0.8	0.8	0.8	0.9	0.9
Community & Social Services	3.5	5	8.7	11.4	12.9	13.1	13.2	13.3	13.4	13.4	13.5	13.9	14.3	14.5	14.9
Government Services	22.5	31.2	44.3	67.4	73.7	83.5	77.5	79.7	80.1	80.6	81.3	84.1	84.5	86.2	87.5

Source: Adapted by Anthony H. Cordesman from Ministry of Planning, *Achievements of the Development Plans, 1390–1421 (1970–2001), Facts and Figures* (Riyadh: Ministry of Planning, 19th Edition, 2002), Tables 11 and 12.

Chart 6.34
SAMA Estimate of Nonpetroleum Activity in the Saudi Economy (in Billions of Riyals at Constant 1970 Prices)

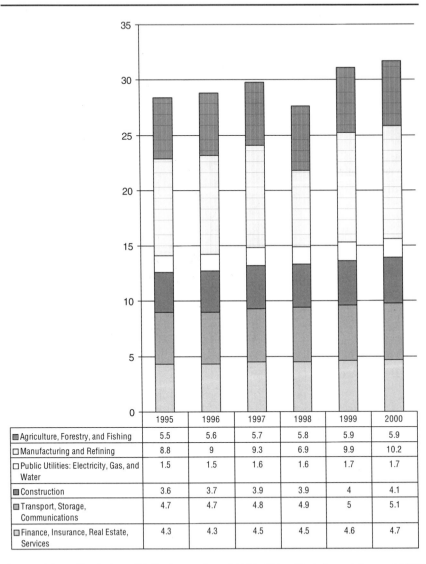

	1995	1996	1997	1998	1999	2000
■ Agriculture, Forestry, and Fishing	5.5	5.6	5.7	5.8	5.9	5.9
□ Manufacturing and Refining	8.8	9	9.3	6.9	9.9	10.2
□ Public Utilities: Electricity, Gas, and Water	1.5	1.5	1.6	1.6	1.7	1.7
■ Construction	3.6	3.7	3.9	3.9	4	4.1
■ Transport, Storage, Communications	4.7	4.7	4.8	4.9	5	5.1
□ Finance, Insurance, Real Estate, Services	4.3	4.3	4.5	4.5	4.6	4.7

Source: Adapted by Anthony H. Cordesman from SAMA, *Thirty-Sixth Annual Report, 1421H (2000G)* (Riyadh: SAMA, 2001), pp. 193–194; *Thirty-Seventh Annual Report, 1422H (2001G)* (Riyadh: SAMA, 2001), pp. 182, 356–358.

Chart 6.35

Saudi Industrial and Agricultural Activity as Share of GDP (in Billions of Riyals at Current Prices)

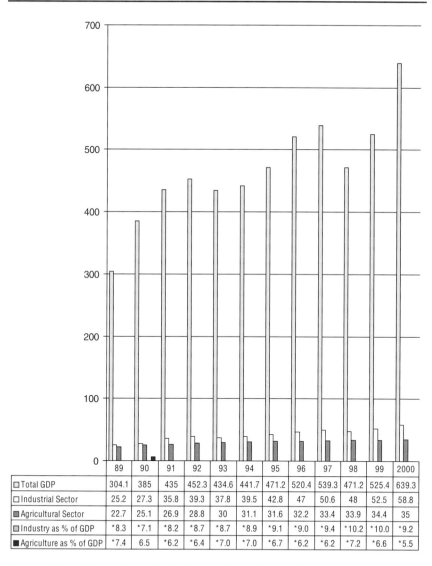

	89	90	91	92	93	94	95	96	97	98	99	2000
☐ Total GDP	304.1	385	435	452.3	434.6	441.7	471.2	520.4	539.3	471.2	525.4	639.3
☐ Industrial Sector	25.2	27.3	35.8	39.3	37.8	39.5	42.8	47	50.6	48	52.5	58.8
■ Agricultural Sector	22.7	25.1	26.9	28.8	30	31.1	31.6	32.2	33.4	33.9	34.4	35
☐ Industry as % of GDP	*8.3	*7.1	*8.2	*8.7	*8.7	*8.9	*9.1	*9.0	*9.4	*10.2	*10.0	*9.2
■ Agriculture as % of GDP	*7.4	6.5	*6.2	*6.4	*7.0	*7.0	*6.7	*6.2	*6.2	*7.2	*6.6	*5.5

Sources: Adapted by Anthony H. Cordesman from SAMA, *Thirty-Sixth Annual Report, 1421H (2000G)* (Riyadh: SAMA, 2001), pp. 194–196; *Thirty-Seventh Annual Report, 1422H (2001G)* (Riyadh: SAMA, 2001), pp. 184–183.

- Mining and quarrying other than the petroleum and gas sector, increased from SR 186 to SR 214 million (+17%), but this growth had negligible impact on an economy whose real growth increased from SR 62,265 million to SR 68,586 million (+10.2%).

- Manufacturing other than refining grew from SR 3,445 million to SR 4,451 million (29%), but this was dominated by government investment in industries like plastics.

- Wholesale and retail trade restaurants and hotels grew from SR 8,203 million to SR 8,932 million (+8.9%).

- Finance, insurance, real estate, and business services grew from SR 4,289 million to SR 4,710 million (+9.8%).

- Construction (much of which is government-funded petroleum and infrastructure construction) grew from SR 3,649 million to SR 5,087 million (+12.3%).

- Transport, storage, and communication (most of which is also government-funded) grew from SR 4,621 million to SR 5,087 million (+10.1%).

- In contrast, the government-controlled petroleum, gas, and refinery sector increased from SR 23,564 million to SR 24,201 million This was only an increase of 2.7% over eight years, but affected 35% to 40% of the GDP.

- Other clearly government-dominated activity include government services; community, social, and personal services; and electricity, gas, and water. Their value grew from SR 8,434 million to SR 9,473 million (+12.3%). This rate of growth, however, was about half the roughly 25.6% growth in the Saudi population.

While there is no exact way to use the SAMA data to fully separate government and private activity in the total Saudi GDP, the total of government petroleum activity and direct government services rose from SR 31.998 million in 1993 to SR 33.674 million in 2000 (+5.2%). The value of these categories amounted to 51% of the GDP in 1993 and 49.1% in 2000. This scarcely reflected a major move toward diversification, and none of the supporting data in the SAMA annual reports through 2001 as yet reflected serious structural progress in the areas where Saudi Arabia will need to move forward.[187] Similarly, if one looks at SAMA data only on the private sector role in the nonoil portion of the GDP, the private sector role only increased from SR 28.9 billion in 1991 to 32.9 billion in 2000 in constant 1970 prices, a total increase of 14% over ten years and an average annual real increase of less than 1.2%.[188]

The Seventh Development Plan and Meeting the Challenge of Diversification

It is too soon to know whether Saudi Arabia's slow rate of past progress is a clear indication of future Saudi actions. The economic reforms discussed at the start of this chapter only began to be implemented in late 1999, and many key measures are still being worked out. It is difficult to restructure an economy to achieve the necessary level of major structural change in this period of time, and even to carry out enough reform to gather decisive momentum. Saudi success or failure will play out over a period of at least a decade, and it may well take at least three five-year plans to evaluate Saudi success.

Unfortunately, the Kingdom's Seventh Development Plan is most vague where it needs to be most specific. It does not really present a detailed plan for achieving economic reform and diversification. Instead, it sets some broad goals and benchmarks. These goals may be summarized as follows:

- Achieve an average annual real GDP growth of 3.16%
- Emphasize a private sector that is expected to grow at average annual rate of 5.04%.
  - However, population growth rate is at least 3.0%. Plan essentially calls for zero increase in real per capita income during 2000–2004.
- Achieve an average annual nonoil growth rate of 4.01%
- Increase the share of nonoil sectors in GDP from 68.4% in 1999 to 71.6% by late 2004.
- Achieve an average annual growth rate of 3.44% in the services sector, 3.05% in agriculture, 8.34% in nonmining, and 5.14% in the industrial sector.
- Electricity, gas, and water sector should grow by an average annual rate of 4.62% and construction by 6.17%.
- Achieve an average annual growth rate of 8.29% in petrochemicals and 7.16% in other manufacturing.
  - No goals are set for increased oil and gas production or maintaining surplus capacity. Saudi officials discuss raising capacity to 13 MMBD; maintaining a 2 MMBD cushion of surplus production.
- Plan calls for increased gas production and developing reserves and domestic use in order to serve development objectives and contribute in the diversification of income sources.
  - Enhance private sector's participation in petroleum industries.
  - Consolidate efficiency in production, refining, and distribution.
- Achieve an average annual real growth rate of 6.85% in investment; increase investment from 22.7% of GDP in 2000 to 25.4% in 2004.
- Reduce the state budget deficit as percent of GDP from –10.8% in 1999 to zero by 2004 by increasing government nonoil revenues and rationalizing government expenditures.
- Improve the current account balance and go from a deficit equal to 3% of GDP in 1999 to surplus of 6.9% in 2004.

What is clear is that even if all of these broad goals are met, the Kingdom would still not achieve major progress in macroeconomic terms during

2000–2004. Meeting these goals would at best create the conditions to achieve such progress in the next development plan while making important progress in some selected areas.

The Growth of the Private Sector

Saudi Arabia does have a base to build on despite its past failures. The Kingdom may not have taken all the steps it should, but it does have its successes. It has long provided loans to finance up to 50% of new ventures in industry, agriculture, and commerce. It set up a Saudi Industrial Development Fund as early as 1974 to provide start-up loans for new industrial ventures and to spur the growth of existing ones. By the end of 2000, this fund had provided loans worth more than SR 35 billion ($9.33 billion) and funded the creation of some 1,700 factories and small manufacturing ventures. Saudi Arabia had some 199 factories in 1970, with a total capital of SR 2.78 billion ($741.33 million. In 2000, it had more than 2,500 factories with a total capital of over SR 170 billion ($45.33 billion).[189] The SIDF reports that it has a 96% recoupment rate on these loans. Further, in spite of increased public borrowing, Saudi banks show very high private sector earnings, and are steadily increasing their loans to the private sector.[190]

The top 100 Saudi companies had sales volume in excess of SR 260 billion in 2001, and pharmaceuticals, electronic components, food processing, packaging, mining, tourism, and construction are all seen as important areas for the further expansion of private sector activity. A substantial amount of this expansion should take place.[191]

As Chart 6.36 shows, the private sector now accounts for around 40% of the Kingdom's gross final consumption and well over 60% of its gross capital formation. Saudi Arabia estimates that the value of the private sector reached 42% of the GDP in 2000, or SR 618 billion ($164.8 billion).[192] As Chart 6.37 shows, however, gross fixed capital formation was largely static during the 1990s—a trend that reinforces the previous analysis of the slow rate of real growth in critical aspects of the Saudi economy. It is also clear from Chart 6.37 that any increase in private capital formation has been largely offset by a decline in government capital formation, reinforcing the data on government's tendency to deal with its budget problems by funding operations and entitlements at the expense of investment and investment-intensive, high-cost renovation and maintenance activities.

If the Kingdom is to succeed in diversifying and restructuring its economy at the required levels and rates, however, it must achieve the following goals:

- *Persuade Saudis to investment a large part of the private capital they now have overseas in domestic businesses.* According to one estimate, this totals around $250 billion in foreign banks, and another $600 billion in investments. The true total may be closer to $300 to $400 billion, rather than $850 billion.

Chart 6.36
Private versus Public Sector Share of Gross Domestic Expenditure and Gross Capital
Formation—Part One: The SAMA Estimate (in Billions of Riyals at Current Prices)

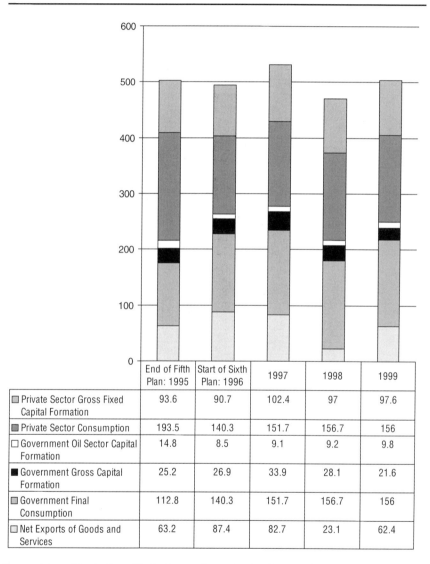

	End of Fifth Plan: 1995	Start of Sixth Plan: 1996	1997	1998	1999
▨ Private Sector Gross Fixed Capital Formation	93.6	90.7	102.4	97	97.6
▨ Private Sector Consumption	193.5	140.3	151.7	156.7	156
□ Government Oil Sector Capital Formation	14.8	8.5	9.1	9.2	9.8
■ Government Gross Capital Formation	25.2	26.9	33.9	28.1	21.6
▨ Government Final Consumption	112.8	140.3	151.7	156.7	156
□ Net Exports of Goods and Services	63.2	87.4	82.7	23.1	62.4

Source: Adapted by Anthony H. Cordesman from SAMA, *Thirty-Sixth Annual Report, 1421H
(2000G)* (Riyadh: SAMA, 2001), pp. 193–194.

Chart 6.37
Private versus Public Sector Share of Gross Domestic Expenditure and Gross Capital Formation—Part Two: The Ministry of Planning Estimate (in Billions of Riyals at Constant Prices)

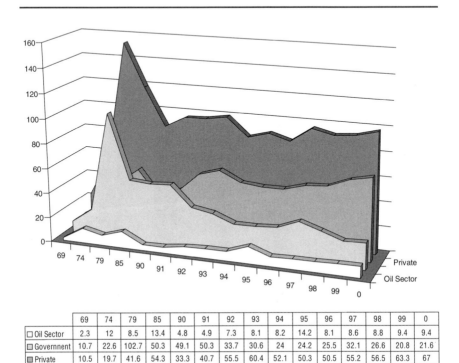

	69	74	79	85	90	91	92	93	94	95	96	97	98	99	0
☐ Oil Sector	2.3	12	8.5	13.4	4.8	4.9	7.3	8.1	8.2	14.2	8.1	8.6	8.8	9.4	9.4
☐ Government	10.7	22.6	102.7	50.3	49.1	50.3	33.7	30.6	24	24.2	25.5	32.1	26.6	20.8	21.6
☐ Private	10.5	19.7	41.6	54.3	33.3	40.7	55.5	60.4	52.1	50.3	50.5	55.2	56.5	63.3	67
☐ Total	23.5	54.2	152.8	118.1	87.1	96	96.5	99.1	84.2	88.7	84.1	95.8	91.9	93.4	98

Source: Adapted by Anthony H. Cordesman from SAMA, *Thirty-Sixth Annual Report, 1421H (2000G)* (Riyadh: SAMA, 2001), pp. 193–194.

Nevertheless, this is still a vast amount of capital that could go into the domestic private sector.

- Ironically, a combination of a massive drop in Western stock markets from 2000 on and tensions with the United States after September 11 may help. The lack of attractive and secure investment options in the West led Saudis to repatriate as much as $100 billion in 2001–2002. At the same time, Saudis also lost as much due to the drop in foreign stock values and found few attractive domestic investment opportunities beyond banks and stocks centered around large existing enterprises.

- *Develop an effective approach to privatization—one that does more than simply try to shift the burden of government capital investment in existing areas like infrastructure and the petroleum sector to the private sector and foreign investment.* This both means transforming state entities into viable businesses that sell at market prices, or at least at minimal levels of subsidy, and creating major new private industries.

- *Develop a true stock market and banking system free enough to both attract capital and produce productive investments.*

- *Attract foreign capital on the basis of the ability to compete in the global capital market and at global rates of return on investment.*

- *Over time, move the government as far out of the economy as possible, allowing the private sector to grow through domestic and foreign investment with as little government intervention and subsidy as possible.*

The Success of Privatization by Firm and Sector

Saudi efforts at privatization are beginning to move ahead in several important areas.[193] In addition to the creation of the Supreme Economic Council, the Supreme Council for Petroleum and Ministerial Affairs, the General Investment Authority, and the Supreme Tourist Authority, the government created a Fund for National Manpower Training in 2000. It also approved amendments to the social insurance system to make it easier to transfer workers between government and private sector jobs, and it issued regulations allowing the private sector to finance and operate private colleges. As noted earlier, on June 2, 2001, it also gave the SEC the mission of coordinating and supervising privatization and of creating a plan and time schedule to privatize sectors like communications and postal services, the electricity sector (after consolidating and marginalizing the regional power companies into one company), the General Railway Organization, and a number of facilities of the General Port Sector.[194]

The Privatization of SABIC and SIPC

Saudi Arabia's most significant accomplishment to date has been the partial privatization of the Saudi Basic Industries Corporation (SABIC). The Kingdom created SABIC in 1976 to diversify into heavy industries that then required more capital and management expertise for private entrepreneurs and that could create the feedstocks and materials for private ventures in medium and light industries. These investments poured tens of billions of U.S. dollars into major industrial complexes in Jubail, Yanbu, and Jeddah, producing feedstocks for fertilizers, chemicals, and resins, and diversification into secondary industries.

SABIC is now one of two large state corporations—along with the state oil firm, Saudi Aramco—that dominate the Saudi economy (70%).[195] SABIC is the Middle East's largest nonoil industrial company, and it now accounts for around 10% of world petrochemical production. Current plans will expand this capacity to 48 million tons by 2010.[196] In February 2001,

SABIC completed a $1 billion expansion at the Yanbu petrochemical facility, making it the largest polyethylene plant in the world. These measures raised the value of private sector and public sector nonoil industrial exports (roughly 90% of all Saudi nonoil exports) to SR 24.8 billion ($6.6 billion) in 2000.[197]

In 2001, SABIC had a capitalization of around SR 13.3 billion and was a complex of some sixteen basic, downstream, and support industries—producing around 28 million metric tons of petrochemical, plastics, fertilizers, metals, and industrial gases. It employed roughly 14,4000 personnel, 75% of whom were said to be Saudi nationals. SABIC also had a 20% share in Bahrain's two main aluminum companies and a 25% share in its marketing company. It exported around SR 16 billion worth of nonoil exports, and its primary markets were in Southeast Asia, the Far East, North America, and Western Europe.[198]

In December 1994, the government approved the sale of three-quarters of its 70% share in SABIC.[199] SABIC is the Middle East's largest nonoil industrial company, and has been soliciting additional foreign investment in private petrochemical projects, such as a proposed $800-million plant proposed for Jubail.[200]

The success of Saudi privatization and foreign investment plans depends heavily on selling off the government's share of SABIC and a number of other government ventures, although it is unclear how successful the government will be in the near future. These other ventures include the Saudi Petrochemical Company (Sadaf), which is a joint venture between SABIC and Shell Oil. In February 1997, Sadaf launched a $1 billion expansion program that includes a new 700,000-metric-ton/year plant for methyl tertiary butyl ether (MTBE). Sadaf also is looking at setting up Saudi Arabia's first independent power plant (IPP) at its petrochemical complex in Jubail.

The Ministry of Commerce approved the establishment of another joint-stock company, the Saudi International Petrochemical Company (SIPC), on October 25, 1999. The Al-Zamil Group owns 15% of the Riyadh-based company, with the remaining 85% of shares issued for private placement among Saudi and GCC member-state companies.[201] The SIPC is capitalized at SR 500 million ($133 million), and will have 10 million shares, each with a nominal value of SR50 divided among seventy-three shareholders. However, the company's shares will not be traded for another two years.[202] The SIPC is slated to act as a holding company, with plans to form three separate petrochemical ventures in Jubail Industrial City. Total value of the plants is put at around $730 million.[203]

The Saudi government is seeking to establish a joint-stock utilities company to provide services to the industrial cities of Jubail and Yanbu. One such step is the formation of the Utility Company (UCO), which will be formed by the Saudi government.[204] A board of directors will manage the company for the first three years, after which management will be turned over to an independent administrative body. At that time, shares will also be opened to the general public.[205]

The Privatization of Natural Gas

As discussed in more detail in Chapter 7, Saudi Arabia has a massive program underway to convert the Kingdom to the use of natural gas and exploit natural gas feedstocks, both to free more petroleum for export and to create new and more labor intensive downstream industries. In May 2000, foreign oil companies were invited to secure proposals for investment in Saudi Arabia, which paved the way to create memorandums of understanding dealing particularly with upstream gas projects. A seven-man council, headed by Foreign Minister Prince Saud al-Faisal, engaged in three major negotiations with international oil companies (IOCs), and the Supreme Petroleum Council was given the right to conclude contracts for "exploration, drilling and production of gas" with IOCs. It reiterates previous edicts in retaining exclusivity to Saudi Aramco.[206]

In May 2001, Saudi Arabia selected companies to participate in a "Saudi Gas Initiative" with a potential value of $25 billion. This was the first major reopening of Saudi Arabia's upstream hydrocarbons sector to foreign investment since it had been nationalized in the 1970s. The Saudi Gas Initiative will integrate upstream gas development with downstream petrochemicals and power generation, and is by far the Kingdom's most important effort to attract foreign investment.

The companies that Saudi Arabia selected for the three "core ventures" of the Saudi Gas Initiative were, by area of development:

- Core Venture 1—South Ghawar: ExxonMobil, Shell, BP, Phillips;
- Core Venture 2—Red Sea: Exxon plus Marathon and Occidental;
- Core Venture 3—Shaybah: Shell, TotalFinaElf, and Conoco.

A report by the EIA describes these efforts are follows:

The Core Venture 1, in South Ghawar, will be one of the world's largest ($15 billion) integrated natural gas projects, including exploration, pipelines, two gas-fired power plants, two petrochemical plants, two desalination units, and more. Core Venture 2 will involve exploration in the Red Sea, development of the Barqan and Midyan fields on the Red Sea coast in northwestern Saudi Arabia, as well as construction of a petrochemical plant, a power station, desalination capacity, etc., at a cost of $4 billion. Core Venture 3 will involve exploration near Shaybah in the Rub al-Khali ("Empty Quarter") of southeastern Saudi Arabia, development of the Kidan gas field, laying of pipelines from Shaybah to the Haradh and Hawiyah natural gas treatment plants east of Riyadh, and construction of a petrochemical plant in Jubail, at a cost of $4 billion.[207]

Saudi Arabia and the foreign oil companies failed to meet an initial December 1, 2001, deadline for an agreement on the "Saudi Gas Initiative." Part of the reason for the delay was disagreement over the price of the natural gas to be produced from the project, and part was the quality of the acreage offered.

The sheer scale of the effort has also, however, proved to be a problem since developing plans, contracts, and regulations for the effort is the largest single program in the Saudi government's history and is part of a broader gas development program that the Kingdom estimates at $45 billion over the next twenty-five years.

The Privatization of Telecommunications

The government has announced that Saudi Arabia's telecommunications services will be privatized and a joint stock company will be set up to run the Kingdom's telephone and telex facilities. In September 1999, the Saudi Telecommunications Company (STC) took over from Saudi Telecom, which is operated by the Ministry of Posts, Telephones, and Telegraphs. Although it is financially independent of the government, the STC is headed by the PTT minister and is 100% owned by the state.[208] Plans for privatizing the company have been delayed since it was established in April 1998, partly due to financial difficulties. In early June 1999, four Saudi banks—the Riyadh Bank, National Commercial Bank, Saudi British Bank and Arab National Bank—agreed to provide a syndicated loan of SR 2.25 billion to STC to be used to make payments on arrears.[209]

There is a clear need for improved services. The Kingdom has around 3 million land lines, 2 million mobile phone users, and some 200,000 Internet subscribers (600,000 users), but has some 21 million people.

The Ministerial Committee on Privatization directed that a series of nine study groups be created in 2001 to determine how to privatize Saudi telecommunications activity. These included an information and technology team, a network work team, and teams to handle financing, personnel, and other issues. Work is underway to create a specialized body with the administrative and financial autonomy to organize the telecommunications sector and provide the rules and regulations to ensure fair competition among private firms. It will also control digital and frequency management, monitor the quality of services, and set goals for the overall development of the national system.[210]

The privatization process is accelerating; the Majlis al-Shura proposed a bill on May 15, 2001.[211] It also has examined what stake the government should retain in the company, and what percentage will be offered to foreign investors.[212] Valuations of STC normally range from $10 to $15 billion.[213] A new telecommunications law was passed in the summer of 2001. STC also helped to show that it was a viable private entity when it reported an annual profit of SR 3,479,000 in 2001.

It now seems like that 30% of the company will be sold to the public in late 2002, based on a valuation of ten times its earnings of $1 billion in 2001.[214] This would mean a sale of some $3 billion worth of shares. The government is also discussing plans to open the Saudi GSM market up to competition in 2003. In theory, the sale of STC is one of several major sales that will allow the government to reduce its domestic debt to the General Organization for Social Insurance, although some such sales could involve a swap of shares rather than cash repayment.[215]

The Privatization of Saudi Airlines

King Fahd first advanced the idea of privatizing Saudi Arabian Airlines (Saudia) in 1994. Since that time, Saudia has been slowly restructured to make it more viable as a commercial entity; in September 1999, Saudia's board gave instructions to form a committee to obtain the consulting services necessary for a detailed privatization plan. In May 2000, Saudia invited investment banks to prepare bids for privatization of the state-owned carrier, although the scale of privatization—whether it is to be a full-scale sell-off or a partial sale of the airline's services such as its catering, in-flight sales, and international sales offices—was not clarified. Saudia signed contracts with the consulting firms it selected on August 10, 2000, and work began on October 30, 2000. These studies are still in progress, but the goal is to float Saudia on the Saudi stock market for public subscription.[216]

The Privatization of Postal Services

The government has permitted the private sector to invest in postal agencies. The initial goal is 100 agencies, and contracts for 73 were signed by the end of 2000. Investment has been allowed in surface and mobile postal services since 1995, and twenty-six services were under contract by 2001. The government is also privatizing the maintenance of postal buildings—some 137 construction projects at a cost of SR 1.2 billion—and the renovation of postal buildings. Tentative royal approval has been given to converting the entire postal service to an autonomous public corporation, and the World Bank is assisting in derating the required administrative and postal regulations. [217]

The Privatization of Electricity

As has been discussed earlier, Saudi Arabia needs about $120 billion for power generation projects over the next twenty years, with the annual demand growth for electricity in the Kingdom estimated at 4.5%. To meet this demand the country must increase its power generation capacity to 70,000 megawatts by the year 2020—from 21,000 megawatts at present—at a cost of more than $4.5 billion per year. As discussed in the previous chapter, most of this investment is expected to come from the private sector, possibly including foreign investors. The vast majority of this capacity is to be natural gas–fired or combined cycle, as part of the government's plans to expand gas utilization in the power sector.[218]

The government has already acted to restructure and merge the Kingdom's electricity companies into one company, This led the government to create the Saudi Electric Company (SEC) by consolidating the country's eleven regional power companies (including the four SCECOs—East, West, Central, and South—which controlled 85% of the country's power supplies. Electricity Minister Dr. Hashem bin Abdullah al-Yamani signed the merger agreement between Saudi Arabia's ten existing power companies on February 16, 2000, and the SEC was established as a joint-stock company, owned in large part by the Saudi government, on April 5, 2000.

The company's initial capital was set at SR 33.8 billion based on its asset value. It was divided into 675.2 million shares at SR50 each. A statute provides for increasing the company's capital by an amount equal to the net value of the dissolved General Electricity Corporation and raising money through an increase in the fees collected and receivables of the Electricity Tariff Fund. [219]

The U.S. Department of Energy reports that a key reason for the Saudi government action was that the four SCECO companies had long operated at a loss because they were required to sell power far below cost to Saudi consumers, as well as due to inefficiencies and difficulties with nonpayment of bills. The government had subsidized the cost of electricity since at least the early 1970s, and had paid a guaranteed dividend to private shareholders without regard to earnings.

The restructuring of the SCECO system was intended to lead to a more general streamlining/privatization of the Saudi power sector, such as a further splitting of SEC into units dealing with generation, transmission, and distribution companies. Although 85% of the company was initially owned by the government, the idea was to open the electricity market to independent power producers who could sell power to the transmission and generating arms of SEC. The SEC was expected to develop three separate sector companies for generation, transmission, and distribution.

The implementation of the proposed merger plans was slow. The SEC initially became more of a holding company for the four key power authorities and the SCECOs. Each company initially remained more or less autonomous, and each of the four main executives reported back to the main executive of the SEC who was yet to be named. No overall strategy was laid out, and each company pursued its own interest. The delay in building SCECO-Central's 1,800-megawatt PP-9 plant being a case in point. There were no new projects in 2000, despite pressure on the national grid.

By 2001, however, Saudi Arabia had largely consolidated the smaller companies into the Saudi Electric Company (SEC), which started active trading in July 2002. The SEC was also reported to now have a capital in excess of SR 90.6 billion. The SEC also made a profit—in theory—although this profit only totaled SR 711 million in 2001, after the payment of zakat. It was largely unreal since it did not include a fair price for gas fuel or facilities.

The SEC is seeking higher electricity tariffs to allow for private sector competition in power generation, and is seeking to unbundle its generating, transmitting, and distribution structure to allow for such competition. Several projects are also already underway that employ financing mechanisms that are new to Saudi Arabia's electric power sector.

For example, the 1,200-megawatt, PP-9 power station north of Riyadh has been funded with extra revenues generated by a special tariff imposed on heavy users since January 1995. The $1.7-billion Ghazlan II power project is being financed by an internationally syndicated $500-million commercial loan (the first such loan in Saudi history), and being built by a consortium led by Mitsubishi and Bechtel. Ghazlan II consists of four 600-megawatt steam turbine units, which are expected to come online, approximately one unit per year, through 2002. Combined with the existing 1,600-megawatt Ghazlan I facility located on the Gulf coast north of Dammam, the entire complex—when completed—will have power generating capacity of 4,000 megawatts and will supply Saudi Arabia's Eastern Province. In March 2001, Ghazlan I temporarily halted operations following a fire.

Saudi plans for a $1.7 billion, 1,100-megawatt gas-fired power plant at Shuaiba on the Red Sea coast are moving ahead, and Crown Prince Abdullah attended a groundbreaking ceremony in May 2000. Asea Brown Boveri had been awarded the contract on a turnkey basis, and the plant is to be constructed in three stages. The SEC also signed a $419 million contract with the Anglo-French engineering company Alstom to expand the Shuaiba oil-fired power plant—Phase 1 of which is nearly complete—by 780 megawatts (units 4 and 5). These two new units should enter service in late 2003 or early 2004. Finally, in May 2001, CMS Energy, along with joint venture partner A.H. al Zamil Group, was chosen to build Saudi Arabia's 230-megawatt, Sadaf cogeneration power project. This project represents Saudi Arabia's first privately owned IPP.

On October 9, 2000, Saudi Arabia approved plans for setting up a new utility company (UCO) in the twin industrial cities of Yanbu and Jubail. The company, named Marafeq, is being founded by the Royal Commission, the Public Investments Fund, Saudi Aramco, and SABIC, with local investors also holding a stake in the company. The UCO may be privatized when it becomes profitable, but its establishment of UCO may not signify a big step forward. The four shareholders are all state-owned or affiliated in some way, and shares will not be offered to the public for another three years, therefore making UCO a company that is not truly privately-owned. Originally, UCO was meant to be a limited liabilities company with American firms Bechtel and Parsons Corporation taking 10% each. However, in

October 1997, Saudi officials announced that foreign investors would not be included, although the two firms would be offered an advisory role in the company.[220]

The U.S. Department of Energy reports that creation of the SEC also could open the door to private sector construction of new power plants on BOO (Build-Own-Operate) and BOT (Build-Own-Transfer) bases.

The future of IPPs (Independent Power Producers) in Saudi Arabia remains uncertain, however, and major challenges remain—including: tariffs, legal and operating framework, taxation, and fuel supply. The failure to bring electricity prices closer to market prices is a key example. Saudi Arabia introduced a new tariff structure for electricity charges in April 2000. The resulting charges remained far below the market cost—including return on investment and recapitalization charges. The increases in tariffs also focused on customers using 10,000 kilowatts a month, who faced a doubling of charges. They did not affect some 93% of Saudi households, who consume less than 5,000 kilowatt-hours per month.[221] Even so, the SEC announced on October 9, 2000, that it was rescinding these increases (effective October 28) in the face of widespread resistance. Rescinding a small step forward that only affected the very richest consumers is scarcely a move toward privatization and reform of the Saudi power sector, and will reduce SEC revenues and potential profitability.

Other projects have been delayed.[222] The SEC received only two bids for the second-phase 700-megawatt expansion of the Shuaiba plant. The BOO option met with even less success, even though the deadline was extended to May 1999. The lack of financial regulation was attributed to be one of the chief reasons for the lack of interest in power projects.[223]

The government proposes that a separate transmission company will be created that can buy electricity from a variety of suppliers when a unified national power grid is completed. This could be another important step in the commercialization of the power sector. Only two of the country's four power regions are now connected. Creating a unified national grid could require over 20,000 miles of additional power transmission lines, and Saudi Arabia requires major additional investment in power transmission.

The Privatization of the General Railway Organization

The Kingdom has long sought to expand the railway system it created in eastern Saudi Arabia in 1946 to link its ports in the Gulf to Riyadh. It sees an expanded rail system as essential to developing its mining industry in the Jalamid region in the northwest with a route through Al-Jawf, Ha'il, and Al-Qasim; and to handling the growing transport problems of the Hajj and the expansion of a tourist industry by linking Riyadh to Mecca, Medina, and the Red Sea port of Jeddah. Other links would expand the system to Jubail. While Saudi Arabia developed plans to do this through government funding, and also tried to make rail development a part of oil deals with nations like Japan, the government has never found the capital to build such railways, or a foreign partner willing to take the risk. It has, however, faced problems both in developing a mining industry and in creating an efficient commercial transportation system. During the 1990s, freight shipments by rail declined from a peak of 1.017 billion ton kilometers in 1991 to 821.9 million in 2000, and freight from 2,093 thousand tons to 1,623, although passenger kilometers did increase from 129 million to 288 million. During this same period, the number of registered trucks nearly doubled from 84,056 to 145,410, and more than doubled in capacity, and the number of buses increased from 1,984 to 10,726. The length of paved roads, however, only increased from 39,500 kilometers to 46,300. An improved rail system cannot possibly cover Saudi Arabia but it might reduce the problems it faces in terms of road construction costs and moving bulk cargo.[224]

As result, the Kingdom has shifted to a plan to have the private sector participate on the basis of "build, operate, and transfer" (BOT), and has studied the feasibility of covering the cost of expansion, operation, and maintenance through this method. This study led to a Royal Court Directive being issued on June 17, 2000, which called for a formal study plan to be developed by the Ministerial Committee on Privatization, which in turn instructed the Public Investment Fund to prepare an implementation plan in coordination with the Ministry of Transport, Ministry of Finance and National Economy, Ministry of Planning, and General Port Authority.[225]

The Privatization of the General Port Authority

Saudi Arabia had eight major ports in 2000—six commercial and two industrial—with 183 berths and an annual design capacity of 251.5 million tons. These ports were overbuilt, with an average utilization rate of 48.5%, and the Kingdom had a major incentive to try to make them more efficient through privatization.[226]

Some ports are already being run by the private sector on an income-sharing basis under ten-year lease contracts.[227] The General Port Authority awarded twenty-one ten-to-twenty-year contracts for projects during 1998–2000 involving services at the Kingdom's eight ports. These contracts involved direct investments of SR 18.7 to 484.6 million. All the awards have gone to Saudi companies or joint ventures. The total private direct investment as of late 2001 was SR 2,140 million, affecting operations with annual revenues of SR 1,021 million.[228]

The state owns the port assets but the private sector operates them. The tasks to be performed include handling of general goods, containers, bulk grain, roll-on cargo, chilled and frozen goods, and providing maritime services such as the operation of piers and goods-handling equipment. Contracts have also been issued to lease the King Fahd Vessel Repair Yards and two reexport areas in the ports at Jeddah and Dammam.

Overall Progress in Privatization

The Saudi government is actively encouraging private investment in metals industries, downstream industries, and similar manufactures. While SABIC is primarily a petrochemical conglomerate with sixteen affiliates and subsidiaries and a market capitalization of nearly $10 billion, it does involve other industrial activity. One affiliate, Saudi Iron and Steel, is able to invest in $1 billion rolling mills. Saudi private steel mills and aluminum products companies also involve large-scale businesses.[229]

Unfortunately, the government's actions to date have only been partly market-driven and some seem more of an effort to shift the investment burden away from the government rather than seriously privatize functions now operated by the state sector on a commercial basis. Privatization can only have the required impact on growth and reform if it means the conversion of state-held functions to truly competitive private enterprises that can charge market prices, and reduce labor and overhead costs to become more productive and profitable.

Work by Brad Bourland of the Saudi American Bank shows the scale of the future effort that is still needed:[230]

- The Kingdom's electrification plan calls for capacity to increase from 23,000 megawatts in 2001 to 60,000 megawatts in 2023, at a cost of 433 billion Riyals, or $115 billion. This requires average annual expenditures of $4.6 billion a year, and average annual expenditures of $5.3 billion during 2000-2005. The Saudi Electricity Company alone estimates investment needs of $4.6 billion a year from the private sector.[231]

- The average annual cost of upgrading telecommunications is $3 billion a year from 2000 to 2005.

- The new gas initiative described in the next chapter will require expenditures of about $25 billion over the five to ten year period following 2001. This requires a minimum annual average expenditure of $2.5 billion a year.

- The Kingdom spent around 15 billion Riyals ($4 billion) a year on petrochemicals during 1988–1998. The Seventh Development Plan calls for 8 percent growth, which would mean spending roughly $4 billion a year.

- Desalination is expected to meet a goal of 50% of average personal consumption of 300 liters per day. This would cost 46.5 billion Riyals ($12.4 billion) between 2001 and 2020. This is an average of 2.3 billion Riyals a year, or $620 million.

- Mining is seen as a major source of diversification. One key project is a $1.2 billion phosphate mine, but this requires a $1.2 billion railroad. At present no real investment is taking place, but a major expansion of the mining sector could easily require $10–25 billion in future investment over a decade of intensive development activity.

Bourland estimates that if the investment cost of privatizations are ignored, the required government capital expenditures would total about $15 billion a year, or up to 10% of the GDP. Funding all of the required investment could bring the total up to 25% of the GDP, and $15 to $20 billion would then have to come from the private sector. This is a very significant level of investment; even if 30% was financed through equities, there would still be a requirement for some $10 billion a year in financing, which compares with $7.5 billion a year in current lending by foreign and domestic banks. This means a significant increase in both domestic and foreign lending, as well as domestic and foreign investment. Saudi Arabia has so little real-world experience with privatization that it is difficult to tell what can and cannot be done. Charts 6.38 and 6.39 also send a mixed message. They show that the Middle East as a whole has had a terrible record in this area in comparison with faster-developing regions in the world. At the same time, they show that rapid change has been possible in other regions.

PRIVATE AND FOREIGN INVESTMENT AND BANKING REFORM

If Saudi Arabia is to attract and keep the foreign and private domestic investment it needs, it must fully reform its economy to have suitable investment laws for both foreign and domestic investors, create a legal system that can fully enforce contracts and debt collection, create the equivalent of a strong merchant banking and investment banking sector, and have a fully functional stock market.

The Saudi government has called for the banking sector to steadily improve its equity and its share of loans to the private sector.[232] So far, however, the banking system has been slow to develop. Despite being the largest economy in the Arab Middle East, Saudi Arabia still has relatively few banks. In 1997, it had only nine private commercial banks, far less than the UAE's forty or so institutions and Lebanon's seventy-plus. As of October 2001, Saudi Arabia had ten local and one foreign commercial bank (International Gulf Bank of Bahrain, which opened in 2000), with combined assets of $124.8 billion. There were nine banks listed in the Saudi stock market, which controlled 50% of the market's capitalization and had some 1,000 branches. The commercial banking sector is also becoming more modern: retail banking is becoming the focus of most banks and the credit card and ATM business is booming. There is a joint credit card venture between American Express and Saudi Investment Bank.[233]

Chart 6.38
Privatization Revenues Have Lagged Badly Behind Other Regions, 1990–1999
(Transfer of Productive Assets from State to Private Investors in $US Current Millions)

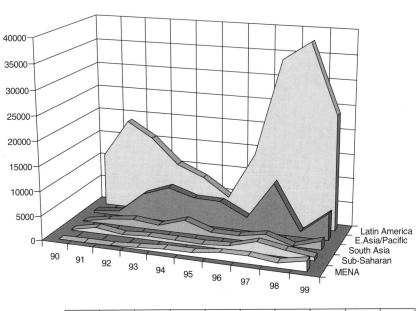

	90	91	92	93	94	95	96	97	98	99
☐ MENA	2	17	69	417	782	746	1478	1612	1000	2074
☐ Sub-Saharan	74	1121	307	641	605	473	745	2348	1356	694
☐ South Asia	29	996	1557	974	2666	916	889	1794	174	1859
☐ E.Asia/Pacific	376	834	5161	7155	5508	5410	2680	10385	1091	5500
☐ Latin America	10915	18723	15560	10488	8199	4616	14142	33897	37685	23614

Source: Adapted by Anthony H. Cordesman from World Bank, Global Development Finance, 2001 (Washington: World Bank, 2001), pp. 180–190.

The Saudi banking sector seems financially sound except for government domestic borrowing, but as has already been discussed, commercial banks are not really investment-oriented. The banking industry is still very much the creature of the state and is being used to fund the government's debt and budget deficits. As Chart 6.40 shows, Saudi investment in treasury bills and development bonds rose from SR 43.5 billion after the Gulf War to SR 102.3 billion by 1999.[234]

SAMA reports that total commercial bank claims on the private sector were only SR 172.2 billion in 2000—a comparatively low figure—and increased by only 1% between 1999 and 2000. Out of this total, only

Chart 6.39

Negligible Regional Foreign Participation in Privatization, 1990–1999 (Transfer of Productive Assets from State to Private Investors in $US Current Millions)

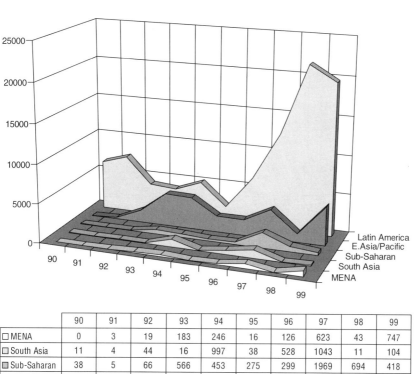

	90	91	92	93	94	95	96	97	98	99
☐ MENA	0	3	19	183	246	16	126	623	43	747
☐ South Asia	11	4	44	16	997	38	528	1043	11	104
☐ Sub-Saharan	38	5	66	566	453	275	299	1969	694	418
■ E.Asia/Pacific	1	102	1556	4156	4036	2026	1990	3775	1082	4982
☐ Latin America	6358	7384	4037	3765	5058	2206	6448	12486	21535	19567

Source: Adapted by Anthony H. Cordesman from World Bank, *Global Development Finance, 2001* (Washington: World Bank, 2001), p. 190.

SR 8.3 billion were investments in private securities, and SR 160.1 billion were in the form of loans. Out of the 164.3 billion in such loans, less than 25 billion were for manufacturing, processing, mining, and quarrying. In contrast, 58 billion were for commerce, services, and finance.[235] At the same time, there has been a steady increase in the percentage of total assets in bank investment funds invested abroad, and total foreign assets increased to SR 101.2 billion in 2000, and have recently been increasing by 5% to10% per year.[236] Investments in domestic mutual funds increased from SR 5.3 billion in 1992 to SR 14.7 billion in 2000, but investments in foreign funds increased from SR 7.1 to SR 22.9 billion. There were 138 such

Chart 6.40
Saudi Bank Investment in Government Securities, 1993–1999 (in Billions of Riyals)

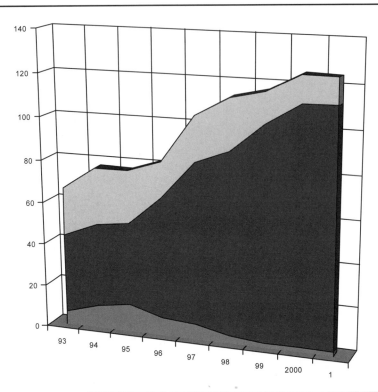

	93	94	95	96	97	98	99	2000	1
■ Total	*66.1	*77	*76.7	*82	*104.1	*113	*116.6	*124.7	*124.4
□ Bank credit to Public Service Enterprises	22.6	26.9	24.5	16.7	20.9	23.6	14.4	12.4	12
□ Sub-Total	*43.5	*50.0	*52.3	*65.3	*83.2	*89.5	*102.3	*112.3	*112.4
■ Development Bonds	37.1	39	39.2	56.6	75.9	85.8	100	110.1	110.4
▣ Treasury Bills	6.4	11	13.1	8.7	7.3	3.6	2.3	2.2	2

Sources: Adapted by Anthony H. Cordesman from SAMA, *Thirty-Sixth Annual Report, 1421H (2000G)*, Research and Statistics Department, September 2000, p. 95; and *Thirty-Seventh Annual Report, 1422H (2001G)*, Research and Statistics Department, December 2001, p. 300.

funds in 2000, with total assets of SR 38.6 billion, but 22.0 billion—or 57%—were invested overseas.[237]

The Kingdom also has several government-owned banks: The Saudi Agricultural Fund, the Public Investment Fund, the Saudi Industrial Development Fund, the Saudi Credit Bank, and the Real Estate Development Fund. These government-owned banks do provide funds for development.

The Public Investment Fund grants loans and equity participation on a medium- and long-term basis for industrial and commercial purposes, such as electric power development. The Saudi Industrial Development Fund provides medium- and long-term loans up of to 50% of the cost of an industrial project as well as marketing, financial, and technical advice.[238]

The government-owned banks had granted outstanding loans of $39.3 billion as of October 2001, but much of this was in the form of housing and real estate loans or loans granted on nonmarket terms. The total disbursements of the Saudi Industrial Development Fund were SR 27.8 billion at the end of 2000, for 2,320 loans, and the annual rate of loans was SR 1.1 to 1.2 billion. The Public Investment Fund had SR 20.8 billion in dispersed loans, but the amount dropped by 4.8% in 2001, and the total number of loans outstanding dropped from 1,185 to 1,077.5, or by 9.1%. In contrast, the Real Estate Development Fund had outstanding loans of SR 69.5 billion.[239]

Investment and Stock Market Reform

The growth of the Saudi stock market is shown in Charts 6.41 and 6.42.[240] The first Saudi shares started trading as early as 1935. SAMA was given supervision and control of all share-trading activity in 1984, and a modern Electronic Share Information System was introduced in 1984.[241] In 1965, the Saudi stock market had a total capitalization of nearly $60 billion, although only seventy-one firms were traded, largely by major banks, and little disclosure was required of a company's financial position. Because the government controlled the banks and forced them to finance Saudi Arabia's debt, there were other problems that affected Saudi investment in the private sector. Some estimates indicate that lending to the government accounted for about 25% of banks total assets.

The total value of shares traded reached SR 25.4 billion ($6.77 billion) in 1996 and $16.56 billion in 1997. The turnover of shares remained relatively low due to the extent of government ownership of quoted shares, which was estimated to account for about 25%. The banking sector owned slightly over another 40%. SABIC was the most heavily capitalized entity and accounted for 21% of the total market. The market reached a total market capitalization of SR 172 billion ($45.86 billion) in 1996, a rise of more than 12% over 1995. Market capitalization reached $58.6 billion by 1997.[242] The Saudi stock market was so heavily dominated by Saudi banks, however, that it had little liquidity—its annual turnover averaged only 15% of total capitalization. Furthermore, the government placed severe limits on foreign investment and the ability of the Saudi private sector to diversify into the capital-intensive private sector that Saudi Arabia so badly needed.[243]

Significant growth took place in the late 1990s. The Saudi stock market had a total capitalization of $173.1 billion in 2000. It accounted for 45.3%

Chart 6.41
Saudi Stock Market Regional Growth During 1990–1998 ($US Current Billions)

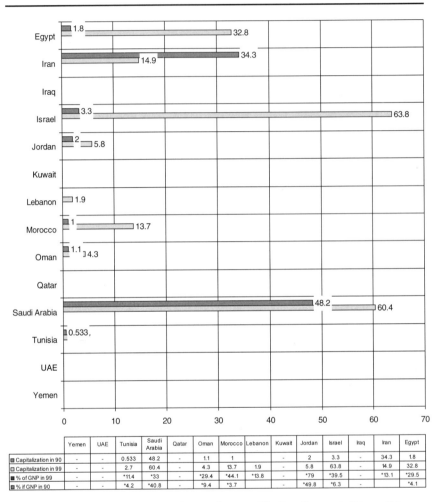

	Yemen	UAE	Tunisia	Saudi Arabia	Qatar	Oman	Morocco	Lebanon	Kuwait	Jordan	Israel	Iraq	Iran	Egypt
Capitalization in 90	-	-	0.533	48.2	-	1.1	1		-	2	3.3	-	34.3	1.8
Capitalization in 99	-	-	2.7	60.4	-	4.3	13.7	1.9	-	5.8	63.8	-	14.9	32.8
% of GNP in 99	-	-	*11.4	*33	-	*29.4	*44.1	*13.8	-	*79	*39.5	-	*13.1	*29.5
% if GNP in 90	-	-	*4.2	*40.8	-	*9.4	*3.7		-	*49.8	*6.3	-		*4.1

Source: Adapted by Anthony H. Cordesman from *Middle East Economic Digest*, February 13, 1998, p. 10.

of the total capitalization of shares in the Arab Monetary Fund Index, versus 20.8% for Egypt and 13.4% for Kuwait. No other Arab country has more than 10% of the total.[244] The Saudi American Bank reports that the market rose by 43% in current dollars in 1999, 11.3% in 2000, and 7.6% in 2001—showing a rough correlation to Saudi oil export revenues and their impact on the health of the Saudi economy.[245]

Chart 6.42

Growth of the Saudi and Other MENA Stock Markets Fell Far Below the Rise in U.S. and European Markets During 1994–2000 (Capitalization in Local Currency)

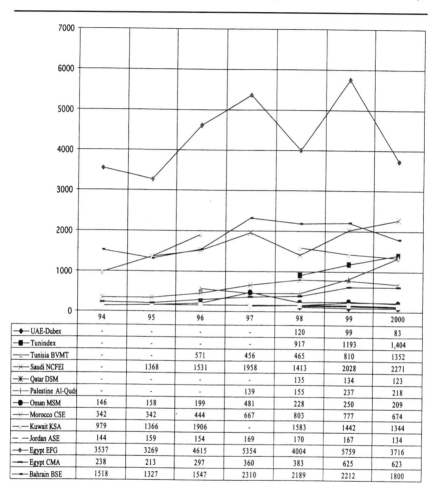

	94	95	96	97	98	99	2000
UAE-Dubex	-	-	-	-	120	99	83
Tunindex	-	-	-	-	917	1193	1,404
Tunisia BVMT	-	-	571	456	465	810	1352
Saudi NCFEI	-	1368	1531	1958	1413	2028	2271
Qatar DSM	-	-	-	-	135	134	123
Palestine Al-Quds	-	-	-	139	155	237	218
Oman MSM	146	158	199	481	228	250	209
Morocco CSE	342	342	444	667	803	777	674
Kuwait KSA	979	1366	1906	-	1583	1442	1344
Jordan ASE	144	159	154	169	170	167	134
Egypt EFG	3537	3269	4615	5354	4004	5759	3716
Egypt CMA	238	213	297	360	383	625	623
Bahrain BSE	1518	1327	1547	2310	2189	2212	1800

Source: Adapted by Anthony H. Cordesman from *Middle East Economic Digest*, December 15, 2000.

SAMA statistics indicate that the total value of shares trade in current riyals rose by 15.4% during 1999–2000, from SR 56.6 billion to SR 65.3 billion. It also reports that market capitalization grew by 12.1% in 1996, 29.7% in 1997, dropped by 28.3% in 1998, and grew by 43.1% in 1999 and by 10.9% in 2000. The value of trade shares grew by 93% in 1996, 144.4% in 1997, dropped by 17.0% in 1998, and grew by 9.8% in 1999 and by 15.4% in 2000.[246]

This growth was led by the construction sector—the value of cement shares rose 58.7% in 2001. The services sector rose by 19.1% in 2001, electricity by 13.4%, banks by 7.9%, and agriculture by 2.6%. The industrial sector, however, was down by 9.6%, again illustrating Saudi vulnerability due to a lack of diversity. SABIC's value dropped by 26.6% due to low oil prices, and SABIC alone accounted for 17% of the total capitalization of the market.[247]

Nevertheless, Saudi Arabia was slow to restructure its stock market to encourage private domestic investment on a free market basis, and the Saudi stock market remained more a government-controlled banking consortium than a real stock market. It is still largely an over-the counter market in which the commercial banks buy and sell shares by means of an electronic trading system that was established by SAMA in 1990. Commercial bank shares still accounted for 35% of the value of the total bank shares trade in 2001, although industry now accounted for 43.5%.[248]

The rise in industry's share of the stock market has helped development, but many Saudi companies are virtually closed joint-stock companies and many of their shares are unavailable for trading. Many of the largest family-run businesses are not traded on the market, and investment outside Saudi Arabia is often far more attractive for both Saudis and foreigners.[249] The failure to change public attitudes to treat local stocks for what they are—as low cost instruments to raise money—also led Saudis to continue to invest abroad. It is estimated that Saudi capital overseas amounted to sums between $500 and $800 billion before September 11, 2001, and some estimates go much higher.[250]

The performance of the Saudi market improved in 1999–2002, despite these problems. Saudi Arabia has seen a shift back toward investment in Saudi stock market since September 11, in part from fear of U.S. efforts to seize or control assets, resentment of U.S. and Western policy on terrorism, and a major drop in the value of Western and Asian stocks.

Lifting of restrictions on foreigners taking equity positions in 1999 failed to produce the expected increase in capital flow. However, the stock market rose as a result of the increase in oil prices and a related 10% rise in spending over the year's projected budget. The NFFEI index broke the 2000 mark, making a swift recovery from a 28% drop in 1999, which was a result of the fall in oil prices and knock-on effect of the Southeast Asian financial crisis.[251] High oil revenues led to a 43% increase in the stock index by the start of 2000, another 11.3% rise in 2000, and a rise of 7.6% in 2001. Daily trading volumes averaged between 2 and 3 million shares per day.[252]

Capital flows also shifted, although with mixed results. Fear of staying invested in the West; the backlash against the Second Intifada, and the collapse of Western stock markets led to significant repatriation of private and government capital and or reinvestment outside the United States after the beginning of 2000. This was helped by the fact that Saudi Tadawuli All-Share Index (TAS) was up 14.6% in the first half of 2002, while world stock markets continued to experience major losses. This rise was driven by speculation over more realistic electric prices and restructuring of the industry, a 10.6% rise in the shares of nine banks that make up 50% of stock market capitalization, and a 10.8% rise in the value of industrial shares like SABIC.[253]

The Saudi market also moved toward greater risk-taking with mutual funds offered by domestic banks rising by 68% over the last two years.[254] Institutions such as SAMA, Saudi Holland Bank, and Bank al-Jazira opened mutual funds to foreign investors in the wake of the change in regulations for foreign investors.

However, the drop in the value of oversea investments led to a decline in private and government capital resources invested overseas. A Saudi American Bank estimate of Saudi losses in Western stock markets during 2000–2002 goes as high as $160 billion, and indicates that Saudi central bank foreign assets dropped by $6.2 billion in 2001 alone, declining to $42 billion versus $56.9 billion in 1997. (Even so, the Saudi government still had total foreign assets of $77 billion in mid-2002. This total was about 84% of the domestic money supply, thirty-four months worth of imports, and 2.4 times the private sector–held public debt, and still gave the Kingdom good liquidity compared to most nations.)[255]

These trends show that the Saudi stock market has great potential, but now has a structure that fails to attract enough private and foreign investment to act as an adequate indicator for economic change and growth. Its performance and market capitalization may be good by Middle Eastern standards, but it remains low by the standards of other regions. It is clear that a major degree of liberalization and true privatization is still needed if the market is to play its proper role in economic growth. The Saudi government needs to restructure capital market regulations from the current structure dominated by SAMA and the Commerce Ministry to develop a formal stock exchange with an independent regulator

The fundamental changes required in the form of a new capital markets law have dragged on for several years, and the law is still in draft. The lesser reforms the government announced in June 1997 seemed to be designed more to avoid a repetition of the kind of speculation that went on in Kuwait's "camel market" than to encourage serious investment. Companies that wished to convert to public joint-stock companies had to be at least ten years old, have made a profit in the previous year, offer at least 51% of the shares to the public, have minimum assets and partner equity of $20 million, show a profit of 10% in each of the five years preceding an application to convert to joint stock status, and project a 10% of larger profit for each of the coming five years.[256]

Opening Up Saudi Arabia to Foreign Investment

As discussed at the start of this chapter, Saudi government was slow to open capital markets to foreigners but has changed its polices since 2000. While Charts 6.43 and 6.44 show the Kingdom has been more successful than other Middle Eastern states, it has failed to attract foreign direct investment (FDI) in anything like the proportion that matches the size of the economy. Between 1984 and 1997 the FDI for Saudi Arabia was $4.32 billion, while Singapore achieved $51.4 billion, Malaysia $36 billion and South Korea $14.6 billion.[257] Foreign corporations were taxed at a rate of 25% on the first SR 100,000 ($26,666) of profits, 35% on anything above that amount, up to SR 500,000 ($133,333), 40% on profits above SR 500,000 up to SR 1 million ($266,666), and 45% on everything above this amount.

Chart 6.43
Foreign Direct Investment Since the New Oil Boom in 1999 (in $US billions)

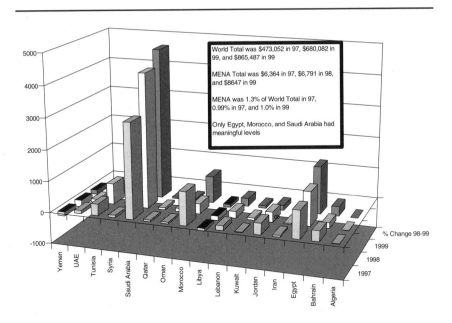

	Yemen	UAE	Tunisia	Syria	Saudi Arabia	Qatar	Oman	Morocco	Libya	Lebanon	Kuwait	Jordan	Iran	Egypt	Bahrain	Algeria
☐ 1997	-139	100	366	80	3,044	55	53	1,079	-82	150	20	361	53	888	329	7
☐ 1998	-210	100	670	80	4,289	70	106	329	-152	200	59	310	24	1,077	181	5
▣ 1999	-150	160	368	75	4,800	50	70	847	-100	250	72	151	85	1,500	300	6
☐ % Change 98-99	*-28.6	*60	*-45.1	*-6.3	*11.9	*-28.6	*-34.0	*157.4	*-34.2	*25	*22	*-51.3	*254.2	*39.3	*65.7	*20.0

Sources: Adapted by Anthony H. Cordesman from *Middle East Economic Digest*, November 10, 2000, p. 26; and *World Investment Report 2000* (Geneva: UNCTAD, 2000).

Chart 6.44
Gulf FDI Levels, 1997–1999 (in $US billions)

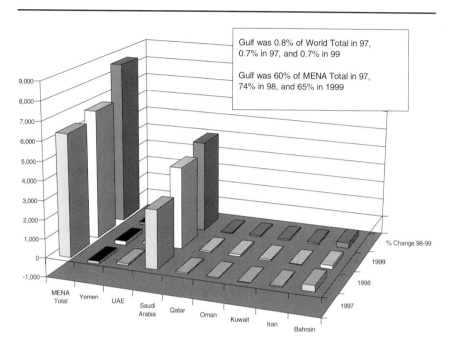

Gulf was 0.8% of World Total in 97, 0.7% in 97, and 0.7% in 99

Gulf was 60% of MENA Total in 97, 74% in 98, and 65% in 1999

	MENA Total	Yemen	UAE	Saudi Arabia	Qatar	Oman	Kuwait	Iran	Bahrain
☐ 1997	6,364	-139	100	3,044	55	53	20	53	329
☐ 1998	6,791	-210	100	4,289	70	106	59	24	181
▣ 1999	8,647	-150	160	4,800	50	70	72	85	300
▣ % Change 98-99		*-28.6	*60	*11.9	*-28.6	*-34.0	*22	*254.2	*65.7

Sources: Adapted by Anthony H. Cordesman from *Middle East Economic Digest*, November 10, 2000, p. 26; and *World Investment Report 2000*, (Geneva: UNCTAD, 2000).

The new Foreign Direct Investment Code announced on May 10, 2000, allows foreigners to own property either independently or with a Saudi partner. It allows investors to remit funds abroad, and reduces taxes by 15% for foreign companies with an annual profit in excess of SR 100,000 ($26,700).[258] It also reduces the country's tax rates on foreign business profits to a limit of 30% (versus the previous ceiling of 45%) and allows foreign companies 100% ownership of projects and property ownership—upfrom the previous limit of 49% stake in joint ventures requiring a Saudi sponsor.

Foreign businesses now qualify for Saudi Industrial Development Fund (SIDF) soft loans even if the corporation is 100% foreign-owned, and the real estate law has been amended to allow foreigners to own real estate.

Saudi visa rules for American businessmen were also changed to make it easier and cheaper to visit Saudi Arabia.[259] Amending the system of local sponsorship for doing business in the country is also under consideration, with a special committee set up by the government to prepare a report on the possibilities for modification.[260] Prince Abdullah has also announced tax incentives for foreign investors for research, development and Saudisation.[261]

Finance Minister Ibrahim bin Abdulaziz al-Assaf announced plans to allow direct foreign investment in the Saudi stock market on November 8, 1999, but made it clear that the complete liberalization of investment and the stock market was not foreseen in the immediate future.[262] The government also issued another directive in early November 1999 authorizing Saudi banks to open their unit trusts, focusing on local stocks, to foreign investors.[263] These included twelve unit trusts valued at SR 2.2 billion ($587 million).

The creation of the Saudi Arabian General Investment Authority (SAGIA) on April 10, 2000, provided a centralized body to create new incentives for foreign investment.[264] As has been discussed earlier, the SAGIA is intended to provide "one-stop-shopping" for foreign investors, and has representatives from sixteen government agencies. Its goal is to make a single agency responsible for approving and overseeing each foreign investment project, and to reduce the time for approving a foreign investment to thirty days.[265]

The SAGIA submitted its list of activities that would not be covered by the new foreign investment laws to the Supreme Economic Council in July 2000.[266] The final SAGIA list was approved by the SEC on February 12, 2001. As discussed earlier, however, the list still presents major barriers to effective foreign investment in many areas, although Saudi Arabia will probably reduce this list even further if it succeeds in joining the WTO.[267] The following areas were excluded:

- *Industrial Sector:* Exploration for and production of petroleum and petroleum products, except for services relating to mining; the manufacture of military equipment, machinery, and uniforms; and the manufacture of explosives for civilian use.

- *Services Sector:* Provision of relations for the armed forces; investigative and security work; insurance services; real estate investment in Mecca and Medina; tourist guidance services related to the Hajj and Umrah pilgrimages; manpower agencies and those dealing with recruitment from overseas; real estate brokerage; printing and publications; wholesale and retail distribution including medical retail such as private pharmacies; and commercial agencies—with the exception of concession rights services—provided that foreign ownership does not exceed 49%, there is a special need, and no more than one such investment is made per province.

- *Other Areas:* Education services at the elementary, secondary, and adult levels; telecommunications services; land and air transport; delivery and distribution of electric power within the general grid; space transport services; delivery of products through pipelines; services provided by midwives, nurses, physiotherapists, and paramedics; services related to fisheries; and poison centers, blood banks, and quarantine facilities.

Nevertheless, the SAGIA reported in January 2001 that foreign investment commitments had reached $1.6 billion, including fifty-three licenses (twenty-nine industrial, tenty-four nonindustrial).[268] It is also important to note that there are sectors where the Kingdom has increasingly encouraged foreign investment. These include oil and gas equipment and services, auto parts and service equipment, telecommunications services, electrical power systems, chemical production equipment, computer software and services, franchising, air-conditioning and refrigeration equipment, building products, cosmetics, toiletries, pharmaceuticals, operation and maintenance services, medical equipment, and clothing.[269]

SAGIA reported in April 2002 that it had granted a total of 784 licenses to foreign investors over the last two years for projects worth $10.2 billion. Some $8.3 billion (SR 31 billion) were for 467 projects owned only by foreign investors. The remaining 317 projects ($1.9 billion or SR 7.2 billion) were for joint ventures, with Saudis having a $1 billion stake.[270]

An example of SAGIA activities is the issuing of three industrial licenses for a world-scale petrochemical project to be built in Jubail Industrial City by a newly established U.S.-Saudi joint venture, Jubail Chevron Phillips. The project is estimated cost SR 3.776 billion (over $1 billion), including an expansion of the group's existing plant in Jubail. The capital is to be raised through equity investment of SR 1.2 billion (about $320 million) and a low-interest loan from the Saudi Industrial Development Fund (SIDF). The first such joint venture between Chevron and the Saudi group was established in 1996 and began manufacturing operations in 2000. It was the Kingdom's first privately financed basic petrochemical industry, with an investment of about SR 2.5 billion ($650 million), and uses CPChem's proprietary Aromax technology to produce benzene. As discussed earlier, the government is also opening up new areas in the Saudi energy sector.

Once again, however, existing reforms are not enough.[271] U.S. experts report that SAGIA can still present problems for Saudi investors and is a challenge for foreign investors. They indicate that there is still some internal confusion over the project approval process resulting from an overly centralized authority structure. This means that small-scale deals that do not have multijurisdictional facets are comparatively simple; however, the lack of centralization requires that the investor engage in serious bureaucratic acrobatics to gain approval. These problems are further compounded by the need to deal with actors outside of SAGIA, such as the Ministry of Industry, to obtain permits for electricity and water. Just because investors can invest does not mean that they will invest, if it difficult and overly bureaucratic to do so. Nonetheless, SAMBA estimates that the reforms Saudi Arabia has already taken will strengthen the nonenergy sectors by half a percent annually to steady growth rate of 6% annually. [272]

Saudi Arabia has been too slow to open up its markets to provide transparency; adopt modern accounting methods; and reform its commercial code, regulations, and legal procedures. The Saudi tax code is still a nightmare that interferes with foreign investment without raising revenue. Saudi and GCC nationals only pay zakat, a modest wealth tax that averages 2.5% of the nonfixed capital employed. Foreign corporations sometimes enjoy an initial tax holiday, but then pay taxes four to five times higher. In late 1997 steps to "level the playing field" were undertaken. Among measures introduced were deep reductions in the top marginal rate paid by foreign companies. The tax reforms announced by Prince Abdullah in October 1999 may reduce these barriers to foreign businesses, but it is too early to tell.

Despite higher oil revenues in 1999–2000, Saudi government payments can still lag from six to fifteen months. Tariffs average 12%, and reach 20% for infant industries—some of which are defined in ways that amount to favoritism for given firms. The 30% set aside for Saudi nationals in government contracts and other offset provisions are often administered in ways that make it extremely difficult to use the money efficiently. In many cases, the money is allocated on the basis of favoritism and corruption, and often in ways that simply recycles imports and the efforts by foreign workers without benefiting the Saudi economy.

The concept of intellectual property protection is relatively new to Saudi Arabia, and efforts to protect intellectual property rights are uneven. In April 1996 the U.S. government moved Saudi Arabia to Watch List status from the Priority Watch List, in recognition of progress made in intellectual property right over the previous year. The Saudi patent office has a backlog of several thousand cases, and losses to computer software companies due to illegal copying are considered significant.

Saudi Arabia also continues to move slowly in fully implementing a new foreign capital investment regime. The Minister of Industry and Electricity stated that the "modernization" of the investment regime is "in the final stages" and that the new legislation would be announced by the end of 1999, but had not done so as of January 2003.[273] Yet incremental increases in foreign investment simply will not meet the Kingdom's needs. Former Saudi Minister of Industry and Electricity Salih al-Husaini stated that Saudi Arabia would need "30 billion Saudi Riyals (8 billion US dollars) annually over the next 20 years to turn the Kingdom into a semi-industrial state."[274]

BROADER GOALS FOR ECONOMIC AND SOCIAL REFORM

It is difficult to sum up the trends in Saudi Arabia's search for structural economic reform without either appearing overoptimistic and Panglossian, or appearing overcritical and joining the Cassandras that have predicted one Saudi crisis after another that never materialized. Perhaps the best answer is to let the previous trends speak for themselves and note that everything depends on the consistency and intensity of the government's future actions.

It cannot be stressed too firmly that none of the structural economic and demographic challenges the Kingdom faces are likely to prove critical in the near-to-mid-term. The Saudi government has time. It may still be acting too slowly, but it has recognized virtually all of the nation's economic problems except the need to reduce the rate of population growth.

Many of the solutions the government has identified will be workable *if* the government aggressively implements them, and Saudi Arabia has ample time in which to take decisive action. As the previous analysis has shown, Saudi Arabia's budget deficit has already been reduced by a combination of higher oil prices and austerity measures. Saudi Arabia has been able to repay its foreign debt and has already financed much of the infrastructure needed to modernize the country. It is unlikely that Saudi Arabia will have to pay for another Gulf War, and many Saudi arms purchases have been frontloaded so that arms imports in the late 1990s and early 2000s will cost substantially less than in the aftermath of the Gulf War.

Nevertheless, the analysis in Chapter 5 and the analysis in this chapter have shown that Saudi Arabia does face serious structural economic problems. It has also shown that the problems will be compounded by the impact of constant social change, high birth rates, internal political divisions, and a "youth explosion." No one outside Saudi Arabia, and probably no one within it, can be certain of just how serious the impact of the resulting tensions within Saudi society will prove to be over time. None currently seem to threaten the government, and there are few signs that a cohesive opposition is beginning to emerge. Nevertheless, the Saudi government can scarcely ignore the importance of such tensions, and it faces the added problem of dealing with a highly conservative Islamic revival at a time when it must move toward internal reform, modernize Saudi society, and deal with the West.

Saudi Arabia traditionally moves slowly. It advances ideas long before they are really implemented, experiments with different approaches to implementation, discusses and coordinates, and partially implements its decisions. This approach has often worked for the Kingdom in the past. It is doubtful, however, that this pace of action can succeed in the future. Reform must match the pace of the challenges it attempts to resolve and the seriousness of these challenges is clearly accelerating faster than the present pace of reform.

The Kingdom must also look beyond economic considerations as it intensifies its efforts at reform. Economics are always tied to politics, and society and the structure of government must also evolve along with the economy if Saudi Arabia is to preserve its internal stability. The government must build an informed consensus around economic reform, which is another reason that it must continue to expand the role of the Majlis and find ways to allow peaceful debate of social and economic issues and the need for modernism and reform versus the need to preserve traditional values. It must provide increasing popular control of national resources. It must come to grips with the issue of defining a uniform commercial code and rule of law that applies to all its citizens, including the royal family.

At some point in the mid-term, the Kingdom must tackle the issue of taxes and entitlements. Saudi economic reform cannot ignore the political realities created by its existing welfare and entitlements programs and must continue to ensure that wealth is shared throughout its society. In the process, Saudi Arabia must redefine its "social contract."

Saudi Arabia cannot afford the cost of remaining a patriarchical welfare state, and its increasingly well-educated youth is unlikely to tolerate the social role such a state gives them. Saudi Arabia must look beyond oil exports to ensure its budgets are brought into better balance and that its society and economy develop. It needs to increase revenues by directly taxing wealthier citizens. It should reduce state spending and create a more balanced economy by eliminating most subsidies and converting to market prices. It must make a full commitment to privatization and reform of the educational system, as well as social attitudes, to produce Saudi citizens able and willing to fill the places of expatriate workers.

NOTES

1. These estimates have been summarized in Table 1.1, Chart 1.2 Chart 1.3, Chart 1.4, Chart 1.6, Chart 4.5, Chart 4.7, and Chart 4.8.

2. CIA, *World Factbook, 1996, 1999, 2000, 2001,* and *2002,* "Saudi Arabia."

3. World Bank, *World Bank Atlas, 199,* (Washington: World Bank, 1997); World Bank, *World Development Indicators, 2002* (Washington: World Bank, 2002), p. 20.

4. *Saudi Arabia* (June 1997), p. 2.

5. Reuters, August 14, 1996, 1202.

6. *Saudi Arabia* (February 1997), p. 3.

7. Ibid.

8. See International Monetary Fund (IMF), *1988–1995 International Financial Statistics* (Washington: IMF, 1996); and *Middle East Economic Digest,* June 13, 1997, p. 24.

9. Energy Information Agency (EIA) *Saudi Arabia* (Washington: Department of Energy, January 2000), URL: *www.eia.doe.gov/emeu/cabs/saudi.html.*

10. *Saudi Arabia* (June 1997), pp. 1–2.

11. *Saudi Commerce and Economic Review* (February 1996), No. 22.

12. Kingdom of Saudi Arabia, Ministry of Planning, *Seventh Development Plan 1420/21–1424/25 AH (2000–2004 AD)* (Riyadh: Ministry of Planning, 2001), pp. 118–120.

13. Taken from Brad C. Bourland, *The Saudi Economy in 2002* (Riyadh: Saudi American Bank, February 2002), pp. 8–9.

14. EIA, *Saudi Arabia* (Washington: Department of Energy, January 2000), URL: *www.eia.doe.gov/emeu/cabs/saudi.html*; *Middle East Economic Digest*, May 9, 2000, p. 18, May 26, 2000, p. 17.

15. Date of the Royal Order. For a full statement of responsibility, see Saudi Arabia Monetary Agency (SAMA), *Thirty-Seventh Annual Report, 1422H (2001G)* (Riyadh: SAMA, September 2001), pp. 44–46.

16. *Monthly Newsletter of the Royal Embassy of Saudi Arabia,* "Formation of New Economic Council" (September 1999), p. 1.

17. *US-Saudi Business Brief,* Vol. 6, No. 1 (2001), p. 3; SAMA, *Thirty-Seventh Annual Report, 1422H (2001G),* pp. 44–46.

18. Saudi Embassy in the United States, press release /01 spa/09-23-econ.html.

19. SAMA, *Thirty-Seventh Annual Report, 1422H (2001G),* pp. 44–46.

20. Saudi Press Agency Information Release, "16-member Economic Consultative Commission formed in Saudi Arabia," September 23, 1999.

21. *Monthly Newsletter of the Royal Embassy of Saudi Arabia,* "Formation of new Economic Council," p. 1.

22. Drawn from comments by St. John Armitage.

23. *Middle East Economic Survey,* November 1, 1999.

24. Ibid.; SAMA, *Thirty-Seventh Annual Report, 1422H (2001G),* pp. 47–48.

25. Brad C. Bourland, *The Saudi Economy: Mid-Year 2000 Update* (Riyadh: Saudi American Bank, August 2000), p. 10; *Saudi Arabia,* Vol. 18, No. 1 (Spring 2001), pp. 7–10; SAMA, *Thirty-Seventh Annual Report, 1422H (2001G),* pp. 47-48.

26. EIA, *Saudi Arabia* (Washington: Department of Energy, January 2000), *www.eia.doe.gov/emeu/cabs/saudi.html*; SAMA, *Thirty-Seventh Annual Report, 1422H (2001G),* pp. 46–49.

27. "Information Office of the Royal Embassy of Saudi Arabia Ushering in a New Era of Foreign Investment," *Saudi Arabia,* Vol. 17, No. 2 (Summer 2000), p. 7.

28. See his interview in *Gulf Business,* Vol. 6, No. 12 (April 2002).

29. Associated Press, May 9, 2001, 1435; *Saudi Arabia,* Vol. 18, No. 1 (Spring 2001), p. 12.

30. SAMA, *Thirty-Seventh Annual Report, 1422H (2001G),* pp. 49–50.

31. *Saudi Arabia,* Vol. 18, No. 1 (Spring 2001), pp. 7–8.

32. Ibid., pp. 9-10. The full text of the Foreign Investment Act may be found at SAGIA's Web site (URL: *www.sagia.org/THE_FOREIGN_INVESTMENT_ACT.htm*).

33. Additional details are taken from SAMA, *Thirty-Seventh Annual Report, 1422H (2001G),* pp. 48–49.

34. Ibid., pp. 50–51.

35. Saudi Embassy in the US, press release /00 spa/04-15-econ.html.

36. SAMA, *Thirty-Seventh Annual Report, 1422H (2001G),* p. 52.

37. *Arab News,* April 15, 2002, URL: *www.arabnew.com/article.asp?ID=14435.*

38. Ministry of Planning, *Achievements of the Development Plans 1970–2001, Facts and Figures* (Riyadh: Ministry of Planning, 2002),19th Issue, pp. 212–215.

39. Ibid., p. 285.

40. Ibid., p. 288.

41. Bourland, *The Saudi Economy in 2002*, pp. 26–27.

42. Bloomberg, April 18, 2001, 1151.

43. *Arab News*, April 20, 2001, URL: *www.arabnew.com/article.asp?sct= WTO&ID=1300*.

44. Reuters, April 21, 2001, 0835, April 22, 2001, 0829; Bloomberg, April 18, 2001, 1151.

45. *Middle East Economic Survey*, July 3, 2000; Interviews, April 16, 2002.

46. Office of the SAMBA Chief Economist, *The Saudi Economy at Mid-Year 2002* (Riyadh: Saudi American Bank, August 2002).

47. Interviews in Saudi Arabia in 2000.

48. SAMA, *Thirty-Seventh Annual Report, 1422H (2001G)*, pp. 49–50.

49. Bourland, *The Saudi Economy: Mid-Year 2000 Update*, , p. 10.

50. *Arab News*, April 24, 2002, URL: *www.arabnew.com/article.asp?ID=14625*.

51. *Middle East Economic Survey*, June 5, 2000.

52. Ibid.

53. SAMA, *Thirty-Sixth Annual Report, 1421H (2000G)* (Riyadh: SAMA, 2000), pp. 152–166.

54. Reuters, April 23, 2001, 1616, May 7, 2001, 1053.

55. Bourland, *The Saudi Economy in 2002*, p. 9.

56. Much of this list is taken from Bourland, *The Saudi Economy: Mid-Year 2000 Update* and *The Saudi Economy in 2002*, pp. 8–9.

57. *Middle East Economic Digest*, July 14, 2000, July 21, 2000.

58. Ministry of Planning, *Achievements of the Development Plans, 1390–1420 (1970–2000), Facts and Figures* (Riyadh: Ministry of Planning, 2001), 18th Edition, Tables 7 and 17; and Kingdom of Saudi Arabia, Ministry of Planning, *Achievements of the Development Plans 1970–2001, Facts and Figures*.

59. Ministry of Planning, *Achievements of the Development Plans, 1390–1420 (1970–2000), Facts and Figures*, Table 11; and Kingdom of Saudi Arabia, Ministry of Planning, *Achievements of the Development Plans 1970–2001, Facts and Figures*.

60. World Bank, *Forging a Partnership for Environmental Action* (Washington: World Bank, December 1994), p. 24.

61. World Bank, *World Bank Atlas, 1997* (Washington: World Bank, 1997). Saudi Arabia does not publish detailed data on per capita income. SAMA claims that the total GDP rose by 1.4% during 1994, 4.3% during 1995, and 6% during 1996, but these figures present definitional problems that make them impossible to compare with World Bank data. *Saudi Arabia*, Vol. 14 (January 1997), pp. 1–2.

62. CIA, *World Factbook, 2000, 2001,* and *2002*, "Saudi Arabia"; "Saudi Arabia 2000 Economic Trends," U.S. Embassy, Riyadh. April 2000.

63. *Saudi Arabia*, Vol. 14 (January 1997), pp. 1–2; *Middle East Economic Digest*, May 16, 1997, p. 3.

64. *Saudi Commerce and Economic Review*, No. 22 (February 1996), p. 14. The difficulty of estimating the Saudi GDP in meaningful terms is illustrated by the fact that Saudi finance minister used an entirely different definition in summarizing the Sixth Development Plan. He called for an increase from a GDP of $101.5 billion (SR 380.8 billion) in 1995 to a GDP of $122.3 billion (SR 458.6 billion) by 2000. Reuters, August 14, 1996, 1202.

65. The term "real" implies constant riyals or dollars. In practice, the "real" growth estimated by Middle Eastern governments tends to consistently exaggerate actual growth.

66. *Saudi Commerce and Economic Review*, No. 22 (February 1996), pp. 10–19.

67. Ibid.; and *Middle East Economic Digest*, "Special Report: Saudi Arabia," April 5, 1996, pp. 35–49.

68. Ibid.

69. Ibid.

70. Ministry of Planning, *Achievements of the Development Plans, 1390–1420 (1970–2000), Facts and Figures*, Tables 7 and 17; and Kingdom of Saudi Arabia, Ministry of Planning, *Achievements of the Development Plans 1970–2001, Facts and Figures*.

71. Ministry of Planning, *Achievements of the Development Plans, 1390–1420 (1970–2000), Facts and Figures*, Table 11; and Kingdom of Saudi Arabia, Ministry of Planning, *Achievements of the Development Plans 1970–2001, Facts and Figures*.

72. *Saudi Commerce and Economic Review*, No. 22 (February 1996), pp. 10–19.

73. Reuters, December 28, 1998, 1728; Information Office, Royal Embassy of Saudi Arabia, Vol. 16, November 1 1999, p. 1; National Commercial Bank Economist 2000, p. 3.

74. The figures in this analysis are based on briefings by the Ministry of Planning and on the English-language version of the *Seventh Development Plan 1420/21–1424/25 AH (2000–2004 AD)*, plus material provided on the Ministry of Planning Web site.

75. English-language version of the *Seventh Development Plan 1420/21–1424/25 AH (2000–2004 AD)*, p. 131.

76. *Monthly Newsletter of Royal Embassy of Saudi Arabia*, "Objective of Seventh Development Plan Outlined" (August 1999), p. 5; English-language version of the *Seventh Development Plan 1420/21–1424/25 AH (2000–2004 AD)*.

77. *Middle East Economic Digest*, June 30, 2000, pp. 22–37.

78. *Saudi Arabia*, Vol.17, No. 12, pp. 1–2; and EIA country report on Saudi Arabia, URL: *http://www.eia.doe.gov/cabs/saudi.html*, June 8, 2001.

79. DOE/EIA, Internet country database on Saudi Arabia, accessed August 26, 1997.

80. Kingdom of Saudi Arabia, Ministry of Planning, *Achievements of the Development Plans 1970–2001, Facts and Figures,* pp. 198–202.

81. Ministry of Planning, *Achievements of the Development Plans, 1390–1420 (1970–2000), Facts and Figures*, Table 11; SAMA, *Thirty-Seventh Annual Report*; Bourland, *The Saudi Economy in 2002*, pp. 32–25; and Kingdom of Saudi Arabia, Ministry of Planning, *Achievements of the Development Plans 1970–2001, Facts and Figures*, p. 205.

82. SAMA, *Thirty-Seventh Annual Report*; Bourland, *The Saudi Economy in 2002*, pp. 32–25; and Kingdom of Saudi Arabia, Ministry of Planning, *Achievements of the Development Plans 1970–2001, Facts and Figures*.

83. Ministry of Planning, *Achievements of the Development Plans, 1390–1420 (1970–2000), Facts and Figures*, Table 11; SAMA, *Thirty-Seventh Annual Report*;

Bourland, *The Saudi Economy in 2002*, pp. 32–25; and Kingdom of Saudi Arabia, Ministry of Planning, *Achievements of the Development Plans 1970–2001, Facts and Figures*.

84. Ibid.

85. Ministry of Planning, *Achievements of the Development Plans, 1390–1420 (1970–2000), Facts and Figures*, Tables 11, 12, and 14; SAMA, *Thirty-Seventh Annual Report*; Bourland, *The Saudi Economy in 2002*, pp. 32–25; and Kingdom of Saudi Arabia, Ministry of Planning, *Achievements of the Development Plans 1970–2001, Facts and Figures*.

86. CIA, *World Fact Book, 1996*, "Saudi Arabia."

87. Ministry of Planning, *Achievements of the Development Plans, 1390–1420 (1970–2000), Facts and Figures*, Tables 11 and 12; SAMA, *Thirty-Seventh Annual Report*; Bourland, *The Saudi Economy in 2002*, pp. 32–25; and Kingdom of Saudi Arabia, Ministry of Planning, *Achievements of the Development Plans 1970–2001, Facts and Figures*.

88. Ministry of Planning, *Achievements of the Development Plans, 1390–1420 (1970–2000), Facts and Figures*, Tables 11, 12, and 14; SAMA, *Thirty-Seventh Annual Report*; Bourland, *The Saudi Economy in 2002*, pp. 32–25.

89. Interviews in Saudi Arabia in February, 2001; and Kingdom of Saudi Arabia, Ministry of Planning, *Achievements of the Development Plans 1970–2001, Facts and Figures*.

90. Ministry of Planning, *Achievements of the Development Plans, 1390–1420 (1970–2000), Facts and Figures*, Table 14; SAMA, *Thirty-Seventh Annual Report*; Bourland, *The Saudi Economy in 2002*, pp. 32–25; and Kingdom of Saudi Arabia, Ministry of Planning, *Achievements of the Development Plans 1970–2001, Facts and Figures*.

91. CIA, *World Factbook, 1996, , 2000, 2001*, and *2002*, "Saudi Arabia"; *Middle East Economic Digest*, June 13, 1997, pp. 23–35.

92. This analysis is based on Said al-Shaikh, "Kingdom's Non-Oil Exports Cross $25B," *Arab News*, April 17, 2002. The author is chief economist at National Commercial Bank in Jeddah.

93. Congressional Quarterly, *The Middle East*, 7th ed. (Washington: Congressional Quarterly, 1990), p. 117.

94. EIA, online database on Saudi Arabia, accessed August 26, 1997.

95. Reuters, August 8, 1994, 1013; *Middle East Economic Digest*, August 18, 1995, p. 3, June 16, 1996, p. 5, October 18, 1996, p. 6, June 13, 1997, pp. 23–25; Bourland, *The Saudi Economy in 2002*, p. 37; *SAMA Monthly Bulletin* (November 2001); SAMA, *Thirty-Seventh Annual Report*.

96. *Middle East Economic Digest*, "Special Report: Saudi Arabia", March 10, 1995, pp. 28–30, April 5, 1996, pp. 35–49, June 13, 1997, pp. 23–25; *Saudi Arabia* (February 1996), p. 3; and interviews with U.S. experts.

97. Brad C. Bourland, *The Saudi Economy: 2000 Performance, 2001 Forecast* (Riyadh: Saudi American Bank, February 2001), p. 2; Bourland, *The Saudi Economy in 2002*, p. 2.

98. *U.S.-Saudi Business Brief*, Vol. 4, No.1 (1999), p. 2.

99. Bourland, *The Saudi Economy: 2000 Performance, 2001 Forecast*, p. 13; *The Saudi Economy in 2002*, p. 37.

100. EIA, "OPEC," April 8, 2002, URL: *www.eia.doe.ov/emeu/cabs/opec2.html*.

101. As should already be apparent, very different estimates of oil export revenues exist, depending on who is doing the calculation and the definition involved. These differences do not, however, affect the macroeconomic and structural issues addressed.

102. *Middle East Economic Digest*, July 3, 1998, p. 3.

103. *Middle East Economic Digest*, March 26, 1999, p. 5.

104. Reuters, March 9, 1999.

105. *Middle East Economic Digest*, July 3, 1998, p. 3.

106. EIA, "OPEC Revenues Fact Sheet," March 2000, URL: *http://www.eia.doe.gov/emeu/cabs/opecrev.html*.

107. Bourland, *The Saudi Economy: 2000 Performance, 2001 Forecast*, p. 1.

108. *The Washington Post*, March 13, 1999, p. B1.

109. EIA, "OPEC Revenues Fact Sheet", *Middle East Economic Digest*, August 4, 2000, p. 20.

110. U.S. Embassy, *Saudi Arabia 2000 Economic Trends* (Riyadh: U.S. Embassy, April 2000), p. 4; Bourland, *The Saudi Economy in 2002*, pp. 2–37.

111. Bourland, *The Saudi Economy: 2000 Performance, 2001 Forecast*, p. 1.

112. *Middle East Economic Survey*, February 26, 2001.

113. Bourland, *The Saudi Economy: 2000 Performance, 2001 Forecast*, p. 2, and *The Saudi Economy in 2002*, p. 32.

114. Brad Bourland, *The Saudi Economy: 2000 Performance, 2001 Forecast*, p. 2.

115. The best long-term models are those presented in the EIA section of the U.S. Department of Energy (DOE) Web page (URL: *eia.gov*) as part of the material on the EIA's *International Energy Outlook*. The work of the International Energy Agency is somewhat similar, and is presented in its annual edition of the *World Energy Outlook*. The IEA data and assumptions and modeling effort, however, are much less transparent than those of the EIA. OPEC does not publicly release its modeling, but an examination of OPEC confidential documents indicates that its modeling effort and conclusions are very similar to those of the IEA. One of the best analyses of the limits to any increases in alternatives to global use of oil can be found in Office of Analysis and Integrated Forecasting, EIA, *Impacts of the Kyoto Protocol on US Energy Markets and Economic Activity* (Washington: Department of Energy, SR/OIAF/98-03, October 1998).

116. Bureau of Verification and Compliance, *World Military Expenditures and Arms Transfers, 1998* (Washington: U.S. State Department, 2000), Table I, p. 101.

117. An effort to impose taxes of up to 30% on foreigners was withdrawn shortly after it was proposed. Nearly two-thirds of the bonds were bought by the Saudi Arabian government. *Wall Street Journal*, December 31, 1987, p. 4, January 5, 1988, p. 21, January 6, 1988, p. 12, January 7, 1988, p. 16, January 12, 1988, p. 2; *Washington Post*, December 31, 1987, p. E-3, January 12, 1988, p. C-3; *Economist*, January 16–22, 1988, p. 59; *New York Times*, January 6, 1988, p. A-1; *Chicago Tribune*, January 27, 1988, p. 3-7.

118. *New York Times*, August 22, 1993; *Washington Post*, August 29, 1993, p. C-2.

119. *Middle East Economic Digest*, January 12, 1996, p. 15; *Saudi Arabia*, Vol. 14 (January 1997), pp. 1–2.

456 Saudi Arabia Enters the Twenty-First Century

Saudi Arabia Enters the Twenty-First Century

120. Data are taken from working papers distributed during the Royal Institute of International Affairs conference on Saudi Arabia in October 4–5, 1993.

121. Bourland, *The Saudi Economy: 2000 Performance, 2001 Forecast*, p. 2, and *The Saudi Economy in 2002*, p. 2.

122. *Jane's Defence Weekly*, December 5, 1992, p. 5; *Business Week*, February 15, 1993, p. 50.

123. U.S. State Department, *World Military Expenditures and Arms Transfers, 1999–2000* (Washington: Bureau of Verification and Compliance, 2002), Table I, p. 41.

124. *Middle East Economic Digest*, January 17, 1992, pp. 4–5, March 20, 1992, pp. 10–16.

125. Bourland, *The Saudi Economy in 2002*, p. 2.

126. *Jane's Defence Weekly*, December 5, 1992, p. 5; *Business Week*, February 15, 1993, p. 50.

127. *New York Times*, June 19, 1995, p. D-2; IMF Article 4 Report, 1994; *Middle East Economic Digest*, "Special Report: Saudi Arabia," March 10, 1995, pp. 28–30; Reuters, August 7, 1995, 0552, 1420; Executive News Service, July 31, 1995, 0905; *Middle East Economic Digest*, January 12, 1996, pp. 15–16; *Middle East Economic Digest*, November 3, 1995, p. 38.

128. IMF; *Middle East Economic Digest*, April 5, 1996, p. 43, October 18, 1996, p. 6.

129. IMF Article 4 Report, 1995; *Middle East Economic Digest*, April 5, 1996, pp. 30–43.

130. IMF Article 4 Report, 1994 and 1995; *Middle East Economic Digest*, "Special Report: Saudi Arabia," March 10, 1995, pp. 28–30, April 5, 1996, pp. 30–43; Reuters, August 7, 1995, 0552, 1420; Executive News Service, July 31, 1995, 0905; *Middle East Economic Digest*, August 18, 1995, p. 3, January 12, 1996, pp. 15–16.

131. *Middle East Economic Digest*, January 12, 1996, pp. 15–16, and calculations by the author.

132. Agence France Presse, March 14, 1997; *Middle East Economic Digest*, September 19, 1997, p. 28.

133. Reuters, December 28, 1998, 1728.

134. EIA, Country Brief, "Saudi Arabia," January 1999.

135. *Saudi Arabia*, Vol. 16, No. 1 (January 1999), pp. 1–2; *Middle East Economic Digest*, January 15, 1996, pp. 2–3.

136. *Policywatch*, The Washington Institute for Near East Policy, January 5, 1999.

137. Agence France Presse, "Saudi Plans to levy highway tolls," *Arabia.On.Line*, URL: *http://www.arabia.com*, December 6, 1999.

138. *Policywatch*, The Washington Institute for Near East Policy, January 5, 1999.

139. *Middle East Economic Digest*, June 11, 1999, p. 7.

140. *US-Saudi Business*, Vol. 4, No. 1 (1999), p. 2; *Middle East Economic Digest*, January 15, 1996, pp. 2–3.

141. Bourland, *The Saudi Economy: 1999 Performance, 2000 Forecast*; *Middle East Economic Digest*, March 2, 2000; *Saudi Arabia* (January 2000).

142. "Deficit in Saudi Budget may drop as oil prices rise," *Saudi Gazette*, September 26, 1999. Accessed through Lexis-Nexis.

143. Bourland, *The Saudi Economy: 1999 Performance, 2000 Forecast*, February 2000.

144. Ibid.

145. Ibid.

146. Bourland, *The Saudi Economy: 2000 Performance, 2001 Forecast*, pp. 5–8.

147. Bourland, *The Saudi Economy in 2002*, p. 2.

148. Ibid., p. 11.

149. *Saudi Arabia*, Vol. 18, No. 1 (January 2001), p. 2.

150. Bourland, *The Saudi Economy: 2000 Performance, 2001 Forecast*, Riyadh, Saudi American Bank, February 2001, pp. 5–8.

151. Bourland, *The Saudi Economy in Mid-Year: 2002*, p. 8.

152. Bourland, *The Saudi Economy in 2002*, pp. 10–11.

153. *Saudi Arabia*, Vol. 18, No. 1 (January 2001), p. 2.

154. SAMA, *Thirty-Seventh Annual Report*, p. 142.

155. Bourland, *The Saudi Economy: 2000 Performance, 2001 Forecast*, p. 8, and *The Saudi Economy in 2002*, p. 12.

156. SAMA, *Thirty-Sixth Annual Report, 1421H (2000G)*, pp. 134–135.

157. *Middle East Economic Digest*, January 12, 1996, p. 15, June 14, 1996, p. 5; *Saudi Arabia*, Vol. 14, No. 1 (January 1997), pp. 1–2; *Middle East Economic Survey*, January 6, 1997, p. B-1.

158. IMF Article 4 Report, 1994 and 1995; *Middle East Economic Digest*, "Special Report: Saudi Arabia," March 10, 1995, pp. 28–30, April 5, 1996, pp. 30–43; Reuters, August 7, 1995, 0552, 1420; Executive News Service, July 31, 1995, 0905; *Middle East Economic Digest*, August 18, 1995, p. 3, January 12, 1996, pp. 15–16, and calculations by the author.

159. A Saudi official indicates that the true deficit was $5.9 billion and that arrears exceeded $3 billion if all debt was counted, and the government was not allowed to unilaterally write off debts to contractors and the failure to pay interest on some arrears. See *Middle East Economic Survey*, January 6, 1997, p. B-1; *Saudi Commerce and Economic Review* (February 1996), p. 6.

160. *Middle East Economic Digest*, June 13, 19967, p. 24.

161. *Saudi Arabia* (February 1997), p. 3; *MEM* (February 1997), p. 3.

162. *Middle East Economic Survey*, January 6, 1997, p. B-2.

163. *Wall Street Journal*, September 23, 1996, p. B-10D.

164. SAMA, *Thirty-Sixth Annual Report, 1421H (2000G)*, pp. 134–135.

165. *Middle East Economic Digest*, "Special Report: Saudi Arabia", March 10, 1995, pp. 28–30, November 3, 1995, p. 37.

166. *Middle East Economic Digest*, "Special Report: Saudi Arabia," March 10, 1995, pp. 28–30.

167. Bourland, *The Saudi Economy: 2000 Performance, 2001 Forecast*, p. 1; *The Saudi Economy at Mid-Year 2002*, p. 13.

168. Bourland, *The Saudi Economy in 2002*, pp. 2, 12.

169. *Middle East Economic Digest*, "Special Report: Saudi Arabia," March 10, 1995, pp. 28–30, November 3, 1995, p. 37.

170. *Middle East Economic Digest*, April 5, 1996, p. 48; Saudi American Bank, *The Saudi Economy: 1999 Performance: 2000 Forecast*.

171. Bourland, *The Saudi Economy: 2000 Performance, 2001 Forecast*, p. 7; *The Saudi Economy at Mid-Year 2002*, p. 13.

172. *Neu Zurcher Zeitung*, April 15, 1995; Executive News Service, August 7, 1995, 0552, August 31, 1995, 0942; *Economist*, May 27, 1995.

173. *Middle East Economic Digest*, April 26, 1996, p. 27.

174. Ibid.

175. *Washington Post*, June 6, 1995, p. D-2; *Washington Times*, June 6, 1995, p. B-6; Executive News Service, August 7, 1995, 0552, August 31, 1995, 0942, *Wall Street Journal*, September 22, 1995, p. B-4.

176. *Middle East Economic Survey*, January 6, 1997, p. B-1; *Middle East Economic Digest*, October 18, 1996, p. 6.

177. *Middle East Economic Digest*, January 17, 1997, p. 5, June 13, 1997, p. 24; *Wall Street Journal*, May 29, 1997; *Financial Times*, January 2, 1997, Internet.

178. Saudi American Bank, *The Saudi Economy: 1999 Performance, 2000 Forecast*.

179. *The Financial Times*, January 30, 1996, p. 6.

180. Associated Press, December 5, 1998, 0817; *New York Times*, December 5, 1998, p. A-5; Agence France Press, December 5, 1998.

181. *Middle East Economic Digest*, January 15, 1996, pp. 2–3.

182. *Middle East Economic Digest*, April 5, 1996, p. 48.

183. Saudi American Bank, *The Saudi Economy: 1999 Performance, 2000 Forecast*; *Middle East Economic Digest*, March 24, 2000.

184. *Middle East Economic Digest*, April 5, 1996, p. 48.

185. *Middle East Economic Digest*, April 5, 1996, p. 48; Saudi American Bank, *The Saudi Economy: 1999 Performance: 2000 Forecast*.

186. *Middle East Economic Digest*, April 18, 1997, p. 2.

187. SAMA, *Thirty-Seventh Annual Report*, pp. 356–358. The reader should be aware that these SAMA GDP data seem to consistently understate the fluctuations in the value of the petroleum sector. Other data show that it rose in value in current dollars from $39.4 billion in 1993 to $71.8 billion in 2000, and low Saudi inflation cannot explain the different SAMA figures. See Bourland, *The Saudi Economy in 2002*, p. 34.

188. Ibid.

189. Ibid., p. 35.

190. "Industry: Diversifying in New Directions," *Saudi Arabia*, Vol. 18, No. 1 (Spring 2001), pp. 10–13.

191. *Wall Street Journal*, "Saudi Arabia," September 22, 1995; *Middle East Economic Digest*, August 18, 1995, pp. 2–16, June 13, 1997, pp. 22–26; Executive News Service, August 7, 1995, 1420, September 18, 1995, 1631.

192. RTR0475 3 OVR 504, August 2, 1995, 1936; *Washington Times*, August 5, 1995, p. B-7; DOE/EIA Online database, analysis section, country section. Accessed July 25, 1995; *Wall Street Journal*, "Saudi Arabia," September 22, 1995 and May 29, 1997, Section B; *Saudi Commerce and Economic Review* No. 22 (February 1996); *Middle East Economic Digest*, October 18, 1996. p. 6, June 13, 1997, pp. 22–26; *Financial Times*, January 2, 1997, Internet; *Saudi Arabia* (December 1996), p. 5.

193. "Industry: Diversifying in New Directions," *Saudi Arabia*, Vol. 18, No. 1 (Spring 2001), p. 12.

194. For a good Saudi discussion of privatization see SAMA, *Thirty-Sixth Annual Report, 1421H (2000G)*, pp. 110–132.

195. See the summary in SAMA, *Thirty-Seventh Annual Report, 1422H (2001G)*, pp. 37–38, 55–64.

196. EIA, *Saudi Arabia* (Washington: Department of Energy, June 2001), URL: *http://www.eia.doe.gov/emeu/cabs/saudi.html*.

197. "Industry: Diversifying in New Directions," *Saudi Arabia*, Vol. 18, No. 1 (Spring 2001), pp. 10–13.

198. *SABIC Annual Report, 2001* (Riyadh: SABIC, 2002), URL: *www.sabic.com*; *MEED Quarterly Report—Saudi Arabia*, August 15, 2002, p. 10.

199. Kingdom of Saudi Arabia, Ministry of Planning, *Achievements of the Development Plans: Facts and Figures, 1390–1421H (1970–2001AD)*, pp. 120–121.

200. *Middle East Economic Digest*, June 13, 1997, pp. 34–37, September 19, 1997, p. 29.

201. EIA, *Saudi Arabia* (Washington: Department of Energy, June 2001), URL: *http://www.eia.doe.gov/emeu/cabs/saudi.html*.

202. "Al-Zamil Group Forms Joint-Stock Company," *US-Saudi Business Brief*, Vol. 4, No. 3 (1999).

203. *Middle East Economic Survey*, November 1, 1999.

204. Ibid.

205. *Middle East Business Intelligence*, August 5, 1999. Accessed through Lexis-Nexis.

206. "New Utilities Company Created for Jubail and Yanbu," *US-Saudi Business Brief*, Vol. 4, No. 3 (1999).

207. *Middle East Economic Survey*, June 5 2000; June 26, 2000.

208. EIA, *Saudi Arabia* (Washington: Department of Energy, January 2002), URL: *http://www.eia.doe.gov/emeu/cabs/saudi.html*.

209. Samantha Tomkin, "The state shakes up its role in the economy," *In Focus*, Special advertising supplement on Saudi Arabia, *New York Times*, September 23, 1999, pp. 20–21.

210. "Saudi Arabia Finance: Saudi telecom set for privatization," *Economist Intelligence Unit Views Wire*, September 2, 1999. Accessed through Lexis-Nexis.

211. SAMA, *Thirty-Seventh Annual Report, 1422H (2001G)*, pp. 55–57.

212. "Saudi Arabia Finance: Saudi telecom set for privatization"; Reuters, May 15, 2001, 0539.

213. *Middle East Economic Survey*, November 1, 1999.

214. Bourland, *The Saudi Economy: 2000 Performance, 2001 Forecast*, p. 11.

215. Bourland, *The Saudi Economy at Mid-Year 2000*, pp. 13–14.

216. *MEED Quarterly Report—Saudi Arabia*, August 15, 2002, p. 10.

217. SAMA, *Thirty-Seventh Annual Report, 1422H ((2001G)*, pp. 58–59.

218. Ibid., pp. 59–60.

219. Much of this analysis is drawn from the EIA, *Saudi Arabia* (Washington: Department of Energy, June 2001 and January 2002), URL: *http://www.eia.doe.gov/emeu/cabs/saudi.html*.

220. SAMA, *Thirty-Seventh Annual Report, 1422H (2001G)*, pp. 60–61.

221. *Middle East Business Intelligence*, August 5, 1999. Accessed through Lexis-Nexis.

222. *Middle East Economic Digest*, March 19, 1999, pp. 2–3.

223. *Middle East Economic Digest*, December 4, 1998, p. 22.

224. *Middle East Economic Digest*, August 11, 2000.

225. Kingdom of Saudi Arabia, Ministry of Planning, *Achievements of the Development Plans: Facts and Figures, 1390–1421H (1970–2001AD)*, pp. 120–121, 339.

226. SAMA, *Thirty-Seventh Annual Report, 1422H (2001G)*, pp. 61–62.

227. Kingdom of Saudi Arabia, Ministry of Planning, *Seventh Development Plan 1420/21–1424/25 AH (2000–2004 AD)*, p. 319.

228. *Middle East Economic Digest*, June 13, 1997, pp. 34–37, September 19, 1997, p. 29.

229. SAMA, *Thirty-Seventh Annual Report, 1422H (2001G)*, pp. 61–62.

230. *Wall Street Journal*, "Saudi Arabia," September 22, 1995; *Middle East Economic Digest*, August 18, 1995, pp. 2–16, June 13, 1997, pp. 22–26; Executive News Service, August 7, 1995, 1420, September 18, 1995, 1631.

231. Bourland, *The Saudi Economy: 2000 Performance, 2001 Forecast*, p. 11.

232. Bloomberg News, May 3, 2001, 0258.

233. *Saudi Arabia* (January 1997), pp. 1–3

234. Agence France Presse, "Saudi to Encourage Foreign Investment," *Arabia.On.Line*, URL: *http://www.arabia.com*, October 20, 1999.

235. SAMA, *Thirty-Sixth Annual Report, 1421H (2000G)*, p. 95.

236. SAMA, *Thirty-Seventh Annual Report, 1422H (2001G)*, pp. 74–79.

237. Ibid., pp. 81–82.

238. SAMA, *Thirty-Sixth Annual Report, 1421H (2000G)*, pp. 89–90; *Thirty-Seventh Annual Report, 1422H (2001G)*, pp. 87, 112–121.

239. Bourland, *The Saudi Economy In 2002*, pp. 35–26.

240. SAMA, *Thirty-Seventh Annual Report, 1422H (2001G)*, pp. 122–125.

241. For a good Saudi discussion of the stock market and banking sector see SAMA, *Thirty-Sixth Annual Report, 1421H (2000G)*, pp. 80–105.

242. SAMA, *Thirty-Seventh Annual Report, 1422H (2001G)*, pp. 99–110.

243. Agence France Presse, "Saudi opens bourse to indirect foreign investment," *Arabia.On.Line*,URL: *http://www.arabia.com*, November 1, 1999.

244. *Middle East Economic Digest*, September 19, 1997, pp. 31–32.

245. SAMA, *Thirty-Seventh Annual Report, 1422H (2001G)*, p. 108.

246. Bourland, *The Saudi Economy in 2002*, pp. 27–29.

247. SAMA, *Thirty-Seventh Annual Report, 1422H (2001G)*, pp. 99–110.

248. Bourland, *The Saudi Economy in 2002*, pp. 27–29.

249. SAMA, *Thirty-Seventh Annual Report, 1422H (2001G)*, p. 102

250. *Middle East Economic Digest*, April 18, 1997, pp. 2–3, June 13, 1997, pp. 23–37; *Wall Street Journal*, May 29, 1997, Section B.

251. U.S. Embassy, *Saudi Arabia 2000 Economic Trends* (Riyadh: U.S. Embassy, April 2000), p. 5; Saudi officials, April 17, 2002.

252. *Middle East Economic Digest*, May 12, 2000, p. 5.

253. *Saudi Gazette*, September 26, 2002, p. 5.

254. Bourland, *The Saudi Economy at Mid-Year 2000*, pp. 13–14; *Saudi Gazette*, September 26, 2002, pp. 16–17.

255. *Middle East Economic Survey*, Vol. 43, No.24 (June 12, 2000).

256. Bourland, *The Saudi Economy at Mid-Year 2000*, pp. 13–14; *Saudi Gazette*, September 26, 2002, p. 5.

257. *Middle East Economic Digest*, September 19, 1997, pp. 31–32.

258. *Middle East Economic Survey*, July 3, 2000.

259. *Saudi Arabia* Vol. 18, No. 1 (Spring 2001), pp. 9–10.

260. Under the new deal, visitors from the United States are able to obtain a two-year multiple-entry visa for approximately $52, as opposed to the previously common one-year three-entry visas, which cost three times as much. Reuters, "US, Saudi Arabia to ease visa rules," *Khaleej Times Online*, October 18, 1999, URL: *http://www.khaleejtimes.com*.

261. *Middle East Economic Survey*, November 1, 1999.

262. Saudi Press Agency Information Release, "Incentives for foreign investors announced," October 23, 1999.

263. *Middle East Economic Survey*, November 1, 1999.

264. Agence France Presse, November 8, 1999; Saudi Press Agency Information Release, November 1, 1999.

265. Associated Press, May 9, 2001, 1435; *Saudi Arabia*, Vol. 18, No. 1 (Spring 20010, p. 12.

266. *Saudi Arabia*, Vol. 18, No. 1 (Spring 2001), pp. 7–8.

267. *Middle East Economic Digest*, August 4, 2000, p. 21.

268. *Saudi Arabia* (March 2001), p. 5.

269. EIA, *Saudi Arabia* (Washington: Department of Energy, June 2001), URL: *http://www.eia.doe.gov/emeu/cabs/saudi.html*.

270. *Saudi Arabia*, Vol. 18, No. 1 (Spring 2001), pp. 4–5.

271. *Arab News*, April 15, 2002, URL: *www.arabnew.com/article.asp?ID=14360*.

272. For a good summary discussion, see *The Economist*, June 9, 2001, p. 66.

273. *Middle East Economic Survey*, February 26, 2001.

274. *Middle East Economic Survey*, November 1, 1999.

275. *Middle East Economic Survey*, February 26, 2001.

Chapter 7

Shaping the Future of the Saudi Petroleum Sector

Saudi Arabia's need for economic reform and diversification does not mean that its petroleum sector will lose its importance in Saudi Arabia's future. No matter how successful economic, demographic, and social reforms become, Saudi Arabia's strategic position, economy, and ability to meet the expectations of its people will still depend on the revenues provided by its petroleum sector. While Saudi energy exports cannot by themselves support the Saudi Arabia of the twenty-first century, they will remain the most important source of the Kingdom's income. Saudi Arabia will stay a petroleum sector–driven economy even if it is successful in both diversifying and expanding its private sector. In fact, much of its diversification, and much of the growth in its private sector, will consist of ventures that add value and labor intensity to the Saudi economy through the production of petroleum-related products.[1]

The petroleum sector normally accounts for around 40% of the Saudi GDP by Saudi estimates. The Saudi Arabian Monetary Agency (SAMA) estimates that the total value of crude oil, natural gas, and petroleum refining was $51.7 billion in 1992, out of a GDP of 123.0 billion (42%). It was $48.2 billion out of $127.6 billion in 1995 (39.0%), $39.1 billion out of $128.76 billion in 1997 (30%), and $77.6 billion out of $173.1 billion in 2000 (44.8%).[2] These percentages vary according to world demand for petroleum and the resulting Saudi earnings, but they do not reveal any trend toward reduced dependence.

The Energy Information Agency of the U.S. Department of Energy (DOE) makes similar estimates. It estimated in 2002 that the petroleum sector accounted for some 90% to 95% of total Saudi export earnings in 2002, 80% of state revenues, and 40% of the country's gross domestic product (GDP).[3]

As discussed in the previous chapter, these figures vary sharply according to world demand for petroleum. An estimate by the Saudi American Bank indicates that oil exports accounted for $28.2 billion of total government budget revenues of $39.1 billion in 1995 (72%), $36.3 billion of total government budget revenues of $47.8 billion in 1996 (76%), $42.7 billion of total government budget revenues of $54.8 billion in 1997 (78%), $21.3 billion of total government budget revenues of $38.1 billion in 1998 (56%), $27.6 billion of total government budget revenues of $39.2 billion in 1999 (70%), $57.2 billion of total government budget revenues of $68.8 billion in 2000 (83%), and $49.3 billion of total government budget revenues of $ 61.3 billion in 2001 (80%).[4]

While gross annual Saudi petroleum export revenues varied from lows of $34.2 billion to highs of $75.3 billion during 1991–2001, Saudi Arabia has consistently earned more oil export revenues than any other single member of OPEC.[5] The Saudi share of total OPEC revenues ranged from below 20% in 1972, to over 40% in the early 1980s and around 30% in 2001.[6]

As has also been touched on in the two previous chapters, there are significant differences in the estimates of Saudi oil revenues. The EIA, for example, estimated that Saudi net petroleum exports were worth $68.7 billion in 2000 and $58.2 billion in 2001, and that they would reach $49.6 billion in 2002.[7] Saudi Aramco, however, reports that EIA estimates of petroleum export earnings do not include total income from the entire petroleum sector—including downstream operations, related manufacturing, and domestic earnings—which Aramco put at $70 to $80 billion in 2000.[8]

Cambridge Energy Research Associates uses Saudi data to produce estimates that put total Saudi petroleum revenues, in current dollars, at $44.7 billion in 1990, $47.1 billion in 1995, $654.5 billion in 1997, $44.6 billion in 1999, and $75.3 billion in 2000.[9] SAMA puts the total crude oil and natural gas earnings portion of the Saudi GDP at $53.6 billion in 1997, $35.2 billion in 1998, $46.2 billion in 1999, and $71.8 billion in 2000. If petroleum-refining earnings are added to these totals, Saudi Arabia earned $58.9 billion in 1997, $39.2 billion in 1998, $51.0 billion in 1999, and $77.6 billion in 2000.[10]

These differing estimates illustrate the dangers of trying to make precise estimates of Saudi dependence on petroleum earnings, even if one ignores the notorious volatility of the world oil market. The central fact remains, however, that the previous chapters have shown that even the most successful economic reforms will take well over a decade to make a major reduction in the Kingdom's current level of dependence on crude oil exports, and many forms of diversification and Saudisation will depend on adding value to the petroleum sector by exporting more petroleum-related products.

Saudi Arabia's energy strategy is clearly as critical to its future as its strategy for dealing with population growth and economic reform.

THE CRITICAL GLOBAL IMPORTANCE OF SAUDI OIL RESERVES

The future of Saudi Arabia's petroleum sector will be as important to the world as it is to Saudi Arabia. The Kingdom shapes its energy strategy from a unique position. Its massive oil reserves make up over 25% of the entire world's proven reserves. Estimates of the size and importance of Saudi oil reserves do differ slightly according to source. The U.S. government estimates that Saudi Arabia proper (excluding the Saudi-Kuwaiti "Neutral Zone") contained at least 262 billion barrels of proven oil reserves as of 2002. It estimates that Saudi reserves totaled 264.2 billion barrels when oil from the Saudi half of the Neutral Zone—about 5 billion barrels of proven oil reserves.[11] A comparable Saudi estimate was 261.7 billion barrels.[12]

Virtually all sources agree, however, that estimates of Saudi proven reserves have increased every year since 1962, and that Saudi Arabia has massive additional reserves that are not yet "proven." SAMA estimates the reserves were 56.9 billion barrels in 1962, 96.2 billion in 1973, 113.5 billion barrels in 1980, and 257.8 billion barrels in 1990.[13] Saudi Aramco estimates that Saudi Arabia's recoverable crude oil and condensate reserves rose to 259.1 in 1997, 259.2 in 1998, 259.2 1999, and 259.3 in 2000.[14]

The U.S. Department of Energy estimates that Saudi Arabia has a little over one-quarter of the world's total proven petroleum reserves (25.4%). This compares with 11% for Iraq, 9.6% for the UAE, 9.2% for Kuwait, 8.6% for Iran, 13% for the rest of OPEC, and 22.6% for the rest of the world.[15] BP estimates that Saudi Arabia has 25.0% of the world's total proven reserves, which compares with 10.8% for Iraq, 9.3% for the UAE, 9.2% for Kuwait, 8.7% for Iran, and 37.0% for the rest of the world.[16] Saudi Aramco estimates that Saudi Arabia's 261.7 billion barrels worth of reserves compare to 112.5 billion for Iraq, 97.8 for the UAE, 96.5 for Kuwait, 89.7 for Iran, 76.9 for Venezuela, 48.6 for Russia and 29.7 for the United States.[17]

These are hard numbers to visualize; Chart 7.1 shows how the scale of Saudi reserves compared to those of other nations and regions. Not only does Saudi Arabia have over eighty years of reserves at current average annual production rates (approaching 9 million barrels a day), but its reserves are nearly ten times those of the United States and more than four times those of all of North America. They are well over five times the reserves of Russia, and sixteen times the roughly 17 billion barrels of proven reserves in all of the Caspian Sea and Central Asia. They are larger than all of the roughly 230 billion barrels of proven oil reserves in Latin America, Africa, Asia and the Pacific, and Western and Eastern Europe combined.[18]

Chart 7.1
The Role of Saudi Reserves in Total World Reserves (in Billions of Barrels)

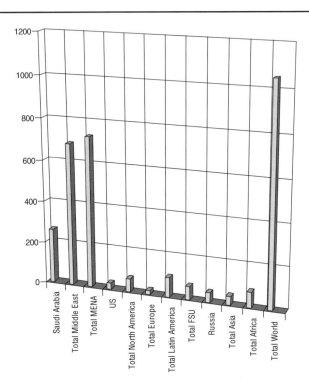

	Saudi Arabia	Total Middle East	Total MENA	US	Total North America	Total Europe	Total Latin America	Total FSU	Russia	Total Asia	Total Africa	Total World
☐ Billions of Barrels	261.8	685.6	727	30.4	63.9	18.7	96	64.4	48.6	43.8	76.7	1050
■ % of World	*24.9	*65.3	*68.9	*2.9	*6.1%	*1.8	*9.1	*6.2	*4.6	*4.2%	*7.3	*100
☐ R/P Ratio	*85.0	*86.8	-	*10.7	*13.5	*7.8	*38.8	*21.1	*19.1	*15.6	*27.4	*40.3

Source: BP Amoco, *Statistical Review of World Energy, 2002*, June 2002, URL: *www.bpamoco.com/alive*.

As Tables 7.1 and 7.2 show, however, many analysts—such as those of the U.S. Geological Service—believe that even these figures sharply underestimate the Kingdom's strategic importance. Saudi Arabia almost certainly has at least another 42 billion barrels of oil, and both the U.S. Department of Energy and unofficial Saudi estimates put the Kingdom's total ultimately recoverable holdings as high as 1 trillion barrels. This total could be even higher with the introduction of more advanced EOR techniques.[19]

Impressive as the figures in Chart 7.1 are, they also gravely understate the importance of Saudi Arabia's strategic position in terms of providing security for world oil reserves. The total Gulf area has some 677 billion barrels—65% of the world total of 1,046 billion barrels. Saudi Arabia's stability and strategic ties to the West underpin the security of roughly two-thirds of all of the world's proven oil reserves. Any effort to contain Iran and Iraq, with roughly 20% of all the world's oil reserves, depends heavily on Western access and military ties to Saudi Arabia. The same is true of any effort to provide security for the other GCC states—Bahrain, Kuwait, Oman, Qatar, and the UAE—with another 20% of the world's oil reserves.

To put Saudi reserves in further perspective, the world has spent more than a quarter of a century since the Arab oil embargo of 1974 trying to find alternative sources of oil and energy. In the process, it has conducted an intense search throughout the world. The net result, however, has been to expose the fact that many areas projected to have major reserves did not. At the same time, new discoveries in Saudi Arabia have steadily increased both estimates of proven Saudi reserves and the Saudi share of the world's total reserves.

The net result is that Saudi Arabia enters the 21st century as an even more important source of petroleum. It also enters the century as a nation with a vast surplus of capacity relative to present and projected domestic demand, and at a time when many nations have begun to seriously deplete their reserves or face steady increases in the cost of extraction. Moreover, despite more than a quarter of a century of efforts to find alternate sources of energy, the U.S. Department of Energy projects that world consumption of oil will rise by an average of 2.3% per year from 2000 to 2020, versus 3.2% for gas, 1.5% for coal, 0.3% for nuclear, and 2.0% for hydropower, solar, geothermal and all other forms of alternative energy combined.[20]

SAUDI OIL PRODUCTION

Saudi Arabia has already produced over 70 billion barrels of oil, and still has a reserve-to-production ratio of 81:1.[21] (The history of Saudi oil production is shown in Chart 7.2.) While Saudi production levels have varied sharply over time, the country has been a critical exporter for at least three decades. Saudi production averaged 8.8 MMBD in 2000, a year of high oil demand. This total included 700,000 barrels per day (bpd) of natural gas liquids and 320,000 bpd from the Neutral Zone.[22]

The History of Saudi Oil Development and the Role of Aramco

A single company—Saudi Aramco—produces all of the crude oil in Saudi Arabia proper. Aramco's origins date back to May 29, 1933, when Saudi Arabia signed an oil exploration concession agreement with the Standard

Table 7.1
Comparative Oil Reserves and Production Levels of the Gulf States—Part One: Comparative Reserves

Country	Identified	Undiscovered	Identified + Undiscovered	Proven	% of World Total
Bahrain	—	—	—	0.2	(−0.05%)
Iran	69.2	19.0	88.2	89.7	8.6%
Iraq	90.8	35.0	125.8	112.5	10.8%
Kuwait	92.6	3.0	95.6	96.5	9.2%
Oman	—	—	—	5.5	0.5%
Qatar	3.9	0	3.9	13.2	1.3%
Saudi Arabia	265.5	51.0	316.5	261.7	25.0%
UAE	61.1	4.2	65.3	97.8	9.3%
Total	583.0	112.2	695.2	677.1	64.7%
Algeria	—	—	—	9.2	0.9%
Egypt	—	—	—	2.9	0.3%
Libya	—	—	—	29.5	2.9%

Syria	2.5	0.2%
Tunisia	0.3	(−0.05%)
Yemen	4.0	0.4%
Total Middle East and North Africa	725.5	69.4%
Rest of World	320.9	31.4%
(US)	29.76	2.8%
(North America)	64.4	6.1%
(Russia)	48.6	4.6%
(FSU)	65.3	6.4%
World	1,046.4	100.0%

Note: Comparative oil reserves in billions of barrels.

Sources: Adapted by Anthony H. Cordesman from estimates in U.S. Geological survey, *World Petroleum Assessment 2000*, URL: *usgs.gov/ energy/WorldEnergy/DDS-60*; and BPAmoco, *Statistical Review of World Energy, 2001*, June 2001, URL: *www.bpamoco.com/alive*.

Table 7.2
Comparative Oil Reserves and Production Levels of the Gulf States—Part Two: Comparative Production and Production Capacity

Country	DOE Reference Case Estimate of Maximum Sustainable Production Capacity							Actual Production		
	1990	1995	2000	2005	2010	2015	2020	1990	1995	2000
Bahrain	—	—	—	—	—	—	—	—	—	—
Iran	3.2	3.9	3.9	4.0	4.4	4.5	4.7	3.2	3.7	3.8
Iraq	2.2	0.6	2.8	3.1	3.9	4.5	5.5	2.2	0.6	2.6
Kuwait	1.7	2.6	2.6	2.8	3.5	4.1	4.8	1.7	2.1	2.5
Oman	—	—	—	—	—	—	—	—	0.9	0.9
Qatar	0.5	0.6	0.6	0.5	0.6	0.7	0.7	0.5	0.5	0.7
Saudi Arabia	8.6	10.6	11.4	12.5	14.6	18.2	22.1	8.6	8.9	9.4
UAE	2.5	2.6	2.7	3.0	3.7	4.4	5.1	2.5	2.5	2.5
Total Gulf	18.7	20.9	24.0	25.9	30.7	36.4	42.9	18.7	19.6	21.7
Other Middle East	1.4	1.6	1.9	2.2	2.4	2.5	2.4	1.4	1.1	2.0
Algeria	1.3	1.4	1.4	1.9	2.2	2.3	2.5	1.3	1.3	1.4
Libya	1.5	1.5	1.5	2.1	2.5	2.8	3.2	1.5	1.4	1.5
Total North Africa	2.8	2.9	2.9	4.0	4.7	5.1	5.7	2.8	2.7	2.9
Total Middle East and North Africa	22.9	25.4	28.8	32.1	37.8	44.0	51.0	22.9	23.4	26.6
World	69.4	73.0	78.7	88.0	98.4	109.8	121.3	69.4	68.0	77.4
(Saudi Arabia as % of World)	12.4%	14.5%	14.5%	14.2%	14.8%	16.5%	18.2%	12.4%	13.0%	12.1%

Note: Comparative oil production capacity (in millions of barrels per day).
Source: Adapted by Anthony H. Cordesman from estimates in DOE/EIA, International Energy Outlook, 2002 (Washington: DOE/EIA, 2002), p. 235.

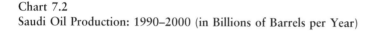

Chart 7.2
Saudi Oil Production: 1990–2000 (in Billions of Barrels per Year)

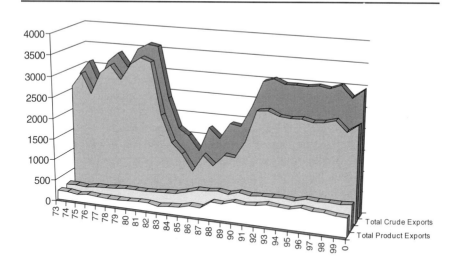

Sources: Adapted by Anthony H. Cordesman from SAMA, *Thirty-Sixth Annual Report,*
1421H (2000G) (Riyadh: SAMA, 2001), pp. 401–404; and *Thirty-Seventh Annual Report,*
1422H (2001G) (Riyadh: SAMA, 2002), pp. 411–416.

Oil Company of California (later Chevron). In 1936, the Texas Company
(later Texaco) joined the enterprise, providing needed capital for expansion
of operations in Saudi Arabia. In 1948, Standard Oil Company (later
Exxon) and Soconoy Vacuum Oil Company (later Mobil) also acquired
shares in Aramco.

The first actual discovery of commercial quantities of oil in Saudi Arabia
took place on March 3, 1938, when Dammam Well Number 7 was deep-
ened to reach what became called the "Arab Zone." In 1939, King Abd
al-Aziz opened a valve to release the nation's first tanker-load of crude oil
from the port of Ras Tanura, which became the site of the Kingdom's first
oil refinery a few years later. A decade after the discovery of oil in Saudi
Arabia, Ghawar and Safaniya—the world's largest onshore and offshore
fields—were discovered. A 1,750-kilometer pipeline linking the oil fields
of the Eastern Province with the Mediterranean Sea opened in 1950. The
development of Ghawar, Safaniya, and other oil fields during the 1960s and
1970s made Aramco the world's largest producer and exporter of crude oil
and liquefied petroleum gas. During the 1970s, the Kingdom developed a
Master Gas system to supply much of its domestic energy needs, and in
1983 it inaugurated the Exploration and Petroleum Engineering Center, one
of the world's most advanced earth science facilities.

From 1973 onward, Saudi Arabia took a series of steps (called the "participation") to purchase back Aramco's assets, eventually reaching full ownership in 1980. In 1988, King Fahd signed a royal decree officially establishing the Saudi Arabian Oil Company, or Saudi Aramco, to replace Aramco and assume its responsibilities. Long before that, however, Aramco had become a largely Saudi company. The employment, training, and professional development of Saudi nationals had been a guiding principle since the earliest days of the venture, and Saudi executives, professionals, and operations personnel were found throughout the company.

Since 1988, Saudi Aramco's responsibilities have grown to include new areas of exploration in the Kingdom, an international marine shipping subsidiary, and the establishment of a series of downstream joint ventures to provide outlets for the Kingdom's crude oil production. Saudi Aramco's responsibilities then grew tremendously. Exploration efforts have been extended to new areas of the Kingdom, and the company expanded into international operations with the creation of a marine shipping subsidiary and the establishment of a series of downstream joint ventures to provide outlets for its enormous crude oil production:

- In 1988, Saudi Aramco entered its first downstream joint venture relationship, creating Star Enterprise in partnership with Texaco. In 1991, Saudi Aramco bought a 35% share of the Sang Yong Oil Refining Company (later S-Oil), South Korea's third largest petroleum refiner.

- In 1993, Saudi Aramco was given responsibility for all of the Kingdom's refining and distribution operations and assumed the Kingdom's interest in several domestic joint ventures from the Saudi Arabian Marketing and Refining Company (Samarec) and the General Petroleum and Minerals Organization (Petromin), consolidating virtually all of the Kingdom's oil-related activities.

- In 1994, Saudi Aramco acquired a 40% stake in Petron, the largest refiner and leading petroleum products marketer in the Philippines.

- In 1995, a program to build fifteen advanced supertankers for Vela International Marine Limited (a company subsidiary) was completed. Rabigh Refinery was integrated into company operations.

- In 1996, Saudi Aramco entered its fourth joint venture, purchasing 50% of Motor Oil (Hellas) Corinth Refineries S.A. and Avinoil Industrial Maritime Oil Company S.A. in Greece.

- In 1998, Saudi Aramco established Motiva Enterprises LLC, a downstream joint venture with Texaco and Shell in the United States, replacing Star Enterprise by adding Shell's assets.

- In 2001, Saudi Aramco and Shell agreed to purchase Texaco's share of Motiva's assets as part of Chevron's purchase of Texaco. Pending completion of the purchase, Saudi Aramco and Shell would each own 50% of Motiva. The acquisition of a further interest in Motiva was intended to strengthen Saudi Aramco's presence in the North American refining and marketing sector and solidify Saudi Aramco's leading position as a supplier of crude oil to North America. Saudi Aramco supplied in excess of 1.5 million barrels of crude oil per day to customers in North America in 2001, including approximately 525,000 bpd of Arabian crude purchased by Motiva for processing in the Motiva refineries.

Saudi Oil Production Today

Today, Saudi Aramco produces more than 95% of all crude oil and natural gas liquids (NGL), and has played a major role in the world oil market. Saudi Aramco is a vertically integrated company with tanker and refinery operations. It has both cut its production levels to maintain its assigned OPEC quota level and raised production to prevent possible price and supply crises or reduce their impact.

The Saudi government's ability to use Aramco as a "swing producer" gives Saudi Arabia still further strategic importance. Saudi production of different types of crude gives Saudi Arabia special flexibility. Unlike Kuwait—which can produce only one type of crude—or the UAE and Iraq—which can produce two each—Saudi Arabia can produce five types ranging from heavy to light.[23] During 1999–2001, for example, Saudi Arabia gave repeated assurances that it would increase production to meet any shortfall from Iraq at a time when Iraq was attempting to use cutting off its oil exports as a threat that could help it break out of UN sanctions.[24]

Since the late 1990s, oil production in Saudi Arabia has taken place in eighteen oil fields in Saudi Arabia proper, and in five oil fields in the Neutral Zone. (See Map 7.1.) Over half of Saudi Arabia's current proven reserves are contained in eight fields, and 90% of all Saudi production comes from the four largest—Ghawar, Safaniyah, Abqaiq, and Berri. The Ghawar field alone has some 70 to 85 billion barrels and is the world's largest onshore oil field. The Safaniyah field has 19 billion barrels and is the world's largest offshore field. The Abqaiq field has 17 billion barrels and Berri has 11 billion barrels. There are a number of other major fields, including Manifa (11 billion barrels), Zuluf (8 billion barrels), Shaybah (with at least 7 billion), Abu Safah (6 billion), and Khursaniyah (3.5 billion).[25]

The Neutral Zone contains 5 billion barrels of proven oil reserves. Japan's Arabian Oil Co. (AOC) used to operate two offshore fields (Khafji and Hout) in the Neutral Zone, producing around 300,000 bpd; 80% of revenue went to AOC while 10% each went to Saudi Arabia and Kuwait. Japan would not, however, meet Saudi demands to invest over $1 billion in railways, minerals, and other aspects of the Saudi economy as the price of renewing its concessions. As a result, the AOC lost the concession in February 2000. The AOC also announced in April 2000 that it had reached an agreement with Aramco's Gulf Operations Company to split output from the Kafji field until January 4, 2003, when AOC's concession on the Kuwaiti

Map 7.1
Saudi Oil Facilities

Source: The CIA.

side of the Neutral Zone expires. Saudi Arabian Texaco continues to produce at the onshore (formerly Getty) field in the Partitioned Zone with Kuwait, and operates three onshore fields in the Neutral Zone (Wafra, South Fawaris, and South Umm Gudair). AOC reportedly will be asked to develop the offshore Dorra gas field now that Saudi Arabia and Kuwait have agreed on a border demarcation.[26]

Saudi Arabia produces a range of crude oil grades from heavy to super light. About 65% to 70% of Saudi Arabia's total oil production capacity is considered light gravity, with the rest either medium or heavy. The lightest grades are produced onshore, while the medium and heavy grades come mainly from offshore. The Ghawar field is the primary producer of 34 API Arab Light crude, while Abqaiq produces 37 API Arab Extra Light crude. Since 1994, the Hawtah Trend, which includes the Hawtah field and smaller satellites, has been producing 45 to 50 API Arab Super Light. Offshore production includes Arab Medium crude from the Zuluf and Marjan fields and Arab Heavy crude from the Safaniya field.[27] The price for Saudi oil varies by grade. For example, the spot price of Berri oil (39 API) varied from a low of $12.61 in 1998 to a high of $27.46 in 2000. The spot price of Arabian light oil (37 API) varied from a low of $12.20 to a high of $21.81. The price of Arabian medium oil (31 API) varied from a low of $11.58 to a high of $25.95, and the price of Arabian heavy (27 API) has recently varied from a low of $10.95 in 1998 to a high of $25.20 in 2000.[28]

As Chart 7.2 shows, Saudi oil production levels have fluctuated sharply over the years, depending largely on the political conditions in the Gulf and the changing world oil market. Saudi production was 7.6 million barrels a day (MMBD) in 1973, when the oil boom began. It rose to a peak of 9.9 MMBD in 1980, driven partly by the fall of the Shah of Iran and the start of the Iran-Iraq War. Production then dropped back to a low of only 3.4 MMBD in 1985, largely because OPEC oil prices reached the point where demand was cut sharply or because new sources outside of OPEC began to enter the market. Saudi Arabia's decision in 1986 to focus on market share rather than high prices raised production back to 4.9 MMBD in 1986. Levels rose slowly, reaching 5.3 MMBD in 1990 before the Iraqi invasion of Kuwait.[29]

The outbreak of the Gulf War in August 1990 drove Iraqi and Kuwaiti oil out of the market, and Saudi production rose to a peak of 8.5 MMBD by December 1990 to compensate for the shortage. Saudi oil production stayed at levels over 8.1 MMBD through the early and mid-1990s, ranging from annual averages of 8.1 to 8.3 MMBD. Saudi Arabia produced an average of 6.41 MMBD in 1990, 8.1 MMBD in 1991, 8.3 MMBD in 1992, 8.2 MMBD in 1993, 8.1 MMBD in 1994, 8.2 MMBD in 1995, 8.2 MMBD in 1996, 8.4 MMBD in 1997, 8.4 MMBD in 1998, 7.8 MMBD in 1999, and 8.6 MMBD in 2000.[30] These production figures compare with a total production capacity of 10.4 to 10.6 MMBD.[31]

These figures, however, only include crude oil production in Saudi Arabia proper. For example, Saudi oil production totaled about 9.3 MMBDbpd in 1997, including 800,000 bpd of NGL and about 270,000 bpd of crude oil produced from its half-share of the Saudi-Kuwaiti Neutral Zone. This compared with what the Department of Energy estimated was a sustainable crude oil production capacity of about 11.3 MMBD and an OPEC crude oil production quota of 8 MMBD (8.76 MMBD as of January 1, 1998). In 2000, Saudi oil production totaled about 9.1 MMBD, of which about 8.4 MMBD was crude oil and 0.7 MMBD was NGL. Saudi Arabia produced around 9.2 MMBD of oil in the first quarter of 2001 (including half of the Saudi-Kuwaiti Neutral Zone's 600,000 bpd), compared to production capacity of around 11.6 MMBD.[32]

Saudi Arabia also constantly adjusts its production of crude types in response to fluctuations in demand. Saudi Arabia has very sophisticated models for predicting the most profitable mix of crude oil exports by type, based on short- and long-term estimates of market demand and the cost-benefits of any given production mix. Such models are necessarily uncertain, but Aramco indicates that they have steadily increased profitability over the years.

Oil Production and Quotas

As discussed in Chapters 4 and 5, Saudi oil production reacts to political and military events and OPEC energy strategy as well as market conditions. At the same time, Saudi production is so important to the world market that it can have a major impact on events like the Gulf War, the oil crash of 1997–1998, the oil boom of 1999–2000, and the world's ability to sustain sanctions on Iraq. The increase in Saudi production helped trigger the market glut and the oil crash; Saudi Arabia concluded in mid-1997 that it faced a hardening world oil market and that it could raise production without suffering a major loss of revenues. It succeeded in persuading OPEC to raise its crude oil production quotas by about 10% at its November 1997 meeting, which raised the Saudi quota from 8 MMBD to 8.76 MMBD. As of early February 1998, Saudi Arabia was reportedly producing close to this amount. A mild winter and a major recession in Asia, however, sharply reduced demand, and the resulting combination of increased supply and reduced demand created the oil crash.[33]

This forced Saudi Arabia to progressively decrease its oil production in an effort to reduce the world oil glut and stabilize prices. Saudi Arabia had an OPEC quota of 8.76 MMBD until the Riyadh Pact of March 1998 led OPEC to make production cuts of 1.860 MMBD, effective in April. This pact was negotiated primarily between Saudi Arabia, Mexico, and Venezuela, and the Saudi quota included the 240,000 bpd it received from the Divided or Neutral Zone. It did not count 700,000 bpd in NGL, which are not counted by any member of OPEC. Saudi Arabia did, however, try to maintain its oil income, insofar as possible, by increasing production of Extra Light and Arab Super Light at the expense of Arab Heavy and Arab Medium crude oil. It shut down some capacity to do so, and used field rotations to minimize reservoir pressure damage and preserve the option of bringing increased production back online within a few months, if needed.[34] During this period, Saudi Arabia supplied about 16% of U.S. crude imports, competing largely with Venezuela and Mexico. [35]

In June 1998, a steady deepening of the Asian recession forced OPEC members to once again cut their quotas, effective July 1998. As a result, oil production in Saudi Arabia fell from 8.62 MMBD to around 8 MMBD. However, these cuts were not enough to improve oil prices as the effects of the Asian financial crisis wore on. In December 1999, oil prices reached a one year low of $9.90 bpd for Brent Crude, leading to the massive drop in oil export revenues discussed earlier. Saudi gross exports fell from $54.7 billion in 1997 to $34.2 billion in 1998.[36] As a result, Saudi Arabia and most other oil producing states faced severe budget crises.[37]

What Saudi Arabia expected to be a mild oil boom had turned into an oil crash, and the slowing global economy further cut into demand for Saudi and other OPEC oil exports. In March 1999, the major members of OPEC met in Amsterdam and agreed to further cut production by 1.411 MMBD, effective on April 1. All OPEC members, with the exception of Iraq, agreed to the cuts, and all OPEC states except Iran cut production by 7.3% from the July 1998 quotas. The agreement of March 1999 brought Saudi Arabia's production substantially below the "floor" of 8 MMBD, which it had tried to defend for the past several years, reducing it to 7.438 MMBD.[38] As of September 1999, MEES estimated that Saudi Arabia was producing 7.5 MMBD.[39] The total OPEC cuts during 1998–1999 amounted to 4.0 MMBD and the non-OPEC cuts to 870,000 bpd. All of the OPEC countries participated except Iraq.

Ironically, the new OPEC agreement of March 1999 occurred at a time when the West's economy was beginning to boom, the Asian economy had recovered, stock levels were exceptionally low, and weather factors increased demand. It had an immediate impact on prices, which rapidly rose to $16 to $18 a barrel by the end of March 1999.[40] Against many expectations, OPEC discipline continued to hold in the following months, with the IEA estimating 96% compliance with cuts for September.

Accordingly, the price of Saudi Arabian Light shot over $23 per barrel by late September, dipping only slightly to $20 to $22 in October.[41] The price movements following each series of cuts varied sharply. The lowest price in 1999 was $10.20 per barrel in February, and the highest price was $25.80 in December. Brent crude rates then rose above $30 per barrel, prices not seen since the 1990 Gulf War. In just eighteen months prices rose from under $10 to over $25 a barrel. Gross Saudi oil export revenues in current dollars rose from $34.2 billion in 1997—the lowest level in the 1990s—to $43.9 billion in 1999.[42]

This rise in oil prices and revenues proved a key factor in the Kingdom's decision to support increases in production at the OPEC meeting in March 2000. OPEC agreed to a Saudi proposal to reverse that latest production cut of 1.4 MMBD made in 1999. As a result, production increased by 1.4 MMBD in April. While Iran objected to the adjustment in production, it took its share of the increase.

In June 2000, OPEC agreed to increase production by 703,000 bpd. Despite the fact that Iraq increased production by 420,000 bpd, prices continued to rise as a result of the high degree to which OPEC members had implemented the previously agreed upon production cuts, and additionally because of the related production restraints imposed by the production decisions of non-OPEC states, such as Mexico, Norway, and Oman. The continued climb in prices led to increasing pressure on OPEC from the United States and other importers to increase production and lower prices. As a result, OPEC, in a June 2000 meeting in Vienna, agreed to increase its production to an official figure of 708,000 bpd. However, the announcement failed to have an effect on prices, which stayed above $30.[43]

The failure of OPEC's production hike to affect high oil prices led Saudi Arabia to announce plans in July 2000 to unilaterally increase production by 500,000 bpd independent of OPEC. Saudi Arabia made this declaration partly for strategic reasons, and partly because it felt that maintaining very high prices would drive consumers toward other sources of energy or non-OPEC exports. In response to the Saudi decision to increase production, the price of Brent crude fell sharply to the high twenties. At the same time, OPEC agreed to pump half a million more barrels if prices for the "OPEC basket" of crude oil failed to fall below $28. This helped lead OPEC members to agree to a further official production increase of 800,000 bpd in September, which allotted Saudi Arabia an additional 162,000 bpd in production and brought the Saudi total quota to 8.253 MMBD.[44]

This still did not cut prices to the point desired by Saudi Arabia, and the Kingdom pushed OPEC to make further cuts to support the informal price band mechanism that OPEC adopted during its March 2000 meetings (and later formally ratified on January 17, 2001). In this system, OPEC basket prices higher than $28 per barrel or lower than $22 per barrel would trigger automatic production adjustments. Prices sustained above the price band's target range for twenty trading days would result in an automatic production increase of 500,000 bpd, while prices below the target range for ten trading days would result in cuts of 500,000 bpd. This led OPEC to increase production by a further 500,000 bpd in November 2000 in an effort to maintain its desired price band and to keep prices from rising too quickly. This was the only time OPEC activated the informal price band mechanism during the rest of 2000, even though the average OPEC basket price stayed above the $28 level for eighty-one consecutive trading days between August 14 and December 4, 2000.

The net effect was that OPEC increased production by a total of 3.4 MMBD in 2000—largely in response to Saudi initiatives—in a bid to re-balance the market and keep it well supplied. During this process, Saudi Arabia increased its production quota to 8.023 MMBD in April, 8.253 MMBD in September, and 8.674 MMBD by the end of the year. Saudi Arabia actually produced an estimated 8.4 MMBD (29% of total OPEC oil production) in December 2001 and was a net exporter of around 7.1 MMBD, versus December 2000 when it produced 9.1 MMBD and exported 7.8 MMBD. Even so, gross Saudi oil export revenues in current dollars rose from $43.9 billion in 1999 to $75.3 billion in 2000—the highest level in a decade.[45]

This situation reversed itself yet again in 2001. Declines in U.S. and world economic output, high Iraqi and non-OPEC oil production, the crash of the U.S. technology sector in early 2001, and the economic impacts of the terrorist attacks on the World Trade Center and the Pentagon on September 11, 2001, led to a major decline in oil demand. As a result, an EIA chronology of OPEC actions during 2001 shows that it had to make three major production quota cuts—totaling 3.5 MMBD—over the course of the year:[46]

- *January 17, 2001:* OPEC agrees to cut production quotas by 1.5 MMBD, effective February 1, 2001. The Saudi quota is cut from 8.674 MMBD in November 2000 to 8.169 MMBD.

- *March 16, 2001:* OPEC agrees to cut production quotas by 1 MMBD, effective April 1, 2001. The Saudi quota is cut to 7.865 MMBD.

- *June 1, 2001:* The ninth phase of the oil-for-food program concludes; the United Nations approves a thirty-day rollover of the program.

- *June 4, 2001:* Iraq halts oil-for-food exports.

- *June 5, 2001:* OPEC holds its 115th meeting to review the state of world oil markets, leaving quotas unchanged.

- *July 3, 2001:* OPEC holds its 116th meeting to discuss the impact of Iraqi oil export cuts, and again leaves quotas unchanged. Also, the one-month rollover of the oil-for-food program ends, and the UN approves another five months of the program with UN Security Council Resolution 1360.

- *July 10, 2001:* Iraq resumes oil-for-food exports.

- *July 25, 2001:* OPEC agrees to cut production quotas by 1 MMBD, effective September 1, 2001. The Saudi quota iscut to 7.541 MMBD.

- *September 11, 2001:* Al-Qaeda terrorists attack the World Trade Center and the Pentagon.

- *September 26, 2001:* OPEC holds its 117th meeting to review world oil markets, leaving production quotas unchanged.

- *October 29, 2001:* OPEC meets with non-OPEC countries in Vienna in an expert's meeting to assess the state of world oil markets.

- *November 14, 2001:* OPEC holds its 118th meeting and decides to cut production quotas by 1.5 million bpd, effective January 1, 2002, contingent on non-OPEC agreement to cut production by 500,000 bpd.

- *November 29, 2001:* The eleventh phase of Iraq's oil-for-food program ss approved for six months (180 days) beginning December 1, according to UN Security Council Resolution 1382.

- *December 28, 2001:* OPEC holds its 119th meeting to review oil markets, confirming a 1.5 MMBD production quota cut, effective January 1, 2002. The Saudi quota is cut to 7.053 MMBD, and Saudi surplus production capacity rises to 3.427 MMBD.[47]

- *March 15, 2002:* OPEC holds its 120th meeting to review oil markets, and, citing a desire to maintain a targeted price of $25 a barrel, leaves production levels unchanged.

- *May 30, 2002:* The eleventh phase of Iraq's oil-for-food ends and is renewed for a twelfth phase. Iraq temporarily halts production to protest Israel's conflict with the Palestinians.

- *June 26, 2002:* OPEC holds its 121st meeting to review oil markets.

Once it made the November 2001 cuts, OPEC indicated to other oil suppliers that a price collapse could result if they did not participate in another round of supply cuts. After much negotiation, OPEC announced on December 28, 2001, that pledges of supply reductions from Angola, Mexico, Norway, Oman, and the Russian Federation totaling 462,500 bpd were not enough to satisfy its needs.

As a result, OPEC announced that it would cut an additional 1.5 MMBD from its production quota beginning January 1, 2002, with announced OPEC/non-OPEC cuts totaling almost 2 MMBD. These cuts forced Saudi Arabian Oil Minister Ali al-Naimi to declare in January 2002 that the OPEC price band had been suspended, as stability in the market was more important than the OPEC price target. OPEC had previously cut the Saudi quota to 7.623 MMBD in the first quarter of 2001 and to 7.3 MMBD by the fourth quarter of 2001, which left it with a quota of 7.053 MMBD on January 2, 2002.[48] The CERA estimate of gross Saudi oil export revenues in current dollars to dropped from $75.3 billion in 2000 to $63.1 billion in 2001, and as a consequence of the additional production cuts, revenues from oil production were projected to be only $44.9 billion in 2002.[49] Similarly, the EIA estimate of net oil export revenues dropped to $58.2 billion for 2001, with an estimate of $49.6 billion for 2002.[50]

By April of 2002, OPEC had cut its quotas by a total of 5 MMBD since January 2001, or nearly 20%. OPEC had a spare production capacity of some 7 MMBD, and Saudi Arabia was operating under a production quota of 7.053 MMBD out of a total OPEC production quota of 21.7 MMBD

(Iraq was excluded). This gave Saudi Arabia 2.784 to 3.284 MMBD of surplus production capacity.[51] These trends seemed likely to cut oil prices below the levels Saudi Arabia had projected in calculating the revenues for its 2002 budget.

Tensions over the possibility of war with Iraq, however, led to a firming of prices in the summer and fall of 2002 despite a steady decline in global economic growth and major cuts in world stock markets. The fact that Iraqi production remained below 1.8 MMBD despite its estimated production capability of 3.05 MMBD was also a factor. As a result, OPEC kept its quotas unchanged at its September 19, 2002, meeting. Instead of trying to enforce its price band, OPEC left markets uncertain as to when the OPEC 10 (OPEC less Iraq) quotas would be realigned to more accurately reflect current production levels and when it would address the issue of rising oil prices. OPEC was able to do so even though the OPEC 10 produced at levels above quota in September 2000 that increased to an estimated 2.2 MMBD.

The fact that rising OPEC and Saudi production was accompanied by rising oil prices and declining commercial oil inventories (particularly in the United States), despite a steady drop in world stock prices and economic activity, also provided a further indication that neither global macroeconomic trends nor OPEC quota levels serve as a good guide as to future prices and OPEC 10 production, and that oil responds as much to security considerations as market demand.[52]

In more narrow terms, this combination of political and economic conditions led to an increase in Saudi oil export earnings that allowed Saudi Arabia to increase its estimate of government income from SR 157 billion to SR 220 billion and to reduce its estimated budget deficit for 2002 from $12.0 billion to $5.06 billion—a reduction from 7.3% of GDP to 2.8%. This reduction would have been even sharper if Saudi Arabia had not again increased spending with oil revenues and raised its estimated budget for 2002 from SR 202 billion to SR 239 billion.[53]

Even if one ignores the impact of major world crises on the global economy, the world oil market, and Saudi Arabia, this history of sudden post–Gulf War "reversals of fortune" illustrates both the overall importance of Saudi oil production strategy and the impact that actual Saudi production can have on world markets. It also is exceedingly unlikely to change in the near future. In the fall of 2002, the prospect of war between the United States and Britain and Iraq left the world oil market for 2003 as uncertain as ever.

The EIA's October 2002 forecast for 2003 indicated that the limiting factors for OPEC 10 production growth in 2003 would be the situation in Iraq and whether world demand for oil would recover as expected. Without a war, the U.S. economy was projected to grow by over 3% annually in 2003 and lead a recovery in the global economy, with China and other non-OECD countries projected to provide another 0.5 MMBD of demand growth next year.[54]

At the same time, the EIA noted that other uncertainties also affected such estimates. The EIA forecast that rising non-OPEC production would meet much of this new demand. About half of the anticipated 1 MMBD increase in non-OPEC supply in 2003 was expected to come from additional oil exports from Russia and the Caspian Sea region. Increases are also expected from offshore Africa, Mexico, and increased Canadian synthetic oil production.[55]

EIA noted that the OPEC 10 production cuts over the past two years, coupled with rising Russian production, had narrowed the gap greatly between the world's two largest oil producers: Saudi Arabia and Russia. Had the OPEC 10 produced at quota levels in 2002, Russia would have passed Saudi Arabia as the world's largest producer of crude oil by February 2002. Russia's Energy Ministry reported that its crude oil production reached 7.84 MMBD in September, and could exceed the Saudi crude oil production numbers reported by OPEC in 2002, although Russia's estimated total crude oil and other liquids production of 8.05 MMBD in September would still trail Saudi Arabia's actual production, which was well above 8.05 MMBD despite its 7.8 MMBD quota.[56]

In practice, however, such trends have limited practical meaning. Russia has well under 20% of Saudi reserves and far higher current and projected domestic demand. The extent to which Russia actually passes Saudi Arabia in short-term oil production cannot be a major factor in shaping the future of world energy supply or Saudi Arabia's mid- and long-term oil revenues. It does, however, show the limits OPEC as a whole faces in the short- and mid-term. Russia, a country with smaller oil reserves than many OPEC countries, has been able to take a share of the world oil market as large or larger than any OPEC country. When OPEC cut quotas by 5 MMBD in 2001 to keep oil prices high, non-OPEC producing countries benefited from the higher prices, increasing their market share at OPEC's expense. [57]

Saudi Arabia is also a unique oil producer in other ways. It has enough oil reserves and low enough marginal production costs that it can size its production capacity at levels substantially higher than its planned production. The fact that Saudi Arabian production capacity is normally much larger than actual Saudi production gives added importance to Saudi oil. Saudi Arabia has long adopted a strategy of trying to maintain a surplus production capacity of 2 MMBD and is one of the few countries that can make sudden major increases in oil production to provide additional supplies in an emergency. This is a role that increases in importance in periods when other OPEC and non-OPEC producers produce at levels closer to their total production capacity. Unlike Russia, Saudi Arabia's reserves are so large that the Kingdom can sustain such a margin of surplus production indefinitely into the future.

This surplus production capacity has long allowed the Kingdom to play a major role as a "swing state" that can increase production to deal with a sudden shortfall or interruption in global oil production and exports. Saudi Arabia had enough surplus production capacity to largely compensate for the fall in oil production in Iran during the fall of the Shah, cuts in Iranian and Iraqi production during the Iran-Iraq War, and cuts in Iraqi and Kuwaiti production during the Gulf War. It has sought to preserve a surplus capacity of around 2.08 MMBD in recent years. In October 2000, all of OPEC had a nominal surplus capacity of 2.48 MMBD; 1.68 MMBD of that capacity (67%) was in Saudi Arabia.[58] In October 2002, the OPEC 10 had a nominal surplus capacity of 4.6 to 5.1 MMBD, and 2.2 to 2.7 MMBD of that capacity was in Saudi Arabia. (OPEC's total surplus capacity was 5.9 to 6.4 MMBD including Iraq.)[59]

Saudi Oil Exports

Chart 7.2 shows that the level of Saudi crude oil exports has varied in much the same way as production, although the production and export of refined product has been more constant because industrial facilities must be operated to a given level of output and because refined product has a more stable market. Saudi Aramco reports that Saudi Arabia exported 2,263,876,508 barrels of crude oil in 2000, and that 10.7% went to Europe, 40.7% to the Far East, 10.3% to the Mediterranean area, 23.3% to the United States, and 15.0% went to other destinations.[60]

Saudi Arabia has consistently been a key oil supplier for the United States, Europe, Japan, and Asia. However, the destination of the Saudi exports shown in Chart 7.2 has varied according to market conditions. Saudi Arabia sells oil as a global commodity at market prices on a relatively free world market, and the destination of its oil is determined largely by current transportation costs and other marginal price differences affecting a given consuming region. The only major exception to this has been the oil that Saudi Arabia supplies to the United Kingdom under a defense procurement agreement under which it obtains advanced aircraft and infrastructure development for the Saudi Air Force.[61] This oil reached a peak of 600,000 bpd, but declined to about half that amount in the late 1990s. It is marketed by Saudi Aramco at market prices and the proceeds enter into an escrow account for the UK-Saudi defense procurement program. Saudi Arabia did, however, provide around 150,000 bpd in oil to Pakistan and Afghanistan in 2000 as foreign aid in lieu of cash (although this oil does not appear to be officially counted in Saudi export figures).[62]

The portion of Saudi oil going to the United States has fluctuated sharply from lows of 132,000 bpd in 1986 (before Saudi Arabia decided to emphasize market share over price) to a high of 1.7 MMBD in 1990—the key year in the Gulf War. It averaged in excess of 1.2 MMBD since 1990, and averaged around 1.4 MMBD in the late 1990s.[63] Saudi Arabia exported 1.57 MMBD of oil (1.52 MMBD of crude) to the United States during 2000. During this time, Saudi Arabia ranked second (after Canada, and just ahead of Venezuela) as a source of total U.S. oil imports (crude plus refined products), and first for crude only (ahead of Canada and Mexico). It provided an average of 17% of all U.S. crude oil imports. [64] The United States was Saudi Arabia's second largest national oil export market, followed by Japan; Asia has long been its largest regional market.[65]

Direct oil exports to the United States and other industrialized nations are, however, only part of the story. The United States *indirectly* imports large additional amounts of Saudi oil from many other countries in the form of manufactured imports and services provided by countries that also import Saudi oil. To put this in perspective, Asia received over half of Saudi Arabia's crude oil exports in 2000, as well as the majority of its refined petroleum product exports.[66] The fact that the United States is critically dependent on world trade, and particularly on energy-intensive Asian manufactured goods, makes the amount of Saudi oil flowing to other nations of major strategic interest to the United States. So does the fact that the United States depends heavily on the overall health of the global economy, which would have been crippled by a major shortfall in Saudi exports, regardless of which nations received the remainder.

The future importance of Saudi oil to the world's global economy is also illustrated by the fact the EIA estimates that about twice as much Saudi oil went to industrialized states in 1995 as went to nonindustrialized states. This ratio will probably virtually reverse itself by 2020, which will actually increase the importance of Saudi oil in terms of "globalization" since today's industrialized states are becoming steadily more dependent on nonindustrialized states for manufactured imports.[67] This growing global economic interdependence again illustrates the importance of the world's overall dependence on Saudi exports.

The portion of Saudi oil that goes to given countries under normal market conditions is of limited strategic importance, however, in indicating what would happen in a war or crisis, or if some other form of interruption or embargo took place. There are some long-term supply contracts, some countries like the United States have large strategic reserves, and the OECD nations are obligated to share a portion of the supply that remains on the world market. However, oil importers must generally compete for the remaining share of world production by paying higher prices and outbidding each other. This quickly changes the share of oil coming to each importer from a given exporter in a crisis, as the total pool of oil exports is treated as a commodity on a global basis.

Past crises have shown that the flow of Saudi oil changes radically in the case of an emergency or oil interruption, that Saudi production shifts accordingly to play a critical role in compensating for any interruption in exports from other countries, and that the flow of Saudi oil suddenly shifts to the countries most needing imports. This has made Saudi oil exports even more critical in energy interruptions and crises, as Saudi production capacity can deter oil interruptions as well as compensate for them. In the spring of 2002, for example, the Kingdom's declaration that it would not join in any oil embargo was a key factor in forcing Iraq to halt its embargo and in persuading Iran that an embargo would not be practical.

In short, the key issue in a crisis or oil interruption is how much Saudi oil flows globally and at what price, rather than which nation is the destination of its exports at any given time. Saudi Arabia produced 12.3% of all the world's oil in 2000, and this percentage is virtually certain to increase over time.[68] The EIA notes that Saudi Arabia provided around 20% of total world oil exports in 1995, and projects it will provide well over 30% by 2020.

Expanding Saudi Oil Production

Saudi Arabia's economy, as well as much of the security of world energy supplies, depends on the rate at which Saudi Arabia increases its oil production and oil production capacity. There is no doubt that the Kingdom can make major increases. Much of Saudi Arabia's oil potential is still unexplored, and drilling rates had been limited through much of the 1990s.[69] Saudi Arabia discovered seven new oil fields in 1990 alone, with potential reserves of between 500 million and 3 billion barrels.[70]

Saudi Arabia carried out major development activity during 1991–1995. It raised the production of fourteen different fields during this period and raised its sustained production capacity from 8.7 MMBD to 10.87 MMBD, with most of the increase occurring in the Ghawar field. Recent explorations have revealed new ultra-light crude oil reserves in the country's central area and additional fields on the northern and southern Red Sea coasts. Another major super-light crude field was found about fifteen miles from Houta (100 miles south of Riyadh) in April 1995.[71]

Important increases in Saudi offshore capacity have occurred in the Zuluf and Marjan fields. Their outputs were boosted to 1.2 MMBD and 600,000 bpd, respectively. Work at Zuluf entailed the completion of two 250,000 bpd gas/oil separation plants (GOSP). Construction of a 270,000 bpd GOSP at the offshore Safaniya field also boosted production in 1994. These fields are the primary producers of Saudi Arabia's Arab Heavy and Arab Medium, which have gravities of around 27 and 31 API, respectively. By mid-1994, total offshore Saudi oil output was estimated at 3.8 MMBD.

Saudi Arabia is continuing to invest in the development of lighter crude reserves. It has given priority to developing its Shaybah field, which is located in the Empty Quarter in an area bordering the United Arab Emirates. The Shaybah field, which has been called Saudi Arabia's "crown jewel," is located 400 miles from Abqaiq. Shaybah came online in 1998, with a capacity of 500,000 bpd. The field contains an estimated 7 to 15.4 billion barrels of 40 to 42 API sweet crude oil, plus twenty-five TCF of gas.

The full development of the Shaybah project cost $2 to $2.5 billion, and included three GOSPs and a 395-mile pipeline to connect the field to Abqaiq, Saudi Arabia's closest gathering center, for blending with Arabian Extra Light crude (Berri and Abqaiq streams).[72] Two U.S. companies played a major role in the Shaybah project: Parsons Corporation (project management) and Bechtel (construction).

The EIA estimates that Saudi Arabia has cut production of Arab Light from overworked parts of the Ghawar reservoir because its water content is rising, as well as cut offshore production of Arab Heavy crude to accommodate light crude production increases at Shaybah of 500,000 bpd.[73] Another project, the $200 million Haradh-2 GOSP for the Ghawar field, appears to be back on track as part of Saudi Arabia's effort to increase production of Arab Light oil by 600,000 bpd.[74] Other projects include a $200 million upgrade of several offshore Arab Heavy and Medium fields. In addition, a new 250,000 GOSP unit for the Ghawar field's Haradh zone is planned, as well as a 75,000 bpd GOSP at the smaller, onshore Nuayyim field.

The EIA reports that Saudi Arabia has plans to increase its oil production capacity, especially of relatively light crudes, to 12.5 MMBD in coming years. One possible project, at the Qatif field, could boost Arab Light and Arab Medium production capacity by 500,000 bpd at a cost of $1.2 to $1.5 billion. Qatif contains extra light and medium quality, 33 to 34 API gravity oil. Another potential project, at the Khurais field, could increase Saudi production capacity by 800,000 bpd by 2005 at a cost of $3 billion. This would involve installation of four GOSPs, with a capacity of 200,000 bpd each, at Khurais, which first came online in the 1960s but was mothballed by Aramco (along with several other fields—Abu Hadriya, Abu Jifan, Harmaliyah, and Khursaniyah) in the 1990s.[75]

For 2001, Saudi Aramco's budget calls for drilling 246 wells (208 onshore, 38 offshore) at a cost of $1 billion, a 25% increase from 2000 and nearly double the 1999 drilling budget of $580 million. For 2002, Aramco plans to drill 292 wells at a cost of $1.2 billion. Many of these wells will be drilled in Ghawar.[76]

As discussed earlier, Japan's AOC operated the Neutral Zone offshore fields (Khafji and Hout), with production capacity of about 350,000 barrels per day, until March 2000, when its rights expired under its concessions with Saudi Arabia. The Saudi half interests in the field were transferred to the control of Saudi Aramco. Aramco's new subsidiary, Aramco Gulf

Operations Company, assumed drilling rights to the Neutral Zone's offshore oil and gas fields.[77] Texaco operates the onshore fields in the Neutral Zone (Wafra, South Fawaris, and South Umm Gudair) with current crude oil production of more than 300,000 bpd. Texaco planned to increase output from its fields and drill three exploration wells in the Neutral Zone in 1998. AOC's concession on the Saudi side expired in 2000, and its concession on the Kuwaiti side of the Neutral Zone will expire in 2003. Texaco's onshore concession lasts until 2010.

The Case For and Against Foreign Investment in Crude Oil Production

These expansion plans raise several issues about privatization and foreign investment. They involve massive government outlays, which the budget analysis in previous chapters indicates may sometimes be substantially higher than the direct costs reported by the government, and which tend to understate related infrastructure costs and life cycle investment costs. They involve the use of significant amounts of foreign labor but they create relatively few jobs per dollar. This has led some to argue that such "upstream" investments should be opened up to foreign oil companies and private investment. In fact, there were indications during the worst days of Saudi Arabia's cash flow problems during the oil crash that the Kingdom was going to seek such foreign investment.

There are a number of reasons for Saudi opposition to any foreign control and ownership of the Kingdom's crude oil production. Two that are often discussed in the Western press are a strong current of nationalism and the memory of colonial and foreign exploitation of oil concessions in other countries. Another is bureaucratic resistance both from within Aramco and among Saudi technocrats in the Ministry of Petroleum and Minerals. At the same time, there are pragmatic arguments as well. No public analysis has yet made it clear that the Kingdom would get enough foreign or Saudi private capital at desirable rates to justify opening up its crude oil sector, nor has it shown that such investment would not come at the cost of investment in other areas the Kingdom needs to finance. It is also not clear that foreign and/or Saudi private ventures would be any more efficient than Aramco.

EXPORT FACILITIES AND DISTRIBUTION

Regardless of what future level of production capacity Saudi Arabia decides upon and can actually finance, it will have to make a matching investment in expanding its export terminals and pipelines. Saudi Arabia has the following major terminals, all of which hold significant strategic importance and pose a key potential target in any future war:[78]

- Ras Tanura has a capacity of 8 MMBD, facilities to load crude oil and Liquid Petroleum Gas (LPG), two piers, and eighteen berths. It can handle ultra-large crude carriers (ULCCs) up to 550,000 dead weight tons (dwt) and has a 35 million metric ton tank farm.

- Ras al Juaymah has a capacity of 4 MMBD, facilities to load crude oil and LPG, six single-buoy moorings, and two berths. It can also separately handle the largest crude carriers (ULCCs and VLCCs) and has a 33 million metric ton tank farm.

- Yanbu has a capacity of 4.2 MMBD, facilities to load crude oil and LPG, one three-berth pier, and a two-berth LPG platform. It can load ULCC and smaller tankers as well as LPG tankers.

- Jubail has four berths and can load petroleum product and petrochemical carriers.

- Ras al-Khafji has four berths located three-to-seven miles off the Neutral Zone and can load 100,000 and 300,000 dwt tankers.

- Rabigh has nine berths and can receive and supply tankers of up to 321,000 dwt with crude oil or product.

Saudi Arabia also has a massive network of domestic pipelines and five pipelines to ports or other countries. It should be noted that these pipelines also represent key areas of potential vulnerability.[79]

- The 4.8 MMBD East-West Crude Oil Pipeline (Petroline) was expanded to its present capacity in 1993. It is used predominantly to transport Arab Light and Super Light to refineries in the Western Province and to Red Sea terminals for direct export to European markets. According to Saudi Oil Minister Naimi, Saudi Arabia has "surplus oil export and pipelines capacity . . . [including the] East-West oil pipeline system [which] can carry and deliver 5 million b/d" but is being run at "only half capacity."[80]

- The 270,000 bpd Abqaiq-Yanbu NGL pipeline runs parallel to the Petroline. It is used to carry NGLs to Yanbu for petrochemical feedstock and to export LPG products to Yanbu.

- The 500,000 bpd Trans-Arabian Pipeline (Tapline) was constructed in 1950 to transport crude oil for export from Lebanon. However, since the 1970s, it has been mothballed and has served only to supply a 60,000 bpd Jordanian refinery. Shipment to Jordan was cut off after the Gulf War and the pipeline remains unused.

- The 1.65 MMBD Iraqi-Saudi Pipelines (IPSA-1 and IPSA-2) were closed indefinitely after the start of the Gulf War. The 500,000 bpd IPSA-1 pipeline transmitted oil from Khor al-Zubair in Southern Iraq to a Petroline pipeline in Saudi Arabia. The 1.65 bpd Iraqi-Saudi Pipeline (IPSA-2) is capable of moving oil from a Petroline pump station in Saudi Arabia to Yanbu.

- The Arabian-Bahrain pipeline connects Abqaiq to Bahrain and has a capacity of roughly 200,000 bpd.

The sheer volume of shipping in and out of Saudi ports also creates maritime vulnerabilities. During 1996–2000, tankers made an average total of 4,200 ship calls to Saudi ports. These involved 1,600 to 1,900 ships carrying product, 1,800 to 2,000 carrying crude, and 380 to 470 carrying refrigerated LPG. These ships carried 2.25 to 2.63 MMBD worth of crude oil and 0.4 to 0.47 MMBD worth of product. Since virtually all Saudi oil and product must move by ship, these numbers increase steadily in proportion to every increase in Saudi exports.[81]

Saudi Arabia is increasing its export capabilities and protecting against market fluctuations and short-term damage to its facilities by acquiring new tankers, increasing its overseas crude oil storage capacities, and buying downstream operations in Europe, Asia, and the United States.[82] In early 1994, Japan's Mitsubishi agreed to provide Saudi Arabia with five new double-hull, 300,000 dwt VLCCs. Saudi Arabia received and additional fifteen VLCCs and ULCCs—built in Japanese, South Korean, and Danish shipyards—at the end of 1997. In 2002, the Saudi fleet included twenty-three crude tankers and four product vessels.[83]

Saudi Arabia maintains a strategic oil reserve and product reserve for its security, and is boosting the size of its overseas storage facilities. In mid-1994, storage capacity was increased dramatically through a 34% acquisition of equity in Texaco's 17-million-barrel Maatschap terminal. This acquisition in Rotterdam represented a move from Saudi Arabia's previous strategy of only leasing storage facilities. In December 1993, Saudi Arabia signed a long-term lease for a 5-million-barrel facility on St. Eustatius in the Caribbean. Saudi Arabia's owned and leased storage facilities now have a capacity of over 30 million barrels.

The Kingdom has also quietly set up strategic reserves of petroleum product near its major cities to cover major accidents, sabotage, and attacks. It seems to have created significant additional strategic crude oil reserves inside Saudi Arabia although Aramco officially denies these exist. Aramco has done some limited stockpiling of spare parts and replacement assemblies to cover damage to its fields and facilities, and has steadily strengthened the security forces and systems covering its fields—although again details are not available.

REFINING

Saudi Arabia realizes that it can utilize its natural advantages in cheap energy and feedstocks to expand its oil and gas industry more easily than other aspects of its economy. It is seeking to expand its real export income by creating massive downstream refining and petrochemical capabilities. Chart 7.3 shows the steady growth in total product output and product exports. Saudi Arabia also invests in overseas downstream joint ventures

Chart 7.3
Saudi Product and Refinery Production: 1973–2000 (in Billions of Barrels per Year)

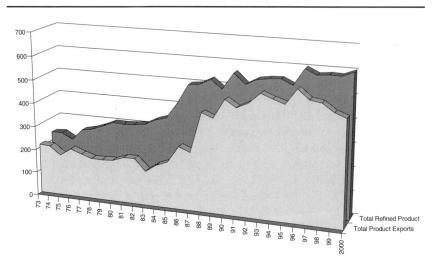

Sources: Adapted by Anthony H. Cordesman from SAMA, *Thirty-Sixth Annual Report, 1421H (2000G)* (Riyadh: SAMA, 2001), pp. 401–404; *Thirty-Seventh Annual Report, 1422H (2001G)* (Riyadh: SAMA, 2002), pp. 413–414.

in order to "lock in" its crude export streams, buying refineries that can economically use its oil as refinery feedstocks. These investments are designed to allow the Kingdom to stabilize its export patterns and participate in the foreign production of downstream products.

Chart 7.4 shows the trends in the value of total Saudi production of refined product, plastics, and chemical products—which are all derived from petroleum—and in the value of total product exports. It is important to note that while unsophisticated product exports tend to vary in value with oil prices, and exhibit the same instability in total value, prices of more sophisticated petrochemical products, refinery output, and plastics fluctuate somewhat less and produce more predictable streams of revenue. In 2000, Saudi domestic and joint venture refineries sold a total of 486.7 million barrels worth of product: 8.5 million barrels worth of LPG, 42.8 million barrels worth of naphtha, 75.9 million worth of gasoline, 44.3 million worth of jet fuel and kerosene, 167.6 million worth of diesel oil, 139.4 million worth of fuel oil, and 8.1 million worth of asphalt and other products.[84]

As is the case with the mix of crude oils it exports, Saudi Arabia has very sophisticated models for predicting the best mix of refined product based on short- and long-term estimates of market demand and the cost-benefits of any given production mix. Such models are necessarily uncer-

Chart 7.4
Value of Saudi Product and Refinery Production: 1970–2000 (in Billions of Riyals)

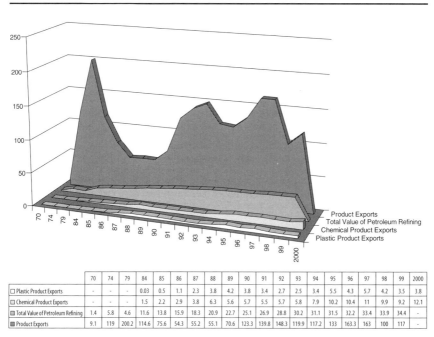

	70	74	79	84	85	86	87	88	89	90	91	92	93	94	95	96	97	98	99	2000
☐ Plastic Product Exports	-	-	-	0.03	0.5	1.1	2.3	3.8	4.2	3.8	3.4	2.7	2.5	3.4	5.5	4.3	5.7	4.2	3.5	3.8
☐ Chemical Product Exports	-	-	-	1.5	2.2	2.9	3.8	6.3	5.6	5.7	5.5	5.7	5.8	7.9	10.2	10.4	11	9.9	9.2	12.1
▨ Total Value of Petroleum Refining	1.4	5.8	4.6	11.6	13.8	15.9	18.3	20.9	22.7	25.1	26.9	28.8	30.2	31.1	31.5	32.2	33.4	33.9	34.4	-
▨ Product Exports	9.1	119	200.2	114.6	75.6	54.3	55.2	55.1	70.6	123.3	139.8	148.3	119.9	117.2	133	163.3	163	100	117	-

Sources: Adapted by Anthony H. Cordesman from SAMA, *Thirty-Sixth Annual Report, 1421H (2000G)* (Riyadh: SAMA, 2001), pp. 344–345; *Thirty-Seventh Annual Report, 1422H (2001G)* (Riyadh: SAMA, 2002), p. 372; Ministry of Planning, *Achievements of the Development Plans, 1390–1420 (1970–2000)* (Riyadh: Ministry of Planning, 2001), Table 29.

tain, but the Kingdom steadily refines them and they have steadily increased profitability over the years.

Refining in Saudi Arabia

The Kingdom has seven Aramco and joint-venture refineries, with a combined crude throughput capacity of around 1.795 MMBD. Two of the seven are joint-venture, export-oriented refineries, with a total capacity of 0.67 MMBD, while the other five are primarily aimed at meeting local needs and have a total capacity of 1.125 MMBD. In addition, Saudi Aramco owns an interest in refining capacity overseas, as well as extensive distribution and marketing operations. Saudi Aramco has around 1.6 MMBD of refining capacity overseas.[85]

Saudi Arabia had two large refineries at Yanbu in 2000, with throughputs of 315,200 and 190,000 bpd. Riyadh had a throughput of 140,000 bpd, and refineries at Jeddah and Ras al-Khafji had throughputs of 87,000 and 30,000 bpd respectively. Saudi Aramco reports that Saudi Arabia exported 175,609,350 barrels of refined products in 2000, and that 3.1% went to Europe, 61.0% to the Far East, 5.8% to the Mediterranean area, 1.5% to the United States, and 28.6% to other destinations.[86]

The Saudi Aramco domestic refineries sold a total of 371.0 million barrels worth of product in 2000: 7.3 million barrels worth of LPG, 30.6 million barrels worth of naphtha, 51.4 million worth of gasoline, 21.7 million worth of jet fuel and kerosene, 137.1 million worth of diesel oil, 114.8 million worth of fuel oil, and 8.1 million worth of asphalt and other products.[87] Saudi domestic joint venture refineries sold more than 20% of total Saudi refinery sales, and sold a total of 115.7 million barrels worth of product in 2000, including: 1.2 million barrels worth of LPG, 12.2 million barrels worth of Naptha, 24.6 million worth of gasoline, 22.6 million worth of jet fuel and kerosene, 30.5 million worth of diesel oil, and 24.6 million worth of fuel oil.[88]

Saudi Arabia continues to invest heavily in downstream operations. In June 1993, Samarec was merged with Saudi Aramco to vertically integrate the country's entire oil industry. This move placed all refineries—except for the 30,000 bpd Mina al-Khafji refinery in the Neutral Zone—under Saudi Aramco's control.[89] Prior to this merger, Samarec had planned to spend $4 billion over a ten-year period to upgrade all of the country's refineries. After the merger, these plans were put on hold, except for the Ras Tanura refinery.[90] This was necessary to meet the increasing domestic demand for gasoline and middle distillates. The work began in late 1994, and was completed in 1999.[91]

When oil prices increased in 1999, Saudi Arabia revived plans for investment in refinery upgrades and expansions. According to the EIA, it developed proposals for downstream oil projects and gas development totaling around $100 billion. The projects included a $1.2 billion upgrade of the 300,000-bpd Ras Tanura refinery. Ras Tanura is Saudi Arabia's oldest refinery and once had a capacity of 530,000 bpd, although a fire in 1990 destroyed one of its distillation towers and reduced this capacity. A 200,000 bpd fractionation unit at Ras Tanura was awarded to Italy's Snamprogetti in 2000.

Saudi plans also call for boosting the capacity at Rabigh refinery on the Red Sea coast, now Saudi Arabia's largest domestic refinery, to production levels as high as 400,000 bpd. These plans were first developed in the mid-1990s, and called for upgrading the refinery's product slate away from low-value heavy products toward gasoline and kerosene at an estimated cost of $1.8 billion. Funding for these plans was scaled back by 60% to $800 million during the oil crash of 1997, but was revived in 2000.[92]

Japan's Chiyoda is carrying out a $284 million expansion of the Saudi Aramco-Mobil refinery (Samref) at Yanbu. Various reports put the yield at this refinery at 360,000 bpd. Yanbu is a primary supplier of gasoline, lubricants, and kerosene for the Western Province, and the government is hoping to expand the Yanbu Industrial City through developing gas supplies that will feed integrated petrochemical projects. Saudi Arabia is studying the expansion of the 305,000 bpd Saudi-Shell refinery (Sasref) at Jubail through de-bottlenecking and hydrocracker modification. The $140 million project will involve the installation of a new thermal gas-oil unit/gas turbine and allow it to generate 30 megawatts of its power requirement of 85 megawatts, rather than the current 5 megawatts.[93] Saudi Arabia plans to modernize the refinery at Riyadh, although without changing its 200,000 bpd capacity.

These Saudi projects should increase the revenue streams from petroleum production, but such investments can present problems. The Kingdom seems to have been relatively efficient in constructing refineries, but the full investment and life-cycle costs of these facilities are not transparent and Saudi ROI and profit margins are unclear. There are some indications that net profitability is not as high as it should be. Investment costs are high, and must now be funded largely through Aramco. It is not clear that the Kingdom would gain in terms of profitability from privatizing refinery operations or opening them up to foreign investment, but it must take on a significant capital burden at a time when Chapters 4 and 5 have shown it faces major capital burdens in other areas.

Like most investments in the petroleum sector, they also have only limited impact on employment. Construction may employ large amounts of foreign labor, but operations require little manpower and involve very little job creation per dollar of investment. As a result, major petroleum projects do little to solve Saudi Arabia's employment problems.

Refining Overseas

Saudi Arabia has taken measures to secure its outlets for refined products in the United States, Europe, and Asia (currently totaling 1.2 MMBD). In 1988, it acquired a 50% stake in Star Enterprise, a joint venture with Texaco. Star Enterprise controlled distribution networks in half of the United States, and had contracts to purchase up to 600,000 bpd of Saudi crude oil for processing at three former Texaco refineries. In July 1997, Aramco went further and announced a merger of Star Enterprise's downstream operations in the eastern and Gulf coast regions of the United States with those of Shell. The new company is 32.5% owned by Aramco, with 35% ownership by Shell and 32.5% by Texaco. It operates four refineries with a capacity of 820,000 bpd, along with 15,000 Texaco- and Shell-branded service stations in twenty-six states.[94]

In 1991, Saudi Arabia bought a 35% share in South Korea's two 300,000 bpd Sangyong refineries.[95] In February 1994, Saudi Arabia made a similar move to buy a 40% equity in a Philippines refinery, and in 1995, Saudi Aramco agreed to acquire a 50% share in Motor Oil Hellas (MOH), a domestic Greek refining company with 700 retail stations and a 100,000 bpd refinery, for $400 million. Saudi Arabia also negotiated for, but did not proceed with a deal for a 30% to 35% stake in Portugal's state oil firm, Petrogal, which had two refineries (totaling a 304,000 bpd capacity) and controlled a major share of Portugal's refined product market. A feasibility study in India for a 120,000 bpd joint venture refinery in the Punjab (with Hindustan Petroleum Corporation) also did not bear fruit.

Saudi Arabia has signed a memorandum of understanding (MOU) with South Africa. Additionally, it continues to look to East Asia for expansion of its downstream oil investments. Saudi Aramco and Petron (in which Aramco has a 40% stake) are planning a 250,000 bpd refinery and are considering a 165,000 bpd grassroots refinery in Limay, Bataan. At the same time, Saudi Arabia is also negotiating new refining joint ventures in China, where it has signed a feasibility study agreement with Exxon and Sihopee for a $3 billion expansion of its existing refinery and added internal petrochemical production.

What is not clear is what the Kingdom's profit margins are on these deals, or whether they really guarantee it any market share it would not win without them. They create few Saudi jobs and they do not expand the Saudi private sector or assist in the government's attempts to invest in diversification. As a result, there are real questions as to whether foreign refineries are of help to the Kingdom or are simply examples of technocratic empire building.

PETROCHEMICALS

As discussed in Chapters 5 and 6, petrochemicals are another way that Saudi Arabia can diversify its petroleum-based economy and have a higher potential profit margin. While a number of Gulf countries are involved in petrochemical operations, Saudi Arabia has created a massive industry. By 1987, Saudi Arabia had a total of ten major projects under consideration or in final design. These had a total capacity of over 3 million tons per year and a cost of well over $5 billion.[96]

In November 1993, a 700,000-ton-per-year plant began operation in Jubail. In July 1994, a 700,000-ton-per-year complex at Ibn Sina started operations. By the end of 1996, the Kingdom had invested $29.5 billion (SR 110.5 billion) in such industries. As a result, Saudi petrochemical companies were producing more than 20 million tons of products a year, and exported to more than seventy-five countries. The Sixth Development Plan called for the further expansion of the petrochemical industry, and for growth at an annual average rate of 8.3% a year during 1996–2000. The plan also called for total capacity to increase from 23 million tons in 1997 to 28 million tons in 2000.[97] Saudi Arabia did not quite meet this goal. Nevertheless, in 2001, the Kingdom was the leading producer of petrochemicals in the Middle East, with 20 million tons of petrochemical and polymer production and 4.5 million tons of fertilizer production. That same year, Aramco reported that it had reached annual sales totaling $7 billion.

Saudi Basic Industries Corporation (SABIC)

Saudi Basic Industries Corporation (SABIC) has become the largest exporter of Saudi Arabian petrochemicals and the third largest petrochemical producer in the world. The Department of Energy reports that SABIC is the largest nonoil industrial company in the Middle East, and is expected to become one of the world's top five ethylene producers by 2005. It already accounts for around 10% of world petrochemical production.[98]

SABIC's profits reached $1 billion a year for the first time in 1994 and approached $2 billion in 1995. SABIC increased production by 35% in 1994, and plans to increase its production of methyl tertiary butyl ether (MTBE) from its current levels of 2 million tons per year to 2.7 million tons per year by the end of 1996.[99] Its profits have since been further enhanced by the December 1995 privatization of SABIC's Arabian Industrial Fibre Company.[100]

SABIC continued to expand despite the oil crash that began in late 1997, and accounted for 5% of world petrochemical production by the end of that year. In the process, SABIC became so important that reduced tariff barriers for SABIC's exports were a major force behind Saudi Arabia's pursuit of membership in the World Trade Organization. SABIC also became involved in joint ventures.

The oil crash of late 1997 cut Saudi petrochemical revenues as well as oil export revenues. In 1998, petrochemical prices dropped below 1997 prices by 20% to 35%, cutting SABIC's profits by 56% in 1998.[101] First-quarter profits for SABIC fell by 73% in 1999. Although Middle East ethane-based petrochemical firms have a potential advantage over their naphtha-based European competitors, low oil prices cut costs dramatically for European producers. As a result, product prices for Middle Eastern companies did not to recover until 2000, although profits edged up during the latter half of 1999 due to the boosting of oil prices by OPEC cutbacks.[102]

The oil boom that began in 1999 led Saudi Arabia to formulate new plans for expanding petrochemical production using natural gas as a feedstock. In February 2001, SABIC completed a $1 billion expansion at the Yanbu petrochemical facility, making it the largest polyethylene plant in the world. In early January 2002, SABIC agreed to a $1.15 billion loan to fund a new petrochemicals plant in the eastern industrial city of Jubail. The complex is scheduled to come online in 2004 and to produce 1 million tons per year of ethylene, plus olefins, polyethylene, and glycol ethylene. It is uncertain at the present time whether or not the Saudi government will sell off more of its 70% stake in SABIC in the near future.[103]

As discussed in the previous chapter, SABIC's success has made it a natural target for privatization and foreign investment, and the government has set a goal of reducing its share of the corporation to 25%.[104] The government has sold 30% of SABIC's shares to the public since 1987, and SABIC is now a private company whose shares are traded on the Saudi stock exchange. As such, it is run on commercial grounds, and the price of its feedstock (methane and ethane) is the same to all users and industries. It has renegotiated the price of LPG with Aramco to end a 30% reduction from the export price, in order to make it easier for the Kingdom to accede to the WTO. The government is considering selling off more of its stake in SABIC in the future, and SABIC has been soliciting foreign investors in private petrochemical projects, such as an $800 million plant proposed for Jubail.

Petrochemicals, Privatization, and Foreign Investment

There has long been foreign private sector investment in other petrochemical firms. Mobil Corporation signed a contract in May 1996 to invest $1 billion in a joint venture with the Saudi government to create a major new petrochemical complex in Yanbu (Yanpet). The operation is 70% Saudi owned and a complex capable of producing more than 1.6 million metric tons of ethylene per year and 2 million metric tons of petroleum derivatives per year. Unlike some other Saudi petrochemical projects, it is expected to be fully competitive by world standards and to become one of the most efficient plants in the world. About 70% of the facility is to be debt-financed.[105]

In February 1997, Saudi Petrochemical Company (Sadaf), a joint venture between SABIC and Shell Oil Company of the United States, launched a $1 billion expansion program that includes a new 700,000 metric ton/year plant for MTBE. The plant's opening boosts SABIC's total MTBE production capacity to 2.7 million metric tons/year.[106] Expansion plans include a new 700,000-metric-ton/year plant for MTBE. Sadaf also is looking at setting up Saudi Arabia's first independent power plant (IPP) at its petrochemical complex in Jubail.[107]

In January 1998, Saudi Alujain Company, the Italian Ikofiol Company, and the Finnish Nesti Oy Company signed a partnership to set up a factory for the production of MTBE in Yanbu, which will be the largest MTBE project of its kind in the world. In February 1998, South Korea's Daelim Engineering Co. agreed to build a chemical plant in Al-Jubayl for $170 million. The plant began producing 500,000 tons of ethyl-benzene and styrene monomer in March 2000. In January 1998, Japan's Chiyoda Corp. won a $500 million order from Saudi Arabia's Eastern Petrochemical Corp. to build an ethylene glycol plant in Saudi Arabia's Jubail Industrial area. The plant is to produce 500,000 tons per year, mainly for export to Southeast Asia.

Saudi investment has also proceeded despite the reductions in some other areas of investment during the oil crash. A Cyclar process aromatics complex, owned by SABIC affiliate Ibn Rushd, came online at Yanbu in 1999. The complex will consume nearly 1 million tons of propane per year, but will be able to run on butane as well. A joint venture between SABIC and Mobil's Yanbu Petrochemicals subsidiary located near Ibn Rushd at Yanpet is in the process of installing additional ethylene capacity. This expansion project is known as Yanpet-2, and involves the construction of an ethylene cracker that can run on a mix of ethane, propane, and light naphtha; it will utilize 820,000 tons of propane per year. The project cost was about $2.8 billion and enhanced polyethylene and ethylene glycol production capacity. The Crown Prince inaugurated Yanpet-2 in October 1999.[108]

Two projects in the eastern area of Jubail are operational. Kemya, a joint venture between SABIC and Exxon, is constructing Petrokemya III, a flexible feedstock cracker that will run on a mix of both propane and ethane and will initially require between 1 and 2 million tons of propane per year. A second ethylene cracker under construction by Kemya is scheduled to come online in mid-2001, and will consume 1.6 million tons per year of propane. Aramco has also committed to supply a propane dehydrogenation unit planned at Jubail by a private sector company known as the National Industrialization Company. The new unit, which is designed to produce some 450,000 tons per year of propylene, should require nearly 600,000 tons per year of propane.[109]

Still more plants are expected to come online as a result of joint ventures with Chevron and European companies. In June 2000, Chevron and Philips Petroleum announced a joint venture to run a $650 million petrochemicals complex in Jubail, replacing the joint venture of Saudi Chevron Petroleum that ran the complex.

Al-Khobar-based National Pipe Company (NPC) is building a new mill to meet growing demand for heavier duty pipelines in the gas industry in Saudi Arabia and the rest of the GCC. The company will invest over $80 million in the project, which will double its capacity, and awarded the equipment supply and construction contracts in early 2000. NPC says the new mill will produce straight seam submerged arc weld (SAW) pipe. It will have a capacity of 180,000 tons a year, which is the same as the company's existing mill. The company says that development of non-associated gas fields is creating a growing demand for the heavier grade of pipe.[110]

In spite of this progress, it is important to note that Saudi investments in refineries and petrochemicals do present most of the same economic risks, as oil exports have limited value in terms of diversification. The Saudi petrochemical industry as a whole experienced grave problems during the oil crisis. The Asian economic crisis and the resulting loss of demand, as well as increased competition from Asian producers, hit hard at external suppliers. During that time, Asia accounted for 20% of world demand, giving developments there a major influence over the fortunes of the industry.

NATURAL GAS

Saudi Arabia estimates that the Kingdom's natural gas reserves stood at 222.5 trillion cubic feet (TCF) at the start of 2001—an increase of 20% since the mid-1990s—due to the discovery of nonassociated gas in Aramco areas of operation. Much of this increase in Saudi gas reserves has been recent. Aramco estimates that Saudi Arabia's recoverable gas reserves rose from 197.4 TCF in 1996, to 204.0 in 1997, 210.8 in 1998, 213.3 in 1999, and 219.0 in 2000.[111] This compares with 1,700 TCF for Russia, 812.3 for Iran, 393.9 for Qatar, 212.1 for the UAE, 167.4 for the US, 159.7 for Algeria, and 109.8 for Iraq.[112]

The EIA estimates Saudi Arabia's proven gas reserves at 219.5 TCF, ranking them fourth largest in the world—after Russia, Iran, and Qatar.[113] Other estimates give Saudi Arabia at least 214 TCF of natural gas reserves, without the reserves in the Neutral Zone, and 217 TCF including these reserves. This would be about 4% of the world's reserves, which ranks Saudi Arabia fifth in the world.[114]

British Petroleum estimates that Saudi Arabia has 213.8 TCF (6.05 trillion cubic meters) of natural gas reserves, which is also 4% of the world's total.[115] Saudi reserves compare with Russia reserves of 1,700 TCF, Iranian reserves of 812 TCF, Qatari reserves of 394 TCF, and UAE reserves of 212 TCF. The United States, by comparison, has reserves of 167 TCF.[116] An IEA estimate of the relative size and ranking of Saudi gas reserves is shown in Table 7.3 and Charts 7.5 and 7.6.

The EIA reports that roughly two-thirds of Saudi Arabia's currently proven gas reserves consist of associated gas, mainly from the onshore Ghawar field and the offshore Safaniya and Zuluf fields. The Ghawar oil field alone accounts for one-third of the country's total gas reserves. Most new associated gas reserves discovered in the 1990s have been in fields that contain light crude oil, especially in the Najd region south of Riyadh. Most of Saudi Arabia's nonassociated gas reserves (Mazalij, Al-Manjoura, Shaden, Niban, Tinat, Al-Waar, etc.) are located in the deep Khuff reservoir that

Table 7.3
Gulf and World Gas Reserves and Production

| Nation | Reserves in 2001 | | Percent of World Reserves | Production in 2001 (% of World) |
	TCM	TCF		
Bahrain	0.09	3.2	0.1	0.4
Iran	23.00	812.3	14.8	2.5
Iraq	3.11	109.8	2.0	—
Kuwait	1.49	52.7	1.0	0.4
Oman	0.83	29.3	0.5	0.5
Qatar	14.40	508.5	9.3	1.3
Saudi Arabia	6.22	219.5	4.0	2.2
UAE	6.01	212.1	3.9	1.7
Yemen	0.29	10.2	0.2	—
Gulf	55.78	1964.4	35.9	—
Total Middle East	55.91	1,974.6	36.1	9.3
Algeria	4.52	159.7	2.9	3.2
Libya	1.31	46.4	0.8	0.2
Egypt	1.00	35.2	0.6	0.9
Total MENA	61.74	2,3150.9	40.4	13.6
Russia	47.57	1,680.0	30.7	22.0
US	5.02	177.4	3.2	22.5
EU	14.87	525.0	9.6	8.6
Asia/Pacific	12.27	443.3	7.9	11.4
World Total	155.08	5,476.1	100.0%	100%

Source: The reserve and production data are adapted by Anthony H. Cordesman from British Petroleum, *BP Statistical Review of World Energy, 2002* (London: British Petroleum June 2002), pp. 20–23.

Chart 7.5
Saudi Arabia versus Total Proven Gas Reserves of the Other Gulf States, 1979–2001: BP Estimate (in Trillions of Cubic Meters)

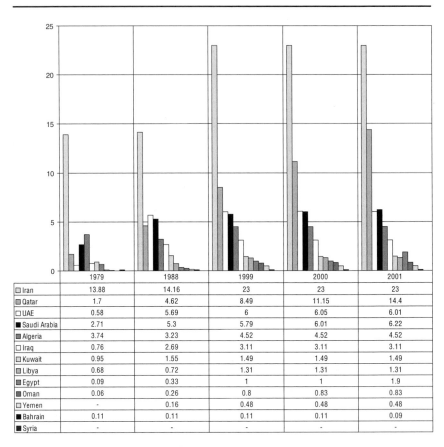

	1979	1988	1999	2000	2001
☐ Iran	13.88	14.16	23	23	23
☐ Qatar	1.7	4.62	8.49	11.15	14.4
☐ UAE	0.58	5.69	6	6.05	6.01
■ Saudi Arabia	2.71	5.3	5.79	6.01	6.22
☐ Algeria	3.74	3.23	4.52	4.52	4.52
☐ Iraq	0.76	2.69	3.11	3.11	3.11
☐ Kuwait	0.95	1.55	1.49	1.49	1.49
☐ Libya	0.68	0.72	1.31	1.31	1.31
☐ Egypt	0.09	0.33	1	1	1.9
☐ Oman	0.06	0.26	0.8	0.83	0.83
☐ Yemen	-	0.16	0.48	0.48	0.48
■ Bahrain	0.11	0.11	0.11	0.11	0.09
■ Syria	-	-	-	-	-

Source: British Petroleum, *BP Statistical Review of World Energy, 2002* (London: British Petroleum, June 2002), pp. 20–21.

underlies the Ghawar oil field. Another gas field, called Dorra, is located near the Khafji oil field in the Neutral Zone and may be developed by Japan's AOC. Gas also is located in the Rub al-Khali and the extreme northwest, at Midyan.[117]

In early 2000, Saudi Arabia reportedly decided not to move ahead with development of Midyan, which included provision of gas to the Tabuk power station. However, Saudi Arabia has announced plans to add some

Chart 7.6
Saudi Arabia versus Other States as Percent of Total Proven World Gas Reserves in 2001

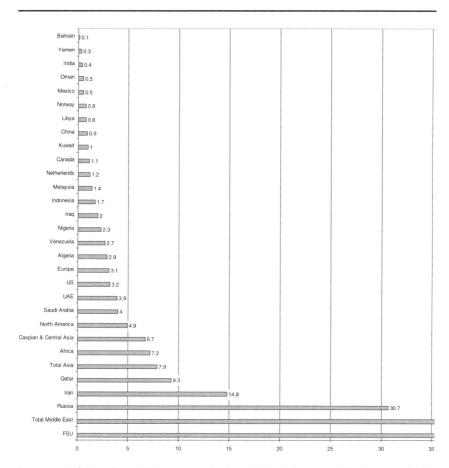

Source: British Petroleum, *BP Statistical Review of World Energy, 2002* (London: British Petroleum, June 2002), pp. 20–21.

5 TCF of recoverable gas to its reserves each year. In September 2000, tests at Ghazal No. 1, located on the southern tip of the giant Ghawar oil field and west of the Haradh gas field, indicated a significant gas discovery, and represented the eighth gas or condensate discovery in the area under Saudi Arabia's stepped-up gas exploration program.[118]

SAUDI GAS PRODUCTION

Global energy trends toward cleaner energy have made gas increasingly popular as a fuel and have made gas exports more lucrative for the Gulf region as a whole. Qatar and Oman have taken the greatest advantage of the growing LNG market, and the UAE is becoming steadily more export-oriented. Saudi Arabia, however, can use most of its gas production to meet domestic energy demands and reduce its dependence on crude oil—which provides higher profitability than gas exports. As a result, it is focusing on the development of gas to provide a nationwide energy source, as well as feedstock for product and petrochemicals. The EIA reports that Saudi Arabia has not expressed great interest in liquefied natural gas because it is more cost-effective to use it as feedstock or fuel.

Gas production has done much to meet domestic energy needs and to reduce the domestic demand for oil, which is easier and more economical to export. Saudi gas production now accounts for roughly 2% of all world output. It rose from 1.43 million tons of oil equivalent (MTOE) in 1971, to 3.101 MTOE in 1975, 8.51 MTOE in 1980, 15.75 MTOE in 1985, 25.36 MTOE in 1990, and 29.32 MTOE in 1993. More recent estimates indicate that production rose from 33.5 billion cubic meters (BCM) in 1990 to 42.9 in 1995, 44.5 in 1996, 45.8 in 1997, 46.7 in 1998, 46.2 in 1999, and 47.0 in 2000. Virtually all this gas production was consumed in Saudi Arabia, and domestic demand for gas is expected to increase at an average rate of 7% a year for at least the next decade.[119]

If gas production is broken out into type, delivered sales gas production rose from 3.097 billion BTUs per day in 1996 to 3.708 in 2000. Ethane sales dropped from 0.724 billion BTUs per day in 1996 to 0.689 in 2000. The sale of raw gas-to-gas plants rose from 4.13 billions of SCFD in 1996 to 4.80 in 2000. The sale of NGL from hydrocarbon gas rose from 276, 749, 751 million barrels in 1996 to 285,007,720 in 2000.[120] Saudi Aramco reports that Saudi Arabia exported 237,803,981 barrels of crude oil in 2000; of that amount, 62.6% went to the Far East, 4.7% went to the Mediterranean area, 0.4% went to the United States, and 32.3% went to other destinations.[121]

Most of Saudi Arabia's natural gas was flared prior to the start-up of the Kingdom's Master Gas System (MGS), which was completed in 1982. This system cost some $13 billion and was created primarily to meet domestic demand and to provide most of the 0.7 MMBD of LPG that makes Saudi Arabia the world's largest exporter. The MGS currently gathers about 5 BCF per day of raw gas, primarily from the Ghawar field and the offshore Safaniyah and Zuluf fields. Associated gas accounts for 4.1 BCF per day of this amount and nonassociated gas for 0.9 BCF per day. Three processing facilities at Berri, Shedgum, and Uthmaniya are able to process up to 5.8 BCF per day.[122] Saudi Arabia has reduced its flaring and reinjection of gas to the point where these activities accounted for only 0.36 BCM out of 48.69 BDC produced in 1999. Even with all other losses, including handling, the total was reduced to only 2.49 BCM out of 48.69 BCM produced.[123]

The need to meet domestic demand is driving a $4.5 billion expansion of Saudi Arabia's MGS. The MGS feeds gas to the industrial cities of Yanbu and Jubail, which, when combined, account for 10% of the world's petrochemical production. Additionally, the MGS feeds gas to electric power plants, desalination plants, and cement plants in the Eastern Province and Riyadh.[124] There are also fractionalization plants at Juaymah and Yanbu.[125]

In October 1997, the Saudi oil minister announced plans to boost its gas processing capacity in five years to 10 BCF a day. Substantial work on this project is ongoing. Foster Wheeler is managing a $2.6 billion project to build a new gas processing plant at Haradh. The Haradah plant alone is expected to process 1.6 BCF a day from the Ghawar and Khuff gas wells when it goes on stream in December 2003.[126]

In November 1996, a project management contract was signed with U.S.-based Parsons Corp. for construction of a $2 billion, 2.4 BCF-per-day gas processing plant at Hawiyah. Other corporations involved at Hawiyah (located south of Dhahran and east of Riyadh) include Japan's JGC, Argentina's Techint, and Italy's Technip. Hawiyah represents the largest Saudi gas project in more than ten years. It was 98% complete in 2001 and began delivering gas some four months ahead of its scheduled completion date in 2002. Initial production began at 260 MCF per day and the plant will have a capacity of 1.4 BCF per day when it is finished. The Hawiyah plant—plus the debottlenecking of three other existing plants (Berri, Haradh, Ras Tanura)—will boost Saudi Arabia's gas processing capacity to 6.3 BCF per day by 2002.[127]

In 2000, Saudi gas production totaled about 6% of Saudi primary energy production, including crude oil. In June 2000, a key pipeline project was completed that extended the MGS from the Eastern Province (which contains large potential gas and condensate reserves) to the capital, Riyadh, in the Central Province, where it will replace crude oil in power generation. This is part of a broader expansion of the existing gas transmission system in Saudi Arabia.[128] Saudi gas production capacity is expected to increase to 7,500 cubic feet a day when the new processing plant at Haradh is completed. Over 6,000 MCF of gas reserves have been discovered over the last five years.[129]

The Parsons Corporation has also worked with a local partner on debottlenecking of the existing Uthmaniyah gas processing plant. Contracts for debottlenecking on the Kingdom's other existing gas processing plants (Berri and Shedgum) were awarded in 1997. Canada's Delta Hudson is carrying out basic engineering and preparing tender documents for the $500 million Berri upgrade. At present there is no ethane recovery at Berri, which could supply up to 240 MCFD.[130] The new plant plus the debottlenecking of the three existing plants will boost capacity to 6.3 BCF per day by 2002.

Saudi Aramco has spent $200 million to build a third fractionalization plant at Juaymah, and plans a $100 million upgrade of the Berri plant, and a similar upgrade at Uthmaniya.[131] This increase in the processing capacity of the MGS will require expansion of transportation facilities.

In another major project announced recently, the Uthamaniyah plant is to be linked with Juaymah and Berri by an underground gas pipeline. The planned 1,400 MCFD gas processing plant in Haradh has been opened up for bids from both international and local contractors. The project is split into three packages, the largest of which is the downstream pipeline of 350 to 400 kilometers, which has been demarcated for international contractors only. The second package includes a central processing plant valued at $600 to $700 million, which will process 770,000 CFD of sour gas. The third and final package comprises plant and offsite utilities, including gas compression facilities and fuel gas systems, all amounting to some $500 million.

Saudi Domestic Gas Use

Chart 7.7 shows the trends in Saudi gas production and utilization. Chart 7.8 shows the steady rise in Saudi domestic consumption of petroleum and natural gas liquids. The Kingdom determined as early as the 1970s that domestic use of gas would be more commercially feasible and have more strategic value that exporting it in the form of LNG. This decision has been validated during the last few decades, as the MGS has provided gas to Saudi utilities and petrochemical industries and has enabled Saudi Arabia to become the leading producer of petrochemicals in the Middle East.

Domestic natural gas consumption could not keep pace initially with total production, but increased from 500 MCFD in 1980 to 3.4 BCFD in 2000, an annual growth rate of 11% over the period. As the charts show, domestic ability to use total production accelerated sharply in the mid-1990s, as major domestic projects that use gas came online. In the utilities sectors (electricity and desalination), demand for gas grew by an average of 7.3% annually during the 1990s, while demand for gas grew by 7.6% annually in the petrochemical industry. This demand raised Saudi per capita consumption to 180 CFD, one of the highest rates in the world. This growth was partially driven by the increased supply made available by the MGS.

Saudi Aramco projects that domestic gas consumption will increase at an average annual rate of 5.2% over the next twenty-five years—with a 9% growth rate until 2010—due to fuel substitution for gas in power generation. As a result, domestic demand is projected to rise from 3.4 BCFD in 2000, to 6.8 BCFD in 2005 and 12.2 BCFD in 2025. Most of this increase in demand will come from the manufacturing sector, including petro-

Chart 7.7
Saudi Gas Production and Utilization: 1970–1998 (in Billions of Cubic Meters)

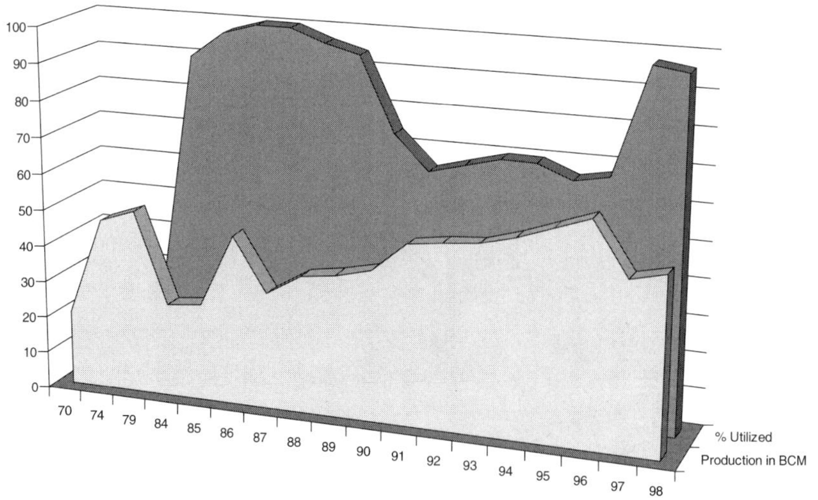

	70	74	79	84	85	86	87	88	89	90	91	92	93	94	95	96	97	98
☐ Production in BCM	20.6	47.3	50.6	25.7	26.8	46.9	32	37.7	39.1	41.4	49.5	50.7	51.6	54.3	57.8	61.3	46.6	48.9
▨ % Utilized	11	13.1	23.1	90.4	97.4	100	100	96.5	94	73.7	64.6	67.1	69.6	69.4	65.8	67.4	97.2	95.8

Source: Adapted by Anthony H. Cordesman from Saudi Ministry of Planning, *Achievements of the Development Plans, 1390–1420 (1970–2000)* (Riyadh: Ministry of Planning, 2001), Table 53.

chemicals, which will account for 57% of the increase. This is due to the projected expansion of the petrochemical industry, which is expected to use the favorable comparative advantage that Saudi Arabia has in terms of feedstock prices and investment in production and advanced industrial infrastructure. Most of the increased demand in these sectors will be for ethane and NGL; it is projected that annual demand for ethane will rise by 4.3% until 2025, and that demand for NGL will rise 10% annually.

The incremental increase in demand will be mostly from nonassociated gas, the production of which will increase over the coming years. The MGS, which is now capable of processing 6.1 BCFD of gas and of delivering 4.2 BCFD of sales gas, will be expanded to handle 9.3 BCFD of processing capability (7.2 BCFD of supply) by 2004, with the completion of the Hawiyah gas plant at 1.4 BCFD capacity in 2002 and the Haradh gas plant at 1.5 BCFD capacity in 2004.

In the past, the Kingdom tended to treat gas prices the way it treated electricity: as something that is more of a subsidy or entitlement than a market commodity. It sharply underpriced gas to both the ordinary

Chart 7.8

Saudi Domestic Consumption of Refined Products and Natural Gas: 1970–2000 (in Millions of U.S. Barrels of Oil Equivalent)

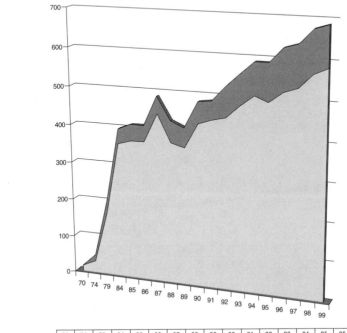

	70	74	79	84	85	86	87	88	89	90	91	92	93	94	95	96	97	98	99
▣ Oil Industry	-	17.5	33.9	38.5	42.7	41.6	45.4	56.3	51	56.1	48.4	79	78.8	82.2	96.5	106.5	105.8	107.2	101.9
▢ Public and Utility Use	15.5	32	165.8	356.8	366.4	367.5	441.7	370.8	361.1	424.8	437.2	445.3	478.1	505.5	491.8	519	531	566.7	583.4

Source: Adapted by Anthony H. Cordesman from Saudi Ministry of Planning, *Achievements of the Development Plans, 1390–1420 (1970–2000)* (Riyadh: Ministry of Planning, 2001), Table 53.

consumers and power and petrochemical plants. It now, however, is seeking to both expand the MGS and to gradually raise gas prices to market levels.[132] It increased the price for gas from 50 cents to 75 cents per million BTU in January 1999. In early 1999, key Aramco officials warned LPG customers that the impending increase in domestic demand could reduce exports from the Kingdom by some 30% by the year 2001.

It is far from clear, however, that the Kingdom has a realistic strategy to set consumer gas prices at levels that will force energy efficiency, and to ensure that both state and industrial users will pay a fair market price for gas, passing this price onto their consumers. There are also strong indicators that past projects involved underpriced gas, unrealistic returns on investments, and false assumptions about Saudisation and other indirect benefits. The problems in making cost-effective use of gas have also sometimes been compounded by technocratic and bureaucratic empire-building, hidden kickbacks, and a tendency to confuse optimism with planning. The Kingdom has many real opportunities to use gas, as well as expand upstream and downstream operations for both oil and gas. The Kingdom does, however, need to do more to put gas use on a solid market footing and review how cost-effective each deal will be, in addition to reviewing how effective the ongoing investment activity and the resulting operations and sales really are.

Foreign Investment in the Gas Sector

Increasing gas production is such a high priority for the Saudi government that gas development is slated to consume a large share of Aramco's budget. (In late 1999, Aramco decided to invest $45 billion over twenty-five years on upstream gas development and processing facilities.) Unlike crude oil production, however, Saudi Arabia has decided that it cannot meet its development objectives without major transfers of foreign investment capital.[133]

Ten IOCs engaged in negotiations with the Saudi government in the summer of 2000 in an effort to develop upstream and integrated gas-based projects. In its July briefings with the IOCs, the government presented three proposals for integrated gas projects: the Haradh gas development project; an integrated refinery and petrochemicals project at Rabigh; and gas development in the southeast in Kidan and Shaybah. Aramco was to be a partner in all these projects.[134]

In May 2001, Saudi Arabia selected a mix of eight companies to participate in the huge ($25 billion) "Saudi Gas Initiative," the first major reopening of Saudi Arabia's upstream hydrocarbons sector to foreign investment since they were nationalized in the 1970s. The Saudi Gas Initiative seeks to integrate upstream gas development with downstream petrochemicals, power generation, and desalination, and is seen as the key to Saudi Arabia's entire foreign investment strategy. The companies selected for the three "core ventures" under the Saudi Gas Initiative were:[135]

- Core Venture 1: South Ghawar—North Rub al-Khali (Empty Quarter) project. Venture 1 will be one of the world's largest integrated gas projects, and includes gas development in a 70,000-square-kilometer area. Activity includes exploration, pipelines, a gas plant including ethane recovery, two gas-fired power plants with 400 megawatts of capacity, a petrochemical plant with two million tons of annual production, two desalination units with an output of 300 million gallons per day, and more. The estimated cost of the project is $8 billion and the consortium involves ExxonMobil (35%), Shell (25%), BP (25%), and Phillips (15%).

- Core Venture 2: North Red Sea: This venture will involve exploration in the Red Sea and exploration and development of three offshore fields on the Red Sea coast in northwestern Saudi Arabia—Midyan, Al-Wajh, and Umluj—plus the Barqan onshore field. It includes a gas processing plant, a gas pipeline, and a power plant in Dhuba, plus a possible petrochemical plant with a total cost of $4 billion. This project involves ExxonMobil (60%), Occidental ($20%), and Marathon (20%).

- Core Venture 3: Shaybah/Kidan Gas Project, consisting of exploration and development of gas fields and processing plants at Shaybah and Kidan in the Rub al-Khali ("Empty Quarter") of southeastern Saudi Arabia. It will involve development of the Kidan gas field and future laying of pipelines from Shaybah to the Hawiyah "straddle" gas treatment plant and the Haradh plant east of Riyadh, construction of a petrochemical plant in Jubail, and petrochemical, power, and desalination plants, with an estimated cost of $7 billion. The consortium for this project is led by Shell (40%) and Conoco (40%), while Total/Fina has a smaller share (30%).

After four years of talks, highlighted by thirteen months of intense negotiations ending in early 2002, the eight IOCs involved in the three "core ventures" submitted their final proposals in July of that year. Submitting these final proposals, coupled with prospects of reentering the Saudi Arabian oil market for the first time since the 1970s, should have resulted in a wave of enthusiasm among international oil executives. However, impasses have occurred due to growing fears of regional destabilization because of problems in U.S.-Saudi relations and a possible conflict between the United States and Iraq.[136]

The main point of contention concerns the rates of return from the joint ventures and how these returns would be distributed among the parties involved. ExxonMobil and Royal Dutch/Shell had sought to receive returns of between 16% and 18% from each project. Lower returns, both firms claim, would not justify the risk or the outlay for the petrochemical plants, power stations, and desalinization facilities they would build as part of the deal. Additionally, the Western corporations sought concessions from the Saudis on the amount of land that would be open for gas exploration and on the size of the role that Saudi Arabia's state-run oil-related industries would have in any joint-projects.[137]

During meetings held that same month in Los Angeles, between a group of Saudi ministers, led by Prince Saud al-Faisal and Lee Raymond, chief executive of ExxonMobil, both sides indicated a willingness to continue talks in the hope that a final agreement could be reached by a previously self-imposed deadline of March 2. Reports of a breakdown in dialogue led Saudi Oil Minister Ali al-Naimi to comment, "The companies have their demands, and the state has its demands. . . . We are trying to sort out these demands into an agreement." Al-Naimi appeared optimistic and declined to characterize that state of the talks as "a dispute."[138]

By April 2002, talks between the Western companies and Saudi officials were reported to have broken down. While the delay was partially attributed to Saudi government leaders' focus on more pressing matters, including the Israeli-Palestinian situation, little progress had been made on the issue of the investment returns. Western firms continued to demand a minimum rate of return of 15%, but the Saudis sought to establish an investment return level of no more than 10%. Other differences remained. ExxonMobil, which was selected to lead the Ghawar venture, remained displeased with the amount of potential gas resources that were offered for exploration. Also, the Core Venture 2 project was reported to be on hold. While progress had been made in negotiations over the third Core Venture project in the "Empty Quarter," Royal Dutch/Shell remained concerned that the level of actual gas reserves in the target region was, in reality, much lower than Saudi predictions suggested. As insurance, Royal Dutch/Shell sought "guaranteed substitutes," for the reserves that it was being allocated.[139]

Some Western executives also had the sense that the rising tide of anti-American feelings throughout Saudi Arabia and the Middle East had placed additional pressure on the Saudi government to further delay the development of final guidelines for each project. Some experts believe that as anti-American sentiment continues to rise, Western oil companies will incur greater political and economic risks from their business dealings in the Kingdom, and therefore will be less willing to concede to Saudi demands for a lower rate of investment return.[140]

Despite these concerns, Oil Minister al-Naimi continued to project an optimistic outlook on the status of the investment talks. In comments that he delivered on April 22 to a Washington meeting of the Petroleum Industry Research Foundation, U.S.-Saudi Business Council Conference, and the Council of Foreign Relations, al-Naimi referred to the historic "partnership" that has existed for decades between American oil companies and Saudi Arabia.[141] In his remarks, Naimi touched on the subject of Saudi Arabia's attempts at economic diversification, stating: "Today Saudi Arabia is undertaking an ambitious plan to restructure its economy—a massive effort that will not only bring strong economic growth in coming years, but will also create excellent investment opportunities, including [for] those from the United States."

On the subject of the Saudi gas initiatives, al-Naimi reaffirmed the Kingdom's desire to see "eight multinational oil companies . . . invest over $25 billion over the next five years in gas exploration and production, as well as power generation, desalination and chemical facilities." He also specifically responded to reports that the talks between both sides had broken down, stating that the media was "inaccurate in its statements" and that "there are no political setbacks in the initiative."[142] He further reiterated this stance at the conclusion of his speech, commenting that the gas initiatives and other diversification projects "hold a great promise for the future of Saudi Arabia and for creating excellent opportunities for U.S. and other international companies to invest in the Kingdom."[143]

Under the terms of the preliminary agreements between the Saudis and the Western oil companies, the IOCs' exclusive right to the projects expired in March.[144] In June 2002, Saudi sources indicated that Crown Prince Abdullah was set to meet with the heads of ExxonMobil and Royal Dutch/ Shell in an effort to resolve the differences over the investments that remained.[145] If these talks with Abdullah fail to yield any progress the Saudis may announce that they are opening up the projects to additional bidders. Saudi economist Ihsan by Hlaika underscored this belief, commenting that while "the gas initiative will give tremendous support for the industrial sector . . . in terms of higher growth, new jobs and development of . . . infrastructure," time is increasingly a factor, "and the window of opportunity [for reaching an agreement] will not last forever."[146]

While a successful resolution to the current negotiations is uncertain, several key factors indicate that a positive outcome remains possible. Even though some Saudi ministers and technocrats continue to oppose providing IOCs direct access to Saudi Arabia's natural gas reserves on more preferential terms (or any terms in some cases), Crown Prince Abdullah and Prince Saud have shown a willingness to negotiate over the matter. Both recognize that Saudi Arabia needs significant foreign investment to offset a rapidly growing population and rising unemployment. Despite improvements in oil revenues since the oil crash of 1997, the conditions that led Prince Abdullah to create the SGI (and the risk of growing social and economic unrest) still loom on the horizon. Regional and domestic concerns may hinder an immediate response to the recently submitted proposals, but may not stand in the way of an eventual negotiated deal. As put by one Saudi analyst, "This initiative is really needed and will not fail. The price of failure is too high to contemplate."[147]

One must be careful, however, about taking the success or failure of such deals too seriously. If these gas development projects are successful, they will sharply reduce Saudi domestic consumption of crude oil and provide the Kingdom with an environmentally safe fuel supply for electricity generation, desalination, industrial and home use, and diversification into gas products for at least three to four decades. Much will, however, depend on whether the Kingdom can handle the most ambitious single investment project in its history with the necessary speed and efficiency and whether it will apply a market pricing strategy that ensures gas is used wisely. Much of the Kingdom's discussion of gas strategy now seems to focus too much on finding sources of investment and too little on the need to introduce a rational pricing strategy as soon as possible. This is necessary both to ensure an allocation and conservation of resources and to ensure that ventures have suitable profitability.

It is equally important to note that the Kingdom's approach to foreign investment in this area is not really privatization in the classic sense, but rather one of granting major concessions to large consortiums in return for foreign capital. There is no present way to determine such operations will be more cost-effective and efficient than state investment in and operation by Aramco. As is the case with petroleum production, upstream gas production also involves only limited Saudi labor during the construction phase and is one of the least labor-intensive uses of capital once the system becomes operational.

SAUDI ENERGY STRATEGY IN THE TWENTY-FIRST CENTURY

Saudi energy strategy has long been oriented toward creating a stable long-term market in which it can achieve the highest possible short-term oil export revenues without jeopardizing long-term demand for oil. It has stressed the role of being a reliable supplier, and consequently has maintained a high level of surplus production, enabling it to guard against emergencies in any given field, and allowing it the ability to capitalize on major increases in demand or supply emergencies in other countries and increase its economic and political leverage. Saudi Arabia has not attempted to use oil embargoes, or use oil as a political weapon, since the Arab oil embargo in 1974.

The Saudis fully understand their efforts cannot bind world markets or, in creating a high degree of predictability regarding future demand, future prices, future revenues, and future investment income. Crown Prince Abdullah cited the fact that oil reserves will always be uncertain as a key reason why Saudi Arabia needed to reduce its dependence on oil export revenues and diversify its economy in a speech to the GCC summit meeting on November 6, 1998:[148]

> Our revenues have been affected by what you call the fall in oil prices. However, we in the Kingdom are making big efforts to maintain equilibrium and mitigate the negative impacts. The state is serious about controlling spending and approving practical plans for providing vital alternatives for the national income. This does not mean dispensing with oil or underestimating its importance. Rather, it means looking vigorously for other sources to back up and consolidate the national income. We will do our utmost so as to not overburden our citizens—especially those of limited or medium income. Our first and foremost concern is the well-being and prosperity of our citizens. It is the duty of the state to strike a balance between the policy of rationalizing spending to curb inflation or recession and between reducing the impact of these necessary measures on the lives of citizens.

The Strategy in the Seventh Development Plan

Saudi development plans do not attempt to set specific goals for future oil and gas production, exports, and revenues. Saudi Arabia realizes that it can control market forces, which is why Saudi plans have called for diversification of the economy away from oil ever since the First Development Plan. The Seventh Development Plan does observe that international estimates indicate that total world crude oil production may increase from about 78 MMBD in 1999 to around 115 MMBD in 2020. It notes that demand for natural gas is projected to account for one-third of world primary energy production by 2020, and that it is estimated to grow at three times the average rate of the overall demand for all types of energy. It also notes a rise in Asian demand that indicates that about 50% of the increase in total world energy demand and 40% of the increase in demand for oil between 2000 and 2020 will come from South and East Asian countries, and that the share of OPEC countries in total world production is projected to rise from 39% in 1999 to more than 50% by 2020.[149] These projections, however, are little more than a repetition of OPEC, IEA, and EIA estimates.

The Seventh Development Plan does set one tangible goal by calling for an increase in production capacity of 1.5% to 2% per year, but qualifies even this vague goal by noting that significant structural changes are taking place in the world oil market, that environmental issues are having a steadily great impact on oil and gas use, and that no one can predict the impact of the changes taking place in energy supply and utilization technology and the rate of future dependence on oil. Its only references to a longer-term oil strategy (through 2020) are to call for:[150]

- Maintaining the position of the Kingdom in world energy markets commensurate with its share of world oil reserves.
- Optimizing production levels and maximizing crude oil revenues while using such revenues to finance investment programs.
- Developing the Kingdom's natural gas resources and enhancing their role in the long-term strategy for suitable development.

As for future policies, the Seventh Development Plan sets out seven broad policy activities:[151]

- Monitoring and analyzing world energy development in a continuous and regular manner through developing an advanced system for carrying out this task. This system becomes of great significant due to the growing impact of environmental and technological policies on world energy markets, a matter that entails precise follow-up and in-depth analysis of the rational and future directions of these policies.
- The objective of strengthening cooperation and consultation between OPEC and non-OPEC producers will remain among the Kingdom's strategic priorities. The issue of discriminatory and high taxes is considered to be among the important topics for consultation. The Kingdom will, in collaboration with other oil producing countries, exert efforts aimed at including the oil trade

within the WTO as the existing exception is discriminatory and unfair to the oil producing countries.

- The Kingdom will strive to confirm its role and active partnership in energy and environmental affairs, as well as its support and contribution to scientific research and technological development in the domain of energy and environmental conservation.

- Because of the gap between the Kingdom's share in world oil reserves (25%) on the one hand and its share in world oil production (12%) on the other hand, and in light of the comparative advantage of Saudi oil, arguments for economic efficiency call for closing this gap while maintaining oil market stability.

- Continuing to develop natural gas supply sources and its local and regional markets. In this context, a national grid covering all parts of the Kingdom will be developed with the aim of support industrial sectors and services.

- Assigning a substantial role to the domestic and foreign private sector to invest in programs designed to increase natural gas production and develop its uses.

- Developing oil markets within a strategy for maintaining the role of oil in world energy markets as a means for maintaining the share of oil in these markets.

The net result is a pragmatic, market-driven strategy that emphasizes the search to maximize long-term oil revenues and market stability rather than maximize short-term profits. In short, it is a pragmatic strategy that fully recognizes what the Kingdom can and cannot do, given global market forces.

The Statements of the Saudi Oil Minister

The Saudi oil ministry has continued to state its commitment to this strategy. Saudi Oil Minister Ali al-Naimi maintained in October 1999 that Saudi oil policy was based on four facts: maintenance of the largest oil reserves and among the lowest production costs—around $1.50 per barrel—in the world; maintenance of significant spare oil production capacity; a national economy closely linked to the oil industry; and a stable political and economic system. Al-Naimi also stressed the importance of "a stable international oil market" where "wide and rapid swings in prices are undesirable." Reportedly, the SPC has approved Aramco's spending of $15 billion per year between 2000 and 2004 to boost oil production capacity and increase gas output.[152]

Al-Naimi amplified these points in 2001 at a conference on energy policy in Norway. He noted that oil was seen as "an extension of our governing system . . . as a tool to help achieve our economic and social prosperity, and to make meaningful contributions toward peace and economic development at the regional and global levels—especially to less fortunate societies." He described Saudi oil strategy as follows:[153]

[O]il policy is [determined by] our position on the world's oil map. We have about 25 percent of all proven conventional reserves, currently more than 260 billion barrels. If you add the reserves of our neighbors in the Gulf . . . the total comes to around 500 billion barrels. It is natural, therefore, that we work not only to expand the use of, but also prolong the life of, oil, far into the future. I feel we are succeeding; yet we face problems from within the oil business and from outsiders. Within our business, there are those who have doubts about the future of our commodity. Others may look only at short-term interests, where in the end they might not see the long-term issues.

And from the outsiders, there are those whom we might call the anti-oil groups, who are using every tactic to discredit oil. Sometimes they talk about the insecurity of supply or independence from foreign sources. Other times they are disguised under the guise of environmental protection or restriction of globalization, which they fear multinational enterprises.

The debate can often rise to highly emotional levels. We in Saudi Arabia and, I believe, the majority of all oil producers feel it is unwise to be guided by emotions. Rather, we consider it a duty to protect our long-term interests from any influence that might impair our ability to function as major oil suppliers to the world. Only by remaining focused on such a mission will stability prevail.

The Saudi government is working diligently to reduce the level of [economic] dependency on oil. . . . The Kingdom is currently undertaking major steps toward economic and financial reforms, which will eventually facilitate diversification of the economy and lessen our dependence on a single depleting natural resource.

. . . To summarize, Saudi Arabia's oil policies are grounded in the prudent management of an abundant and valuable natural resource. We share with our GCC neighbors the desire to conduct business worldwide in a very competitive market economy. And we have been working hard to create a stable environment for a much-needed commodity—oil—while promoting a better understanding of the challenges and risks that its delivery entails. Our goal is a stable market, a reasonable price for our commodity and the realization of prosperity for ourselves and those we serve.

Al-Naimi made it clear in September 2002 that the Kingdom planned to maintain a stable source of oil supplies, and use its surplus capacity, in the event of a war with Iraq. He stated at the meeting of the International Energy Forum in Osaka, Japan on September 21, 2002 that,[154]

Saudi Arabia is committed to maintaining a stable worldwide oil market, free of disruptive price swings yet responsive to changing conditions. . . . I can't think of any producing nation that has gone to the extent of the Kingdom in servicing its dedicated customers and shoring up any weakness in the global oil market. We certainly don't claim to shoulder all efforts in this regard, but we do have a significant track record. . . . We have invested billions of dollars to build production capacity and to construct export routes . . . we continue to keep some 30 percent of our production capacity unutilized to be ready in times of supply interruption.

In addition to the over 10 million barrels per day export facilities in the Eastern Province ports, we have five million barrels of production capacity from the Red Sea ports to contribute to oil supply and security.

He then gave an interview after the meeting—on September 23, 2002—in which he said that Saudi Arabia had a surplus capacity of 3.0 MMBD which was ready for use in a crisis, and that he supported stockpiling to prevent price surges and panics in the event of a crisis. He also rejected suggestions to broaden the OPEC price band from $22 to $28 per barrel to $10 to $30 a barrel.[155]

Longer-Term Saudi Strategy

Up to now, Saudi Arabia has been successful in developing its existing oil fields in the most economically efficient manner, bringing new ones on line when needed, creating efficient refineries, and creating a large petrochemical industry. Unlike many other oil- and gas-exporting states, Saudi Arabia also has invested in the kind of production capacity, refining output, and downstream operations that are suited to a strategy of maintaining moderate prices and high long-term demand. Saudi Arabia has demonstrated its commitment to securing its markets indefinitely into the future by keeping production high and prices at levels that ensure that it can steadily expand its exports.

The key issues affecting Saudi Arabia's future strategy do not involve any concern over whether it will continue to be a major oil and gas producer, but focus rather how large a producer and exporter it will be, and whether it can obtain all of the investment capital it needs to pursue its desired strategy and price oil and gas at the proper level while managing the expansion of state and private oil and gas along efficient, market-driven lines. Virtually any Saudi energy strategy will be based on the need to export large quantities of oil to maintain high oil export revenues. At the same time, Saudi Arabia has considerable discretion in choosing just how quickly and how much it will increase oil and gas production capacity, how to diversify, how much to rely on market forces, and how to deal with the problem of Saudisation.

As is clear from Oil Minister al-Naimi's public remarks and interviews with senior Saudis, however, Saudi energy strategy must consider additional factors that sometimes involve competing priorities:

- Saudi Arabia's overall national investment strategy must make increasingly difficult choices between state investment in the energy sector, Saudi economic reform and diversification, paying for social and entitlement programs, funding infrastructure, and paying for national defense.

- As discussed in Chapters 4 and 5, as well as earlier in this chapter, the future role of privatization, foreign investment, and domestic private investment in upstream operations, downstream operations, product production, and petroleum-related manufacturing are all critical issues.

- Saudi Arabia must make very expensive investments in new production capacity, both to maintain a cash flow capable of keeping up with its population growth and meet world demand. The long lead times involved, however, make it extremely difficult to predict what capacity will be needed in any given time period and the oil export revenues that will result.

- As discussed in Chapter 2, oil has a major security dimension. The steady expansion of Saudi oil and gas facilities, and related electricity and desalination facilities, is changing the Kingdom's military vulnerability as well as the importance of such facilities to the global economy.

- Saudi Arabia must take account of the diplomatic and strategic implications of its production capacity and actual production on potential threat nations like Iran and Iraq, as well as on the support it can obtain from its allies in the GCC.

- The Kingdom must deal with other members of OPEC outside the Gulf; some members of OPEC, both inside and outside the Gulf, feel that Saudi Arabia should reduce production to allow them to increase their oil export revenues. OPEC is both an aid to Saudi Arabia and a threat. Its interests may coincide with OPEC at any given time, or it may gain more from shaping its production levels to maximize revenues to the Kingdom, even if this means other OPEC states obtain less revenue.

- Saudi pricing strategy must ensure both significant current market share and high current revenues without pushing consumer states to find alternative sources of energy in the mid-to-long-term.

- Saudi Arabia must make decisions about whether to retain a significant margin of surplus capacity, allowing it to continue to act as the world's primary "swing" state that can increase production in an emergency. While surplus capacity allows Saudi Arabia to gain revenues in a crisis, it is also costly and leads to consumer pressure on the Kingdom to increase production for political reasons.

- The Kingdom cannot ignore the risk that another Arab-Israeli conflict, or some other major crisis, could lead to some form of future energy embargo.

It is obvious that there are many exogenous factors in this list that the Kingdom can neither control nor predict. Once again, Saudi strategy must constantly be adjusted to suit the conditions imposed by the global economy, war, and political considerations. At the same time, the Kingdom's decisions do have a major impact on total world supply and the global economy. As a result, Saudi Arabia's willingness and ability to increase its exports and invest in surplus production capacity, also play a critical role in determining whether world oil supplies and prices remain relatively stable.

Shaping Future Saudi Oil Production Capacity and Exports: Western Estimates and Projections

The West sees Saudi Arabia as the major source of new oil production capacity that will meet growing world demand through at least 2020. It also seems increasingly unlikely that Iran and Iraq can achieve the production capacity increases currently forecasted, and there are growing uncertainties regarding future Russian and Central Asian oil production and the rate of increase in Asian demand.

The EIA and IEA both project massive increases in Saudi production capacity through 2020 in ways that track broadly with the previous estimates referred to in the Saudi Seventh Development Plan. As is shown in Chart 7.9, the EIA reference case for 2002 projects that Saudi production capacity will rise from 10.6 MMBD in 1995 and 11.4 MMBD in 2000, to 12.5 MMBD by 2005, 14.6 MMBD by 2010, 18.2 MMBD by 2015, and 22.1MMBD by 2020.[156] This is an increase of 94% between 2000 and 2020.[157]

To put these figures in perspective, the EIA estimates that Saudi production capacity made up roughly 50% of total Gulf capacity in 1997, and roughly 15% of world production capacity. Chart 7.10 shows that the EIA projects that Saudi production capacity will provide 48% of total Gulf capacity in 2010, and over 14% of world production capacity. It estimates that Saudi production capacity will provide 52% of total Gulf capacity, and over 18% of world production capacity, in 2020.[158] Put differently, Saudi Arabia provided over 20% of all world oil exports in 1995. The EIA projects that it will provide well over 30% of all world oil exports, in 2020.[159] IEA projections indicate that Saudi production will rise somewhat faster than the EIA projections estimate, but both sets of data reach similar conclusions regarding production levels in 2020; the same is true of OPEC projections.

Neither the EIA nor IEA make projections of actual future exports by country. Chart 7.11 shows, however, that the EIA projects that total Gulf oil exports will rise from 14.8 MMBD in 2000, to 33.5 MMBD in 2020. This is an increase of over 125% between 2000 and 2020.

Table 7.4 and Chart 7.12 show that Gulf oil exports will also be even more "globalized" in 2020 than they are today. They are projected to remain at 33% of the industrialized world's imports in 2020, but will rise from 39% of the nonindustrialized world's imports to 66%—an increase of 15.2 MMBD. In 1998, the Gulf exported 2.2 MMBD to North America, 4.0 MMBD to Western Europe, and 8.7 MMBD to all of Asia. In 2020, it is projected to export 4.9 MMBD to North America, 3.5 MMBD to

Chart 7.9

The "Swing State": Saudi Petroleum Production Capacity Relative to Gulf and World Capacity During 1990–2020—Part One (EIA Reference Case in MMBD)

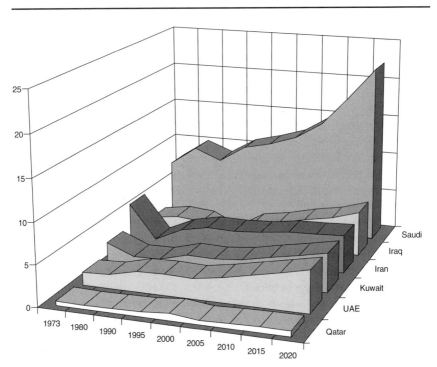

	1973	1980	1990	1995	2000	2005	2010	2015	2020
☐ Qatar	0.57	0.472	0.5	0.6	0.9	0.5	0.6	0.7	0.7
☐ UAE	1.533	1.709	2.5	2.6	2.5	3	3.7	4.4	5.1
▣ Kuwait	3.02	1.656	1.7	2.6	2.5	2.8	3.5	4.1	4.8
■ Iran	5.8	1.662	3.2	3.9	3.8	4	4.4	4.5	4.7
☐ Iraq	2.018	2.514	2.2	0.6	2.6	3.1	3.9	4.5	5.5
▣ Saudi	7.596	9.9	8.6	10.6	11.4	12.5	14.6	18.2	22.1

Total Gulf		—	18.7	—	21.7	25.9	30.7	36.4	42.9
Saudi Arabia as % of Total		—	45.95	—	43.35	48.2	47.6	50.0	51.53
Total OPEC		—	27.2	—	31.4	38.4	44.8	52.0	60.2
Total World		—	69.4	—	77.4	88.0	98.4	109.8	121.3
Saudi Arabia as % of Total		—	12.4	—	12.1	14.25	14.8	16.6	18.21

Sources: Adapted by Anthony H. Cordesman from EIA, International Energy Outlook, 1997 (Washington: DOE/EIA-0484 [97], April 1997), pp. 157—160; and EIA, International Energy Outlook, 2002 (Washington: DOE/EIA-0484 [2002], March 2002), Table D1.

Chart 7.10
Saudi Petroleum Production Capacity Relative to Gulf and World Capacity During 1990–2020—Part Two (EIA Reference Case in MMBD)

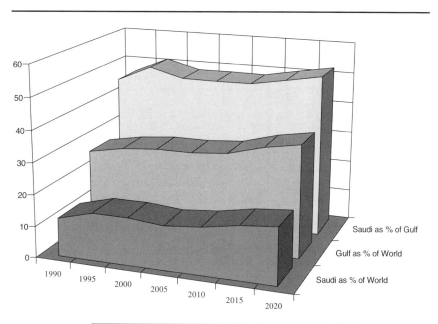

	1990	1995	2000	2005	2010	2015	2020
■ Saudi as % of World	12	15	15	14	15	17	18
▨ Gulf as % of World	27	29	30	30	31	34	36
□ Saudi as % of Gulf	46	51	48	48	48	50	52

Sources: Adapted by Anthony H. Cordesman from EIA, *International Energy Outlook, 1997* (Washington: DOE/EIA-0484 [97], April 1997), pp. 157–160; *International Energy Outlook, 2002* (Washington: DOE/EIA-0484 [2002], March 2002), Table D1;and *International Energy Outlook, 2002* (Washington: DOE/EIA-0484 [2002], March 2002), Table D1, p. 239.

Western Europe, and 20.8 MMBD to all of Asia.[160] Since most of the increase in Gulf exports is projected to go to East Asia, the total volume that must move by tanker would have to increase by over 150%, requiring a stable, on-time flow of tanker traffic from the Gulf, Red Sea, and Indian Ocean area that would be well over 2.5 times today's capacity.[161]

Shaping Future Saudi Oil Production Capacity and Exports: The Saudi Approach

These Western estimates of increased Saudi production capacity, however, are based on computer models of estimated global demand, not on

Table 7.4
Estimated Trends in World Oil Exports by Supplier and Destination (in Millions of Barrels Per Day)

Exporting Region	Importing Region								
	Industrialized				Non-Industrialized			
	North America	Western Europe	Asia	Total Industrial	Pacific Rim	China	Rest of World	Total Nonindustrial
2000								
OPEC								
Persian Gulf	2.6	3.2	4.1	9.9	2.7	0.7	1.5	4.9
North Africa	0.3	2.0	0	2.3	0	0	0.1	0.1
West Africa	0.9	0.5	0	1.4	0.1	0	0.1	0.2
South America	1.6	0.2	0	1.8	0.1	0	0.8	0.9
Asia	0.1	0	0.3	0.4	0.2	0	0	0.2
Total OPEC	5.4	5.9	4.5	15.8	3.2	0.7	2.5	6.4
Non-OPEC								
North Sea	0.6	4.7	0	5.3	0	0	2.2	2.5
Caribbean Basin	1.8	0.2	0	2.1	0.3	0	0.1	0.3
FSU	0	1.6	0	1.7	0.2	0	0.1	0.3
Other Non-OPEC	2.9	1.3	0.9	5.1	1.9	0.4	1.1	3.4
Total Non-OPEC	5.3	7.8	1.0	14.1	2.4	0.4	3.4	6.2
World Total	10.7	13.7	5.4	29.9	5.6	1.1	5.9	12.5

2020

OPEC								
Persian Gulf	4.9	3.5	5.0	13.4	8.7	7.1	4.3	20.1
North Africa	0.5	2.3	0	2.7	0.1	0	0.4	0.6
West Africa	0.9	0.9	0.2	2.0	0.1	0	0.9	1.0
South America	3.3	0.3	0.1	3.7	0.1	0	1.4	1.5
Asia	0.1	0	0.1	0.2	0.2	0.1	0	0.3
Total OPEC	9.7	6.9	5.5	22.0	9.3	7.2	7.0	23.4
Non-OPEC								
North Sea	0.5	3.9	0	4.4	0.1	0	0	0.1
Caribbean Basin	3.4	0.4	0.1	3.9	0.2	0	1.5	1.6
FSU	0.4	3.1	0.5	4.0	1.4	0.1	0.2	1.7
Other Non-OPEC	4.2	1.3	0.4	5.9	2.2	0.3	1.2	3.7
Total Non-OPEC	8.4	8.8	1.0	18.2	3.9	0.4	2.9	7.2
World Total	18.2	15.6	6.5	40.3	13.1	7.6	9.9	30.6

Source: Adapted by Anthony H. Cordesman from estimates in EIA, *International Energy Outlook, 2002* (Washington: DOE/EIA-0484 [2002], March 2002), Table D1, p. 38.

Chart 7.11
The Rising Importance of Saudi and Gulf Exports Relative to Other Exports in
Meeting World Demand, 2000 versus 2020 (EIA Reference Case in MMBD)

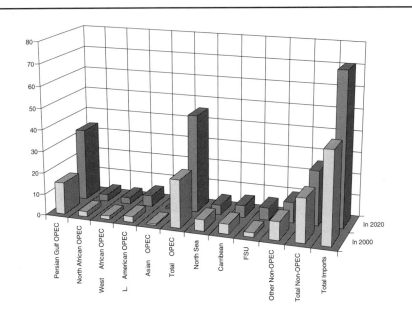

	Persian Gulf OPEC	North African OPEC	West African OPEC	L. American OPEC	Asian OPEC	Total OPEC	North Sea	Carribean	FSU	Other Non-OPEC	Total Non-OPEC	Total Imports
☐ In 2000	14.8	2.4	1.6	2.7	0.6	22.2	5.3	4.6	2	8.5	20.3	42.4
■ In 2020	33.5	3.3	3	5.2	0.5	45.4	4.5	5.5	5.7	9.6	25.4	70.9

Source: Adapted by Anthony H. Cordesman from EIA, *International Energy Outlook, 2002*
(Washington: DOE/EIA-0484 [2002], March 2002), Table 11, p. 38.

Saudi plans. As might be expected from the previous description of Saudi
strategy, Saudi Arabia's longer-term goals for expanding oil production
capacity and exports are market-driven and evolutionary, rather than tied
to some model of the world's future need for oil production capacity and
exports. Saudi Arabia also is constantly reconsidering how best to implement its energy strategy.

In early 1991, Saudi Aramco announced new plans to increase capacity
to 10 MMBD. In April 1995, former Saudi Oil Minister Hisham Nazer
stated that the country's oil industry was undergoing a "restructuring" in
an effort to ensure "stable petroleum revenues" and "an efficient oil industry capable of a timely response to the changing market." The new expansion plans he announced included five projects that ultimately could cost

Chart 7.12
The Globalization of Gulf Oil Exports in 2020 (in MMBD)

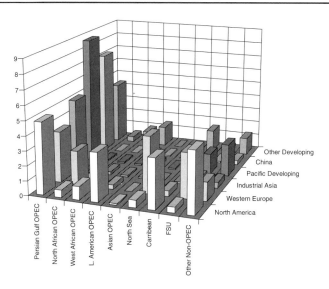

	Persian Gulf OPEC	North African OPEC	West African OPEC	L. American OPEC	Asian OPEC	North Sea	Carribean	FSU	Other Non-OPEC
☐ North America	4.9	0.5	0.9	3.3	0.1	0.5	3.4	0.4	4.2
☐ Western Europe	3.5	2.3	0.9	0.3	0	3.9	0.4	3.1	1.3
▦ Industrial Asia	5	0	0.2	0.1	0.1	0	0.1	0.5	0.4
▪ Pacific Developing	8.7	0.1	0.1	0.1	0.2	0.1	0.2	1.4	2.2
☐ China	7.1	0	0	0	0.1	0	0	0.1	0.3
▦ Other Developing	4.3	0.4	0.9	1.4	0	0	1.5	0.2	1.2

Source: Adapted by Anthony H. Cordesman from EIA, *International Energy Outlook, 2002* (Washington: DOE/EIA-0484 [2002], March 2002), Table 11, p. 38.

$3 billion. At the same time, Saudi Arabia continued to invest heavily in the development of lighter crude reserves.

Saudi Arabia announced plans in 1997 to keep its production capacity at 10 to 11 MMBD through 2005, while maintaining a cushion of at least 2.0 MMBD in surplus capacity. It has not announced longer-term goals for production or surplus capacity. Various officials discussed plans to increase the volume and share of light crude oil production, increase the vertical integration of its oil companies, and carry 50% of its exports in Saudi-owned tankers. The Kingdom also said it planned to keep expanding its petrochemical production and marketing, and has issued plans to spend a total of $34 to $50 billion on such projects during the period between 1995 and 2007.[162]

In mid-2000, the Saudi Ministry of Petroleum and Minerals projected no increase in capacity in Saudi Arabia proper beyond their current estimate of 10.2 MMBD before 2005. It said the Kingdom had no firm goal for future increases in capacity, beyond a broad goal of maintaining 2 MMBD in surplus capacity above the average level of actual production. Saudi officials denied, however, that they were seeking to preserve their role as a "swing producer," which they felt implied maintaining a very expensive investment in overcapacity that other OPEC nations would pressure Saudi Arabia not to use.

Saudi officials did acknowledge, however, that the country "did not object" to OPEC forecasts that called for major increases in oil production from 2005 onward. These plans require OPEC production capacity to increase from 29.0 MMBD in 1998 to 54.6 MMBD in 2020—a level similar to that projected by the EIA and IEA. The Saudi officials also noted that Saudi Arabia would probably continue to provide one third of all OPEC production, and that OPEC production would increasingly come from the Gulf, with as much as 85% of all OPEC production expected to be from Iraq, Kuwait, Saudi Arabia, and the UAE by 2020. Saudi Arabia announced plans in 2001 to increase its oil production capacity, especially of relatively light crudes, allowing for some decline in capacity at other fields; Qatif already had 750,000 barrels of shut-in capacity.[163] Minister al-Naimi stated that Saudi Arabia would "continue to maintain excess capacity to moderate price spikes whenever disruptions to supplies occur."[164]

Saudi Ability to Meet Long-Term Increases in Demand

The EIA, IEA, and oil company experts feel that Saudi Arabia can easily continue to steadily expand its production capacity if it chooses to do so and can find the required capital. Saudi Arabia has been effective in developing its oil reserves. Several experts feel that Saudi Arabia is the only Gulf country that currently invests its money efficiently in modern exploration and production capacity and that draws effectively on advanced Western oil production technology. They also feel that the Kingdom will never have a problem in obtaining suitable investment capital because it can always turn to foreign investors, or get foreign loans, if it cannot finance its own production capacity increases, as long as it is clear that the increase in demand will be sustained. As the world's lowest-cost mass-producer, the Kingdom will always be an attractive investment.

Other experts are concerned, however, that Saudi Arabia will need to make truly massive investments if it is to expand production to the levels needed to keep world prices moderate, and that the Kingdom can no longer finance these improvements with government capital. Some are concerned that Saudi Arabia's growing population and low prices (Saudi Arabia charges only $1 a gallon at the pump, although it also does not tax gas and this Saudi charge for gas alone is often higher than the U.S. charge before taxes) have already sharply increased domestic demand for crude oil as well as gas. As a result, future increases in domestic demand might offset a substantial part of Saudi Arabia's planned increase in oil production unless it can make a major increase in its gas production and distribution to substitute for oil.

It is too soon to resolve these differences, and they certainly involve issues that will provide years of warning in which to act. It is important to note, however, that Saudi Arabia's long-term expansion of capacity will be more uncertain in other areas of energy production. There are no meaningful forecasts of long-term Gulf gas-production capacity, actual gas production, domestic consumption, or direct and product exports. For the Gulf region, however, the early 2000s are expected to be the last years of a gas surplus.

Some experts have predicted that Saudi Arabia will have an average growth rate of 6.5% in domestic gas use, but that the supply/demand deficit will rise to 4.5 BCFD in 2005, 6 BCFD in 2010, and 8 BCFD in 2015 unless the Kingdom finances major increases in gas production capacity. While Saudi Arabia has total gas reserves amounting to between 170 and 215 TCF, much is associated gas and therefore is tied to the Saudi level of oil production. While upstream exploration is likely to lead to significant increases in Saudi Arabia's estimated reserves, it is not possible to estimate the impact of any such discoveries on Saudi production.[165]

CHANGES IN SAUDI ENERGY STRATEGY AND INVESTMENT POLICIES

Much of the Kingdom's ability to finance its energy strategy depends on whether Saudi Arabia can get most of the investment funds it needs from its petroleum revenues, assumptions about the efficiency of foreign versus state oil operations, and the merits of opening up the Saudi oil sector to foreign investment. At the same time, much also depends on the security of the Gulf and the extent to which Saudi Arabia will have to make political decisions about oil policy and production based on such factors as its need to maintain its rapprochement with Iran, the threat from Iraq, and political pressures from various Arab and Islamic countries.

The Problem of Oil Prices

The previous chapter pointed out that there is no way to meaningfully estimate future price trends. Chart 7.13 supplements that analysis by showing how sharp the variations in Saudi oil export revenues have been in the recent past. For what it is worth, those "experts" who do attempt to predict oil prices, despite the fact that there is no analytically meaningful way to do so, tend to divide into two conflicting camps.

Chart 7.13
The Value of Saudi Oil Exports versus Total OPEC Exports, 1992–2002 (in $US Current Billions)

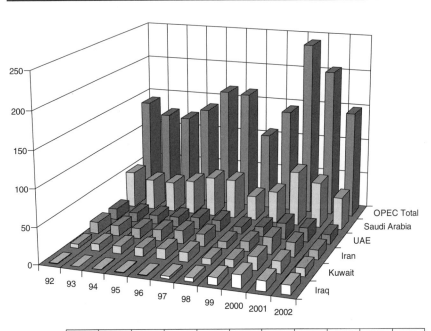

	92	93	94	95	96	97	98	99	2000	2001	2002
☐ Iraq	0.5	0.4	0.4	0.5	0.7	3.5	5.6	9.9	17.2	13.9	12.3
☐ Kuwait	5.9	9.4	10.3	11.7	13.5	13.3	8.2	10.9	18.9	16.6	11.5
▨ Iran	15.5	14	13.8	15.4	18	16.3	10.1	13.9	23	19.9	13.6
▧ UAE	15.2	12.7	12.6	13.5	16.1	15.8	10.2	13.3	21.9	18.9	13.4
☐ Saudi Arabia	50.7	42.5	41.9	46.9	54.9	54.7	34.2	43.9	75.3	63.1	44.9
▨ OPEC Total	140.4	124.3	121.4	136.3	165.5	163.5	106.2	143.2	241.2	204.2	148.1

Source: Cambridge Energy Research Associates Advisory Services, "OPEC Tilts to Market Share," *World Oil Watch*(Winter 2002), p. 28.

On the one hand, there are experts who argue that production capacity will rise sharply, and that low-cost producers like Saudi Arabia will have to meet their economic needs by maximizing production and driving higher cost producers to reduce their production. This same set of arguments leads some experts to believe that the oil crash may actually have served Saudi Arabia's longer-term interests by deterring the development of alternative energy sources, including increasingly economical "unconventional" oil sources, such as Canadian tar sands and Venezuelan orimulsion, and by discouraging marginal, non-OPEC oil production investment.

On the other hand, there are experts who feel that current estimates of the world's oil reserves are overstated, as are estimates of the probable future increases in proved oil reserves that will be made in areas outside of the OPEC countries. These experts predict a future where the ratio of supply to demand will decrease steadily in the mid-term, producing a significant increase in oil prices from 2010 to 2020. Work by the IEA, for example, includes a study of the risk that technology gain and the discovery of new reserves may decline sharply during the next few years. The IEA projects a much more rapid increase in the mid-term demand for Gulf oil than the US. Department of Energy and the EIA.[166]

Saudi oil experts have never believed that it is possible to make such forecasts. As a result of the oil crash and oil boom, however, Saudi Arabia has become more proactive in trying to stabilize oil prices within a band that can ease both its current cash flow problems and provide a more stable basis for investment planning. Saudi Oil Minister al-Naimi has been a leading spokesman for such a price band:[167]

> [A]fter careful study and analysis, we in Saudi Arabia and within OPEC arrived at the conclusion that the right price for oil is about $25 dollars per barrel for the OPEC basket. We realize, however this cannot or should not be fixed for all times. In truth, the market decides what the price of oil will be at any given day and moment.
>
> For Saudi Arabia, $25 dollars per barrel is a desirable goal that would be durable. To achieve this target, we created a band of $22 to $28 dollars per barrel, either side of which would trigger an immediate need for correction. We believe there is a general support from the majority of participants in the oil markets, including OPEC and non-OPEC producers, the oil companies and the major consumers.

As part of this effort, Saudi Arabia has called for the creation of a permanent body to promote a dialogue between oil exporters and importers. Crown Prince Abdullah set forth this idea in some detail in a speech to the Seventh International Energy Forum in Riyadh on November 17, 2001.[168]

> To achieve these goals, the Kingdom suggests considering the establishment of a permanent secretariat for the energy forum to work toward promoting a continuous dialogue between producers and consumers. This dialogue should include the industry and all other parties interested in energy matters. The establishment of such a secretariat will enhance our dialogue and make it more regular and more conducive to achieving our goals.
>
> Our efforts to ensure oil market stability and oil supply continuity require similar efforts by consumers because of the importance of cooperation among all parties to achieve this objective. We are concerned as more calls are made to discriminate against oil, or when doubt is cast on the continuity of its supplies. It worries us when we are blamed for the rise of oil prices to the final consumers.

Saudi Oil Minister al-Naimi explained the need for dialogue as follows:[169]

> The world oil market has witnessed successive developments that were of major concern not only to producers, but also to consumers, governments, and people. The fluctuations in crude oil prices, the supply and demand situation of certain products, taxation policies and inventory management in major consumption areas, as well as environmental specifications and restrictions ... have highlighted the urgent need for dialogue between producing and consuming countries to reach acceptable formulas to ensure the stability of prices, the continuity of supplies and the transparency of demand.
>
> They have also shown the urgent need for detailed information about supply and demand in order to make an accurate assessment of the market and its future course and adopt suitable policies necessary for market stability. It is important in this context to enlarge the scope of cooperation to set up a global energy database starting with data exchange among the various concerned world organizations ... and to hold periodic meetings to obtain timely and accurate information. The availability of such information is a necessary condition for market stability.

This announcement was followed by the creation of a committee to study proposals for the creation of a new permanent secretariat to the International Energy Forum headed by Prince Abdulaziz bin Salman bin Abdulaziz in February 2001. Al-Naimi announced on April 7, 2002, that such a secretariat would be established by the end of the year, once its final structure was approved at the meeting of the International Energy Forum in Osaka in September 2002.

The Saudi proposal led to numerous debates over the role such a secretariat should play relative to the IEA and OPEC, the role of various exporting and importing governments, the views of oil companies versus consumers, and how to finance the group. Nevertheless, the International Energy Forum agreed to create such a group at its meeting on September 22, 2002. The new body was to be funded on a voluntary basis and be led by a secretary general, executive director, and advisory board. It was agreed that it would help coordinate monthly reporting, organize and facilitate the meetings of the International Energy Forum, and seek to create a database and models that would help producers and consumers agree on suitable production and stock levels and bands of prices.[170]

The Saudi Debate Over Investment Strategy

The uncertainties over the Kingdom's ability to finance both the massive investments it must make in the petroleum sector and the development of the rest of the economy have led to a debate over the need for increased near-term foreign and private investment in its energy sectors. As has already been discussed, there was little debate over potential the value of such investment in gas. However, there was a debate over whether foreign investment should be allowed in upstream oil development or only in gas and downstream production of oil products.

In the fall of 1998, Saudi Arabia publicly indicated that it was considering changes in its energy policies that would open up the national oil industry to foreign investment and allow it to fund long-term increases in oil production capacity, which would ensure that Saudi Arabia remains a dominant swing producer. It did not then explicitly distinguish between investment in oil and gas sectors.

Crown Prince Abdullah met with several major oil companies during a September 26, 1998, visit to Washington, including Mobil, Texaco, Exxon, Chevron, Arco, Phillips Petroleum, and Conoco, and invited them to make suggestions for cooperating in the development of Saudi Arabia's massive oil resources.[171] He held similar meetings with a number of European companies in Riyadh. These firms included British Petroleum, the Royal Dutch Shell Group, ENI, Elf, and Total.[172] This round of meetings was followed by a number of media reports that the Kingdom was considering foreign investment in upstream crude oil production, as well as downstream crude oil products and both upstream and downstream gas.[173]

The crown prince called for proposals by November 10, 1998, and a number of international oil companies quickly made it clear that they were interested in the projects that the Kingdom had already opened to foreign investment. Atlantic Richfield Co., Conoco Inc., and Phillips Petroleum Co. announced that they planned to submit project proposals to the Saudis. ExxonMobil also said they were interested in exploring for and extracting oil in Saudi Arabia.[174]

It soon became clear, however, that there was a debate within Saudi Arabia over what kind of energy development strategy the Kingdom should pursue, and what kind of foreign investment was desirable.[175] The main incentives for private and foreign investors to make large-scale investments were access to Saudi Arabia's massive oil reserves, coupled with its low extraction costs. On the other hand, Saudi Arabia's incentives in opening up its oil sector were the need for major investment funds for virtually every aspect of its energy sector, particularly the gas sector, and the need to find ways to reduce the broader financial pressures that had caused a long series of budget deficits. At the time the crown prince made his initiatives, the Kingdom's oil export revenues had dropped by over 50% from their 1996 level, and Saudi Arabia had a projected budget deficit of close to $8 billion. There were reports in October 1998 that Saudi Arabia had arranged a private $5 billion "bridge" loan from Abu Dhabi.

It also became clear that some in Saudi Arabia felt the Kingdom needed outside investment to modernize Aramco's operating procedures and technology base. The key question in this debate was what parts of its energy sector Saudi Arabia would open to foreign investment, and whether these investment opportunities would include upstream oil production, or only downstream oil and gas production activities.

One major argument for opening up the oil sector was that the Kingdom could then use its oil export revenues to fund other programs and eliminate its budget deficits. Another argument was that Aramco suffered from a lack of cash flow for exploration and development. Other arguments were that efforts at Saudisation have created some problems because skilled foreign managers and technicians had to be replaced with Saudis who lack their experience. Consequently, some felt that Aramco's management lacked experience, and that its employees' real skills were still inadequate.[176]

These views were opposed by Aramco, some in the Ministry of Petroleum, and by many other Saudis. Some of the opposition was nationalistic or the result of bureaucratic turf battles, but there were strong substantive arguments as well: Aramco is an efficient producer with a long history of operating in the Kingdom and of using some of the best technology and practices of American companies. Roughly 85% of the current Aramco workforce is Saudi, and it is unlikely that any foreign firm will hire equal percentages. Aramco can respond to the political and strategic needs of the Kingdom, and can accept a lower rate of return. Many of these Saudis have excellent training and experience, and as part of its efforts to increase the skills of domestic workers, Aramco trains 300 to 350 Saudis a year in graduate and postgraduate programs in the United States. Finally, Aramco does have the economies of scale it has gained over twenty-five years of experience in integrating oil and gas operations, and it is not clear that other firms or joint ventures can be as or more efficient.[177]

The views of the late Abdullah Dabbagh, then a member of Saudi Arabia's consultative Majlis al-Shura and a member of the council's economic and finance committee, illustrate the attitudes of many leading Saudis regarding these questions. Dabbagh was influential in business circles and was then the chief advisor to the board of the Council of Saudi Chambers of Commerce and Industry, which he headed for fifteen years. On November 19, 1998, Dabbagh gave an interview on foreign investment in Saudi Arabia's strategic upstream energy sector.[178] Dabbagh said that he believed the Kingdom would consider opening its gas fields to foreign investors, but not oil. "I would say it's a fair possibility that the government would look seriously at suggestions of investing in upstream gas projects. Gas will be limited because [investment in] upstream oil is out of the question. But I see a possibility that the government might consider favorably a participation by foreign companies [in upstream gas]."

Dabbagh said he would "definitely" support the opening of the upstream gas sector to foreign investors, and predicted that low-to-moderate oil prices, the need for advanced technology, and rising Saudi electricity demand would create opportunities in upstream gas. "For the time being, with the decline in oil income, and so on, it might be very hard for us to go it alone. The technology in gas has changed a great deal in the last 10 years or so. Gas is very important. We have to generate a great deal of electricity in the next 20 years." Dabbagh mentioned that Saudi businessmen had told him they would seek joint venture opportunities if foreign investors were given access to upstream gas projects. "A lot of businessmen would be interested in that. I am talking about deep-pocket businessmen. The majority of businessmen would like to see the country open up."

At the same time, Dabbagh stated that a number of senior Saudis opposed opening the upstream sector of Saudi oil production to foreign firms at a time when it had substantial surplus production capacity. These officials sought to avoid the entry of foreign firms into upstream oil production until it was clear that major new investment was needed to increase Saudi capacity and/or that the Kingdom really needed foreign funds. He said that Prince Abdullah had merely asked U.S. executives for ideas on developing Saudi Arabia's energy sector: "The prince opened the door for ideas. He did not commit himself to anything. We are rational enough to accept good ideas if they come along." Dabbagh added that it would not make sense to allow foreign investment in upstream oil projects in a country that already had more than 2 MMBD of unused capacity. He stated that Crown Prince Abdullah had held a question-and-answer session in early November with members of the Shura Council about his overseas tour, parts of which were televised. However, the council had not been formally consulted on the issue of foreign investment in the upstream energy sector.

In contrast, the United States, other Western governments and major international oil companies made it clear that they had great interest in opening up the oil production sector. On November 17, 1998, U.S. Energy Secretary Bill Richardson issued a statement publicly supporting an expansion of U.S. energy investment in Saudi Arabia, and announced he would visit to Saudi Arabia to encourage U.S. investment contacts. Richardson suggested that this would involve the Saudi upstream exploration and production sector.

Richardson told a news conference he understood some form of involvement in Saudi Arabia's upstream was possible.

> My understanding is that Saudi leaders want to see upstream investment and joint projects. They haven't been specific entirely yet. I think there are discussions going on with companies. Saudi Arabia's interest in opening its upstream market has been widely reported—hailed by industry as a potential major breakthrough. The U.S. government views this as a healthy development. We will encourage it and that will be one of the main purposes of my trip, to encourage this joint upstream investment in both Saudi Arabia and Kuwait.

Richardson seems to have reacted to both what Prince Abdullah had said and to guidance from the Saudi embassy in Washington. By the time

Richardson visited Saudi Arabia in early February 1999, however, a rise in oil export revenues had eased the Kingdom's investment problems. Richardson was told that the Saudis wished to avoid any foreign investment in oil production in the near-term.[179] Saudi Arabia's oil minister, Ali al-Naimi, publicly invited U.S. oil companies to submit proposals to utilize the Kingdom's natural gas reserves for industrial development, but he ruled out any access to its oil reserves for the time being. Al-Naimi spoke at a press conference in Riyadh after his meeting with Secretary Richardson and said that, "a successful proposal would be the one on the development of our industrial base being fueled by natural gas." He added,

> [T]hose companies who invest today to develop the industrial base of Saudi Arabia will probably be the ones that will participate in the exploitation of our upstream oil if and when it opens up. We are looking for concepts and proposals that deal with integrated projects, which as far as gas is concerned will give us an end product such as desalinated water, megawatts for increased power, and petrochemicals. In the area of oil we are looking at improving the efficiencies of our refineries, and we are looking for an improved production of lubricants . . . reasonable people do reasonable things—we have 261 billion barrels of reserves, we have over 80 oil fields and we are only producing from 8 or 9, we have 2 million barrels of oil per day extra capacity—we do not need to expand our oil capacity right now.[180]

During Richardson's visit, Saudi officials also raised the issue of foreign investment in electricity. They noted that Saudi Arabia needed about $120 billion for power generation projects over the next twenty years, with the annual demand growth for electricity in the Kingdom estimated at 4.5%. To meet this demand, the country must increase its power generation capacity from the current rate of 21,000 megawatts to 70,000 megawatts by the year 2020.

Oil Crash Becomes Oil Boom, and Oil Boom Turns to Oil Crunch

There is no way to tell what would have happened if the oil crash had continued deep into 1999, but this debate over foreign investment in the upstream oil sector took place at a time when the oil crash was about to turn into the oil boom. This may have decided the outcome within the Saudi government—although many Saudis feel that the West misinterpreted what Crown Prince Abdullah was seeking to do—and saw an immediate opening up of the oil sector where the Crown Prince saw a need for foreign investment in gas and oil as only a future option.

In any case, Saudi Arabia's opening up of the gas sector still attracted considerable interest from potential foreign investors, which led to the investments discussed earlier. Beginning in December 1998, a number of international oil companies submitted gas and downstream oil investment proposals to the Saudi government. Texaco Chairman Peter Bijur flew to Saudi Arabia to present a natural gas development proposal. Chevron Chief Executive Kenneth Derr said that his firm submitted plans for the development of all areas of Saudi Arabia's energy industry and was "very encouraged" by his meetings with Saudi oil officials. Arco, Chevron, Conoco, ExxonMobil, Phillips Petroleum (U.S.), Elf Aquitaine (France), Royal Dutch-Shell, and ENI (Italy) also made proposals for investments in the gas and downstream oil sectors. In July 1999, the Franco-Belgian TotalFina coupled proposals for upstream gas development and water desalination, with an offer to take over oil production in the Neutral Zone.

The Saudi response to these proposals was methodical and deliberate, reflecting a relaxation of financial pressure due to high oil prices. For months following al-Naimi's comments in February, little word was forthcoming from the Saudi government, and an Aramco technical committee gave a negative review to the proposals that had been submitted in May 1999. In late August 1999, however, Foreign Affairs Minister Prince Saud al-Faisal sent a letter to the chief executives of companies that had submitted proposals, assuring them that Saudi Arabia would begin taking bids by the end of 1999 or early 2000.[181] On September 27, the prince announced that the ministerial petroleum committee in charge of reviewing the proposals would submit a "strategic evaluation" to Crown Prince Abdullah by the end of October. "Once it is approved, the Kingdom will renew its call to global companies who presented investment offers to start negotiations."[182] Saudi Arabia also hired the American investment bank Morgan Stanley to advise it on negotiating foreign investment in the energy sector, including financing options and technological issues.[183]

On October 21, 1999, when Crown Prince Abdullah announced a broad package of legal reforms designed to encourage foreign investment, no mention was made of upstream oil. The fact that Oil Minister al-Naimi remained in office after a June 16 cabinet reshuffle also suggested that the Saudis would continue to rule out any near-term foreign investment in oil prospecting and production, although it is important to note that al-Naimi did not rule out such investment in the future.

Al-Naimi made his view clear in a speech at the Houston Forum on October 20, 1999:

> In philosophy and principle, Saudi Arabia is not against foreign investment in crude oil production and exploration. Thus, it is not an issue of principle, but an issue of whether foreign company participation can be mutually beneficial at this time. . . .
>
> The benefit of such investment for Saudi Arabia would not be in the finding of new oil or increasing our production or capacity. We already have plenty of reserves and idle capacity, and any production increase is subject to our commitments with other producers, especially within OPEC. What we

need, then, is not somebody to come along and produce oil or gas and sell it to others. We need integrated projects, where each chain of the link adds value. These projects could involve petrochemicals, electricity, water desalinization and so on. In other words, the needed investments are those which complement our industries, our national companies, not replace them.

I am happy to tell you today that many of the proposals which we have received do fit within our needs and within the criteria we have just mentioned. We are looking into these proposals carefully, with each receiving close consideration. Equally important, we are considering other new ideas and possible projects. We expect soon, therefore, to see the commencement of negotiations with companies to formalize the needed projects. In this regard, I would like this opportunity to make it clear that the concerned companies will have an equal and fair chance. Moreover, the proposals and information supplied by each will be kept completely confidential.[184]

In early January 2000, King Fahd set up the Supreme Petroleum and Minerals Council (SPMC) to review the various proposals submitted by international oil companies seeking participation in the Saudi oil and gas sector.[185] On February 15, 2000, he issued a royal edict authorizing Saudi Arabia's SPMC to approve agreements and contracts with specialized companies concerned with exploration, drilling, and production of gas and other hydrocarbons, with the exception of oil. The edict opened the way for the Supreme Council to award contracts either to Saudi Aramco or international oil companies (IOCs).

The council's second meeting was held on February 20, 2000. It was chaired by King Fahd, with Crown Prince Abdullah, and vice-chairman of the council, also present. In an effort to expedite gas-based projects and upstream gas development, the Supreme Council appointed the foreign minister, Prince Saud al-Faisal, to head a committee to contact IOCs to initiate negotiations in late March and early April.[186]

In April 2001, eleven IOCs, including Shell, Phillips, Chevron and ExxonMobil, held preliminary talks on upstream and integrated oil projects with the ministerial negotiating committee of the Supreme Council for Petroleum and Mineral Affairs. However, the talks focused on investments to develop known gas reserves and discover and develop new gas fields. This was followed up by the appointment of a full-time team to negotiate with IOCs, and a decision that Prince Saud would supervise negotiations. As a result, it was made clear that investment in the gas sector would now be permitted in the following cases:

- In areas where Aramco is already producing gas, foreign companies could invest in the postproduction phase.
- In areas where gas has been discovered, but not exploited, foreign investment is permitted in the development and postproduction phases.

- In areas where gas has yet to be discovered foreign companies can invest in exploration, development, production and postproduction phases.

On October 18, 2000, Aramco was placed under the direct control of the SPCM, chaired by the King. The council replaced Aramco's Supreme Petroleum Council, established in 1989, which had also been headed by the King. The SPCM became the main policy body overseeing the petroleum sector, and included key members of the Saudi government, such as the foreign minister, minister of petroleum, minister of finance, and CEO of Aramco.

At the same time, the Saudi Ministerial Committee for the Kingdom's Natural Gas Initiative made it clear that it was considering the three ventures by the IOCs described earlier. The ministerial committee provided the following clarifications regarding Saudi Arabia's policy on foreign investment in gas:

- The Kingdom is fully committed to offering IOCs world-class rewards for their investments in world-class projects. Furthermore, it will make sure that the fiscal terms to be applied to the core ventures (CVs) are appropriate to produce acceptable economic growth from exploration and production activities, as well as the midstream and downstream segments of integrated core ventures.
- IOCs will be free to produce and market all gas liquids associated with natural gas discoveries, but not crude oil.
- Long-term supplies of feedstock gas for the straddle plant project in CV 1 are guaranteed.
- Long-term supplies of feedstock (gas and liquids) for downstream projects are guaranteed until IOCs discover their own gas resources.
- Saudi Aramco will be a participant in IOC projects, not a competitor.
- Some of the power, desalination, and petrochemical projects that were previously described as satellite projects, have been included in the CVs.
- Additional data on CV 1 will be made available to IOCs.
- Details of a regulatory system will be officially published after approval by the Supreme Petroleum Council.[187]

This activity demonstrated the seriousness of Saudi Arabia's interest in foreign investment, and played a key role in the creation of the three awards the Kingdom made in the spring of 2001.[188] It did not, however, lead to final deals in the gas sector or provide any indication that the Kingdom would open up its upstream oil sector.

Future Need for Foreign Investment in Upstream Oil

The case for and against opening up Saudi oil fields to private and foreign investment has ideological advocates on both sides, as well as opposing groups with obvious sets of conflicting profit motives. Regardless of the interests of the IOCs, however, Saudi Arabia seems to be correct in calculating that it benefits most from opening up other areas, such as its gas sector. At least on the surface, Aramco seems to be a relatively efficient oil company and appears to manage its investments well. Given the economies of scale involved, it also is not clear that competition per se will give the Kingdom higher levels of efficiency and profitability. While Aramco may overemploy Saudis, it seems unlikely that any future private investors will not have to do the same. It also is unclear whether marginal reductions in the Saudi labor force are a form of efficiency that can give the Kingdom benefits that outweigh the social and political costs.

Ideological arguments that pit nationalism against idealized free enterprise confuse the issue rather than illuminate it, and resolving these uncertainties requires Saudi Arabia to base its energy strategy on analysis rather than ideology. The Kingdom must, however, perform two types of analysis that it never seems to have performed. One is a detailed venture analysis of the cost-benefits to the Kingdom of foreign investment versus reliance on Aramco. The second is a risk analysis of the Kingdom's total capital needs and the marginal benefit of foreign investment in oil production.

As a guess, the case for foreign investment in Saudi Arabia's upstream oil sector is likely to be marginal if real oil prices average $25 per barrel or more in constant 2002 dollars, but the Kingdom may well need to shift its capital resources elsewhere if average prices fall much lower. This is, however, a guess at best. There simply are not enough public data available to make such a judgment, or even model the issue in the most general terms.

It also is not clear that it can convincingly resolve the issue even if every possible form of analysis is performed. Not only are future oil revenues impossible to forecast, but also (as the previous chapters have shown) Saudi five-year plans and economic data do not permit more than the most generalized estimates of future investment needs.

Saudi Oil Production Capacity Strategy

Saudi Arabia has no clear need to depart from its present strategy for linking the size of its total production capacity to the trends reflected in market-driven forces, rather than shaping it on the basis of some kind of effort to predict the future. Stable increases in global demand have long lead times, and Chart 7.14 shows just how much the need for Saudi oil production capacity can vary, even if market forces are the only major factor at work. The highest estimate of the required production capacity in 2020 is nearly twice the lowest estimate, and shows just how serious all of the previous uncertainties and debates over price and investment really are. The

Chart 7.14
EIA Estimate of Different Levels of Saudi Production Capacity Resulting from Different Market and Production Strategy Conditions (EIA Reference Case in MMBD)

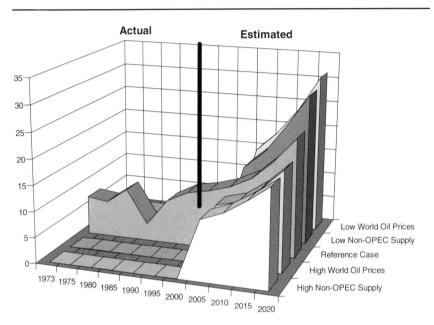

	1973	1975	1980	1985	1990	1995	2000	2005	2010	2015	2020
☐ High Non-OPEC Supply								11.7	13.3	15.9	18.9
☐ High World Oil Prices								11.6	12.7	15.6	19.5
▦ Reference Case	7.596	7.075	9.9	3.388	8.5	10.6	11.4	12.6	14.7	18.4	23.1
▣ Low Non-OPEC Supply								14.1	17.7	23.2	29.3
☐ Low World Oil Prices								15.4	19.3	24.4	31.1

Sources: Adapted by Anthony H. Cordesman from EIA, *International Energy Outlook, 1997* (Washington: DOE/EIA-0484 [97], April 1997), pp. 157–160; and *International Energy Outlook, 2001* (Washington: DOE/EIA-0484 [2001], March 2001), Table D1.

fact remains, however, that Saudi Arabia's decisions regarding the expansion of Saudi oil production capacity and exports are critical to both the Kingdom's future and the stability of world energy supplies.

There are three broad energy strategies that Saudi Arabia can pursue:

- *Limiting production in an effort to maintain high prices and maximize oil export revenues.* This strategy depends on the Kingdom's being able to persuade enough competing oil exporters to limit their production to levels that will produce more of a marginal increase in oil prices over time than would normal market forces. It also depends on Saudi and other oil exporters' ability to create a new equilibrium between supply and demand so that the net real oil export revenues to the Kingdom will actually be higher than if Saudi Arabia maximized production. Saudi Arabia pursued some aspects of this strategy in response to the oil crash of 1998.

- *Maximizing production capacity to recapture market share and marginalize high cost producers.* This strategy is both the most radical option and the most theoretical. It would require Saudi Arabia to accept a cut in near-term oil export revenues, but it would potentially change the oil industry by driving out higher cost producers. As a result, it would increase Saudi Arabia's mid- and long-term market share and future Saudi oil export revenues.

- *Responding to market forces by increasing oil production capacity to try to maintain both moderate prices and a high output of oil to maximize oil export revenues, while maintaining a margin of surplus production capacity to ensure the stability of both future prices and a high volume of demand for Saudi oil.* This strategy calls for a major rise in oil production capacity to provide exports and in gas production to meet domestic private and industrial demand. It also requires increasing Saudi and foreign investment in downstream operations and product output to maximize value added sales from oil.

It seems likely that Saudi Arabia's future choices will be pragmatic and based on market conditions—as they have been in the past—and that the Kingdom will shift its plans in whatever direction is required. The previous two chapters have, however, shown that Saudi Arabia does not seek to make major steady increases in its oil export revenues, and has no practical hope of diversifying to the extent that it can afford not to increase production capacity as long as this path leads to such increases in oil export revenues.

The Impact of Limiting Production to Maintain High Prices and Maximize Oil Export Revenues

More radical production and production capacity strategies do not seem to offer the Kingdom any clear benefit and could create massive new problems. A production strategy of limiting production to maintain high prices and maximize oil export revenues depends so heavily on the Kingdom's being able to persuade enough competing oil exporters to limit their production that it simply is not practical. In fact, it is a strategy that makes much more sense for countries with much smaller petroleum reserves, lower production capacity, and higher production costs that may try to impose on Saudi Arabia.

OPEC already provides Saudi Arabia with about as many benefits as it is ever likely to get from trying to raise prices by limiting production. As has been noted earlier, however, the end result has often been the opposite of what Saudi Arabia desires. Saudi Arabia is forced to cut production disproportionately, and the net real oil export revenues to the Kingdom would actually be higher if Saudi Arabia was not a member of OPEC. Saudi Arabia pursued some aspects of this strategy in response to the oil crash of 1998.

It would be virtually impossible for the Kingdom to do more than OPEC can to persuade other exporting countries to reduce their marginal output to levels that would actually give Saudi Arabia more of a marginal increase in oil revenues over time than would normal market forces. Unlike OPEC, success would also depend on Saudi and other oil exporters' ability to create a lasting new equilibrium between supply and demand over time and precisely adapt the production level to keep supply marginally under global demand. As OPEC demonstrated to its detriment during the oil crash of 1997–1998, it is far easier to model the proper level of production quotas on a spreadsheet than it is to execute them even in the short-term.

The Impact of a Maximum Market Share Strategy

Again, in theory Saudi Arabia would have potential advantage in pursuing a maximum market share strategy because its oil is so cheap to produce. Saudi Arabia can produce five different grades of crude oil and meet a wide range of demands. When oil prices fall, it caps production of some of its lower-grade Arabian Heavy crude, and instead pumps the more valuable Arab Extra Light crude from fields like its new Shaybah field in the Empty Quarter. This not only allows the Kingdom to keep production costs low, but also produces higher value oil products per barrel when refined. Additionally, Shaybah, which began production in July 1998, pumps 500,000 barrels of oil a day and has production costs of less than $2 barrel. Shaybah, which cost nearly $3 billion to develop, has proven reserves of 14.3 billion barrels of oil and an estimated life of seventy-five years. As Saudi Aramco's CEO, Abdullah Jum'ah, put it, "We will be here for a long time. When the oil runs out, the field will remain active for another 75 years producing gas."[189]

If Saudi Arabia maximized its production to near capacity to increase its market share in a period of low prices, this would price oil at levels that would be so low that other producers would have to shut in high-cost wells. The marginal return on investment in other regions would be far less attractive and cause massive restructuring throughout the oil industry. It would put severe pressure on the ability of high-cost producers in other regions like the Caspian, the United States, and Western Canada. To maintain production, it would tend to freeze production in North Sea and West Africa to compete and attract investment in increasing their volume of production, although Mexico, Venezuela, Libya, and Algeria are also estimated to be low-cost producers and would benefit in terms of increased production.[190]

The problem with such a theoretical market share strategy is that it is so dependent on political factors, global economic conditions, and Saudi ability to manipulate global access and demand over time that it might well not work in practice. It would be extremely costly to attempt in the short run, and Saudi Arabia might find it to be unaffordable to even attempt it. Such an attempt would mean much lower revenues for the Kingdom and much higher investment cost over a short-term period. It would also mean further short-to-mid-term cuts in the Saudi budget and taking the political risks inherent in economic reforms.

Such strategy would mean serious tension with Iran, which is a relatively high-cost producer. It could worsen relations with Iraq because Iraq needs to maximize its oil export revenues and cannot take advantage of its status as a potential high-volume, low-cost producer for at least half a decade because of sanctions and limited production capacity.[191]

The other problems with such a strategy are several-fold:

- First, it involves a massive sustained Saudi gamble in macroeconomics over half a decade that is acutely sensitive to the future marginal impact of advances in exploration and production strategy in other regions.
- Second, it requires major efforts at true economic reform, plus considerable budget austerity and additional private investment.
- Third, it means a potential confrontation with Northern Gulf states.[192]
- Fourth, competitors may react by finding much more economic ways to shut in production and ride out the Saudi effort.
- Fifth, it would create a strong new motive for importers to substitute other sources of energy.

Finally, such a strategy might prove to be based on false assumptions about how easily Saudi Arabia can achieve and maintain the level of production required. One U.S. study estimates the need for sustained Saudi production levels at 11.0 MMBD.[193] These are much higher production levels than the 8 MMBD that Saudi Arabia has averaged in recent years.[194] At the same time, the investment required to provide the level of exports necessary to implement the "market share" strategy might have to be much higher, and could lead Saudi Arabia into the trap of massive spending on new capacity that would still fail to restructure the world oil market.

LIVING WITH UNCERTAINTY, AND DOING SO WITH AS LITTLE IDEOLOGY, AND AS MUCH PRAGMATISM, AS POSSIBLE

In summary, nothing the Kingdom does can eliminate major uncertainties over the cost-benefits of given Saudi decisions regarding its energy and production strategies, the future oil price Saudi Arabia can achieve at any given level of actual production at any given time, over the oil export revenues that result, and over whether maximizing production does in fact increase net revenues.

Good fortune during any given period can also lead to problems later. If world demand is relatively high, Saudi Arabia can maintain high net revenues without costly increases in production capacity. A strategy may lower net revenues if demand and prices drop. If world demand is moderate, it may drive higher-cost producers who are desperate for revenues to produce at a lower profit margin to compete with Saudi production, leading to lower Saudi net revenues. If demand is truly low, a Saudi effort to drive high-cost producers virtually out of the market could create a massive confrontation with Iran and other security problems, which would offset any economic benefits.

Saudi Arabia's combination of massive reserves, high existing production capacity, and low production costs does mean, however, that it will benefit over time from any major depletion of reserves in other countries that could raise oil prices, production problems caused by political or economic reasons, slow-downs in technology gain, declines in the finding of new reserves, or major increases in economic growth in any region. Only major new discoveries of alternative fuels or new technologies can prevent Saudi Arabia from receiving some combination of these benefits over time.

It is also far from clear that the outside world has much to teach Saudi Arabia about managing its oil and gas resources. So far, the Kingdom has always chosen pragmatism over ideology, and has balanced its risks rather than choosing extremes. All of the issues raised in this chapter are ones that are being debated by Saudi planners and oil experts, and it is clear from the previous examples that these debates take place with considerable sophistication. The one major area of future uncertainty is foreign investment in the oil sector, and the real-world answer is that the Kingdom is likely to seek this if it feels a clear case emerges for such investment and that such investment will benefit the Kingdom.

Saudi Arabia does not face the same investment problems in its energy sector that it does in diversifying its economy. Foreign and private investment in the energy sector should not be made on the basis of theory or ideology, but on bottom-line calculations based on cost benefit and the Kingdom's overall financial needs. It seems likely that the Kingdom may need to turn to foreign investors even in its upstream oil sector over time, but it is not yet clear it needs to do so—and it will always be able to attract such investment if the world oil market reflects a steady increase in demand. It should also be noted that it is one thing to seek such investment to free Saudi resources for investment in diversification and development, and quite another to fall into the trap of using foreign investment in the Kingdom's energy sector to make unsustainable expenditures on operations and maintenance or entitlement programs.

Uncertainty is the only thing that is certain. No effort by any government or combination of governments can bring true stability to world oil prices or the flow of oil revenues. The macroeconomic forces involved are far too great and the end result will be the same as trying to halt icebergs with the *Titanic*. There does, however, seem to be a good case for the broader exporter-importer (producer-consumer) dialogue of the kind proposed by Crown Prince Abdullah, which is now institutionalized in the secretariat of the International Energy Forum.

Having a formal, institutionalized dialogue on plans to increase future capacity, ensure safe export routes and infrastructure, and guarantee that investment takes place on mutually advantageous terms is likely to help reduce the kinds of swings in oil prices and revenues documented in this chapter, as well as reduce the tensions and misunderstanding that now exist over oil strategy and production plans. Such a dialogue cannot and should not prevent constant competition and adjustment to market forces. It can, however, allow nations like Saudi Arabia to develop as realistic a picture of future demand as possible and to react accordingly. This is almost certainly the best energy strategy from the Kingdom's viewpoint, as well as from the viewpoint of most other exporters, consumers and importers.

NOTES

1. Much of this text is adapted from the U.S. Department of Energy, Energy Information Agency (EIA) online database, analysis section, country analysis as of June 2001. Other sources include IEA, *Middle East Oil and Gas* (Paris: OECD/IEA, 1995), Annexes 1E and 2K; EIA, *Annual Energy Outlook* (Washington: Department of Energy, various editions); and EIA, *International Energy Outlook* (Washington: Department of Energy, various editions). The IEA estimates the Saudi share of world reserves as 25.7%; British Petroleum estimates them at 261.7 billion barrels, or 25.0% of total world proved reserves: BP, *Statistical Review of World Energy* (June 2001), pp. 4–5.

2. Conversions based on SAMA data. For the latest published reported in Saudi Riyals see SAMA, *Thirty-Seventh Annual Report* (Riyadh: SAMA, 2002), pp. 361–364.

3. EIA, *Saudi Arabia* (Washington: Department of Energy, January 2002), URL: *http://www.eia.doe.gov/emeu/cabs/saudi.html*.

4. Brad C. Bourland, *The Saudi Economy in 2002* (Riyadh: Saudi American Bank, February 2002), pp. 1, 32, 34.

5. Cambridge Energy Resource Associates Advisory Services, "OPEC Tilts to Market Share," *World Oil Watch* (Winter 2002), p. 28.

6. EIA, "OPEC Revenues Fact Sheet," December 2001, URL: *http://www.eia.doe.gov/emeu/cabs/opecrev.html*; CERA Advisory Services, "OPEC Tilts to Market Share," p. 28.

7. EIA, "OPEC Country Revenues," December 12, 2001, URL: *www.eia.doe.gov/emeu/cabs/orevcoun.html*, and EIA, *Country Report on Saudi Arabia*, URL: *http://www.eia.doe.gov/cabs/saudi.html*, June 8, 2001, and January 2002.

8. Letter from David D. Bosch, Aramco Services Company, November 15, 2001.

9. CERA Advisory Services, "OPEC Tilts to Market Share," p. 28.

10. SAMA, *Thirty-Seventh Annual Report*, as calculated by Bourland in *The Saudi Economy in 2002*, p. 34.

11. EIA, *Country Report on Saudi Arabia*, January, 2002.

12. Saudi Aramco, *Facts and Figures 2000*, URL: *saudiaramco.com*, January 30, 2001.

13. SAMA, *Thirty-Seventh Annual Report*, p. 417.

14. Saudi Aramco, *Annual Review, 2000* (Dammam: Altraiki Press, 2001); SAMA, *Thirty-Seventh Annual Report*, p. 417.

15. EIA, *Country Report on Saudi Arabia*, June 8, 2001, and January 25, 2002.

16. Ibid.; BP, *Statistical Review of World Energy*, pp. 4–5.

17. BP, *Statistical Review of World Energy*, pp. 4–5.

18. EIA, *Country Report on Saudi Arabia*, June 8, 2001, and January 25, 2002.

19. EIA, "Saudi Arabia," June 2001 and January 2002.

20. EIA, *International Energy Outlook, 2001*, Table A2.

21. *Oil and Gas Journal*, September 23, 1991, p. 62; "Special Report on Oil and Gas," *Middle East Economic Digest*, September 22, 1995, pp. 20–22; and BP, *Statistical Review of World Energy*, June 2001.

22. EIA, *Country Report on Saudi Arabia*, January 25, 2002.

23. IEA, *Middle East Oil and Gas*, Annex 1E; EIA, online database, analysis section, country analysis.

24. For example, see Bloomberg, April 12, 2001, 1050, April 25, 2001, 0512; Reuters, June 2, 2001, 0736; New York Times on the Web, June 11, 2001.

25. IEA, *Middle East Oil and Gas*, Annex 1E; EIA, *International Energy Outlook, 1997* (Washington: DOE/EIA-0484 [97], April 1997); EIA online database, analysis section, country analysis.

26. EIA, "Saudi Arabia," June 2001 and January 2002.

27. EIA, *Country Report on Saudi Arabia*, EIA onlinedatabase, accessed August 26, 1997.

28. SAMA, *Thirty-Seventh Annual Report*, p. 419.

29. DOE/EIA, *Monthly Energy Review* (Washington: DOE/EIA-0035 [99/03], March 1999), pp. 130–131.

30. EIA online fact sheet, accessed January 1, 1999; BP, *Statistical Review of World Energy*, pp. 6–7.

31. These figures include some product. Aramco reports that crude oil production was 8.1 MMBD in 1996, 8.0 in 1997, 8.28 in 1998, 7.565 in 1999, and 8.248 in 2000. Saudi Aramco, *Facts and Figures 2000*, URL: *saudiaramco.com*, January 30, 2002.

32. EIA, *Country Report on Saudi Arabia*, June 8, 2001, and January 25, 2002; DOE/EIA, *International Energy Outlook, 2001*, Table D.

33. Edmund O' Sullivan, "The Kingdom Faces the Future," *Middle East Economic Digest*, January 22, 1999, pp. 16–17, 33–41.

34. EIA, *Country Report on Saudi Arabia*, EIA online database, accessed August 26, 1997.

35. O' Sullivan, "The Kingdom Faces the Future," pp. 16–17, 33–41.

36. CERA Advisory Services, "OPEC Tilts to Market Share," p. 28.

37. BBC news, March 24, 1999, URL: *bbc.co.uk.*

38. *The Washington Post,* March 13, 1999, p. B1.

39. *Middle East Economic Survey,* October 18, 1999.

40. *Middle East Economic Digest,* March 26, 1999, pp. 4–5.

41. Xinhua, October 13, 1999. This section is from Garner's section in the "Geopolitics" manuscript.

42. CERA Advisory Services, "OPEC Tilts to Market Share," p. 28.

43. BBC news, March 24, 1999, URL: *bbc.co.uk; Middle East Economic Survey,* June 26, 2000.

44. *Middle East Economic Survey,* June 26, 2000.

45. CERA Advisory Services, "OPEC Tilts to Market Share," p. 28; *Wall Street Journal,* March 18, 2002, p. A-2.

46. EIA, "OPEC Fact Sheet," January 8, 2002.

47. CERA Advisory Services, "OPEC Tilts to Market Share," p. 6.

48. EIA, "OPEC," URL: *http://www.eia.doe.gov/emeu/cabs/opec.html,* July 6. 2001; "OPEC Fact Sheet," January 8, 2002.

49. CERA Advisory Services, "OPEC Tilts to Market Share," p. 28.

50. EIA, *Country Report on Saudi Arabia,* June 8, 2001, and January 25, 2002.

51. EIA, "OPEC," May 6, 2002.

52. EIA, "OPEC Fact Sheet," October 2002.

53. Brad C. Bourland, *The Saudi Economy at Mid Year 2002* (Riyadh: Saudi American Bank, 2002), pp. 8, 12; EIA, OPEC Fact Sheet," October 2002.

54. EIA, "OPEC Fact Sheet," October 2002.

55. Ibid.

56. Ibid.

57. Ibid.

58. EIA, "Persian Gulf Fact Sheet," URL: *http://www.eia.doe.gov/emeu/cabs/ opec.html,* February 2001.

59. EIA, "OPEC Fact Sheet," October 2002.

60. Saudi Aramco, *Annual Review, 2000.*

61. Reuters, March 4, 1997, 1337; EIA, *Country Report on Saudi Arabia,* EIA online database, accessed August 26, 1997.

62. EIA, "Saudi Arabia," June 2001, January 2002, and January 2002; , and online data in Table 1.1a, "World Crude Oil Production," URL: *http:// www.eia.doe.gov/emeu/ipsr/t11a.text.*

63. DOE/EIA, *Monthly Energy Review,* March 1999, pp. 48–50.

64. EIA, "Saudi Arabia," June 2001 and January 2002; and online data in Table 1.1a, "World Crude Oil Production."

65. Ibid.

66. Ibid.

67. EIA, *International Energy Outlook, 2002,* pp. 37–40.

68. BP, *Statistical Review of World Energy,* pp. 4–5.

69. EIA, *Country Report on Saudi Arabia,* accessed August 20, 1997.

70. IEA, *Middle East Oil and Gas,* Annex 1E; and EIA, *International Energy Outlook, 1997;* EIA online database, analysis section, country analysis.

71. *New York Times,* April 28, 1995, p. D-6.

72. EIA, "Saudi Arabia," June 2001 and January 2002.

73. Ibid.

74. *Wall Street Journal*, May 29, 1997, Special Section; *Hart's Middle East Oil and Gas*, Vol. 2, No. 5 (March 7, 2000); EIA, "Saudi Arabia," June 2001 and January 2002.

75. EIA, "Saudi Arabia," June 2001 and January 2002.

76. Ibid.

77. *Middle East Economic Survey*, Vol. 43, No.16 (April 17, 2000).

78. Estimates based on EIA and IEA working data; letter from David Bosch, Aramco Services Company, November 15, 2001.

79. Estimates based on EIA and IEA working data.

80. EIA, "Saudi Arabia," June 2001 and January 2002.

81. Saudi Aramco, *Facts and Figures 2000*.

82. "Special Report on Oil and Gas," *Middle East Economic Digest*, pp. 20–22; IEA, *Middle East Oil and Gas*, Annexes 1E and 2K.

83. EIA, "Saudi Arabia," June 2001 and January 2002.

84. Saudi Aramco, *Annual Review, 2000*.

85. EIA, *International Energy Outlook, 1994* (Washington: DOE/EIA 0484[94], July 1994), pp. 14–26; EIA, *International Petroleum Status Report* (Washington: DOE/EIA 0520[94]1, November 1994), pp. 6–7; EIA, *International Energy Outlook, 1997* (Washington: DOE/EIA-0484[97], April 1997); IEA, *Middle East Oil and Gas*, Annexes 1E and 2K; *International Petroleum Encyclopedia, 1993* (Tulsa: PennWell Press, 1993), p. 280; "Special Report on Oil and Gas," *Middle East Economic Digest*, pp. 20–22; Saudi Aramco, *Annual Review, 2000*; Saudi Aramco, *Facts and Figures 2000*, January 30, 2002; EIA, "Saudi Arabia," June 2001 and January 2002. Estimates of reserves have become increasingly more political in recent years as each major producer in the Gulf has tried to exaggerate its reserves and relative importance.

86. Saudi Aramco, *Annual Review, 2000*.

87. Ibid.

88. Ibid.

89. IEA, *Middle East Oil and Gas*, Annex 1E; EIA online database, analysis section, country analysis; "Special Report on Oil and Gas," *Middle East Economic Digest*, April 11, 1997, pp. 12, 16–17; Saudi Aramco, *1999 Annual Review* (Riyadh: Aramco, 2000); EIA, "Saudi Arabia," June 2001 and January 2002.

90. "Royal Visits Inaugurate Shaybah, Upgrade Projects," *Saudi Aramco Dimensions* (Special Issue/Royal Visits 1999), p. 13; Saudi Aramco, *1999 Annual Review*; EIA, "Saudi Arabia," June 2001 and January 2002.

91. "Special Report on Oil and Gas," *Middle East Economic Digest*, April 11, 1997, pp. 12, 16–17; *Wall Street Journal*, May 29, 1997, Special Section.

92. EIA, "Saudi Arabia," June 2001 and January 2002.

93. *Middle East Economic Digest*, September 19, 1997, p. 32. EIA, *Country Report on Saudi Arabia*, EIA online database, accessed August 26, 1997; "Special Report on Oil and Gas," *Middle East Economic Digest*, April 11, 1997, pp. 12, 16–17.

94. *Middle East Economic Digest*, September 19, 1997, p. 34.

95. *Saudi Arabia* (June 1997), p. 3.

96. *Washington Post*, May 14, 1996, p. D-1; *New York Times*, May 14, 1996, p. D-12; *Middle East Economic Digest*, November 29, 1996, p. 28, April 25, 1997, pp. 12–13; Reuters, September 25, 1997, 0746, *Middle East Economic Survey*, Volume 43, No.22 (May 29, 2000).

97. *Saudi Arabia* (December 1996), p. 4; *Saudi Commerce and Economic Review* (February 1996), pp. 13, 20–22; *Middle East Economic Digest*, March 21, 1997, pp. 11, 30–31.

98. EIA, "Saudi Arabia," June 2001 and January 2002.

99. *Middle East Economic Digest*, August 18, 1995, p. 3, March 21, 1997, pp. 11, 30–31, April 11, 1997, pp. 12, 16–17.

100. *Saudi Arabia*, Vol. 13, No. 1 (January 1996), p. 5.

101. See "Saudi Arabia's Petrochemical Industry Diversifies to Face Challenges," *The Oil and Gas Journal*, Vol. 97, No. 33 (August 16, 1999), p. 65+.

102. *Middle East Economic Digest*, June 4, 1999, p. 2.

103. EIA, "Saudi Arabia," June 2001 and January 2002.

104. *Washington Post*, May 14, 1996, p. D-1; *New York Times*, May 14, 1996, p. D-12; *Middle East Economic Digest*, April 25, 1997, pp. 12–13.

105. Ibid.

106. EIA, *Country Report on Saudi Arabia*, EIA online database, accessed August 26, 1997; "Special Report on Oil and Gas," *Middle East Economic Digest*, April 11, 1997, pp. 12, 16–17.

107. EIA, "Saudi Arabia," June 2001 and January 2002.

108. *Middle East Economic Survey*, November 1, 1999.

109. *Middle East Economic Survey*, Vol.42, No.15 (April 12, 1999), p. A7.

110. *Middle East Economic Digest*, Vol. 43, No. 45 (November 12, 1999), p. 32.

111. Saudi Aramco, *Annual Review, 2000*.

112. Saudi Aramco, *Facts and Figures 2000*, January 30, 2001.

113. EIA, "Saudi Arabia," June 2001 and January 2002.

114. EIA, *International Energy Outlook, 1994*, pp. 14–26; EIA, *Country Report on Saudi Arabia*, EIA online database, accessed August 26, 1997; IEA, *Middle East Oil and Gas*, Annexes 1E and 2K; EIA, *International Petroleum Status Report* November 1994, pp. 6–7; *International Petroleum Encyclopedia, 1993*, p. 280; "Special Report on Oil and Gas," *Middle East Economic Digest*, September 22, 1995, pp. 20–22. Estimates of reserves have become increasingly more political in recent years as each major producer in the Gulf has tried to exaggerate its reserves and relative importance.

115. BP, *BP Statistical Review of World Energy, 2001*, pp. 20–21.

116. EIA, *International Energy Outlook, 2000*, p. 46; IEA, *Middle East Oil and Gas*, Annexes 1E and 2K; BP, *BP Statistical Review of World Energy, 2001*, pp. 20–21.

117. EIA, "Saudi Arabia," June 2001 and January 2002.

118. Ibid.

119. British Petroleum, *BP Statistical Review of World Energy, 2001*, pp. 22–23; Reuters, May 14, 2001, 1027.

120. Saudi Aramco, *Annual Review, 2000*.

121. Ibid.

122. IEA, *Middle East Oil and Gas*, Annex 1E; EIA online database, analysis section, country analysis, accessed August 26, 1997.

123. IEA, *Middle East Oil and Gas*, Annex 1E; EIA pnline database, analysis section, country analysis, accessed August 26, 1997.

124. EIA, "Saudi Arabia," June 2001 and January 2002.

125. IEA, *Middle East Oil and Gas*, Annex 1E; EIA online database, analysis section, country analysis, accessed August 26, 1997.

126. Ibid.; *Middle East Economic Digest*, June 30, 2000, p. 10.

127. EIA, "Saudi Arabia," June 2001 and January 2002; Reuters, April 18, 2001, 0814; *The Arabian Sun*, September 19, 2001, p. 1, October 10, 2001, p. 1.

128. EIA, "Saudi Arabia," June 2001 and January 2002.

129. IEA, *Middle East Oil and Gas*, p. 307; EIA online database, analysis section, country analysis, accessed August 26, 1997, *Middle East Economic Digest*, June 30, 2000, p. 10.

130. *Middle East Economic Digest*, January 22, 1999, p. 16.

131. EIA, *Country Report on Saudi Arabia*, EIA online database, accessed August 26, 1997.

132. *Middle East Economic Digest*, September 13, 1996, pp. 2–3; IEA, *Middle East Oil and Gas*, Annex 1E; EIA online database, analysis section, country analysis, accessed August 26, 1997; *Wall Street Journal*, May 29, 1997, B-1.

133. EIA, "Saudi Arabia," June 2001 and January 2002.

134. *Middle East Economic Digest*, August 4, 2000, p. 28.

135. Reuters, May 14, 2001, 1027, June 2, 2001, 1345; Bloomberg, April 17, 2001, 1629, April 17, 2001, 0804, April 17, 2001, 0720, April 17, 2001, 0523; *Saudi Arabia* (May 2001), p. 5; New York Times on the Web, June 3, 2001; Associated Press, June 3, 2001, 17:57.

136. Energy Intelligence Group, *The Oil Daily*, Vol. 52, No. 139 (July 23, 2002).

137. *Wall Street Journal*, February 19, 2002, p. A-12.

138. Ibid.

139. *Wall Street Journal*, April 22, 2002, p. A-15.

140. Ibid.

141. Remarks by Saudi Minister of Petroleum and Mineral Resources Ali al-Naimi to the Council on Foreign Relations, Petroleum Industry Research Foundation, and U.S.-Saudi Business Council Conference, April 22, 2002, Washington, D.C.

142. Ibid.

143. Ibid.

144. "Saudis, oil group likely to sign mega deal," *Gulf News*, June 6, 2002.

145. "Prince Abdullah to meet with Exxon Shell on gas deals," *MENAFN*, June 7, 2002.

146. "Saudis, oil group likely to sign mega deal," *Gulf News*.

147. GrahamAllen, *The Financial Times*, August 1, 2002, p. 7.

148. Reuters, November 7, 1998, 0541; *Middle East Economic Digest*, January 22, 1999, p. 16–17; *Middle East Economic Survey*, January 18, 1999, pp. D-1–D-11.

149. Kingdom of Saudi Arabia, Ministry of Planning, *Seventh Development Plan* (Riyadh: Ministry of Planning, 2001), pp. 88–90.

150. Ibid.

151. Ibid.

152. EIA, "Saudi Arabia," June 2001 and January 2002.

153. *Saudi Arabia*, Vol. 18, No. 3 (March 2001), pp. 1, 3.

154. *Riyadh Daily*, September 22, 2002, p. 1.

155. Ibid.

156. EIA, *International Energy Outlook, 1999*, pp. 201–202; and *International*

Energy Outlook, 2001 (Washington: DOE/EIA-0484[2001], March, 2001, Internet edition.

157. It is important to note that these DOE/EIA estimates are based on computer models that are heavily driven by the optimization of production to meet estimated world demand at moderate oil prices. These models are demand-driven, rather than supply-driven, and this represents a critical weakness in U.S energy planning, which is matched by equally unrealistic planning by OPEC and the EIA. The models are not predictive, but rather estimate potential market demand at a given price and then creates the "supply" necessary to meet that demand. As a result, the models create estimates of future Saudi production capacity. The estimates are not based on any estimate of actual Saudi plans and intentions. Further, these DOE/EIA forecasts of Saudi production have been heavily driven in recent years by cutbacks in the estimates of the production capacity of Iran, Iraq, and Libya because of U.S. sanctions that lead the modelers to assume more production comes from Saudi Arabia.

Most oil industry experts feel it is extremely doubtful that Saudi Arabia will increase production and the rate estimated by DOE/EIA, or the very similar modeling efforts of the IEA and OPEC. Most oil companies keep their forecasts of Saudi production proprietary, but an examination of the working data on several companies indicates that their estimates now fall below the lowest range of the DOE/EIA forecasts. Discussions with Saudi government and Saudi officials indicate that Saudi Arabia has no firm plans at present to raise production above its present 10.2 MMBD worth of capacity. Unfortunately, no one can forecast either the impact of market forces on Saudi Arabia's efforts to increase oil production capacity, or its resulting production investments and exports with any accuracy.

158. EIA, *International Energy Outlook, 1999*, pp. 201–202; *International Energy Outlook, 2001*, Internet edition; and *International Energy Outlook, 2002*, Internet edition.

159. Ibid.

160. EIA, *International Energy Outlook, 2001*, Internet edition, p. 39.

161. EIA, *International Energy Outlook, 1999*, pp. 201202; *International Energy Outlook, 2001*, Internet edition; and *International Energy Outlook, 2002*, Internet edition.

162. IEA, *Middle East Oil and Gas*, Annex 1E; and EIA, *International Energy Outlook, 1997*.

163. Reuters, May 9, 2001, 1140.

164. Bloomberg, May 7, 2001, 2341.

165. *Middle East Economic Survey*, May 29, 2000.

166. EIA, *International Energy Outlook, 1999*, pp. 32–34, 201–207; EIA, *International Energy Outlook, 2001*, Internet edition; and EIA, *International Energy Outlook, 2002*, Internet edition, pp. 25–26.

167. *Saudi Arabia*, Vol. 18, No. 3 (March 2001), pp. 1, 3. Also see Bloomberg, April 25, 2001, 0512; *MEED Quarterly Report—Saudi Arabia*, March 28, 2000, p. 19.

168. *Saudi Arabia*, Vol. 17, No. 12 (December 2000), p. 5; *The Oil Daily*, November 20, 2000; *Platt's Oilgram News*, November 21, 2000; *BBC Broadcast Summary*, ME/W0668/S1, November 25, 2000.

169. *Saudi Arabia*, Vol. 17, No. 12 (December 2000), p. 5; *Petroleum Economist*, January 16, 2001; *Middle East Newsfile*, January 22, 2001.

170. *Middle East Newsfile*, January 22, 2001; *Middle East Economic Digest*, February 9, 2001, p. 12; *Energy Compass*, April 18, 2002; Canada News Wire, May 14, 2002; M2 Presswire, May 27, 2002; Kyodo News Service, September 23, 2002; Jiji Press Ticker Service, September 23, 2002.

171. *Business Week*, November 2, 1998, p. 58; *Wall Street Journal*, November 12, 1998.

172. Reuters, November 17, 1998, 1227.

173. *New York Times*, December 3, 1998, p. C-6.

174. Bloomberg, February 7, 1999, 0403.

175. Reuters, November 17, 1998, 1227.

176. *Business Week*, November 2, 1998, p. 58; *Wall Street Journal*, November 12, 1998.

177. Reuters, November 17, 1998, 1227.

178. Reuters, November 17, 1998, 0218.

179. Reuters, January 9, 1999, 0336.

180. Bloomberg, February 6, 1999, 1048.

181. *The Oil Daily*, Vol. 49, No. 162 (August 24, 1999).

182. Agence France Presse, September 28, 1999, 11:13.

183. *Hart's Middle East Oil and Gas*, Vol. 1, No. 3 (October 19, 1999).

184. *Middle East Economic Survey*, October 25, 1999, pp. D1–D4.

185. Simon Henderson, "Crucial Tests Await New Saudi Oil Council," *Policywatch*, January 24, 2000.

186. *Middle East Economic Survey*, Vol. 43, No. 8 (February 21, 2000), p. A5.

187. *Middle East Economic Survey* Vol. 44, no. 8 26 (February 26, 2001), p. A2.

188. Saudi American Bank, *The Saudi Economy: 2000 Performance, 2001 Forecast* (Riyadh: Saudi American Bank, February 2001).

189. Bloomberg, February 8, 1998, 0420.

190. Petroleum Finance Corporation, "Saudi Oil Policy Options—Time to Choose: Market Share or Price Defense?" Washington, December 1998.

191. Ibid.

192. Ibid.

193. Ibid.

194. EIA, *International Energy Outlook, 1999*, pp. 201205; EIA, *International Energy Outlook, 2001*, Internet edition.

Chapter 8

Saudi Arabia at the Start of the Twenty-First Century: Key Conclusions

Saudi Arabia faces a wide range of challenges as it enters the twenty-first century. These problems include foreign policy and security, internal political stability, Islamic extremism, demographics and overdependence on foreign labor, restructuring and diversifying the economy, and developing the oil and gas sectors in ways that meet the domestic challenges that are most likely to challenge Kingdom's long-term needs. All of these challenges are important, but Saudi Arabia is scarcely a fragile state or one without allies.

It is not foreign threats but internal challenges that pose the most serious threat to the Kingdom's future. The Saudi Arabia of the twenty-first century must evolve into a very different state from the Saudi Arabia of today. It must move from oil wealth to a more diversified economy or it eventually will sink into oil poverty. It may not need Western-style democracy, but it does need political reform, modernization of its government, and more advanced forms of consultation. Saudi Arabia can only deal with Islamic extremism if it reshapes its Islamic practices to make them more tolerant and more flexible and evolves a clearer picture of what Saudi society should become.

Saudi Arabia must deal with major population problems, sharply reduce its dependence on foreign workers, and shift its youth from dependence on the state to a competitive role in the global economy. Saudi Arabia must also shift its energy sector from one dependent on state investment to one with enough private investment to reduce the strains on the budget while steadily expanding production to meet world demand.

POLITICAL CHANGE

Although Saudi Arabia must remain sensitive to its Islamic character, it must also ensure that Islamic extremism cannot challenge the legitimacy of the government or block social and economic change. Saudi religious practices now make far too many concessions to hard-liners and extremists, and live in the past rather than adapt to the future—they oppose, rather than propose.

Saudi Arabia's political system must evolve if it is to preserve its internal stability. The Kingdom should continue to expand the role of the Majlis, and find ways of allowing peaceful debate of social and economic issues. It must preserve the almost-universal Islamic character of the Saudi state and society while resolving the differences between modernism and traditionalism. It needs to allow popular debate and increasing popular control of its national resources. It must come to grips with the issue of defining a rule of law that applies to all its citizens, and to the royal family as well as ordinary citizens. It should create better legal protection of human rights and provide for a uniform commercial code and fully competitive privatization, while resolving the inevitable tensions and conflicts between religious and civil law.

The leadership of the royal family should set clear limits to the future benefits its members receive from the state and phase out special privileges and commissions. It needs to transfer all revenues from oil and gas to the state budget, rather than allow some to be treated differently by members of the royal family and to ensure that princes obey the rule of law and are not seen as "corrupt" or abusing the powers of the state. The royal family already has the wealth to do this, and it does not take much vision to see that the Saudi monarchy cannot give 15,000 princes the same rights and privileges it once gave several hundred. The vast majority of the royal family will have to be cast loose from state support and forced to earn its own living.

The Majlis al-Shura needs to be steadily expanded in power, and in regional and sectarian representation, to provide an evolution toward a more representative form of government. The Majlis has made a good beginning, but it needs younger members, members who are moderate critics of the royal family, and some Shi'ites who are permitted to speak for this ethnic group. It must play a more direct role in reviewing the Saudi budget, and its debates need to be more open and reported in the media. It may be some years before Saudi Arabia is ready for an elected Majlis or National Assembly, but the Saudi government needs to be more open, and somebody other than the royal family needs to be seen as playing a major role in decision-making. The present closed, overcentralized process of government breeds extremist opposition.

Saudi Arabia must be given a "rule of law" that protects human rights and guarantees the right of peaceful opposition to openly criticize the government. A lack of repression is certainly more important in the near-term than a formal movement toward stronger representative government. While Saudi Arabia has never been particularly repressive, it must improve it's policies and place firm limits on its legal abuses by its Islamists and religious police.

A modern commercial rule of law is equally important. The private sector and foreign investment need to operate in a secure environment that makes Saudi commercial practices competitive on a global basis. The occasional legal abuses of princes, ministers, and the privileged, and the tolerance of excessive corruption, are dated remnants of the past.

POPULATION, YOUTH, AND A VISION OF THE FUTURE

Saudi Arabia should face the fact that its most serious threat is its own population growth. The failure of the Arab and Islamic world to confront demographic realities has been an act of continuing intellectual cowardice and one of the great disgraces of the twentieth century. This cowardice cannot be allowed to continue into the twenty-first century.

The royal family, government, and the people of Saudi Arabia must come to grips with the fact that the Kingdom's oil wealth is limited, that economic reform and diversification can only evolve slowly and face serious structural limits, and that Saudi Arabia faces a potential demographic crisis. Strong leadership is needed to persuade the Wahhabi Ulema that voluntary population control is needed and to convince Saudi families that they should limit their number of children. There needs to be a firm understanding that even the best economic development plan cannot maintain the present standard of real per capita wealth in Saudi Arabia without a sharper decline in the birth rate, and that population growth is a major factor affecting political stability.

At the same time, these same demographic pressures illustrate why the government cannot succeed in dealing with Islamic extremism by a combination of accommodating the most fundamental and regressive Wahhabi practices while forcibly repressing Islamic extremists that actively criticize the government. These policies are dragging Saudi Arabia back into a past that cannot be viable in the future and that makes the problems young Saudis face in finding rewarding careers and a valid place in society even more difficult. The royal family and government need to face the problem of social alienation and religion much more directly, and push for slow but steady reform. They need to realize that the present cost of such efforts is likely to be much lower than waiting and relying on the present policy.

Social reform requires religious reform and evolution. Islam is more than flexible enough to deal with any pace of social and technological change, but Saudi Arabia must encourage such change. The government, royal family, and all educated Saudis need to start asking existential questions about the future of Saudi social customs and religious practices, and about the role of young Saudis in an evolving society. Even today, most educated Saudi women face a dead end at the end of their education and most young men graduate into purposeless jobs that offer little real future or productive value to the economy.

The impact of the Kingdom's religious practices and demographics on Saudi society and its job market has been partially disguised by the fact that half of the population is still under eighteen and living with an extended family. Within the next half decade, however, something like 20% of the present native population want to acquire real jobs and careers. Unless Saudi Arabia succeeds in reform, it will have nowhere to go. Only radical efforts to stimulate the private sector and remove foreign labor can begin to deal with this problem.

This need for steady evolutionary reform does not mean Saudi Arabia should be an imitation of the West. Saudi Arabia must find its own path within these constraints. It is unrealistic and impractical for the Kingdom to attempt to adopt Western standards of human rights. The West needs to be careful not to be trapped into supporting the efforts of Islamic extremists who claim to advocate human rights and democracy as a way of attacking the Saudi regime. At the same time, Saudi Arabia does need to give its Shi'ites a special religious status and proper economic rights, emphasize the protections of the individual already granted under Saudi law, and sharply rein in the growing abuses of the religious police. The government must reestablish public faith in the Saudi legal process and the rule of law.

THE NEED FOR A NEW SOCIAL CONTRACT

Saudi Arabia's present structural and economic problems must be kept in careful perspective. None of its near- to mid-term financial problems are critical. The government may be acting slowly, but it has recognized virtually all of the nation's economic problems except the overwhelming population growth. Many of the solutions the government has identified are workable, and Saudi Arabia has ample time in which to take decisive action.

Oil Wealth or Oil Poverty?

As the previous analysis has shown, Saudi Arabia's budget deficit has already been reduced by a combination of higher oil prices and austerity measures. Saudi Arabia has been able to repay its foreign debt and has already financed much of the infrastructure needed to modernize the country. It is unlikely that the Kingdom will have to pay for another Gulf War, and many Saudi arms purchases have been "front loaded" so that arms imports in the late 1990s and early 2000s will cost substantially less than in the aftermath of the Gulf War.

There are many positive trends in the Saudi economy. Some of the increase in the governments domestic civil debt has gone into investment, rather than paying for services, the deficit, and foreign loans. These expenditures will eventually be repaid in the form of added future revenues. Foreign debt has been reduced to low levels, although at the cost of rising central government domestic debt.[1]

Nevertheless, Saudi Arabia faces serious economic problems that greatly compound the impact of constant social change, high birth rates, internal political divisions, and a "youth explosion." No one outside Saudi Arabia—and probably no one within it—can be certain of just how serious an impact the resulting tensions will have within Saudi society. None currently seem to threaten the government and there are few signs that a cohesive opposition is beginning to emerge. Nevertheless, the government can scarcely ignore the importance of such tensions, and it faces the added problem of dealing with a highly conservative Islamic revival at a time when it must move toward internal reform in modernizing Saudi society and dealing with the West.

Creating the Need for a New Social Contract

Saudi Arabia cannot live in the past or stay in the present. Society, government, and the economy must evolve relatively rapidly if Saudi Arabia is to preserve its internal stability. The government must continue to expand the role of the Majlis, and find ways of modernizing the economy and society that can win the tolerance of most of its traditionalists. It must replace "statism" with a dominant private sector, which means it must provide for a uniform commercial code and fully competitive privatization while resolving the inevitable tensions and conflicts between religious and civil law.

Saudi Arabia cannot ignore the political realities created by its welfare and entitlements programs. It should continue to ensure that oil wealth is shared throughout its society. At the same time, it must move beyond a petroleum- and service-based economy and a subsidized welfare state. This is not simply a matter of dealing with declining oil revenues per capita—it is a matter of creating a work ethic and economy that employs young Saudis, giving them a real career and share in the future of the nation, and steadily reducing Saudi Arabia's dependence on foreign labor.

Saudi Arabia must redefine its "social contract." It needs to look beyond oil exports to ensure that its budgets are brought into better balance and that its society and economy develop. It must increase revenues by directly taxing wealthier citizens, reduce state spending, and create a more balanced economy by eliminating most subsidies and converting to market prices. It needs to make a full commitment to privatization and adopt much more stringent restrictions on foreign labor that put far more native citizens to work. In an effort to tighten restrictions on foreign labor, the Kingdom is considering a proposal to double the cost of work permits for foreign laborers, increasing the fee from 1,000 riyals to 2,000 riyals ($533). The London-based Saudi paper *Al-Hayat* reported that the Kingdom expects to make 80 million riyals ($21.3 million) from the work permit fees.[2]

The State Budget, Subsidies, and Welfare

The government must reform the structure of the national budget, find new sources of revenue by reforming the tax system, and tax earnings and sales with progressive rates that reduce or eliminate budget deficits. At the same time, it needs to make the budget open and transparent and allow an effective debate over both the preparation of the budget and future five-year plans within Saudi Arabia's consultative bodies.

It should ensure that all income from enterprises with state financing is reflected in the national budget and is integrated into the national economic development and planning program, and make certain that all of the nation's revenues and foreign reserves are integrated into the national budget and into the planning process. It needs to reduce the amount of money going directly to royal accounts and clearly separate royal and national income and investment holdings. It should place limits on the transfer of state funds to princes and members of the royal family outside the actual ruling family, as well as transfers of unearned income to members of other leading families.

National security spending should be placed on the same basis as other state spending and be integrated fully into the national budget, including investment and equipment purchases. The government should also replace the present emphasis on judging purchases on the basis of initial procurement costs and technical features with a full assessment of life-cycle costs, including training, maintenance, and facilities, and implement specific procedures for evaluating the value of standardization and interoperability with existing national equipment and facilities, those of other Gulf states, and those of the United States and other power-projection forces.

Privatization and Encouraging the Private Sector

The private sector is the only force that can create real jobs and career opportunities for native Saudis and open opportunities to a wider range of investors. Saudi Arabia needs to carry out much more rapid and extensive privatization to increase the efficiency of its investments in both downstream and upstream operations. At the same time, privatization must be managed in ways that ensure all Saudis have an opportunity to share in the privatization process and that the changeover is not conducted in a manner that benefits a small, elite group of investors and discourages popular confidence and willingness to invest in Saudi Arabia.

Where Saudi Arabia does continue to rely on a major public sector, it should establish market criteria for all major state and state-supported investments. There may still be a case for a major state role in some aspects of oil and gas production and utilities, but the government should require detailed and independent risk assessment and projections of comparative return on these investments, with a substantial penalty for state versus privately funded projects and ventures. It should downsize the scale of programs to reduce investment and cash flow costs and the risk of cost-escalation. It should remove distortions in its economy and reform the underpricing of water, oil, and gas. It needs to enforce a firm rule of law for all property, contract, permit, and business activity and reduce state bureaucratic and permitting barriers to private investment.

The Kingdom needs to come to grips with the fact that no nation can isolate itself from the global economy and the growing role of multinational corporations. The government should encourage foreign investment and allow such investment on more competitive terms. Saudi Arabia currently allows only limited foreign investment in certain sectors of the economy, in minority partnerships, and on terms compatible with continued Saudi Arabian control of all basic economic activities.

Reform is measured solely in macroeconomic success, never in intentions, plans, decrees, or rhetoric. Some sectors of the economy—including oil and gas, banking, insurance and real estate—have been virtually closed to foreign investment. Foreigners (with the exception of nationals from some GCC states) are not permitted to trade in Saudi Arabia, except through Saudi firms. Protection should not extend to the point where it prevents investment in upstream or downstream operations, eliminates efficiency and competitiveness, and restricts economic expansion. Saudi Arabia needs to act decisively on proposals such as allowing foreign equity participation in the banking sector and in the upstream oil sector.

The government should consider creating new incentives to invest in local industries and business and disincentives for the expatriation of capital. At the same time, it must put an end to the present kind of "offset requirements" that often simply create disguised unemployment or noncompetitive ventures that act as a further state-sponsored distortion of the economy. Some Saudi firms and businesses are now subsidized in ways that prevent economic growth and development and that deprive the government of revenue.

Saudis need to learn to be truly competitive. Policies that strongly favor Saudi citizens and Saudi-owned companies in ways that block constructive foreign investment should be amended. Income taxes are levied only on foreign corporations and foreign interests in Saudi Arabian corporations, at rates that may range as high as 55% of net income. Individuals are not subject to income taxes, eliminating a key source of revenue as well as a means of ensuring the more equitable distribution of income. Saudi Arabia needs to tax its citizens and companies and ensure that wealthier Saudis make a proper contribution to social services and defense.

Population and Foreign Workers

The government must make good on its attempts to force radical reductions in the number of foreign workers, with priority for reductions in servants and in trades that allow the most rapid conversion to native labor. It must create economic incentives for employers hiring native labor and establish disincentives for hiring foreign labor. Saudi Arabia's young and well-educated population needs to replace its foreign workers as quickly as possible and will only develop a work ethic and suitable skills once it is thrust into the labor market.

State efforts to encourage Saudis to work and develop a work ethic are useful, but creating a climate where Saudis must work for a living on market terms and restructuring the educational system to focus on job training and competitiveness is key to the success of these measures. The government needs to create strong new incentives for faculty and students to focus on job-related education, sharply downsize other forms of educational funding and activity, and eliminate high overhead educational activities without economic benefits.

THE WEST AND THE PACE OF SAUDI MODERNIZATION

It is always far easier to call for reform that it is to implement it, and Saudi society does not make reform easy. The West needs to understand that most Gulf royal families can only make such changes as fast as their societies can accept them. In Saudi Arabia, for example, there is already a major fundamentalist reaction to the existing rate of change. Over-accelerating the pace of change would lead to conservative reaction rather than actual progress.

The West can only help Saudi Arabia if it accepts these facts and if it pays more attention to the Kingdom's needs for economic and social reform and makes fewer vacuous calls for instant democracy. Quiet progress is also more important than noisy gestures. The Saudi government often prefers to use private and informal methods in modernizing, supporting the Arab-Israeli peace process, and limiting the influence of Arab and Islamic radicals; the West and Israel prefer formal and visible arrangements. Israel has often made the mistake of treating Saudi Arabia and other moderate and conservative Arab states as enemies, insisting on formal arrangements as signs of progress.

Saudi Arabia cannot survive allowing Islamic conservatives and hard-liners to dictate the future structure of Saudi society. At the same time, it is important for both the West and Israel to understand that Saudi Arabia must preserve its Islamic character, avoid provoking Arab radicals, and minimize the risk of confrontation with Iran, Iraq, and Syria. For the Saudis, informal success is always preferable to formal failure—which is a lesson that the United States and Israel have found very difficult to learn.

Partnership is also based on respect and a clear understanding that any partner must give priority to its own national interests. Crown Prince Abdullah made this point quite clearly in an interview in the Lebanese newspaper *As-Safir* in June 1997,[3]

> We are friends with the Americans, this is known. But we are the ones who know our interests. We can't give precedence to their interests over our interests. We are Arabs and our interests are those of Arabs and Muslims everywhere. On many occasions we have to tell the Americans . . . you have your policy and we have our policy . . . you have your interest and we have our interests? Do you want weak friends who are of no benefit and burden you, or do you want strong friends?

The United States and the West also need to understand that Saudi Arabia has the right to make different choices about foreign and security policy and its approach to key issues like the Arab-Israeli conflict and Iran and Iraq. Such differences do not mean that underlying common security interests do not remain—the United States needs to maintain strong ties of friendship with Saudi Arabia. Its grand strategic and economic interests all depend on Saudi Arabia's continuing development as the lynchpin of any effort to create stability in the Gulf. At the same time, much depends on Saudi willingness to work with the United States and show flexibility in supporting U.S. interests as well as its own. No nation likes to admit its dependence on another, but the success of Saudi military forces ultimately depends on the effectiveness of U.S. power-projection capabilities. Saudi Arabia will remain as dependent on the West for security as the West is dependent on Saudi Arabia for oil.

NOTES

1. Data are taken from working papers distributed during the Royal Institute of International Affairs conference on Saudi Arabia in October 4–5, 1993.

2. Reuters, May 6, 1999.

3. *Middle East Economic Digest*, September 19, 1997, p. 25.

Bibliography

Abir, Mordechai. *Saudi Arabia: Government, Society and the Gulf Crisis*. London: Routeledge, 1993.

Abir, Mordechai. *Oil, Power, and Politics: Conflict in Arabia, the Red Sea and The Gulf*. London: Frank Cass, 1974.

Aburish, Said K. *The Rise, Corruption, and Coming Fall of the House of Saud*. New York: St. Martin's Griffin, 1996.

Ajami, Fouad. *The Dream Palace of the Arabs: A Generation's Odyssey*. New York: Pantheon Books, 1998.

Ajami, Fouad. "The Sentry's Solitude." *Foreign Affairs* (November/December 2001), pp. 2–16.

Al-Deeb, Khalid. "Gadhafi Calls for Libyan Withdrawal from Arab League, Criticizes Saudi Peace Proposal." *AP Worldstream*, March 2, 2002.

al-Farsy, Foud. *Saudi Arabia: A Case Study in Development*. London: Stacey International, 1978.

Al-Yassini, Ayman. *Religion and State in the Kingdom of Saudi Arabia*. Boulder: Westview Press, 1985.

Ali, Mohammad Said AlHaj. *Saudi Arabian Monetary Agency: A Review of Its Accomplishments, 1372–1411 AH/1952–1991 AD*. Riyadh: Saudi Arabian Ministry of Information, Safar 1412/August 1991.

Ali Sheikh Rustum. *Saudi Arabia and Oil Diplomacy*. New York: Praeger, 1976.

Ali, Tariq. *Clash of Fundamentalisms: Crusades, Jihads and Modernity*. London: Verso, 2002.

Alexander, Yonah and Michael S. Swetnam. *Usama Bin Laden's al-Qaida: Profile of a Terrorist Network*. Ardsley: Transnational Publishers Inc. 2001.

Amery, Hussein A. and Aaron T. Wolfe. *Water in the Middle East: A Geography of Peace*. Austin: University of Texas Press, 2000.

Amuzegar, Jahangir. *Managing the Oil Wealth: OPEC's Windfalls and Pitfalls.* London: I.B. Tauris, 2001.

Anthony, John Duke. "A Changing of the Guard in Saudi Arabia: A Personal Perspective." *Gulf Wire—Perspectives,* September 3–9, 2001, *http://arabialink.com/GulfWire/GULFWIRE.htm.*

Anthony, John Duke. "Saudi-Yemeni Relations: Implications for US Policy." *Middle East Policy,* vol. 7, no. 3 (June 2000), pp. 78–96.

Arab News, various editions.

Associated Press. "Syrian President Backs Saudi Peace Proposal," *The Desert News,* March 6, 2002, p. 4.

Badeeb, Saeed M. *Saudi-Iranian Relations 1932–1982.* London: Centre for Arab and Iranian Studies, 1993.

Bakheet, Beshr. "Developing GCC Stock Markets: The Private Sector Role." *Middle East Policy,* vol. 6, no. 3 (February 1999), pp. 72–77.

Baltimore Sun, various editions.

Barr, Cameron W. "Arab Peace Plan Faces First Round." *The Christian Science Monitor,* March 26, 2002, p. 1.

Beling, Willard A., ed. *King Faisal and the Modernization of Saudi Arabia.* Boulder, CO: Westview Press, 1980.

Benjamon, Daniel and Steven Simon. *The Age of Sacred Terror.* New York: Random House, 2002.

Bergen, Peter. *Holy War Inc.: Inside the Secret World of Usama Bin Laden.* New York: The Free Press, 2001.

Bin Sultan, Khaled. *Desert Warrior.* New York: Harpers, 1995.

Bligh, A. and S. Plant. "Saudi Modernization in Oil and Foreign Policies in the Post-AWACS Sale Period." *Middle East Review,* 14 (Spring–Summer 1982).

Boston Globe, various editions.

Bourland, Bradley C. *The Saudi Economy at Mid-Year 2002.* Riyadh: Saudi American Bank, 2002.

BP Statistical Review of World Energy, June 2002. Bournemouth, England: BP Distribution Services, 2002.

Brossard, E.B. *Petroleum, Politics, and Power.* Boston: Allyn and Bacon, 1974.

Brown, Anthony Cave. *Oil, God, and Gold: the Story of Aramco and the Saudi Kings.* Boston: Houghton Mifflin Company, 1999.

Central Intelligence Agency (CIA). *Handbook of Economic Statistics.* Washington, DC: GPO, various editions.

Central Intelligence Agency (CIA). *World Factbook,* various editions.

Chaudhry, Kiren Aziz. *The Price of Wealth: Economies and Institutions in the Middle East.* Ithaca: Cornell University Press, 1997.

Chicago Tribune, various editions.

Chowdhury, Abdul Quader. "Saudi Middle East Peace Vision," *The Independent,* March 5, 2002.

Christian Science Monitor, various editions.

Clawson, Patrick. *Iran's Challenge to the West, How, When, and Why.* Policy Papers, Number 33. Washington, DC: The Washington Institute, 1993.

Cleron, Jean Paul. *Saudi Arabia 2000.* London: Croom Helm, 1978.

Collins, John N. *Military Geography.* Washington, DC: National Defense University, 1998.

Collins, John M. and Clyde R. Mark. *Petroleum Imports from the Persian Gulf: Use of US Armed Force to Ensure Supplies.* Issue Brief IB 79046. Washington, DC: Library of Congress, Congressional Research Service, 1979.

Congressional Budget Office. *Limiting Conventional Arms Transfers to the Middle East.* Washington, DC: A CBO Study, September 1992.

Cordesman, Anthony H. *The Threat from the Northern Gulf.* Boulder, CO: Westview, 1994.

Cordesman, Anthony H. "After AWACS: Establishing Western Security Throughout Southwest Asia." *Armed Forces Journal* (December 1981), pp. 64–68.

Cordesman, Anthony H. *After the Storm: The Changing Military Balance in the Middle East.* Boulder, CO: Westview, 1993.

Cordesman, Anthony H. *Bahrain, Oman, Qatar and the UAE: Challenges of Security.* Boulder, CO: Westview, 1997.

Cordesman, Anthony H. *Iran in Transition: Conventional Threats and Weapons of Mass Destruction.* Westport, CT: Praeger, 1999.

Cordesman, Anthony H. *Iraq and the War of the Sanctions: Conventional Threats and Weapons of Mass Destruction.* Westport, CT: Praeger, 1999.

Cordesman, Anthony H. *Kuwait: Recovery and Security After the Gulf War.* Boulder, CO: Westview, 1997.

Cordesman, Anthony H. *Peace and War.* Westport, CT: Praeger, 2001.

Cordesman, Anthony H. *Saudi Arabia: Guarding the Desert Kingdom.* Boulder, CO: Westview, 1997.

Cordesman, Anthony H. *The Gulf and the Search for Strategic Stability.* Boulder, CO: Westview, 1984.

Cordesman, Anthony H. *The Gulf and the West.* Boulder, CO: Westview, 1988.

Cordesman, Anthony H. *Transnational Threats from the Middle East.* Carlisle, PA: U.S. Army War College, 1999.

Cordesman, Anthony H. *Western Strategic Interests and Saudi Arabia.* London: Croom Helm, 1986.

Dagget, Stephen T. and Gary J. Pagliano. *Persian Gulf War: US Costs and Allied Financial Contributions.* Washington, DC: Congressional Research Service IB91019, September 21, 1992.

Dawisha, Adeed I. *Saudi Arabia's Search for Security.* Adelphi Paper Number 158. London: International Institute for Strategic Studies, Winter 1979–1980.

De Gaury, Gerald. *Faisal: King of Saudi Arabia.* New York: Praeger, 1966.

Dekmejian, R. Harir. *Islam in Revolution: Fundamentalism in the Arab World.* 2nd ed. Syracuse, NY: Syracuse University Press, 1995.

Denoeux, Guilain. "The Forgotten Swamp: Navigating Political Islam." *Middle East Policy*, vol. 9, no. 2 (June 2002), pp. 56–81.

Department of State. *World Military Expenditures and Arms Transfers.* Washington, DC: GPO, various editions.

Dimensions, various editions.

Drake, C.J.M. *Terrorist's Target Selection.* New York: St. Martin's Press, 1998.

Dunn, Michael Collins. "Is the Sky Falling? Saudi Arabia's Economic Problems and Political Stability." *Middle East Policy*, vol. 3, no. 4 (April 1995), pp. 29–39.

Economist, various editions.

Economist Intelligence Unit, various country reports.

EIA. *Persian Gulf Factsheet.* March 2002. URL: *http://www.eia.doe.gov/cabs/ pgulf.html.*

Esposito, John L. *Unholy War: Terror in the Name of Islam.* New York: Oxford University Press, 1978.

Executive News Service. Online database.

Fandy, Mamoun. *Saudi Arabia and the Politics of Dissent.* New York: St. Martin's Press, 1999.

Financial Times, various editions.

Fisher, Earleen. "Syria Endorses Saudi Peace Proposal, But Faces Obstacles." *AP Worldstream,* March 6, 2002.

Flight International, various editions.

Friedman, Thomas. "An Intriguing Signal from the Saudi Crown Prince." *The New York Times,* February 17, 2002, sec. 4, p. 11.

Fromkin, David. *A Peace to End All Peace: The Fall of the Ottoman Empire and the Creation of the Modern Middle East.* New York: Avon Books, 1989.

Fuller, Graham E. "The Saudi Peace Plan: How Serious?" *Middle East Policy,* vol. 9, no. 2 (June 2002), pp. 27–30.

Gause, F. Gregory, III. *Oil Monarchies: Domestic and Security Challenges in the Arab Gulf States.* New York: Council on Foreign Relations Press, 1994.

GulfWire, *www.ArabiaLink.com,* various editions.

Guthrie, Andrew. "Saudi Peace Proposal." *World Opinion Roundup,* February 28, 2002. URL: *http://www.globalsecurity.org/military/library/news/2002/02/ mil-020228-252e5879.htm.* Accessed on August 21, 2002.

Halliday, Fred. *Arabia Without Sultans.* London: Pelican, 1975.

Hart, Parker T. *Saudi Arabia and the United States: Birth of a Security Partnership.* Bloomington: Indiana University Press, 1998.

Held, Colbert. *Middle East Patterns.* Boulder, CO: Westview, 1989.

Helms, Christian Moss. *The Cohesion of Saudi Arabia.* Baltimore, MD: Johns Hopkins University Press, 1981.

Holden, David, and Johns, Richard. *The House of Saud.* London: Sidgwick and Jackson, 1981.

Hunter, Shireen, ed. *The Politics of Islamic Revivalism: Diversity and Unity.* Washington, DC: Center for Strategic and International Studies, 1988.

Husband, Mark. *Warriors of the Prophet: The Struggle for Islam.* Boulder, CO: Westview Press, 1999.

Ibrahim, Saad Eddin. *The New Arab Social Order: A Study of the Social Impact of Oil Wealth.* Boulder, CO: Westview Press, 1982.

Insight, various editions.

International Institute of Strategic Studies (IISS), *Military Balance,* various editions.

International Institute of Strategic Studies (IISS), *Strategic Survey,* various editions.

International Monetary Fund, *Direction of Trade Statistics,* various editions

International Monetary Fund, *Direction of Trade Yearbook,* various years.

Jerichow, Anders. *The Saudi File: People, Power, Politics.* New York: St. Martin's Press, 1998.

Johany, Ali D. *The Myth of the OPEC Cartel: The Role of Saudi Arabia.* New York: John Wiley, 1982.

Kalicki, Jan H. "A Vision for the US-Saudi and US-Gulf Commercial Relationship." *Middle East Policy,* vol. 5, no. 2 (May 1997), pp. 73–78.

Kechichian, Joseph A. *Succession in Saudi Arabia*. New York: Palgrave, 2001.

Kelly, J. B. *Arabia, the Gulf and the West: A Critical View of the Arabs and Their Oil Policy*. New York: Basic Books, 1980.

Kemp, Geoffrey and Robert E. Harkavy. *Strategic Geography and the Changing Middle East*. Washington, DC: Carnegie Endowment/Brookings, 1997.

Kemp, Jack. "Saudi Arabian Peace Plan a Snow Job." *The Seattle Post-Intelligencer*, March 6, 2002, p. B5.

Kepel, Giles. *Jihad: The Trial of Political Islam*, Cambridge, MA: Belknap Press of Harvard University Press, 2002.

Kramer, Martin, ed. *The Islamism Debate*. Dayan Center Papers 120. Tel Aviv: Tel Aviv University, 1997.

Lacey, Robert. *The Kingdom*. London: Hutchinson and Company, 1981.

Lackner, Helen. *A House Built on Sand: The Political Economy of Saudi Arabia*. London: Ithaca Press, 1978.

Laffin, John L. *The Dagger of Islam*. London: Sphere, 1979.

Laffin, John. *The World in Conflict or War Annual*. London: Brassey's, various editions.

Lesch, Ann M. "Osama Bin Laden: Embedded in the Middle East Crisis." *Middle East Policy*, vol. 9, no. 2 (June 2002), pp. 82–91.

London Financial Times, various editions.

London *Sunday Times*, various editions.

Long, David E. *The Kingdom of Saudi Arabia*. Gainesville: University Press of Florida, 1997.

Looney, Robert E. *Saudi Arabia's Development Potential*. Lexington, MA: Lexington Books, 1982.

Macleod, Scott. "Anatomy of a Peace Plan." *TIME Europe*, March 26, 2002.

Majarian, Lynda. "Saudi Peace Proposal Is Public Relations Move to Raise Country's Image in American Eyes," March 4, 2002.

El Mallakh, Ragaei. *Saudi Arabia: Rush to Development*. London: Croom Helm, 1982.

El Mallakh, Ragaei, and Dorothea H. El Mallakh. *Saudi Arabia: Energy, Development Planning, and Industrialization*. Lexington, MA: Lexington Books, 1982.

Mansur, Abdul Kasim (pseud.). "The American Threat to Saudi Arabia." *Armed Forces Journal International* (September 1980), pp. 47–60.

Masud, Muhammad Khalid, Brinkley Messick, and David S. Powers. *Islamic Legal Interpretation: Muftis and Their Fatwas*. Cambridge, MA: Harvard University Press, 1996.

Matinuddin, Kamal. *The Taliban Phenomenon: Afghanistan 1994–1997*. New York: Oxford University Press, 1999.

McMillan, Joseph, Anthony H. Cordesman, Mamoun Fandy and Fareed Mohamedi. "The United States and Saudi Arabia: American Interests and Challenges to the Kingdom in 2002." *Middle East Policy*, vol. 9, no. 1, (March 2002), pp. 1–28.

Metz, Helen Chapin. *Saudi Arabia: A Country Study*. Washington, DC: Congressional Research Service, December 1992. URL: *http://lcweb2.loc.gov/cgibin/query/r?frd/cstdy:@field-(DOCID+sa0000*.

Middle East Economic Digest, various editions.

Middle East Economic Survey, various editions.

Middle East Policy (formerly *Arab-American Affairs*), various editions.

Miller, Aaron David. *Search for Security: Saudi Arabian Oil and American Foreign Policy, 1939–1949.* Chapel Hill: University of North Carolina Press, 1980.

Moyston, Trevor. *Saudi Arabia.* London: MEED, 1981.

Nevo, Joseph. "The Saudi Royal Family: The Third Generation." *Jerusalem Quarterly,* no. 31 (Spring 1984).

New York Times, various editions.

Newsweek, various editions.

Niblock, Tim, ed. *State, Society, and the Economy in Saudi Arabia.* London: Croom Helm, 1982.

Nimir, S.A. and M. Palmer. "Bureaucracy and Development in Saudi Arabia: A Behavioral Analysis." *Public Administration and Development* (April–June 1982).

Noyes, James H. *The Clouded Lens.* Stanford, CA: Hoover Institution, 1982.

Obaid, Nawaf E. *The Oil Kingdom at 100: Petroleum Policymaking in Saudi Arabia.* Washington, DC: The Washington Institute for Near East Policy, 2000.

Ochsenwald, William. "Saudi Arabia and the Islamic Revival." *International Journal of Middle East Studies,* vol. 13, no. 3 (August 1981), pp. 271–286.

Organization of Petroleum Exporting Countries (OPEC). *Annual Report.* Vienna, various years.

Peterson, J.E. *Saudi Arabia and the Illusion of Security.* New York: Oxford University Press, 2002.

Philadelphia Inquirer, various editions.

Policywatch, various editions.

Quandt, William B. "Riyadh between the Superpowers." *Foreign Policy,* no. 44 (Fall 1981).

Quandt, William B. *Saudi Arabia in the 1980s: Foreign Policy, Security and Oil.* Washington, DC: Brookings Institution, 1982

Quandt, William B. *Saudi Arabia's Oil Policy: A Staff Paper.* Washington, DC: Brookings Institution, 1982.

Rashid, Ahmed. *Taliban: Militant Islam, Oil, and Fundamentalism in Central Asia.* New Haven, CT: Yale University Press, 2000.

Rashid, Ahmed. *Jihad: The Rise of Militant Islam in Central Asia.* New Haven, CT: Yale University Press, 2002.

Reeves, Phil. "Bush Backs Saudi Plan for Peace in the Middle East." *The Independent,* February 27, 2002, p. 16.

Reuters, Online access.

Richards, Alan. "Economic Roots of Instability in the Middle East." *Middle East Policy,* vol. 4, nos. 1 and 2 (September 1995), pp. 175–187.

Richards, Alan. "The Global Financial Crisis and Economic Reform in the Middle East." *Middle East Policy,* vol. 6, no. 3 (February 1999), pp. 62–71.

Roule, Trifin J. Jeremy Kinsell, and Brian Joyce. "Investigators seek to break up Al-Qaida's financial structure." *Jane's Intelligence Review* (November 2001), pp. 8–11.

Rubin, Barry. *Crises in the Contemporary Persian Gulf*. Portland, OR: Frank Cass Publishers, 2002.

Rubin, Daniel and Warren P. Strobel. "Saudi Plan Interesting, Sharon Tells UN Chief." *The Philadelphia Inquirer*, February 27, 2002.

Rugh, William A. "Education in Saudi Arabia: Choices and Constraints." *Middle East Policy*, vol. 9, no. 2 (June 2002), pp. 40–55.

Sabini, John. *Armies in the Sand: The Struggle for Mecca and Medina*. New York: W. W. Norton, 1981.

Safran, Nadav. *Saudi Arabia: The Ceaseless Quest for Security*. Cambridge, MA: Belknap Press of Harvard University Press, 1985.

Salameh, Mamdouh G. "A Third Oil Crisis?" *Survival*, vol. 43, no. 3 (Autumn 2001), pp. 129–144.

Salem, Paul. "The Rise and Fall of Secularism." *Middle East Policy*, vol. 4, no. 3 (March 1996), pp. 147–160.

Saudi Arabia, various editions.

Saudi American Bank, Office of the SAMBA Chief Economist. *The Saudi Economy*. Riyadh: SAMBA, various editions.

Saudi American Bank. *Saudi Arabia Investor's Guide 2002*. Riyadh: MEED, 2002.

Saudi Arabia, Kingdom of. *Annual Report of the Saudi Fund for Development, 1984–1985*. Saudi Arabia, 1985.

Saudi Arabia, Kingdom of, Royal Embassy. "Government Officials' Biographies: His Royal Highness Prince Sultan bin Abdul Aziz Al Saud." URL: *http://www.saudiembassy.net-/gov-profile/bio_sultan.html*. Accessed on May 30, 2002.

Saudi Arabia, Kingdom of, Royal Embassy. "Kingdom's Aid to Palestinians Nears 10 Billion Riyals." May 2, 2002. URL: *http://www.saudiembassy.net/press_release/02-spa/05-02-aid.htm*. Accessed on May 26, 2002.

Saudi Arabia, Kingdom of, Royal Embassy. "Red Crescent Confirms Kingdom's Humanitarian Aid to Palestine." April 10, 2002. URL: *http://www.saudiembassy.net/pressrelease/02-spa/04-11-mideast.htm*. Accessed on May 26, 2002.

Saudi Arabia, Kingdom of, Royal Embassy, Information Office. "Press Release: The Kingdom of Saudi Arabia Responds to False Israeli Charges." May 6, 2002. URL: *http://www.saudi-embassy.net/press_release/releases/02-PR-0506-bandar-mideast.htm*. Accessed on May 26, 2002.

Saudi Arabia, Kingdom of, Ministry of Education. *Education in the Kingdom of Saudi Arabia, Within the Last Hundred Years*. Riyadh: Ministry of Education, 2001.

Saudi Arabia, Kingdom of, Ministry of Finance and National Economy, Central Department of Statistics. *Population Census*, Volume 14. Dammam, 1977.

Saudi Arabia, Kingdom of, Ministry of Finance and National Economy. *Statistical Yearbook*. Jidda, various years.

Saudi Arabia, Kingdom of, Ministry of Planning. *Second Development Plan, 1975–1980*. Springfield, VA: U.S. Department of Commerce, Bureau of International Commerce, 1975.

Saudi Arabia, Kingdom of, Saudi Arabian Monetary Agency, Research and Statistics Department. *Statistical Summary*. Riyadh, various years.

Saudi Arabia, Kingdom of, Ministry of Planning. *Third Development Plan, 1980–85*. Riyadh: Ministry of Planning Press, 1980.

Saudi Arabia, Kingdom of, Ministry of Planning. *Seventh Development Plan, 2000–2004*. Riyadh: Ministry of Planning Press, 2000.

Saudi Arabia, Kingdom of, Ministry of Planning. *Achievements of the Development Plans: Facts and Figures*. Riyadh, Ministry of Planning Press, various editions, especially the 19th ed. (2002).

Saudi Arabia, Kingdom of, Saudi Arabian Monetary Agency (SAMA). *Thirty-Sixth Annual Report*, 1421H.

Saudi Arabia, Kingdom of, Saudi Arabian Monetary Agency (SAMA). *Thirty-Seventh Annual Report*, 1422H.

Saudi Aramco, online database. URL: *www.saudiaramco.com*.

Saudi Aramco. *Saudi Aramco 2001: Transformation: Energy to the World*. Dhahran: Saudi Aramco, 2002.

Saudi Aramco. *Saudi Aramco 2001: Facts and Figures*. Dhahran: Saudi Aramco, 2002.

Saudi Aramco. *Saudi Aramco and Its World: Arabia and the Middle East*. Dhahran: Saudi Aramco, 1995.

Saudi Aramco. *Saudi Aramco and Its People: A History of Training*. Dhahran: Saudi Aramco, 1998.

Saudi Aramco. *Annual Review*. Dhahran: Saudi Aramco, various editions.

Saudi Basic Industries Corporation (SABIC), online database. URL: *www.Sabic.com*.

Saudi Basic Industries Corporation (SABIC). *Annual Report*. Riyadh: SABIC, various editions, especially the 2001 edition.

Saudi Commerce and Economic Review, various editions.

Shadid, Anthony. *Legacy of the Prophet: Despots, Democrats, and the New Politics of Islam*. Boulder, CO: Westview Press, 2001.

Shaw, John A. and David E. Long. *Saudi Arabian Modernization*. Washington Papers 89. New York: Praeger, 1982.

Strobel, Warren P. and Daniel Rubin. "Saudis to Seek Arab Support for Their Mideast Plan." *The Miami Herald*, February 28, 2002, Part A, p. 1.

Survival, various editions.

Taecker, Kevin. "Saudi Arabia and the GCC in a Troubled Global Economy." *Middle East Policy*, vol. 6, no. 2 (October 1998), pp. 29–35.

Tanks of the World (Bernard and Grafe), various editions.

Teitelbaum, Joshua. *Holier than Thou: Saudi Arabia's Islamic Opposition*. Washington, DC: The Washington Institute for Near East Policy, 2000.

The Estimate, various editions.

Thomas, Troy S. and Stephen D. Kiser. *Lords of the Silk Route: Violent Non-State Actors in Central Asia*. Occasional Paper 43. Colorado: United States Air Force Institute for National Security Studies (INSS), May 2002.

Turner, Louis, and James M. Bedore. *Middle East Industrialization: A Study of Saudi and Iranian Downstream Investments*. London: Saxon House, 1979.

United Nations Development Program. *Arab Human Development Report 2002*. New York: United Nations Development Program/Arab Fund for Economic and Social Development, 2002.

USA Today, various editions.

U.S. Department of Defense. *Report on Allied Contributions to the Common Defense*, Report to the U.S. Congress by the Secretary of Defense, March 2001.

U.S. Department of State, "Patterns of Global Terrorism." URL: *http://www.state.gov/www/global-/terrorism/*.

U.S. Department of State. *Annual Report on Military Expenditures*. Submitted to the Committee on Appropriations of the U.S. Senate and the Committee on Appropriations of the U.S. House of Representatives, in accordance with section 511(b) of the Foreign Operations, Export Financing, and Related Programs Appropriations Act, 1993.

U.S. Department of State. *Country Report on Human Rights Practices*. URL: *http://www.state.-gov/www/global/human_rights/l*.

U.S. Department of State. *Congressional Presentation for Security Assistance Programs, Fiscal Year 1996*. Washington, DC: Department of State, 1995.

U.S. Department of State. *Congressional Presentation: Foreign Operations*, various editions.

U.S. Energy Information Administration. *Impacts of World Oil Market Shocks on the US Economy*. Washington, DC: Department of Energy/EIA-0411, July 1983.

U.S. Energy Information Administration. *International Energy Outlook*. Washington, DC: Department of Energy, various editions.

U.S. Energy Information Administration. *Monthly Energy Review*. Washington, DC: Government Printing Office, various editions.

U.S. Library of Congress, Congressional Research Service, Foreign Affairs and National Defense Division. *Saudi Arabia and the United States: The New Context in an Evolving "Special Relationship."* Report prepared for the Subcommittee on Europe and the Middle East, Committee on Foreign Affairs, U.S. House of Representatives, 1981.

U.S. Library of Congress, Congressional Research Service, Foreign Affairs and National Defense Division. *Western Vulnerability to a Disruption of Persian Gulf Oil Supplies: US Interests and Options*, 1983.

U.S. National Intelligence Council. *Foreign Missile Developments and the Ballistic Missile Threat to the United States Through 2015*. Washington, DC: NIC, September 1999.

U.S.-Saudi Arabian Business Council. *A Business Guide to Saudi Arabia*. 4th ed. Riyadh, 2001. URL: *www.us-saudi-business.org*.

Vassiliev, Alexei, and A. M. Vasil'ev. *A History of Saudi Arabia*. New York: New York University Press, 2000.

Viorst, Milton. *In the Shadow of the Prophet: The Struggle for the Soul of Islam*. New York: Doubleday, 1998.

Washington Post, various editions.

Washington Times, various editions.

Weinbaum, Marvin G. *Food Development, and Politics in the Middle East*. Boulder, CO: Westview Press, 1982.

Weizman, Steve. "Israeli Prime Minister Said Ready to Meet Saudis on New Mideast Peace Proposal." *Associated Press*, International News Section, February 26, 2002.

Wells, Donald A. *Saudi Arabian Development Strategy*. Washington, DC: American Enterprise Institute, 1976.

Whelan, John, ed. *Saudi Arabia*. London: MEED, 1981.

Wiley, Marshall W. "American Security Concerns in the Gulf." *Orbis*, vol. 28, no. 3 (Fall 1984), pp. 456–464.

Wilkinson, Tracey and Michael Slackman. "Unlikely Olive Branch Takes Root; Mideast: Saudi Peace Proposal, Though Vague, Sets the Stage for the Kingdom's Involvement in Possible Talks." *Los Angeles Times*, February 28, 2002, Part A, p. 1.

Wolfe, Ronald G., ed. *The United States, Arabia, and the Gulf*. Washington, DC: Georgetown University Center for Contemporary Arab Studies, 1980.

World Bank. *A Population Perspective on Development in the Middle East and North Africa*. Washington, DC: World Bank, August 1994.

World Bank. *Atlas*, various editions.

World Bank. *Claiming the Future: Choosing Prosperity in the Middle East and North Africa*. Washington, DC: World Bank, 1995.

World Bank. *Global Development Prospects*, various editions.

World Bank. *Will Arab Workers Prosper or Be Left Out in the Twenty-First Century?* Washington, DC: World Bank, 1995.

World Bank. *World Development Indicators*, various editions.

Yisraeli, Sarah. *The Remaking of Saudi Arabia: The Struggle between King Saud and Crown Prince Faysal, 1953–1962*. Tel Aviv: Moshe Dayan Center for Middle Eastern and African Studies, Tel Aviv University, 1997.

Yodfat, Aryeh Y. *The Soviet Union and the Arabian Peninsula: Soviet Policy towards the Persian Gulf and Arabia*. New York: St. Martin's Press, 1983.

Zogby, James. "What Arabs Think: Values, Beliefs and Concerns." Report by Zogby International, Commissioned the Arab Thought Foundation, September 2002.

Index

Note: Page numbers in *italics* refer to illustrations.

About the Author

ANTHONY H. CORDESMAN is a Senior Fellow and the Arleigh A. Burke Chair in Strategy at the Center for Strategic and International Studies, and a military analyst for ABC News. The author of numerous books on Middle Eastern security issues, he has served in senior positions for the office of the Secretary of Defense, NATO, and the U.S. Senate.